LIGHT *on the* HILL

A HISTORY OF TUFTS COLLEGE
1852–1952

LIGHT on the HILL

A History of
Tufts College 1852-1952

RUSSELL E. MILLER
Professor of History
Tufts University

BEACON PRESS　　　BOSTON

TO NILS YNGVE WESSELL
President of Tufts, 1953-1966

Foreword

THIS HISTORY OF TUFTS speaks for itself and does so eloquently. The author has brought objectivity to his task without neglecting the human side of the story; he has combined a most readable style with the exacting standards of historical scholarship. While the first appeal of this volume will be to Tufts alumni and other members of the vast Tufts family, it is also a model for those who might essay the same task on behalf of other colleges and universities and for all who would achieve for themselves the combined goals of lucid expression and scholarship of a high order.

It is a source of great pride to me that it was during my tenure as president of Tufts University that an historical work so well done and so significant was written. I know that among the author's rewards will be the appreciation of Tufts men and women everywhere who read the results of his happy labor.

When the record of the second century of Tufts history is written, may it be done as well and may those who will have created it be as deserving of commendation as are the leaders of the first hundred years.

Nils Y. Wessell
PRESIDENT
TUFTS UNIVERSITY

Contents

Contents

Illustrations

Preface

THIS HISTORY OF AN INSTITUTION OF HIGHER LEARNING is undoubtedly typical in many ways of dozens of others that have appeared in the past and presumably will continue to appear in ever-increasing numbers. Yet in some ways the writer believes (and hopes) that, if it is not superior to some of its prototypes, it is at least in some respects unique in both its conception and execution. The idea, of which this work is the concrete expression, was suggested by the author rather than by the officers of the institution. It was not commissioned in any sense as an "official" history, although it received a welcome blessing. The decade of the 1960's witnessed a veritable cascade of histories of public educational institutions, on the occasion of the celebration of the centennial of the Morrill Act of 1862, which made possible the land-grant college and university. This particular history is of a private, independent, non-sectarian school and was not written to commemorate any particular event or anniversary. It was not intended even to raise money. The author is not an alumnus of the institution and in fact had not laid eyes on it until 1948. The story is also brought, by the canons of most writers of history, perilously close to the date of its publication. No one is more aware than the author of the snares and pitfalls that are built into any attempt to record what is usually called "contemporary history," involving as it does the consideration of events still fresh in mind, and personalities that have not yet retired from the academic stage on which the history of this particular institution has been played. There is also the danger of implying that, once recorded, the history of an educational institution has come to an end. Nothing could be farther from the truth in the case of Tufts.

The year 1952 was selected as a terminal date for this work because it marks the centennial of the chartering of the College, because it marks the end of the presidential administration of one of its most prominent alumni, and because it gave an opportunity to record some of the manifold changes that occurred in one of the most significant periods in Tufts' history.

A word should be said about the use of the terms "college" and "university." Tufts officially became a "university" in 1955, when its charter was amended in order to describe most accurately what the institution had been in actuality since it opened an engineering department in 1865, a theological school in 1869, a graduate school in 1892, a medical school in 1893, a dental school in 1899, a graduate school of international law and diplomacy in 1933, and added a number of associated undergraduate professional schools thereafter. But to many generations of alumni, faculty, officers, and friends, it has always been, and will probably remain, "Tufts College."

The writing of this history, like most such endeavors, brought both satisfactions and frustrations. One of the most gratifying experiences was the enthusiastic and wholehearted response of President Nils Y. Wessell to the suggestion that Tufts had had a sufficiently long and distinguished history to make it a worthy subject of a formal account. His willingness to make accessible any and all information that might be relevant may not have been surprising, but it was most certainly a great source of satisfaction. His faith in the author's ability to use the material wisely probably represented a calculated risk. It is the author's sincere hope that the risk was worth taking.

Likewise most heartwarming both to the University and to the writer was the generous and completely unsolicited contribution of the Class of 1959. The members of this group demonstrated their enthusiasm by donating toward the publication of this history the money remaining in their class treasury when they departed from the Hill as alumni. It was not only the gift but the spirit which prompted it that merits a special note of appreciation.

The policy of the administrative officers of the University in throwing open the files of the institution also generated its own problems. There is too much material rather than too little. The collegiate Founding Fathers, and their successors, were excellent record-keepers. The passage of time, the accidents of fate, and the

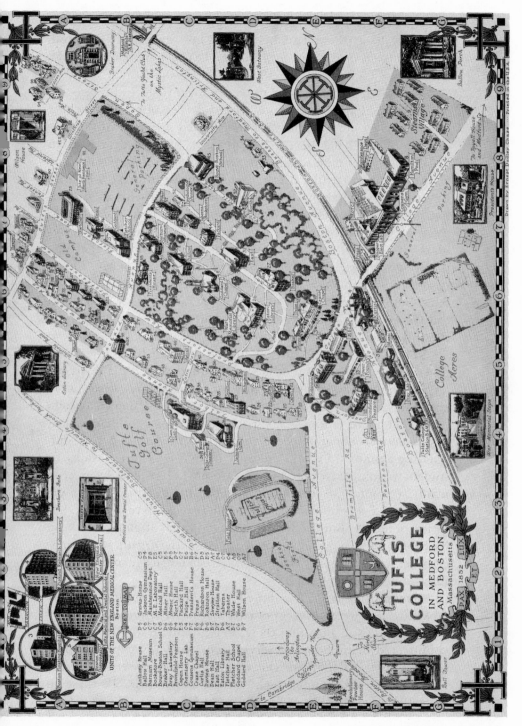

Centennial Map, 1852–1952

ravages of flood (but, fortunately, not of fire) have taken their toll. But what has remained for the historian has been more than ample. So the story has been put together from the many sources available.

Compilers of college and university histories are also faced by the basic problem of selection of material. Too often they include not only trivia but material of such localized interest that the general reader is, if not bored close to tears, frightened away from works that might have some value beyond institutional walls. The author of this particular history has attempted to strike a balance between the general and the specific that is admittedly difficult, if not impossible, to achieve. How successful has been the attempt, the reader must judge. The writer hopes that, if this history serves no other purpose, it will give an enhanced awareness of the complexities of an academic enterprise, regardless of size or age. This is not meant to imply that Tufts has had more than its share of problems, but certainly it has not escaped the fate of other colleges in this respect. Hopefully, its story may be instructive to some outside its walls as well as to some within.

The writer knows that this history may not be to everyone's taste. There may be those who wish to quarrel with the relatively large amount of space devoted to what is commonly called "background," especially evident in the early chapters. Others may complain that there is too much space devoted to "problems"; still others may be unhappy because some favorite professors, or outstanding alumni (of whom there are many) , or winning teams, or student pranks, have not been mentioned. It would have been manifestly unfair to have omitted them all; this would have dehumanized a very human institution and would have distorted historical actuality. But the writer throughout has attempted to keep his focus on the main functions of a college: the organization, preservation, transmission, and promotion of knowledge and learning in a community of scholars.

Among those who contributed to the finished product, directly or indirectly, were three graduates of Tufts who heard of the project while still pursuing their undergraduate studies and who volunteered many hours of service, not with any expectation of compensation in dollars and cents, but because they were interested and because they thought the effort was worthwhile. To these go special thanks: Carol Sudalter Herman, A.B., Jackson, 1954; Harriet Weitzman Rosen, A.B., Jackson, 1961; and Warren Wheeler Baker, B.S. in Chemical Engineering, 1962. It would be impossible to list all of those associated with the University who furnished encouragement, advice, materials, and facilities, but the following should be singled out for special mention: Leonard C. Mead, the University Provost; Miss Marie Donnelly, Assistant Secretary of the Board of Trustees; Miss Margaret Lovejoy, of the Provost's office; Professor Albert H. Imlah, of the History Department; and Professor Joseph Komidar, University Librarian, and his staff. Besides a long-suffering spouse and various colleagues upon whom were inflicted varying quantities of manuscript, the author owes an incalculable debt to Mrs. Ruth H. Stirling, who devoted, on a part-time basis, over five years to assist in organizing and filing the archival material out of which much of this history has been written; and to Mrs. Carolyn MacVicar, for secretarial (and editorial) services that extended well beyond the line of duty.

§   §   §

In 1896, the junior class of Tufts College wrote a history of the institution. They felt it had "reached a point in its career when its history is worth writing. . . . At some future day . . . someone will take up the work and give to it the time and care which it deserves. Both time and care will indeed be requisite fifty years from now, for history is being made almost faster than it can be written." The author hopes that he has complied with the wishes expressed there, even though more than half a century has passed since those words were put on paper.

Russell E. Miller

MEDFORD, MASSACHUSETTS
OCTOBER, 1965

A NOTE ABOUT DOCUMENTATION

This work is intended to be a scholarly presentation. Footnotes are one of the outward manifestations of such an effort and exist to serve certain well-defined purposes. Theoretically, every sentence or paragraph of a work not derived from an author's direct experience ought to be accompanied by one or more footnotes indicating source or authority. Unfortunately, the trappings of scholarship can be overdone. One result may be a veritable meadow of footnotes intersected by a thin trickle of text — a device which serves only to irritate and distract the reader. At the risk of requiring a great act of faith on the part of said reader, sources that seem obvious from context or common sense have been omitted or explained in blanket footnotes. The interests of continuity, simplicity, and economy (of both verbiage and what the nineteenth century was wont to call "pecuniary expenditure") seem to be best served in this fashion. Secondary works which have proved helpful in compiling or interpreting the narrative, or matters which have seemed especially worth calling to the attention of the reader or requiring citation by their very nature, have been indicated in the usual way. The writer, whenever he has interjected his own judgments or introduced material which he has felt needed authority to back it up, has done his best to make this clear.

The reader who wishes further information is assured that a fully documented draft of this work reposes in the University Archives and is available to shed light on the dark and dusty corners from which this material was gathered. A Bibliographical Note at the end of the work gives detailed information about the principal sources from which this account has been drawn.

R. E. M.

LIGHT *on the* HILL
A HISTORY OF TUFTS COLLEGE
1852–1952

1. *"Almost Altogether an Uphill Business"*

TUESDAY, JULY 19, 1853, was a typically warm midsummer day in the Boston area. By midmorning the thermometer registered almost 90° in the valleys, and a bright sun shimmered on a large tent pitched on a rocky and treeless hilltop a few miles northwest of the city. Beneath the tent, from the top of which three American ensigns floated lazily in a light breeze, sat more than 1,500 men and women. They had just listened to an "able and eminently appropriate" address by a prominent Boston clergyman and were watching attentively a diminutive gentleman in a frock coat and with a fringe of graying hair. Silhouetted against the sky was a section of red brick wall about twenty feet high, and at one corner a few feet away lay a block of Connecticut sandstone. The aforementioned gentleman made sure that the stone was placed "plum, level, and square; and then standing upon it, he pronounced it properly laid."[1] The location was Walnut Hill, on the outskirts of the town of Medford, Massachusetts; from this eminence, the highest in the Boston area, the Bunker Hill monument was clearly visible, and it was said that seventeen towns and villages could be distinguished in the distance. The occasion was the laying of the cornerstone of the main building for "a literary institution devoted to the higher cultivation of the mind," already christened Tufts College by its Board of Trustees. The occupants of the tent were clergymen and laymen of the Universalist Church, who watched with pride and satisfaction the tangible results of almost twenty years of effort. The gentleman who had delivered the principal address was the Rev. Alonzo Ames Miner, one of the prime movers in the establishment of the College. The clergyman standing on the cornerstone that

[1] See the Note About Documentation.

3

summer day was the Rev. Hosea Ballou 2d, D.D., first president of the new institution. Somewhat belatedly (nearly half a century later) the building, of which only a part of the wall had been erected in 1853, was to bear his name. Prominent in the assemblage was Charles Tufts, who had donated the land on which the College Edifice was being constructed; "though incapacitated by reason of deafness from enjoying the services, he seemed to look upon the scene before him with feelings of peculiar pleasure and interest."

§　　§　　§

The institution that was being constructed on that New England hilltop in 1853 was the first venture into higher education by one of the diverse offshoots of Protestantism. Although, like many American religious groups, the Universalist Church could and did trace its origins back into the European past, it was basically a New World phenomenon. Universalism had appeared as a recognizable sect in late eighteenth-century and early nineteenth-century America and represented a small part of the larger movement of revolt against the Calvinist predestinarianism which the majority of colonists had inherited. It offered, through its teachings of the universal Fatherhood of God and the universal brotherhood and ultimate salvation of all men, an optimistic, humane ethic characteristic of the democratic strivings of a new nation in the making. From its American beginnings, usually traced back to John Murray, who arrived from England in 1770 and who served for a time as chaplain of the Rhode Island Revolutionary regiments under George Washington, the sect was suspicious of aristocratic privilege and of a monolithic church or state in any form.[2] Early Universalists, who

2 The definitive history of Universalism has yet to be written. The most recent summary is a sketch by Clinton Lee Scott, *The Universalist Chuch of America* (Boston: Universalist Historical Society, 1957), from which considerable background material has been drawn by this writer. The European origins of Universalism are traced in Hosea Ballou 2d's *Ancient History of Universalism* (Boston: Marsh and Capen, 1829), which commences the story at the time of the Christian apostles and carries it to the condemnation of Universalism at the Fifth General Council of the Western Church in 553; there is an appendix tracing the doctrine down to the era of the Protestant Reformation of the sixteenth century. The narrative was continued, but never completed, by Thomas Whittemore's *Modern History of Universalism* (Boston: A. Tompkins, 1860), of which only three chapters deal with America.

4

organized their first church in Gloucester, Massachusetts, in 1779, had to do prolonged battle through the courts for recognition of their rights as a separate religious body.

Universalism, as a religious ideal, grew slowly, for it was a movement with theological ideas quite at variance with those of the orthodox Protestant majority represented by American Congregationalism. Much of its early activity, largely in the New England backcountry, was carried on by circuit riders, who delivered their message of a benevolent Deity, and of the hope of salvation for all, in town halls or private homes, or on village greens. Universalists were constrained, like members of many dissident sects, to gain their first numbers and strength by attracting "come-outers" who were dissatisfied with what they found in existing denominations. Many Universalists had Baptist origins, and an occasional Methodist or disgruntled Congregationalist joined the ranks. With their aversion to building up "a mammoth and central power," their emphasis on moral suasion, their professed search for untrammeled truth, and their opposition to the "hellfire and damnation" approach to theology, the Universalists may be compared in many respects with the Quakers. Because of the individualistic character of the early adherents to Universalism, there was even an avoidance of terminology conventionally associated with religious bodies. They labeled the Congregationalists "Orthodox" or "Partialists" and avoided among themselves even the term "church," preferring "parish," "society," and "meeting house." Their spiritual leaders were more often "preachers" than "clergymen." Reluctance to join forces was a chronic weakness of the Universalists, inherent in their very philosophy, and goes far to explain the failure of the sect to take organized form early in its history.

As Societies were formed, informal associations of neighboring parishes did begin to appear late in the eighteenth century. The rigors of isolation and the need to share preachers and meeting places were among the reasons. The Societies followed a strictly congregational form of church government, which meant that each

The most comprehensive and detailed coverage, now over seventy-five years old, is Richard Eddy's *Universalism in America* (2 vols., Boston: Universalist Publishing House, 1884–1886).

local group controlled its own destiny. They were accountable to no other body for the choice, settlement, or dismissal of their pastors and in every other way exercised complete autonomy. The first general meeting out of which was born the Universalist Church took place in Oxford, Massachusetts, in 1785. Delegates from seven Societies in New England agreed, somewhat like their forebears in 1620, on a "Charter of Compact," and Universalism became a separate denomination, with a distinctive name and set of beliefs. The Oxford body, originally known as the New England Convention, decided to hold annual meetings. Thereafter, under the rather cumbersome and overly ambitious title adopted in 1804, "The General Convention of Universalists in the New England States and others" met for some thirty years. In 1833 the parent organization became the "United States Convention of Universalists," but only after it was clearly provided that its functions would be advisory only, and that it would in no way attempt to legislate for the local units.

An attempt to organize on a large scale had been made in 1790 in Philadelphia, with the adoption of a Declaration of Faith and a Plan of Church Government. The principal author was Benjamin Rush, talented physician and social reformer, and a convert to Universalism. But the denomination was not yet ready for a national organization, in which all Societies would be united in one body, so the plan came to naught. Instead, local and regional groupings reflecting the atomistic character of Universalism began to appear, and New England became the focal point for the denomination. Boston was eventually a sort of headquarters, but the historical strength of the group always remained in the rural areas. A Union Association which included central and western Massachusetts was organized in 1816. The Old Colony Association, created in 1827, embraced southeastern Massachusetts. And in 1829 the Boston Association came into being, representing four counties and fifty-one Societies and including originally some thirty-seven preachers. Similar organizations appeared in Vermont, New Hampshire, Maine, Connecticut, and Rhode Island, as well as in New York State.

Not until the 1830's were state-wide associations formed, such as the one organized in Massachusetts in 1834. It was the Boston Association that assumed the leadership in organizing the State

Convention. Even then the various local groups continued to lead quite separate lives. The annual meetings, operating through the Universalist General Convention, were little more than periodic gatherings for clergy and interested laity, who renewed acquaintances, exchanged experiences, and heard sermons. Seldom was any significant business transacted, for the sovereignty of the local Societies and organizations was too jealously guarded.[3] This reluctance to countenance a centralized authority helps explain the chronic delay in launching any movement requiring united denominational effort. Tufts College might have been created much sooner under other circumstances.

Until the 1830's and 1840's the Universalists remained very much on the defensive as an "heretical" Protestant sect. In 1795 there were probably no more than twenty professed Universalist preachers in the country; in 1820, no more than fifty. The Societies remained small, scattered, largely uncoordinated, and often "spoken against." Committed as they were to liberal religious views, Universalists were often lumped together with "Sceptics, Deists, Atheists and other libertines" but, with a hint of Christian martyrdom, felt that they "must reconcile themselves to bear every species of reproach." As late as 1829, because of their religious convictions, they were barred in several states (including Massachusetts and Connecticut) from testifying under oath in court proceedings. Because they were for many decades a minority group, and most of their energies and resources were devoted to assuring their survival as a denomination, they paid scant attention at first to most social issues. However, on one matter they were outspoken and uncompromising from the beginning: they championed separation of church and state in season and out, and challenged the preferential position of Congregationalism in Massachusetts. As they matured as an organization and attracted larger numbers and gained greater respectability, Universalists became more socially conscious than in their formative days. They took a strong stand against slavery, advocated temperance, and even organized a General Reform Association in the 1840's through which they could express themselves

[3] It was not until 1942 that the Universalist General Convention officially became "The Universalist Church of America," which in turn merged with the American Unitarian Association in May 1961 to form the Unitarian Universalist Association.

and act on the various movements permeating the Jacksonian era that were intended to better the lot of mankind. Rather to the embarrassment of Universalists who deplored some of the extreme "enthusiasms" of the period, one of their own number, Adin Ballou, became a Christian pacifist and believer in "the fraternization of property." It was Ballou who in 1842 launched the utopian experiment of the Hopedale Community in Massachusetts, which lasted some fourteen years. It attracted the attention both of his contemporaries and of scholars of a later day who have been interested in the various blueprints for making over American society a century or more ago.

Universalists were by no means pioneers in establishing institutions of learning, at any level. They were finally forced by their convictions into establishing academies, seminaries, theological schools, and even colleges, to counteract the alleged sectarianism that they found in other educational establishments. They delayed their educational efforts partly because for many years they were concerned with what in their view were more pressing matters. In their origins, furthermore, the bulk of Universalist preachers and parishioners were thrifty, hard-working farmers and small businessmen who considered formal education, beyond minimum literacy, a luxury or downright dangerous. Typical of the older generation of preachers who distrusted book learning was the elder Hosea Ballou. Ballou, great-uncle of the first president of Tufts (and often confused with him), has often been considered "the father of Universalism in America." With less than three years of formal schooling, he was largely self-educated and was especially suspicious of training obtained in theological schools. The call of the Spirit, a Bible, and a group of listeners were all that were needed to spread the glad tidings of Universalism. It was the proselyting sectarianism characteristic of nineteenth-century American education that Universalists deplored and eventually tried to remedy.[4]

The first experiments in Universalist-sponsored education were at the secondary school level. The greatest debates and, correspondingly, the longest delays in taking concrete action occurred in the realm of collegiate education and the professional training of the

[4] The present writer has dealt with this general subject at some length in "Universalism and Sectarian Education before 1860," *Annual Journal,* Universalist Historical Society, Vol. III (1962), pp. 30–53.

Universalist clergy. The story, in spite of interruptions, struggles, disagreements, and even failures, and in spite of long-standing indecision as to what type of schools should be established and supported, was one of growing momentum. The result, by the time Tufts College was chartered in 1852, was the establishment of over a dozen academies. Not all prospered, or even survived, but more succeeded than failed.

Nichols Academy, in Dudley, Massachusetts, was the first educational enterprise established wholly under Universalist auspices. The idea was planted by a circular issued in 1814 calling for the establishment of a seminary "embracing the united interests of Literature and Religion." In the following year, the Universalist General Convention agreed to direct and patronize the proposed school and undertook to raise a subscription of $5,000. The project was thought likely to succeed, for Amasa Nichols, a local merchant, had erected an academy building at his own expense in 1815. Unfortunately, it had been destroyed by fire soon after the school began operation, but he wanted to rebuild. In order to reopen the school, he proposed that his fellow Universalists take over its sponsorship. A charter was obtained in 1819, and the academy was opened as a coeducational school (as was every secondary school founded under Universalist auspices), and without any religious instruction included in the curriculum (also true of all other Universalist-sponsored academies and preparatory schools).

But Nichols Academy was a failure, so far as the Universalists were concerned, in spite of the fact that it opened auspiciously with over sixty students and had the support of a wealthy Universalist. The Convention was unable to support the school after Nichols turned it over to the fifteen Trustees and left it as their responsibility. Only $1,000 of the $5,000 subscription was ever raised, and the school was opened even before the building was completed. Without funds, and supported only by inadequate tuition fees and the personal contributions of the Trustees, the school almost foundered before being rescued by state aid. More fundamental than this, perhaps, as a problem was the philosophy under which the Trustees operated. When the Convention voted in 1819 "to receive the Nichols' Academy under their patronage," it was with the proviso that the Trustees be Universalists. But a majority of that body were so intent on making the school truly non-sectarian that they

9

disregarded the mandate of the Convention and voted to open their ranks to other denominations. When two non-Universalists were elected to fill vacancies, Nichols withdrew his support, resigned as a Trustee, and lost all interest in the academy. In consequence, the school fell into Congregational hands, which meant, in Universalist eyes, that it had fallen victim to "sectarian maneuvering."[5]

The brief experience with Nichols Academy taught the supporters of the idea of Universalist schools more than a lesson about the principle of permissiveness in the administration of an educational institution. It indicated that, from a practical standpoint, Universalists were not yet ready to support their own schools. Over a decade passed before another attempt was made, and it was much more successful.

The second school established by Universalists was the product of their growing strength in upstate New York. The movement that resulted in Clinton Liberal Institute was spearheaded by Rev. Dolphus Skinner, through the columns of the *Evangelical Magazine and Gospel Advocate,* one of the numerous denominational newspapers that appeared in the 1820's and 1830's. With the endorsement and aid of various local and regional associations, the school opened in the fall of 1831 after subscriptions of between $7,000 and $8,000 had been raised. Accommodations were provided for 100 boys and girls, and by 1833 ninety students were already enrolled. The number exceeded 100 the next year, and within a short time consideration had to be given to expanding facilities to provide for even more students. Following in rapid succession the establishment of Clinton Liberal Institute were three schools in the Midwest (none of which had an independent existence for very long) and a large number in New England.[6]

Among the academies, seminaries, and institutes appearing in

[5] In 1931, long after losing any denominational connection it might have had, Nichols Academy became a junior college, restricted to men, with a business administration curriculum. It was awarded degree-granting privileges in 1938 and, after being closed during the Second World War, reopened in 1946 as Nichols College of Business Administration, with a four-year degree program for men.

[6] No attempt is made here to detail the complex history of each of these academies. Only those that related directly to Tufts College are included. The mortality rate was high, for many were opened with insufficient endowment or none at all; several were combined, renamed, or fell into other hands.

the 1830's and 1840's which survived long enough to exert some influence, and in some cases to provide both students and faculty for Tufts College, were Westbrook Seminary, Westbrook, Maine (1834); Waterville Liberal Institute, Waterville, Maine (1836); and Green Mountain Liberal Institute (later Perkins), South Woodstock, Vermont (1848).[7] Two of the most important Universalist preparatory schools which served as "feeders" for Tufts and in which, for decades, Tufts maintained a proprietary interest were Green Mountain Central Institute (later Goddard Seminary and now Goddard College), Barre, Vermont (1836), and Dean Academy (later Dean Junior College), Franklin, Massachusetts (1866). Oddly enough, Massachusetts, which contained a comparatively large number of Universalists in the pre-Civil War period, was the only New England state in which Universalist schools did not flourish. Several attempts were made to establish schools, such as the ill-fated Methuen Liberal Institute (1839), but during the 1840's and 1850's an academy in Reading was the only school at all in the state that could claim any direct Universalist connection. One reason for this peculiar situation was the rapid expansion of the public school system, in which Massachusetts was a pioneer.

In respect to curriculum, the "literary and scientific institutions," as the academies were frequently called, followed very much the same pattern both among themselves and as compared with other private schools. The academic year was usually divided into four twelve-week terms, and the course might extend from one to four years, depending on the facilities offered by the school and the goals of the students. A typical Universalist academy which offered college preparatory subjects as well as a general secondary education would list "the common English branches" (including arithmetic, grammar, geometry, and rhetoric); Latin and Greek; several modern languages (French, German, Italian, and Spanish were frequently available and were often taught by the same person); and certain "ornamental" subjects, such as piano, voice and diction (both elocution and singing), freehand drawing, penmanship, and

[7] The actual dates for many schools in this period of the nineteenth century, regardless of sponsorship, are difficult to determine. In every case possible, the date indicates actual opening rather than chartering, for often many years elapsed before the school came into existence, or the school changed hands.

art (both oil and watercolor). Curricula changed slowly, and the "English branches," in spite of occasional variations, were very much standardized. Languages were particularly emphasized for those planning to enter teaching, college, or the ministry. English literature was usually included in some form in the college preparatory course, as were algebra and geography (especially ancient). The classical period of Greco-Roman history always received prominence.[8]

The one feature which both bound Universalist academies together and set them apart from most other church-related schools established before the Civil War was their conscious attempt to maintain a non-sectarian character. This did not mean that they were anti-religious; in fact, Universalists were as sure as any nineteenth-century Christians that religion could and should be "taught." It was "something inseparable from our nature, being derived immediately from the laws which govern our being." More specifically, "the religion of the Bible, revealed in all its beauty in the New Testament, *must be,* from the constitution of man, the great perfecting principle of human nature." Probably few Universalists were aware of the dilemma they posed for themselves in trying to distinguish between religious instruction and sectarianism *per se.* They themselves were merely expressing one variation of Protestant Christianity. But somehow they believed that their principles were more liberal than those of other denominations. They insisted that, by contrast, other religious bodies propagandized so blatantly that Universalist children were unable to receive an education not colored with some form of religious prejudice. A comprehensive public school system was established in Massachusetts in 1827 which included the famous "Textbook Law" forbidding the use of schoolbooks favoring any particular religious sect or tenet. Horace Mann, beginning in 1837, worked unceasingly to separate education and religious indoctrination in the common schools. But even these steps did not completely satisfy Universalists, much as they approved of both. So they believed that setting up their own schools was one of the answers. Meanwhile, they watched with an eagle eye for any indication of sectarianism in the public schools.

[8] The collegiate curricula, which often overlapped the preparatory school work, are dealt with at some length in Chapter 3.

Universalists never regarded their academic and "literary institutions" as competitors of the public schools. In a way, they considered themselves trustees of education, as it were, contributing in a modest way to the non-sectarian training of youth until the public school system could be firmly established. When a southern newspaper took occasion in the 1830's to praise the New England public school system, the leading Universalist newspaper enthusiastically agreed: "Of her public schools, above all her other admirable institutions, her people have just cause to be proud." Universalists lavished praise on Mann's efforts as secretary of the state Board of Education and referred repeatedly to the public schools as one of "the glories of the Commonwealth." They reiterated with almost tiresome regularity the idea that the schools were for gaining knowledge and not for adding to the ranks of the Methodists, Baptists, or any other religious group. As one Universalist expressed it, schools "are to educate children for *time,* not for *eternity*; children are sent to these useful Seminaries not to experience religion, but to fill their minds with the elements of worldly sciences."

From the evidence available, it seems clear that the Universalists attempted to practice what they preached about keeping sectarian religion out of their own schools. This naturally reduced potential school enrollments, for few non-Universalists would subscribe to such a radical departure from accepted educational practice. But Universalists stuck to their principles in this respect and published their views for all to read and to ponder. Clinton Liberal Institute was advertised as "an unsectarian English and Classical Seminary of education." The school was debarred by its charter from holding any religious services in the buildings during class hours or interfering with the religious opinions of the pupils. No minister of any sect was allowed to hold meetings at the school. The Institute carried its non-sectarian practices even further: it rejected the well-nigh universal practice of church-related schools of employing only those who professed the same religious faith as the sponsors of the school. The first principal of Clinton Liberal Institute was a German Lutheran; in the "Female Department," the first teacher was a Presbyterian, "in habits, prejudices and association," if not in membership. Her successor had been educated under Episcopalian supervision; and the next teacher was in fact an Episcopalian. The 1850 catalogue of Green Mountain Liberal Institute in Vermont stated explicitly that "one object of this Institution is to secure to the youth who come to it, perfect freedom of conscience and freedom of opinion which some institutions fail to do. Non-conformity in religious sentiments is not made the unpardonable sin of the student."

Whether or not members of other denominations looked askance at this unorthodox approach, the Universalists continued to maintain that religion and education were separate spheres, at least for instructional purposes. This is why no religious indoctrination as such was ever included in Universalist curricula. Even at the college level, theological training was kept separate from instruction in the arts and sciences. Tufts College offered no theological courses for almost twenty years after it was chartered, and when a divinity school was finally established, its faculty, and to a large extent its student body, maintained a separate existence from the rest of the College despite their location on the same campus. When St. Lawrence University was created in 1856, Universalists went so far as to provide separate Boards of Trustees for the liberal arts college and the theological school.

The statistical evidence makes it clear that both the denomination and its educational efforts grew apace after 1830. Over twenty schools of various kinds had come into existence as a result of Universalist activities by 1870. One reason for the flurry of educational enthusiasm, slow as it was in coming, can be found in the faith in the efficacy of education which an increasing number of Universalists were beginning to share with their fellow Americans, regardless of religious persuasion. There was a firm belief both in its value and in the need of extending opportunity for it. When the opening of a "People's Literary Institute and Gymnasium" (not under Universalist supervision) in Pembroke, New Hampshire, was announced, for the particular benefit of the "laboring classes," the largely self-educated Thomas Whittemore, editor of the *Trumpet and Universalist Magazine,* greeted the new school with enthusiasm. "We go for a universal education of the people — the poor and the rich — the farmer and the mechanic and the seaman, as well as the lawyer, the physician and the clergyman. Let all the people be educated. The universal diffusion of knowledge, is the only safeguard of our republican institutions."

§　　§　　§

Forces outside the denomination certainly had their influence in generating interest in education. But the Universalists would never have had either the will to attempt as much as they did or the organizational strength they had achieved by the 1840's and 1850's if competent and devoted leadership had not existed within their own ranks. Hosea Ballou 2d, the first president of Tufts College, helped furnish that leadership; his biography is in a sense the biography of much of the Universalist denomination in the first half of the nineteenth century. Gentle and retiring to the point of self-effacement, studious and meticulously thorough, he was active, in his quiet way, in most Universalist affairs during the crucial early period. In his lifetime he was overshadowed by his great-uncle Hosea Ballou, twenty-five years his senior, who helped shape the theology of American Universalism.[9] The younger Ballou added the "2d" to his name early in life in order to avoid confusion with his great-uncle. Many people have assumed erroneously, both now and then, that they were father and son. The older Ballou spent some forty years spreading the Gospel and zestfully tackling any religious controversy that arose. By contrast, his great-nephew, an equally dedicated Universalist, exhibited his talents and expended his energies in other directions. He was, above all, the scholar of American Universalism, both by temperament and by accomplishment. He was no polemicist, and when he became a writer and editor, he used his position to counsel "union and peace." When doctrinal squabbles erupted, frequently resulting in recriminatory language and even threatening to disrupt the denomination, he served as peacemaker. He seldom made forays onto the well-populated theological battlefield of his day, preferring to leave such activities to others.

Born in Guilford, Vermont, in 1796, Hosea 2d early showed a love for books. At the age of fifteen, while himself a student of the Rev. Thomas H. Wood, under whose guidance he learned his Latin so well, Hosea 2d became a teacher. For three winters he "boarded around," and during the summer months he worked on the family farm and continued his studies. There were family hopes that he might be able to receive a college education, and with this possibility in view he received excellent basic training in classical subjects.

[9] See Ernest Cassara, *Hosea Ballou: The Challenge to Orthodoxy* (Boston: Universalist Historical Society, 1961).

His later phenomenal proficiency in languages was an outgrowth and a reflection of his lifelong literary inclinations, although he never received the formal higher education which might have directed his intellectual development. During the 1820's he perfected his earlier knowledge of Latin, learned to read "with ease" French, German, and Greek, and acquired "considerable knowledge" of Hebrew.[10]

Following his decision to enter the Universalist ministry, Hosea 2d studied theology under the elder Ballou. After the great-uncle accepted a call to Portsmouth, New Hampshire, Hosea 2d assisted him in the operation of a private school which augmented a meager pastoral income. When he held his own pastorates later, Hosea 2d likewise conducted a private school, at first assisted by his younger brother Levi. In the days before formal theological training was provided, or even considered necessary, by the denomination, candidates for the ministry who had "heard the Call" followed the tradition which Hosea 2d himself had followed of apprenticing under an older and more experienced minister. During his seventeen-year pastorate in Roxbury, Massachusetts, Hosea 2d guided many students in their theological preparation. He worked out a three-year "home-study" course for his students. Among his pupils who became outstanding leaders in the denomination was John Stebbins Lee, the first president of St. Lawrence University, which was founded under Universalist auspices in 1856.[11]

Throughout his life, Hosea 2d was intensely interested in furthering public education, and he supported it at every opportunity. Clerical influence still dominated the American educational system at all levels, so it was expected that all clergymen in a community would serve on the local school board or committee of visitors. While in Roxbury and Medford, Hosea 2d performed his duty conscientiously, and after his initial appointments were over, he served in elective capacities for many years. For almost five years, from 1854, he was on the eight-man state Board of Education, created in

[10] Most of the books in his extensive personal library, now in the Tufts University Library and consisting of a large proportion of foreign language works, are extensively annotated in the language in which the books were written.

[11] For further information about Hosea 2d's students, and for detailed biographical data not included here, see Hosea Starr Ballou, *Hosea Ballou 2d* (Boston: E. P. Guild, 1896).

1837. While on the Board he was a member of its Executive Committee for three years and was also one of the two state visitors to the Massachusetts Normal School at Bridgewater.

Meanwhile, Hosea 2d's participation in the activities of organized Universalism had begun in 1817. For over forty years he served in almost every post that a Universalist could hold in his denomination. His first assignment came at the age of twenty, just after he had accepted his first pastorate, in Stafford, Connecticut. He was appointed a member of a committee of the General Convention to obtain subscriptions for what became Nichols Academy in 1819. It was in that year that he preached the first of many Convention sermons. Within the next decade he had, among other activities, served on committees to visit the regional Associations being organized; been moderator of the General Convention several times; helped review letters of fellowship and ordination; and become "omnipresent at dedications, installations, and associations." Hosea 2d's facility with the written word, his accuracy, his attention to detail, and his willingness to accept responsibility made him a logical choice to do the "paper work" so necessary in any organization. For some fifteen years he was alternate or standing clerk of the General Convention. When the Boston Association of Universalists was organized he became its first secretary. At the General Convention in 1829 he was appointed chairman of a special committee to compile the constitution, by-laws, and other rules for the government of the Convention. When it was necessary to gather statistics on the general state of Universalism in the United States, Hosea 2d was usually appointed to the task. It was quite fitting also that he should serve on committees "to inquire into the literary qualifications of candidates for the ministry." When the proposal was made in 1832 to enlarge the jurisdiction of the General Convention to include the entire denomination rather than the New England region alone, Hosea 2d was one of the two delegates selected to represent Massachusetts on a special committee to consider the feasibility of the plan.

During the more than thirty years that Hosea 2d held pastorates in various Universalist churches in Connecticut and Massachusetts, and in fact throughout his lifetime, he manifested scholarly propensities. He contributed over 100 articles and reviews to Universalist periodicals, co-edited at various times two Universalist papers, edited a scholarly journal which he had founded, edited the first American edition of a European work in religious history, and published a collection of psalms and hymns for Universalist use.[12] His major research contribution was a history of Universalism during the first six centuries of the Christian era which probably did more than anything else to establish the author's reputation as a Universalist scholar.

Hosea 2d's career as a writer had begun as a youth when he wrote, by his own admission, bad poetry. His first significant prose efforts appeared in 1820 in the *Universalist Magazine*. This had been established the previous year by his great-uncle for the purpose of expounding and defending Universalist principles and for publishing sermons, and it was the first Universalist paper regularly published in the United States. For four years (1822–26) Hosea 2d was co-editor, together with Hosea the elder and Thomas Whittemore. Hosea 2d's active mind was constantly at work planning projects of an historical bent which would shore up the foundations of Universalism. He hoped, for example, that someone would undertake to collect a Universalist theological library of primary sources. As it turned out, he became one of the organizers of the Universalist Historical Society at the General Convention in 1834, served as its first president, and was later corresponding secretary for the Society in Massachusetts.

In 1830 there existed over half a dozen Universalist serial publications, mostly in the form of the weekly newspapers so popular before the Civil War. The best known, and probably the most widely read, was the *Trumpet and Universalist Magazine,* published on Cornhill in Boston. Like so many similar publications, the *Trumpet* went through numerous changes of title and format after it had been started as the *Universalist Magazine* in 1819; it lasted for almost half a century. But something seemed lacking among denominational publications. There was no organ that served "as a safe depository for the more labored Essays, for systematic Disquisitions on doctrine, and for occasional Reviews of such works as are peculiarly interesting to Universalists." In short, a journal was needed to supplement existing publications and to

[12] The European work was J. C. L. Simonde de Sismondi's *History of the Crusades against the Albigenses in the Thirteenth Century* (Boston: B. B. Mussey, 1835).

traverse ground more esoteric and less popular than was covered in weekly newspapers or other publications for the family circle. The result was the *Universalist Expositor,* which made its first appearance in the summer of 1830. The character of the new publication was made clear in the first issue: It was to consist chiefly of "dissertations on points of Biblical Literature, critical interpretations of texts, explanations of Scriptural phrases and subjects; doctrinal Dissertations; and Expositions, both illustrative and historical, of Religious Truth in general." When occasion demanded, there might also be included reviews of religious works, "such Sermons as shall be judged of lasting as well as of immediate interest"; even "the embellishments of Poetry" would not be entirely neglected. Contributions were solicited, with the promise that as soon as the list of subscribers was sufficient, "a suitable reward" would be paid.

The man behind this experiment in scholarly publication was Hosea 2d. He felt certain that a bimonthly or quarterly journal was appropriate for a denomination that had been well established and was spreading with gratifying rapidity. The elder Ballou's name was carried as co-editor on the title page of the first volume, but it was Hosea 2d that carried the initial burden of the magazine. Appropriately enough, he wrote the first article, complete with extended footnotes.[13] Tucked away in the middle of the first issue was also a poem from his pen, inspired by a verse from Habakkuk. His other contribution to the first volume was an article on "Observance of Sunday among the Primitive Christians." Unfortunately, publication was suspended after the second volume for lack of patronage. Nothing daunted, Hosea 2d revived the journal as the *Expositor and Universalist Review* in 1833. A second revival became necessary in 1838, and this effort lasted only two years, making six volumes in all. Hosea 2d's ministerial colleagues seem to have been unprepared for the profundity of his scholarship. The launching in 1844 of the *Universalist Quarterly,* the lineal descendant of the *Expositor,* was more successful. This publication, of which

[13] "A Dissertation on the Phrase, Kingdom of Heaven, as used in the New Testament." His articles were the most fully documented of any to appear in the journal. He was also responsible for most of the book reviews, and it was evident that he read carefully the books he reviewed.

Hosea 2d was editor for twelve years, lasted thirty years beyond his death in 1861.

Through the columns of such newspapers and periodicals as have been mentioned can be traced the growing interest in and concern for education among Universalists. It was, for example, in the *Expositor* that a handful of persistent Universalists called for the elimination of sectarianism in the public schools and for augmented Universalist efforts to do something about the problem. Even more significant in many ways was the use of Universalist publications as a vehicle for advertising the need for an educated clergy and for the establishment of one or more institutions of higher learning under denominational sponsorship.

§ § §

The movement out of which Tufts College, as a liberal arts institution, was born, actually arose out of a demand for a theological school, although the two aims were often intertwined. In fact, Universalists were originally divided among themselves as to what kind of higher education to sponsor — literary or theological, or a combination. When the patronage of the denomination had been requested in 1819 for Nichols Academy, which was described as a "Seminary of Science" and a purely "Literary Institution," the hope was expressed that "whenever there shall arise a surplus income, it [would] be expended in the free education of young men, of indigent circumstances, but moral and pious habits, designing to enter the gospel ministry." But objections were immediately raised to such a proposal, and for over a quarter of a century Universalists debated the merits of providing formal theological training. The idea of a free education for ministerial candidates was thought undesirable for reasons of principle as well as economy, for it might attract unworthy candidates — those who lacked sincere religious convictions and were merely intrigued by the possibility of "getting something for nothing." But the obstacles persistently encountered were the apathy of the denomination and the stubborn prejudice against theological schools. The latter was particularly evident among the older generation, who were sensitive about sectarianism anyway, and who were sure that no formal theological training, Universalist or otherwise, could result in other than indoctrination in more or less undesirable dogmas.

At the 1833 meeting of the Connecticut State Convention, the Executive Committee unanimously disapproved the suggestion of establishing a theological school, on the grounds that such was "unnecessary, uncalled for, and useless — yea worse — opposed to the spirit and genius of the Gospel, at variance with the principles of our faith and most highly deleterious in its influence." Theological schools were condemned by one Universalist because the preachers thus trained "would not precisely resemble the Apostles" because they would not be coming directly from the workshops and the fields. Others were convinced that theological schools would probably be mismanaged anyway and would fall prey to the aggrandizing tendencies of self-seeking individuals; that they would somehow produce "clerical domination"; that they would make preaching a "trade." When the Southern Convention of Universalists met in Portsmouth, Virginia, in 1836, one of its principal accomplishments was to pass a resolution declaring that theological seminaries were "alike dangerous, inconsistent and inexpedient; equally injurious to the cause of pure religion, and destructive of Christian liberty."

No wonder Thomas Whittemore, outspoken champion of education in all its forms, wrote that getting Universalists to see the light was "almost altogether an *uphill* business." In his view the age of miracles had passed, whereby men were prepared for the ministry solely "by immediate communication from heaven"; in a later day it was recognized that "we must use human means, in hope that the divine blessing will render them successful." Hosea 2d was in favor of establishing theological institutions as necessary elements in professional preparation, but he sensed the strength of the opposition and tried to play the part of mediator and peacemaker in a situation which threatened to split the denomination. Although he could not help feeling "that the fears which many of our brethren entertain on this point are, to a great degree, unfounded in the nature of the case, and in the matter of historical fact," he cautioned the supporters not to "urge the measure in opposition to the wishes of others." Whatever other arguments may have been used to discourage the founding of theological schools, the recurrent theme, and probably the most telling criticism of the proposal, was that such institutions might develop a sophisticated intellectual aristocracy who would "become ashamed of the simple yet profound teachings of Jesus, and would become vain speculative philosophers." It was arguments like these that Universalist supporters of both theological and secular education had to overcome.

At first, it appeared that the opponents of theological schools, on one ground or another, would win the day, for efforts to establish such a school were halting and largely unsuccessful for many decades. Yet a start had to be made, and it came in 1826 with the recognition that some kind of formal education was requisite for the clergy. It took the form of a resolution offered by the General Convention "that no candidate for the ministry shall be entitled to a letter of fellowship, from any association in this connexion, until he shall have obtained a competent knowledge of the common branches of English Literature, and devoted, at least one year, exclusively, to the study of Theology." At the 1827 Convention, Hosea 2d was selected to head a committee to examine ministerial applicants "in secular and sacred learning . . . with special regard to their literary and theological requirements." This was an important step forward. But the next step turned out to have been manifestly premature, and it came to grief. A committee (of which Hosea 2d was a member) was appointed to report at the next session "the most practicable plan for establishing a Theological Seminary." Its report, made in 1828, was still to have a familiar ring ten years later: "An interesting discussion took place on this subject, which was discontinued without any resolution."

After three years of silence on the subject, the editor of the *Trumpet* raised the question again. He admitted that opposition was strong, and that the minimum sum needed to establish a theological school (first set at $20,000) was too great to be raised by a single individual. So, estimating that forty contributors were necessary, he offered to be one of the forty, provided thirty-nine others could be found. He recommended that tuition be charged and that "an academical department" might be opened to help defray expenses. He pointed out that young men who wished to prepare for the ministry were obliged to do so "under great disadvantage" and was positive that many were discouraged or actually prevented from "coming forward" because no training institution existed. Further, Whittemore felt that it would be much better to invest money permanently "in land, and brick walls, and a library for the benefit of the ministry than to contribute to the thousand schemes for raising money to be sent to Asia for the propagation of orthodoxy."

At this point a leader in the movement to establish a theological school stepped forward in the person of Thomas Jefferson Sawyer, dedicated Universalist clergyman and educator, destined to be the longtime head of the Clinton Liberal Institute, operator of a small theological school of his own, and finally a professor in the Tufts Divinity School. At the General Convention in 1835 he offered a resolution that "the propriety and expediency of establishing a Theological Seminary" be recommended to the consideration of the denomination at large. As a result, the various local and regional associations were requested to instruct their delegates to the next General Convention as to "the views and wishes of our brethren throughout the Union." A lively discussion ensued at the 1835 Convention before Sawyer's resolution was finally adopted, and there was considerable "disapprobation" of the whole scheme. The Boston Association and numerous other lay and clerical bodies acceded to the request and debated the issue with more or less enthusiasm. Consent was considerably short of unanimous, for opponents raised their voices in almost every organization. The best the General Convention could do in 1836 was recommend "a continued consideration of the subject" and urge that some means of raising the standards of ministerial qualifications be found so that an "enlightened and educated" as well as a "virtuous" clergy could be assured. The Boston Association, under Hosea 2d's leadership, cautiously approved the idea of one or more theological schools, and the wording of their resolution — ambivalent to say the least — was adopted substantially by the Massachusetts State Convention in 1837 but only after "much discussion." The resolution acknowledged that "schools for instruction in those branches of learning proper for young men entering the ministry" were desirable but would be established only if, when, and where "circumstances render it convenient."

After this inconclusive result, Thomas Whittemore became increasingly irritated with the do-nothing policies of his denomination and used the columns of his *Trumpet* for the next two years to prod his co-religionists. He argued that the Universalists had fallen behind the times, and tried to shame them into action by pointing out that "almost all denominations . . . are awake to this subject, except Universalists. It is a deep disgrace to us, that we are doing *nothing*, just *nothing,* on this important matter." The Methodists, for example, were forging ahead with dramatic rapidity. They had already established four literary institutions in New England and had announced a plan to establish a Wesleyan Institute in Massachusetts for clerical training to supplement their other schools. He also pointed to the success of the Baptist theological school in Newton, Massachusetts. The time had long since passed, wrote Whittemore, when Universalists need be deluded into believing that one or more theological schools would mean the creation of "a whole host of Universalist professors, — then . . . synods, and at last Universalist bishops, and a Universalist Pope." Universalists in the 1830's were living "in another age, — a different age, — an age of more light, — of greater literature, — of a higher standard of preaching."

Whittemore's agitation began to bear fruit. Letters trickled into the *Trumpet* office agreeing with his contentions. But even though more Universalists came to support the idea of theological seminaries in principle, there were serious differences of opinion over the optimum number, location, and endowment. He optimistically suggested that $10,000 would be sufficient to establish such a school, but many felt that even that modest figure was excessive. One Universalist suggested that the training facilities of other denominations be used, in order to save money. The Congregational school at Andover, Massachusetts, and the Unitarian school in Cambridge were proposed as possibilities. After all, the fact that most were "orthodox" was of no moment, for "the student must learn those very doctrines and come in daily contact with men professing them; he may as well learn them there as elsewhere. And if a student cannot pass that ordeal and come out unscorched, he can poorly defend the faith when he mingles with the world." But Whittemore discarded this plan immediately; it was a "wild scheme," fraught with danger. "If it be necessary for us to have our own Sunday Schools for our children, it is no less necessary to have our own Institution for the preparation of candidates for the ministry."

Another alternative was to establish a theological school, or at least endow a professorship of theology at an existing school such as Westbrook Seminary or Clinton Liberal Institute. The non-religious character of Clinton did not preclude the founding of a separate school there, specifically for preparation of clergymen. Many Universalists saw nothing wrong in continuing the long-standing system of apprenticeship under an ordained minister who could supplement informal teaching with classes conducted in his home. Sawyer replied to this by arguing that both self-education and the apprenticeship system were clearly inadequate. Not only was the pastor unable to spend sufficient time in systematic instruction, but he did not have the library resources indispensable to a well-educated minister. Universalists must realize that "theological knowledge is to be attained by laborious and painstaking study like all other kinds of knowledge. . . . A clergyman needs a good general education, and besides, a thorough professional one." Even with all the advantages of a liberal education as a base, and under the most favorable circumstances, three years was not too long to devote to formal theological training. Although Sawyer set his sights high, he recognized the practical limitations under which the denomination would be working and so was willing to start anywhere—so long as a start was made. To those who complained of the long preparatory period needed and of the great expense entailed in formal instruction, the reply was that, even though only ten out of one hundred might be able to attend, the school would still be worthwhile in view of the long-run advantage of having it. Further, if subscriptions could be raised, with pledges of $5.00 and up, a theological school would in no way saddle the denomination with a great burden.

In the meantime, the need for some kind of facilities became more and more pressing. So many young men wished to receive instruction under Hosea 2d that in 1840 he was forced to establish stated times throughout the year when persons could be admitted and taught in classes rather than individually. He required formal application and testimonials of satisfactory moral and religious character. He offered Biblical training, with either a Greek or English basis. Tuition, board, and washing in Medford were set at $3.25 a week, payable at the end of each quarter.

As the discussions continued, and as it became clearer than ever that the leaders in the movement were determined to set up a theological school of some sort, somewhere, upstate New York and the Boston area became the two logical choices. It was the Massachusetts State Convention that took the first step to bring a school nearer reality. Calvin Gardiner of Waterville, Maine, had proposed early in 1839 that a special meeting be called in Boston to consider setting up a school. The result was a meeting of the Convention in June of that year which was attended by approximately one-half of the one hundred Universalist clergy in the state and made such a school its principal item of business. The outcome was not only a resolution favoring a theological school in Massachusetts but the appointment of a committee to report a concrete plan at the next session. Quite appropriately, Thomas Whittemore was one of the committee.

The 1840 State Convention took a further step forward. It followed the recommendation of the committee previously appointed, and it authorized the creation of a Board of Trustees, which was to select a site, raise funds, erect a suitable building, appoint a principal and other officers, hold the property in trust, and generally take charge of the school.[14] The committee chosen to appoint the Trustees included the two well-known Ballous — Hosea the elder and Hosea 2d. The latter served as clerk of the committee and was probably responsible for the set of rules drawn up to govern the school. But even before that had been done, a prominent Universalist in Charlestown came forward with an offer to make a gift of ten acres of land which he held in Medford and Somerville. Because of the site selected, the institution was to be known as the "Walnut Hill Evangelical Seminary." The Board of Trustees was to consist only of men who subscribed to the Universalist Profession of Faith adopted in 1803 and known as the Winchester Confession. Five of the nine Trustees reappeared on the Tufts Board of Trustees some ten years later; Oliver Dean, president of the Walnut Hill Trustees, was also the first president of the Tufts Trustees. There was no requirement that the Trustees be clergymen. The Board was to be self-perpetuating, and its members were to hold office for life except in cases of "voluntary resignation, immoral conduct, mental imbecility, or want of belief, or interest" in Universalist principles. All financial affairs were to be audited by a committee of the State Convention.

[14] Unless otherwise noted, the material about the proposed seminary is derived from the Trustee records in the possession of the Universalist Historical Society.

The Trustees held their first meeting in January 1841, and within the next few weeks had committed themselves to raising $50,000 by subscription. Calvin Gardiner, strong advocate of Universalist education, agreed to act as agent to obtain subscriptions. In order to assure as broad a patronage as possible, provisions were made for Trustee representation from every state in New England, and two from New York. At the last meeting the Board held, in May 1841, Trustees had been nominated from every state. Sawyer had been asked to serve as a representative from New York and to recommend one other. He managed to find one individual who would accept, but declined himself to serve because, among other reasons, he was "about to embark on a grand enterprise in our own state — the establishment of a College or University that will successfully compete with any institution in this Empire State." (Sawyer was referring to a plan to turn Clinton Liberal Institute into a collegiate institution. The plan never materialized.) This, he thought, would require all of his time and energy to carry through.

Gardiner, who had had no experience in fund-raising, undertook his task with some trepidation. Long before the summer of 1841 was over, he was discouraged. He wrote Whittemore, secretary of the Trustees, that "I do not see the interest manifested in the subject, which the circumstances of the case seem to me to require." In October the same report was made; Gardiner was sure that "the public mind did not seem to be properly prepared" for his services. Because there was "too much indifference among the great mass of the people," he requested that he be relieved of his assignment. Gardiner and the Trustees had cause for discouragement, for the previous month the support hoped for from the General Convention had not been forthcoming. The best the delegates would do was pass a vague and noncommittal resolution "that the interests of the denomination seem to render it important that Institutions be established for the purpose of assisting young men, who contemplate entering the gospel ministry. . . ."

The active little band of supporters and Trustees, with one notable exception, worked hard to get the institution off the drawing board and onto Walnut Hill. Each of the officers of the Trustees pledged $1,000. B. B. Mussey, a Boston publisher, also pledged $1,000. Whittemore kept the readers of the *Trumpet* posted on every development and pushed the project as much as possible. With one eye on the proposed seminary and the other on good business, he pledged an additional $1,000. He announced that if interested individuals would increase the subscription list of his newspaper by six hundred after January 1, 1841, the *Trumpet* would donate the fees from the new subscribers. When a pledge of $100 was made by "a young man of modest circumstances" in Philadelphia who averred that he would pay it, if necessary, "by abstaining from a portion of my daily food, and clothing myself with homespun," Whittemore lauded his zeal and indicated that if all showed the same enthusiasm, the subscription would be raised in no time at all. Whittemore considered the very honor of the denomination at stake and insisted that, if the seminary were not established, Universalists would be forced to blush with shame and would lay themselves open to "reproach and sarcasm" heaped on them by their critics. Although Hosea 2d served in no official capacity after he had helped select the Trustees and had drawn up the rules and regulations, he undertook to raise subscriptions in Medford. He could contribute little if any himself, for his salary was only $600 a year, but he managed to solicit $1,200 in a few days. Whittemore pointedly remarked that three Universalist Societies in Boston paid their ministers $1,200 apiece, and each should easily be able to raise $4,000. There is no evidence that any of them contributed to the subscription.

There were scattered expressions of approval of the project from various Societies. Circulars (some of them written by Hosea 2d) were published in Universalist newspapers, and the supporters organized meetings in a few towns. Hosea 2d and others addressed a group in Worcester, where $700 was subscribed. Supporters were also urged to hold "auxiliary meetings" in adjoining states to awaken interest. It was at the Worcester meeting that the first (and only) references were made to the curriculum and conduct of the proposed school. The audience was assured that complete academic freedom for the student would prevail, and that, while he would be given assistance in the acquisition of knowledge of the Scriptures, "no student shall be bound to receive the opinions of his teacher without a solemn conviction of their truth; nor held under obligation to adopt any creed of human origin which may be offered for his consideration." The course of study was to include

"Moral Philosophy, the art of Composition and of Speaking, and every branch of study which may be deemed necessary to the student, that he may be a man thoroughly furnished for the work of a Christian minister."

Throughout the campaign, one powerful dissenting voice was heard. Although Hosea Ballou the elder was on the Walnut Hill Board of Trustees, he remained dubious to the very end about the merits of the whole idea. He insisted on dredging up all the well-worn objections that had been heard from the very first time a theological school had been proposed. He engaged in a prolonged newspaper debate with Calvin Gardiner in the columns of the *Trumpet* and certainly did the cause no good. What was wrong, asked "Father" Ballou, as he was solemnly and affectionately called by his many disciples, with the preaching of the so-called unlettered earlier generations of Universalist preachers? What evidence was there that formal theological training would produce better Christians than the old apprenticeship system? It might be conceded that "solid learning" was an advantage to the minister, but this was likely to be overbalanced by the danger inherent in all theological schools — that they were likely to inculcate false doctrines, and by their very existence impose a rigidity on theological training that was not consonant with Universalist permissiveness and freedom of conscience. Gardiner's well-reasoned argument that nearly all existing institutions to which Universalists could go were under religious influences unacceptable to Universalist sentiments apparently made no impression on the venerable Ballou; neither did Gardiner's argument that undue reliance on past tradition would make the denomination static and out of tune with the times. At the last meeting held to drum up interest in the seminary, in Boston in October 1841, Hosea 2d spoke fervently in favor. His great-uncle, on the other hand, "suggested certain queries, which will doubtless be profitable to reflect upon." When at the same meeting E. H. Chapin, a strong advocate of the school, gave the principal address and called for general donations to the cause, the elder Ballou rose to say that times were hard and that it was "an unfavorable period to commence the undertaking."

There is no way, of course, of knowing how influential Ballou the elder was in killing the plan for the Walnut Hill Evangelical

Seminary. But there can be no doubt that many shared his reluctance to embark on such an experiment. Heard again and again was the argument that the setting up of a theological school would be undemocratic, for it would create an overweening clerical class elevated above the laity. "Give the people the New Testament and they can learn from that all theology necessary for them to know without having to pay a self-created aristocratic priesthood." Certainly the views of the beloved "elder statesman" in the denomination were not to be taken lightly. The State Convention in 1841 was made so aware of the strength of his opposition that it adopted a resolution insisting that the arguments would not deter the proponents of a theological school from pursuing their goal.

In any case, after more than three years of travail, the infant refused to be born. Less than one-fifth of the subscription was ever pledged. The *Universalist Register* in 1842, and again in 1843, reported that "measures are still pursued to establish a Theological School, at Walnut Hill, in Medford," but no evidence was presented that any progress was really being made. When a report was submitted on the state of Universalism in Massachusetts in 1844, the academy in Reading was its only educational institution, and "our Theological Seminary is *not* yet."

When Gardiner had agreed to serve as agent for the seminary, he had asked the Trustees to take a long, hard look at the project, to be sure that the "signs of the times" were favorable for such an enterprise. If it were to be successful, it would have to represent the prompt, energetic, and united effort of its supporters. The work must not be left solely to the agent. Ministers throughout the denomination would have to be "active and persevering in the business of endeavor to prepare the minds of the community." The Universalist public was obviously not yet prepared. Indifference and apathy, skepticism and absolute opposition, had taken their toll, at least in Massachusetts. It appeared that if a theological school were ever to be established, the next move would have to come from the New York Universalists.

Sawyer left New York City in the summer of 1845 to take over the principalship of Clinton Liberal Institute. At the same time, he announced the opening of a theological school on his own responsibility. It was to be operated under his supervision by four clergymen and was to be separate from Clinton and not a department of the Institute. At the General Convention in 1845, the usual resolutions were adopted favoring the idea of a theological school, but this time they called specifically for support of Sawyer's undertaking. An endowment of $10,000 was sought. Simultaneously the decision was made to turn Clinton into a college, with an endowment of $50,000. Hosea 2d found himself deeply involved in all this activity. It was he who drew up the resolutions for the 1845 Convention and chaired a committee which recommended that an agent be appointed to raise funds for both projects. A fourteen-man Board of Trustees (seven laymen and seven clergymen) was selected for the theological school at the New York State Convention. All were from New York State. Sawyer explained that this situation had come about for two reasons: the practical problem of distance, when it became necessary to convene; and the failure of the New England Universalists to do anything about a school. New Yorkers had to take the initiative.

Sawyer soon realized (by the fall of 1846) that he had taken on too much; the duties of supervising both the Institute and the theological school were more than one man could handle. He saw no course but to resign the principalship of the theological school as soon as a successor could be found. The Trustees immediately selected Hosea 2d; if he accepted, he was to take office as soon as the funds could be raised for his support. Otis A. Skinner was to be in charge of money-raising.

In the midst of this renewed effort to get a theological school under way, preparations were being made for the General Convention to be held in New York City in the fall of 1847. A mass meeting was announced, to be held in Boston in May to stir up enthusiasm for the Clinton Theological School. Hosea 2d had declined to serve as its principal; after using his greatest persuasive powers, he was able to get Sawyer to continue, at least temporarily. In the face of the incessant talk about the problems of the theological school, many feared that what to them was the equally important task of establishing a college might be neglected. It was such men as Calvin Gardiner and Hosea Ballou 2d who were instrumental in keeping the idea of a college alive. And one of the most important accomplishments of the 1847 General Convention was to make the creation of a theological school and of a college separate projects. The question of whether the two endeavors should be combined had

31

agitated and divided Universalists for years. Perhaps, however, some lessons had been learned from the abortive attempts to establish a theological school that would make the project of launching a college more of a certainty.

2. "That Bleak Hill Over in Medford"

THE MOVEMENT that eventually resulted in the establishment of a Universalist college followed much the same pattern that was seen in the evolution of academies and the attempts to set up a theological school before 1850: a slow beginning, many haltings and delays, the overcoming of apathy and opposition, and initial failures but ultimate success of sorts. The first attempt to found a college — not alone for the ministry but for those who desired for themselves and their posterity a liberal training in the arts and sciences — dates from 1841. The leadership was not that of one man but of several. In the matter of establishing educational institutions in general, Hosea 2d, Thomas Whittemore, and T. J. Sawyer have been called the "three musketeers." It would be manifestly unfair to his contemporaries to say that Hosea 2d was himself responsible for what became Tufts College. The other members of the trio, and literally dozens more, certainly deserve much credit. But it can honestly be stated that, among Universalist leaders, Hosea 2d had the clearest vision of the educational needs and opportunities of his denomination and of how they could best contribute within the larger framework of American culture. Whittemore, in his blunt and forceful way, assessed Hosea 2d's contributions quite correctly, if not in the most polished literary style. "Dr. Ballou took an active part in preparing the Universalists to get up a literary institution among themselves. He knew they were able to do it in a pecuniary point of view; and that they would do it, when they saw their duty plainly."

For over twenty years Hosea 2d devoted much of his energies to convincing Universalists that only a well-conceived system of schools and seminaries, competently operated, adequately financed, and strategically located, could satisfactorily serve both the de-

33

nomination and a larger public.[1] He served in some capacity, beginning in 1827, on every important committee appointed by the Universalist Conventions, both state and general, that dealt with the
educational needs of the denomination. By the 1840's he had seen
Universalist academies established in considerable numbers, but
often supported with little more than enthusiasm; he had watched
some languish and close their doors. In 1846 he acted as chairman
of a committee to solicit subscriptions for the $50,000 to transform
Clinton Liberal Institute into a college or university and watched
sorrowfully the failure of the attempt. He had wisely stayed in
Medford when not even sufficient funds could be raised to pay him
the salary of $800 he had been promised as principal of the theologi-
cal school at Clinton.

Hosea 2d made his first extended plea for the establishment of
schools in the columns of his *Expositor and Universalist Review* in
1839. It was considered so eloquent and so well reasoned that one
subscriber to the *Trumpet* wrote that the article should be "graved
on the heart of every Universalist." Sufficient momentum was generated by 1841, through the efforts of Hosea 2d and men like him,
to take a first step toward creating a college. After the General Convention had been adjourned that year, those interested in education remained to organize and to see what could be done about a
college. Hosea 2d was on the committee that drafted the resolutions
that were adopted. The preamble stated the case succinctly: "It is
well known that the Academies and Colleges in our country are
generally under the control or influence of sects opposed to the
cause in which we are engaged; it is highly desirable that our denomination, now so rapidly growing, should be provided with institutions under its own care, for the instruction of our youth in the
higher branches of literature and science." After determining to
carry this out by "immediate, concerted, and efficient action," an
eleven-man committee, representing Universalists from all over the
United States, was directed to make recommendations regarding
both literary and theological institutions. News of this provoked
widespread discussion. Most of the reaction to the idea of opening a
college was at first negative; the possibility of a theological school
seems to have been received more favorably. The objections to es-

[1] His personal correspondence, much of which is in the Tufts University
Archives, is full of his hopes and plans for education.

tablishing a college or university were quite nicely summed up by one critic in the following words: "The proper sphere of a University lies in the department of general science and learning, and it should be the organ of no religious tenets, nor sectarian influences and prejudices. It ought never to be established or managed by any religious denomination *as such,* but rather by those who are interested in the cause of science and letters, of all denominations, for thus the influence of sectarian motives and feelings would be neutralized." The same writer offered a second argument: there were too many "puny Universities" already. "We should only create a feeble institution, doomed to languish on through a life-long consumption, and die at last a lingering, painful death." The most practical solution was to support "the best existing institutions" rather than to found new ones. Universalists in New England were urged "to direct their patronage and exert their influence" on Harvard. The learning of two centuries had been accumulated there; moreover, sectarian influences were "studiously excluded. There is no way in which we could do half so much service to the cause of learning in our country as by contributing to render this institution still more adequate to its purpose, and inspiring into it a more liberal, republican and earnest spirit."

The Harvard University of the 1840's had long since lost its "orthodox" Congregational inheritance, and for much of the early nineteenth century both the Overseers and the Corporation were dominated by Unitarians. The Harvard Corporation, comprising the President, Treasurer, and five other Fellows, served as an executive committee, responsible for actual operation of the institution. The Board of Overseers, a large body consisting of the Governor, the Council, the Senate, the Speaker of the House, and thirty others (fifteen clergymen and fifteen laymen) served as the equivalent of a Board of Trustees. Suspicious as they then were of Unitarians, Universalists considered them less objectionable than the "orthodox," and hence more acceptable than Congregationalists, Episcopalians, or the like.

It had not always been so. According to a tradition in the Ballou family, Hosea 2d had been destined for some New England college, but when Grandfather Benjamin Ballou heard of this in 1812, he warned the family, with vivid examples, that the youth would be exposed to the proselyting activities of other denominations, which in his estimation would have calamitous results. Hosea 2d never found out what might have been in store for him as a candidate for an earned degree at one of these institutions, but his contact with Harvard in later years was frequent and close. Much of the research for his *Ancient History of Universalism* was done in the Harvard College Library, and he counted Josiah Quincy, president of Harvard from 1829 to 1846, and a Unitarian, among his most congenial friends. In 1843 Hosea 2d was given an opportunity to gain valuable academic and administrative experience, for he was elected to the Harvard Board of Overseers to replace William Ellery Channing, who had died the previous year. Hosea 2d performed his duties so faithfully that he served, by re-election, for fifteen years and through four Harvard presidential administrations. He resigned in 1858 because his other duties, including the presidency of Tufts, had become so great. In 1844 and 1845 he received additional recognition from Harvard. In the former year he was one of five (including the distinguished botanist Asa Gray) to receive an honorary Master of Arts degree. A year later, he received the honorary degree of Doctor of Sacred Theology (referred to interchangeably in the records as Doctor of Divinity). These honors had a double significance. They signalized the unusual attainments of a man who had never had the opportunity for a formal college education but who in learning, experience, and character had won a deserved reputation outside Universalist circles. The bestowal of the honorary Divinity degree for the first time on a member of the Universalist clergy also signified the increasing respect for liberal religion. Within a few years Harvard conferred several honorary degrees on Universalists. Otis A. Skinner and Benjamin Franklin Tweed, who was to be on the original faculty of Tufts College, were among the recipients.

While Hosea 2d was being honored by Harvard, it appeared that his denomination had again come to a standstill in its efforts on behalf of higher education. Six years elapsed before activity was resumed. But at least something tangible was to come out of the efforts of 1847. The impetus came from a decision by Sawyer to thrash out once and for all the whole problem of Universalist-sponsored schools. None of the projects that had so far been started had really amounted to anything. The plan to turn Clinton Liberal Institute into a college had evaporated. Even the attempt to raise

$10,000 to endow a theological school at Clinton had been an abysmal failure; and Sawyer, with virtually no salary and no real facilities at all, struggled along with a few students whom he attempted to train for the ministry. He and others equally dissatisfied with the lack of progress determined that something had to be done. In April 1847, there appeared over Sawyer's signature a call for an Educational Convention to meet in New York the next month, several weeks before the General Convention to be held in the same city. The circular was as forthright as Sawyer could make it. It posed three questions that demanded answers. Did Universalists need a well-endowed college and theological seminary? If so, where should they be located? And how could sufficient funds be raised? If this effort were not successful, then the denomination might as well surrender "to hopeless ignorance and stupidity for another generation."

Sawyer's circular had the effect intended. The largest group interested in education that had yet assembled duly met in New York and answered the first question with a rousing affirmative. It was resolved, first, "that it is expedient that means be at once devised for the establishment of a College to meet the wants of our denomination." It was further resolved that the college be located in the valley of the Hudson or the Mohawk river, the exact location to be left to a Board of Trustees to be selected by a five-man committee of which Hosea 2d was a member. Fifteen Trustees were promptly nominated while the Convention was in session. They represented eight states, and included Calvin Gardiner of Maine, T. J. Sawyer of New York, and B. B. Mussey and Thomas Whittemore of Massachusetts. Besides the New England area and New York, Pennsylvania and Ohio were represented. The intent was obvious: to draw on the greatest possible potential resources and at the same time make the proposed institution more than a New England effort. The Convention further proceeded to appoint a committee (again including Hosea 2d) to obtain an agent to secure funds. The target, $100,000, was set by Hosea 2d, who had already seen too many Universalist efforts come to grief because of inadequate financing. The subscriptions would be binding only if the total amount were pledged. A resolution was also offered to found and finance, as a separate entity, a permanent theological school, and a committee was set up to solicit reactions from the denomination at large and to recommend the best method of raising funds for that specific purpose. It was hoped that in this way the two educational projects could be kept sufficiently distinct to avoid the difficulties of both confusion and diffusion of effort that had plagued the denomination before. The Massachusetts State Convention endorsed both resolutions but agreed to concentrate on the accomplishment of the first goal, namely, the creation of a college. It was largely the efforts of this organization that reversed the original expectation of the Educational Convention that the theological school would be located in eastern New England and the college in western Massachusetts or New York State.

The General Convention met in New York in September 1847, and the keynote address that would make this meeting so important in the history of the denomination was delivered by Hosea 2d in the customary form of a sermon. It was a sober and lengthy presentation (almost an hour and a half) delivered to an overflow audience at the Orchard Street Church. The Biblical text selected, from the Book of Luke, was intended as a challenge: "Unto whomsoever much is given, of him shall much be required; and to whom men have committed much, of him shall much be required; and to whom men have committed much, of him they will ask the more." Appropriately, the Rev. Dr. Ballou entitled his subject "The Responsibilities of Universalists." Listeners acknowledged the address to have been one of the most powerful ever delivered by the quiet and scholarly clergyman.

Among the themes he pursued was the need for more serious attention to education than had so far been manifested by Universalists. Further neglect, he said, would be most dangerous. Ballou told his hearers, almost plaintively, that "I once indulged the confident expectation that I should live to see Universalists doing their duty, in this cause — founding well-endowed Academies, and at least one College, placed on a permanent basis. I have so long solaced myself with the anticipation of sharing in the work, that it is hard . . . to part with all hope. But the night is coming down, in which no man can work. — The shadows of age are already on these eyes; and nothing is done." His closing remarks were coldly factual. He reminded his audience that the Universalists had been an organized body for well over half a century, with 18 state conventions, 80 associations, and 700 clergymen, and an estimated strength of 700,000 souls. It was high time that the denomination took positive action to aid intellectual progress.[2]

Following the regular sessions of the Convention, a special session was devoted to a review and discussion of the decision made at the Educational Convention the previous May to proceed with plans for a college. They were confirmed with a minimum of debate and disagreement.

After the Convention was adjourned, the next task was to select an agent and to start a subscription list. While Universalists waited for the announcement that an agent had been appointed, the supporters of the college plan kept the advantages of such an institution constantly before their public. They returned to the durable contention that all existing colleges were under "strong sectarian influences." For this reason the students, exposed as they were to revival meetings and other devices for proselyting, tended to become either bigots or infidels. At the same time Universalists staunchly asserted the right of any sect, faith, or denomination (including themselves, of course) to establish their own schools. They came to the defense of the College of the Holy Cross, which had been founded in 1843 and which until 1865 vainly sought to be incorporated as a degree-granting institution by the state legislature. In 1849 such a petition was rejected on the ground that the legislature would not incorporate an educational institution for the benefit of any one religious group. Universalists challenged this reasoning. Existing colleges, such as Harvard, Amherst, and Williams, were certainly sectarian in both origin and character; the legislature had better reform these three if the lawmakers were going to be consistent. Universalists had "no more fellowship for the Papal religion distinctively than for Calvinism, but if sectarian Colleges are to be allowed, then the Catholics have as good a claim to one as any other sect."

Several months went by before any news was received that an agent had been selected. Whittemore and Sawyer chastised their fellow Universalists for their inactivity. The former complained that so much had been said about the plans for a college and so little had

[2] The sermon was reprinted in the *Trumpet,* Vol. 20 (October 2, 1847), pp. 61–62; and in Hosea Ballou 2d, *Counsel and Encouragement* (Boston: Universalist Publishing House, 1866), pp. 382–407. The original manuscript is in the Tufts Archives.

been actually accomplished that he was going to refuse to publish *anything* about it until some concrete action had been taken. Sawyer expressed the sanguine belief that, if a determined effort were made, sufficient funds could be raised within a month. In 1848 the announcement was finally made that Otis A. Skinner (who previously was to have raised money for Clinton) had been employed as agent, and that he would receive nothing for his services unless the $100,000 were fully subscribed. No time limit was set (fortunately, as it turned out), but Skinner immediately set to work. Even so, it was almost three years before his mission was accomplished. An occasional notice would appear in Universalist newspapers that he was in some town or village in New England, but only fragmentary news came out of his travels until late in 1849 and early in 1850.

Sawyer and Hosea 2d watched every development closely, exchanging letters sometimes as often as two or three times a week between Clinton and Medford. Sawyer was discouraged; he wrote Hosea 2d that Universalists would probably have to chalk up still another failure. Hosea 2d tried to bolster his colleague's sagging morale. On the last day of 1849 he wrote his friend in New York State that "as for the College, Brother Skinner has got on to the last $25,000; and this he will obtain, and no mistake." A few days later he assured Sawyer that "we shall have a College yet, and we shall slowly grow into a well informed and cultivated people, though not until after a good many temporary relapses, that are yet to come. I think, however, that we have already sowed our worst crop of wild oats." But even Hosea 2d had doubts at times. He too became discouraged, although he usually managed to retain his dry and puckish sense of humor. "I have often had the hypochondria . . . when observing the practical indifference of our folks with respect to education, their contempt of systematic culture, their magnetic attraction to foolish hobby-horses. I have spent half my life thinking that I was a gone goose."

Until the spring of 1851, Universalists had to be satisfied with occasional tantalizing notices from the agent. He had had moderate success in Chicopee, Massachusetts; he had received pledges of $1,009 in Nashua, New Hampshire; prospects were still bright, and before long he hoped to begin collections. In the summer of 1850 he reported to the New Hampshire State Convention that he had secured pledges of $90,000. Then for a six-month period nothing was heard at all of fund-raising activities, and the *Trumpet* office was deluged with inquiries. Skinner was urged to make a public report and remove the aura of mystery that seemed to surround his activities. The good news was finally announced. Skinner gave public notice in April that he was ready to collect the subscriptions pledged for the college. He confessed that the last $10,000 had been the hardest to obtain and that some skeptical souls had promised to pledge only *after* collections had actually begun. Skinner also admitted that, as a matter of fact, he was still actually $3,000 short of the goal but would pledge the rest himself, confident that others would contribute so that he would not be out of pocket. The goal had been reached, it seemed. One jubilant correspondent in the *Trumpet* wrote: "The great work which has, heretofore, filled so many minds with anxiety, and some with much doubt, has been nearly accomplished. So nearly, indeed, that we can say beyond reasonable peradventure, the WE ARE TO HAVE A COLLEGE!"

In accordance with a call from the Executive Committee of the temporary Board of Trustees created at the 1847 Convention, a meeting of the subscribers was arranged in Boston for September 1851, timed so that it coincided with the Annual General Convention. The Convention, the largest in the history of the denomination, was attended by 220 clergy and "many hundreds" of laymen. It was quite evident that the possibility of actually establishing a college occupied a prominent place in the minds of those present. Skinner reported that he had succeeded in obtaining the subscriptions, and the Executive Committee assured themselves that the terms had been complied with. It was ascertained that $60,000 had been subscribed unconditionally and was immediately collectible. Of the remainder, a bond promising $20,000 after his death had been provided by "a wealthy individual in the City of Boston" who turned out to be Sylvanus Packard, one of the most generous benefactors the College was to have. He agreed to pay $1,000 annually during his lifetime on condition that at least $50,000 of subscriptions had been paid in. The remaining pledge was in the form of a deed to a parcel of twenty acres of land valued at $20,000 and straddling the towns of Medford and Somerville. Those who remembered the earlier attempt to establish Walnut Hill Evangelical

Seminary recognized both the location and the name of the donor
— Charles Tufts.

The college would not have been possible if any of the pledges
had not been made, large or small. But the backbone of the subscriptions was the contributions of dozens of Universalists who had
just a little to give but who wanted to do their share. Although
there were few donations of $1,000 or more, the greatest number
were below $100. Many people gave as little as $5.00. The original
plan had been to have one agent do the collecting, but there were
so many small donors scattered over such a wide area that Skinner
finally had to obtain assistance. Authorized agents, whose names
were announced in Universalist newspapers, were equipped with
printed receipt forms signed in advance by Skinner. Occasionally,
a touch of humor was associated with the collections. One donor,
who had promised to give $100 for each of his nephews, arranged
that each youngster would hand his allotted share to the collector
when he came around. The plan was carried out in good faith, except that between the time of the pledge and the collection another
nephew had been born; so the uncle gave an additional $100.
When the collector arrived, even the three-week-old nephew was
clutching a 100-dollar bill in his hand.

The subscribers who met in Boston that September day in
1851 had a long and important agenda. After it was determined
that they would "establish a college with all convenient dispatch,"
the subscribers made arrangements to nominate a Board of Trustees to replace the one created in 1847, and to obtain an act of incorporation from the state legislature. The new Trustees were
empowered by the subscribers to select a site and to draw up the
necessary rules for governing the new institution. A slate of twenty-
three Trustees representing nine states was duly nominated "with
great unanimity." Less than half (nine) were clergymen.

Probably the best-known member of the Board of Trustees selected in 1851 was Phineas Taylor Barnum, who had already
achieved considerable fame as a showman. Barnum was never formally a member of any church, but it was "well known," according
to Barnum himself, "that my sympathies are with the Universalists"
and that they deserved support. He let it be known on more than
one occasion that he was once imprisoned for defending religious
liberty with such vigor that some of his remarks were considered

libelous by certain Connecticut judges of less liberal religious persuasion.[3] At the time of his election as a Trustee Barnum was a very busy man. He operated out of his Connecticut headquarters of "Iranistan," the pseudo-Moorish palace near Bridgeport from which he commuted daily to New York. Besides his "American Museum" in Boston, he owned a "Travelling Menagerie"; managed the Phillips Patent Fire Annihilator Company For The United States; and served as president of both the Poquonock Bank in Bridgeport and the Fairfield Agricultural Society. He was currently engaged in "getting up an immense Panorama" of the Crystal Palace Exhibition of the World's Fair celebration in London. It was asserted that his life had already "been written in a dozen languages."[4] Barnum paid close attention to Universalist affairs. When the announcement had been made that the General Convention was to meet in Boston in 1851, with charactertisic showmanship he suggested that the sessions be held under a large tent in the center of Boston Common.

Many of the names of the other Trustees were already familiar to most Universalists, if not to the larger world. Calvin Gardiner, Benjamin B. Mussey, Oliver Dean, Otis A. Skinner, Sylvanus Packard, Thomas Whittemore, Hosea Ballou 2d, and T. J. Sawyer had been leaders for many years.[5]

[3] Barnum was a frequent contributor to Universalist newspapers, including the *Trumpet,* and often wrote under pseudonyms that were complete transparencies.

[4] The latter statement was made in a lengthy biographical sketch in the *Trumpet* signed "One Who Knows." Anyone familiar with any of the numerous editions of Barnum's autobiography can identify the author of the *Trumpet* article without undue effort.

[5] The remaining original Trustees were Israel Washburn (Orono, Me.), T. J. Greenwood (Dover, N.H.), L. C. Browne (Nashua, N.H.), Eli Ballou (Montpelier, Vt.), John Chase (Chicopee, Mass.), Christopher Robinson (Woonsocket, R.I.), Thomas Crane (New York City), Caleb Barstow (Buffalo, N.Y.), Josiah Barber (Auburn, N.Y.), John Hollister (Brooklyn, N.Y.), Charles H. Rogers (Philadelphia, Pa.), John Galbraith (Erie, Pa.), and John A. Gurley (Cincinnati, Ohio). Some were dropped when the Board of Trustees was reorganized in 1852; some played no important role on the Board; a few were prominent because of activities not related directly to the college (such as Israel Washburn, governor of Maine); and a scattering of others, such as Rev. T. J. Greenwood, were later to become closely associated with the affairs of the college.

The new Trustees promptly undertook the tasks assigned them by the subscribers. The first was to select a location. Theoretically, several sites were possible, and originally the plan had been to give every person who subscribed $10 to the college one vote on the choice. However, the decision of the subscribers to make the selection a responsibility of the Trustees changed the situation. This in no way precluded an extended discussion about the matter within the denomination, and some of the arguments for or against one location or another, or for a rural or an urban setting, shed considerable light on mid-nineteenth-century conceptions of the role of a college and its responsibility to its constituency.

Some thought that it made no difference at all where the institution was situated. Its success and its stature "must depend upon *what* it is, rather than *where* it is. . . . If properly endowed and wisely maintained, and impartial in its influences, it will build quickly for itself a reputation, even though pushed to an inland forest, adjacent only to one of our small villages; and if *poorly* endowed and *badly* managed, it would fail of support though placed in the centre of one of our largest cities." Skinner was expressing a widely held rural prejudice when he wrote that "all colleges should be remote from cities, where temptations press not so heavily upon a young man." Sawyer recognized the practical problem that a country location posed: "Some might prefer to have the College located [away] from a large city, but it is obvious that it must be placed where we can obtain funds to build and endow it."

During the period when the question was being actively considered, numerous towns had indicated their desire to be considered; Brattleboro, Vermont, and Worcester and Springfield, Massachusetts, were among the contenders.[6] When the matter had been considered in a very preliminary way in the 1840's, western Massachusetts or upstate New York had seemed to be the most popular choices. Hosea 2d had not felt strongly about it then, and considered Clinton, New York, a good possible midpoint between New England and areas west of the Hudson River. He could see some advantages for a New England location, but they were not sufficient to counterbalance other possibilities. The important thing was to

[6] The town of Brattleboro offered to give $3,766 if the Trustees would locate the college there. A "very beautiful" site of twenty acres could be obtained at about $100 an acre; this would leave a cash contribution of $1,766.

create "a respectable college, wherever it might be." After the 1847 convention had proposed the Hudson or Mohawk Valley, Hosea 2d still felt "perfectly indifferent." He suggested to Sawyer that the latter might look over Springfield, but if that place were chosen, the site for the college should be "about a town's width" away from the center of population.

From 1849 until a site was finally selected late in 1851, the New England region seemed to be gaining in favor. There were certain very concrete reasons for this eastward shift in sentiment. Sylvanus Packard's subscription of $20,000 was contingent on the college's being located in Massachusetts. The summer of 1851 brought even more specific recommendations. With the wisdom that is said to come from hindsight, one newspaper editor had expressed his dissatisfaction with the site selected for Harvard. That institution should have been placed "among the West Cambridge hills" instead of on flat terrain. Whittemore immediately suggested that Universalists should capitalize on the opportunity lost by Harvard. If the new college was to be located in the Boston area, there would be no better place than the hills of Somerville or Medford. Whittemore was quite aware of another consideration that was likely to govern the ultimate choice of location; he knew that Charles Tufts' gift of twenty acres of land was subject to the condition that the college be located on that land.

As Medford and Somerville became more and more talked about as a site, Hosea 2d became more and more concerned. When Walnut Hill began to be mentioned, he became thoroughly disturbed and marshaled an impressive list of objections. He saw no reason why a theological school would be inappropriate, but a college was another matter. There were the usual objections that proximity to a large city would make living expenses high and would expose the students to "an unhealthy moral atmosphere." But other considerations caused him the greatest concern. There was "no need of another college on merely *literary* grounds . . . and it would be felt by the community at large as an attempt at a sort of rival institution to Harvard." The Universalist college would inevitably be compared with Harvard "— and what a comparison, especially for the first years! — with our two or three professors, of name unknown in the literary or scientific world, with our library perhaps two or three thousand volumes at most, with but the embryo of a philosophical apparatus, — in contrast with the oldest, richest, best-appointed university on this side of the Atlantic." And in spite of all that could be done, students who might otherwise go to a Universalist school would be attracted by Harvard and its faculty. Recruiting and retaining a respectable student body would be a chronic problem. In short, an institution on Walnut Hill would always be overshadowed by its neighbor in Cambridge and suffer by unfavorable comparison. In view of all this, there was a certain irony in the appointment of Hosea 2d to the Committee on Location.

The probable site when the Trustees met in the fall of 1851 had been narrowed to two: Walnut Hill, in Medford and Somerville; and the village of Franklin, about twenty-five miles south of Boston. The latter location had been offered by a wealthy Universalist physician and member of the Board of Trustees, Oliver Dean, who was willing to donate twenty acres of land and the sum of $20,000. The committee visited both sites, and Hosea 2d gave "at considerable length" his reasons for favoring Franklin. When the five-man committee voted in favor of Walnut Hill, unanimity did not prevail: Hosea 2d cast the lone negative vote. He was as aware as anyone that the principal reason for placing the college at so "unfortunate" a place was the conditional gift of Charles Tufts, but he argued that "it would be better even to sacrifice the donation than to incur the disadvantages which seem to be attached."

Several reasons seem to have prompted the committee's decision in favor of Walnut Hill and make it appear that the discussion over eventual location was really only academic after all. Mr. Tufts would not give his property if the college were located elsewhere, and it was understood that Dr. Dean "would ultimately do about the same for the College in one place as in the other." It was also a matter of pleasing Mr. Tufts, for from the time the Medford and Somerville property had come into his possession in 1840, he had determined to found an educational institution of some sort on it. He made out three legal instruments to that effect before 1848, one of which had been intended for the ill-fated Walnut Hill Seminary. Practical considerations were also involved in the decision. There was a good deal of adjacent property owned by Mr. Tufts which might very well be deeded to the college sometime in the future. Furthermore, the college proper might not need more than ten

Charles Tufts (1781–1876)
Donor of the land on which the College was built

acres of the proffered twenty, and the surplus could be sold off at a comfortable profit. The college land was valued at $1,000 an acre in 1858. The surrounding land was worth from $200 to $300 an acre before the college was located. Thereafter, the valuation jumped to about $500 an acre. Even in 1851 there were residents of Somerville who had offered to buy over ten acres of the Tufts gift at $2,000 an acre. It was estimated by the Trustees that such offers would total $24,000 and still leave sufficient land for the college buildings.

One other less mercenary consideration undoubtedly entered into the choice of location. The metaphorical association of "light" and "education" is an ancient one. There are frequent Biblical references to the value of light in dispelling darkness of various kinds, and the Universalists concerned with establishing the college knew their Bible well. What more effective means was there of spreading the light of education than placing a college on the highest hilltop in the vicinity of Boston? One of the traditions at Tufts, recorded in innumerable variant versions, is that Charles Tufts, when asked by a relative what he would do with the land he had inherited, and more particularly with "that bleak hill over in Medford," replied, "I will put a light on it." At a Universalist festival in Faneuil Hall in June 1855, a toast to the recently opened college was offered. Hosea Ballou 2d's reply either echoed or anticipated Charles Tufts' statement, for the president of the new institution said, "For if Tufts College is to be a source of illumination, as a beacon standing on a hill, where its light cannot be hidden, its influence will naturally work like all light; it will be diffusive." [7] The "beauty and the grandeur" of the site constantly impressed visitors (as it still does in some degree), and those associated with the institution from the beginning have pointed to its location with pride. Elmer Hewitt Capen, president of Tufts from 1875 to 1906, frequently alluded in his writings and speeches to the remarks purported to have been made by Charles Dickens when he first visited Boston in 1842 and was taken on a tour that included Walnut Hill. "He said that there was not, probably, more than one other hill-top in the world from which one could see such a combination of natural beauty in the landscape, and, at the same time, survey such an accumulation of wealth and culture." The pride seemed to have been enforced when Cardinal Newman pronounced a hilltop location one of the essentials of a university.

With the problem of location settled, the next step was to obtain a charter. A premature attempt had been made in 1850, when the "Tufts Institution of Learning" had been created, with Benjamin B. Mussey, Timothy Cotting, and Richard Frothingham, Jr., as the incorporators. But the charter had lapsed because the corporation had not been organized within the time provided by state

[7] There was a certain appropriateness in the title, *Candle in the Wilderness,* selected for the historical essays which comprise the centennial history of St. Lawrence University, published in 1957. St. Lawrence is sometimes called Tufts' "sister institution" because of their common Universalist origins.

Thomas Jefferson Sawyer
Elected first President in July 1852, but declined to serve

law. The charter which did become operative was obtained without difficulty and was approved April 21, 1852, under the corporate name of the Trustees of Tufts College which has been retained to the present day. The Board was made self-perpetuating, and no religious restrictions of any kind were imposed on the composition of the Board. The original charter stipulated that the institution was to be located in Medford. Because of the peculiar location of the Tufts gift, spread as it was across town lines, a month after the original charter was granted, an additional act was necessary to apply the same charter to the Somerville location.

Fourteen of the twenty-three Provisional Board of Trustees of

1851 were retained under the 1852 charter. Timothy Cotting of Medford and Richard Frothingham, Jr., of Charlestown were new to the Board. The name most conspicuously absent from the reconstituted Board was that of Thomas Jefferson Sawyer, who meanwhile had returned to Clinton, New York, to resume his duties in connection with the Universalist school there. Whether he refused to serve as a Trustee because he was piqued that the institution to be established on Walnut Hill was literary rather than theological or because he preferred to confine his activities to strengthening denominational education in New York State is a matter of conjecture. There can be no doubt that some sectional rivalry did exist between Universalists in New England and in New York. In any case, the Trustees unanimously elected him as first president of Tufts College, and a committee (including Hosea 2d) was appointed to "confer with him in relation to the same." The committee returned with the disturbing news that Sawyer would accept the presidency only on the condition that his salary be no less than $2,500 per annum. The Trustees had no alternative but to declare vacant the office of president. Much effort and sacrifice had been expended to raise the initial subscription, and they felt that it was not in their power to make a commitment for such a generous salary, which might have jeopardized the existence of the college before it had even become a physical fact. Fortunately, the Trustees had among their own number a man eminently qualified to fill the post.

Hosea 2d was unanimously elected president in May 1853 and reluctantly agreed to serve. He confided to his brother Levi the doubts he entertained about taking on such a responsibility so late in life. There was also the danger of "pecuniary ruin" for him if the College failed. He defended Sawyer's right to decline the post "for prudential reasons" and told his brother he would have done the same if he had allowed financial considerations to enter into his decision. When he agreed to serve as president, the matter of salary was left open. Hosea 2d requested only that it be equal to what he had been receiving from his Medford parish. The Trustees honored his request and initially agreed on $800; in 1855 the annual stipend was increased to $1,000. It was only his hope to see the College come alive that motivated him to accept. He agreed to hold the office "not on the ground of being fit for it, which the Lord knows I

Hosea Ballou 2d
President, 1853–61

am not, but because I do not know who they can get that is fit for it. But I shut my eyes to the consequences, and rush forward . . . I am in for it, and if I come out ground into powder, I hope it will bring the price of flour down."

Another reason for Hosea 2d's pessimism was what seemed to him the untoward delay and difficulty in getting things under way, Even by May 1853, no by-laws had been adopted even for the governance of the Trustees of the institution, although officers had been selected, with Oliver Dean as the first president of the Board. A building committee had been instructed in the summer of 1852 "to proceed immediately to erect a building for the use of the College," but excavation for the foundation was not begun until mid-November, and work was almost immediately suspended until the following spring. Expenditures by the building committee were originally limited to $20,000; they soon found that figure woefully inadequate and had to request more than twice what was originally allocated. The revised total of $50,000 was then supposed to have been stretched sufficiently to complete the main structure and to provide boarding houses and other facilities in addition. A deficit could be seen even before the first building took shape. Nonetheless, the Trustees proceeded with their plans. Otis Skinner, who had supervised the business arrangements for several months without compensation, was formally employed to oversee construction and the laying out of the grounds. The ceremony of laying the cornerstone was arranged, and with all the trials and tribulations of getting under way, at least a beginning had been made. As Rev. A. A. Miner reminded his audience on that summer day in July 1853 when the cornerstone was laid, "the occasion which has assembled us, is one of mutual congratulation." The *Boston Journal,* recounting the events of the day, also looked on the optimistic side. The prospects of the new College "now are bright and cheerful, and its future progress and prosperity will be watched with interest not only by the members of the denomination of which it is the organ, but by all friends of a wise and liberal education."

§   §   §

While Tufts was coming into being as a liberal arts college, there was still a very vocal contingent who continued to work for the establishment of a separate theological school. The gestures toward establishing such a school made at the 1847 Convention lay fallow for two years, until the New York State Universalists took the leadership in the movement. The effort made by Sawyer to provide theological training as an extracurricular activity had become too great a burden for him and he had been forced to close up shop. When the New York Convention in 1850 called on Universalists to support both Clinton Liberal Institute and the proposed college which became Tufts, they simultaneously urged the reestablishment of the theological school operated by Sawyer. They were even willing to recommend the charging of $30 a year tuition if it would guarantee the existence of the school. Sawyer was requested to draw up a circular on education to be distributed in the state, and Societies were urged to take up special collections to support the project. But nothing happened, in spite of constant urging. It was estimated that there was a shortage of fifty clergymen in New York State alone, and the Midwest — notably Ohio — was desperately lacking in Universalist clergymen. An eloquent plea for a Universalist school was made by a student attending the theological school in Meadville, Pennsylvania, which had been established by the sect known as Christians but had had to accept aid from Unitarians in order to keep their school open. The continued shortage of clergy in the denomination finally prompted the New York State Convention to form an Education Society to solicit donations, and Sawyer agreed to train ministers without charge under its patronage.

For the next three years the New York representatives at the General Convention managed to get the problem of a theological school on the agenda and to get resolutions adopted supporting the idea. The New York group did obtain pledges of $2,100 at one of its meetings in 1853, but it was not until two years later that anything tangible was accomplished. In 1855 the town of Canton offered $15,000 if the school would locate there. The result was the chartering of St. Lawrence University in April 1856.[8] The establishment of a liberal arts college beside the theological school was not the intention of the Universalist founders, but the residents of Canton made this a *quid pro quo* for raising the $15,000. If Sawyer and his colleagues wanted a theological school at all, they had no alternative but to accept the offer. Sawyer found himself elected president of the St. Lawrence University Corporation; he reluctantly held the post until 1868, positive throughout that the denomination had overextended itself. Further, Sawyer was certain that by establishing two colleges within the same decade, without really adequate endowment for either, the denomination had endangered the existence of both and had set into motion an unfortunate rivalry within its own household that would create conflicts of

[8] See Andrew K. Peters, "The Founding of the University," in L. H. Pink and R. E. Delmage (eds.), *Candle in the Wilderness: A Centennial History of the St. Lawrence University, 1856–1956* (New York: Appleton-Century-Crofts, 1957), Chapter 2.

loyalties and disperse desperately needed funds. Many New York Universalists resented the failure of their New England counterparts to support the proposition of the theological school, while many New England supporters of Tufts resented equally the establishment of another liberal arts college in New York State. One result was the insistence in the East that Tufts, even without a theological curriculum, could serve the needs of both the ministerial and the general student. It was this possibly misplaced emphasis on Tufts' role in preparing clergy for the denomination that for several decades was to plague the liberal arts students, who time and time again tried to disabuse the public of the idea that the college was a theological institution. The problem was aggravated after a divinity school was actually created at Tufts in the late 1860's.

One of the Universalists responsible for defending Tufts as an institution capable of producing clergymen was Thomas Whittemore. The editor of the *Trumpet* insisted that "one of the principal objects in establishing Tufts College was to give aspirants to the ministry an opportunity to obtain a competent education." He pointed to the fact that, only a year after the institution had been formally opened, six Tufts students were holding part-time pastorates while engaged in their college studies. There were, said Whittemore, two classes of young men seeking an education at Tufts: prospective clergy and "those who design to follow other pursuits." The College was thus "a great blessing to the Universalist community and ministry." It seems clear that Whittemore was not particularly enthusiastic about seeing potential denominational funds sorely needed by Tufts diverted to the theological school and college at Canton.

It was certainly unfair to place all the blame for financial stringencies on the establishment of St. Lawrence University. Yet economics were uppermost in the minds of a good many people associated with Tufts. Even before the College was a year old, the specter of financial crisis hovered over it. It was estimated that current operating expenses would exceed receipts from fees by $3,500 a year for the period 1856–61, of which only $1,000 could be counted on from the permanent fund. To raise the remaining $2,500 annually a fund-raising committee, headed by John D. W. Joy, was appointed at the meeting in August 1856 celebrating the first anniversary of the College. One result was the taking up of collections in behalf of the College at the Sunday services of several Universalist churches in the Boston area. The General Convention of 1856 solicited material aid for all Universalist educational enterprises but probably strengthened no friendships it might have had at Tufts, for it singled out for "the *special* regard of our Brotherhood . . . our Theological Seminary, now in progress of establishment in Canton, St. Lawrence Co., N.Y."

Finances were a vital consideration in the early years of Tufts, as of most privately endowed institutions, but getting the College actually under way was also an immediate concern of the Trustees. In May 1853, on the same day that Hosea 2d had been elected to fill the vacancy in the presidency created by Sawyer's refusal to accept the position, Hosea 2d was placed on a committee to arrange the course of studies and report what professorships were necessary and what persons were suitable to fill them. And how does one prepare to be a college president? What are his duties and responsibilities? How did one go about running a college? Hosea 2d had all of these questions to answer, and many more. In spite of his academic turn of mind, his scholarly accomplishments, his ten years on the Harvard Board of Overseers, and his two honorary degrees, there is nothing to indicate that he had even seen the inside of a college classroom. Promptly and methodically he set about gaining as much knowledge as possible. The College was far from ready to receive students in the summer of 1853, for its main building was still under construction. So, at his request, Hosea 2d received a year's leave of absence to prepare himself for his new responsibilities. Between September and December 1853, he visited "the principal Colleges of New England, in order that he might combine in the system of Instruction and Government of Tufts College, as many of the excellencies of the different Colleges, as possible." The remainder of his leave was spent in Europe.

Hosea 2d covered an amazing amount of academic ground in four months. He visited Harvard, Williams, Yale, and Brown. He attended classes in mathematics, history, English and declamation, foreign languages, and the sciences; he conferred with instructors on teaching techniques and problems, noted texts used and subjects discussed in the classroom. At Providence he spent considerable time with Brown's notable president, Francis Wayland. He attended President Walker's class in Evidences of Revealed Religion at Harvard. He inquired about grading systems, the handling of disciplinary cases. What, he asked Williams' president, Mark Hopkins, should the teacher do if he disagreed with the textbook? The answer: "Say so, & vindicate." He attended prayers at chapel at Williams at 6:30 A.M. and a few hours later was discussing instructional salaries. He asked the president of Yale how often faculty meetings were held and was apparently relieved to discover that there was "not so much machinery in the Gov't. of Yale as in that of Harvard." He found out how examinations for admission and for courses were conducted. In short, Hosea 2d discovered as much as he could about administering a college.

Returned from Europe the last week in September 1854, he found the College already in operation, although not yet formally opened. An Executive Committee of the Trustees had been created in the summer of 1854. Their first act had been to authorize William P. Drew to use the recently completed building, "known as Tufts College," for one year, beginning after September 1, 1854. The purpose was "to give instruction in the Latin and Greek languages and in Mathematics to such young men as desire to pursue those studies." In October four students appeared — two freshmen and two sophomores. The College had finally acquired a student body, and by the end of the academic year three more freshmen had been enrolled. The original intention of the Trustees had been to postpone the actual opening until the fall of 1855, for the funds raised by the agent had long since been exhausted in building the College Edifice. But Benjamin Mussey, the treasurer, and Otis Skinner, the secretary of the Board, had agreed to assume all responsibility, Mussey guaranteeing the payment of the salaries of the instructors. Accordingly, a notice had appeared in the *Trumpet* that the College would receive students in September 1854, and that professors would be provided to give instruction "in all the studies usually pursued by Freshman and Sophomore classes of the principal colleges of our country."

The next step was to arrange a formal opening, and at the suggestion of the faculty, the Trustee Executive Committee voted to hold "appropriate exercises at the commencement of the College year — August 22, 1855," provided such arrangements could be made "without any expense to the College." The occasion was a great success. It is true that the special train from Boston, carrying

Mr. and Mrs. Tufts among its passengers, either overshot the depot in Somerville or failed to stop as scheduled. Proceedings had to be delayed until a fast horse and carriage could be dispatched to retrieve these important guests. It also happened that there was an unexpectedly large attendance. The formal program was scheduled to take place in the chapel on the second floor of the College Edifice, but the number of people was so great that they overflowed the stairways, hallways, and adjacent rooms, and many were unable to either see or hear the speakers. Only 900 plates had been set for the dinner following the exercises, and many of the over 1,000 who appeared could not be served. But these were minor matters. The addresses were eloquent, the toasts were appropriate, and a dramatic appeal for funds by Sylvanus Packard, accompanied by a pledge of $5,000 beyond what he had already given, brought an additional $4,000 on the spot. The formal installation of the president and faculty was duly conducted by Thomas Whittemore, vice-president of the Trustees.

President Ballou's Inaugural Address was brief, general, and simply stated.[9] He called attention first to the fact that the new College was entering a field already occupied by other institutions; it was their very success that prompted another. "It was the manifest good which they have achieved, it was the powerful influences which they have so widely exerted, and the satisfaction they have given to all competent judges, that moved us to emulate their example, at humble distance." He then proceeded to outline the function of a college, which was more than imparting "a given amount of knowledge and accomplishments to any select number of persons . . . the College works out abroad from itself, beyond the circle of its graduates, sending its energies forth through all other institutions, and down through all classes, even the most unlettered." In short, a college is a leavening force in society — from the common school through public affairs and the professions, and down to the lives of the everyday citizen.

He acknowledged the labor and sacrifice that his co-religionists had already put into their educational effort; he also recognized that "under the present condition of public sentiment in this coun-

[9] It was published in the *Universalist Quarterly,* Vol. 12 (October 1855), pp. 329–344. He made over twenty editorial changes in the page proofs, but for some reason the original version was printed.

try, all institutions of the kind are virtually in charge of some specific denomination, or classes of men, who feel that their own success and reputation are identified with the success and reputation of their respective seats of learning." Ballou never once mentioned the Universalist Church in his address; the closest he came was to refer to "that class of Christians, at whose desire this institution arose." But he suggested that the College might also "reasonably hope for a degree of patronage from all quarters, if it have the requisite merit." Founded under religious auspices or not, no colleges professing to offer a liberal education in the true sense could afford to be "sectarian in their regulations and conduct; they cannot very well be so, for any long period; there is something, in the very tendency of liberal studies, opposed to a narrow bigotry. Narrow, clannish prejudices, exclusiveness, — and a liberal course of learning will always be found irreconcilable." Universalists, in founding a college, were serving more than themselves: they were elevating the whole tone of society and fostering "general improvement in intellect and taste." Their contributions were likely to be modest, particularly until their new creation had gotten itself established. But the task of the College for all time could, said Ballou, be summed up this way: "We consecrate it to the work of instruction in sound learning and science, under the influence of Christian principles."

The first formal term of the infant institution opened the next day, with over thirty students in attendance. Its prospects for survival looked promising, on that "bleak hill over in Medford."

3. *"One Building, Four Professors, Seven Students"*

THOSE FAMILIAR with the vast and sprawling campuses, intricate administrative machinery, impressive faculties, bulging enrollments, and huge endowments and other resources of a later day would be inclined to chuckle at the sight of Tufts College when Hosea 2d began his presidential duties. Judging from reminiscences and contemporary accounts of the opening years, it was not a very prepossessing place. The hill on which the lone building stood in the fall of 1854 had had important and interesting historical associations but had lost its tree-covered beauty long before the College appeared on it.

Walnut Tree Hill was originally upland pasture for residents of Charlestown in the seventeenth century and was densely wooded. That part of the hill on which the first College buildings were constructed was part of a large area annexed by the village of Medford in 1754. Tradition has it that the hill was stripped of many of its trees for firewood by Hessian soldiers captured as an aftermath of the Battle of Saratoga during the American Revolution and temporarily stationed in the area northwest of Boston until they could be transported overseas. The remaining trees were apparently cut down by Medford residents for firewood, or possibly for the shipbuilding business that flourished in the early nineteenth century along the Mystic River, which flows not far from the campus.

The southerly part of what later was to become "College Hill" and still later simply "the Hill" was transferred from Charlestown to Somerville in 1842. Charles Tufts, the fifth generation of his family in the Boston area, inherited several hundred acres of Medford and Somerville land and added to a rather princely domain by numerous purchases. It was from this large acreage that he donated

59

land on which Tufts College was built.[1] The nearest house on the Medford side of the Hill was the mansion of George L. Stearns of Medford, about a quarter of a mile away.[2] On other sides could be seen a scattering of farmhouses surrounded by apple orchards and outbuildings mingled with patches of woodland, rocky pastures, and winding cow paths and cart roads. Tumbledown stone fences stretched across the Hill in all directions, and boulders were scattered over the hilltop. One end of the College Edifice was partially hidden behind a lofty pile of old lumber; the ground was so overgrown with weeds and strewn with rubbish that gaining entrance to the building was a major challenge.

No well-defined road to the campus had yet been laid out. Those who had occasion to come to the College reached it "by crossing the fields by any route that suited the fancy of the visitor." For over a year after the College opened, and before a house was built for him on campus, President Ballou had to tramp some four miles each day to and from his home on Washington Street in Medford, through pastures, woodlands, and orchards. For many years the College, located as it was on the outermost fringes of the Boston area, was considered isolated and in fact inaccessible. However, there was a main link with the city via the (then) Boston and Lowell Railroad. In the 1850's and 1860's trains terminating in Woburn stopped at what was described as "the College Station." In 1860–61, the institution received the post-office designation of College Hill, Medford, and another link was forged with the outside world.

For several years faculty, students, and Medford townsfolk undertook to beautify the barren hilltop by planting trees of all kinds. Pleas for gifts of trees were made in Universalist newspapers, and in the spring of 1858 the campus could boast 300 such plantings. However, the tree-planting project seemed never ending because of the constant addition of land to the original twenty acres.

[1] Further details may be found in Richard B. Coolidge, "Walnut Tree Hill," *Medford Historical Register,* Vol. 39 (June 1936), pp. 21–36; there is an abbreviated version of this article in the *Tuftonian,* Vol. 2, n.s. (May 1942), pp. 164 ff.

[2] Stearns was one of the "Secret Six" who helped finance John Brown's famous raid on Harper's Ferry, Virginia, in 1859. Stearns' home was for a period the Medford headquarters of a branch of the "underground railroad" organized before the Civil War to assist fugitive slaves from the South to escape. Many of those who were assisted by the Medford organization fled to Canada.

Ballou Hall in its 19th-century pastoral setting

Charles Tufts made two additions to his original gift: in 1856, forty-seven acres; in 1864, thirty-six acres. Between 1862 and 1866 the College purchased about sixteen acres from various individuals. By 1866 the campus comprised 120 acres. One donor contributed 104 trees, but the great majority came in small numbers from many individuals. Perhaps the efforts of some generous individuals were not always appreciated at the time, for in 1856 the faculty saw fit "to admonish and solemnly warn" one student for using "indecent language" in the presence of a group of Medford ladies who had come to plant trees. Later generations were to esteem these nineteenth-century efforts at beautification. Unfortunately the ravages of time, weather (including the destructive hurricane of 1938), and building needs took down many of the trees so laboriously set out during the first decades of the College's history.

The exterior of the College Edifice presented a more imposing appearance than its surroundings. It was designed in what was rather loosely called "Italian Renaissance" style, three stories high with walls of red brick; the basement story, corner quoins, and window and door trimmings were of brown sandstone. The main entrance, facing south toward what later became Professors Row, was equipped with a "Roman Ionic" portico surmounted, like the roof, with a balustrade. Six chimneys rose above the slate roof. It was intended originally that the building would house only academic and administrative facilities; there were to be separate boarding houses for the students. But the exigencies of the situation demanded that for a brief period the first-floor rooms served as dormitories. Externally, the building changed very little over the years. The major alteration was made in 1939, with the addition of a matching portico on the side facing the main campus drive. This portico was the gift of Eugene Bowen, Class of 1876. Internally, the main building was completely remodeled in 1955–56, in a combination of modernization and restoration.[3]

The Trustees had felt from the beginning that the College should be as residential in character as location and finances would permit. The public was even invited, via newspaper advertisements, to purchase land from the College on which to build living accommodations for students. In the spring of 1855 the College itself set about remedying this deficiency. The result was a three-story brick structure designated for a time merely as "Building A" but known from completion in 1856 until 1872 as "West Hall." The erection in the latter year of another dormitory, also christened "West Hall," necessitated another name for the older building. It remained "Middle Hall" until 1886, when the simple designation "Library" was chiseled over the entrance. The name "Packard Hall," familiar to later generations, was attached to the building in 1910 as a belated gesture toward Sylvanus Packard, the benefactor of half a century before.

The uses to which this second College building were put were

[3] Edwin B. Rollins, Class of 1901, Professor of Electrical Engineering Emeritus, devoted the better part of a decade following his retirement to compiling histories of the physical aspects of the Hill campus. In 1960 he generously donated to the University Archives eleven volumes of illustrated notebooks detailing the stories of every important building, gate, walk, and set of steps and containing other valuable historical information. The writer, and many users of these notebooks, have appreciated the great effort and care that went into their compilation.

as various as its names. It was built to accommodate twenty-six students and included dining facilities and housing for the steward and his family in the basement.[4] The second president, A. A. Miner, developed an unalterable aversion to Middle Hall. It had suffered from structural defects from the time it was built, and tie rods had to be inserted to restrain the bulging walls before the structure was a decade old. The damage from moisture seepage through the brick walls called for frequent repairs and redecoration. After one such round of repairs in the 1870's Miner reported to the Trustees that the time could not be far distant when "that edifice must give place to a more substantial structure" and recommended that repairs in the future be held to a minimum. A short time later he expressed the hope that a new dormitory could "replace the unsightly and unsuitable building known as Middle Hall." Miner did not have his way. Between 1886 and 1908 two floors were used to house the College library, while students continued to live on the top floor until 1901. They were removed because of the potential danger to the library from fires in stoves and fireplaces in the days before central heating. After brief service as headquarters for the theological school beginning in 1910, the structure was remodeled for classrooms and faculty offices. A large room used earlier as a chapel by the theological school served for faculty meetings and other gatherings until Ballou Hall was remodeled. In 1955–56, during the latter activity, Packard Hall served as temporary headquarters for the administrative offices of the institution.

The third academic structure to appear on the Hill was a wooden building erected in 1857 and intended also as a dormitory. The College officers gave this addition to the campus the rather unimaginative designation "Building B." Unlike the first two, it never received a name. For three years it served its original purpose and then became a dwelling for two of the original faculty. Even another dormitory (East Hall), completed for use during the academic year 1860–61, failed to provide adequate student accommodations for long. East Hall was originally a rather grim-looking

---

[4] In this basement was born the only child known to have come into the world on the hilltop section of the campus. She was the daughter of Patrick Burns, a man-of-all-work around the campus for many years.

West Hall, at the height of its architectural glory in the 1870's

edifice, for it was covered with a brown mastic (stucco) which eventually began to peel off. Several paintings, sand-blastings, and repaintings were subsequently necessary to make the rough brick walls attractive. After East Hall was completed, the dining hall was moved from Middle (Packard) Hall and installed in the basement of the new building. Known as the "Dive," the Commons remained in East Hall until a new multi-purpose structure (Curtis Hall) was built in the 1890's.

"Building B" was removed from the top of the Hill in 1870 and relocated on what became known as "Professors Row" paralleling the south side of the hilltop. After serving as a faculty residence for years, the structure became the western half of Richardson House, a girls' dormitory. On the original site of "Building B" was constructed the largest, most ornate, and most luxurious dormitory on the campus up to that time — West Hall. This structure, completed in 1872 with four stories and a basement, and replete with Gothic-type windows, towers, cupolas, ironwork roof decoration, and dormers of various dimensions, stood proudly as the best (or worst) example on the Hill of "collegiate gingerbread" in the overdressed Gilded Age following the Civil War.

Less than ten years after the College opened, the Trustees were approached by officials of Charlestown who wanted to construct a water storage facility on the highest point of the Hill.[5] The result was a brick and stone reservoir with four and one-half acres of water surface over twenty feet deep, built between 1862 and 1864. Known to generations of Tufts students and alumni as the "Rez," and the scene of uncounted extracurricular activities, the facility was razed many years after it had ceased to serve its original purpose. The area became College property after World War II and was filled in to provide additional space for the growing campus. Many of the bricks were used to construct the Bray Mechanical Laboratory in 1946. The late *Boston Post* mistakenly announced that the "Rez" had been removed in order to build homes for Tufts faculty. Instead, the fringes of the old reservoir site became locations for three men's dormitories. The College long drew its water supply from the Rez, a privilege obtained in exchange for rights-of-way granted by the College for access roads and the laying of water pipes. Fragments of the old pipes were disinterred when the foundations were dug for the Lincoln Filene Center in 1962–63.

Those who live in an era of urban congestion and mechanization may find it difficult to realize how rural, and even pastoral, a college could be in the nineteenth century. From its opening until the late 1880's and early 1890's, both the College and its residential faculty engaged in extensive farming operations. Beginning in 1856, part of the pastureland which still comprised most of the Hill was let out at $60 per year. The College also operated its own farm for many years and raised a crop of hay so bountiful that the surplus that would not go into the barn then standing behind Middle (Packard) Hall was sold. As late as 1880 the Executive Committee of the Trustees reported that "a considerable portion of the college lands in Somerville has been cultivated . . . and four milch cows have been kept; the proceeds of the farm having been used, under the direction of the President, in the College boarding house, securing thereby board for students at a much cheaper rate."

[5] The land was not at that time part of College property, but certain access rights had to be obtained from the College.

A 19th-century panorama of "The Hill"
showing farming operations and the "Artificial"

The faculty were also allocated land for cultivation and grazing of cattle. For eight years one professor kept sufficient cows to furnish twenty quarts of milk a day to seven College families, and so expanded his agricultural activities that he had to hire student help and to rent a barn from another faculty member. The College owned several barns besides the one which remained behind Middle Hall until 1876, and as changes took place on the Hill the barns migrated from place to place or were torn down. Many of the old barns remaining on Professors Row were later converted into garages. The Trustees finally decided that farming operations, either by the College or by its faculty, were not in harmony with the dignity and purposes of the institution, and the last cow officially departed from the Tufts campus in 1893.

§ § §

The seven students who reported in 1854–55 for academic duty were presumably impressed with the faculty-student ratio. With a president (who doubled as a teacher) and three colleagues, the new institution might have seemed ridiculously overstaffed. Yet by the time of Hosea 2d's untimely death in 1861 the College had graduated thirty-six young men and could boast of fifty-three students in attendance. The interior of "College Hall," as the main building was sometimes called, at first bore few of the visible appurtenances of an institution of learning, higher or otherwise. "Not a map or drawing, or even a blackboard, adorned the bare walls. There was no library, no laboratory, no philosophical apparatus, no museum, — nothing but a building, four professors, and seven students. Probably no college has ever begun operations with fewer resources than Tufts College had at the start of 1854." Hosea 2d was perfectly aware of all this, but his hopes were high; two months after the College opened, he wrote his brother Levi that "our principle is to *work, work,* and to let the work speak for itself before the world. With only the germ of a library, and with no philosophical apparatus, I am still persuaded that we are making our students more thorough scholars than those of other colleges which I have visited. The smallness of our classes gives us a peculiarly favorable opportunity for effecting this result." He also noted that he had "full reason to be perfectly satisfied with the plan of instruction, and with the thoroughness and promptness of the Professors."

The three colleagues who embarked with Hosea 2d on the Universalist experiment in higher education were William A. Drew, Benjamin Franklin Tweed, and John P. Marshall.[6] Drew, who taught ancient languages (Greek and Latin) and classical literature, and was the first secretary of the faculty until he resigned from the College in 1857, was a graduate of Bowdoin College and the son of a clergyman in Maine who edited the *Gospel Banner,* a Universalist newspaper.[7] Drew was lame and had to use crutches to make his way about the Hill. During his first year he occupied the College Edifice with the seven students living there, then moved to Medford. He accepted his teaching position with two provisos: that he receive one-sixth of all tuition paid by students in his classes in excess of the number of thirty (which never happened), and that he

[6] Enoch C. Rolf, M.D., was originally to have taught Hygiene and Physiology, which was listed as a requirement for sophomores. However, there is no evidence that he ever had any association with the College.

[7] Detailed and generally accurate biographies of the faculty and administration for the first forty years of the College are to be found in the *History of Tufts College,* published in 1896. For further information about this *History,* see the Bibliographical Note at the end of this work.

have permission to engage in outside activities to supplement his income, provided such activities did not interfere with his College duties. The Trustees accepted both conditions. He resigned when he found his salary (to have been increased from $800 to $900 a year in 1857) inadequate.

B. F. Tweed, born in Reading, Massachusetts, had been a public school teacher and principal in the Boston area. He became a member of the Tufts faculty the same year that he received an honorary M.A. degree from Harvard in recognition of his outstanding work as a teacher. Until his resignation in 1864 he served as Professor of Rhetoric, Logic, and English Literature. He was popular as a lecturer and much in demand as a speaker both before and during his stay at Tufts. He started out with the modest salary of $400 a year, additional compensation having been offered him in 1855 in the form of a house lot on which to build. In 1856 his salary was doubled after he threatened to take a better-paying job. Tufts retained his services until he accepted a professorship in Washington University, St. Louis.

The member of the original faculty destined to serve the longest was John P. Marshall, who first held the title of Professor of Mathematics and Natural Science and then the Professorship of Chemistry, Mineralogy, and Geology and served the College until his retirement in 1898. He was made Professor Emeritus in that year and was the first faculty member to receive a retirement pension ($1,000) from Tufts until his death in 1901. He had been principal of Lebanon Liberal Institute, a Universalist academy in New Hampshire, and had held various teaching and administrative posts in several school systems in New England. When the College was opened, he at first commuted from Chelsea. His name will reappear more than once, for he was acting president after Ballou's death and served in many other capacities.

By tradition and usage in Hosea 2d's day, college presidents had teaching as well as administrative tasks. In pre-Civil War America they customarily taught either Intellectual Philosophy, or Moral Science and Political Economy, or their equivalents, to the senior class.[8] Hosea 2d actually taught in three areas, under two

[8] See George P. Schmidt, *The Old-Time College President* (New York: Columbia University, 1930), for a lively account of the typical nineteenth-century college executive.

professorships. During his presidency no Professor of Moral Science and Political Economy was appointed, so he combined as much of those disciplines as he could into his course in Intellectual Philosophy. In addition, he was Professor of History. Hosea 2d's love of language was equaled only by his devotion to history as an academic discipline. He taught both ancient and American history, and Tufts College thereby became one of the few institutions of higher learning in the United States before 1860 to include this subject in its curriculum.

Others of the early faculty of the College should also be mentioned. Alpheus Augustus Keen, who succeeded Drew as teacher of ancient languages and classical literature, was also the secretary of the faculty until his death in 1864. With a salary raised to $1,200 by 1860, Keen was the only member of the early Tufts faculty to have received more money than the president of the institution. Jerome Schneider, the first holder of a Ph.D. on the faculty, was employed by Hosea 2d to teach foreign languages. He was a European by birth and education, having come to the United States from Basle, Switzerland, and was originally employed in 1856 on a part-time basis. In 1858 he became a full-time faculty member and throughout his long stay at Tufts (he became Professor Emeritus in 1906), he taught Greek and Latin as well as French and German at one time or another. Until housing was provided for him on the Hill, he commuted from his home in Boston and was reimbursed for traveling expenses. For many decades faculty taking a leave were required to arrange for a substitute whom it was their responsibility to compensate. Professor Schneider gave the president and Trustees no end of trouble when he departed suddenly for Europe in 1881, made no provision for the teaching of his classes, and then neglected to pay the substitute that the College was compelled to hire. It was only after the Trustees threatened first to withhold his salary and then to dispense with his services that a species of settlement was made, in 1885. Thereafter, Schneider's salary was reduced and he was required, over his protest, to share the work in the Department of Greek with a new colleague.

Another faculty member in the early days of the College was William R. Shipman, chosen in 1864 to fill the post of Professor of Rhetoric, Logic, and English Literature vacated by Tweed. Like Marshall and Schneider, Shipman was long associated with Tufts

69

and held many responsible positions. He was particularly active in Universalist educational efforts and had been principal of Green Mountain Liberal Institute in South Woodstock, Vermont. He had also been instrumental in the establishment of Goddard Seminary in Barre, Vermont, in 1863, serving for many years as president of its Board of Trustees and as the academy's chief fund-raiser.

In 1864–65 Heman A. Dearborn, of the Class of 1857 and the first alumnus of the College on the faculty, was appointed Professor of Latin Languages and Literature so that Schneider could concentrate his efforts on Greek and modern languages. In the same year that Shipman was appointed, Benjamin Graves Brown, a Harvard graduate who had been employed in 1861 as Tutor in Mathematics, was appointed to the first endowed chair in the College, the Walker Professorship of Mathematics, and served until 1903. Dr. William J. Walker, a wealthy physician of Newport, Rhode Island (and not a Universalist), was a strong supporter of collegiate mathematical instruction and gave substantial amounts to Harvard, Amherst, and Williams as well as to Tufts. He gave approximately $200,000 to the College in several installments, invested in four separate funds. The bulk of the income was used to support the professorship; part was used to establish five scholarships in his honor.

§   §   §

After students, buildings, and faculty were obtained, the next task was to provide a library and what the nineteenth century called "philosophical apparatus." To Hosea 2d the library was the heart of the College, and every spare moment was devoted to creating a collection. He wrote literally hundreds of letters to his wide circle of friends and acquaintances begging for donations. He made pleas for gifts in Universalist newspapers. He personally accessioned most of the books received during his presidency, attached a bookplate to each, and wrote a personal letter of thanks to each donor. Proof of his persuasiveness can be found in the dozens of gifts received from some of the leading figures in the literary life of New England. Typical was the gift to the Tufts Library by Henry Wadsworth Longfellow of a complete set of his works in 1861. One of the most generous donors in the early history of the library was John Langdon Sibley, for thirty-six years associated with the Library of Harvard University. Hosea 2d drew in numerous dupli-

Rules.

1. This Room is held for the purposes exclusively of a Reading-Room; i.e. there shall be no Conversation in it, nor Meetings for business, consultation, or amusement.

2. There shall be no Smoking in the Room.

3. No one shall wear hat, or cap, in the Room.

4. A violation of any of the three foregoing Rules shall be just ground for declaring the use of the Room forfeited. ——————

5. The Officers of the Reading-Room shall, at the end of each ten weeks of a Term, make to the Faculty a written Report of the observance of those Three Rules during such period.

6. A Copy of these Rules shall be kept posted, in some conspicuous place in the Room, for the notice of all who enter.

Oct. 22. 1860.

Rules written by President Ballou in 1860

cates and items of ephemeral value or of no worth at all with the dragnet he spread over New England. As he wrote Sawyer in the spring of 1861, "we have been wonderfully favored in the accumulation of books, — quite miscellaneous on the whole, — but still containing a large number of valuable works. In one word, we have

71

a splendid *Appendage* to a College Library." But Hosea 2d's discriminating taste and his good judgment made the College library unique in its day. The collection, which amounted to over 6,000 volumes by the end of his career in 1861, had been obtained at practically no expense to the Trustees. In most colleges of his time, undergraduate literary societies accumulated substantial group libraries to supplement the chronically inadequate and overzealously guarded college facilities.[9] Tufts was the only nineteenth-century New England college before the Civil War in which literary societies did not build up their own collections. Although it was far from perfect, the College library was considered sufficient for student needs. Hosea 2d was in an ideal position to assess the reading needs and interests of his student body and faculty, for it was he personally who usually checked out the library books.

The library was at first housed in Hosea 2d's office on the second floor of the College Edifice, but after two or three years it had grown so rapidly that it required a separate room. The collection remained in the main College building until 1887, when it was given larger quarters in Middle (Packard) Hall, which was extensively remodeled in 1886 for the purpose. When first established, the library was open only one hour a week (on Saturday afternoon), and a student was employed at the munificent sum of $20 a year to assist users. Aside from this rather nominal expense, Hosea 2d proudly informed the Trustees that almost the only cost of the library during his administration had been to install bookshelves.

Just prior to Hosea 2d's death in 1861, Rev. John Stetson Barry of Medford was employed as a part-time librarian for one year. Because the Trustees could not provide the compensation desired, Barry was replaced by Professor Keen, who serviced the collection as an additional duty. His wife was also employed as an assistant, and through Mrs. Keen's efforts the first attempt was made to catalogue the collection, using the Harvard system of separate author and subject listings in bound ledgers. Mrs. Keen agreed to work five hours a day for a total wage of $4.00 a week. In 1864 her salary was raised to $400 a year after her husband's death. For almost twenty years Professor Shipman acted as part-time librarian, while teaching rhetoric, logic and English literature. In 1884 Miss

[9] See Henry D. Sheldon, *Student Life and Customs* (New York: D. Appleton, 1901).

Helen L. Mellen, who had been employed as an assistant librarian in 1869, became the first full-time librarian at Tufts. She served until retirement in 1907, when the library was moved for the third time, into the structure made possible by a gift from Andrew Carnegie, and into the first building intended exclusively for the library.

"Two or three thousand dollars, for the purchase of books to fill out certain departments, would put us on a level with the Libraries of most of our old Colleges in New England." These words were written by Hosea 2d in 1861, and they expressed a wish that was a long time in being even partially fulfilled. In the days when research activities by either faculty or students were the exception rather than the rule in American colleges, and when textbooks had an authority even greater than they do today, libraries were not necessarily considered vital to an institution's existence. There were always a few individuals, fortunately, who realized the value of a library collection, but after the initial momentum generated by Hosea 2d's efforts had subsided, the library grew so imperceptibly in the next twenty-five years that when Professor Shipman resigned as part-time librarian in the winter of 1883–84 he saw "no sufficient reason for maintaining two officers in connection with it." Miss Mellen could serve very well as librarian, with occasional student assistance. The first major expenditure was the purchase of Hosea 2d's personal library of almost 1,600 volumes from the family. The Trustees voted $1,200 for the acquisition, after Hosea 2d's successor, Alonzo Ames Miner, obtained expert advice on the collection.[10] The first cash donation for the purchase of books was made in 1870, when a Miss M. E. Bacon gave $200 "for the purchase of books for the Department of Modern Languages."

Until the Trustees authorized "no more than $500 for the benefit of the College Library" in 1866, the library had no funds, except for a student assessment, dropped in 1870, and it was years before as much as $500 was spent in any one year. The librarian made repeated pleas for money both to acquire books (particularly current ones) and to bind and repair those already on the shelves. Dozens of books considered indispensable for student use were purchased by the faculty from their own pockets and donated to the

[10] The Ballou library has been maintained as a Special Collection in the University Library.

library, usually without reimbursement. There was no such thing as an annual budget for the library for decades, and the librarian had to hope that special requests from time to time would be honored by the Trustees. For example, in 1874 the president was authorized to spend up to $250 for "the purchase of books for the Library and the Chapel." Presumably this included the acquisition of hymnals.

The first fund established specifically for library use was a gift of $1,200 by John D. W. Joy in 1875. The income was to "be appropriated to the purchase of books for the Library of the College, — preference being given to the department of Philology." The president of the College was to supervise the purchases. In 1886 the Joy Library Fund was increased to $20,000. The income, which was made available immediately, was almost the sole source for library funds for many years. In the 1870's other important donations of both books and money were made, including the library of Thomas Whittemore and a portion of the library of E. H. Chapin. The gift in 1889 of over 1,500 books and pamphlets, including Civil War (Confederate) documents from the widow of W. H. Ryder, was so extensive that a separate room to house it was required in Middle Hall.

One collection which swelled the number of volumes in the College library was the property of the Universalist Historical Society. T. J. Sawyer had long been secretary and librarian of the Society. When he moved from Clinton, New York, to Medford in 1869 to become the first professor in the Tufts Divinity School, he brought the Society library with him. Although it was housed on separate shelves in the College library, it was available for use by both the faculty and students. It comprised about 1,500 volumes in the 1870's, "some of rare interest and value." Over the years, the Society collection migrated from Miner Hall to Eaton Memorial Library to the Crane Library. In 1965 it was given new headquarters in the Wessell Library.

The College Library had become so necessary to both students and faculty by the 1880's that it remained open during daytime hours while the College was in session and in 1893 began to be open at night. The Trustees also found it desirable to create a standing committee on the library in 1886 which was to "be the final authority on the purchase of all books, and auditing accounts for the Library." A corresponding committee was created in the faculty to make recommendations for book purchases to the Trustees. However, this system did not appear to work satisfactorily. Some members of the faculty complained that acquisitions were too long delayed and requested that the privilege of purchasing books for the library be given directly to the teaching staff. The Trustees responded by creating a standing subcommittee on library within the Executive Committee, which met more frequently than the parent body. This may have expedited library acquisitions, but the Trustees maintained control over purchases. Slow and uneven as the growth of the library had been, by the time it was moved from the main College building to Middle Hall in 1887 it consisted of some 20,000 volumes and almost 9,000 pamphlets (most of which were still in the process of being catalogued). The library and other teaching equipment had been insured for a total of $3,000 in 1856. In 1889 the contents of the library alone were insured for $12,000.

While President Ballou was busy establishing a library for the College, Professor Marshall made the collection of "philosophical apparatus" his special province. He too sought gifts and donations, as well as funds from the Trustees. The first piece of teaching equipment acquired was a theodolite, purchased by the Trustees for use in surveying and for computing angles. Two years later (in 1857) the First Universalist Sabbath School in Boston raised $75 with which to buy a chemical balance.[11] Money also trickled in from various donors. A combination of gifts and purchases in the first thirty years resulted in a most variegated collection of mineral specimens, stuffed birds and animals, shells, fossils, and other items. Even a steam engine and boiler were acquired, and a "manikin to illustrate the great facts of Physiology and Natural Theology." So much had been accumulated even by 1869 that Professor Marshall undertook to compile a catalogue of the collections, and an entire "Cabinet Room" in the main College building was devoted to specimens of natural history. By 1876 the laboratory equipment included two microscopes, but a telescope was still lacking. Laboratory facilities were so limited for half a century that the students had to be content to watch demonstra-

[11] This instrument, in its mahogany, glass, and marble case, has been retained as a museum piece by the University.

tions rather than conduct their own experiments. Nevertheless, Professor Marshall made every effort to use his limited resources and space to the maximum. It was in the 1880's that the College received from P. T. Barnum major contributions of money, buildings, and equipment that enabled it to offer *bona fide* laboratory work and even advanced degrees in some of the sciences.

§   §   §

The institution of higher learning brought into being on a rural hilltop by the valiant efforts of a handful of Universalists met virtually all of the specifications of a nineteenth-century denominational college. As its third president frequently explained, Tufts was "of the standard New England type." Presided over by four clergymen in turn, Tufts at first offered to young men the prevailing classical curriculum of four years leading to the degree of Bachelor of Arts. Officially, the program of study was known as the "Regular Course" to distinguish it from the "Partial Course" for non-degree students. There was not a word in the first catalogue about the purposes of this particular institution, or of higher education in general. This was not an oversight, for everyone knew what colleges were intended to accomplish. They were to offer to selected young gentlemen the foundations that would enable them to become leaders in church, state, and the professions — notably teaching. The curriculum in general was set by ancient and honorable usage, for all literate men knew that there was a fixed body of knowledge to be transmitted — knowledge that any educated citizen should acquire. It sharpened and furnished the mind, elevated the character, and promoted piety and virtue.

There were admission requirements, for certain standards of achievement were expected. At the head of the list was the stipulation that each applicant was to produce a certificate of "good moral character." If the young scholar came from another college (possible before the beginning of the senior year), a certificate of "regular dismission therefrom" was likewise required. For admission to the freshman class, an examination had to be "well sustained" in the following studies: Latin, Greek, mathematics, and history. Although substitutions could be approved, certain textbooks were expected to have been used (and were so specified in the catalogue for the benefit of the applicant), and a certain degree of proficiency was supposed to have been attained. In Latin, Arnold's *Latin Prose Composition* was to have been mastered (up to the dative case), as well as Virgil's *Bucolics and Georgics,* and six books of the *Aeneid.* Four books of Homer's *Iliad* and three books of Xenophon's *Anabasis* were basic in Greek. Mathematics included arithmetic and algebra (to equations of the second degree). Preparation in history presupposed a knowledge of modern geography, Worcester's *Ancient Geography,* and Goodrich's *History of the United States.* Admission examinations were held on the day following Commencement and on a fixed day preceding the beginning of the fall term. Examinations began at eight o'clock in the morning and continued for as long as was thought necessary.

The academic year was originally divided into two terms of twenty weeks each, the first beginning toward the end of August ("six weeks after the 2d Wednesday of July") and ending in early January. The second term began in late February and ended on the second Wednesday of July. There was a six-week vacation at the end of each term, as well as special holidays, and many students who were in good standing were allowed to use up to twelve weeks (including the winter vacation) to teach school in neighboring towns. They were, however, to continue their collegiate studies "the mean while." The Thanksgiving recess provided a long weekend, but the Christmas holiday comprised that day only. Fast Day, part of the Anniversary Week in the spring, and the Fourth of July completed the list of vacations. The first catalogue was issued for the opening year (1854–55), but for the only time in the history of the institution the next year's catalogue was omitted; thereafter, the catalogues became a record of what the past year had provided rather than a projection of the next year's arrangements. The first major change in the academic year was inaugurated in 1875–76, when the faculty voted to abolish the winter vacation and to have instead, so far as possible, an undivided year of work. Since written examinations were now required at least monthly, it was considered desirable that final examinations be given at the end of major topics rather than at the end of each term. President Capen, and many of the faculty, felt that only in this way could be avoided "the evils of the cramming process, which from immemorial time has been the bane of colleges." The experiment in abolishing the semester system lasted only a few years. Except during wartime,

77

the College retained the two-term pattern for the regular academic year.

Freshmen encountered Latin, Greek, mathematics, history, and Rhetoric, with Natural Theology added during the second term. Sophomores continued their five-course regimen in the same subjects, except that in the second term they progressed from Natural Theology to Revealed Religion, using Paley's *Evidences of Christianity* — the standard text of the time. The second term was to have required physiology as the sixth subject, to be continued by hygiene when the student had earned upperclass status, but these courses were not actually offered during the early years of the College. Juniors and seniors could take advantage of the luxury of certain electives (as additions to their prescribed work). In the third year mathematics (analytical geometry, including conic sections) became an option, and physics (using Olmsted's *Mechanics*) was taken in its place. Moral Science and Intellectual Philosophy continued the ethical emphasis in the curriculum. Other electives included advanced Latin and Greek, French, Italian, and Lectures on Natural History. The number of electives was increased for seniors (and the required subjects correspondingly decreased). Physics, Intellectual Philosophy and Natural and Revealed Religion, Political Economy, and Rhetoric were required, and the remainder of the student's program was drawn from an arsenal of the aforementioned electives, plus German and Spanish.

Changes in curriculum and textbook occurred with glacial slowness. Literally for decades no alterations appeared in some areas. This was not at all unusual, for it reflected a tendency toward basic conservatism in all nineteenth-century collegiate education. Although an occasional new subject, textbook, or required reading crept into the academic offerings, no substantial change was made in the regular Tufts course of study for some forty years. Lectures on inorganic and organic chemistry appeared in 1864–65 for the sophomores, and botany and zoology made the seventh course required of juniors the same year. Political Economy was also introduced for seniors, including "Lectures on Mercantile Usages"; science received considerable attention, with lectures and demonstrations in geology, mineralogy, and astronomy. A year of French for juniors and German for seniors supplemented the Greek and Latin of the first three years.

In order to be advanced from one class to the next, an examination had to be "well sustained," both in the preparatory studies and "in the studies through which such class shall have already passed." Part-time or "Special" students were a part of institutional enrollment from the beginning of the College, consisting of those who could qualify for specific courses but who did not intend to earn a degree. If a student were a degree candidate, he had certain academic exercises to which he could look forward. A public examination of all classes was scheduled for a four-day period before the end of each term. At first all examinations were oral, conducted by formal Committees of Examination which were listed by name in the catalogue and were drawn from alumni, clergymen, Trustees, and other likely manpower convenient to the College. In 1864–65 separate examining committees were provided for Latin, Greek, mathematics, physics, Natural Theology, Rhetoric and Logic, modern languages, history, and Moral and Intellectual Philosophy. Juniors participated in a Public Exhibition in May, for which parts were assigned, according to the "general Scale of Merit" of each student.

The Junior Exhibition was a very formal and very serious academic ceremony, complete with an elaborate printed program. It took place in the College chapel during Anniversary Week, and classes were dismissed for the occasion. For several years those students selected to participate in the program were excused from recitations for a short time preceding the exercises in order to prepare their parts. A strict hierarchy of Exhibition assignments was established, to correspond to the customary ranks of Valedictory, Salutatory, and below. The parts were delivered by the students in descending order of class standing. First came the Latin Oration, followed by a Dissertation, and an assortment of English Orations, Disquisitions, and Philosophical Orations. Original plans called also for a Colloquy and a Poem, but neither materialized; however, there were occasional Greek Orations. When classes were small there was ordinarily a part for each member of the class, which meant that by 1862 there were thirteen speakers. It can easily be imagined that 3:00 P.M. was none too early to start the programs, for music was interspersed among the addresses, furnished by the Boston Brigade Band. An opening prayer and benediction were a normal part of each program. The topics were broad, gen-

79

erally inspirational, and occasionally practical, and were chosen after consultation with the faculty. A typical Exhibition might include presentations on "Mathematics as a Mental Discipline," "Elements of Success," "Revolutions," "Iron-Clad Ships," and "Our Obligations to Ancient Greece." An abortive attempt was made by the faculty in 1863 to have all Orations delivered in English; but the classical heritage prevailed, and a Latin Oration (*summa cum laude*) was duly delivered that year on Catiline. The students considered the Junior Exhibitions of sufficient importance to petition the faculty in 1863 that nominal parts be assigned those students away on active duty during the Civil War, so that their names (and class standing) might appear on the program. But the faculty ruled that students had to be in residence if their names were to appear on the printed program.

Such an important occasion as the Junior Exhibition required — at least according to the students — a social event following the formal exercises. So in 1858 the junior class petitioned "for liberty to have a social gathering" at American Hall in Medford on the evening of Exhibition Day. After understandable hesitation and due deliberation, the faculty gave its assent, but with certain reservations that would "relieve the College of all responsibility, and not establish a precedent from which evils might arise in future time." The "precedent" was set, however, for the annual festivities in Medford, and President Ballou saw fit in 1859 to issue a "Special Order" giving permission but under certain restrictions as to behavior. No intoxicating drinks were to be permitted on the premises where the social event was being held.

A second by-product of Junior Exhibitions was the surreptitious appearance of so-called Mock Programmes, prepared by fun-loving students. These, too, were elaborately printed, but their contents were far from sedate. Their exaggeration or distortion of both faculty and student personalities made their creators likely candidates for legal action for libel, slander, and defamation of character. The first false program appeared in 1858, only one year after Junior Exhibitions began, and was headed "Second Irregular Commencement of Tough College," with contents to match. A subsequent mock program labeled the institution the "Tufts Foundling Hospital" and inferred that it was for juveniles only. The faculty naturally discouraged the publication and dis-

The original chapel (now the Coolidge Room) in Ballou Hall

tribution of mock programs and eventually forbade their appearance. Suspension from the College was automatically provided for any student detected authoring these spurious editions. Aside from their sometimes scurrilous contents, the faculty feared that the programs might fall into the wrong hands and leave an erroneous impression of what went on within college walls.

The situation had become so serious by 1864 that the Trustees took a hand and suspended a student for several months "for being concerned in the preparation of a false program of the exercises at the annual exhibition." The faculty finally saw fit to discontinue the Annual Exhibitions, the last one being held in the spring of 1871. But the students were not to be so easily discouraged and found other outlets for youthful energy. Among them was the conduct, from 1872 until 1879, of mock funerals (complete with printed program and processions through the campus) of Ana Lytics. These gleeful celebrations marked the end, for seniors at least, of formal training in mathematics. Junior Day ceremonies, Junior "Horribles" (in costume) , and campus Mayoralty campaigns of later days bear witness to the simultaneous arrival of spring and of final examinations and term paper deadlines.

Students and faculty alike were required to attend religious observances. At first, attendance in the College chapel at both morning and evening prayers and the hearing of readings from the Scriptures were expected of all. Evening prayers were abandoned after the first year, but public worship in the chapel on Sundays, Thanksgiving, and Fast Day was mandatory. However, from the time the College opened, students were allowed to go to the church of their choice according to an election made by them or their parents at the beginning of each school year. An optional religious activity was attendance each Saturday evening at a "Biblical Exercise." In order to provide effective supervision over students attending public religious services off campus, for a brief period beginning in 1860–61 it was specified that the students were to attend Medford and Somerville churches. This limitation was soon dropped because so many students came from other towns in the Boston area. Although geographical boundaries may have been set, the policy remained quite liberal. This permission covered attendance at the services of "any other denomination of Christians . . . such worship being that in which [the students] have been educated, or which from conscientious motives they are desirous of attending."

Besides maintaining their class standing and attending religious services, students had certain other obligations to fulfill. Even before admission, every degree candidate was required to give a bond of $200, "with two sureties," to protect the College's investment while the student was in attendance. Tuition was $35 per year (two terms) until 1870–71, when it was raised to $60, and room rent ranged at first from $7.50 to $15 per year, then up to $20 by 1864–65. A fee of $1.00 was levied for a brief period for the privilege of using the library. Board (not including washing and fuel) was $2.50 a week when the College opened but was reduced to $2.00 within two years and varied up to more than $3.00 as the cost of living fluctuated. Students were allowed at first to make private arrangements for board if they chose. They were responsible for furnishing their own rooms. By 1864–65 the estimated annual total College expenses, exclusive of personal necessities and fuel, amounted to $187, including a levy of $1.00 for the privilege of being called to academic duty by a paid bell-ringer and of being supervised by a dormitory monitor. Wear and tear on College property required "average damages" assessments from time to time. Members of the Class of 1868 were assessed $1.00 each in their senior year. The Trustees disclaimed any responsibility, legal or otherwise, for loss of clothing or other articles by students. Minimum estimated annual expenses in 1874–75 were $244, with board at $3.50 a week. The treasurer's paper work was complicated from the very first by the fact that, except for the second term of the senior year, College charges were payable in two installments in 1875–76. Seniors had up to twenty-four hours before Commencement to settle their accounts.

Providing boarding facilities satisfactory to both the students and the College proved to be a chronic problem. A series of private families was employed at various times to supply food service, with uneven success. The annual deficit, ranging in the early 1860's from $600 to over $1,500, made the Trustees unhappy; the allegedly plain and monotonous fare, "permanently seasoned with the contingency of increased charges" made the students equally unhappy. This problem was by no means confined to a minority of the student body; in 1864–65, forty-four of the forty-six students boarded at the College. President Ballou once commented on the uninspiring diet in a delightful poem, "Salt Fish," which begins:

> Staple Food on Walnut Hill!
> Victual fund for drafts at will!
> Ready in all exigents,
> Minute-man of esculents!
> Substitute for every dish, —
> Hail, all hail to thee, Salt Fish.

The students then took matters into their own hands and organized their own system for board in the spring of 1870. The College was delighted to have them assume responsibility for a thankless task. "The experiment of the students boarding themselves in a club has proved a marked success. It has cured most of the evils formerly complained of." The Adams Club, as the organization was known from its student founder, J. C. Adams, lasted less than a decade, for it encountered the same problems faced previously by the College. In 1878 an alumnus (U. H. Squires, of the Class of 1878) undertook to provide boarding facilities. From time to time thereafter the College provided meals, but when a Commons Building (Curtis Hall) was constructed in 1894, the Trustees ceased their direct responsibilities for boarding the men and leased part of the building to private individuals and firms who agreed to operate the dining halls. After Tufts became coeducational in 1892, a somewhat different arrangement was made for the women, whereby the College furnished a separate dining hall under management distinct from that for the men's facility. In 1893 the Trustees found it necessary to forbid "under any circumstances . . . the maintenance of clubs for the purpose of providing board or lodging for men and women together."

Student expenses climbed slowly but inexorably over the years. In 1875–76 the combined tuition and incidentals fee reached $74. Like the increase in 1870, this one was initiated by the faculty rather than by the Trustees. Only two years later the combined fees were increased to $100, reflecting a period of financial stringency which was more than local in character. The Panic of 1873 had nation-wide reverberations.[12] In an attempt to soften the blow of increased student costs, a note was inserted in the College catalogue for 1879–80 that "the College is, practically, free to those whose circumstances necessitate it." Except for divinity school students, who did receive free tuition for many years but paid most other expenses, this was not literally true; in 1885 the Trustees voted that the statement be deleted. Nonetheless, some of the Trustees had from time to time considered the "feasibility of making the college free of tuition to all its students." But the financial condition of the institution never warranted such generosity. Every fund-raising drive on behalf of the College included pleas for scholarship assistance for meritorious students.

By and large, the economic status of the early student bodies at Tufts was as modest as the College which had been established to serve their intellectual needs. Most came from what are usually called "middle-class" homes and promptly applied for whatever financial help might be available. There were several sources of assistance by the 1860's. The first was three annual scholarships of $50 each, established as a part of the agreement by which Tufts

[12] At no time in the history of Tufts, or of comparable privately endowed institutions known to the writer, has tuition paid more than a fraction of the operating expenses. An analysis of the Tufts Treasurer's Reports for the ten-year period 1857–67 can be taken as typical of the ratio in the nineteenth century. In 1858, operating expenses (with the figures rounded off) were $6,400 and tuition receipts were $1,850; in 1866, $14,000 and $3,400 respectively.

received a portion of the proceeds from the sale of the filled-in Back Bay lands in Boston. The three state scholarships were increased to $100 in 1869 when tuition was raised from $35 to $60. These so-called "state scholarships," like all others awarded, covered the past year rather than the current one. The second source was a revolving loan fund of $1,000 donated to the College, the income of which was, for a few years, lent to deserving students in individual sums not exceeding $30. Student employment was also provided wherever possible, and the first such positions were as monitors in the dormitories and as bell-ringer. By 1864–65 they garnered annual stipends of $20 and $40 respectively and were much sought after. Satisfactory academic progress and avoidance of "grave College censure" were among the prerequisites for eligibility for these posts, as well as for scholarships and other financial aid.

Four scholarships of $50 each were provided in 1865–66 from a bequest of $10,000 made by Edwin Howland, Esq., of South Africa, and five mathematical scholarships of $100 each were established in honor of Dr. William J. Walker. By the time tuition was raised to $100 in 1877–78, there were twenty-seven scholarships "in the gift of the College," ranging from $60 to $100 each. In view of the fact that only eighty-three students were enrolled in the College proper that year, student needs seem to have been fairly adequately covered. Other efforts were made to recognize the financial problems of students (and their parents), for in 1889 the treasurer was authorized to accept the notes of any student for balances due on term bills, as long as the president certified the need. There were, of course, a few students who let their unpaid bills accumulate rather alarmingly, and authority was given by the Trustees to place some cases in the hands of an attorney for collection. It was reported to the Executive Committee in the spring of 1896 that $5,000 was owed by students who had left the College since 1892. At one time in the 1890's an annual fee of $10 was levied "for the rent of space for study purposes" on all students not residing in a dormitory or fraternity on the Hill or not living with their families. This levy was soon rescinded.

There was another way besides loans and scholarships by which students could be assisted or at least rewarded, even if not always in cash or credit. Student prizes were first announced in the catalogue in 1862–63, after the Goddard Prize Fund was established. The first prizes provided, one for a member of each class, consisted of books of scholarly character. Motley's *Rise of the Dutch Republic* and *History of New Netherlands* were given to the senior who wrote the best dissertation on "The Comparative Value of Contemporary and Subsequent Narrations of Historical Events." The junior prize, a copy of Muller and Donaldson's *History of the Literature of Ancient Greece,* was awarded for the best prose composition (in Greek) on "De Origine et Usu Oraculorum." The sophomore prize, the two-volume set of Smiles' *Engineers,* was to be earned for the best examination in algebra, geometry, and trigonometry. The winning freshman received Smith's *Dictionary of Greek and Roman Biography* for the best Latin translation of a particular chapter in Gibbon's *History of Rome* (Boston edition, 1864) ending on page 413. A ceiling was placed on the length of the dissertation and the Greek prose composition. The first was not to exceed the equivalent of fifteen pages of the *North American Review,* and the second was to be limited to three pages comparable to those in Felton's *Greek Historians.* Vagueness played no part in academic assignments, for prizes or otherwise. The monetary equivalent was awarded in books, and of course the subjects of the dissertations and compositions varied from year to year. "The Social Problem in England" might be assigned for a senior dissertation, or a Latin translation of extracts from William Pitt's "Abolition of the Slave Trade" for the freshman prize. Frequently the faculty, who selected the winners, considered no one worthy of one prize or another, so not all awards were made in any given year.

§   §   §

The climax of the academic year came at public Commencement, which for many years was scheduled for the second Wednesday in July. The first such program was planned for 1856, although none of the thirty students then enrolled had achieved the rank of seniors or had completed the degree requirements. Nevertheless, the first anniversary of the formal "commencement" of the College was celebrated in August 1856, with a public dinner and addresses by T. J. Sawyer and E. H. Chapin at which various "eminent friends of Education" were present.

The first Commencement at which degrees were conferred

took place on July 8, 1857, when three candidates were graduated. The pattern was set on this occasion for similar exercises for years to come. Students were assigned Commencement parts, in accordance with their class rank, and delivered appropriate addresses. From 1857 through 1878 the first address delivered was the Salutatory. Then came, in descending order of rank, Disquisitions, English Orations, Dissertations, and Philosophical Orations, with as many of each as the size and rank of the graduating classes warranted. The high point came with the Valedictory Oration, delivered as the last speech on the program.

Until 1878 there was a part on the program for every degree candidate. But after sixteen addresses were scheduled for Commencement in 1877, the practice was inaugurated of choosing six orations on a competitive basis from those with the highest overall average, and those with the highest grades in Composition and Oratory. Until 1879 the degree candidates were listed alphabetically on the Commencement program. The faculty then considered the idea of placing after each name the percentage grade-rank of the candidate. But this means of airing the students' private academic life was discarded, and a compromise was worked out. From 1879 through 1889 the candidates were listed "in the order of scholarship" for each degree, rather than alphabetically, but without a box score of their individual grades.

Until 1875 the morning Commencement exercises were followed by a formal program in the afternoon under the auspices of the Mathetican Society, the leading undergraduate literary and debating club. The order of exercises consisted usually of an Oration and a Poem delivered by prominent citizens such as Ralph Waldo Emerson, who spoke on the dangers of militarism and the need for "revival and elevation of the intellect" at exercises in 1861. In 1874 Walt Whitman was scheduled to deliver the Poem but was unable to attend because of illness. In 1875 the afternoon exercises were conducted by the Association of Alumni and marked their increasing interest in the affairs of their Alma Mater. Usually a special "Committee of Arrangements" was appointed from within the Trustees to make the necessary preparations for Commencement Day. Printed circulars of the first Commencement were sent to all Universalist pastors to read to their congregations, and special notice was given that ladies were invited to all the festivities. Music was provided both for the Commencement programs proper and for the exercises of the Mathetican Society. Dinner followed the formal programs, and the caterer was authorized "to furnish refreshments for sale" during the day.

Some of the ancient traditions and appurtenances associated with academic exercises were to be found in Tufts Commencements from the beginning. The first marshal was appointed by the faculty in 1861; from 1870 on, the seniors elected marshals to serve on Commencement Day. Rev. W. S. Balch of New York attended the 1857 exercises, and the ceremonies produced from this outspoken clergyman both a caustic extemporaneous speech and a lengthy series of complaints in the columns of the *Trumpet*. Latin was used in announcing the speakers and their subjects and bestowing the degrees, and both Valedictory and Salutatory were delivered in that tongue. When called upon to say a few words after the formal program was over, the Rev. Mr. Balch startled the assemblage by lambasting the practice of using "a language fifteen hundred years dead" which made the orations "a miserable gibberish" that might as well have been delivered in Choctaw or Sanskrit so far as the majority of the audience was concerned. Balch congratulated the Valedictorian for having the courage to appear upon the platform "in plain citizen's dress." Such antiquated customs as dressing up "young graduates in Roman togas and putting Latin phrases on their tongues" did not accord with "the living spirit" of the nineteenth century. These practices, said Balch, "might do for old institutions founded in other times, or for colleges born in Puritanic days," but no excuse could be found "for young American colleges, just learning to talk, to follow such superstitious nonsense."

Balch might have been mollified if he knew that the addresses were delivered in English beginning with the 1868 Commencement, but he would have been most unhappy to discover that "sonorous Latin" continued for many years to be used in conferring degrees, and that the citations for honorary degrees were recorded in Latin until 1916. He might also have taken some comfort from the fact that upperclassmen did not wear "Oxford caps" and gowns until 1881–82. The faculty, it might be added, did not appear in robes, hoods, and mortarboards until the 1903 Commencement.[13]

Other tokens of formal academic existence were added to Tufts at irregular intervals. The Trustees adopted an official seal in 1857, in accordance with the authority granted in the College charter. The simple motto "Pax et Lux" has endured, but one significant alteration was made in the seal. In 1909, while Latin was going out of style in many circles, the words "Holy Bible," prominently displayed on the seal, became "Biblia Sacra." In 1939, an heraldic shield was designed for general use, on the initiative of President Leonard Carmichael, to be used for catalogues, stationery, and the like, and for various public purposes, both official and unofficial. The previous year a mace was designed by the Gorham Company of New York City for use during important academic ceremonies and was donated by the Alumni Council. It is an unusual mace because the College seal, not ordinarily used on such objects, is included as the finial, or crowning ornament.

§ § §

A physical plant, a faculty and administration, a student body, a curriculum, library, and laboratory equipment, and academic exercises and traditions are all recognized parts of an institution of higher learning. Not always so obvious but equally important is a corporate existence and a governing and directing body, however designated. Even though at times a shadowy part of the institution in the minds of students, faculty, and even the public at large, boards of trustees help shape and determine the character and reputation, not to mention the very existence, of an academic institution. Tufts was fortunate from the day it was born in having a competent, interested, and, above all, sympathetic governing body that kept its records scrupulously, exercised its delegated authority with wisdom, and maintained generally harmonious relationships with its faculty and administration that some other institutions might have envied. This in no sense implies the absence of problems, clashes over or between personalities or policies, frustrations, or failures.

[13] The rules followed for academic costume at Tufts were those established in 1902 by the Intercollegiate Bureau of Academic Costume.

One of the matters early confronting the Trustees of Tufts had to do with their own organization. After a delay of four years, a set of by-laws authorized by the charter was adopted in 1856 which proved workable in spite of occasional changes.[14] At first the annual meeting of the Trustees was held in October, with regular meetings in December, March, and June. Special meetings were convened frequently, especially when the problem of finance was involved. Meetings were held for many years on Cornhill in Boston, at the offices of Whittemore's *Trumpet* or in the vestry of the Second Universalist Society. On occasion, the Trustees convened on the Hill, usually before or immediately after Commencement exercises, but no regular pattern was followed. An Executive Committee was provided in the original by-laws to oversee the "housekeeping" operations of the College, and its membership was sufficiently representative and it met frequently enough to conduct a large proportion of the business.[15] No person other than the president of the College was to be at the same time a Trustee and a member of the instructional staff; acceptance of either position was deemed an automatic resignation from the other.

The first problem faced by the Trustees within their own group was staffing. When the Board was formally constituted in 1852, only sixteen members were selected of the twenty-three authorized. The average total was only eighteen until 1878. In that year, when the charter was amended to provide a maximum of thirty Trustees, there were only twenty-one on the Board. Not until 1891–92 did the Trustees reach their authorized number. The basic reason for the manpower difficulty was reluctance of individuals to serve rather than wholesale resignations. A. A. Miner reported his failure to obtain the services of one individual who "peremptorily refused to allow himself to be considered a candidate." In fact, the membership of the Trustees remained surprisingly stable during the first fifty years.

A second problem, faced even before the by-laws were adopted,

[14] The first printed copy of the by-laws was issued in pamphlet form in 1866, as an appendix to the charter. The charter did not appear in the College catalogue until 1891–92, which also carried for the first time a brief historical account of the institution.

[15] For years the Executive Committee met weekly; beginning in the 1890's it met monthly.

was absenteeism. In more than one instance meetings had to be adjourned for lack of a quorum. The by-laws provided that "the place of any Trustee, who shall neglect to attend the meetings of the Corporation for the period of one year, may be declared vacant." The principal culprit which made necessary this provision was geography rather than apathy; as might be expected, some of the Trustees found their duties on the Board too demanding and resigned because they felt they could not do justice to the interests of the College.[16] After two Trustees had resigned in 1856 because they lived too far away to attend meetings, that body considered "the expediency of removing those Trustees who reside so far from the College, as to prevent their attendance at the meetings of the Board."[17] The 1856 edition of the by-laws provided, instead, that in case any member of the Board moved from the state in which he resided when originally elected his place would be declared vacant.[18] Although they were eligible for immediate reelection, such Trustees frequently moved too far out of range.[19] The case of P. T. Barnum, of circus fame, posed a particular problem. Although one of the Trustees under both the provisional organization of 1851 and the 1852 charter, Barnum was unable to attend a single Trustee meeting. In 1853 the Trustees received a letter of resignation from the showman, prompted by his inability to attend meetings "in consequence of his numerous engagements." The Trustees unanimously declined to accept the resignation, "feeling very unwilling to lose his services." It was not until 1857 that this oft-repeated attempt to resign was reluctantly

[16] Throughout the nineteenth century only two officers of the Trustees were compensated for their services: the treasurer, whose salary of $1,500 set in 1870 was reduced to $1,200 in 1876; and the chairman of the Finance Committee, who by 1898 had to devote two days a week to College affairs and was paid $500 a year. Newton Talbot made an unsuccessful attempt in 1898 to have the Trustees reimbursed for their rail fare to and from meetings if they lived more than ten miles from Boston. A mileage allowance "equal to 4¢ per mile, one way" was provided in 1900.

[17] One of the two who resigned that year was Rev. Calvin Gardiner of Waterville, Maine, who had endeavored to raise money for Clinton Liberal Institute and Walnut Hill Evangelical Seminary.

[18] Eli Ballou of Montpelier, Vermont, who had been a member of the original Board, was forced to resign under this provision.

[19] Rev. W. H. Ryder, who moved to Chicago, was a case in point.

honored, when he informed them that he was then "absent from the country." He was in England exhibiting General Tom Thumb and "little Cordelia Howard," who had gained a national reputation as Little Eva in an adaptation of Harriet Beecher Stowe's *Uncle Tom's Cabin.*

The internal organization of the Trustees remained quite simple and informal for almost thirty years, with the Executive Committee continuing to take care of routine matters while special committees handled unusual problems. By 1880, however, the College had expanded sufficiently to require increased attention, and the complexity of Trustee operations grew correspondingly. The first standing committee was created, on Finance, to assist the Treasurer.[20] The Executive Committee first set up its own standing subcommittees when, in 1881, it provided for one on Schools, on Land and Buildings, and on Finance; a committee on the Library was added in 1886. The Library committee functioned so quietly that the Executive Committee apparently forgot it existed, for a Library committee was again constituted in 1891.[21]

Of all the responsibilities which devolved upon the Trustees, the most recurrent one and the one most likely to spell survival or extinction for the young institution was finance. The item most often found on the agenda of Trustees meetings was the devising of "measures to raise money for the use of the College." The Trustees were warned by the ever-vigilant editor of the *Trumpet* before the College had been in operation for a year not to allow their fledgling educational offspring to fall into the financial toils that had engulfed such schools as Antioch College because of unrealistically low tuition and too-generous scholarship aid. Hosea 2d insisted from beginning to end that expenses should not exceed income; one of his greatest fears was that the College would not be self-supporting. His fear was justified immediately. Before the College had graduated its first class in 1857, indebtedness incurred in constructing the first two buildings and settling with Otis A. Skinner, the agent hired to raise the initial subscriptions, was over $10,000. The balance for operating expenses of slightly over $400 in

[20] An assistant to the treasurer was authorized in 1895. The Finance Committee was enlarged from three to five in 1896.

[21] The Committee on Schools was redesignated as the Committee on Education in 1897.

1857 was more than wiped out by an operating deficit of over $3,000 a year later, partly because estimated receipts had been based on an expected enrollment of sixty-five which turned out to be barely fifty. The budget was balanced only by drawing on notes and installments on subscriptions due which were to have been set aside as a sinking fund, and by contributions quietly made by Treasurer Thomas A. Goddard out of his own pocket.[22]

The Universalists were just not a wealthy denomination to begin with. As T. J. Sawyer expressed it in 1852, "we are composed not of the wealthiest nor the poorest, but of the thrifty middle class who earn their bread by the sweat of the brow." When the Universalist Society in Taunton, Massachusetts, sent in a donation of $35 in 1855, the money was accompanied by a note which included these comments: "As you know, perhaps, we have not a *rich man* among us — not in money, I mean. . . . Men, women, and children contributed . . . and to the extent of our limited means we shall hold ourselves ever ready to help when help is needed." The timing of the opening of the College added a complicating factor to the financial situation, for the nation-wide Panic of 1857 had its effect. Yet the Trustees insisted on expressing an optimism that was associated with so many mid-nineteenth-century efforts. They thought they had "great cause for congratulation that we stand as well as we do, when we consider through what a pecuniary crisis the whole business world has passed, and how adversely almost every educational interest has been affected by it."

Throughout the 1850's the College depended on loans, sometimes made on the personal notes of such benefactors as Sylvanus Packard, and on denominational aid. Bequests began to be made to the College as early as 1858, but they were usually not collectible until several years after they were announced, or consisted of unimproved land or other property that required additional expenditure to make salable. Col. John Wade left approximately $45,000 worth of property in Woburn to the College in 1858, but it was years before it could be improved and sold at what the Trustees considered a fair price. Among the "doubtful assets" was a gift of

[22] The distinction must be borne in mind here between operating expenses and endowment; the latter amounted to slightly under $100,000 in mid-1855, but to have touched the principal would have threatened the College with the loss of its charter.

a bond of the Penobscot and Kennebec Rail Road in Maine; it turned out to be security for a third mortgage on which no interest was paid. The Trustees looked constantly to the denomination for support, and Universalist papers circularized appeals for funds time and time again. Typical was an appeal for $2,500 to pay the expenses for instruction the year the College opened. A group did come forward in 1855 to offer assistance. They organized themselves as the Tufts College Educational Association with A. A. Miner as president, and set out to accomplish a double purpose: to secure the funds for current expenses and to establish resources with which to aid needy students. Universalist Societies were urged not only to contribute what they could individually but to organize special auxiliary money-raising associations. The first $35 raised by each auxiliary association entitled the donors to select one student who would receive free tuition; a $50 contribution would entitle the student to all expenses for one year; and each $50 collected thereafter would be used in the same way.

This device for raising funds was successful, at least as a temporary expedient, for by the spring of 1856 over $1,600 had been collected and turned over to the College. In the next two or three years several hundred dollars were collected by "Committees of Young Men" who volunteered on behalf of the Educational Association to solicit aid from the "larger and stronger societies." But these donations and many like them, generously made as they were, fell far short of the continuing needs of the institution. During 1857–58 the treasurer "hired" almost $8,000, and the estimated deficit for the next year was in excess of $2,600. Such a state of affairs could not continue. The next step was to renew an appeal for state aid made in 1856, which the Trustees confidently expected to receive and in fact did obtain after a certain amount of delay.

At first glance, the idea of public aid for an institution ostensibly private in character and endowment, and under the supervision of a religious denomination, might seem quite contrary both to logic and to the tradition of the distinction between private and public (tax-supported) education so widely recognized today. The Trustees' decision to appeal for public funds might seem even more unusual if one reads the final section of the College charter, which specified that its granting "shall never be considered as any pledge on the part of the Government, that pecuniary aid shall hereafter be granted to the college." Yet a brief review of the historical facts shows that state aid had been both assumed and granted frequently, from the early days of America's colonial period.[23] The establishment of Harvard College furnished the classic example in colonial times of the combined efforts of church and state to provide educational facilities. It had received almost $500,000 in public aid, either direct or indirect, by about 1830. Harvard had been founded in effect as a community enterprise, and its first endowment had been given by the Massachusetts Bay Colony rather than by private individuals. Land was a prevalent type of public gift to educational institutions. Harvard received from Massachusetts out-of-state holdings in Maine before that area was made into a separate state in 1820; the sale of the lands brought Harvard approximately $15,000. Public funds helped construct five of Harvard's original buildings. The same story can be told for other institutions about the country; so-called private schools and academies below the college level in Massachusetts and elsewhere also benefited extensively from this policy of state aid.[24] Universalists were quite in accord with their contemporaries in the 1840's and 1850's in considering Harvard a public institution, whether under sectarian control or not. When Hosea 2d had been elected to the Board of Overseers in 1843, it was pointed out that the legislative members of the Board (the state Senate) believed "that the College is a State Institution; that it should not be under the exclusive jurisdiction of any particular sect; and that as the Board is constituted in part of clergy, they should be selected from the different sects among us." Harvard did not belong "exclusively to the Unitarians"; it was "the property of the State of Massachusetts," and all citizens had "an equal interest in that College." Any *bona fide* educational enterprise had the right to expect state assistance. So the matter of obtaining public aid for Tufts was a matter not of breaking a precedent but of profiting by one that had long existed. A scattering of staunch individual-

[23] See Frank W. Blackmar, *The History of Federal and State Aid to Higher Education in the United States,* Bureau of Education, Whole Number 161 (Washington: Government Printing Office, 1890).

[24] See Sherman M. Smith, *The Relation of the State to Religious Education in Massachusetts* (Syracuse, N.Y.: Syracuse Union Bookstore, 1926).

ists like Thomas Goddard preferred not "to lean upon the State. Tufts College ought to be supported by the Universalist public." But the realities of the situation dictated otherwise.

A Trustee committee was appointed in the winter of 1856 "to prepare a memorial to the Legislature and present the same." The intent was to use at least part of the money so obtained to construct a "large brick dormitory" to supplement the College Edifice and the Boarding House (Middle Hall). Miner presented the petition on behalf of the Trustees, with a detailed and fervent plea for assistance. The House Committee on Education was very complimentary of the College and its aims, and particularly impressed by the fact that "religious freedom is enjoyed by its pupils, and in this respect no college is more free from the objections that would lie against a merely denominational college." But "recognizing [Tufts'] claim and breathing a spirit of general good will" was no substitute for money. The legislative committee reported adversely on the petition, citing the unfavorable condition of the state treasury. It was for this reason that "Building B" on the campus turned out to be a wooden structure costing less than $4,000 and intended to serve only temporarily as a dormitory. A second try for state aid was reported favorably out of committee but came to grief on the floor of the House. The bill, if passed, would have given the College $30,000 in aid, payable in six annual installments of $5,000. The defeat of this bill was particularly painful to Tufts' supporters because in the same year St. Lawrence University received a $50,000 grant from the New York legislature.

The third attempt by the Trustees to gain assistance was successful, for a new source of revenue had been added to the state's resources. In 1857 the legislature authorized the sale of part of the low and swampy area in Boston known as the Back Bay. Up to half of the proceeds were to be used "to fill up said land belonging to the Commonwealth, with good and solid earth and clean gravel." This land in turn was to be sold after having been improved, and all proceeds from both sales were designated as the "Bay Lands Fund." It was announced in 1859 that, after certain state obligations were paid, the remainder of the proceeds (52 per cent of the total) was to be divided among five educational institutions. Tufts received the second largest grant (12 per cent), which amounted to $50,000. The other institutions that benefited were the Museum of Comparative Zoology at Harvard, Williams College, Amherst College, and Wesleyan Academy in Wilbraham. The success of Tufts in obtaining so generous an allotment was due to the persistent efforts of Miner and W. H. Ryder. The Trustees had reason to rejoice, but there were two conditions upon which the state grant was made. The first, the creation by the College of three annual free state scholarships, was accomplished in 1863. The second proviso constituted a real challenge to the College and its supporters, for no payment of state funds was to be made until private subscriptions had been secured equaling the $50,000 state grant. The Trustees admitted that matching this offer would be "a difficult task" but considered it a stimulus to renewed effort.

Slightly more than a year after the announcement was made by the state legislature (in 1860), the requisite sum had been raised by the College. Oliver Dean, president of the Trustees, was among the more generous donors; he pledged $10,000. Now the College had to wait, more or less impatiently, for sufficient Back Bay land to be sold to make possible the state payments. Meanwhile, the Trustees had spent the money many times over, on paper. Treasurer Goddard, reluctant as he was to receive public aid for what he thought should be a denominational responsibility, realized its necessity. He had recommended in 1858 that, whatever the amount of the grant might be, it be used first to pay off the indebtedness of the College; the remainder should be funded, while Universalists continued to help make up the annual operating deficits. The Executive Committee had even more grandiose plans when it became known that the state contribution would be $50,000. The erection of a new boarding house, which had become "a positive necessity," could be planned at once; then the Trustees would be "obliged to lay out some thousands of dollars in the construction of roads; and it is necessary that the Library should be added to, by expending some thousands of dollars." The Trustees proceeded at once to build the new dormitory (East Hall) before even a dollar had been received from the state. In September 1861 the first installment ($12,393.96) arrived, but then it appeared that further payments would be indefinitely postponed. The nation was about to go to war with itself. Fort Sumter, South Carolina, had been fired upon, the President of the United States had issued a call for the militia of the states loyal to the Union, and two months before the

East Hall in the 1870's

first installment of state funds had arrived at Tufts, President Lincoln had ordered Congress to convene in special session. Tension and uncertainty prevailed everywhere. The Executive Committee in May had recognized "the present unfortunate state of our public affairs" and was sure that under the circumstances the sale of Back Bay lands would come to an abrupt halt. The opportunity the College had of using a combination of public and private funds to pay for the new boarding house and "all our debts," and even leave something toward paying the annual deficit, seemed to have gone glimmering.

As soon as the promise of state aid had been made in 1859, the Tufts College Educational Association had disbanded. In 1860 the treasurer had been authorized to borrow up to $12,000 on a combination of personal notes of the Executive Committee and certain bonds and mortgages held by the Corporation. By the end of 1860 the Corporation was paying out $1,200 a year in interest on various obligations. Even with the $12,000 from the state, the indebtedness by the end of the fiscal year 1861–62 was over $17,000, and the estimated operating deficiency for 1862–63 was $4,000. Plans were made to sell off some of the valuable rental property in the greater Boston area in which part of the endowment had been invested, or which had been willed to the College. To make matters worse, Tufts lost its first president in this critical period. It was no wonder that the Trustees felt they could not employ Sawyer as Hosea 2d's successor, even at the modest salary of $1,200, and that they breathed a sigh of relief when Miner indicated his willingness to accept the post without compensation.

The chairman of the Executive Committee wryly remarked at the Trustees' regular meeting in May 1863 that it would be nice some day to "see the Treasurer's account denuded of its hitherto stereotyped finis: 'Balance due the Treasurer.'" The Trustees could tolerate at this point what might have seemed a rather flippant remark at the serious juncture in the College's financial affairs. Word had just come that "the sales of Back Bay Lands by the State have been so successful that we have reason to hope we shall receive the balance of the State grant to us of $50,000 very soon." The hopes were justified, although another year elapsed between the promise and the fulfillment. The hoped-for check for $37,-606.04 arrived in May 1864, and the promise of the state had been vindicated, down to the very last cent. It seemed that the College might survive after all. As it turned out, Tufts not only survived but expanded its academic horizons in the 1860's by departing from its exclusively classical curriculum and venturing into other areas.

99

4. "A Sound and Generous Culture"

IN THE DECADE OF THE 1860's, Tufts College embarked on three
new degree programs. Two of them, the philosophical course and
the engineering curriculum, were intended to meet the growing
needs of the College and of the student body. The third, a theological department which became the divinity school and eventually
Crane Theological School, was the outgrowth of several impulses
that had been felt long before the College was founded.

But Hosea 2d was not to see any of these come into being during his lifetime. In the fall of 1859 his health began to fail. When
one reviews the extent and strenuousness of his activities on behalf
of the College, it was no wonder. He sensed that his association with
Tufts would soon be over when he wrote his brother Levi, after a
particularly arduous term of school work, that his "labors here
might come to their end ere long." In 1860 his loyal and understanding faculty readjusted and reduced his teaching and administrative load by taking over some of his duties. Little more than a
month before a kidney ailment cut short his career at the age of
sixty-four, Hosea 2d wrote his devoted friend Sawyer that his life
was wearing away, his energies were failing, and so much remained
to be done. His passing was a blow to all, and the resolutions on his
death, which occurred at his College home on May 27, 1861, elic-
ited simple and moving tributes from faculty, students, and Trustees, and from the denomination at large. The day following President Ballou's death, the Trustees held their regular meeting scheduled long before. The usual reports had already been prepared,
and that of the Executive Committee seemed a fitting epitaph for
the man who had labored so diligently. They found the progress
and conduct of the students, and student relations with the faculty,

John Potter Marshall
Acting President, 1861–62

never better. The general state of the College, even with many unfinished tasks at hand, was "eminently satisfactory."

But the business of the College had to go on. The fifth Commencement had to be planned, diplomas had to be signed, and examining committees had to be appointed to select an entering class for the next term. Professor Tweed was selected to preside on Commencement Day and confer the degrees, and Professor Marshall was made acting president until a successor could be found.

The Trustees immediately set about finding a head for their institution, but over a year went by before any success was achieved.

The first committee appointed to make a selection failed to nominate a candidate, and another committee had the same results. The problem was finally referred to the Executive Committee, which contacted "several gentlemen," none of whom was willing to accept the office. Rev. James P. Weston, president of Lombard University, Galesburg, Illinois, from 1860 to 1872, was suggested by Sylvanus Packard, but Weston preferred to stay where he was.[1] Both the faculty and students suggested T. J. Sawyer, who had declined the presidency in 1853. After extended discussion, Sawyer declined a second time. He argued "pressure of other duties," including management of a large farm for which he had recently assumed responsibility. But in the last analysis, the old question of salary was the real stumbling block. The Trustees were unable to meet his request for $1,200, for it would increase the existing annual deficiency to over $5,000. One alternative was to "dispense with one of the Professors or the Tutor now employed."[2] However, this would only create new complications. In view of "all the circumstances, the state of our country, the limited means at our command, and the little probability of any immediate increase in our income," the Executive Committee had a real problem on its hands. To continue indefinitely with an interim president solved nothing; selecting a president from the faculty would solve one manpower dilemma, only to create another. The final decision was to select "some gentleman of established reputation, whose interest in the College would lead him to devote a portion of his time to it without salary, the College paying his expenses and disbursements."

The Trustees were as fortunate in 1862 as they had been a decade earlier in having qualified presidential material within their own ranks. The man unanimously selected was Alonzo Ames Miner, associate of and later successor to Hosea Ballou the elder as pastor of the School Street Universalist Society in Boston, and a man active in the denomination from the time he preached his first sermon in 1838. He had held pastorates in Vermont, New Hamp-

[1] Lombard University, chartered as a collegiate institution in 1853, was founded as a Universalist academy in 1831. After many vicissitudes, Knox College absorbed all but Lombard's Ryder Divinity School, which was united with the Meadville Theological School in Chicago.

[2] Benjamin Graves Brown, Tutor in Mathematics from 1861 to 1865. He continued as a permanent member of the faculty.

Alonzo Ames Miner
President, 1862–75

shire, and two towns in Massachusetts before his arrival in Boston
in 1848, and very soon achieved a considerable reputation not only
as an eloquent preacher but as an able polemicist. He was probably
as conservative religiously as a Universalist could be and still stay
within the denomination, and he expended much ink, paper, and
effort in challenging what he considered to be the non-Christian
teachings of the brilliant Unitarian social reformer Theodore Parker. Miner was an uncompromising opponent of the use of alcohol,
served as president of the Massachusetts Temperance Alliance for
some twenty years, and at one time was a gubernatorial candidate
on the Prohibition ticket. He loved a good fight on the issues of the

day and had an excellent opportunity to demonstrate both his ideas and his eloquence when he was called upon in 1884 to deliver the annual Election Sermon before the state legislature. This sermon was a tradition established in colonial times; a clergyman was selected to deliver what usually turned out to be a mildly inspirational and platitudinous address before the incoming and outgoing public officers. Miner's peroration comprised such a scathing attack on the consumption of alcoholic beverages and on the "liquor interests" in general that the annoyed legislators soon thereafter dispensed with the Election Sermon entirely.

Miner's experience as an educator was already impressive when the Trustees, as a measure of desperation, asked him to take over the presidency of Tufts. Like Hosea 2d, Miner was a self-educated man whose college degrees were all honorary but whose devotion to the cause of education was unswerving. He had taught school as a youth in Vermont and New Hampshire and subsequently served on the school boards of Methuen, Lowell, and Boston. He too was a member of the Harvard Board of Overseers, and of the state Board of Education. For twenty years he was chairman of the Board of Visitors of the State Normal Art School. Miner was one of the numerous Universalists in the 1850's and 1860's on whom Harvard University conferred an honorary Divinity degree. His range of activities on behalf of the denomination was second only to that of Hosea 2d. His activities in the organization and social reform efforts of the Universalists made his name a familiar one. He was one of the founders of the Universalist Publishing House, incorporated in Massachusetts in 1872. He was also president of the Trustees of the Bromfield School at Harvard, Massachusetts. Miner served as trustee of the estate of Henry Bromfield Pearson that made possible the establishment of a preparatory school for engineering at Tufts. His efforts on behalf of Universalist academies were equally important. He was both a benefactor and Trustee of Dean Academy and a donor to other Universalist preparatory schools. It might be added that most of these activities (only a partial listing) were carried on simultaneously with ministering to a parish and guiding the College.[3]

Miner's direct connection with Tufts began when he was

[3] The standard biography is George H. Emerson, *Life of Alonzo Ames Miner* (Boston: Universalist Publishing House, 1896).

elected a Trustee in 1855. He was immediately placed on the Executive Committee, served on numerous special committees, and was secretary and also treasurer of the Corporation for many years. The Trustees selected from their number the man most intimately associated with the College and probably the man most aware of its needs. They were obviously pleased that Miner accepted the presidency, but there was concern expressed immediately that his clerical post might take a disproportionate share of his time and energies, and that the two jobs would prove too demanding. This problem of "divided allegiance," as it were, was to plague him for most of his thirteen years as Tufts' chief executive, but he accepted the office on the terms outlined by his fellow Trustees and became the first (and only) non-resident, non-salaried president in the history of the institution.

The Executive Committee recognized the obligations Miner had undertaken but explained that the facts had to be faced: the question was "not what *would be* best under *other* circumstances, but what *is* best under *existing* circumstances." If the Second Universalist Society had not paid Miner a full salary, it is difficult to imagine what the fate of the College might have been. When he assumed office in the late summer of 1862, after having been duly inaugurated on July 9, the country was already rent asunder by its most tragic internecine conflict, and Tufts was in a precarious, if not desperate, financial condition. It was already burdened with an indebtedness of $18,000, and annual operating deficits were far outrunning income. The treasury was so low in the summer of 1862 that Sylvanus Packard and Charles Tufts volunteered to make up out of their own pockets any deficit arising from the dinner held in connection with Miner's inauguration. It was a tribute to Miner's abilities as an executive that when he tendered his resignation in 1874 the assets of the institution were nearly $1,000,000.

There was one bright spot in an otherwise gloomy picture in 1862. The faculty and the students shared the Trustees' enthusiasm for Miner. When the students were informed that Sawyer had declined the post, a petition bearing the name of every student in the College present the day it was circulated was transmitted to the Trustees asking them to select Miner. A Trustee subcommittee had solicited faculty reaction, and the result was "hearty approbation," backed up with a letter from the faculty informing the Trustees that the instructional staff had unanimously voted that they would "receive with *great pleasure*" the announcement of Miner's election. The considerable evidence available indicates that both faculty and students were aware of the stresses and strains under which the College was operating in 1861–62 and expressed what the Trustees considered a commendable and truly heartwarming loyalty to the young institution.

§ § §

The first steps taken in Miner's administration to strengthen the College resulted from a combination of principle and expediency. The introduction of a "Philosophical Course" and the creation of an Engineeering Department had several purposes. They reinforced Miner's conviction that educational opportunity should be increased and that the College's social and intellectual base should be broadened to insure that the institution was serving societal needs in the most effective fashion possible. At the same time, it was hoped that the introduction of new curricula would appeal to sufficient applicants to help fill the near-empty coffers of the College.

In 1863–64 the faculty adopted and the Trustees approved a so-called Philosophical Course of Study as a parallel alternative to the "Classical" or "Academic" curriculum. It was originally announced as a "partial Course of Instruction," for three years, to lead to the degree of Bachelor of Philosophy (B.Ph.). Entrance examinations were to be "well sustained" in mathematics, geography, and history, as required for the regular course, and in English grammar in place of ancient languages. The subjects required for the degree were substantially the same as for the A.B., except that French and German were used to fulfill the foreign language requirement. The new degree was introduced in part to meet the needs of increasing numbers of applicants who had insufficient preparation in Greek and Latin, and was for that reason considered an "inferior" degree by both faculty and A.B. candidates. After two years' experimentation, the philosophical curriculum lost its designation as a "partial course" and became a "Special Course of Instruction" of two years. The requirements for admission were also increased by raising the standards in mathematics to include geometry and algebra. But the philosophical course was never considered satisfactory. Despite the existence of the program, students were encouraged by a catalogue statement to complete the "full Collegiate Course" whenever possible as the better alternative. In 1875–76 a reconstruction of the philosophical course was undertaken, for as a degree program it had failed either to gain favor among students or to accomplish the results originally expected of it. The faculty also considered the possibility of abolishing the course in that year, since only two students were enrolled in the program at the time. Giving a Bachelor's degree for only two years of collegiate work was thought "altogether incompatible with the dignity of the College" and inconsistent with the standard of scholarship it sought to maintain. Judging from faculty records and especially the "Proficiency" reports, less able students tended to enroll in the philosophical course prior to 1875. It was possible for students in that course to become candidates for the A.B. by making up the work in the "regular" course by arrangements with their instructors, but very few apparently availed themselves of the opportunity at first. The result was the establishment of a four-year curriculum in 1875–76 running parallel to the A.B. program, the only difference being the substitution in the philosophical course of modern languages for Greek. To insure that the language requirement was adequate it was stipulated that the student should have had the equivalent of one year's preparation in French before admission. This requirement not only provided a respectable criterion for admission but helped answer, said the president, "a crying reproach of American college education in general": namely, that too little attention was being paid to modern languages, especially French and German. Even then, the outcome was far from satisfactory. The freshmen were so deficient in French that they were "disqualified from pursuing the work that was laid down for them when the course was established." Such students had to be put in a special class and treated as though they had never studied the language. The only way the deficiency could be overcome, said President Capen, was "rigid adherence to our standard of admission."

The revised philosophical curriculum after 1875 was actually identical to the classical program except for the foreign language requirement, which represented the first major concession to modern languages and the first significant retreat in the position of

ancient languages in the curriculum. As the faculty themselves
pointed out, the substitution of French for Greek and the offering
of a relatively wide range of electives were "best adapted alike to
the circumstances of the College and the needs of a large body of
young men desiring an extended curriculum which shall be rather
literary than scientific." Only one major change was made in the
program before it was abandoned in 1902. Students were allowed
to substitute German for French beginning in 1884. The philosophical curriculum was so much like the regular course that several times in the 1880's and 1890's the faculty considered the awarding of the A.B. degree for either course of study. When several students requested transfer from the B.Ph. to the A.B. program in
1896–97, a procedure was worked out so that it could be effected by
taking six additional term hours in modern languages.

The reorganization of the philosophical course to bring it
more into line with conventional collegiate-level expectations did
not attract the "large body of young men" to whom it was intended
to appeal. Only fifteen men had graduated under the pre-1875 programs. There was a slight increase after the four-year course was
introduced, and forty-four students received the B.Ph. degree between 1879 and 1900. But the number of enrollees in the program
thereafter declined while overall enrollment expanded, and only
twelve more had been graduated when the last philosophical degree was awarded in 1905. On several occasions there were no B.Ph.
graduates at all in a given year. The last two such degrees, awarded
in 1908 and 1909 respectively, were *extra ordinem,* as of previous
classes. In some ways the post-1874 course was more "modern" and
more permissive than its "classical" counterpart, but it lacked the
prestigiousness of the latter course. One reason certainly for the
ultimate failure of the program was the tendency to set aside the
"Philosophicals" (as the students in the program were called by
the faculty) as an inferior breed. They were at the bottom of the
list of underclassmen even in drawings for dormitory rooms, and
they were not admitted to competitions for prizes. The next departure from the traditional classical curriculum was more successful.

§   §   §

Tufts embarked in 1865–66 on a degree program combining
liberal arts and professional training. A three-year course of in-

struction in civil engineering was introduced which led to the degree of Civil Engineer (C.E.) , with the requirements for admission the same as for the philosophical program. At first the faculty considered granting either the A.B. or the B.Ph. degree because of the substantial liberal arts content of the engineering curriculum; however, the first degree actually awarded under the new program was designated "Civil Engineer." The instruction in engineering was made possible by the Walker donations intended to strengthen the field of mathematics, particularly in its practical applications. The engineering curriculum included "most of the branches of an English education," but with a greater emphasis on mathematics. French was the designated foreign language and Rhetoric was required throughout the course. Chemistry (both inorganic and organic), botany, mineralogy, geology, and physics were included, together with the customary Intellectual and Moral Philosophy, Logic, and Political Economy. Mathematics included trigonometry, surveying, descriptive and analytical geometry, differential and integral calculus, and mechanics. Drawing was required throughout the program. The same recommendation was made for engineering as for the philosophical course, namely, that the full collegiate course should be taken if possible, although the engineering program would offer "means of valuable discipline, and of a substantial practical education." Emphasis throughout the engineering course was on application of textbook principles. Hence much time was spent in surveying, drafting, and field work, which was concentrated in the second and third years. In 1871 the engineering classes under Instructor Charles Durlin Bray were given permission to be absent from the Hill approximately one month "to engage in the practical work of laying out a Rail Road." A course in iron manufacture included visits to the Bay State Iron Works in South Boston. Another special project in "field engineering" was the construction by students of a topographic map of the College grounds to be shown at the Centennial Exhibition in Philadelphia in 1876. Among the other displays at the Exhibition was a Tufts catalogue in an elegant embossed leather binding.

The Engineering Department started without fanfare and with only tolerable success. Both equipment and library facilities in this new branch of instruction were inadequate, and for many years a large amount of ingenuity and effort went to improvisation by both faculty and students. But this was turned to good advantage in the educational process. Until an actual steam engine could be obtained, students were required to design a complete engine in the drafting room. In 1894 the Electrical Engineering Department constructed, at a cost of less than $700, a Morday Alternating Current dynamo weighing approximately three tons. It would have cost some $2,000 if acquired from a commercial firm.

In the spring of 1870 the engineering student body was far from overwhelming in numbers. Five students had enrolled in September 1869 (one in the first year and four in the second year). But three of the five had dropped out before the academic year was over. Of these, one had resigned from school, one had transferred to the philosophical course, and one had been dropped because of inability to do the work. The two remaining students were handicapped by poor preparation and were having difficulty in maintaining passing grades.

Nothing daunted, the College in the 1870's attempted to make the program more attractive and at the same time appeal to more competent students. The three-year curriculum was retained, but in 1876–77 a notice was inserted in the catalogue that a fourth year of study was provided "for those graduate Engineers who wish to take up work in some branch of Engineering and in other departments of the College." Two years later it was provided that students in the "regular" course could so arrange electives that they could obtain the degree of Civil Engineer by a one-year postgraduate course in the Engineering Department. This opportunity to blend liberal arts and engineering training was extended in 1879–80 to those in the philosophical course. The blurring of lines between the "literary" and the engineering curricula is illustrated by the fact that "knowledge of the metric system" was added to the admissions requirements for the engineering course two years after it was required for the "regular" course.

The College had sufficient facilities by 1883 to announce another degree program in engineering. If demand warranted it, a three-year program in "Electrical Science" was to be offered, with emphasis on commercial applications in the fields of telegraphy, telephony, and electric lighting. Graduates of the electrical engineering program were promised a distinctive degree although, as it turned out, by the time the Department of Electrical Engineering was formally created in 1890, the engineering degrees had been re-designated. The degree of Civil Engineer became Bachelor of Mechanic Arts in 1883–84 and the designation of "Civil" and "Electrical" was to appear on the diploma, depending on which course was completed. This degree gave way to the two separate degrees of Bachelor of Civil Engineering and Bachelor of Electrical Engineering when the engineering curricula were extended to four years in 1892–93. The faculty considered the possibility of allowing students to complete the program in three years, providing they maintained an average of 75 per cent, but this plan was not adopted. With the inception of the four-year program, the students, previously referred to as "first year," etc., received the same label (freshman, etc.) as the students in the College of Letters. The "Engineers" were never set apart as were the "Philosophicals" from the rank and file of the student body, being, for example, always assigned Commencement parts. A group of engineering students who presumably did not appreciate the classical tradition petitioned the faculty in 1900 that their diplomas be written in English, and a faculty committee was appointed to confer with the Trustees on the matter, but with no immediate results.

In rapid succession Mechanical and Chemical Engineering Departments were established (the first in 1894–95 and the second in 1898–99). To avoid proliferation of undergraduate engineering degrees and to minimize confusion, the uniform degree of Bachelor of Science in Engineering was awarded beginning in 1895–96, with the diploma stating the particular curriculum followed. The new degrees were actually authorized to be used the previous year, but habit was apparently too strong, for the Commencement program in 1894–95 still carried the old designations. The basic programs for the first two years of each of the four curricula were substantially the same. It was provided in some instances that students could take both electrical and civil engineering courses "with a view to taking degrees from both departments." The engineering departments had come a long way by the turn of the century from the faltering beginning made in the 1860's.

§ § §

The third new degree program established by the College during Miner's administration was in reality not new at all in view of the antecedents of the institution. The divinity school, which opened in the fall of 1869 with four students and two teachers, represented the realization of the hopes of some Universalists over a quarter of a century before. The very first agitation to found a theological school had assumed one located in Massachusetts, and when the parallel demand for a college was voiced, the latter was to have been located in New York State. The events of the 1850's had reversed these original intentions, and Tufts had opened as a strictly "literary" institution, with no formal theology offered in its curriculum. The event which brought the Tufts Divinity School into existence was the death of Sylvanus Packard in 1866. A provision in his will stipulated that part of the proceeds from his estate was to be used to establish a Professorship of Christian Theology in the College. Tufts, as the residuary legatee of Packard's substantial estate, was expected to receive approximately $300,000 in all. This posed a problem for the Trustees. They wished to keep anything that smacked of sectarianism — even of the Universalist variety — out of the curriculum. On the other hand, they had every intention of honoring the wishes of one of Tufts' most generous benefactors. The result was a decision to build a separate and quasi-independent theological school around the Professorship of Christian Theology required by Packard's will. The first conversations among the Trustees as to how to solve the problem were held in 1866. After much discussion they determined to establish the divinity school "in connection with Tufts College" but with a faculty and course of instruction distinct from the rest of the institution.

Pending the settlement of the Packard estate, no concrete action was taken until the early summer of 1869, except to establish the Packard Professorship and offer it to the Rev. T. J. Sawyer. Sawyer waited well over a year before he made up his mind. After having declined the presidency of Tufts twice, he this time accepted the theological post, with what for that day was the rather substantial salary of $2,500. Even then, he assumed the task with great hesitation. As he pointed out to Miner, he had served the denomination over forty years and had thought himself done with public responsibilities. But his devotion to Universalism was stronger than his concern for "temporal affairs," as he expressed it.

He knew that, in the last analysis, he could have obtained "much larger pecuniary returns" than Tufts College could offer him but he saw where his duty lay.

Sawyer promptly cautioned the denomination that the Packard bequest, however large it might be, was not to be interpreted as relieving Universalists of their obligation to support the new theological school. All that Packard had intended was to lay a foundation on which such a school could be built. It was up to the denomination to build the superstructure. Sawyer enumerated three immediate needs of the school. First on the list was an adequate library. The College library was respectable, "considering the circumstances under which it was gathered," but there were many deficiencies in the collection on theology, where the results of "the best scholarship of the day" ought to be available. Further, the great preponderance of theological students were, "if rich in faith, still poor as relates to this world's goods." Financial assistance to such students was indispensable. Finally, the shortage of ministers, no matter how trained, was chronic and becoming more critical as Universalism expanded.

Plans were outlined for opening the divinity school at the beginning of the academic year 1869–70, and the Rev. Charles H. Leonard of Chelsea was selected as the second faculty member. Leonard, grandfather of Leonard Carmichael, seventh president of Tufts, was highly regarded in the denomination. Elmer H. Capen, although thirty-one at the time, offered Leonard's name with some trepidation because Capen was "one of the younger members of the Denomination" and his suggestion might have been regarded as "impertinent or presumptuous." How much influence Capen had cannot be known for a certainty, but it is true that Leonard was elected Goddard Professor of Sacred Rhetoric and Pastoral Theology just a few weeks after Capen wrote his letter. Leonard had studied for the ministry under Sawyer at Clinton, New York, and when he came to Tufts had held his Chelsea pastorate for twenty-three years and achieved an exceptional reputation for his Sunday School work.

Before the divinity school was two years old, Sawyer requested additional staff, for by the end of the 1870–71 academic year the enrollment had increased to twelve, and twenty-one students had applied for admission the following year. Sawyer pointed out that even with a new man the school was not as adequately staffed as the theological school at St. Lawrence University. His request was complied with, for the Rev. William G. Tousey was employed as Instructor in Psychology and Natural Theology in 1871. Tousey had been graduated from Tufts in 1869 and was a member of the first class in the divinity school. He jumped from instructor to professor in 1873, only one year after receiving his Divinity degree. It should be noted that he was twenty-three when he entered Tufts as a freshman in 1865 and had already had several years of teaching experience before entering college. He was also one of the many Tufts undergraduates who spent their winters between terms "keeping school" before that custom was abolished.

The school's offerings were expanded after 1875 with the addition of Rev. George T. Knight to its faculty. Knight, the second Tufts alumnus to serve on the divinity school staff, taught Rhetoric, Biblical History, Church History, and Greek. In the next year Moses True Brown, who taught Oratory in the regular curriculum, began to offer a similar course for the divinity school students.

Under the unofficial headship of Sawyer (he was given the title of dean in 1882) the school was fortunate in being able to supplement its classroom offerings by drawing upon a rich variety of ministerial talent off the campus. Each year lectures were given by leading clergymen who shared their ideas, learning, and experience with the students. The College was able to obtain the services of the majority at almost no cost except for travel. In accord with the liberal philosophy of the entire College, the divinity school not infrequently went outside its traditional Universalist ranks and brought in men from other denominations and faiths. For part of 1879–80 a Jewish scholar, Bernard Maimon, served as Instructor (without pay) of Hebrew Language and Literature. Students were also encouraged to take advantage of the "important instrumentalities of culture in the Boston area, including attendance at services conducted by the most noted Divines of New England."

The first curriculum established in the divinity school represented an attempt to provide theological training for students with a wide variety of backgrounds. The two requirements to be met by all students were that they furnish testimonials of Christian character and that they "believe in the Christian Religion, and have a sincere purpose to devote their lives to the Christian ministry." The

114

second requirement created considerable embarrassment when the faculty came to vote degrees in 1883. One candidate had completed the prescribed work but announced just as he was about to be graduated that he was not a believer in Christianity. If his attitude were allowed to influence the faculty's decision, they could do nothing else but withhold their recommendation for a degree. In their judgment the candidate was "not fit to be a minister of the Gospel in any Christian Church." The problem was dumped in the laps of the Trustees. The recommendation that the candidate receive a degree was tabled for one year; the student received his degree in 1884, after a clergyman who had know him for many years interceded in his behalf.

A three-year course of study for holders of the Bachelor's degree was provided, leading to the Bachelor of Divinity (B.D.) degree. Such candidates were admitted to the divinity school without examination. Those who were unable, in the judgment of the faculty, to pursue the full course were "examined in those branches of learning which are usually taught in the best High Schools and Academies" and were placed in classes appropriate to their degree of attainment. They received a certificate instead of a diploma upon completion of three years of work. A fourth year of study under faculty direction was provided for such students, who could then become candidates for the B.D. In 1871–72 the "Junior" (first) class of six students elected to stay four years and did extra work in Greek, Logic, Rhetoric, and Natural Theology. By 1879–80 the elective subjects available to all students in the school totaled thirteen; the Syriac language and Egyptian hieroglyphics were among the offerings. In 1871 a "partial course" was authorized for those desiring to attend less than four years.

Students who entered the regular three-year program ("Junior," "Middle," and "Senior" years respectively) received a comprehensive training for their chosen calling. First-year students were instructed in the Hebrew language; Biblical archeology and geography; the Gospels (including Greek exegesis, using the books of Matthew and Mark in the New Testament); Hebrew history and law; and Evidences of Christianity. "Middle Year" students reviewed the literature and interpretations of the Old Testament; continued Greek exegesis (Luke and John); studied ecclesiastical history, systematic theology, and the history of doctrines; and were instructed in the office and work of the Christian ministry. In this second year the students had their first experience in composing and delivering sermons. The senior year continued most of the work of the second year but also included instruction in church polity and administration, Christian Ethics, and pastoral theology. The "conditional" studies for those not able to pursue the regular program included logic, rhetoric, Intellectual and Moral Philosophy, Greek, and work in Elocution (Oratory). German and French were available in the "academical" (collegiate) part of the College. It was "earnestly recommended" in 1871 that all applicants for admission be able to read "some of the Latin Classical Authors, and the Greek text of the Gospels."

All theological students were required to attend daily devotional services and weekly prayer meetings, and to listen to each other's efforts at delivering sermons. One privilege set the divinity school students apart from their "collegiate" brethren: they paid no tuition or room rent, although the usual charges were made for board. It was universally assumed, as Sawyer had emphasized, that candidates for the ministry would be of modest circumstances, if not penniless. To assist needy students the Board of Trustees of the Universalist General Convention provided full scholarships (originally $160) in the form of loans payable to the students in three installments. The recipients of such aid (their names were never divulged) were to repay in five annual installments, without interest, after graduation. If they failed to enter the divinity school after being given aid, withdrew before completing the course, or decided not to enter the Universalist ministry after receiving aid, such recipients were expected to repay whatever amount had been lent them. At the end of each year the divinity school was required to make a report on each scholarship holder "as to piety, talents, diligence, scholarship, prudence, health, and general influence." Mere evidence of need was soon found to be inadequate as a basis for providing scholarship-loans, and in 1871 candidates for financial assistance were required to pass creditably an examination in Rhetoric, Mental and Moral Science, and English prose composition. A religious test was also added: each candidate had to affirm his acceptance of the Winchester Confession of Faith.

When the divinity school opened, its classroom facilities consisted of a small room on the second floor of the College Edifice.

The western half of the West Hall was assigned to the school when the dormitory was built in 1872. The first floor was used for classes and one room was fitted up as a chapel. The rooms on the upper floors provided housing accommodations. This location prevailed until the divinity school received a home of its own in Miner and Paige Halls in 1891–92. With no tuition or room rent to pay, divinity school student expenses were not expected to exceed $300 a year. Board was available through the College facilities, which in the 1870's and most of the 1880's were furnished through a student eating club. Theological students showing "sufficient maturity" were permitted to preach, under faculty supervision, for the last year and a half and in this way could "add to their pecuniary resources."

The creation of the divinity school met with immediate favor with the denomination. It seemed to be "admirably suited to the purpose," and clergymen who did not enjoy the advantage of systematic theological training were realizing how much they had missed. There was no longer any excuse for "young men rushing into the ministry, half prepared." One writer optimistically stated that the new divinity school marked "a new era" in the history of the Universalist Church, particularly in allowing those with no formal preparation for the ministry at all to avail themselves of the services of the school.

The liberal policy of opening the divinity school to practically all comers caused academic complications from the outset. Before the school was five years old a four-year curriculum was provided which attempted to combine a liberal arts foundation with ministerial training. Prospective students were strongly urged, however, to take "a full Collegiate course of study" before they enrolled in the school. As the catalogue statement put the matter, "the call is for men of liberal culture, and it has been found that Academic discipline is a great value as a preparation for professional studies." The faculty did not yet (in 1873–74) think it desirable to make an A.B. degree a prerequisite, largely because of the financial burdens it would impose on the students, but they did offer what they considered the equivalent of a collegiate course as the next best thing. In actuality, the new four-year program did not differ basically from the existing three-year sequence or from the optional additional fourth year offered in 1871–72, except for increased emphasis on

Homiletics and Pastoral Theology. The three-year program temporarily remained the regimen for those who held the first degree. The new four-year course apparently met a real need, for in 1876–77, three years after it was announced, seven of the thirty-one students were enrolled in it.

When the financial situation of the College became precarious in the late 1870's and continued so into the 1880's, the divinity school was as vulnerable as the "academical" departments. No action was taken at the time, but the Executive Committee of the Trustees recommended in 1877 that the school's new four-year program be cut back to three and suggested that standards of admission also be raised. Between 1877–78 and 1883–84, divinity school enrollment suffered a slow but steady decline, which was an additional source of concern to the Trustees. In the former year there were twenty-five students; in the latter, only eighteen. The Trustees established the Professorship of Church History in 1883, to which the Rev. George T. Knight was promoted (but without increase in salary). It was decided at first that the resulting vacancy in the instructorship would not be filled. However, the faculty of the school insisted that its needs required a replacement, particularly as Sawyer was forced to reduce his teaching and administrative load because of failing eyesight and other infirmities that came with advancing age. The Trustees again bowed to the wishes of the school by employing Rev. George M. Harmon in 1883, but only by following the rather drastic financial expedient of reducing the salaries of Tousey and Sawyer sufficiently to make up the new faculty member's salary. Sawyer was left with a college-owned residence and a salary of $650. As can be readily imagined, this evoked a lengthy protest from the elderly clergyman, who had come to Tufts as the first Packard Professor. Less than a year later, when he was relieved of all academic duties, his salary was further reduced, although he was permitted to live in his house rent-free.[4]

Even before the financial difficulties facing both the College

[4] The house itself was old, and apparently needed constant repairs. It had been the residence of the Teele farm, which had been purchased by the College in 1863. On one occasion Mrs. Sawyer requested a new floor in the dining room, which had been the old kitchen. For over sixteen years the kitchen had been used for canning and pickling for market, and there is no doubt that the floor had been well seasoned.

and the divinity school were noticeably eased, the faculty of the school undertook to heed the recommendation of the Trustees to elevate "the standards of ministerial scholarship." Their resolutions, submitted to the Trustees in the winter of 1883, suggested that after a two-year transition period, "only graduates of some College, or persons who in the judgment of the Faculty have received an equivalent education, shall be admitted to the Divinity School as candidates for the degree of B.D." No person was to be admitted even as a "Special" student who did not have an education equivalent to that required for college. Accepting the general principles embodied in the divinity school recommendations, the Trustees added the requirement that all candidates for admission, degree holders or not, had to "pass such an examination as, in the judgment of the Faculty shall show that they are prepared to take up the work of the School with profit." The aims of the divinity school faculty were worthy, but the accomplishments of the students apparently continued to fall short of the ideal. There was continuing concern in the 1890's over the lack of maturity and preparedness of many entering students which dogged them even after graduation. The effect, according to one visitor to the school, was "to lower the theological school in the estimation of students in other departments of the College, and of educated men who see that these men are not fitted to cope with the problems which surround them." A special Trustee committee investigated the criticisms of the school and came to its defense. The committee found that the catalogue requirements were so strictly adhered to that many clergy complained. The fact that in 1896 degrees were recommended to less than half of the senior class was evidence that the faculty were attempting to maintain standards; but the high academic mortality rate reflected the basic weakness of an admissions policy that still allowed students with no college training to enroll in the school.

It is clear that the Trustees intended the divinity school to be kept as separate as possible from the rest of the College; it is equally clear that the attempt was far from successful for at least thirty years. The divinity school faculty was administratively distinct from the general faculty, kept separate records, and made its recommendations for degrees directly to the Trustees. When the Trustees provided Visiting Committees in 1869–70, a separate one was provided for the divinity school. The curriculum was independent and led to the distinctive degree of Bachelor of Divinity. At first even the academic calendar was different from that of the College, and the students in the divinity school had their own "literary association" (the Zetagathean Society) corresponding to the Mathetican Society. Tufts undergraduates went to great pains to explain to the denominational journals that "young men from this institution who preach are not members of the College, but of the Divinity School." The students tried to disabuse anyone of "the idea that the College is a sort of Divinity School" and felt it "but justice to the few former professors to relieve them from the imputation of having attempted to give theological instruction in addition to their regular programs." The faculty "did not approve of any student thus dividing his time and attention between the College and the pulpit." President Ballou had been the only member of the early faculty qualified to teach theology, and he had "confined himself scrupulously to the duties of the presidency and to teaching the branches assigned to him in the college curriculum. The institution from the start was of no doubtful character, but strictly a college, in the true New England sense."

The divinity school did receive money earmarked for its own use. The Greenwood Scholarship was established in 1878–79 (from an income of $1,000) to be awarded for "excellence in such department of work as the Faculty of that School shall determine." In 1882 a gift of $500 was made to strengthen the library; the income was to be spent for books relating to subjects taught in the Department of Homiletics. Other early gifts included the Dockstader Fund of $6,000, which was established in 1889 "in aid of indigent and deserving young men, preparing for the Universalist ministry"; and the Warren S. Woodbridge Professorship of Applied Christianity, which was provided with the understanding that the donor would be the first incumbent. The divinity school also received a life insurance policy assigned to the College in 1894, of which $2,000 was to be used to establish the Benjamin H. Davis Scholarship for students who would take the prescribed course in the College and then enroll in the divinity school.

But no matter how distinct the divinity school might have been in theory, in practice the relationship to the College was inevitably close. The school and the College had a common Board of Trustees, and the students and faculty shared the same campus, including the library facilities. The divinity school periodically used the services of the College faculty, as in the case of Moses True Brown and his Oratory courses. For many years, President Capen taught Christian Ethics in the divinity school, although without compensation. The experiment of having an academic calendar different from that of the rest of the College was abandoned after one year. The divinity school started out with its own Anniversary exercises, but they were combined with the College Commencement exercises in 1882. The divinity school students in 1897–98 even lost their tuition-free status and were charged the same fee of $100 as the other students. They did, however, receive rent-free rooms, and if they were unable to live in the dormitory provided for them, half of their tuition was remitted. When the new charges were announced, they applied even to those already in the divinity school. The students so affected immediately protested, but the Trustees denied their petition to be excused from paying the tuition. The Trustees did, however, vote them $50 a year from the Dockstader Fund until they had completed their course.

The decision to levy tuition charges on divinity school students was based on two arguments. Free tuition was thought to be bad on principle, for it created a privileged class of students who might not always deserve or appreciate such generosity or the advantages they were receiving. More immediate was the hard fact that the College had to support the school largely out of its general funds because the denomination had not stepped forth to support the theological school on the scale that had been hoped. In the nineteenth century the school never paid its own way. The finance Committee of the Trustees made a special report in 1896 indicating that the school had cost the College over $180,000 since it had been established. The income of the school itself in 1896 was only $5,000, and the operating expenses were estimated at $11,000. The $6,000 loss that year increased the total College deficit to over $18,000. The services of Anson B. Curtis, who had been employed as Professor of Hebrew and Old Testament in 1894, had to be dispensed with only two years later as an economy move. The device used was to abolish the professorship and distribute the work among the remaining faculty. When divinity school alumni inquired whether it would be proper to raise money to reinstate Curtis, the Executive

Committee replied that the financial condition of the school was such that if any appeals for money were to be made, they should be for the general endowment of the school and not for any one department within it.

The idea of a separate endowment for the divinity school was first recommended in 1884, after the Rev. Henry Rugg had surveyed the situation and had found the school severely handicapped by inadequate resources. The Trustees devoted much time in 1889 to discussions about the relationship between the school and the College, and approved a proposal that "at an early date" the school should be given "a distinctive name . . . in order that there may be not only a real but also an apparent separation of that school from the College of Letters."[5] The Trustees echoed the sentiments expressed by the students almost fifteen years before, when they justified their proposal on the grounds that there had been "in the minds of many persons an erroneous idea that Tufts College was only an institution for the education of young men for the ministry." Although this misconception was not as prevalent as before, there was "no doubt that at the present time it operates somewhat prejudicially to the college proper and does not advance the interests of the divinity school." The school, it was argued, should have not only "a particular name of its own, but it should also have funds specially appropriated and set apart for its maintenance." A special Committee on Finances did not, however, feel that the Trustees themselves should undertake to raise any large amount of money for such purposes, as it was apparent that "the needs of the school will not keep pace with the demands of the college itself." The money-raising should be a project for persons especially interested in the school. If they could raise "a perpetual endowment fund" of $100,000 for the benefit of the school (the income to be expended by the Trustees at their discretion), the Trustees would agree to furnish a separate building for the school "unless sooner provided."

Miner thoroughly agreed that separate housing should be pro-

[5] The designation "College of Letters" began to be used in 1882, after the by-laws of the Trustees were revised and a "General Faculty" had been created. The term "General Faculty" was only temporary, for the expression "Faculty of the College of Letters" prevailed; it did not, of course, include the divinity school.

vided for the school. It was not so much a matter, he said, of anticipating a great increase in divinity school enrollment as of alleviating the pressing needs of the College for accommodating its own students. Further, "a wider separation of the School of Theology from the other departments of the institution" was "on many grounds greatly to be desired." It was Miner himself who was to provide the funds for the construction of a headquarters for the school during the 1890's, when the College greatly expanded both its academic activities and its physical plant.

§   §   §

While the engineering curriculum was being developed in the 1870's and the relationship between the divinity school and the College was being discussed, Miner submitted his resignation to the Trustees, effective in February 1875. This act was taken after much deliberation and was in no way unexpected. From the time of his election in June 1862, doubt had been expressed as to his ability to hold both a full-time pastorate and the presidency. For over a year he tried to serve both his church and the College full-time. Early in 1864 a delegation from the Second Universalist Society (School Street) conferred with the Executive Committee of the Trustees, arguing that Miner's duties "were more than ought to be performed by any one man, and more than he could do." He was preaching in the morning at the College and in the afternoon at his church. The result of the discussion was compromise whereby the Society would require his services only half of each Sunday. The College, in return, agreed to defray the expense of his services half the day at the College and to employ another clergyman to handle half the School Street assignment on Sundays. Miner was still responsible as a pastor for the multitude of other duties that fell to a clergyman. It was also agreed that the College would reimburse Miner, as a non-resident president, for the expenses of his horse and chaise in commuting on Sundays. Miner's transportation facilities, while he was on the campus, were housed in the barn behind Middle (Packard) Hall. The Treasurer's Reports contain precise records of the cost of this "fringe benefit" over the years of Miner's presidency.

Miner found his double job a demanding one, for in the summer of 1865 he expressed doubts to the Trustees as to how much

Middle (Packard) Hall
with the barn that housed President Miner's horse and carriage

longer he could continue "to serve two masters." The reaction of the Trustees was not only to give him a vote of confidence but to impress upon him the prejudicial effect the termination of his services would have on the College. They agreed to take whatever measures were necessary to retain him; the most tangible step was the decision to pay him a salary ($3,000), effective January 1, 1866. His academic assignments were also lightened somewhat; his classes were strictly limited to seniors, and during 1866–67 he supplied the College pulpit only one Sunday in four during the first term, and every other Sunday during the second term. Even then, he found it necessary to be absent much of the time on church business, especially during 1871–72, and his activities that year were further curtailed by illness; for several weeks, Professor Shipman conducted the president's classes while he was on leave of absence to recover his health.

The first step that led to Miner's eventual resignation was a

124

request from the Second Universalist Society to the Trustees in the fall of 1874 that he devote himself entirely to the service of the Society, which had moved into new quarters on Columbus Avenue in 1872. For several weeks a veritable tug-of-war ensued between the Society and the College to retain his services. In October he resigned his pastorate, but he was so urgently requested to reconsider that he acceded and announced his plans to resign the presidency. The decision was enthusiastically received by his parish, which immediately voted him a salary of $6,000. The resignation was accepted "with unfeigned reluctance" by the Trustees and was accompanied by an extensive Minute of Appreciation that appeared in several newspapers. In order to clear accounts, Miner was reimbursed by the College for $338.16 that he had personally lent various students to help them pay College bills. However, the College did not lose Miner's services. He continued as a very active Trustee until his death in 1895 and contributed in many ways to the strengthening of the institution.

Less than a month before his resignation from the presidency of the College was to take effect, Miner transmitted to the Trustees the first Annual Report to have been printed and made available for public distribution. He had seen Tufts graduate its eighteenth class and could report that these men were filling, "with credit to themselves and honor to the College," prominent and responsible positions in many professions — theology, law, medicine, and business. A high proportion had entered teaching; some had become principals of academies and others were masters of high schools and grammar schools. The internal order of the College had been "highly satisfactory," in spite of an occasional lapse of student deportment. Academic standards had been not only maintained but improved, and the basic purpose of the College had not been lost sight of: Not so much to train men for particular positions as "to build up such intelligent, manly, and well-rounded character as shall be an adequate foundation for preparation for any position." This was being achieved "not by following tradition and blind custom, but by conforming to the growing light and generous spirit of the age."

The College under Miner's leadership had not departed markedly from the traditions established, however shortly before, by his predecessor and the original faculty. True, an engineering course had been established, and a divinity school had been organized, but the core of the College remained its classical curriculum. When President Miner offered his resignation in 1874, the work of the freshman and sophomore years was still prescribed; limited electives were permitted upperclassmen. The academic offerings were organized into nine departments, exclusive of the divinity school. There was considerable overlapping within departments because so many subjects were frequently taught by the same instructor; in fact, few departments consisted of more than one man. Professor Marshall's Department of Chemistry also included work in mineralogy, botany, and geology, with lectures on the side in Animal and Vegetable Physiology, and zoology. The geological features in the neighborhood of the College were exploited, and excursions were made during the spring term to study formations and collect specimens. Much attention had to be paid to elementary chemistry, for most entering students had no acquaintance with the subject.

Professor Schneider's classes in Greek for freshman and sophomores read from Thucydides, Plato, Lucian, Herodotus, and Sophocles and periodically wrote short prose compositions. A handful of students elected Greek in their upperclass years. The professor of Latin Language and Literature, whose course included Roman History and Antiquities, was pleased with the quality of the work done by the freshmen with their assignments from Livy and Horace but less happy with the performance by the sophomores, particularly in Latin composition. Their study of Horace and Tacitus was satisfactory, and three upperclassmen elected advanced Latin and read from Juvenal and Cicero. Throughout the Latin assignments, emphasis was put on thorough understanding of selected readings — grammatical analysis, etymology, idiom, and allusions — rather than on extensive and superficial coverage.

The two-man Mathematical Department offered plane and solid geometry, and algebra, to the freshmen; trigonometry (including surveying) to the sophomores. Examinations lasting from three to four hours climaxed each semester's work, and reasoning rather than blind memorization was stressed. S. W. Sutton, Walker Special Instructor in Mathematics, and a graduate of the Class of 1872, was convinced that much more was being accomplished than in his own undergraduate days. The Walker Professor of Mathematics, Benjamin Graves Brown, taught physics to the juniors and seniors and repeatedly called attention to the lack of a laboratory in which demonstrations and experiments in mechanics, hydrostatics, pneumatics, heat, and static electricity could be provided. Work on optics for the seniors was severely limited because the room fitted for experiments in that field was unheated. The second half of the term was devoted to astronomy — but with no observatory available to show how astronomical instruments were used or to view the heavens.

The Department of Rhetoric, Logic, and English Literature, to which Intellectual Philosophy was added (as an upperclass requirement), consisted, administratively, of Professor William R. Shipman, who doubled as librarian. Intensive study of grammar, an average of six themes per year, and introduction to the masterpieces of English literature were included in the freshman and sophomore courses. Intellectual Philosophy ("a mental science rather than metaphysics") and logic were included in the upperclass course of study. The most popular elective, and the natural carry-over from theme-writing, was Declamation and Oratory. Professor Moses True Brown, who presided over this department, was proud of the fact that Tufts had established the first full Professorship in Elocution in any New England college when he was appointed in 1866. However, Oratory was offered for only half of the academic year. He was equally proud of the fact that Oratory was considered a separate department at Tufts and was not *"attached* to the department of English Literature or Rhetoric, to be persistently ignored by the professors." He insisted that Oratory, systematically taught, was as much of an art to be cultivated as music or painting. An analysis of the three-page outline of the course which Professor Brown submitted to the Trustees is evidence of the thoroughness with which he dealt with the subject. With missionary fervor, he recommended that Oratory be allotted as much time as other studies, and that it be made a regular elective. J. W. Adams of Boston also gave instruction twice a week "in the culture of the voice and in vocal Music"; the side benefits reflected favorably in reading, elocution, and in pronunciation of foreign languages by those students taking advantage of his services. The program for seniors was rounded out by lectures in Political Economy, given by the president; the customary Evidences of Christianity was still a regular part of the presidential offering.

German, French, and Italian comprised the offerings of the Department of Modern Languages. The first two were required for both the philosophical and engineering curricula. Italian was elective, beginning in the junior year. Although some attention was given to pronunciation, no direct effort was made to develop oral facility in any of the foreign languages. Language teachers of a later era would certainly challenge the statement that "the futility of such endeavor in a college course has been demonstrated by a general experience." Introduction to the literature in these languages and a venture into comparative philology were all that was attempted after grammar and sentence structure were mastered. Professor Charles E. Fay considered the greatest deficiency to be the lack of French and German in the preparatory schools; as a result, valuable time was wasted in college learning the elements of those languages. He felt strongly that a college-level course should presuppose secondary school preparation and that the teaching of a language at the elementary level should not have to be the task of the College. Many an educator since has supported this contention.

President Miner had made it clear in his Inaugural Address, delivered on July 9, 1862, that he was not going to be an innovator. He did "not propose to ask . . . acceptance of any new doctrines in regard to education. . . . Our work is not revolutionary, but regenerative. We have not founded here a New School in Science and Literature, but a new instrumentality for the furtherance of the Old Schools. We pay our homage to the older institutions. . . . We aim to secure for our own young men . . . the same benefits which other institutions are securing to the young men of other sects." At the same time, President Miner had made a bid for the patronage of that segment of the population who professed no formal religious faith and attended no place of worship, but whose sentiments were likely to coincide with those of the Universalists. Tufts College could thereby serve the "very large portion" of citizenry who did not find the orthodoxy of other sects congenial.

Much of Miner's address had been taken up with stressing the value of "a sound and generous culture" as a foundation for professional life. As he put the matter, "a liberal education is the best investment, financially considered, that the passing generation can make for the next." He referred his hearers to "the masterly discussion" of liberal education in his predecessor's Inaugural and insisted that he (Miner) was "contented to be but a gleaner on the borders of the field" which Ballou had "so thoroughly harvested." Miner recognized that Tufts was, as yet, only a junior partner among the institutions of the educational world. But the time had already come, he said, "when a young man is asked, at least by the wise, not where he graduated, but what he can do. Sound learning consents to wear no local brand." Tufts, he was convinced, was doing its share in offering a worthwhile liberal education.

If the Trustees wished that a man with these sentiments could continue to serve the College, their next president fulfilled that wish, and more. Under President Elmer Hewitt Capen, Tufts ceased to be "only a junior partner among the institutions of the educational world" and began to assume a position more akin to the conception of the university held by those conversant with the changing face of higher education in late-nineteenth-century America.

5. Capen at the Helm

FINDING A SUCCESSOR TO MINER in 1875 posed almost as much of a problem as the Trustees had faced in 1861–62 at the death of President Ballou. The most likely candidate seemed to be Israel Washburn, Jr., a long-time member of the Board of Trustees and ex-governor of Maine. Before his name was formally proposed, he wrote the Trustees that, much to his distress, he had seen his name mentioned in the papers as a candidate. He insisted that he was not qualified for the position and would not, if elected, dare accept it. He requested that no one vote for him if anyone placed his name in nomination. The Trustees did not take him at his word. They elected him to the presidency anyway, and sent a committee to Portland, Maine, to inform him in person. He declined promptly and with finality. Washburn claimed, among other things, insufficient time to devote to College affairs. His attendance record at Trustee meetings seems to support this; he seldom came. One of the few times he was present was the meeting at which his letter of refusal of the presidency was read.

The faculty took a hand in recommending the next candidate. This body transmitted to the Trustees a lengthy communication signed by all thirteen members outlining several requirements for the ideal president. The candidate should be a "college man"; that is, "one of college education, & therefore familiar with college life & college work." The next president should also be an alumnus, "with a sincere love for his *Alma Mater*, a just pride in her good name, & an earnest desire for her prosperity." Although some of the faculty demurred, the majority agreed that the president of Tufts should also be "a clergyman, especially a *Universalist* clergyman." It was further considered "a *sine qua non* that he should reside on College Hill." The final recommendation was unanimous: that the

Elmer Hewitt Capen
President, 1875–1905

Rev. Elmer Hewitt Capen was the best choice. It is impossible to know whether the Trustees would have chosen otherwise without faculty urging, but it is clear that they agreed with the faculty in every respect. The report of the Trustee nominating committee was merely a paraphrase of the faculty letter, which went on to say that Capen's "scholarship and his fitness for the high duties of the office" made him a most appropriate candidate. The nominating committee added that the faculty communication indicated "the cordiality with which he would be welcomed," and pointed out his active role on the Board of Trustees. Capen's nomination and election were unanimous. He was inaugurated on June 2, 1875, purchased property from the College on Professors Row on which to erect a residence, and assumed his new duties with such smoothness that there was no break at all in the administration of the College.[1]

The first paragraph of Capen's Inaugural Address made it a certainty that continuity was to be the watchword of his administration.[2] "I am no revolutionist or iconoclast; if I were I should not have ventured to respond to the summons which has placed me in this chair." He would not have taken on the responsibility, he said, if he had been asked to do otherwise than carry out "the wise intentions of the projectors and founders of this seat of learning." He underlined his basically conservative philosophy with the statement that it was the task of an institution of higher learning "to hold with a tenacious grasp whatever the experience of ages has approved, and to enter the portals of the future by those ancient and established ways over which the sages and philosophers of every time have successfully travelled." This comment is particularly interesting in view of the fact that some of the most dramatic changes in the history of the College came during the latter half of his administration.

Capen's prospectus for Tufts College was reminiscent of one of the ancient Greek ideals of a university: "culture, — pure and simple, and this, too, for its own sake." In fact, he envisioned the institution as another *studium generale* which took all knowledge to be its province, and rejected as a collegiate goal the providing of practical education in the narrow vocational sense. He would not have the course of study already established curtailed in any of its departments but, on the contrary, would have it expanded and enlarged in all respects. He would restore history (originally taught by President Ballou) to the curriculum, and add jurisprudence. He championed not only the continuance but the strengthening of "the classic languages of Greece and Rome," announced that he would resist any attempt to reduce such instruction, and went so far

[1] Capen sold the house to the Trustees in 1894 and rented it until his death in 1905.

[2] The address was reprinted in E. H. Capen, *Occasional Addresses* (Medford: Tufts College Press, 1902), pp. 1–39. This work, which Capen personally paid to have printed, was one of several publications that came from the Tufts College Press, operated by H. W. Whittemore (Class of 1886). The story of the Press is given elsewhere in this history.

as to recommend that Latin and Greek be added to the curriculum of every elementary school. The College also needed additional students, who he wished would flock to the institution "in overwhelming numbers, as they went after Abelard at Paris in the twelfth century . . . as they went in the same epoch by thousands and tens of thousands to Oxford and Bologna." The enrollment at the time he delivered his address was fifty-six (exclusive of the divinity school); only eleven students were graduated in June 1875 (nine in the A.B. program and two in the engineering program).

The man who had been selected to serve as the third president of Tufts and who had delivered such an eloquent Inaugural Address had already exhibited unusual talents when he was called to head his Alma Mater. Born in Stoughton, Massachusetts, in 1838, he received his preparatory education at Pierce Academy in Middleborough and at Green Mountain Institute in South Woodstock, Vermont. He had enrolled in the College in 1856 but interrupted his undergraduate studies in 1859 to serve a term in the Massachusetts legislature as a representative from his native town. In so doing he became, at twenty-one, the youngest member of that body when he took his seat. At the expiration of his term, he resumed his college studies and was able to graduate with his class in 1860, with the expectation that he would become a lawyer. Instead, he decided to enter the Universalist ministry, and when he resigned his third pastorate (in Providence, Rhode Island) to accept the presidency of Tufts, he had already made clear his devotion to the cause of education.

Like his predecessor, Capen was instrumental in the establishment of Dean Academy in 1865 and served as the first secretary of its Board of Trustees. Before he took up his official duties on the Hill, he had been president of the New England Commission on Admission Examinations, and during part of his thirty-year tenure as Tufts' president was chairman of the Massachusetts Board of Education. He also served as chairman of various educational groups, including the Board of Visitors of the Salem Normal School and the school building committee of the town of Fitchburg. His political activities included service as a delegate to the Republican National Convention in 1888, which nominated Benjamin Harrison for the presidency of the nation. Within his denomination Capen was a Trustee of the Universalist General Convention for some twenty years. It was from Capen's able and active pen that came the articles on Universalism and on Tufts College in the ninth edition of the *Encyclopaedia Britannica.* The history of the College during his long service bore witness to the wisdom of the Trustees in selecting the first alumnus to serve as president. Aside from an unusual ability to get along with everybody, from Trustees to students, Capen was able to prevail in his insistence that the development of Tufts must be balanced among and within its increasingly numerous divisions, departments, and schools.

§   §   §

The new president did not confine his Inaugural Address in 1875 to abstractions and classical allusions, although they abounded. With a deft change of pace, he outlined the brick-and-mortar needs of the College. Among them were a separate home on the campus for the divinity school; a scientific building; "a library, new-created, almost, from the bottom" ("even a million dollars would not be too large a foundation for such a collection as every first-class university should have"); a gymnasium; and, above all, "a comely and commodious chapel." President Capen saw three of these — the chapel, the gymnasium, and the science building — completed during the first ten years of his administration. In the next decade, not one but two buildings rose for the divinity school. The money with which to build a new library was received, as Capen expressed it, "as a sort of Christmas present" in December 1904, a few months before his death.

In his first annual report to the Trustees in 1875–76 Capen put the "very pressing necessity" of a chapel at the top of his priority list for buildings. Four years later a joint committee of the Massachusetts Universalist Convention and the Boston Sabbath School Union proposed that a Sunday School and church be provided on the Hill. If the College would furnish $5,000 for a "temporary chapel" and the land on which to construct it, the two organizations would create and staff a parish for the College community. Income from pew rentals could be used to help defray operating expenses. After a permanent chapel was provided, the temporary building could be used "for literary exercises, the anniversaries of college societies, concerts and the like, and so still remain useful." The Trustees felt they were in no position to follow up this idea, particularly

*The Tufts campus in its rural splendor in 1875
viewed from what became Powderhouse Square*

as the authors of the proposal had carefully refrained from suggesting the source from which money might come to finance such a venture.

The problem of obtaining a chapel was solved in 1881 when Mary T. Goddard, widow of Thomas A. Goddard, a Trustee and early benefactor of the College who had died in 1868, offered $25,000 for a permanent building as a memorial to her husband. Goddard Chapel was built in 1882–83 and by the fall of 1883 had been dedicated and put to use. The structure, with an exterior of bluish Somerville slate, was in Romanesque style, with rounded arches and a barrel ceiling, all topped with a contrasting red slate roof. A 100-foot tower at one corner dominated the Hill and could be seen from miles around. The new chapel was considered an architectural masterpiece when it was built, and attracted hundreds of visitors. Even in the 1930's the firm of Andrews, Jones, Biscoe, and Whitmore, for many years the College Architects, considered the chapel and its tower "one of the most picturesque buildings of

Goddard Chapel, showing its Bell Tower

the sort in the country." Goddard Chapel actually cost almost $35,000 to construct and to furnish. Part of the extra expense was defrayed by numerous contributions for memorial windows. Mrs. Goddard also farsightedly established a special fund to provide for maintenance. Picturesque or not, Goddard Chapel became a building of many uses; Commencement ceremonies were held there for many years, until the student body had outgrown it.

Another long-felt need of the College was supplied by the same donor who provided the funds for Goddard Chapel, and almost at the same time. In 1883 Mrs. Mary Goddard presented a check for $15,000 to help "satisfy a want so greatly felt by the undergraduates" for a gymnasium. The result was a substantial red brick structure with a rather forbidding fortress-like exterior, with Romanesque tendencies and a minaret on each corner. Goddard Gymnasium, like the chapel, became a multi-purpose building and was used for social occasions and for Commencement dinners as well as athletics. The building was enlarged in 1899. It was renamed Goddard Hall when it was replaced by the much larger

136

Barnum Museum in 1887 (before it sprouted wings)

Cousens Gymnasium and was renovated in 1932–33 to become the home of the Fletcher School of Law and Diplomacy.

The only academic building on the campus that was constructed with the express stipulation that it be named after its donor was completed in 1884. The "friend of the College" who offered $50,000 for the purpose was identified more than a year after his gift as none other than P. T. Barnum, the busy showman who had been unable to attend the meetings of the Board of Trustees to which he had been elected before the College had officially opened. The Trustees immediately agreed to comply with Barnum's desire to have the building named after him, and with his intent that it be used for the Department of Natural History. The main structure was designed by the same architect who planned Goddard Chapel and was also faced with slate quarried in Somerville. The two buildings flanked the College Edifice and added to the architectural variety that was already so evident on the Hill. The original building cost slightly less than $31,000. Three wings were added: a west wing in 1894, an east wing in 1934–35, and a north wing at right angles to the west wing, in 1963–64. Barnum had bequeathed an additional $40,000 to the College which was used to construct the first two wings. The Dana Foundation, the National Science Foundation, and contributors to the Tufts University Program (successfully completed in June 1963) made possible the third wing. The original structure, christened the Barnum Museum of Natural History, gave Professor Marshall, the long-time teacher of the natural sciences, the space for laboratory work and for displays that had been lacking in the main College building.

Barnum Museum also served for years as a home for dozens of stuffed animals and miscellaneous flora and fauna donated from time to time by Barnum and put on public display at his request. He further contributed $5,000 for the purchase of natural history specimens. Most of the Barnum collection migrated to other quarters over the years, and very little of it remained in the building by the 1960's. In the late 1880's the collection was considered sufficiently valuable to have been insured for $20,000. The best-known item, housed on the main floor of Barnum Museum, becoming a permanent fixture, was Jumbo, the College mascot. During the elephant's lifetime Jumbo was one of the prime attractions of Barnum's far-flung entertainment empire. The mounted skin of this huge pachyderm was placed on exhibition in the Museum in 1889 and remained to awe and delight school children from near and far and serve as a source of pride for generations of Tufts students and alumni. Jumbo has been the subject of a vast and constantly growing literature; the stories about him, apocryphal and otherwise, are legion.[3]

President Capen could view with satisfaction the construction of three major buildings early in his administration. He encountered, simultaneously, a less happy aspect of educational operations, namely, that most durable of all academic problems — finance. Few presidents of the institution faced more complications than he in

---

[3] Authentic details are to be found in articles by Professor Russell L. Carpenter, who in 1941 was largely responsible for transforming the "Jumbo Room" in the Museum into a lounge and treasure room for Jumbo and Barnum memorabilia. The University possesses considerable Barnum correspondence as well as autographed copies of several editions of his famous autobiography, which he periodically updated and distributed widely to an admiring public.

Jumbo, the famous Tufts mascot
before he met an untimely death in 1885

Jumbo at home in Barnum Museum, with a portrait of his donor

attempting to expand a college with limited resources and at the same time keep it on an even keel.

§   §   §

The financial tide had seemed to turn in favor of the College in the mid-1860's, after it had weathered the uncertain period of the Civil War and had received state assistance in the proverbial nick of time. It appeared in 1864–65 that for once the ordinary anticipated income would meet ordinary expenditures. If this turned out to be the case, the Executive Committee was ready with a long list of ways to spend whatever surplus there was. There could be "a regular appropriation for the increase of the Library, . . . the adorning of our grounds," a salary for the president, and even possibly a gymnasium. The goal was not achieved that year, but in 1865–66 there was actually a balance of over $2,000, and the estimated surplus for the following year was over $7,000.[4] This desirable excess of receipts over outgo continued all too briefly. A disastrous conflagration in Boston on November 8, 1872, known as the "Great Fire," destroyed approximately $25,000 of the College's endowment in investment property and stocks. Much of the business property was rebuilt with partial reimbursement from insurance, the amounts determined by rulings of the state Supreme Court. Other College-held properties were mortgaged to cover the balance of the extraordinary expenditures. One investment of $7,500 in insurance stocks (one of the Walker Funds) was completely wiped out, for obvious reasons.

The sharp decrease in College income from these sources meant a corresponding decline in scholarship and gratuity aid, which had been derived almost exclusively from profit on Boston investments. In fact, in their attempt to assist worthy students, the Trustees and faculty had actually gone so far beyond the regular scholarship grants that costs for student assistance came close to canceling out income from student fees. This was one reason that for four consecutive years (1873–77) expenses again exceeded income. On top of everything else, the College's investments were hard hit by another downturn of the national economy known in American history as the Panic of 1873. As a result, the stocks in

[4] Of the $37,000 received in 1865–66, less than $3,400 came from student term bills.

which the remaining Walker Funds ($175,000) were invested were either worthless or badly depreciated. "Ledger value" and "real value" no longer bore much resemblance to each other.

What could and should the College do to meet this new threat to its financial welfare? William H. Finney, who had become treasurer in the midst of this unhappy period, reviewed all of the assets and liabilities, opened a new set of books in 1876, and rearranged the accounts so that principal and income could be perceived at a glance. The modernizing of the system was justified on the ground that the days when the financial transactions were comparatively small and the accounts few in number had long since passed, and the situation required an overhauling.[5] While the hard-working treasurer was reorganizing his books, the Executive Committee undertook to find ways of economizing and keeping expenses within income. After considering several possibilities, the Trustees agreed in 1877 on the following: to give no more aid to students beyond regular scholarships, to increase student charges (including tuition) from $75 to $100, and to reduce the salaries of the president and the faculty by 20 per cent for one year.[6]

The outcome of this "general economical management" was merely a slight reduction in the deficit. Retrenchment alone was not enough. Clearly the permanent solution had to be an increase in the endowment. By 1879 the situation had become so serious that, if all attempts at soliciting funds failed, the Trustees saw no other path before them than to (1) abolish the divinity school "in part or in whole" (except for the Packard Professorship, which had to be maintained because of the provisions in the donor's will), (2) eliminate the Department of Oratory, and (3) reduce and/or consolidate existing departments. At the same time, it was voted to notitfy all faculty that, effective December 31, 1879, all obligations of the College toward them would terminate pending renegotia-

[5] The treasurer, as an economy move, was authorized by the Trustees in 1879 to declare the property on the Hill tax exempt when making annual reports for assessment purposes. The question of exemption for College property had not been previously raised.

[6] The salaries for instructional staff at this time ranged from $800 to $2,625. The librarian received $500. In 1878–79 total salaries amounted to $32,000, paid out of an income of $85,000; the net from tuition that year was only $2,050.

tion, which was, in turn, dependent on the financial prospects by then. Only eight days before the deadline, the faculty were notified that their salaries would continue. Although matters had improved somewhat by the end of the year, a special Trustee committee was appointed to conduct an on-the-spot investigation of the College to see whether instructional expenses could be reduced. Consideration was also given to selling off College land on the fringes of the Hill, but that drastic step was not taken; instead, properties in Chelsea were sold.[7]

In the 1880's the Trustees launched the first capital funds drive since the College had opened, first by deciding to issue a circular calling for aid and then by proposing to hire a fund-raising agent. His task was to be threefold: to secure funds for current expenses, to seek additions to permanent endowment through gifts and bequests, and to devise and develop plans for increasing enrollment. There were 102 students enrolled in all departments of the College in 1879–80, eight less than in 1877–78. This trend was a matter of continuing concern to President Capen, who called attention in almost every one of his annual reports to the failure of enrollment to increase. In his report for 1879–80 he insisted that the College could double the number of students without materially increasing the teaching force.

Finding an agent was no small problem, for the demands of such a post required an additional member of the staff and increased financial outlay. But the time had come, said the Trustees, when Tufts had to face up to the fact that it was living in a rapidly changing world.

> The spirit of competition which is now so fierce in every branch of business, extends even to our educational institutions. Neighboring colleges are straining every nerve to obtain students; established courses of instruction are extended, and new ones are introduced, important experiments in instruction and in discipline are making; attractions unknown in our New England Colleges a quarter of a century ago are presented to the young man who contemplates entering an institution of learning. . . . Although it would be neither wise nor dignified for us to enter into this

[7] One by-product of the difficulties of the 1870's was the adoption of a budget based on appropriations, beginning in 1880, so that "ways and means will be considered *before* disbursements instead of afterwards."

scramble, the fact still remains that we must be progressive and aggressive if we expect Tufts College to maintain the rank it has gained among New England institutions.

It was first proposed that the fund-raiser be an alumnus of the College and have academic rank as Professor of "Ethics" in addition to the title of "General Secretary," at a salary of $2,500.[8] The Trustees felt, however, that this would be too elaborate and too expensive an undertaking. They compromised temporarily by relieving President Capen of his teaching duties for 1881–82, at an expense not to exceed $500, and giving him a mandate to raise $150,000. He reported in March 1882 that he had secured subscriptions of $139,000, and the Trustees decided that the sum was so close to the goal that the subscriptions could be called in by May 1. The sum of $12,000 had been added by January 1883. The financial plight of the College might have been alleviated by the endowment drive, but it certainly had not been solved. Service on indebtedness alone outran general expenses (exclusive of salaries) by $500. The Executive Committee was authorized in the summer of 1883 to sell off additional investment property, including holdings in Winchester and Woburn and, if necessary, part of the land in Medford acquired many years before from Timothy Cotting. Trustee Wilmot L. Warren filed a vigorous objection to what he considered a shortsighted policy, and recommended that the Trustees retain the properties, leasing or renting them subject to periodic renewal and first option of the lessees to buy the buildings and other improvements. He cited the success that Columbia College (later University) had had with such a policy. But the majority decision of the Trustees prevailed, and the Cotting land northwest of the College across the Boston and Maine Railroad was sold.[9]

Financial conditions were improving to some extent by the late 1880's, but deficits in operating costs continued to plague the College. President Capen was again selected to head a two-pronged campaign to obtain pledges for current expenses and for endowment, and particularly to obtain $2,000 cash for fifty scholarships.

[8] Before the plan was submitted to the Trustees, the title was changed to "General Agent," and the proposals that the new officer be a member of the faculty and reside on the Hill were dropped.

[9] Marshall and Cotting Streets, in that area, commemorated two names prominently associated with Tufts' early history.

The idea of employing a "canvassing agent for the College" was also resurrected in 1888, and the Trustees secured the services of the Rev. A. P. Patterson, who worked with President Capen. Sufficient money had been pledged by 1891 to create twenty-seven new scholarships and to increase the total scholarship funds of the College to $54,000. New permanent scholarships were established in many names, including Miner, Travelli, and Talbot. Besides these and some scholarships established by endowments for a term of years, there were eight provided by that many Universalist parishes by means of annual payments. The College also received in 1890 over $32,000 from the estate of Rev. W. H. Ryder, and part of this was earmarked for the hard-pressed divinity school.

President Capen could report to the Trustees in 1890 that the total increase in funds for the one year had been more than $130,-000. If this rate of increase could have been maintained for a period of years, the Trustees would have soon been "relieved of the anxiety under which they have labored for some time in carrying on the work of the institution." But even this impressive addition to the College's resources failed to meet its long-range needs. The Trustees sold the improved land in Woburn for $60,000 and early in 1890 disposed of sizable holdings in Boston from the Packard estate. They were reminded in 1895 of the unhappy fact that the annual operating deficit for the preceding five years averaged over $12,000, and the unrestricted funds left to meet it were almost exhausted. There seemed no alternative but to employ on a permanent basis "the best financial officer available." The appeal, said President Capen, must be made "to all, in or out of the ranks of the Universalist Church." In view of the straitened circumstances of the institution, "no increase of salaries of teachers and employees should be considered, but every decrease possible should be availed of."[10]

Rev. Benjamin F. Eaton was employed in 1896 to solicit funds, on a commission basis. Even with an agent, funds trickled in so slowly that a special Trustee committee spent six months in 1897 inventorying the entire College. They came to the gloomy conclusion that any reduction in instructional staff or teaching equipment

[10] At this time the improved property on the Hill was estimated to be worth $1,268,000 (exclusive of land); over $230,000 of that had been donated to erect five buildings which were constructed after 1880.

would impair the effectiveness of the institution and its standing in the educational world. Unless whole divisions or departments were closed down, the only choice was to employ additional agents. Eaton tried hard, but it was a discouraging business. The 1890's were a time of economic unrest throughout the nation, and the agent ran into it at every turn. "Promises to do something for the College when 'the times permit' " he received "almost without number," but tangible results were very slim. Eaton collected less than $3,000 in cash and subscriptions in the second of his two years as agent. He put the blame on three circumstances: the economic uncertainties of the times; the disruption of the Spanish-American War, which siphoned off many prospective students; and the failure of the College to offer sufficient financial inducements. He considered Dartmouth College one of Tufts' greatest competitors in the latter respect. Eaton resigned in 1898 because he could not earn an adequate livelihood as agent and because he seemed unable to "do the most good for the College" under the circumstances.

In view of the disappointing results of Eaton's efforts, the Trustees undertook still another retrenchment campaign at the College. If all of the recommendations had been adopted, the institution would, among other things, have lost three faculty members. As it was, one of the three was hurried into retirement, one was given a greatly increased load at a slight increase in compensation, and the third exchanged a promotion in rank for a reduced salary.[11] The Trustees began negotiations in 1899 with another prospective financial agent, Rev. Henry W. Rugg, to take Eaton's place and hoped the new year (and the new century) would brighten Tufts' prospects.

§   §   §

One area of administration which did not involve the knotty problems of finance but about which President Capen felt very strongly was "bringing the College into intelligent contact with the outside public." One of the best ways, he thought, that the public could be informed of how well the standards of the institution were being maintained and could be apprised of its progress was the creation of Boards of Visitors. Such boards, drawn both from the

[11] The third person referred to was Frank W. Durkee, who was promoted to the Professorship of Inorganic Chemistry created especially for him, at a salary of $1,200.

wider community and from those with some association with the College, could also serve as a stimulus to teachers and students and could awaken "a fresh interest" in intellectual activity. The result of Capen's efforts was the establishment in the winter of 1881–82 of two Boards of Visitors, one for the college of letters and one for the divinity school, both appointed by the Trustees. Article 9 of the by-laws adopted in 1884 provided that at least three of the nine Visitors to the college of letters were to be graduates of the College, and at least two of the seven to the divinity school were to be alumni of that school. In a sense, the creation of these boards did not represent a radical departure from existing practices, for precedents could easily be traced back to the early years of the College.

The idea of having individuals outside the instructional staff review the work of the College had taken form in 1855 with the practice of holding public exercises in the form of oral examinations for all classes twice a year (at the end of each term). The Trustees were notified of the exact date. Occasionally the examinations scheduled for midyear had to be postponed because such a high proportion of the students were away teaching school. In 1856 the Trustees began to appoint "Committees of Examination," consisting of at least three Trustees, the requisite number of alumni, and a sprinkling of outside talent (usually clergymen). Even after written examinations were introduced by some teachers in 1857 (with Trustee approval), oral examinations were continued, and the examiners were required to make a report to the Trustees. There were frequently as many as fifteen examiners, with two to five assigned to each subject. Beginning in 1863–64 the names of the examiners were printed in the catalogue. From time to time the tasks of the examiners were lightened by conditions at the College. The examinations were omitted in the second term of 1867 and 1868, in the first instance because of "over-working of the Sophomore class, and ill-health of the Junior class."

Written examinations were adopted by the faculty in all departments in 1867–68 "with highly satisfactory results." As a consequence, the last recitation day in each course was devoted to such examinations, and in 1869 outside Committees of Examination were abandoned and were replaced by "Visiting Committees" of eight for the "Academic Department" and six for the divinity school. They were "invited to visit the several departments of instruction at any time and without previous notice; also to inspect the papers at the Annual and Semi-Annual Examinations."

Many of the Committees of Examination discharged their responsibilities "with great fidelity and perseverance" and left for later generations some interesting and occasionally amusing reports of their reactions. As might be expected, their findings were rather mixed. Occasionally they were couched in the broadest of generalities; conversely, some dealt in minute detail with the academic work and the personalities involved. One committee was "highly gratified with the results" they had observed and departed "satisfied that in this institution there is no reason to fear a decline in the study of the Ancient Languages . . . [which were] an essential part of a thorough education." One observer in a class in English grammar came to the circumspect and ambiguous conclusion that "while there were no failures, it may not be expedient to report the names of one or two members, who, if judged solely by the examination, would rank below the average merit of the class." One class in mathematics received a "special commendation" because its written work in geometry and trigonometry was done "with exactness and elegance." One department received a "highly unfavorable report" because the student responses were inaccurate, the written work was carelessly done, the questions prepared by the instructor were too elementary, and the students were allowed to use their texts while the examinations were in progress.

The greatest difficulty in administering the plan of Committees of Examination was finding sufficient individuals willing to serve. The Executive Committee of the Trustees often had to use "much persuasion" and often "without entire success." In more than one instance, only one of the members assigned to examine the class appeared, and after the system had been in operation for only a few years there were so many resignations from committees that the Trustees requested the Executive Committee to review "the whole subject of appointing the usual Committees of Examination."

The system of a Board of Visitors for each part of the College, which was instituted in 1881–82, likewise worked with only moderate success. Some conscientious members did visit the College occasionally and made elaborate reports reflecting considerable thought and attention. Byron Groce, a graduate of the Class of

1867 and master in the Boston Latin School in the 1880's, was forth-right in his recommendations. He was critical of the quality of academic performance and called for higher standards in examinations both for admission and for meeting degree requirements. He urged greater attention to English composition and believed the subject should be required for each year until graduation. The experimental work in the chemistry and physics laboratories encouraged by Professors Dolbear and Michael was thoroughly approved by some of the Visitors; on the other hand, some were concerned that graduate-level research was being carried on to the detriment of undergraduate instruction and were particularly disturbed to discover that Professor Michael was interested only in supervising the work of three or four graduate students and "relegated" the instruction of undergraduates to those with lesser academic rank. Another member of the Board of Visitors (in 1885) would "be sorry to see Tufts take on too much the nature of a university; it ought to be sufficient glory for her to be a first class college." [12]

Several difficulties arose in regard to the Board of Visitors, and President Capen used his personal influence as much as possible to alleviate them. One was the often-repeated complaint that the Board members, drawn as they were from many professions and locations, did not feel competent to evaluate the work of the College without being experts in higher education, and had little or no opportunity to know what other institutions did; so it was difficult to compare Tufts with other schools. Other Board members complained that their reports, often containing specific recommendations worthy of consideration, were merely "placed on file." As Samuel W. Mendum of the Class of 1885 expressed it in a report made in 1897, "the fate of the reports . . . seems to be a speedy assignment to a cavity in the archives . . . from which they never emerge to the light of day. The honor of having our names in the pages of the Tufts College Catalogue is great but it is too dearly purchased as the price of days of visitation at the college, if our reports are ignored and consigned to oblivion before the ink with which they are written has time to dry." The chairman of one Board of Visitors to the college of letters complained that interest

[12] Most of the reports of members of the Boards dealt explicitly with the departments or divisions to which the Visitors were assigned and have been referred to elsewhere in this work.

in its task was so minimal that "it was almost impossible to get a quorum of Visitors together to visit the College." One reason he gave for this negative attitude was the widespread feeling that "their labors or suggestions did not count for anything."

Several recommendations were made for improving the situation. One called for the printing and distribution of Visitors' reports as part of the president's annual report. The Executive Committee, spearheaded by President Capen, came to the defense of the system and, in a circular distributed to the Trustees and the Visitors, pointed out that the reports were not ignored. The College was not always able to act, but the reports were referred to various standing committees and to the president of the institution. The point was added that much of the material contained in the reports was confidential and dealt by name with individuals. The information certainly should not be made public property. One result of the complaint that no one paid any attention to the Visitors' reports was the appointment, beginning in 1898, of a special Trustee committee to review them and report any matters requiring comment or action. In 1899 a Board of Overseers was created consisting exclusively of alumni, and the function of appointing Boards of Visitors was transferred from the Trustees to that body.

§   §   §

The Board of Overseers created in 1899 represented a significant recognition of the growing importance of the alumni in the affairs of the College. President Capen, quite appropriately as an alumnus himself, was the first president of the institution to make a distinct bid for alumni support. His predecessors had made occasional remarks indicating their awareness of the great potential that would eventually be built up as the number of alumni increased, but it was Capen who saw the full implications of alumni support. He addressed a considerable portion of his Inaugural Address to the alumni. He listed four agencies needed to "best secure the ends of the University." They were: location (situation); living teachers; dead teachers ("books, *books,* BOOKS — not simply a limited collection of them, however well selected, but in boundless profusion"); and finally, "loyal children." The alumni, he said, had the power in their own hands to make or break the reputation of the College. Among the many things of which Tufts could already be proud in its brief history up to 1875 was its alumni. They were important "for what they have already accomplished, and for the abundant promise which they give of future eminence and renown." Capen went a step further. "Especially do I invite the frank counsel and confidential friendship of my brethren of the Alumni. In a peculiar and very important sense, the College is theirs; and it is within their power to exert a greater influence than any other body of men whatever over its achievements and destiny. By wisdom and prudence they can easily direct its action and shape its policy."

The most systematic way that the alumni could exert their influence effectively was through organization. In later years graduates of the institution could look back with justifiable pride to the "Association of the Alumni of Tufts College" which was created in 1860 — pride not only in its accomplishments, modest as they might have been, but in its very existence. The alumni of Williams College waited half a century to organize; the alumni of Yale, over a century; and the alumni of Harvard, over two centuries.[13] The alumni of Tufts adopted a constitution when the College had graduated only five classes. It was peculiarly fitting that Capen should have stressed the role of the alumni, for he had been selected as one of the two vice-presidents of the Alumni Association when it was organized the very week he received his A.B. degree.

The possibility of alumni participation in the government of the College was first voiced formally by the Association in 1869, when an appeal to the Trustees was prepared urging that the alumni be permitted to nominate candidates when vacancies occurred on the Board. This effort having received no encouragement, an enlarged committee of the Association was created in 1871 to consider the best method of giving the alumni a share in the management of the institution. The result was the selection in 1873 of a five-man delegation to confer with the Trustees "on the subject of giving to representatives elected by the Alumni Association a place on their board." The columns of the *Tufts Collegian* were also used to publicize the idea and obtain alumni support. The committee wanted it made clear that their desire for formal representation was not to be taken as a criticism of the Trustees or as an

[13] Charles F. Thwing, *A History of Higher Education in America* (New York: D. Appleton, 1906), p. 402.

intimation that sudden or sweeping changes were in the offing. It was simply a matter of recognition that the ultimate responsibility for the College rested with the alumni "as a natural trust." The Trustees had already recognized the importance of the alumni by filling the last three vacancies on their Board with graduates of Tufts. This was a step in the right direction but did not solve the problem. The selection of replacements should be made by the alumni themselves. The interest of the graduate in his Alma Mater had to "rest upon something more substantial than the fleeting memory of his college days."

This proposal, in turn, raised another problem. The Association in 1874 comprised scarcely 50 per cent of the alumni. This was not an adequate basis on which to move with any degree of assurance. Two possibilities seemed to exist: abandon the informal organization as it then stood and make the alumni a corporate body, or greatly enlarge the scope and membership of the existing organization to make it both influential and truly representative.

No visible progress was made for several years toward the goal of either formal alumni representation on the Board of Trustees or reorganization of the Association. But two proposals made in 1878 testified to the continuing interest of the alumni in the College's affairs. One was to consider the feasibility of raising an annual sum of $1,000 for the use of the College, to be raised by five-dollar shares bought by the alumni. Thus was born the Alumni Fund, familiar in some form and in some degree to every graduate of Tufts. The start was unspectacular, to say the least. As the Committee on the Alumni Fund put the matter in 1879, they "had not met with the result they hoped." In one year, they had secured $140 from alumni and the same amount from one other source. Thereupon the Rev. George M. Harmon was made special agent for the raising of the fund. The entire $1,000 of this initial attempt was never secured, but the money that was collected was turned over to the College treasurer.

The other testimony to the concern of the alumni for the welfare of the College was consideration of the advisability of appointing annually "a Visiting Committee whose duty it shall be to visit the College recitations and examinations and report its condition to the alumni." This suggestion was undoubtedly influential in the decision of the Trustees to create the Board of Visitors three years later.

After several years of inaction another move was begun (in 1891) to inquire into alumni representation on the Trustees, with a view toward a closer association of the two groups. The Executive Committee of the Trustees in that year invited a group from the Alumni Association to confer with them as to "the number, elections, etc., of the Trustees." The proposed meeting had to be postponed because the Association had not been convened soon enough to choose representatives. A committee to confer with the Trustees was finally created in 1894. The result was a circular sent by the Trustees to all alumni in 1898 to ascertain their reaction to the idea of creating a Board of Overseers. The consensus was sufficiently favorable to encourage the Trustees to work out a plan in consultation with the alumni.

The proposal offered to the Trustees in the spring of 1899 recommended the creation of a Board of sixteen men and the president of the College, *ex officio.* All sixteen were to be holders of Tufts degrees, but not officers of instruction. No more than four could be Trustees. The members of the Board were to be elected by the alumni for four-year terms and would be eligible for one re-election. Their functions were to ratify all faculty appointments involving the rank of instructor or above made by the Trustees, and to pass on all changes or additions of personnel. They also had power under the original proposal to recommend to the Trustees "such action in any matter of college management or government, not purely financial, as may seem to them advisable, including the power to nominate officers of instruction and government." Action on the plan was postponed until the alumni could again be consulted. Several suggestions were received, although not all were incorporated into the final version. One recommendation made by the Alumni Association on which no action was taken by the Trustees would have provided that alumni would vote only for nominees representing the division of the College (e.g., college of letters, divinity school) of which the voting alumni themselves were graduates. The alumni felt that representation of the college of letters should constitute a majority on such a board.

The plan finally worked out was substantially the same as the original version, except that no Trustee was to be a member aside from the president of the College, and that members had to have been alumni (holding one or more degrees in course) for at least ten years prior to election. Alumni, to be eligible to vote for Board members, must have been degree holders (in course or honorary) at least five years prior to casting their first vote. In order to bring the Board into existence, a nominating committee was provided, five selected by the Trustees and five by the Alumni Association. They were to nominate thirty-two candidates; the sixteen with the largest number of votes were declared elected and were chosen by lot for staggered terms of from one to four years. The Executive Committee of the Alumni Association was responsibile for nominating two candidates for each regular vacancy on the Overseers. Ballots were then to be printed and sent to each graduate eligible to vote. A Committee on Elections was provided to count the ballots and certify the elections.

One change made in the original proposal theoretically strengthened the hand of the Overseers but in actual operation complicated and sometimes delayed the selection of teaching staff. The Board was not merely to ratify elections by the Trustees but was to approve "all nominations for officers of instruction in all departments of the College, whether permanent or temporary, of or above the grade of instructor, together with all votes providing for changes in or additions to departments of instruction." Fortunately, the provision was made that failure of the Overseers to communicate their decisions promptly to the Trustees could be taken as approval, for in actuality the Overseers in some instances failed to transact business because they lacked a quorum. The Overseers, as formally constituted, retained the authority outlined in the original proposal both to recommend policy changes to the Trustees and to nominate officers of instruction and government on their own. As noted earlier, the provision that the Overseers would also appoint the Boards of Visitors was added after the Board of Overseers had been created.

The newly constituted Board held its first meeting on October 9, 1899, and proceeded to organize, with President Capen and ten members present.[14] Very few changes were made in the personnel of

[14] Henry Blanchard (1859), Edwin Ginn (1862), Roland Hammond (1868), Minton Warren (1870), William B. French (1870), Frank M. Hawes (1872), Walter P. Beckwith (1876), Charles W. Parmenter (1877), Arthur W.

the Board of Overseers during its existence of less than eight years. Although the president and secretary could have been changed annually according to the by-laws, Charles W. Parmenter served as secretary until the fall of 1904, and his successor, Arthur W. Peirce, wrote the word "Finis" in a firm hand at the end of the minutes of the last meeting on June 17, 1907. Walter P. Beckwith, principal of the State Normal School at Salem, served as president until his death in 1905 and was succeeded by Edward H. Clement. Most of the Overseers were reelected and in some years, barring an occasional death or resignation, there were no new faces on the Board.[15]

Even before the Overseers had had an opportunity to select their own officers they were plunged into their work. They were asked at their very first meeting to approve the establishment of Professorships of History, and Greek Language and Literature; to approve the nominations of men to fill the new positions; and to fill two other professorships. The Overseers approved the two new posts but asked for time to investigate the four nominations. Lacking sufficient knowledge of the men involved to allow an intelligent vote, they requested time for a special committee to investigate the candidates. This became a chronic problem which was alluded to in almost every exchange with the Trustees. In their annual report for 1902 the Overseers in the very first paragraph mentioned their "inability to perform these duties with such thoroughness and efficiency as to make evident both our desire to promote the prosperity of our Alma Mater and the success of our efforts." The committees to whom nominations were referred uniformly expressed the feeling that it was "out of the question to make any adequate investigation." A second problem immediately arose. The by-laws of the Overseers, adopted at their second meeting, provided for an annual meeting in October and two other stated meetings (one before Commencement Day and another in January). Experience soon

---

Peirce (1882), and Samuel W. Mendum (1885). The following Overseers were not present at the organization meeting: Charles H. Eaton (1874), Edward H. Clement (1864), Seldon Connor (1859), William D. T. Trefry (1878), Francis B. Harrington (1877), and Frank O. Melcher (1887).

[15] The following men served at some time as Overseers in addition to the original group: Frank T. Daniels (1890), Milton G. Starrett (1886), Alphonsus H. Carvill (1866), Fred Gowing (1881), H. Austin Tuttle (1891), Arthur W. DeGoosh (1893), William Fuller (1879), and Frederick W. Perkins (1891).

indicated that if the Overseers were to keep up with the business assigned them they would have to meet more frequently. But distance, time, and professional commitments of the members precluded frequent consultation as a group. In numerous instances action required of them necessitated a hurried conference between the president and the secretary and whatever other Overseers could be contacted on short notice without benefit of a formal scheduled meeting. The provision that nominations for permanent faculty had to lie over for one meeting also made for delays and complications.

Committees (Boards) of Visitors were provided for each of the components of the College existing in 1899 (college of letters, divinity school, medical school, and dental school), to be appointed by a three-man committee of the Overseers and to consist of five members each, three of whom were to be members of the Board of Overseers. Their duties were "to learn what are the methods of government and instruction in the College, and to take such measures as in their judgment will best enable them to report in full on the conditions, wants, and prospects of the College." One of their additional functions was to collect information whenever possible on nominees in the course of their visitations to the campus, so that special committees would not have to be appointed.

The approval by the Overseers of nominations by the Trustees for faculty positions might have appeared routine and a mere formality if one did not look beyond the official records of votes, for the great majority of nominations were approved without question. But inspection of the Overseers' files shows how seriously they took their obligations and how thoroughly and conscientiously they investigated the nominees. Correspondingly, in virtually all instances involving personnel decisions the Trustees heeded the recommendations of the alumni. In the first group of individuals they were called upon to consider, the Overseers found one candidate about whom they had reservations, and the Trustees honored their decision that the appointment (involving a promotion) be delayed at least to the end of the academic year, until the person had proved himself. One matter on which the Overseers were insistent was that no one should be appointed to the rank of full professor until he had clearly demonstrated his fitness for the title. Ordinarily, they considered the practice of promoting teachers from instructorships to professorships unwise. A term of service as assistant professor was desirable as a rule first. This principle was applied in a case in 1900, and the Trustees followed the Overseers' recommendations.

One of the principal duties of the Overseers was to receive the annual reports of the Boards of Visitors, make abstracts of them to be presented to the Trustees, and forward their own observations. The first such report was prepared in the fall of 1901 and touched on many problems that seem to recur in the area of academic affairs. The Overseers recommended that departmental work be organized in such a way that the ablest and most experienced instructors were assigned to the elementary and basic courses, for "beginnings are most vital and important." A revised elective system introduced in the 1890's was beginning to result in such a proliferation of courses that the money for increased salaries deserved by the senior members of the faculty was being diverted into the employment of numerous instructors. Restricting the range of curricular choice and offering courses in alternate years could result both in a checking of the increase in instructors and in enhanced incomes for the permanent faculty. The Overseers were informed by the Trustees that their report had received "very careful" attention and that it showed "a thoughtful consideration and wise appreciation of the educational needs of the College." As to the recommendations of the Overseers, the Trustees found most of them already a part of College policy or concurred "substantially" with the propositions offered by the alumni. During their existence the Overseers commented on everything from the sad state of the divinity school enrollment to student behavior and with only a few notable exceptions received the same reply from the Trustees: The ideas were commendable, the College was already attempting to carry them out, or financial limitations prevented putting them into effect. The refrain became a bit monotonous to some of the more impatient alumni.

The Overseers almost immediately expressed doubts about the feasibility of continuing the visitation system. In 1901 they reported to the Trustees that "there seems to be strong reason for believing that the present method of supervision by Boards of Visitors is not likely to be greatly useful, from the exceeding difficulty, if not actual impossibility, of securing suitable persons of sufficient leisure to undertake the task." The Trustee Committee on Education to which the reports of the Overseers were submitted disagreed with the Overseers as to the value of the Visitors. In their opinion the discontinuance of the Visitors would be a mistake. Yet even the Overseers themselves were reluctant or unable to serve as Visitors, for in 1903 their by-laws were suspended so that Boards of Visitors could include as many persons not members of the Overseers as was deemed advisable. In 1903 the requirement that Overseers be represented on the Boards of Visitors was completely abandoned.

There was so much criticism of the Trustees for alleged failure to pay attention to the lengthy and painstaking reports of the Boards of Visitors and to keep the alumni properly informed that the Executive Committee printed and distributed to the entire alumni body a summary of the reports for 1904–5. The Executive Committee hoped "that the alumni of the College will find this communication of sufficient interest and importance to desire the publication of similar bulletins in the future." So far as the records indicate, this was the only such bulletin published, although reports of individual Visiting Committees continued to appear in the *Tufts College Graduate* (the alumni magazine) from time to time.

The Overseers also began to question the value of their own existence as an organized body. After four years of operation they looked back on their accomplishments and found them wanting. They had been disposed to take their duties seriously and to strive earnestly to be of genuine service to the College, which they loved. But even after making allowance for whatever intangible contributions they might have made, they had developed a keen sense of "the apparent inadequacy and unfruitfulness" of their efforts. It could hardly be otherwise when the Overseers were engaging in activities for which they actually had no ultimate responsibility. The responsibility rested with persons whom they did not meet face-to-face and with whom they could hardly be said to have had "a thorough working understanding." Positive action in regard to nominations of faculty was "difficult and rare." Consideration of financial matters was explicitly excluded from Overseer jurisdiction. Many of the topics discussed by the Overseers were already dealt with by the faculties of the College and resulted in needless duplication of effort unless each group was informed of the views of the other. It was therefore recommended that the reports of the

Overseers be submitted to the appropriate faculty, with replies returned to the Overseers by way of the Trustees. In short, it was desirable that "the closest possible relationship" be established between the faculties and the Overseers.

The problem of establishing a closer tie with the Trustees was
at least partially met in the fall of 1903, when the Executive Committee of the Trustees voted to arrange for joint meetings with the
Overseers or a committee of them, at least annually. The arrangement for ratifying nominations to the faculty was never worked out
satisfactorily. As they pointed out repeatedly to the Trustees, the
Overseers entered the picture only after persons were already nominated, and they were hesitant to express an unfavorable opinion
at that stage of the proceedings. If that function of the Overseers
was to be meaningful, their participation should be in the preliminary rather than in the final stages of the process. Provision for
consultation with the president of the College and the chairmen
of the departments involved was suggested. The Trustees had never
explained to the Overseers the reasons for the system of ratifications
of nominations in the first place.

There was another matter that still required consideration
and appeared periodically on the agenda of Overseers' meetings,
namely, alumni representation on the governing body of the College. The Overseers, in their annual report for 1903, inquired of
the Trustees whether any steps could be taken "looking to a more
formal recognition of the alumni through their organized representatives." Three more years went by before another step was
taken. The recommendations of a special committee of the Overseers appointed in 1906 to investigate the possibility spelled the
doom of their own organization. They inquired into the precedents
and practices of the older New England colleges and found that a
substantial majority provided for some form of alumni representation on their boards of trustees or overseers, or both, when both
existed. The committee reminded the Tufts Overseers that the
Trustees were a self-perpetuating body that by the original charter
was to consist of twenty-three members, enlarged to thirty by legislative act in 1878. The Board of Overseers, which could have been
created by the same device of charter amendment, actually existed
merely by virtue of a by-law of the Trustees. Hence the Overseers
had no such legal existence as would give the alumni any guaran-

teed representation in the management of the College and could be abolished at any time by an amendment to the Trustee by-laws.

In view of the manner in which the Overseers had been brought into existence, the meagerness of their authority, and the constantly growing body of alumni worthy of having "a substantial voice in the management of the College," the committee made a series of recommendations unanimously adopted by the Overseers and transmitted to the Trustees. The recommendations were as follows: that an enactment be secured at the next session of the legislature providing for the election of ten members of the Board by the alumni of three to five years' standing. Two were to be elected each year for five-year terms. The Board of Overseers was to be abolished as soon as the charter change was made. The number of Trustees provided by the revised charter was sufficiently large so that ten alumni would be about in proportion to the number of trustees on the boards of "several of the other New England colleges."

A joint meeting of representatives of the Trustees and the Overseers confirmed the basic agreement of the two bodies as to the course of action proposed by the Overseers. The recognition of the principle of alumni representation was unanimously voted by the Trustees and the number agreed upon was ten, two to be elected by the alumni each year for five years as vacancies occurred on the Board, until the entire ten places were filled. The question of whether, under such a plan, the alumni should also have a voice in filling vacancies among the other twenty Board members (who held unlimited tenure) was submitted to the alumni for consideration.

The last meeting of the Overseers was held, as was the custom, in Young's Hotel in Boston, on June 17, 1907. After receiving the reports of the Boards of Visitors to be transmitted to the Trustees, and after confirming a whole host of nominations to the faculty (mostly medical and dental), the Overseers in effect voted themselves out of existence. In view of the change which had taken place in the College charter on March 29, 1907, providing formal alumni representation on the Board of Trustees, the Overseers recommended the repeal of the by-law that had created them. The Trustees acted accordingly at their fall meeting.

After existing for nearly eight years, the Board of Overseers willingly bowed out in favor of machinery that would insure a closer relationship between the College and its alumni. Even though there had been practical difficulties, and the Overseers had not always agreed with the decisions or policies of the Trustees, their experiences had given them a more intimate view of the College. While this "nearer view point" had revealed many ideals unrealized, the Overseers had come to believe "more fully than ever in the present strength of the institution and to have a better grounded hope for its future prosperity." The Overseers themselves had served a valuable purpose in providing a transitional stage in alumni representation. Many of the procedural details, such as the eligibility for alumni Trustee membership and selection, were almost identical to the system prevailing under the rules and regulations of the Overseers. All persons who for five years had held a degree (in course or honorary) were eligible to vote for the ten alumni members. Any person who for ten years had held a degree in course was eligible for membership on the Trustees, provided that at all times at least seven of the ten members so elected should hold the first degree in arts or sciences. Except for the first election, alumni were to serve for five years and be eligible for reelection. The filling of vacancies on the Board by the alumni was to be limited to those positions that had been held by alumni Trustees. When Jackson College was chartered in 1910, alumnae received the same franchise rights as the alumni and the same opportunity to be elected to the Board of Trustees. In 1919 it was further provided that the nominations and elections of alumni Trustees were to be conducted in accordance with the rules and regulations of the Alumni Association. No further charter changes were made until 1934, after the Alumni Council had been created and the alumni were empowered to delegate their voting rights for alumni Trustees to a representative group rather than to act directly.

With the demise of the Overseers the Trustees resumed their authority to appoint Boards (Committees) of Visitors, and the matter was placed in the hands of the Executive Committee. The system differed only slightly from that of preceding years. The committees, appointed annually by the Executive Committee, were originally to have consisted of three persons, one of them a Trustee who was to be responsible as chairman for preparing a report to submit to the annual meeting of the Trustees. In actuality, the number of members of Boards of Visitors assigned to the various divisions of the College varied from two to six. In order to get as many points of view as possible and to involve the largest possible number of persons who it was believed should become acquainted with the work of the College, the policy was inaugurated in 1909 (at President Hamilton's suggestion) of changing the personnel annually. The policy of rotation was not consistently followed, but it did represent a recognition of the dangers of inbreeding and of the possibility (unfortunate as it might have been) that Visitors would refuse to serve for prolonged periods.

Whatever the doubts might have been about the utility of Boards of Visitors, they continued to exist and continued to play the same rather ambiguous role that had been assigned them when they had been first appointed by the Trustees in 1881–82. When the medical and dental schools were added in the 1890's and Jackson College for Women was created in 1910, Boards of Visitors were promptly provided for them. As other major divisions were added to the institution, such as the Fletcher School of Law and Diplomacy in 1933, they too had Boards of Visitors assigned to them. Mrs. Cora Polk Dewick, who was serving as chairman of the Committee of Visitors to Jackson College in 1924 and was in the process of preparing her report to the Trustees, commented rather acidly that "my observations at past meetings have led me to decide that nobody listens to the reports anyway, so I cannot hope to make much of an impression." President John A. Cousens, in a letter in 1931 to the man destined to succeed him, recognized the problem and commented that "of late years the reports have tended to be more and more perfunctory." He solicited suggestions for improving the system, which was apparently moribund. No matter at what period they existed, the value of the Boards of Visitors depended on such variables as their composition from year to year, the state of the general administration of the affairs of the College, and the role that the alumni and others ostensibly interested in the College saw fit to play.

It was in the midst of the economic insecurity of the 1890's and the discussions over the merits of such devices as Boards of Visitors that the College assumed new responsibilities and reorganized many of its internal operations in response both to local pressures and to an enlarged awareness of its educational obligations. In this decade the College opened its doors to women (after great debate and delay), added a medical school and a dental school, broadened the base of its engineering curriculum and opened a technical preparatory school, expanded its graduate department to offer the Ph.D. degree, completely revamped its undergraduate liberal arts program and reviewed its admissions policies, and reorganized its faculty and administrative structure. Tufts in the 1890's became a university *de facto,* although it persisted in calling itself a college.

6. "A Fair Chance for the Girls": Coeducation and Segregation

WHEN TUFTS COLLEGE OPENED ITS DOORS in 1854, the Universalist Church had established sixteen academies or seminaries. The College was unique for the denomination in two respects: it was the Universalists' first venture into higher education, and it was the only school of any kind under their auspices that was not coeducational in some degree when it was created. Twenty years after Tufts began to receive students, the Universalists had added three more colleges to the educational scene, and all of them were coeducational from the beginning.[1] Meanwhile, Tufts clung to a policy labeled "For Men Only."

The Trustees were made aware of this deficiency while the College was still in its infancy and were reminded of it with mounting vehemence for the next thirty-odd years until the pressure was too great to be resisted any longer. In view of the advanced ideas about the rights of women already held by most Universalists, it was not surprising that women should apply for admission almost immediately.[2] The first such application was received by the faculty in the summer of 1856, only two years after the College opened. A young lady from South Reading (Wakefield), Massachusetts, had made the first move. The faculty was completely at a loss as to how to handle the problem, for there is no record that the

[1] The institutions were St. Lawrence University, Lombard University, and Buchtel College.

[2] For biographical sketches of the leading Universalist women of the nineteenth century see Phebe A. Hanaford, *Daughters of America; or Women of the Century* (Augusta, Maine; True and Company, n.d.); and E. R. Hanson, *Our Women Workers: Biographical Sketches of Women Eminent in the Universalist Church for Literary, Philanthropic and Christian Work* (Chicago: The Star and Covenant Office, 1881).

possibility of making Tufts coeducational when it was founded was ever discussed in official circles, and there were no facilities of any kind providing for this contingency. So the only alternative was to refer the matter to the Executive Committee of the Trustees. There is no record that this body took positive action either.

Although Tufts pioneered in New England by encouraging all qualified applicants to apply regardless of race or religious creed, thereby practicing what its charter preached, it had, in fact, been founded under the auspices of Universalists, and it was they who felt a sense of responsibility for its policies and its future. In 1855, even before the young lady from South Reading applied for admission, the Massachusetts Universalist Convention had resolved that "the institution known as Tufts College, in arranging the basis of its operations, consider the propriety of opening it to both sexes alike, and of awarding its honors according to proficiency in study, irrespective of sex." When Tufts' first Commencement was held in 1857, special comment was made about the large number of ladies who "graced the occasion with their cheering presence." It was somewhat archly noted that only their forbearance and liberality made their presence possible at an institution which was "pandering to old fogey prejudices" by following the narrow and unenlightened policy of not admitting women to its privileges and advantages. The denominational press was full of communications complaining that women had fully expected to enter Tufts when it opened but had been unable to do so. Their only alternative, except to wait until the College saw the light, was to enter such institutions as Oberlin or Antioch, where they would be welcomed.[3] It was a crushing blow to see one-half the potential student population deprived of its rights to higher learning. Who was to blame? Obviously, it was "a limited minority of conservative minds . . .[who] . . . could see nothing but chaos, ruin, destruction in the mingling of the sexes in halls for highest culture."

The situation was in no way bettered for another two decades. When Dean Academy at Franklin, Massachusetts, which had been chartered in 1865 as a preparatory school for Tufts, announced in 1870 that it was inaugurating a collegiate curriculum for women

[3] Oberlin, opened in 1833, admitted women only four years later and thus became the first coeducational college in the United States. Antioch had opened as a coeducational institution in 1853.

only, separate from the existing coeducational academy, the suggestion was immediately made that Tufts become coeducational. It seemed foolish to operate two separate sets of college facilities within fifty miles of each other, especially when Dean was planning to use the Tufts curriculum as a model. A writer in the *Christian Ambassador* commented rather tartly that "This old, fossilized idea of herding only men together in college for educational purposes" had already proved unsatisfactory in some instances. Furthermore, men had "proved themselves far less proficient in pursuit of their studies than as if they had been stimulated by the presence and ambition of lady students." To show that this desire to make Tufts coeducational was no idle threat, one of the faculty of Dean Academy presented to President Miner in 1873 the credentials of two promising young ladies who were completing their preparatory course at Dean. He asked the Tufts president point-blank if the two candidates should report to Tufts to take the entrance examinations scheduled the week after the letter was sent. If President Miner answered, the reply is not recorded.

Pressure was soon exerted from another quarter. In the course of a discussion on coeducation at a Boston club in the same year, according to a report in the *Boston Globe,* a clergyman had asserted that "at the time of the foundation of Tufts College he had predicted that it would never come to anything unless it admitted women to its privileges, and now he found it perfectly dead when it might have been a live institution," possibly with a woman at its head. In fact, according to the report of the clergyman's remarks in the *Boston Advertiser,* Tufts "might have been one of the most powerful educational institutions in the country" if it had recognized the rights of women. It was probably inevitable that someone should suggest at the same time that those who repeatedly criticized such institutions as Tufts and Harvard for not admitting women should turn their siege guns on schools like Vassar, "which slams its doors in the face of boys."

Throughout the 1870's the controversy continued to wax in fervor and intensity. Many Universalists insisted that one's sex had no more to do with the question of who should be educated than whether one's hair was red or black. The issue was not whether the individual was male or female but whether women had the physical and mental equipment necessary to be admitted to and pursue successfully a collegiate program. If that issue was resolved in the affirmative, then logically the next question was: "Should females have the same textbooks, the same lessons, the same training, that males should have?" Even granted that a difference in kind of education was desirable, assurance had to be given that the quality would be the same as that of the education received by men. The next question, regardless of the kind of education to be made available, was a crucial one: "Should females be in the same classes with males — the two sexes having the same lessons, and reciting in common?" The answer of most Universalists was a categorical "yes"; the absolute separation of the sexes in the educating process was a poor policy for either sex.

Collegiate coeducation was urged as part of a larger goal: the elevation of the position of women at large. It would help assure that they would be reading something besides trivia and that they would talk about something more profound than the latest fashions. It was hoped that a woman, as a result of higher educational opportunity, would "indignantly revolt" at being asked to be no more than a "walking advertisement of millinery." If no more, higher education might result in respectful acceptance on the public platform, from which women had so long been excluded. The supporter of this particular point may have had in mind the experience of the first coeds at Oberlin. In spite of the vaunted "equality of the sexes" there, the young ladies who had been assigned Commencement parts had to sit meekly and mutely on the platform while a male classmate read their speeches for them.

Long before the Tufts Trustees took their first vote on coeducation, every important argument ever offered for or against the higher education of women had reverberated across the land.[4] Half a century before, the common opinion seemed to have been that women were mentally incapable of being educated in "the higher branches." After the women had effectively disproved this, the argument shifted and the question became: "Can a woman stand the pressure of an intellectual life on her physical constitution?"

[4] A substantial literature has been accumulating on the subject. Two representative works are Mabel Newcomer, *A Century of Higher Education for American Women* (New York: Harper, 1959), and Thomas Woody, *A History of Women's Education in the United States* (2 vols., Lancaster, Pa.: Science Press, 1929).

There was no one answer. President Eliot of Harvard strongly opposed coeducation; one of his arguments centered around the presumed inability of women "to bear the nervous strain of collegiate study." Simultaneously, President Andrew D. White of Cornell and President James B. Angell of the University of Michigan were arguing just the contrary. The latter reported that his institution's experiment in coeducation had been an unqualified success. "Any lady," he asserted, "who can endure the draft that modern dress and modern society make upon her, can certainly endure any college course so far as physical endurance is concerned."

While the controversy over coeducation became more vocal and attracted more public attention, Tufts College remained silent, at least officially. Certain enterprising Universalists thereupon decided to press for a decision. At the Massachusetts Universalist Convention in the fall of 1873, Mrs. E. M. Bruce of Melrose offered a preamble and four resolutions calling for forthright action to promote coeducation at Tufts. Her wording was spiced with a certain amount of righteous indignation. First of all, it was clear, at least to her, that there was no obstacle to the introduction of the system at Tufts so far as the Trustees, the faculy, and the students were concerned. Her conclusion was derived from remarks made by President Miner in the course of a public speech during the Commencement festivities earlier in the year. The Trustees, she gathered, "had never taken ground against coeducation of the sexes at Tufts"; the presence of women "would not be disagreeable to the students"; furthermore, the faculty, it appeared, "would find delight in giving them instruction." What irked her was the fact that "the President of our first College . . . proceeded openly and squarely to shift the burden of responsibility for the exclusion of female students from the shoulders of the College management to the shoulders of the people" by declaring that "the doors of the College were closed to women solely on account of, and in deference to the backward state of public opinion." The resolutions therefore included a declaration that the State Convention, at least, disclaimed all responsibility for whatever backwardness existed in public opinion; that the Universalist leaders were pioneers in advocating and practicing coeducation in their schools; that a denial of the principle was a violation of the theories, declarations, and convictions of Universalists; and finally, that suitable pro-

167

vision should be made for the reception of young women at Tufts in the near future. All of Mrs. Bruce's efforts were tabled by the Convention, but it was voted that they be considered again at the next meeting.

The annual State Convention in 1874 was faithful to its charge. So it was not surprising that Dr. Miner referred to the subject when he was called upon to speak on the general topic of the responsibility of the church in promoting reform movements. He "believed in a higher education for women" and had, for example, preached the first sermon in favor of a high school for girls in Boston. But this did not necessarily mean coeducation. "He was growing in his distrust of the policy of putting boys and girls into the same school and the same classes," and raised the question whether "separate schools for the sexes" might not be advisable. After all, he said, "a man is not a woman, a woman is not a man; and if education attempts to make either the other, it will fail." He had come to believe that Tufts College had better remain as it was for a while, "till its fruits can be compared with the fruits of the mixed policy."

Rev. John Coleman Adams of Newtonville, Massachusetts, a Tufts graduate of the Class of 1870 and later a member of the Board of Trustees, contributed to the discussion by arguing that "he would go as far as any one. He would give his sister just as good an opportunity as he had enjoyed himself." But he was not prepared at that time to say he believed in coeducation. Equality of of the sexes did not necessarily call for that. As yet, experience with coeducation was insufficient. It was too early for a mature judgment; it was "the part of prudence to wait."

With the stage thus set, the previously tabled resolutions bearing on coeducation at Tufts were brought up for discussion. According to the reporter at this session, "there were many speakers." They fell into three classifications: those in favor of coeducation, those opposed to coeducation, and those in doubt. The upshot of the discussion was that the preamble and first three resolutions were stricken out and the last resolution, expressing the hope that "suitable provision" for coeducation at Tufts would be made eventually, was indefinitely postponed. The vote was by no means unanimous, but the size of the majority was unquestioned. Dr. Miner completed the lowering of the boom on the possibility of coeducation, at least for the immediate future, by objecting to the assumptions made in the preamble about the willingness of the College to embark on the experiment. He argued that they were unwarranted and had been based merely "upon sportive remarks which he had made at a commencement dinner" and not upon any official pronouncement.

Until the fall of 1874 the students in the all-male institution on Walnut Hill had not expressed any opinions on coeducation of which there is any record. But a vehicle for the dissemination of student opinion on all kinds of subjects was created with the *Tufts Collegian,* the first all-campus student publication. The first student magazine had been the *Tuftonian,* which appeared in 1864 and was published at irregular intervals until 1872. It was sponsored jointly by Zeta Psi and Theta Delta Chi, the first national fraternities to have chapters on the Tufts campus. In 1874 the *Tufts Collegian* appeared, under the auspices of the Tufts College Publishing Association, and four years later appropriated the name of the *Tuftonian.* Until the turn of the twentieth century the *Tuftonian* was a combination campus newssheet, literary magazine, and alumni reporting agency. Some of its coverage was transferred to the *Tufts Weekly* in 1895 and to an alumni magazine in 1903.

The very first issue of the *Tufts Collegian* carried an article entitled "The Co-Education Question." The editors did not, however, fling caution to the winds and take up the cudgels for coeducation then and there. Instead, they took a cautious approach and in two successive issues presented summary reviews of current literature on the subject, with a view to educating rather than converting the student body. Judgment would be reserved, it was emphasized, until more of the returns were in. The editors, in fact, deplored a situation that apparently existed regarding the whole subject of coeducation, in which "the formation of opinion has preceded the collection of evidence." The *Collegian* first reviewed the work of the Harvard physician Dr. Edward H. Clarke, *Sex in Education; or, A Fair Chance for the Girls,* published in 1873. The burden of his argument against coeducation was that, from a biological viewpoint, the system would jeopardize the health of the delicate young ladies who would be seeking to acquire higher education. Mrs. Julia Ward Howe rejoined in 1874 with a bundle of essays which she had collected, entitled *Sex and Education*. In the same year Anna C. Brackett's selection of essays from various sources, *The Education of American Girls,* tended likewise to defend coeducation and to criticize Dr. Clarke. Rev. Giles Bailey, a Universalist clergyman and staunch supporter of Tufts, added his voice to the proponents of coeducation in an early issue of the *Tufts Collegian.* As an outsider looking in, he had come to the conclusion that the College was "a little too conservative" in its exclusion of young women and had expressed the wish that the experiment with coeducation be tried.

Simultaneously, another interested Universalist clergyman, Rev. James Eastwood, offered in a prominently displayed article in one of the denominational papers not only an eloquent plea for coeducation but the first practical plan for financing such a program. He doubted that the College would be flooded with female applicants, but the principle was more important — the opportunity for them should be available. No less than $1,000,000 would be needed, he thought, to build and endow a separate college for women. Yet no more than $100,000 would be required to make Tufts coeducational, and that amount was within the realm of reason. He had no doubt, furthermore, that most young women likely to apply for admission had the ability to master the curriculum. Bringing the sexes together in the classroom would create a competitive situation in which both men and women would do their best, and academic achievement would permit standards to rise rather than force them down. He ruled out as completely fallacious the often-heard argument about the physical disadvantages under which women allegedly operated in a collegiate situation. After all, he pointed out, the young women at Vassar seemed to be surviving the academic ordeal, and statistical evidence could be produced that the percentage of prolonged absenteeism for reasons of health was no higher at Vassar than at Amherst, an all-men's college.

As to problems of morality and discipline which might arise if coeducation were introduced, Eastwood saw no reason to believe that the virtue of the Tufts student body was any higher without coeds than it would be with women on the campus. "Nobody believes that the average college student altogether eschews female society for four years; and it is obvious how much better it is for a young man to associate with women whose culture and aims are like his own than with those of an indifferent or bad character." Any dangers allegedly stemming from coeducation on grounds of social relations would be minimized by certain other factors. There would be, he was convinced, a relatively small number of qualified women sufficiently interested in higher education who would apply. Certainly there would not be the danger incipient in a situation where the sexes were numerically equal. It was then that the maximum opportunity would be afforded to "that strong tendency in human nature, 'to pair off.'" Then too, some trust had to be put in the ability of the women to take care of themselves. They would be "of such age and probity as to be a law unto themselves." There was no validity in the argument that because Tufts was established as a men's college women had no right to attend. Women had been just as active as men in supporting the institution and raising money for it and had just as much vested interest in Tufts as the men. Why, he asked, should Tufts stand by and watch other coeducational schools like Wesleyan and Boston University forge ahead? Why make a virtue out of the *status quo* and continue to live on and in the past?

After 1875 the movement to make Tufts coeducational began to accelerate. When Capen became president, following Miner's resignation, his stand on the question was much less equivocal. It was Capen who made the first official recommendation in 1883. By that time, if public opinion had ever been "backward" on the subject of education of both sexes, it had progressed significantly. Further, there was tangible evidence that higher education for women was here to stay. Such institutions as Mount Holyoke, Vassar, Smith, and Wellesley had long since vindicated their right to exist as women's colleges. Both private and state-supported institutions, ranging from Oberlin and Antioch to the State University of Iowa and the Universities of Michigan and Wisconsin, had survived the coeducational struggle. The experiment in coordinate colleges for women, attached in some degree to existing all-male campuses, had even been tried when the "Annex," later to be known as Radcliffe, was born just outside the Harvard Yard in 1879. The steadily growing impact of feminine influence outside college walls was being felt simultaneously. In that same year (1879) women in Boston, under the leadership of such champions as

Mrs. Julia Ward Howe of the New England Suffrage Association, obtained the privilege of voting for school board members and 989 women registered.

President Capen was very much aware of these developments about the country when he composed his annual report to the Trustees for 1882–83. As to the principle of coeducation, he noted, there was admittedly a diversity of opinion not only among the Trustees and faculty but among the patrons and constituents of the College as well. "Nevertheless, the trend of public opinion appears to be, for the present at least, unmistakably towards co-education." It might, he admitted, be years before "the most conservative institutions of the country" swung about to some type of coeducation, but the trend seemed inevitable. He took pains to point out to the Trustees that "in a movement of such vast importance, there are those who think Tufts should lead rather than follow." He also emphasized, and reaffirmed many times later, the difficulties inherent in financing such an endeavor as coeducation. He stated the problem quite bluntly. "In the present condition of the College, before any step could be taken toward opening its doors to the other sex, it would be necessary that ample provision should be made for their separate lodging and oversight."

The Trustees were impressed by the president's recommendations, for in the spring of 1883 a special five-man committee was appointed "to consider the expediency of opening the College to women." Quite logically, President Capen was made chairman. The Committee on the Admission of Women made its first report in September and regretfully came to the conclusion that, regardless of the merits of coeducation, the material increase in expenditures for dormitory and other facilities made the move impracticable at that time. It was recommended, however, that the special committee be continued, in the hope that someone might be found to finance such a project. Almost a year went by before the committee was prepared to report again. In his annual report for 1883–84 the president again alluded to the subject of coeducation, noting that "a portion of our constituency is insisting that it is the duty of the Trustees to afford the same facilities for education to young women as to young men." Capen repeated the point made a decade before by one of the denominational journals: mere zealousness of purpose and high idealism were inadequate of themselves. Money was needed to underwrite the proposed change of policy, and it was fruitless to exhort and to give gratuitous advice without providing the necessary financial support. Rev. Mr. Eastwood had used the same argument in 1874. President Capen believed that the often-mentioned sum of $100,000 was "certainly needed to do this work with dignity and decency." He made it very clear that "the friends of co-education, therefore, ought not to complain that doors of the College are closed against women, until they are prepared to tender the requisite sum for this purpose." He repeated his strong belief that, no matter what the objections to coeducation, they would be eventually overcome "by the spirit of the age," which inexorably demanded the admission of both sexes to institutions of learning.

The next step was taken as a direct result of these comments by the president and came from outside the College. In June 1885 the Trusteees received a letter from Mrs. Lena C. Start. She represented a committee of women and interested alumni who were prepared to launch a drive to raise the requisite $100,000, provided the Trustees made it clear by official action beforehand that they were favorable to the admission of women. The letter was duly referred to the Trustee Committee on the Admission of Women for report at the next annual meeting. The secretary of the Trustees was, in the meantime, to obtain "the individual opinions of the General Faculty of the College upon the question of co-education of the sexes in Tufts College" and to circularize the alumni for their views. Mrs. Start's letter was printed and distributed among the alumni, and ninety-three replies were received. Although the majority (fifty-one) were in favor, thirty-three were "strongly opposed," and the remaining nine were "doubtful in regard to the policy." Most of those who approved did so only on condition that sufficient funds could be raised so that coeducation could be introduced "without detriment to the work of the College as at present carried on."

Meanwhile, some of the Trustees had done a bit of research into the status of coeducation in New England. They compiled statistics for the six institutions which admitted women (Bates, Boston University, Colby, the University of Vermont, Wesleyan, and Middlebury) and found that Middlebury, which had just opened its doors to women in 1882–83, was the only New England college since 1874 to adopt coeducation — "a period of *eleven years*." This presumably proved that the movement to make existing institutions coeducational was noticeably declining. It was also noted that most of the women attending coeducational colleges resided in the vicinty of the institution and very few came from a distance.

Although the matter of the admission of women was placed on the agenda of the regular October meeting of the Trustees, the committee requested further time, and its report was heard at a special meeting in December 1885. President Capen presented the majority report. The consensus was that it was inexpedient to open the College to women at that time. The committee's vote had not been unanimous, for a lengthy and vigorous dissent was filed with the Trustees by Wilmot L. Warren, who as a busy newspaperman associated with the influential *Springfield Republican* had been unable to attend the committee meetings. He was most indignant and considered the failure of the committee to recommend coeducation a breach of trust and a blow to the cause of human enlightenment.

Neither the determination of Mrs. Start and her supporters nor the eloquence of Mr. Warren prevailed. On former President Miner's motion, the Trustees, while appreciating the importance of collegiate education for women in general, deemed it "inexpedient, all things considered, at the present time to open the College to them." The vote was a decisive twelve to two; President Capen voted in favor of the motion. The Trustee Committee on the Admission of Women had taken its responsibility seriously and had explored the problem conscientiously and deliberately before making its negative recommendation to the Trustees. As President Capen pointed out repeatedly in subsequent months, the decision not to admit women had been made reluctantly but realistically. The crux of the matter was the financial inability of the College to provide the facilities for coeducation. The committee assumed that if women were admitted they had to be placed "on an absolute equality with young men." Nothing less would do. It would not be fair or just to deprive either sex of the privilege of scholarships, gratuities, and prizes. Aside from the additional housing and other arrangements necessary, augmented instruction would have to be provided in at least four departments (Ancient Languages, Modern Languages, Psychology, and English). The committee also feared that such a shock would be produced among the male undergraduates by the admission of women that "some young men would doubtless leave. Others would be deterred in their purpose to come and for a time at least there would be a diminution in the attendance of young men." This would naturally shrink income from tuition and would require more time and patience than could be afforded "to recover from the shock and adjust to the altered circumstances." Finally, the committee was "decidedly of the opinion" that $100,000 was completely inadequate to finance "so important and radical a change in the policy of the College"; no less than double that amount would be necessary.

No further formal action on coeducation was taken by the College until the spring of 1892. This did not mean, however, that interest in coeducation had appreciably diminished. The undergraduate editors of the *Tuftonian* devoted considerable space to the topic, faithfully presented pros and cons, and reported the official decisions of the Trustees as the years went by. In the spring of 1882 the subject was reviewed in the *Tuftonian* in some detail, and it appeared that the "time-honored prejudice that young men and women should not be educated together" was crumbling away. Sufficient experience had by then been accumulated from other institutions to allow some tentative judgments to be made. It appeared to the editors, at least, that it had been convincingly demonstrated not only that women were entitled to greater educational advantages than they were then enjoying but that they were fully as intelligent and capable as men and would add tone and gentility to any campus. During 1883–84 both sides of the coeducation question were aired at some length, and it is difficult to determine which set of arguments had the upper hand. The following year the opponents of coeducation seemed, at least temporarily, to have come off with the better of the debate.

The burden of the opposition to coeducation appeared to rest on the twofold fear that the admission of women would lower the "literary standard" of the College and would turn the Hill into a playboy's paradise. Somewhat contradictorily, it was simultaneously argued that stringent rules for conduct would be necessary to prevent the deterioration of morality, and the rules would in turn make Tufts like a prison. A six-point rejoinder a month later ended the student skirmishing, at least in print. The defenders of the principle of coeducation took particular umbrage at the implication that Tufts men found it difficult to be gentlemen except under duress.

While the members of the Tufts Club of Boston discussed the merits and demerits of coeducation at their Alma Mater in the fall of 1885 and heard President Capen speak in favor, the undergraduates conducted their own opinion poll. The sentiment of the student body was strongly against the admission of women; in fact, many of the men refused to take even the possibility seriously. Of the ninety-six students who voted, seventy-three expressed their opposition and only two were undecided. Under these circumstances, it seemed that the *Springfield Republican,* in urging at the time that Tufts could not "in justice refuse to admit women," was a voice crying in the wilderness. As one member of the Class of 1889 explained, he did not want to be driven to the desperate expedient of washing his face and putting on a clean collar every day.

President Capen returned to the subject in his annual report for 1885–86. He made much of the fact that the negative Trustee action of 1885 was not intended as an expression of opposition on principle, or even on grounds of practicability if the circumstances changed. And he thought the circumstances were rapidly changing. Since the Trustees had voted, Columbia had joined the ranks of co-educational colleges and Brown was actively considering undergraduate instruction for women, although in separate classes. He was convinced that it would not be long "before Tufts College will of its own motion take the place in the ranks of progress to which the logic of events has assigned it."

President Capen was right. At the December meeting of the Trustees in 1891 the matter of education of women was again placed on the agenda, although action was temporarily postponed in order to give the Executive Committee opportunity to review the matter. On April 26, 1892, the Executive Committee voted unanimously to recommend "that provision be made for the education of women at Tufts College." The recommendation was adopted, and the Executive Committee was charged with preparing and presenting a plan to carry it into effect. Final action was taken on July 15, 1892. It was voted "that the College be opened to women in the undergraduate departments on the same terms and conditions as to men."

This meeting of the Trustees was an important one for the

College. Not only was coeducation approved, but the main College building, which had remained unnamed for almost half a century, was christened Ballou Hall. At the same meeting, the new dormitory for the divinity school became Paige Hall. When former President Miner gave $40,000 to build a separate headquarters for the school (Miner Hall), it was with the understanding that the College would raise at least $12,000 to build "an accompanying dormitory for the students of such school." The dormitory, completed in 1892 with funds raised in part by friends of the divinity school, was named for Lucius R. Paige, Universalist clergyman and a Trustee from 1859 until his death in 1896. He served as secretary to that body for nearly fourteen years. Of equal moment was the Trustees' decision that day to create a graduate school faculty and to offer the Ph.D. degree in biology and chemistry. In a sense, the vote to admit women to Tufts came by way of the graduate school. After the vote to grant the doctorate and to adopt a revised program for the M.A. degree, the Trustees agreed "that graduate courses at the College be opened to candidates of either sex." It was then voted to open the College to women at the undergraduate level as well.

A newspaper reporter stood outside the door of the building in downtown Boston when the Trustees filed out. "President Capen's face," he wrote, "wore a smile. . . . 'At last,' he said, 'the die has been cast.' " If women presented themselves for admission to the regular classes, they would " 'be welcomed, and be allowed to do the same work as the men.' " The president reminisced for a moment. When Tufts was founded, he told the reporter, "there was a strong movement in favor of coeducation, but for some reason it failed to accomplish anything." But he knew it was inevitable. "For ten years I have felt that this must come. The whole growth of the College has been toward a broader field." Tufts had now joined its neighboring institutions in providing the opportunity for women which had been so long denied.

The *Boston Globe* prominently displayed the news in an extended article. "Tufts College," it reported, "is going to admit women. . . . When [the Trustees] took their seats the college was a place to nurture men only. When they arose to depart it was a full-fledged co-educational institution. Its doors had been thrown open to women, and a step had been taken that all present felt was of great moment to the future of the College." Denominational papers reported the news triumphantly, and one pointed out (somewhat inaccurately) that women's rights to higher education had never been disputed; it was only the means that were debatable. Coeducation had now won the day at Tufts. It was confidently asserted that "before another decade passes the matter will no longer be in controversy."

The agitation that had started some forty years before had served its purpose. Women had come into their own. But a multitude of practical problems now confronted the College. If one took the long view, Tufts had come a great way since the Trustees had first discussed coeducation in 1882 and 1883. Its resources had been much strengthened. From a physical plant of four buildings and sixteen instructors it had grown to ten buildings and twenty-seven instructors. Exclusive of certain earmarked special funds, the College had approximately $1,250,000 of income-bearing property and fifty-two free scholarships at its disposal. But there were numerous pressing problems to face and to solve. In view of the lateness of the date in 1892 on which the decision to admit women was made, how many would apply for the opening term in 1892? And where would they be housed and fed? How would their education be financed? How would Tufts men react? How would the faculty react? A partial answer to the latter question was given by the poll of faculty opinion taken by the secretary of the Trustees when coeducation had been discussed in 1885. The results did not augur well for the future. Of the thirteen faculty members of whose views a record was made, only three were favorable to the admission of women (Professors Marshall, Dearborn, and Moses True Brown); six were "unqualifiedly in opposition" (Professors Schneider, Shipman, Leonard, Fay, Amos Dolbear, and Harmon); Professor Tousey expressed opposition "qualifiedly"; and three (Professors Benjamin G. Brown, Bray, and Knight), while "not specially favoring such a change in the policy of the College . . . would not object to it, provided the young women could be lodged and cared for in some manner different from the present dormitory system." Faculty reaction was mixed, to say the least. In fairness to the faculty, it should be stated that many of them who had originally opposed coeducation at Tufts, like Professor Fay, not only changed their minds after the young ladies began to arrive but in several instances became their staunch defenders.

Despite the short time elapsing between the announcement of the Trustees' decision and the opening of the fall term in 1892, nine young ladies took their places in Tufts classrooms on the Hill. The medical school, which was to become a part of Tufts in 1893, was made up in large part of students who had come from the College of Physicians and Surgeons, which was already coeducational. So the students in downtown Boston undoubtedly failed to appreciate the excitement generated on the Medford campus. In fact, President Capen commented that women had shown "excellent capacity" for medical training. Moreover, the teachers in the medical school neither observed nor themselves experienced embarrassment because of the presence of women in lecture room or laboratory.

Of the nine young women who entered the Hill schools, one was a transfer from Boston University at the end of her junior year and could claim many distinctions. In 1893 Henrietta Noble Brown received the first baccalaureate degree conferred on a woman by Tufts College. Her father, Benjamin G. Brown, was Walker Professor of Mathematics at Tufts; she was born in the house at 38 Professors Row, which for several years after 1949 served as headquarters for the Tufts Faculty Club. In 1895 she married Frank W. Durkee, of the Class of 1888, who later was to hold the chairmanship of the Tufts Chemistry Department for almost a quarter of a century. In 1895 Mrs. Durkee also received the first Master's degree conferred on a woman at Tufts. Not content with a higher degree in chemistry, she resumed her graduate work a few years later and in 1918 scored another "first." When her daughter received her A.B., Mrs. Durkee was awarded an M.A. in history.

Of the eight other feminine pioneers, four were in the college of letters and the remaining four were enrolled in the divinity school. Among the graduates of the Class of 1896 were Miss Ethel M. Hayes, who served on the staff of the Tufts Library for half a century, and Miss Cora Alma Polk, known to a later generation as Mrs. Frank A. Dewick and the first woman to be elected as a Trustee.

For Universalists, the entrance of the four women into the divinity school was a fitting and long-anticipated event. Universalism had produced the first ordained clergywoman in the United States: Mrs. Olympia (Brown) Willis, who was graduated from An-

179

tioch in 1860 and received her theological training at St. Lawrence.[5] For over twenty years that denomination had been the one religious body to permit, and in fact to encourage, the ordination of women for the ministry. In spite of all dire predictions to the contrary, the collegiate survival rate of the first group of women at Tufts was rather high. Six of the eight coeds who had received their entire instruction at Tufts obtained their A.B. degree in 1896.

As to the problem of housing for the young ladies upon their arrival on campus, the president had worked out on paper a beautiful scheme. Capen was convinced that as much home life and atmosphere as possible should be carried over into college experience. For that reason, he felt it would be unwise to have large dormitories. Instead, one central building should serve as a nucleus for smaller houses grouped about the main structure, no one containing more than sixteen to twenty young women. This plan could not of course be effected in a few weeks. So for almost three years the new arrivals who did not already reside at home were forced to make housing and dining arrangements as best they could. Several lived at the homes of faculty members and other residents in the immediate vicinity of the College who were willing and able to take in boarders.

As soon as coeducation had become a fact, President Capen swung into action. He made it known that some place would be provided for the young ladies to study, but he also made it clear that there were no dormitory facilities because there was no money to provide them. Although the president quite accurately predicted that there would probably be no more than ten women during the first term of coeducation, he warned that provisions for at least twenty-five would have to be made for 1893–94. This naturally raised the problem of dormitory facilities. Now was the golden opportunity "for the people who have been demanding coeducation at Tufts to come forward and furnish the means to put the women on the same footing as the men."

Someone did come forward. In the spring of 1893 Albert Metcalf of Newton made a gift to the College providing for a building "as a home for women students." Construction was begun at once,

[5] The centennial of her ordination in 1863 was acknowledged by the Universalist Historical Society, which devoted Volume 4 of its *Annual Journal* (1963) to articles by and about her.

Metcalf Hall in 1904

and the expectation was that the building would be completed and ready for use by the academic year 1894–95. Facilities for at least thirty were planned. In actuality, Metcalf Hall, as it was officially named in the fall of 1894, provided housing for twenty-four students on the second and third floors, with dining facilities and a suite for the matron on the first floor. Metcalf Hall, which became 56 Professors Row, was built of yellow brick and was surmounted by a tower on the east side. The College took great pride in the new structure. President Capen described it as a building which "in solidity, durability, and fineness of finish" was "unquestionably one of the very best buildings belonging to the college." He reported to the Trustees that no expense had been spared to make it "a beautiful home for young women [and] an ornament to the College grounds." It was made even more ornamental in a verbal sense, for it was soon dubbed the "Bird Cage" by the Tufts men. Although a delay in preparing the new dormitory for occupancy in 1894–95 resulted in the use of only half the rooms that year, Metcalf served its full complement of students thereafter. The study space promised by President Capen was provided temporarily by carving out a room in overcrowded Ballou Hall.

181

Residential supervision by the College authorities was instituted from the beginning and was made doubly necessary by the high proportion of young ladies who continued to reside in private homes. Metcalf Hall could house only a portion of the coeds. A Women's Advisory Board, consisting largely of faculty and Trustee wives, undertook the general supervision of both College and off-campus women's residences. In 1901 it was given general oversight of all matters not purely academic relating to the health, conduct, and deportment of women students. The printed rules for approved private homes which were listed with the College give some indication of its concern for the welfare of its feminine charges. Householders renting rooms to students were expected to furnish, in addition to light and heat, a parlor or reception room where students might entertain callers. All instances of "indiscreet behavior" were to be reported directly to the president. These rules were enforced, for householders more than once were notified that their rooms had not received the necessary sanction; therefore, the young ladies were obliged to seek other quarters. Women students were expected "to observe in their conduct the usages and restrictions of the best home life." More specifically, they were "to attend evening entertainments away from the Hill only when accompanied by a chaperon." In 1901 Tufts acquired its second women's dormitory, a former faculty residence known as Start House. It had been constructed in 1894 and housed women until 1925, when it became the home for the dean of the engineering school. A third building, known as Allen House, was used as a women's dormitory in the late 1890's and again during the First World War. For several years after 1916 it served as an infirmary for Jackson students.

The fear expressed by many that the policy of coeducation would place an excessive financial burden on the College was not at first borne out. The generosity of Albert Metcalf had provided for the most pressing need requiring a major outlay. The feminine enrollment in the college of letters went up steadily. In 1893–94 there were twenty-two; in the following year there were thirty-nine; in the spring of 1896 there were fifty-six; by the turn of the century, there were ninety-nine. An attempt was made to provide sufficient funds to assure that the women received an equitable share of scholarship and other financial assistance. Much of this was made possible by the supporters of coeducation among Universalist women. Individually, their contributions were small, but the sincerity of spirit in which the gifts were made testified to their devotion to the institution and to the principle of coeducation. The Women's Universalist Missionary Society of Massachusetts had been delighted when Tufts was opened to women, and immediately set about soliciting funds. Mrs. Cornelia B. Skinner, grandmother of Clarence R. Skinner, a well-known dean of the theological school, led the way. In 1886 she had bequeathed her diamond ring and camel's-hair shawl to be converted into money for the cause. When President Capen reported this first contribution specifically for the higher education of women to be $250, he expressed the hope that, modest as it might be, it would attract other and larger donations. In 1893 the Missionary Society invited President Capen to a mass meeting to discuss various ways in which help would be given. The decision was to establish a loan fund for women. It was created on the spot with a contribution of $5.00 presented by a young child on behalf of her widowed grandmother who was present at the meeting. The following day another lady, who had lost not only her husband but three children as well, donated $25 in their memory, and the loan fund was on its way. Some scholarship funds for women were also created in the 1890's. Typical was the John and Lucy H. Stow Scholarship Fund of $5,000 established in 1894; the income was to be paid to two or three girls each year who were deemed both worthy and needy.

The first of the "larger donations" which President Capen hoped for could not be accepted by the College. In 1890 Sarah P. Blake left her farm in Wrentham, Massachusetts, to Tufts, upon the condition that within three years after her death the Trustees would agree "to use said property for erecting and maintaining thereon buildings for educational purposes in connection with said College or for establishing and maintaining thereon a College for the higher education of women only." The Trustees declined to accept the bequest under the conditions attached, even though the will was probated after Tufts had become coeducational. The next donation on behalf of the education of women also had strings attached, but the Trustees saw fit to accept it.

The benefactor who left the largest single amount to further feminine education at Tufts was a relatively obscure person, but little known outside her home city of Providence, Rhode Island.

She was Cornelia Maria Jackson, and her lifelong conviction was that women were entitled to rights and privileges equal to those of men. By the logic of the situation, she was a champion of women's suffrage and an enthusiastic advocate of higher education for women. She had been born in Wrentham, Massachusetts, on December 15, 1822, and died in Providence, Rhode Island, in 1895. She received an unusually large amount of formal education for her day, having attended Attleboro Academy and Bridgewater State Normal School, from which she graduated in 1847. Continuing her residence in southern Massachusetts, she taught school in Wrentham, Mansfield, and Attleboro for several years. In 1862 she married Sylvester R. Jackson, a Providence businessman, and lived thereafter in Providence. Her interest in Tufts can be traced to the influence of her pastor, Rev. Dr. Henry W. Rugg, who was secretary of the Tufts Trustees and a member of the committee that had voted to open Tufts to women in 1892. Albert Metcalf, the donor of the first women's dormitory, had been a student under Mrs. Jackson.

The provisions of Mrs. Jackson's will, dated February 1, 1893, were formally accepted by the Trustees in 1895. In order to help "remove the disabilities of women" she bequeathed $70,000 and half of the residue of her estate to Tufts.[6] Like so many bequests before and since, there were various conditions attached which necessitated the carrying out of the spirit rather than the letter of the will. To make matters more complex in this particular instance, the executor of Mrs. Jackson's estate died before the will could be probated. Resulting legal entanglements and delays made the final settlement a lengthy one, and for several years Tufts could only guess what the final amount of her bequest to the College would be. Estimates, as late as 1910, ran as high as half a million dollars. The actual bequest was considerably less than this; by the spring of 1910 less than $60,000 of the original bequest had been received.

The two special conditions of Mrs. Jackson's bequest were quite natural under the circumstances. First, Tufts was to erect a building to be designated "The Cornelia M. Jackson College for Women." Second, in addition to the regular courses prescribed for the students of the College, women were to receive special instruc-

[6] The other half was willed to the Rhode Island Homeopathic Hospital in Providence.

tion "in the duties and privileges of American citizenship, and in the theory and working of the United States government." In compliance with this provision, the Trustees established, effective in 1898–99, the Cornelia M. Jackson Professorship of Political Science. Dr. Henry C. Metcalf was the first holder of this chair.

When the time came in 1896 to graduate the first group of women who had entered as underclassmen, President Capen took stock of the preceding four years. All seemed to be going well. The enrollment of both men and women had been encouraging. The problem of living quarters for the women had somehow been solved. The College was still surviving financially. Dear to the president's heart was confirmation of the feeling he had expressed shortly after coeducation had been introduced. He had informed the Trustees that the women had "come quietly and unobtrusively into their places, and, so far as their presence in the classes is concerned, have not caused the slightest friction." He could be even more specific in his report for 1896.

> The presence of women . . . has not diminished the interest in the activities or sports which are supposed to belong peculiarly to men's colleges. There has been no friction arising from their presence in the class-rooms, and they have not increased materially the difficulties of administration . . . their work has been as well done as the work of the men. The general testimony of the teachers is that they have raised the tone of the class-room and quickened the serious efforts of student life. Their presence also has brought an element into the social atmosphere of the College, which is very agreeable and very wholesome.

The Commencement festivities of 1893 were especially significant for the College. A woman for the first time in the history of Tufts had an official place in the proceedings. Miss Henrietta Noble Brown delivered the first Commencement Oration by a Tufts woman.[7] At the 1896 Commencement, when the first four-year group of women was graduated, two of the six speakers were women. One, an M.D. candidate, discussed "Antisepsis," and Miss Ethel Munroe Hayes, representing the women on the Hill, discoursed on "The Geographical Situation in Venezuela." The 1896

[7] Her presentation was entitled "Some Aspects of Immigration," erroneously printed on the Commencement program as "Some Aspects of Imagination."

Commencement was a landmark in Tufts' history in another respect. The well-known Universalist Mrs. Mary A. Livermore, writer, feminist leader, and humanitarian, who had done relief work in the Civil War, received the first honorary degree awarded by Tufts to a woman. In acknowledgment of this recognition, she composed a poem entitled "Tufts College" which was widely printed. It was Mrs. Livermore who had been suggested for the presidency of Tufts by the speaker at the Boston club in 1873.

In the meantime, making a place for women among the Tufts undergraduates was more difficult than either the president admitted or the general public probably realized. The female invasion of a previously all-male bailiwick, although only on a small scale, was received far from enthusiastically. Most of the men chose to ignore their new classmates or to treat them with distant respect. But they could not be ignored. Even though 1896 was a red-letter year in the history of the College, when the Commencement proceedings were reported in the new undergraduate newspaper that had been launched the previous year, the *Tufts Weekly* merely listed the names of the women graduates, without editorial comment. The Class History for 1896 did include a clipping from a Boston paper describing "how '96 first meandered over College Hill hand in hand with the co-eds," but that effusion was apparently reproduced with a shrug of the shoulders. For many years it was the custom during Class Day festivities for the students to gather on the Hill and to cheer the Trustees, the president, the faculty, and the buildings in general. At Class Day in 1894 the all-male class of 1895 celebrated "its womanless condition" with these words:

> We thank the Lord we've lived alone
> Without a girl upon the throne:
> The only class that's now alive,
> The glorious class of '95.

Among the cheers on Class Day in 1896 was one grudgingly dedicated merely to "the girls." It was unthinkable that a woman should hold a class office, and feminine participation in such activities as class banquets was considered little less than a horror.

The decade after 1900 brought unsettling developments on the Hill and bade fair to extinguish the flame of coeducation. A reaction set in against the policy. The reasons were many, and possibly not always clear either to the present generation or to earlier ones. Whether myth or reality, they all played their part in the inauguration of a new policy. It was known as "segregation," and it centered about the issue of "separate but equal treatment of the sexes." For more than three years these were the burning issues for Tufts — among the Trustees, administration, faculty, and students alike. Even the outside world put in its bid to be heard.

The first serious questioning of the merits of coeducation came from Eaton, the financial agent of the College in the 1890's. Tours about New England had convinced him that "the fact that girls are admitted to Tufts College is being used to prejudice young men against the College." Members of the graduating class at Goddard Seminary had told him that "not a single young man" from that school would enter Tufts in the fall of 1897 because it was believed that the College was "becoming a girl's school, and that the best and strongest young men would not go there." The subcommittee on education of the Trustee Executive Committee, when asked in 1898 to recommend economies that might be effected in College operations, put part of the blame for financial stress on "the friends of women's education who clamored so loudly for the opening of the College to women" and then failed to support the cause.

In terms of the number of women students, Tufts was "a great success," but in terms of the number of men, it was "a painful fact" that since 1891 the College had made no substantial gains in the number of male students commensurate with the growth of course offerings or improvements in instruction. There were fifty-eight full-time students enrolled in the regular classical or scientific courses in 1891–92, the year before Tufts admitted women. In 1895–96 there were 224 men and 43 women in the regular undergraduate programs; in the year in which the Trustees' investigation was made (1898), there were 259 men and the number of women had jumped to 97. The Trustee committee felt sure that neither the alumni nor the student body had ever really favored coeducation. The situation would become even worse if the rate of increase in feminine enrollment continued; it might very well be that eventually the College would "practically become a school for women." The alternatives, if Tufts was to remain "as much a man's College as a woman's College," were not very happy. It was too late to abolish coeducation; that would be a step backward. There was the possibility of separating the men's and women's educational facilities, but that would necessitate the employment of additional faculty and the erection of at least one building. This alternative seemed to be "an experiment too costly to be prudent" considering the financial situation of the institution. An intermediate course of action seemed the only other possibility. It would require the arbitrary limiting of the number of women to the capacity of Metcalf Hall. Following this path would likewise be unfortunate, for Tufts had already established an excellent reputation as a school that admitted women, and there was a tremendous reservoir of competent female students in the Boston area alone which had not been sufficiently tapped.

The solution decided upon at the time by the Trustees was not to curb coeducation but to make the College more attractive to men. In the last analysis, coeducation was probably not basically to blame for the increasing disproportion in the student body. The fault lay in the twin lack of advertising and insufficient financial inducement. The Trustee committee repeated the oft-made assertion that Tufts had "always been a poor man's College. Many, if not most of our students are of the class that works for an education." If the College could be made more attractive to prospective students by a combination of increased extracurricular activities and augmented financial aid, a partial solution to the problem seemed assured. The Glee Club might be enlarged and improved; a College choir could be established to enliven the chapel services; opportunity in athletics might be increased. Athletics was one of the best ways to make a college known to the outside world, yet Tufts had been doing less in this area than any other New England institution, in the opinion of the Trustees. If athletics were to be encouraged, however, certain safeguards would have to be established. "To hire men to come to our College to play ball would be contemptible, would be condemned by the students, and in the end would injure the institution. To recognize merit in athletic ability, and to encourage it when found with scholarly attainment, is a very different proposition." The committee made such a convincing case for their point of view that in 1899 the Trustees established twenty annual gratuities worth up to $100 each, to be awarded by the president in consultation with the chairman of the Executive Committee. The gratuities were not to be cash awards but would take the form of free room rent, reduced tuition, and the like. The suggestion was made that these gratuities not be considered purely as "athletic scholarships"; in fact, six of the twenty were to be for the benefit of the Glee Club, and the remaining ones for "general athletics."

Creating gratuities for undergraduate men was only a partial remedy for the problems brought by coeducation. The limitations of the physical plant were becoming acute. It seemed in 1902 that President Capen was himself beginning to have doubts about the success of coeducation. He devoted a portion of his annual report for 1901–2 to a plea for a building to be used by women students exclusively, for recitations and assembly, located possibly next to Metcalf Hall on Professors Row. He reminded the Trustees of the provisions of Mrs. Jackson's bequest in 1893. He deplored the fact that "the whole of that portion of her estate" left to Tufts had not been "devoted to the objects specified by her." As Tufts approached its fiftieth anniversary in 1902, he devoted a proportion of his annual report to endowment needs and again urged the provision of "a woman's building to serve at once for assembly, physical training and recitations," which would cost an estimated $75,000.

The individual who precipitated the debate over coeducation at Tufts and who offered the most detailed arguments in favor of segregation of the sexes was Rev. Dr. Frederick W. Hamilton, an alumnus (Class of 1880) and the last Universalist clergyman to serve as a president of Tufts. He assumed his duties at the beginning of the academic year 1905–6 and within two years had roused a storm of controversy and created much opposition both within the College and outside. Two things should be made clear at the outset: he was by no means alone in his opposition to coeducation; and he was sincere and realistic in his approach, for he was the chief executive of a college with limited resources which had to make its way in an increasingly competitive educational world. On June 19, 1906, he delivered an Inaugural Address which contained nothing new or revolutionary. But at the end of the first year, when he made his annual report to the Trustees in 1907, he had reached an unhappy conclusion. With the exception of the theological school, the college of letters was sharing the least in the growth of the College. The Engineering Department, and the medical and dental schools, which had been created in 1893 and 1899 respectively,

189

were filled to capacity and in some cases students were being turned away. But in 1906–07 there was an accelerated decline in liberal arts enrollment. Various factors could explain part of this — an increase in tuition fees from $100 to $125 per year, effective in 1907–8, and a change in financial arrangements which required payment of term bills (tuition and room rent) at the beginning of each half-year rather than at the middle and end of the academic year. But these did not satisfactorily explain the general pattern. Even the increasing demand for technical education accounted only in part for the trend away from liberal arts. After all, the president pointed out, Dartmouth, Brown, and Bowdoin were all experiencing record enrollments at the time.

After an analysis of the situation, President Hamilton came to the conclusion that the cause for Tufts' failure to share in the growth of the liberal arts area could "be found in our system of coeducation." Unlike the state-supported universities of the Middle West, which had a virtual monopoly over education in that area and were not seriously affected by coeducation, the privately endowed New England schools had to compete for patronage, and within substantially the same territory. Hence they could not afford the luxury of coeducation. Why? Because "the average young man will not go to a coeducational institution if other things are anywhere near equal." The Tufts engineering student had, so far as association with women in Tufts classrooms was concerned, a great advantage over the liberal arts student; he could keep such contact at a minimum because he had no reason to associate with women "excepting in a few electives which he takes in the College of Letters. He, therefore, is not disturbed by the presence of women." The corresponding disadvantage for the male liberal arts candidate was the necessity of attending the same classes as women. "He is not comfortable with the women in the class room. In some things he feels that he is at a disadvantage, and I have known some of the best students to say that they often hesitate to recite or to enter into discussion in the mixed classes for fear of making themselves ridiculous before the women." In science courses, the situation was often reversed. Furthermore, "the differences between the feminine mind and the masculine mind, and also between the feminine and masculine avocations of the college student, usually lead to the capturing of a large proportion of the scholastic honors by the women."

Then there was the whole area of sentiment, or even prejudice against women, irrational as it might be. Unreasonable or not, it existed and had to be reckoned with. "It is not possible for Tufts College to conquer it or to reason the masculine youth of New England out of it. If the present state of affairs continued to exist, the College of Letters, which we older graduates know and love as Tufts College, will become a girls' school, and that sooner than most of us realize."

President Hamilton kept hammering away at his theme in newspaper and magazine articles. In 1908 he heartily seconded the sentiments expressed in an article by the prominent psychologist G. Stanley Hall, entitled "The Feminization of Boys." They agreed that there were not enough men in the teaching profession, particularly at the high school level. Hamilton was "strong in the opinion that after graduating from grammar schools, boys and girls should be educated separately."

Coeducation kept away capable women as well as men. The feeling against coeducational institutions was not so strong among women, said the president, but it still existed, and sent many an excellent student whose general prepossessions would be in favor of Tufts to Radcliffe, Smith, or Wellesley. The issue involved no abstract discussion about the rights or capacities of women. It was the very practical problem of the future of an institution which depended largely upon the public for its patronage. "The future of the academic department of Tufts College as a man's college depends upon the immediate segregation of the women into a separate department or college."

This did not mean that Tufts should cease to educate women. For one thing, the gifts already made by Albert Metcalf and Mrs. Cornelia Jackson for the purpose would preclude that. Further, his recommendations regarding segregation were not to be interpreted, he said, as an attempt "to discourage the women in any way" or "to relegate them to any inferior position." On the contrary, the plan would, he felt, "do more by far for the education of women than was done by opening the doors of Tufts to women students." But they should be educated separately, with their own dormitories, lecture rooms, chapel, and dean. Instruction should be given by the Tufts faculty, and the library and laboratory facilties, at least temporarily, could be shared by men and women. Such association as would come to the students from separated departments in the laboratories or in the library would not be harmful. Aside from financial savings in using the same faculty, there was "no doubt" in the president's mind that "the training which women can receive in a college taught by men who are at the same time instructors in a man's college, whose educational views and methods are fixed by the point of view obtained in being educated among men and teaching men, is far superior in depth, in breadth, and in vitality to that which can be obtained by women who are taught by women, who themselves have been taught by women and are working only with women."

In order to bring about segregation, "a considerable expenditure of money" would of course be necessary. A lecture hall would be required as well as a gymnasium with facilities for non-resident students, and additional dormitories would have to be provided. The total outlay for buildings and extra salaries to begin operations would not exceed $250,000. The president considered the matter of segregation of the sexes "the most pressing educational problem" then before the institution. He had no fear that failure to solve the problem would be catastrophic for the College as a whole, but he had no doubt that failure to solve it involved "imminent disaster to the College of Liberal Arts."[8] This may have been an exaggeration, but there is no denying the fact that it was considered a serious problem in the minds of many in the Tufts community, and that statistics seemed to bear out many of President Hamilton's assertions.

In the fifteen years after coeducation had been introduced, the percentage of women in liberal arts had steadily risen. By the fall of 1907, when matters came to a head, women comprised almost 70 per cent of the entering class. For better or worse, it was also an undisputed fact that the enrollment of men in liberal arts was correspondingly decreasing. A writer in the *New Haven Courant* asked the natural question: Why was it that "only a year or two ago the same boys who are so unwilling to have the girls study with them at Wesleyan or Tufts were delighted to have them as fellow-students at the high school?" Rev. John Coleman Adams, a Tufts

[8] The *Boston Globe* made this comment a bit more sweeping by reporting that President Hamilton called coeducation a "national disaster."

Trustee, undertook to supply the answer. For one thing, he wrote, the numerical balance of the sexes was being destroyed at Tufts. If the trend of increased enrollment of women at the expense of the men continued, the liberal arts department would become "wholly feminized." Criticism of coeducation had nothing to do with the failure of women to justify their presence academically. In fact, they had "done their work too well, if anything." The women had become the scapegoat for the unhappy conditions alleged to prevail in other areas of the College, namely, "an unhealthy craze for athletics, the drift away from the broader courses of study, and the conversion of the college into a "social rather than a pedagogical institution."

The *Boston Transcript* reviewed President Hamilton's warning about Tufts and suggested that it was a problem facing most eastern colleges that admitted women. The newspaper's diagnosis of the ailment was economically oriented:

> The difficulty is simply the tendency of the women to drive out the men. A principle similar to Gresham's Law in the economic sphere — that cheap money drives dear money out of circulation — appears to operate in the college world. The weaker sex drives out the stronger. And, as the economists have come to recognize that the maintenance of a bimetallic standard of gold and silver requires an international monetary agreement, so educators seem to be working toward the conclusion that isolated experiments with the double educational standard in the face of the general practice of separate college education are destined to fail.

Again, the cold facts of the case tended to support President Hamilton's arguments. The coeds simply walked off with more than the lion's share of available academic honors. In 1906 the women chalked up another unchallenged victory. For the first time in the history of Tufts all of the seniors (five in number) elected to membership in Phi Beta Kappa were women. Two years later four of the six recipients of that coveted honor were coeds. The tables had been turned; now the men were on the defensive, and *their* quality was being challenged.

President Hamilton's experience and observations in 1908 and 1909 reinforced his conviction that the need for separation of the sexes was urgent, and he was quite willing to have his opinions known. Every Boston paper reported every scrap of information about the subject. Typical was the coverage of the *Boston Transcript,* in which the following series of headlines appeared in the issue of January 28, 1909, over an article concerning the College:

SYSTEM AT TUFTS WRONG
Hamilton Inveighs Against Co-Education
Sexes Should Be Segregated, His Firm Conviction
Future of College of Letters at Stake
Tells Trustees That They Have Grave Problem on Hand

Lack of funds continued to be the major stumbling block. However, Hamilton offered a partial solution which would also alleviate the chronic problem of inadequate faculty salaries. In many cases the separate instruction required by segregation could be conducted by the existing staff, who, by repeating their work, would add to their hours of classroom commitment but would not add materially to the time given to their own study and preparation. The work in Radcliffe was provided for in this way. The Harvard instructors, while still doing full work and receiving full pay from Harvard, repeated their courses at Radcliffe, receiving therefor a compensation adequate for the work done but much less than the amount received from Harvard. In this way "a considerable number" of instructors would have the opportunity to earn larger incomes, at least in the college of letters.

At the October meeting of the Trustees in 1909, President Hamilton sought concrete action by that body. He recommended that a special committee be appointed "to consider and report upon the advisability of immediate action in the matter of segregation of the sexes." Forthwith, a five-man Committee on Segregation was created.[9] The seriousness with which the Trustees tackled this problem is driven home by the fact that the president, the vice-president, and the treasurer of the Corporation all served. The committee made a progress report in December. Although not all the faculty were solicited for their opinions, there was among the eleven senior members who were consulted "an absolute unanimity of sentiment and opinion as to the desirability of the segregation

---

[9] After Arthur W. Peirce and Austin B. Fletcher, both alumni Trustees, had declined to serve, the committee consisted of Arthur E. Mason (chairman), Thomas H. Armstrong, Hosea W. Parker, Henry W. Rugg, and Edward H. Clement.

of women, not only for the sake of the men, but for the women also." At a special meeting on April 12, 1910, the Committee on Segregation was ready with its report and recommendations, which had been circulated among the Trustees in advance. The report was long, elaborate, and impressively documented with statistical tables and the results of consultation with faculty, alumni, and students.

The consensus appeared to be inescapable. Coeducation had not worked well at Tufts. The faculty seemed to be unanimous in feeling that the interests of all would best be served by separating the sexes for instructional purposes. Some faculty admitted that they had reversed their earlier opinions and judgments. As befitted a college faculty, the reasons given in support of segregation varied considerably. Some found that "the delicacy of treating freely a subject where both men and women were present in the same class" was a consideration, although not a major one. Others noted "the invariably different view point (due to the difference in sex) from which men and women approached nearly all the subjects." Still others noted "a natural diffidence on the part of both sexes to enter, during a recitation, into any argument with the other sex over any subject under consideration." Many of the faculty were quick to point out what they felt to be the nub of the problem: "The tendency of women to select courses in which from the nature of the subject and their natural aptitude and ability they will secure high marks, coupled with the general desire of women for high marks." The end product was a measurable weakening of the incentive for the men to work for honors and awards. The men were already convinced of "the approximate certainty of non-success" in the face of feminine competition. The faculty were substantially agreed on one point: The presence of women on the Hill "had served to help the tone of the community — had exercised a sort of refining influence on the men." But there seemed to be "a feeling of sentiment pervading the whole student body . . . that each sex would be better off in their work were the other absent." The Trustee Committee on Segregation reported confirmation of this faculty feeling from other sources, including the president, the remarks of "sundry students," and alumni. This, in turn, did not mean that any hostility existed between the sexes. It had "always

195

been the custom of each sex to treat the other with respect and consideration" although it was recognized that, in view of the long male dominance of the College, women were still considered "an alien element." Justified or not, this feeling was a contributing factor to increasing sentiment against coeducation.

Moreover, both the men and women graduates of the College who opposed coeducation — and there were some — refused to send their sons or daughters to Tufts or failed to recommend the institution to others. Statistics were produced which showed that over the period since 1892 there had been a relative loss of enrollment amounting to 15 per cent for both men and women. It was clear to all that this was an unhealthy sign. While the enrollment of comparable New England men's colleges (Bowdoin, Williams, Amherst) had increased between 43 per cent and 45 per cent in the ten-year period from 1899–1900 to 1909–10, the enrollment of Tufts men had shown a gain of less than 15 per cent. Put another way, if the Tufts gain had been in the same ratio for the same period, the liberal arts male enrollment should have been 198 rather than 116. Stating the matter baldly, the issue of coeducation was in part a simple problem of dollars and cents.

The Committee on Segregation offered four recommendations, which were unanimously adopted by the Trustees on April 12, 1910. At the same meeting, as many of the recommendations as possible were implemented. First, "the best interests of this institution require a separation of the sexes." Second, "the best way of accomplishing this is by the establishment of an independent College for Women." Third, the importance of the matter was "so great that though the financial resources are not at this moment in hand to meet the extra cost, the action should be taken at the earliest possible moment." Finally, an amendment to the College charter was to be secured for the separate college, "to be known as Jackson College for Women." It was recommended that in the interim "a Woman's Department be established which shall be merged into Jackson College for Women as soon as the legislation therefor shall be secured." There was considerable discussion regarding the necessity for a charter amendment and a separate college. Segregation could have been accomplished merely by creating a Department of Women, comparable to existing departments such as Engineering. But there were two good reasons for what might have appeared to be a rather cumbersome and unnecessarily complicated procedure. The Trustees voiced one of the reasons, and President Hamilton made public the other. The Trustees wished above all to prevent misinterpretation of their actions. Segregation, if it was to be undertaken, had to be "full and complete." Furthermore, there should be no possibility that the Trustees' action might be interpreted to mean a lowering of standards or any diminution in the opportunities for women. The women should "be able to say that they have *equal opportunity* with the men." And in order to accomplish this, "a separate institution exclusively for women with a suitable and appropriate name and the right and power to grant its separate degrees should be established. This institution should have its own officers and faculty."

In order to clarify further the status of the new college and to set doubts at rest, sixty questions were prepared for President Hamilton to answer. Although many of the questions and answers were set up in routine fashion in advance at the request of the president by Mrs. Fred D. Lambert, wife of a member of the Biology Department and an active alumna of the Class of 1900, others clearly reflected the fear of those coeds who felt that the College might be planning to relegate the women to an inferior position. The questions (and answers) were published in the *Boston Journal,* May 5, 1910. When asked why the purposes of segregation could not have been more simply accomplished by the creation of a Department of Women, President Hamilton gave the second reason for the Trustees' action. In order to take advantage of "the only definite promise of endowment for Jackson" which had so far been made, it was necessary to comply with the bequest providing the endowment. According to the president's interpretation, Mrs. Jackson's will had specified that a college for women be separately chartered although operated by the Trustees of Tufts College. A reading of the will, it might be noted, does not completely support the president's public statement. The bequest did *not* specify segregation of women as a *quid pro quo.* It should be recalled that Mrs. Jackson's will was made shortly after Tufts became coeducational, and so far as is known, she voiced no objection to the system.

The plan to establish an interim Department of Women (bearing the name Jackson College) pending the approval of charter changes was made unnecessary by the prompt action of the Massachusetts legislature. The petition prepared by the Trustee Committee on Segregation in April was approved by the General Court on June 15, 1910. A separate college, at least on the drawing board, existed effective the following day. As if to reinforce the idea of separateness, Section 3 of the charter amendment provided that the new college could "adopt and use upon diplomas and other written instruments . . . a seal of a design differing from the common seal of the corporation." Alumnae of Jackson were also given both the right to vote for the ten alumni members of the Trustees which had been provided in 1907 and the right to serve on the Board of the Corporation. Their legal equality with all other graduates of Tufts was thereby assured.[10]

The alumnae of Tufts had already been heard from before the legislature had even chartered Jackson College. The Executive Board of the Association of Tufts Alumnae were dissatisfied with the name that had been selected. They were quite willing to "give moral and financial support" to the new women's college, but someone discovered that the name "Jackson" had already been appropriated by an institution in the South. So the alumnae requested that the name be reconsidered. The query about possible confusion with the school in Mississippi also appeared in the list of sixty questions which President Hamilton had publicly answered. He saw no grounds for confusion, as the southern school was not listed in the current report of the United States Commissioner of Education. The Trustees dutifully reconsidered the name, as requested, and, after determining that the other school referred to was listed as a secondary school in spite of the name "Jackson College," unanimously voted that Mrs. Cornelia M. Jackson's memory be perpetuated in Tufts' new college.[11]

§   §   §

In 1892, when Tufts had begun its coeducational experiment, it had been necessary to consider certain pressing problems: How

[10] The by-laws of the Trustees were also amended to provide for separate accounting of Jackson funds by the treasurer of the Corporation.

[11] There *was* a Jackson College in the South. It had been founded in 1877 as a school for Negroes, with the name Natchez Seminary. In 1882 its name was changed to Jackson College, although it did not become a degree-granting institution until 1944, when it was renamed Jackson College for Negro Teachers.

many women would enroll? How would they be housed? Could the project be adequately financed? And how would the Tufts community react? Two of these questions were much more easily answered in 1910 than in 1892, and the answers seemed to express affirmation rather than negation. There was, in the first place, a ready-made student body for Jackson. Beginning June 16, 1910, all women students in liberal arts were automatically registered in Jackson College. As a consequence, there were fifty-four women inherited from the days of coeducation, plus six transfers from other institutions and two special students. In addition, twenty-three women entered the first freshman class in Jackson, making a total of eighty-five. This was "most gratifying" in view of the last-minute announcement of the change of policy, and of the widespread fear that the change would be to the detriment of women. The enrollment in Jackson thereafter increased in a most satisfactory way. By the time the dean of Jackson made her second annual report she was already hinting that additional dormitory space would soon be necessary.

As to the reaction to the new regime, there seemed to be general agreement on all sides that segregation was a good thing. According to President Hamilton, when the policy was being considered in 1909 and 1910, "the Alumni, almost unanimously, heartily endorsed it." The faculty could do little more than approve it in view of the opinions they had already expressed to the Trustees. The male student body, showing no marked enthusiasm for coeducation from the beginning and maintaining a rather equivocal attitude, finally made their feelings clear. They fully approved. Surprisingly little time, space, or attention was devoted to the subject of coeducation by the students in their undergraduate publications between 1892 and 1910. A large proportion of the early coeds chose English as their major field and appeared unobtrusively but effectively on the staff of the *Tuftonian*, the campus literary magazine. The *Tufts Weekly* continued to be dominated by male leadership, and much more attention was devoted to sports events, class rivalries, and fraternities than to the doings of the women. As one undergraduate (male) in the *Tuftonian* casually expressed it, there were three classes of reactions to the women: "co-ed haters, co-ed tolerators, and co-ed lovers. The co-ed tolerators were by far in the majority."

When segregation was announced in the spring of 1910, Tufts-men were galvanized into action. The *Tufts Weekly* on April 21 reported that "great hilarity and celebration" were the order of the day when the news arrived on the campus. A huge bonfire was quickly arranged, and the students marched around the Hill to the accompaniment of the band. At chapel the next morning the juniors who were about to be segregated filed out from the service and were confronted with a double line of men extending from Goddard Chapel to Ballou Hall. The embarrassed young ladies marched to the accompaniment of loud cheering on the part of the masculine contingent. The undergraduate newspaper even de-voted an editorial to the subject of segregation and commended the Trustees for their action. The experiment in coeducation had been a failure. The men were being "crowded out of the department of liberal arts" and had come to feel that the very traditions of the College were being lost, while the freedom of the entire institution was being "pushed into the background."

While all this was taking place, the Trustees and administra-tion were engaged in solving the chronic problems of finance and housing. At the same meeting at which segregation had been voted, the president and secretary of the Corporation were constituted a committee to notify the alumni of the Trustees' decision and to make a plea for financial support. It was calculated that if each alumnus would make an annual pledge of $5.00 for a five-year period, at least $5,000 a year could be raised from that source alone. If coeducation had contributed to the slow growth of liberal arts enrollment, then segregation should bring about increased enroll-ment of both men and women. It was estimated that increased reve-nue from tuition might bring in as much as $2,500 a year, and pos-sibly $10,000 annually by the fifth year. If this expectation seems overly conservative to later generations, it should be remembered that the tuition was $125 a year in 1910. The income from unre-stricted funds (as of 1909) was $5,600. For the past several years, gratuities and scholarships paid out to both men and women had averaged over 25 per cent for each, and these funds were sorely in need of replenishing. In his annual report for 1910–11, President Hamilton called for "special endowments" for Jackson, with first priority to scholarships. If existing funds were assigned fairly among the divisions of the College, Jackson would receive but fourteen. Fortunately, there were already several scholarship and loan funds intended exclusively for women, or which could be used for either men or women. For example, in addition to those cited earlier, the loan fund of the Women's Universalist Missionary Society of Massachusetts, which had been launched by a $5.00 donation in Roxbury in 1893, amounted in 1910 to some $6,000. Loans from this fund in units of $100 at 4 per cent were available to deserving women. A Jackson Building Fund of $18,500 had also been accumulated, and the Jackson Professorship Fund of $40,000 was paying an income of $1,300.

But the most pressing financial needs of all centered about the provision for separate classrooms, laboratories, and administrative headquarters, and the employment of a dean for the new college and an augmented faculty. The only immediate solution was to tighten the College belt, use existing facilities where possible, and hold all expenses to an absolute minimum. Constructing a new building for the specific use of Jackson was out of the question, for the Building Fund established for that purpose was completely inadequate, and Mrs. Jackson's estate was still in such turmoil that nothing could be counted on from that source. So the decision was made to renovate Middle Hall for the use of the theological school and to make Miner Hall the headquarters for Jackson. Middle Hall was vacant in 1910, for its use as the College library had come to an end after Andrew Carnegie had donated sufficient money to Tufts to build Eaton Library, opened in 1908. Middle Hall, although in need of extensive repairs, was easily adaptable for theological school purposes, and it was planned that the exchange of buildings would be only temporary. To that end, a mutual five-year lease arrangement was provided between the theological school for the use of Middle Hall and Jackson for the use of Miner Hall. Middle Hall underwent its scheduled renovation and was christened Packard Hall when the theological school took it over in 1910. All other facilities "necessary to the separate conduct of a College for Women," it was thought, could be arranged at minimal expense.

Miner Hall, which was to serve as the "temporary nucleus" of the Jackson administration while its own buildings were being financed and erected, required only minor alterations. It was

Miner Hall, one-time home of Jackson College

renovated, and a locker room was provided in the basement. The building housed not only the dean's office but also a branch of the bursar's office, part of the College bookstore, and a chapel, which was immediately found to be too small. There were also seven classrooms and a combination reception and study room for the special benefit of students who did not reside on the campus. During registration periods, representatives of each department migrated to Miner Hall to provide necessary services. In short, Miner Hall was destined to be a beehive of academic activity.

Dormitory facilities were another matter that needed immediate attention. Metcalf Hall and Start House still constituted the only college-operated housing for women, and they had long since been outgrown. The situation was not improved by a change of policy regarding residence on campus. When Jackson was established, it was decided that no regular student could be enrolled unless she resided either in a dormitory or with her family. Private homes in the vicinity of the campus were out of bounds, at least temporarily. Housing, in fact, had become so critical that two women were living in Ballou Hall in 1910. It was hoped that additional dormitory space could eventually be provided in buildings already owned by the College, such as converted faculty houses. As it turned out, one of the oldest houses on the campus became the third women's dormitory. This structure, located at 28 Professors Row, had been built in 1857 as a boarding house for men while East Hall was being constructed. It stood on the site of West Hall and was moved in 1870, at which time it was serving as a two-family faculty residence. After extensive remodeling and enlargement by an addition on the east side, it was ready to house eighteen Jacksonites and a matron in October 1910 with the new name of Richardson House. The benefactor after whom the reconstructed building was named was Mrs. Mary A. Richardson, a long-time friend of the College and donor of library books, a scholarship fund, and money for a professorship.

Staffing the new college also required extra expenditure. At the meeting which created Jackson College, the Trustees authorized President Hamilton to nominate candidates for the faculty and administration, including a dean. By using the existing faculty to the maximum, it was anticipated that total extra expense for the new personnel would not exceed $10,000 annually. The Trustees voted to put a ceiling of $12,000 a year on additional expenses for Jackson for the next three years. Fifteen new faculty members were provided. Mrs. Caroline S. Davies was selected as the first dean of Jackson College and served fifteen years until her resignation because of ill health. She was a native of Massachusetts and a person of exceptional scholarly achievement and leadership ability. She was graduated from Wellesley College in 1887 and later attended Newnham College, Cambridge University, where she continued her studies in English literature and in Greek. She served several years as an instructor at Harcourt Place Academy, Gambier, Ohio. Her husband, Rev. Owen John Davies, was for a time the chaplain of Kenyon College. From 1904 through 1909 Mrs. Davies taught in various girls' schools in the Chicago area and served one year as headmistress of St. Peter's School, Bayswater, London. She was an active advocate of women's suffrage, was a member of numerous professional and scholarly organizations, and was included in *Woman's Who's Who of America, 1914–1915*. At the time of her appointment to Jackson College she was living in Boston, but she moved in 1911 to 72 Professors Row, which was then designated as the residence of the dean of Jackson College. Mrs. Davies came to Tufts as both an administrator and a teacher. She carried the title of Professor of Greek and also taught the Jackson freshmen their basic English course when she first arrived. She was both the first woman to hold an administrative post at Tufts and the first woman to teach at the institution. She was also the first and only faculty member to teach courses exclusively for women. Mrs. Davies filled a difficult assignment "quietly, efficiently, and with most remarkable tact, firmness, and patience."

There was still some doubt and a certain amount of confusion about how the new arrangement was intended to operate, and a multitude of administrative decisions still had to be made in 1910. Almost as soon as the Trustees' decision had been announced, President Hamilton was confronted with the sixty questions previously mentioned. In the fall of 1910 he undertook to explain (and to justify) Jackson and to answer some of the recurrent questions. First of all, he assured both men and women that with the separate college there was "no longer any need to sacrifice the interests of either sex to those of the other, or to make any compromise between methods which seem necessarily diverse." The women would be equally entitled with the men to the courses offered by the senior members of the faculty, and he foresaw no possibility that any faculty member, new or old, would refuse to teach women. Except for the courses taught by the dean of Jackson (English and Greek), which were open only to women, all courses on the Hill were to be open irrespective of sex. The requirements for admission, the curricula, and the degree requirements for men and women were identical. Special students who were not degree candidates were to be allowed to enroll, provided they chose a major department. With the exception of the basic course in chemistry, where insufficient laboratory facilities existed, all underclass students were to be segregated in their courses. All courses in which the minimum total enrollment was four would be offered. If upperclass course enrollment was so small as to result in wasteful duplication of facilities, such courses could be taught jointly at the discretion of the instructor, but they would be segregated as soon as the enrollment increased.

Ultimately, President Hamilton told the students, Jackson would have its own buildings, separated from the main group but still sufficiently close to use the library and Goddard Chapel jointly with the men. Until 1909 Goddard Gymnasium was used by both men and women, but on different days. By good fortune, the College had acquired in 1908 a small clubhouse south of the main campus built by the Somerville Golf Club on land leased from the College. This building was enlarged and remodeled and became a women's gymnasium which doubled also as a home for the expanding activities of dramatics. After Jackson Gymnasium for Women was constructed in 1948, the old clubhouse ceased to serve its original dual purpose. It became the home of the Tufts Arena Theatre after extensive and recurrent remodeling.

The creation of Jackson College required no major readjustments in women's physical education, for physical training had become part of the prescribed work for all students in the 1890's, and in 1895–96 a graduate of the Boston Normal School of Gymnastics taught the girls. An advisory committee on outdoor athletics for women had been created in 1901, and in 1906 an athletic commission for women had been organized as a counterpart to the association long in existence for men.

The president was confident that all would work out well under the new system. Increased enrollment of men in liberal arts in the fall of 1910 (a modest increase of five over the previous year) was already evidence to him that "a man's Tufts is more attractive to students than a co-educational Tufts." Likewise, an increased registration of women indicated "a rapidly growing Jackson." If each undergraduate would try to bring one freshman to his college, there would be one hundred liberal arts freshmen in 1911. He felt sure that social relations between the students of the two colleges would adjust themselves naturally and would be more harmonious than ever. In brief, there was "every reason to believe that segregation means greater days for Tufts and Jackson than Tufts has ever known."

There was some discussion about the curriculum for the Jackson students, although in actuality very little concession was made to the presence of women in spite of President Hamilton's pronouncements. He had argued before Jackson was established that it was "not necessary in order to demonstrate the mental equality of women that they should practice medicine or law, or that they should enter the pulpit, or even that they should take exactly the same curriculum in the college as their brothers." Of the seventy-nine academic courses open to women when Jackson was established, only twenty-four were actually segregated. It was not until the crisis of the First World War was upon the nation that a course was introduced exclusively for Jackson students. War emergency courses in shorthand and typing were offered in 1917, as additional electives. Originally offered by a staff member of the Chandler School for Women, they were intended to meet "the ever increasing demand for secretaries of college training and intellectual grasp beyond the power of ordinary stenographers." This meant training not for business office careers but for "intelligent, broadly informed, and efficient secretaries to professional men."

President Hamilton's plans for segregation and the independence of Jackson College were intended to apply even to Commencement arrangements. According to the original blueprint, graduation ceremonies were to be jointly conducted for only three years after 1910. When Jackson graduated an independent class in 1914, the students were to have their own Commencement. However, when 1914 arrived, and seventeen young ladies received the first Bachelor's degrees given by Jackson to a group completing the four-year course, they took their places at the regular exercises. Following precedents set earlier, Jackson, as a division of the College, was represented on the panel of Commencement speakers. Literal segregation was also attempted at first in the designation of degrees but was soon abandoned. The idea of giving separate degrees for women actually went back to the introduction of coeducation in 1892. A young lady graduating between 1896 and 1910 received a Tufts degree but was listed on the records as a "W.A." (Woman of Arts). For the three years from 1911 through 1913 the women were given a choice of Tufts or Jackson degrees. Most elected Tufts. From 1914 to 1916, all women received Jackson degrees. From 1917 until April 1963 they received exclusively Tufts degrees; since the latter date, a compromise has resulted in the identification on the diploma of the separate schools and colleges, but under the Tufts designation.

The experiment in segregation at Tufts, which had not been complete even in 1910, was soon abandoned as an official policy. It was too much of a financial strain for the College to bear, in spite of the glowing future which President Hamilton had foreseen for it. When he resigned the presidency of Tufts in 1912 and returned to the business world with which he had alternated a career as a clergyman, he was sure that Jackson as he envisioned it would be a success. Students and instructors alike, it seemed, had settled into the "new ways speedily and with little friction. Scholarship nowhere suffered. . . . The social relations between the men and women underwent an immediate and marked change for the better." With Dr. Hamilton's departure, the talk of segregation withered away, and by the time the catalogue for 1912–13 was published, all mention of separate classes for women had disappeared from it. But the attempt at segregation left its inheritance: Jackson College, as a corporate entity and a flourishing coordinate institution. The administrative structure of Jackson and the system of joint faculties, as well as other arrangements familiar to a later day, remained virtually unchanged. In a sense, history vindicated the statement in the first catalogue of Jackson College, which stated that the institution offered its students "a combination of the advantages of a women's college and a co-educaional college with comparative freedom from the peculiar disadvantages of each system."

7. *Medical and Dental Education: Beginnings*

NEAR THE END OF OCTOBER 1853 President Ballou received a letter from Dr. Oliver Wendell Holmes in reply to an inquiry. The Massachusetts-born doctor, essayist, and poet was at the time dean of the Harvard Medical School and held the chair of Parkman Professor of Anatomy and Physiology. Dr. Holmes made some suggestions about a medical course that might be included in the curriculum of Tufts College. His recommendations as to texts and branches of study to be undertaken were concise and pointed; he specified also that "clinical attendance at the Hospital from the first and throughout the course of study" was indispensable. Dr. Holmes' advice was to lie fallow for exactly forty years, for Section 2 of the Tufts charter, granted by the state legislature in 1852, authorized the Trustees "to confer such degrees as are usually conferred by colleges in New England, except medical degrees." The reasons for this restrictive clause were embedded in the preferential position that the Harvard Medical College had enjoyed in Massachusetts almost from the time of its founding in 1782. It had achieved through the years a virtual monopoly in the state over the academic training of doctors and was loath to relinquish it. The restrictive clause in question was the result of a law passed in 1818 intended to curb the widespread practice of using the agency of the courts to collect fees levied by "irregular practitioners." Although the law was repealed in 1835, its spirit remained in force. Amherst College, in 1825, was the first Massachusetts institution to have the restrictive clause applied to it, and the College of the Holy Cross, established in 1843, had a similar limitation in its charter. New England colleges outside Massachusetts operated under no such restriction.

In the decades before 1860 the number of medical schools in the United States, most of them unaffiliated with a college or university, had mushroomed with bewildering rapidity. Between 1840 and 1860, for example, the number had skyrocketed from thirty-three to sixty-six, and little systematic effort was made either to establish or to enforce standards of medical education.[1] It was not until after the American Medical Association was organized in 1847 that a nation-wide attempt (although initially unsuccessful) was made both to elevate the standards of the profession and to exert some measure of control over practices (and malpractices) in the field of medicine.[2] Massachusetts had, by the time of the Civil War, contributed its share of medical schools to the fast growing number. Between 1823 and 1836 Williams College had granted medical degrees by means of an affiliation with the Berkshire Medical Institution in Pittsfield. The arrangement was abandoned because it proved unprofitable to Williams.[3] The Worcester Medical Institution, established in 1849, was in the interesting position of being prohibited from conferring degrees or granting licenses to practice medicine.[4] The New England Female Medical College was established in 1848 and was absorbed by Boston University in 1872 as one step in the creation of a coeducational medical school.

The decision of the Tufts Trustees to have the prohibition on the granting of medical degrees removed from the College charter was made in the fall of 1866. This by no means implied that Tufts was about to install a medical curriculum. However, President Miner was no doubt aware that the Boston City Hospital had been opened in 1864 and might be available to furnish clinical facilities.

[1] Irving S. Cutter, "The School of Medicine," in Raymond A. Kent, *Higher Education in America* (Boston: Ginn, 1930), p. 285.

[2] See Henry E. Sigerist, *American Medicine* (New York: Norton, 1934), especially Chapter 5, for background information. There is also a brief historical sketch of medical education in Abraham Flexner, *Medical Education in the United States and Canada* (New York: Carnegie Foundation for the Advancement of Teaching, Bulletin No. 4, 1910), Chapter 1.

[3] See Frederick Rudolph, *Mark Hopkins and the Log: Williams College, 1836–1872* (New Haven: Yale, 1956), p. 12.

[4] Its charter was transferred to the Middlesex College of Medicine and Surgery in Cambridge and Somerville, which was later relocated in Waltham and became the School of Medicine of Middlesex University. It lasted until the Second World War. As late as 1940 it required only a high school diploma and two years of college. Its graduates were licensed to practice only in Massachusetts and the District of Columbia.

He probably knew that at the very time the petition was being presented to the state legislature the Berkshire Medical College was preparing to close its doors. It should be noted also that Oliver Dean, then president of the Tufts Trustees, had been a practicing physician for about a decade and possessed an M.D. degree. He had served an apprenticeship, like so many doctors in the early nineteenth century, and had been awarded his medical degree by the Curators of the Massachusetts Medical Society, which served for many years as an accrediting agency. The intent of the Trustees was to have the restriction removed on broad principle as well as to give the institution a free hand if a determination were at some time made to grant medical degrees. Furthermore, there were other matters relating to the charter that needed attention, and it was thought that all of the requests for amendments might as well be made together to simplify procedure and to avoid delay.[5] The College had reached such a point in the mid-1860's that the ceiling of $20,000 on income from endowments placed in the original document was unrealistic and overly restrictive, and a request was made (and granted) that the figure be revised upward to $100,000.[6]

The petition became a bill in routine fashion and had passed through the customary stages in both branches of the legislature when the faculty of the Harvard Medical College got wind of it and requested its recommittal to the Committee on Education. This would allow objections to be filed against it. President Miner, on behalf of the Tufts Trustees, consented to the recommitment, and a formal hearing followed. The debate was protracted, and Dr. Edward H. Clarke, Professor of Materia Medica at the Harvard school, represented the remonstrants to the petition. The legislative

[5] One editorial correction was to remove the awkward definite article throughout the charter that referred to "the Trustees of the Tufts College."

[6] The petition to have the charter changes made was dated November 20, 1866. The writer is obligated to Dr. Benjamin Spector, Professor of Bioanatomy Emeritus and Professor of the History of Medicine Emeritus of the Tufts University School of Medicine, for the *History of the Tufts College Medical School* which he prepared for the celebration of its semicentennial in 1943. He tracked down in the Archives of the Commonwealth of Massachusetts all of the documents pertaining to the charter changes of 1867. They are reproduced in his *History,* which was published by the Tufts College Medical School Alumni Association. He generously deposited in the University Archives photostatic copies of the important documents.

committee reported the bill back favorably, but it was opposed by some in the lower house. The vote was about two to one in favor of the petitioner, and the Senate passed the bill without debate. Tufts had won a major victory, although whatever corporate ego it had at the time was subjected to a severe bruising and battering at the hands of Dr. Clarke.[7]

The remonstrant from Harvard did not mince words in condemning Tufts' effort to have the restriction on medical degrees removed. There were, he said, already more medical schools in New England than were needed; one physician per 1,000 persons was sufficient. To keep the ranks full, only 150 should enter the profession annually.[8] Graduates totaled 196 in 1867 — forty-six more potential physicians than were needed according to Dr. Clarke's formula. Enrollment in New England's medical schools ranged from Harvard's 303 to Berkshire's 40. Dr. Clarke declared flatly that Tufts had no medical school and no resources to establish one. The cost of educating a Harvard medical student was $111, exclusive of salaries for teachers. Tufts College could "educate cheaper than this only by imparting an inferior education" or by receiving endowments much larger than the $180,000 then available to Harvard. Dr. Clarke argued that "competition between Medical Schools . . . tended to decrease the character and quality of their education. Every new College without liberal endowments increases this danger. When Tufts College has a fully equipped Medical Department, properly endowed and students to graduate, let it have a charter for conferring Medical degrees." If, as Dr. Miner implied in his petition, the right to confer such degrees might attract legacies to the College, a similar right might be sought by every educational institution in the state. The result would be to cheapen the value of a medical degree, and the country would "be overrun with medical incompetence and ignorance." The remonstrant from Harvard asserted that Tufts College had no resources, either then or in future prospect, to do more than "to place the Academic and Undergraduate departments on a proper basis." Any plan to establish a medical school under the circumstances would be ridiculous. Tufts was in

---

[7] The bill became law on March 16, 1867.

[8] There were six medical schools in the area at the time: Bowdoin (Maine), University of Vermont (Burlington), Dartmouth (New Hampshire), Yale (Connecticut); and Harvard and Berkshire (Massachusetts).

no position to acquire competent medical instructors, and such teaching staff as could be assembled would turn out "young men ignorant of the great principles of the profession, to tamper with the health and jeopardize the lives of their patients."

The arguments presented by President Miner were simply and cogently stated. After successfully challenging many of the statistics presented by his opponent, he contended that the charter rights of the College enjoined it to promote learning and allowed it to receive gifts and bequests accordingly, and that the restrictive clause was in conflict with these basic rights. He urged further that it was "absurd for the remonstrants to assume the protectorate of the State, in medical affairs," since medical education was never intended to be placed under the control of one institution. Miner appealed also to the principle of legal equality, arguing that the College was entitled to "stand upon the same basis as other New England colleges . . . & that the community may enjoy the benefits of that honorable & unrestricted competition which is the chief guaranty of excellence." The right to establish a medical school and to confer medical degrees should inhere in the corporate character of the institution and should not be at the whim or caprice of another school that saw its vested interests threatened.

Having obtained the change in the College charter, the next step was to take advantage of the newly acquired right to offer medical degrees. The Trustees promptly followed up the action of the Massachusetts legislature in March 1867 by referring the subject of establishing a medical school to the Executive Committee for investigation and report. Only one alternative was apparently explored at the time. There was a possibility of acquiring the assets of the defunct Berkshire Medical College, which consisted of a building, one acre of grounds, and apparatus and specimens sufficient for twenty-five students. But nothing came of this, and when Capen took over the presidency in 1875 no other steps had been taken. The best he could report in 1882–83 was that a Trustee committee, appointed in March 1883 with Miner at its head, had been engaged "for some months in considering the expediency of establishing a Medical School." Their investigation had progressed sufficiently to indicate that such a school could be established "with a very moderate endowment" and that it would meet with general approval among the New England medical profession and at the same time "meet a want which is not now met by any other school." The committee, a year later, recommended the establishment of such a school "as soon as it can be done without encroachment upon the present resources of the College and a suitable faculty therefore can be organized." The Executive Committee was given the responsibility of taking appropriate action. Still another year went by before the matter of a medical school was taken up again. In 1885 consideration was given to acquiring for $1,000 the equipment and good will of the College of Physicians and Surgeons in Boston and as much of the staff as it was desirable to retain. This would all be done "with the understanding that the school shall not be an annual encumbrance upon the Treasury of the College."

The institution referred to had been incorporated in 1880 under the general laws of Massachusetts and was empowered in 1883 to confer the degree of Doctor of Medicine. In 1884 it had a faculty of ten with professorial rank, all with M.D. degrees, and a roster of some fourteen lecturers on special subjects and three physicians who operated a dispensary in connection with the school. The medical college was headed by Horatio G. Parker, who held no academic or professional degrees. Claiming to be the first independent medical college to be coeducational, it was otherwise typical of many such institutions during the nineteenth century. It offered a three-year course but admitted applicants who were in all stages of training and experience, including college graduates, who could receive a diploma after attending one year of lectures and passing prescribed examinations.[9] The College of Physicians and Surgeons might be said to have represented the second stage through which medical education had progressed in the United States. Early medical education, like most other professional training until well into the nineteenth century, had been largely a matter of individual apprenticeship under experienced practitioners. Aside from a few schools connected with institutions of learning, like the University of Pennsylvania and Harvard, very little was done to extend facilities beyond the opening of literally hundreds of so-called secondary schools. These were operated as combined training and profit-making efforts by a group of physicians who charged fees and divided the income among themselves. The training was usually meager,

[9] This information was derived from Francis H. Brown, *Medical Register for New England,* 2d ed. (Boston: Cupples Upham & Co., 1884).

and laboratory and clinical facilities were inadequate or non-existent.

The initiative that had brought the College of Physicians and Surgeons up for consideration by the Tufts Trustees had been taken by members of that school's faculty. They had offered the properties of their institution for sale to a college or university. Their efforts represented an advance into the third or "university" stage of medical education, whereby a more or less intimate relationship was established which could work to mutual advantage.

The Executive Committee of the Tufts Trustees in 1885 considered the acquisition of the College of Physicians and Surgeons desirable, but at a special meeting called to consider the matter, the Trustees adopted a resolution that it was "inexpedient at the present time" to take such a step. Eight years later (in the summer of 1893) another proposition was presented from the same group of the faculty of the College of Physicians and Surgeons "in regard to operating a Medical School in connection with Tufts College." This effort proved more successful than the one of 1885. The petitioners assured the Trustees that they would bring "a full complement of Lecturers and Instructors, well equipped for the work and earnest, hard working men. We propose to furnish a building, equipment, and everything necessary to carry on the work of a first class medical school without any expense to your institution." Negotiations began immediately, and within a matter of weeks Tufts had acquired a ready-made medical school.

The "original seven," as the first medical faculty came to be called and who had brought all this about, had joined together in 1886 as a group who were also members of the corporation of the College of Physicians and Surgeons. The institution had run into financial and administrative difficulties during its first six years. Between 1886, when the "original seven" took charge of the school, and 1893, matters improved; the enrollment increased from 17 to 101; an indebtedness of $2,000 was paid off; a $500 bond was deposited on a building that was to become the property of the school; and recognition of the school by the Massachusetts Medical Society had been secured.[10] Two circumstances had brought about the

[10] Much of this information, and what follows, was derived from "A Sketch of the Tufts College Medical School during its First Three Years," presented at a meeting of the Medical Alumni Association in 1908 by Dr. Charles

The "original seven," first faculty of the Tufts Medical School in 1893 (left to right: John W. Johnson, Henry W. Dudley, Charles P. Thayer, Walter L. Hall, Albert Nott, Frank Wheatley, and William Chipman)

move to join forces with Tufts. The long-range motivation stemmed from a feeling on the part of the faculty that the standards of the school were too low, that insufficient laboratory and clinical work was being provided, and that in order to do its best work a medical school should not be merely a proprietary institution but should affiliate with a college or university so that its prestige could be raised and necessary educational facilities could be made available. The "original seven" were undoubtedly aware that, in the same year their own request was made, the Johns Hopkins Medical School had been organized, with full university status.

The second series of events which precipitated the petition to the Tufts Trustees arose out of dissatisfaction with the administration of the College of Physicians and Surgeons. The school was governed by a corporation of which the majority were lawyers, clergymen, and teachers "who paid but little attention to its affairs,

P. Thayer, who assumed the leadership in the move to affiliate with Tufts College and who coined the expression "the original seven."

rarely attending even the annual meetings." Actual operation was left in the hands of faculty members who were also corporation members and whose interests frequently diverged from those of the rest of the corporation. At the annual meeting of the corporation in June 1893 matters came to a head. The laymen, apparently in the majority, elected a Board of Directors who were entirely out of sympathy with the faculty. The latter promptly resigned in a body, together with many of the instructors and assistants. The day after what must have been a tumultuous meeting the faculty found the school on Boylston Street securely padlocked.

The summer of 1893 was an anxious one for the ex-faculty, for they were determined that "there was room in Boston for another school." They made an unsuccessful attempt to secure the charter of the old Berkshire Medical College and corresponded with various schools in the state. Because of the favorable attitude of President Capen, the "original seven" had decided to concentrate their efforts on Tufts College. Early in August a Trustee committee reviewed the situation with a committee of the physicians, and the Tufts representatives reported at the next full meeting of the Trustees that they were "satisfied with the character of the memorialists, all of whom are educated physicians, and members in good standing of the Massachusetts Medical Society." Plans were worked out and approved, and the Tufts College Medical School came into official existence on August 22, 1893, by unanimous vote of the Trustees.

The "original seven," who later comprised the Executive Committee of the medical faculty, were an unusually competent and well-educated group and were exceptionally active in community affairs.[11] Dr. Charles Paine Thayer had received his M.D. from the University of Vermont.[12] He served for many years as Health Officer and City Physician of Burlington, Vermont, as well as on the faculty of the University of Vermont Medical School. After he moved to Boston and joined the faculty of the College of Physicians and Sur-

[11] For biographical sketches of the seven, see Spector, *A History of Tufts College Medical School,* Chapter IV.

[12] Thayer's father, Samuel White Thayer, had helped reorganize the medical department there in the 1850's and had served in many academic capacities. See Julian I. Lindsay, *Tradition Looks Forward: The University of Vermont, A History 1791–1904* (Burlington: University of Vermont, 1954), p. 214.

geons he was secretary, purchasing agent, and Professor of General, Descriptive, and Surgical Anatomy. He was secretary, purchasing agent, and Professor of Anatomy at the Tufts Medical School from 1893 to 1905. If any single individual was the originator of the idea of associating a medical school with Tufts College, Thayer was that person. The second of the "big three" within the "original seven" was Albert Nott, also a holder of an M.D. degree from the University of Vermont and a practicing physician in West Newton, Massachusetts, for almost a quarter of a century. He was one of the negotiators in the exploratory talks with the Trustee committee and served as the first dean of the Tufts Medical School (1893–96) as well as Professor of Physiology. John Waldo Johnson, the third physician instrumental in drawing up the preliminary plans for affiliating with Tufts College, held an M.D. from the Harvard Medical School and practiced medicine in Boston for over thirty years. Besides serving as Professor of Obstetrics and Gynecology, and as treasurer of the medical school for its first three years, he operated a private hospital in Boston.

The four other "founding fathers" were equally talented and active in professional affairs. Henry Watson Dudley, Professor of Pathology from 1893 to 1900 and Lecturer on Legal Medicine from 1901 to 1906, completed his formal education at Harvard Medical School. Before his service on the Tufts Medical School faculty he was active in raising standards for admission to the Massachusetts Medical Society. William R. Chipman was also holder of an M.D. from Harvard. He had been Professor of Operative Surgery at the College of Physicians and Surgeons and became the first Professor of Surgery at the Tufts Medical School. Walter Langdon Hall was a graduate of the Bellevue Hospital Medical College in New York. Like Dr. Chipman, Hall spent some time in Europe in postgraduate clinical work. He served as Professor of Theory and Practice of Medicine for four years, and the first faculty meeting of the new medical school was held at his home in Medford. Frank George Wheatley, variously Professor of Materia Medica and Therapeutics, vice-dean and acting dean, and Professor of Pharmacology between 1893 and 1926, received his medical education at the University of Vermont and at Dartmouth Medical School. While on the Tufts Medical School faculty he served for two years in the Massachusetts legislature.

217

The working out of the details for the operation of the new school and the establishment of its relationship to the College took place between August 4 and August 28, 1893, on which date Articles of Agreement were signed. On August 15 the Trustees acted favorably on the recommendations of a five-man Trustee committee. Several of the propositions of the committee representing the "original seven" were included. The Trustees agreed that (1) the by-laws be amended "so as to legally provide for the Medical School"; (2) the new department be designated as the "Medical School of Tufts College"; (3) seven professorships be created, to be occupied by the "original seven"; (4) the dean of the medical school faculty be appointed by the Trustees and the secretary be elected by the medical faculty — both officers to be members of the general faculty of the College; (5) lecturers be nominated and instructors be appointed by the medical faculty, subject to the approval of the Executive Committee of the Trustees; and (6) the special Trustee committee be empowered to work out all contractual arrangements and other details necessary to the operation of the school. The "original seven" were duly nominated for the professorships the same day, and amendments to the College by-laws were submitted. A week later, the recommendations of the special committee were adopted with minor modifications; for example, the new addition to the College became officially the "Tufts College Medical School." Albert Nott was confirmed as the first dean. The nominees for professorships, as the nucleus of the medical school, had met within twenty-four hours after the favorable reaction of the Tufts Trustees on August 15 and had elected Thayer as secretary and Johnson as treasurer. At the same meeting, the medical faculty elected seventeen staff members (lecturers, demonstrators, and assistants), of whom six were graduates of the College of Physicians and Surgeons while it had been under the direction of the "original seven."

The other arrangements made during those busy weeks in August set the pattern of administrative relationships between the medical school and the College. The Tufts Trustees agreed to consider it a department of the College for three years and to appoint the faculty for a corresponding period. The faculty were to serve without compensation and the school was to be operated at no expense to the College. The president of Tufts was to serve as chairman of the medical faculty and was expected to preside at faculty meetings as often as possible. Admission requirements, the course of instruction, the issuance of catalogues, and the provision of accommodations for the school, including a dispensary, were all to be under the control of the medical faculty, subject to the approval of the Trustees. At first only those with professorial rank were members of the medical faculty; instructors and those lower on the teaching scale were "exempted from membership." On recommendation of the Administrative Committee of the medical school in 1902, the position of Demonstrator of Anatomy was elevated to faculty rank. All candidates for the M.D. were to be recommended to the Trustees, subject to their action. The faculty was to receive all tuition and fees paid by the students, except that $10 from the graduation fee of each candidate was to be remitted to the Trustees to defray clerical and other expenses connected with Commencement. A financial report was to be made to the Trustees at the end of each term, and all records were to be turned over to them at the end of the three years. Modifications of the agreements could be made at any time by mutual consent.

Quarters for the new medical school were immediately obtained in the same building on Boylston Street that housed the College of Physicians and Surgeons, which moved to other quarters. This prompt vacating of the Boylston Street location was assured by the fact that Tufts had for many years owned the building as investment property.[13] Two floors were leased and within a year the use of a third floor was acquired. The medical faculty voted to open the school the first week in October 1893, so there was precious little time to make the necessary arrangements. It was thought that $525 would be sufficient to prepare the building, and Thayer, Nott, and Johnson immediately contributed $50 apiece "as a starter." A few weeks before the school opened, an assessment of $50 was levied on each member of the faculty to cover current expenses. The secretary was also authorized to spend $60 for advertising before the

[13] The College of Physicians and Surgeons remained in existence until after the Second World War and graduated its last students in 1949. Like the Middlesex College of Medicine and Surgery, its graduates were licensed to practice only in Massachusetts and the District of Columbia.

opening of the fall term. Somehow the hard-working physicians managed to conduct their medical practice, hold clinics, and have their building ready. The first floor occupied by the school contained the lecture hall, a faculty room, and a study area for women. It might be remarked parenthetically that it was taken for granted that the school, like the College of Physicians and Surgeons, would be coeducational. The Tufts Medical School, in sharp contrast to the portion of the College located in Medford, escaped the years of discussion, doubt, and debate that preceded the opening of the liberal arts divisions to women a year before the medical school was established. The second floor used by the medical school contained a smaller lecture room, the bacteriological laboratory, an office for the Professor of Medical Chemistry (a post created during 1893–94), and a study area for men. When added, the third floor included the general chemistry laboratory. An extension on the outside of this floor was built as a dissecting room and was reached from the inside by steps and a door cut through the wall of the main building. Cadavers for the dissecting room had to be hauled up three flights of stairs. Additional space for the school was soon needed, and consideration was given to acquiring an unused schoolhouse on Tennyson Street. Instead, space was obtained in 1895–96 in a building at the corner of Boylston and Tremont Streets, and at 30 West Street. The latter building was owned by the College, and one of its rooms served as the meeting place of the Trustees for many years.

Admission and graduation requirements had been set by mid-August. Applicants were (like those at the Medford campus) to be of good moral character and had to pass an examination "upon the branches of an English education," including mathematics ("higher arithmetic"), English composition, and elementary physics. Either the translation of "easy Latin prose" or satisfactory knowledge of the derivation of medical terms and medical and pharmaceutical terminology was also necessary. These examinations were required of all applicants except those who had previously matriculated in a regular medical school or were graduates of "a reputable college, high, or normal school." Accredited schools were defined in 1895 as those recognized by the Massachusetts Medical Society, except that students from homeopathic and eclectic schools were required to pass an examination in materia medica and therapeutics.[14] Candidates for the M.D. were required to have studied medicine three full years, attended three courses of medical lectures (the third at the Tufts Medical School), taken a full course in dissection, and passed all of the required examinations. The requirements for graduation followed closely those just established by the Association of American Medical Colleges (of which the Tufts Medical School became a member in 1895) and in fact applied only to those students who matriculated in medical schools after July 1, 1892. Graduates of other medical schools could obtain the Tufts degree by attending one full course of lectures and passing the examinations of the senior year. Annual fees were originally established as follows: general lecture ticket, $90; laboratory, $5.00; matriculation, $5.00; demonstrations, $5.00; graduation, $50; and instruction in special branches of medicine, $40. Two modifications were made in this schedule: The total fees (exclusive of the last two) for the whole three-year course were $250 if paid in advance; and former students of the College of Physicians and Surgeons need pay only $85 for the general lecture ticket and those who graduated were to be charged only $30 instead of $50. Candidates could not receive their degrees until they were twenty-one years of age, and diplomas were frequently withheld for that reason. This meant considerable correspondence and record-keeping by the officers of the College, especially in a day when a sizable proportion of each graduating class went into medical training with only a high school diploma or less than four years of college. The three classes were initially designated Junior, Middle, and Senior.

The freshman class took anatomy, physiology, histology, and general chemistry. The second-year students enrolled in pathology, materia medica and therapeutics, and medical chemistry. The senior year was devoted to obstetrics, gynecology, surgery, theory and practice of medicine, ophthalmology and otology, medical jurisprudence, neurology laryngology, and genito-urinary surgery. If the last year seemed particularly demanding, it should be realized that several subjects were taught by only one or two lectures a

[14] Schools of this type were based on principles of drug use and classification of disease not accepted by the majority of physicians and hence not considered first-class schools.

week for only one of the two terms into which the academic year was divided. For the first year of the school Professor J. Sterling Kingsley of the Tufts Department of Biology lectured at the medical school on histology. This was the first of many instances of cooperation between the school and the College.

The school opened on schedule in October 1893, and President Capen, who had agreed to deliver the opening address, was much surprised to find no less than eighty students present. The explanations for the large number are not difficult to find. A printed circular prepared on August 17 — even before the medical school was formally created by the Trustees — had been addressed personally to a long list of graduating high school students whose names had appeared in current newspapers. The secretary, who had been authorized originally to expend $60 on advertising, was given permission to spend $75 for advertising in the *New York Medical Record*. But the great single source of recruits was the student body of the College of Physicians and Surgeons. Dr. Thayer had been the secretary of the school; after the seven faculty members had seceded from the corporation and he had been ordered to turn over the property of the school to its new Board of Directors, the enterprising doctor had retained the charter and book of records for nearly two months. As he told his listeners at the Medical Alumni Association meeting in 1908 with a chuckle, the corporation officers had not asked for these items specifically, and he had concluded that they had not been missed. While the records were in his possession, he copied the names and addresses of the students who had been in attendance, as well as the results of their examinations and the number of courses they had taken. This information, he thought, "might possibly be of use in the future." So, after the dissident faculty had left the school and arranged their association with Tufts College, Thayer could not only address a circular to each former student but include in it a statement that credit would be allowed for time spent, lectures attended, and examinations passed.[15]

Enrollment in the first three years was most heartening. All

[15] Abraham Flexner, in his report *Medical Education in the United States and Canada,* gave a rather erroneous impression of the first graduating class of the Tufts Medical School. To underline his point about low standards in many medical schools, he cited several instances of senior classes allegedly recruited

twenty-two students (including eight women) who came up for examination were graduated in 1894, and their names duly appeared on the Tufts Commencement program. Four of the first graduating class applied for admission to the Massachusetts Medical Society and were successful in meeting the examination tests for entrance. During the second year, 104 students were in attendance and 19 received degrees. In 1896, 176 students attended and 32 were graduated. Enrollment was so large and the prospects of the school were so encouraging that by the beginning of the second year the faculty was doubled. Chairs in Medical Chemistry, General Chemistry, Ophthalmology and Otology, Neurology, Gynecology, Clinical Medicine, and Diseases of Children were added. By the end of another year, the teaching force had increased to thirty-five; a Professorship of Mental Diseases was among the new positions. To insure efficient administration of a rapidly enlarging faculty, the senior members (the "original seven") were constituted as an Executive Board and given exclusive management of the financial affairs of the school.[16] A clear distinction was maintained between the "faculty" (those of professorial rank) and the teaching force ("Board of Instruction"), which included lecturers, instructors, demonstrators, and assistants in addition to the "faculty."[17] Candidates for the M.D. degree at other institutions were not allowed to serve on the Board of Instruction.

The provision of adequate clinical facilities was a matter of concern from the start, and modest progress was made in the early years. The Suffolk Dispensary, of which Dr. Thayer was treasurer, had been used by the College of Physicians and Surgeons and continued to be available to the medical school staff; use was made of it by the physicians who taught neurology, clinical medicine, and ophthalmology and otology in 1894–95. During the next school

and graduated the same year, and used Tufts as one of five examples. He noted that the Tufts Medical School had opened in 1893 and graduated its first class in 1894 (*Medical Education*, p. 7 n.). He either overlooked or was not aware of the circumstances under which the school was created or the sources from which it drew many of its first students.

[16] The Board was provided for in the by-laws of the school, which were adopted on June 18, 1894.

[17] When the rank of Assistant Professor began to be used in the school in 1896, the holders were considered members of the "faculty."

year the Dispensary came under the complete control of the faculty, who even asked President Capen to raise money to cover a deficit. The first Professor of Clinical Surgery, Dr. Herbert L. Smith, was on the staff of the Boston City Hospital, and Dr. Harold Williams, Professor of Diseases of Children (and later dean of the school) supervised a clinic in the Boston Dispensary. The Professor of Gynecology, Dr. Ernest W. Cushing, operated a private facility near the Charity Club Hospital. Negotiations had been undertaken in 1893 with the Massachusetts General Hospital to allow clinical instruction in its wards for both faculty and students. Material from clinics in the New England Eye and Ear Hospital was offered for the use of Tufts medical students in 1894. The medical faculty as well as extramural teachers were allowed in 1895 the use of the school to give summer courses, with arrangements left up to the individual instructors.

The faculty was pleased by the attitude and morale of the student body, although it did see fit in 1894 to prohibit card-playing in the rooms of the school. Attendance at lectures was good, and the first graduating class immediately formed an alumni association. The women students organized the Alpha Delta Society and the men the Alpha Kappa Kappa Society; both organizations were intended to encourage improvements in medicine. The school year in 1894–95 was increased from seven to eight months, a "Medical Museum of pathological and morbid specimens" was started. Sufficient magazines and pamphlets had been received by the fall of 1894 to "suggest the possibility of a library." The first substantial acquisition of medical books was received from the estate of Howard F. Damon in 1897.

The first major change in the medical curriculum was the establishment of a fourth year, made optional in 1894–95 and compulsory the following year. Dean Nott had suggested the desirability of a lengthened course of study in his first annual report. As he pointed out, there was so much embodied in a medical education, and such a demand for clinical work, that a fourth year was needed to improve medical training and better fit the student for his professional responsibilities. Under the new program the first three years emphasized medical theory and fundamentals and the fourth year provided opportunity for clinical experience. Dr. Nott also dropped the broad hint that too much attention had to be paid to general chemistry and insufficient time was available for medical chemistry; general chemistry should be a field for the preparatory school. The dean was also convinced that the purpose of the Tufts Medical School was to train competent general practitioners and deplored the fact that too much time was devoted to the "so-called specialties."[18] One advantage of the fourth year was the greater opportunity to specialize at the end of the formal degree program rather than throughout the course.

The contract by which the "original seven" had operated the medical school in affiliation with Tufts College expired in August 1896. There was no hesitation on the part of the Trustees when the question of assuming the management and responsibility of the undertaking was put to a vote and the College took over the administration of the school. As Dean Nott put it in his final report, his Executive Committee turned over to the Trustees "a successful Medical School, well equipped, out of debt, thoroughly devoted to the College, and with every prospect of an abundant success in the future. . . . The Medical School is established as a part of a noble New England institution, thoroughly competent to meet the demands of our time in equipping men and women alike to practise successfully the healing art." The Trustees were frank to admit that the financial success of the school was an important factor in their decision. The records of the school amply demonstrated its solvency.

During the three-year period the school had met all its expenses, had paid the Trustees the required $730 to cover graduation fees, and had turned property over to the College valued at more than $1,500. The faculty was able to cancel the $50 individual assessment levied on its members in the uncertain days before the school was opened. By the end of the first year the secretary was authorized to receive a salary of 3 per cent of gross receipts per annum for his services, and there was a balance in the treasury sufficient to pay each member of the faculty $100. In only one respect had the medical faculty failed to comply with the original contract. For the first two years it neglected to file the financial report required to be deposited at the end of each term with the Trustees. When the records were finally received, the Trustees could well have been en-

[18] It was through his efforts that the time for these was reduced from two hours to one hour a week in 1896-97.

vious and possibly a bit wistful when they compared figures with those of the College on the Hill. The income of the medical school its first year was $5,600, of which $5,500 came from student fees; during the second year $6,000 of the $7,000 income had come from students; and the net profit of the school in 1895–96 was no less than $7,000. The net profit of the first year (1893–94) had been over $1,000. The advances of $150 from Thayer, Nott, and Johnson were repaid (with interest) out of this sum. Part of the profit in the third year was accounted for by the practice, begun in 1895, of running laboratory tests as a service to physicians not associated with the school. It was not surprising that President Capen considered the success of the school "most encouraging, and the outlook for the future exceedingly hopeful." The Board of Visitors in 1895 noted that "a good beginning" had been made, in spite of the need for more staff and clinical facilities. As one member expressed it, "you have adopted a child that will always, like your other children, be crying for more," but he was confident that the College would do its best.

The recurrent phrase describing the medical school at the turn of the century was "uninterrupted prosperity." Enrollment steadily advanced, and standards inched up; in 1898–99, nearly 10 per cent of the students held college degrees. New courses in military and mercantile medicine were introduced. Five members of the medical faculty saw military service during the Spanish-American War, and the first mention of research being carried on was made in 1899, accompanied by a plea for funds to assist various projects. Dr. Timothy Leary had already begun to make a deserved name for himself and the medical school in the fields of pathology and bacteriology. During the war with Spain he had taken a leave of absence when he was appointed by the United States Government to investigate and report on contagious diseases in Puerto Rico.

The philosophy on which the school was operating remained the same as it had been from the beginning. As Dean Williams explained when he was in the process of negotiating for the services of Dr. Edward O. Otis to fill the new chair of Climatology and Tuberculosis (Pulmonary Diseases), the aim was "to educate *practical* physicians," as broadly trained as possible. Theory, research, and practical application of medical principles had to go hand in hand.

Staff appointments continued to be made that in turn gave some degree of access to hospitals in the Boston area for Tufts medical students. Clinics of the Massachusetts Charitable Eye and Ear Infirmary, Carney Hospital, the Free Home for Consumptives, and the Good Samaritan Hospital were all made available to some extent in this way. During an outbreak of smallpox in Boston in 1901–2, the medical school dispensary was made a public vaccination station by the state Board of Health, and almost 5,000 persons were treated. When the disease disrupted the work of the Boston City Hospital, the Tufts Dispensary handled many of their surgical out-patients. A surplus continued to appear in the revenues of the medical school, and there were several apportionments in the form of salary among the faculty.

Members of the Boards of Visitors to the medical school hoped that College influence could be increased in the medical school, possibly with the election of a Tufts alumnus to the teaching staff.[19] Relations between the College in Medford and the medical school in Boston were virtually non-existent in the early years.[20] To most of the administrative officers (notably the president), the institution on the Hill and the medical school represented two different worlds. Their separateness seemed to be promoted even by the Trustees when the Executive Committee voted in 1907 that it was inexpedient to allow free tuition in the college of letters to children of the medical and dental faculties. The first direct student link of a formal kind between Medford and Boston came with the establishment of a one-year pre-medical course in 1915–16, but that arrangement involved only part of the student body, and the administration of the program did not contribute materially in bringing the two parts of the College closer together.

At the rate the medical school was growing, expanded accommodations had become a necessity even after overflow space had

[19] Graduates of the Tufts Medical School appeared on the school staff very soon after 1893. One of the first was Charles D. Knowlton, who served as a Demonstrator in Anatomy before he received his degree in 1894, and later as, successively, Assistant, Instructor, and Assistant Professor of Theory and Practice of Medicine. Dr. Olga Cushing Leary became, in 1910, the second appointment of a Tufts Medical School graduate who had completed the entire course; she was also the first woman to join its faculty.

[20] The same had to be said of the dental school after it became a part of Tufts in 1899.

*The second home of the Tufts Medical School
an ex-Baptist Church in downtown Boston acquired in 1896*

been obtained in 1895–96. The Trustees started negotiations that winter for the property of the Free Baptist Society at the corner of Shawmut Avenue and Rutland Street, but the vacant stone church was acquired too late for the opening of the school year. As a temporary expedient, the building near the Boston Public Library in Copley Square belonging to the Chauncy Hall School (which had moved to another location) was leased until the new property could be remodeled for the use of the medical school. It was provided by the Trustees that any net income from the operation of the medical school in 1896 was to be appropriated toward the new building and its equipment. Thereafter, a sum equal to 15 per cent of the gross annual income was to be set aside for the same purpose until the fund was equal to the cost of buildings and equipment.

The ex-Baptist church, bought for $40,000, was transformed into a medical school during the summer of 1897. Except for stairways and walls, it was completely reconstructed, and a fourth floor was squeezed into the space under the roof of part of the building. Room was provided for a dispensary, and an amphitheater seating 200 was built, extending into the new fourth floor and with separate entrances for men and women. The new home for the school was opened with appropriate ceremonies on September 28, 1897. The speeches made at the exercises reflected satisfaction with the present and optimism for the future. Medical education had taken long strides and standards were being steadily raised. Dr. Ernest W. Cushing, Professor of Gynecology and long active in medical affairs, expressed gratification that at long last a state Board of Registration and Examination of Physicians and Surgeons for which he had labored for over a decade had been created to regulate the practice of medicine in Massachusetts.[21] College officials sincerely believed that the converted church would be sufficient for at least a quarter of a century. But no sooner had Tufts assumed the new responsibility of the medical school than the quarters became manifestly inadequate. Another professional school came knocking at the door.

The first official indication that Tufts was about to expand in another direction came in the summer of 1897 when the secretary of the medical faculty reported to the Trustees that the medical school had "received overtures from the Trustees of the Boston Dental College in regard to their students receiving instruction in Anatomy from your Medical faculty, which we strongly recommend."[22] In the fall of 1898 the medical school was authorized to receive such students "at the total special charge aggregating thirty dollars for each student for the current year." The next step was a vote by the Trustees of the Boston Dental College in the same year that their school "be consolidated with some reputable college or university which has a medical department connected therewith." Less than a year later, this had become an accomplished fact. A legislative act authorized the union, and on March 14, 1899, the

21 The Board referred to had been established in 1894. Three years later, the medical school had provided that practicing physicians who had passed the examinations of the state Board could be admitted as fourth-year students and become candidates for the Tufts medical degree.

22 At the same time the dean of the medical school was approached by the Boston Veterinary College, which wished to become a part of Tufts. There is no indication that the College followed up this opportunity to expand in yet another direction.

Tufts Dental School came into existence. The story back of this action was a record not only of negotiations on a local scale but also of a step illustrative of the evolution of dental education in the United States.

§   §   §

American dental education by 1900 had gone through much the same stages that had characterized medical education, with the one exception that it suffered a chronic handicap by being considered an inferior art.[23] One consequence was that public regulation of both dental practice and dental education lagged behind similar developments in medicine. The Boston Dental College became a part of Tufts in the midst of a veritable revolution in the dental profession at the turn of the twentieth century that resulted in higher professional expectations and a greater awareness of the social responsibilities of both the individual dentist and the organizations set up to establish and enforce standards.

Until the mid-nineteenth century, dental disorders were treated as an incidental to medical practice, and extractions and repairs were largely the province of barber-surgeons and goldsmiths. When some attempt was made to systematize dental training, as a supplement to the time-honored apprenticeship system, the dental schools established were, like their companion schools in medicine, proprietary and didactic in character. They were frankly commercial enterprises, and many remained so until after the First World War.[24]

The first professional dental journal was not published until 1839, and the American Society of Dental Surgeons was not organized until 1840. Out of this finally emerged the American Dental Association in 1859. State licensing boards for dentistry were also slow to develop. No real attempt to rate dental schools was

[23] The summary that follows was derived largely from William J. Gies, "The School of Dentistry," in Raymond A. Kent, *Higher Education in America* (Boston: Ginn, 1930), Chapter 5. The same author, editor for many years of the *Journal of Dental Research,* was in charge of the study undertaken by the Carnegie Foundation for the Advancement of Teaching, published as *Dental Education in the United States and Canada,* Bulletin No. 19 (1926). Part I (pp. 23–55) sketches in the historical background.

[24] There were still fourteen proprietary dental schools in the United States in 1921, and the last one (the Cincinnati College of Dental Surgery) did not close until 1929.

made until 1909, when the Dental Educational Council of America undertook the delicate and complicated task. By the same date, three independent bodies had been created, all attempting more or less ineffectively to do the same thing, namely, create a community of interest that might lead to a development of professional spirit and a measure of uniformity of standards in dental theory and practice. The first such organization was the National (American) Association of Dental Faculties (1884), followed by the American Institute of Dental Teachers (1893) and the Dental Faculties Association of American Universities (1908). Not until 1923–24 did the three organizations manage to consolidate and present something approaching a united front as the American Association of Dental Schools. Many of the Boston Dental College faculty belonged to the National Association of Dental Faculties.

The high point in numbers of dental schools was reached in 1900, when fifty-seven existed. Only a handful had any affiliation with a college or university; the great transfer of dental schools from private ownership to university control took place after 1917.[25] In this sense Tufts was one of the pioneers in recognizing, together with the dental college that it absorbed in 1899, the necessity of expanded resources for dental instruction and particularly a close relationship between medicine and dentistry. The number of dental schools had been reduced to forty-six in 1922, and to thirty-eight by 1929, three years after the Carnegie Foundation had investigated national dental practices in the same way as it had looked into medical education in 1910.

Admission requirements in the earliest dental schools were low by any standards, a problem that continued to plague dental educators for generations to come. At first the rudiments of a so-called English education (as contrasted with a Latin or classical education, which was considered superior) were all that was required. This often "meant little more than intelligence enough to arrange for the payment of entrance fees." An average of five months of instruction for one academic year was considered adequate. A model curriculum was first proposed for dental schools in 1899 and re-

[25] The dental department at Harvard was created in 1867. Harvard was the first important institution to give dentistry academic rank. Two courses of four months each were considered adequate to round out previous practical training and experience, of which three years were required.

quired at least the equivalent of a high school education. There-after, advances beyond this point were steadily attempted, although in practice the goals were not always reached.

By 1917 the dental curriculum had been extended in some in-stitutions to four years. The academic year had also been gradually lengthened and was uniformly extended to thirty-two weeks by 1909, thus coinciding with the academic year of universities, with which a few dental schools were coming to be associated. Even with these many advances, however, there were loopholes remaining to be closed. One was the practice, found also in medical education, of accepting "equivalents" for admission. After the Carnegie Re-port of 1926, dental schools who desired to receive the coveted Class A or B rating of the Dental Educational Council of the American Dental Association had to require a minimum of one year of college (or its equivalent) for admission. Paralleling this requirement were increased amounts of basic medical instruction, one result of which was the establishment of numerous pre-dental and pre-medical curricula in colleges and universities.

Progress had been made, but much remained to be done. In respect to the deficiencies that later generations were to uncover in American dental education, the Boston Dental College in the nine-teenth century was no worse than, and in many ways superior to, its contemporaries. Far from becoming a source of embarrassment to Tufts College, it became a department to which the officers of the institution could look with confidence and a measure of pride.

The Boston Dental College that became a part of Tufts in 1899 had been chartered in 1868. It was to be located in Boston and was constituted "for the purpose of teaching dental science and art." A self-perpetuating Board of between eleven and fifteen Trus-tees was provided, authorized to confer the degree of Doctor of Dental Surgery. According to the original charter, candidates were to be of good moral character and twenty-one years of age before they received a diploma. They were to have been examined by the faculty after having devoted three years to the study of dentistry with a dental practitioner who had been approved by the faculty or had been in practice at least eight years. Degree candidates were to have attended "two full courses of lectures" (two years), the second pursued in the dental college. This charter provision shows the persistence of the traditional apprenticeship technique common to most professional training in the nineteenth century. The charter was amended in 1870 to provide more formal instruction, but the in-service idea was retained. Degree candidates were to have "pursued their professional studies three years under competent instructors and [to] have attended two full courses of lectures in the college" if they had had no previous training or experience. A certificate of attendance at one course of lectures "in any respectable dental or medical college, or five years' reputable practice" was considered a satisfactory substitute for the first course of lectures. In addition, candidates had "to maintain a thesis and undergo an examination to the satisfaction of the faculty, and satisfy the professors of operative and mechanical dentistry of their ability to meet satisfactorily the requirements of their art."[26] By-laws adopted by the Trustees in 1878 provided, besides the customary officers, for a combined librarian and curator of a dental museum. At least six professors were to "deliver didactic and clinical lectures on the branches taught in dental colleges; *viz.*, Anatomy, Physiology, Surgery, Chemistry, Operative and Mechanical Dentistry, with such other branches as the Board of Trustees may introduce." An infirmary was provided, and the faculty required that each degree candidate treat at least two patients requiring some dental operation and make one artificial denture. The student also had to produce the patients on whom his work had been done, such work to be approved by the appropriate faculty members. The thesis was to be written "on some subject pertaining to dentistry," and was to include, in addition, an approved specimen of mechanical dentistry to be deposited in the museum.

If an applicant, after presenting his credentials for admission, passed an examination administered by the dean, he paid a $5.00 matriculation fee, $100 for a "full course of lectures" that extended each year for twenty-seven weeks across two terms, a $5.00 demonstrator's fee, and a $30 diploma fee. The college furnished instruments for extracting and all materials used in the operative department, but the student had to supply all other instruments, including laboratory tools for both metallic and rubber work. Stu-

[26] Unless otherwise indicated, all information about the Boston Dental College was derived from an incomplete set of school catalogues and the similarly incomplete set of minutes of the college's Trustees. The story has had to be pieced together from existing records.

dents were informed that all necessary instruments could be purchased for about $50.

The Boston Dental College opened its doors in the fall of 1868 in a rented building on Tremont Street and graduated its first class (of two) the following year. By 1880 the college had produced 152 graduates and could boast of a faculty of eight professors headed by Isaac J. Wetherbee, D.D.S., one of the incorporators of the college, chairman of its Board of Trustees, and Professor of Dental Science and Operative Dentistry. In addition there were five lecturers, six demonstrators, and an instructor in the manufacture of teeth and continuous gums. Judging from the records, much emphasis was placed on the intimate relationship of medicine and dentistry, for four of the eight professors held M.D. degrees, and anatomy and physiology, pathology and therapeutics, and chemistry were prescribed subjects. Dissections were required, and for many years the dean of the college, John A. Follett, M.D., was Professor of Anatomy and Physiology. Students had access to the Massachusetts General Hospital, the Boston City Hospital, and the United States Marine Hospital for observation of "surgical diseases and operations of every kind." Most of the required textbooks were in anatomy, surgery, chemistry, medicine, and pathology. It was this continued stress on the medical aspects of dentistry that led the Boston Dental College eventually to merge with Tufts. A high proportion of the Trustees throughout the history of the dental college were themselves practicing dentists and held either dental degrees, medical degrees, or both. Occasionally a prominent Bostonian like Gamaliel Bradford, the biographer and literary critic, appeared on the Board, but laymen were the exception rather than the rule.

As the Boston Dental College expanded, it underwent several moves in downtown Boston and spilled over into parts of several buildings. It resided briefly on Concord Street and was then located on Montgomery Square off Tremont Street and not far from the Boston City Hospital. In 1893 plans were laid for a new building that could be designed specifically for the needs of the college, and a building fund was established for the purpose that had accumulated $18,000 by 1894 and over $30,000 by the time the school was amalgamated with Tufts College. Sites all over Boston were considered in the next few years, but nothing was settled on, and housing remained critically short throughout the remaining history of the dental college. In the same year (1893), the provision of an oral hospital was recommended by the faculty and rooms were rented for the purpose — an arrangement lasting until 1896, when the building in use was slated for demolition by the owner.

Steadily rising enrollments, reluctance to reduce the size of the student body, and differences of opinion between the faculty and their Trustees over the need for expanded accommodations had by 1895 brought the dental college to a fork in its road. The whole situation of the school was discussed lengthily (and, judging from the record, heatedly) at a joint meeting of faculty and Trustees on October 15, 1895. This failed to bear out the bland remark made by President Capen to the Tufts Trustees in 1899 that the dental college had led a life of "uneventful success" until 1898. Subjects for dissection became difficult and expensive to secure. Conditions in the infirmary were congested and unsanitary. There were only 35 operating chairs for almost 200 students. Faculty morale was being lowered by overcrowded quarters and increased work loads, alumni as well as students were complaining, and Dr. Edward Branigan, the professor in charge, feared that the standards of the college would decline to such an extent that its excellent reputation would be seriously tarnished. The students' programs were so poorly arranged that great quantities of unassigned time were being used in loitering on sidewalks or patronizing neighborhood saloons. The only solution seemed to be the new building, about which there had been so much talk and so little action; or, if not that, a complete reorganization of the college or even affiliation with a medical school. All these possibilities were discussed in 1895.

The first personal link between the Boston Dental College and the Tufts Medical School had been forged in 1894 when Dr. John L. Hildreth, a Cambridge physician (elected to the Board of Trustees of the dental college in 1893) became Professor of Clinical Medicine in the Tufts Medical School. From 1896 to 1898 he served as its dean. His successor as dean of the medical school, Dr. Harold Williams, had likewise been elected to the Board of the Boston Dental College, in 1897. Even before then, a link of another sort had existed between the two schools, although the relationship was not too happy. In order to procure dissecting material, the dental college had to depend on one of two sources for cadavers: local medical schools or supplies from outside the state. The only schools that could dispose of subjects were the College of Physicians and Surgeons, the Harvard Medical School, and the school that became the Tufts Medical School in 1893. Harvard turned its surplus over to its own dental school; it was considered "not advisable to have dealings with the College of Physicians and Surgeons"; so the only source within the locality after 1893 seemed to be the Tufts Medical School. The major drawback there was the price of $40 charged for each subject — a charge considered excessive. So sources from outside the state were explored as well as the possibility of more reasonable prices from the Tufts Medical School. Dr. Hildreth was selected to conduct negotiations. To add to the difficulties posed by limited resources and space, the Trustees of the dental school approved a required course in bacteriology for which there was literally no space in the school.

The problem of obtaining dissecting materials became acute in 1896. Dr. Thayer, of the Tufts Medical School, reported that subjects were "very scarce" that year, and that the dental college had better count on none at all, at least from Tufts. To make matters worse, legislation enacted in 1897 prohibited the interstate shipment of bodies for dissecting purposes. Under the circumstances, the Tufts Medical School was no longer able to secure more than were needed for its own purposes and had nothing to spare for the dental college. It was at this juncture that the Boston Dental College requested permission to have its students receive their anatomical training in the Tufts Medical School. This was done after the dental college had investigated the possibilities at Boston University. Because there was insufficient room in the dental college, the college's officers tried to go a step farther and have the bacteriology course arranged in the same fashion, but apparently nothing came of either that possibility or negotiations to have the Tufts Medical School set up a special course in dissecting for dental students exclusively. The Tufts Medical School did move slightly in the direction of accommodating dental students. The medical faculty voted in 1897 to admit to the second-year class dental students who had completed one full course of lectures. However, such students had to pass an examination in the subjects of the freshman year before graduating.

Some of the Trustees of the dental college in 1898 thought that more could be gained by "turning students over to the Tufts Medical School for instruction in Anatomy, Physiology, Chemistry, Histology, Bacteriology, etc." than by attempting to build, particularly as the fund established to finance a new structure was still several thousand dollars shy of its goal. It was a short step to a decision to consolidate the dental college with an existing medical school. The first serious discussion of this possibility had taken place in 1896, when the system at Harvard of having first-year dental students attend classes in their own medical school was investigated and seemed to have noticeable advantages over the system in the dental college. The events of 1898 turned the possibility of merging with a medical school into a certainty.

The problem of obtaining cadavers for dissection by medical schools was alleviated in 1898 with the passage of a state law "For the promotion of Anatomical Science." Medical schools were allowed to obtain bodies that were subject to burial at public expense in Massachusetts and were not otherwise claimed by friends or relatives. The law merely worsened the plight of the dental college, because it effectively cut off any material it might have had from this source. The act provided for distribution only to medical schools. Hence the Boston Dental College's desire to complete the negotiations begun with the Tufts Trustees the previous summer was reinforced. There was further pressure to make some arrangement with a medical school for provision for instruction in practical anatomy because it was a requirement of the American Association of Dental Faculties, with which the dental college was affiliated. This organization suddenly notified the dental college in the summer of 1898 that it "would leave the College name off the list of reputable colleges unless we have dissection by Jan. 1, 1899."

The Boston Dental College actually had considerable to fear from what amounted to an ultimatum, for no arrangements had yet been completed with the Tufts Trustees for use of the medical school's facilities, and the dental college had not been able for two years to provide dissections. If its records are to be trusted, the crisis for the dental college was a serious one on yet another score. A small but articulate group of disgruntled dentists was conducting a vendetta to drive the dental college out of existence. Most of the dentists in this group had some personal grievance against the college because they had failed to receive appointments or promotions on the faculty or had run afoul of the college because of allegedly unethical practices (including the stealing of college equipment and the unauthorized transfer of dental college patients to their own practice so that higher fees could be charged). Dr. Follett, the panic-stricken dean, had attended the Association meeting in Omaha, Nebraska, and had finally prevailed on the Executive Committee not to suspend the school. He also obtained an extension of the deadline for providing dissections to February 1, 1899. It was pointed out at the Association by dentists friendly to the Boston Dental College that a number of such schools still had no provision for dissecting and had not yet been called to task, and that many members "had always considered the Boston Dental College one of the best."

Events moved rapidly during December 1898 and the following few weeks. A committee of the dental college Trustees conferred with members of a Tufts Trustee committee as to the possibility of a union with Tufts, subject to the approval of the state legislature. Although the dental college committee had been empowered to confer with the officers of colleges or universities other than Tufts, the terms and conditions worked out with Tufts seemed so favorable that they did not consider it advisable to open negotiations with any other institution. Tufts appeared to be the logical choice in other ways, for connections had already been established with it, and Harvard was ruled out because it already had its own medical-dental arrangements.

Many questions had to be settled and multifarious details had to be worked out. As finally agreed, the dental college was to turn over its total assets to Tufts, including more than $30,000 in cash (the bulk of which was the building fund), plus all property and equipment. One dentist was to be elected to the Tufts Trustees, such person in the first instance to be a graduate of the Boston Dental College. A Board of Visitors for the new dental school was to be established, its members to be selected from graduates of the old dental college so far as was compatible with the Trustee by-laws. The Tufts Trustees also undertook "to provide as soon as possible a suitable building to be used in whole or in part by the Dental School." The problem of the name and status of the dental college under the consolidation provoked a certain amount of questioning and even of controversy. The dental college Trustee committee had, in consultation with the Tufts Trustees, recommended that "such a dental school or department shall be known as the 'Tufts College Dental School (formerly Boston Dental College).' " Some of the dental Trustees had questions, and asked what precedents existed for such action. A copy of the legislative act consolidating the New England Female Medical College with Boston University was read as an example. One Trustee objected to the wording and wanted the name of the department changed to "Boston Dental College, Department of Dentistry, Tufts College." The Tufts Trustees rejected this rather awkward wording and pointed out that inasmuch as the dental college was in fact becoming a department of Tufts College, the same system of designation that applied to other professional departments had to be adhered to. It was made clear that the dental school was to stand upon the same general footing as the medical school. So it remained the "Tufts College Dental School," as originally agreed, although the explanatory parenthetical reference, "Formerly Boston Dental College," was authorized for use for three years in the charter amendment approved by the state legislature on February 28, 1899. Consolidation was to be effected by July 1, 1899, so a committee of the Tufts Trustees undertook to work out the details in cooperation with the Trustees of the old dental college, who agreed to continue to meet until formal transfer of all students and properties had been accomplished.

The Tufts Dental School faculty was formally established on June 21, 1899, with a close working relationship provided with the medical school. Harold Williams, already dean of the medical school, was also appointed dean of the new dental school as well as Professor of Theory and Practice of Medicine in the school. Six other professorships were established, for three-year terms, four of the professors likewise to be members of the medical school faculty. The nuclei of the new faculty were Edward W. Branigan, Clinical Dentistry; George A. Bates, Histology and Microscopy; Frederick W. Hemenway, Dental Art and Mechanism (changed in 1900 to Prosthodontia); John C. Monroe, Surgery; Charles P. Thayer, Anatomy; and Timothy Leary, Bacteriology. Salaries of the dean and the faculty were not to "exceed the amount heretofore paid by the Dental School [College] for the same service." An administrative committee was created in 1902 like the one in the medical school and consisted of the president of the College, the dean of the two schools, the secretary of the medical faculty, and two members of the dental school faculty. The Trustees of the old dental college held their last meeting on October 1, 1902, and reported that the transfer of the assets of the institution to Tufts ($42,950 in cash, as well as fixtures and other equipment used by the Boston Dental College) had been completed.

The acquisition of the dental college meant for Tufts even more than increased material and human assets in the way of a co-educational student body of 160, a dental infirmary in which some 24,000 cases were being handled annually, and a total instructional staff of 35. The College also acquired an institution that in its thirty-year history had established its own reputation and had pro-duced 469 graduates. As President Capen informed the Trustees in his annual report in the fall of 1899, it was not only the matter of the anatomy requirement that had brought another family under the Tufts roof. The decision to consolidate represented a recogni-tion of broader developments in dental education that were making traditional ideas obsolete and existing arrangements old-fashioned and inadequate. Curricular requirements unheard of not many decades before had become the order of the day. The College had undertaken new educational responsibilities and had reached an-other milestone in its history. The next few decades were devoted to developing and strengthening the two professional schools and to solving the innumerable problems — academic, technical, and financial — that the new relationships brought in their train.

8. Medical and Dental Education: Problems and Progress

At the time the Boston Dental College was incorporated into Tufts by way of the medical school in 1899, the requirements for admission were very much the same as were to be found in comparable institutions. There were three avenues open: presentation of "a degree in letters, science or medicine from a recognized college or scientific school"; possession of a diploma from a high school of "satisfactory grade"; or passing of written examinations in subjects customarily found in a high school curriculum.

A sequence had been established in the three-year program of the Boston Dental College which included anatomy, physiology, materia medica (introduced in 1895), histology, operative dentistry and dental anatomy, clinical dentistry, mechanical dentistry, dental techniques (introduced in 1896), and chemistry (which was required throughout). Bacteriology had been introduced in 1895, and in the senior year the student received instruction and practice in anesthetics. A review of the curriculum indicates continued stress on medical knowledge and on practical experience. The curriculum looked better on paper, however, than it was in actual operation. As has been indicated, the courses intended to provide a foundation in medical subjects were not always taught as advertised. The facilities for lecture, demonstrations, and laboratory work were so grossly inadequate that these various deficiencies had prompted the union with Tufts.

Opportunity for observation of surgical technique was still provided in 1899; in fact, the Boston Dispensary had been added to the earlier list. But the use of these resources was not systematic, and no schedule of visitation existed. Students were left very much on their own. The total charges had actually been reduced (to $115) by the time the dental college was absorbed by Tufts, as the diploma fee had been abolished. Fees and charges in 1899–1900 increased somewhat (to a total of $150, with the reinstitution of a $30 graduation fee) and were thereafter geared very closely to medical school charges. In 1905–6 the uniform tuition fee for dental school students was $150. The fees remained stable for several years. Even after the First World War total school charges were only $740 for a four-year course. Students were still expected to furnish most of their own instruments, tools, and appliances for both laboratory and operating room as well as all metals used in laboratory work. Affiliation with Tufts most certainly did not automatically solve all the problems of obtaining clinical materials. Prospective students who read the Tufts catalogue for 1900–1901 would have found a note at the bottom of page 229 informing them that "the operations in the Technical Department require a very large number of natural teeth, and a sufficient supply is sometimes difficult to get. It will therefore be to the interest of students if they will bring with them all the extracted teeth they obtain."

No significant changes were made in the entrance requirements inherited from the old Boston Dental College. High school graduation or examination continued to be the minimum expected. After 1910, holders of Regents' Certificates of the State of New York were exempt from entrance examinations, together with those holding a high school diploma or having pursued some amount of college or university work. When the unit system of computing secondary school work came into use in 1911, fourteen such units were required for admission to the dental school (although failure in as many as five units was allowed for conditional admission). Simultaneously, units were grouped into Required and Elective. English, elementary foreign language, elementary physics, elementary algebra, and plane geometry fell into the first category. Those admitted with advanced standing had to complete their last year in the Tufts Dental School. There was something of an effort to preserve a linkage, however tenuous, between professional and classical preparation, for students entering by examination were told to be prepared to demonstrate their knowledge (in writing) of such literary works as William Hickling Prescott's *Conquest of Mexico,* William Makepeace Thackeray's *Henry Esmond,* or Edmund Burke's "Speech on Conciliation with America," not to mention Shakespeare and Sir Walter Scott. Geometry was added to the mathematics requirement, arithmetic was replaced by more advanced algebra, and the required foreign language became Latin (one year's study of part of Caesar's *Commentaries*) as soon as the dental college joined the Tufts ranks. Biology appeared as an optional examination field in 1905–6.

The greatest immediate change in the dental school program was its extension to four years in 1900–1901, effective for all classes in 1902–3. The Tufts Dental School became the second of the fifty-four leading dental schools in the United States to take such a step, the University of Michigan having been the pioneer. Tufts could derive special satisfaction from the fact that the National Association of Dental Faculties voted to demand the same standard of its entire constituency after 1903. The entering class dropped from ninety-nine to forty-three in 1902–3, but immediately climbed again so that records were broken almost every year thereafter. The four-year program made possible new courses in embryology, physiology, and personal hygiene as well as more intensive work in such areas as pathology, orthodontia, and clinical dentistry in general. The first two years of work for dental students were almost the same as the corresponding years in the medical school. This underlined the fact that Tufts was in the forefront of the movement to teach dentistry as a specialty of medicine.

Supporters of the new program were grievously disappointed when, after only one year of the four-year course, the National Association of Dental Faculties reversed itself and returned to a three-year curriculum. This "retrograde step," having been adopted by all dental schools affiliated with the Association, left the Tufts Dental School in the unenviable position of either going along with the majority or attempting to go it alone. The school compromised by leaving the four-year program in its offerings but providing a three-year optional course. There was some feeling, at least at Tufts, that dental schools with university affiliations ought to drop out of the National Association and leave it and the three-year programs to proprietary and commercial schools.

Until the Boston Dental College united with Tufts, graduates received the degree of Doctor of Dental Surgery, as provided in its 1868 charter. After the union was accomplished, graduates obtaining a Tufts degree received the Doctorate of Dental Medicine

(D.M.D.).[1] After the four-year degree program was introduced, the dental school gave holders of the old D.D.S. an opportunity to earn the D.M.D. by taking a postgraduate course, first offered in 1905–6. The curriculum provided lectures, demonstrations, and laboratory exercises in anatomy, physiology, histology and embryology, pathology and bacteriology, and syphilis to holders of degrees from approved dental colleges. After 1907, postgraduate work was available only to graduates of the old Boston Dental College. Tufts became one of only three dental schools in the United States to award the D.M.D. instead of the D.D.S. as the degree for general practitioners of dentistry.[2]

The acquisition of the dental school made new housing imperative. There were 176 students enrolled in the school in 1900–1901, notwithstanding the fact that 30 per cent of the applicants had been rejected on entrance examinations. The College had also agreed to provide the school with a home as part of the arrangements of 1899. In the year before the dental school became formally a part of Tufts, enrollment in the anatomy course in the medical school jumped by fifty students who had come from the Boston Dental College. Anticipating that this might very well be a step in the complete absorption of the dental college, the Tufts Trustees began to look about for new quarters. At first they intended to buy additional land in the same block as the medical school building, but as soon as word got out, the prices of property shot up with astounding rapidity. Checked in this direction, the Trustees decided to purchase land at the corner of Huntington Avenue and Bryant Street across from the Fenway and to erect one building that would serve as a combined medical-dental facility.

One building to serve two schools not only seemed the most economical and efficient solution but was quite in harmony with an educational philosophy which posited the close relationship of the two professions. The very fact that the two schools shared a common dean was a working out of this principle. As President

[1] The legislative act of union of 1899 had made no stipulation about degrees, as this was considered a prerogative of the Corporation.

[2] Gies, "Dental Education," Carnegie Foundation, p. 392. Harvard and North Pacific College of Oregon were the other two. The degree had been originated at Harvard in 1869 as a way of recognizing dentistry to be just as much of a healing art in its way as medicine.

*The headquarters (later razed) of the Tufts Dental School
on Huntington Avenue before it moved
to the New England Medical Center*

Capen explained to the Trustees, dentistry required more than "deft fingers and a good eye." It was "only a branch of medicine after all." He was echoing Dean Williams' belief that dentistry was "a department of medicine instead of an allied branch." The germ theory of disease was applied in the dental infirmary with the introduction of asepsis, including the disinfection of instruments and surgical cleanliness of a high order. The Executive Committee of the Trustees was reflecting this same viewpoint when in 1906 it turned down an offer to establish a scholarship to be awarded to a graduate of the Mechanic Arts High School in Boston or similar manual training schools who showed the highest mechanical proficiency. Dentistry was more than manual dexterity.

Contracts were let in the summer of 1900 for a building to cost $110,000 on land costing slightly over $57,000. The assets received from the old Boston Dental College were applied toward the cost, as well as the sinking fund that had been accumulating in the medical school account. The balance needed was financed by an $80,000 mortgage.[3] The new building, constructed of Jonesport red granite and brick with terra-cotta trimmings and designed by J. Philip Rinn, who had prepared the plans for several other Tufts buildings, was formally opened on October 3, 1901. An additional $35,000 had to be appropriated to complete and furnish it. The Trustees had considerable difficulty in disposing of the reconstructed Baptist church on Shawmut Avenue but in 1902 finally sold it at a loss of several thousand dollars.[4] President Capen found that, after a year at the Huntington Avenue location, where the two schools were "practically one," great satisfaction prevailed. There had been no friction, the new quarters were attractive as well as functional, and a surge of enrollment showed how welcome the new structure was to prospective doctors and dentists.

The close ties already existing between the medical and dental schools in curriculum, use of facilities, and the sharing of a dean were carried over into other areas of administration. One discrepancy that existed at first between the two schools concerned faculty compensation. Teachers with professorial rank in the dental school at the time it became part of Tufts were on salary, which was, of course, a first claim upon income. In the medical school, however, the faculty was, as one person put it, "in a relation of quasi-partnership." Nominally without salary, the medical faculty shared, as has been noted, in the distribution of annual surpluses. The financial arrangement of the dental faculty, coupled with the uncertainties in medical faculty remuneration because of possible increases in fixed charges or decreases of income, brought the adoption of a Trustee policy. The Executive Committee of the Trustees decided in 1901 that the distribution of surplus revenue of the medical school should be discontinued, and that the faculty of both medical and dental schools should be placed on straight salary. This turned out to be not so much of a revolutionary policy as it might have appeared, for the annual salary scale, which ranged from $1,700 down to $50 and averaged less than $500, was still dependent on the

[3] The sum was originally to have been borrowed from the Massachusetts General Hospital at 4 per cent for five years, but for some reason the decision was made to obtain the money from other sources.

[4] One unhappy result was the necessity of transferring much of the medical-dental sinking fund to meet the loss.

surplus available from year to year. But at least a start toward regular salaries had been made. Compensation was equally divided between the two schools for faculty that taught courses such as anatomy in both. In 1903, after $4,500 in surplus had been distributed as under the old system, the Executive Committee decided that the previously determined policy of paying fixed salaries should be strictly adhered to, but this was more of an aspiration than a reality for all but a few of the faculty for the next several years.

The principal source of income from which the medical school faculty was being paid without dipping into the limited resources of the College continued to be student charges. Tuition in the medical school was raised from $125 to $150, effective September 1904. This did not actually mean an increase, for the separate graduation fee of $30 was abolished and made a part of the regular tuition. A corresponding raise was made in the dental school so that tuition was made uniform.

Both medical and dental schools grew so rapidly in the next few decades that quarters previously considered adequate were outgrown time after time. For many years the infirmary connected with the old Boston Dental College had been located in one of the buildings on Tremont Street in which space had been rented. One year after the new facilities had been completed, the infirmary was moved into it. Within four years, the addition of a clinic and expansion of infirmary and laboratory accommodations were being recommended by President Hamilton. Extensive remodeling and the addition of a fourth floor in 1910 to the Huntington Avenue building supplied a chemistry laboratory and new lecture rooms. An anatomical building provided in 1916 for the use of schools was enlarged in 1917 and again in 1920, to include chemical laboratories. An ex-stable on Mechanic Street of unprepossessing appearance, and known officially as the Medical School Annex and unofficially but quite accurately as "the Barn" by several generations of pre-medical and pre-dental students, was leased until mid-1928. The close instructional ties between the two schools were more or less consistently maintained, for in the 1920's, when the Carnegie study of dental education in the United States was made, medicodental subjects were being taught to dental students in separate classes, but by members of the medical faculty, and in laboratories used in common.

Both dental training and service expanded rapidly after 1900. The dental school first offered summer school courses in physiology and histology in 1905. The area of greatest activity and influence was the dental infirmary under the leadership of Dr. Edward W. Branigan, who had been on the faculty of the Boston Dental College and who until his death in 1911 was one of the best-known members of the dental faculty. The practice had been followed for many years of charging only a nominal fee covering no more than the cost of materials, and of quietly treating without charge dozens of patients who could afford to pay nothing. In 1902–3, for example, 120 patients were treated daily, but less than half were charged anything at all. Such a social service was considered doubly worthy, for it extended much-needed benefits to a segment of society not otherwise able to receive them and at the same time exposed advanced dental students to all kinds of clinical material. The infirmary was literally overwhelmed with customers. In 1903 the Executive Committee of the Trustees considered the feasibility of sending out an appeal for funds to subsidize what amounted to a free community service. The sum of $4,000 a year (the income from $100,000) was the goal. Part of the prompting for the decision to make the appeal came from a group of philanthropically inclined citizens interested in free dentistry for the poor. A committee had visited the Tufts Dental School and had been so impressed with it that they recommended "an appeal to the public for a sum sufficient to enlarge very materially the scope of the Infirmary." A decade later, nearly four-fifths of the free dental work in Massachusetts was being done under the direction of the officers of the dental school.

The Tufts Dental School had by 1912 become the twelfth largest such school in the United States. Even more worthy of pride was the fact that in that year its students attained the highest percentage of successful examinations of any school before the state Boards of Examiners.[5]

One of the most important events in the history of the dental school (and, some thought, in the history of dentistry itself) was the establishment of the Forsyth Dental Infirmary for Children. Char-

---

[5] Tufts had less than 5 per cent failures in 1912, according to the report of the National Association of Dental Faculties. Failures of students of other dental schools ran as high as 50 per cent.

tered in 1910, it gave just the facilities and opportunities for the enlargement of the field of charitable dentistry that the dental school wanted. Land, an elegant building following classical lines, and an endowment of approximately $1,000,000 were provided by Thomas Alexander Forsyth and John Hamilton Forsyth in memory of two brothers. The site, on the Fenway in Boston, was admirably suited to dental school purposes, being less than a block from the Tufts building. The intent of the benefactors was to provide care for the school children of Boston and vicinity who were under sixteen years of age. Its establishment not only gave dental school students additional clinical facilities but diverted the children from the badly overcrowded clinics of the school. As a charitable institution, the new infirmary was a pioneer venture of great importance.

The Forsyth Infirmary, with a building dedicated in 1914 and in full operation by January 1, 1915, was an interesting experiment in inter-institutional cooperation. Although technically an independent agency offering complete oral health service for children, it was associated educationally with both Tufts and Harvard. Among the incorporators and Trustees were President Hamilton, Dr. Branigan of the dental school, Dr. Timothy Leary of the medical school, Dean Harold Williams of both schools, and Sumner Robinson, a Tufts Trustee since 1891.[6] At the time the Infirmary was chartered, a proposal was made to give Tufts College exclusive and formal control but rejected because it was deemed advisable, for the best interests of the enterprise and the dental profession at large, to have control shared by more than one educational institution. Harvard conducted advanced work for the Infirmary interns at its own medical and dental schools, engaged in collaborative research, and furnished lecturers from its dental faculty. Members of

[6] President Hamilton served on the Infirmary's Board of Trustees until his resignation from the Tufts presidency in 1912. In anticipation of the educational purposes that the Forsyth Infirmary might serve, and in view of the close relationship between the Infirmary and the College, the Tufts Trustees had the College charter amended to allow the latter to receive gifts and bequests "for the education of men or women in other institutions, incorporated in this commonwealth for that purpose, and associated with it, but not a part of the college now maintained." The amendment was approved February 28, 1910 — *Acts and Resolves,* Commonwealth of Massachusetts, 1910, Chapter 133.

the Tufts dental and medical faculties also gave lectures and supervised demonstrations in advanced work for the Infirmary interns.

The relationships among the Forsyth Infirmary, Tufts, and Harvard were made even more intricate and interlocking by the establishment in 1916 of the Forsyth-Tufts Training School for Dental Hygienists. Members of the Forsyth staff, and of the faculties of the dental schools of both Tufts and Harvard, constituted the Board of Instruction. The Training School was created to prepare young women for oral health service, namely, to teach oral hygiene in the public schools or other institutions, to practice prophylactic cleaning of teeth, and to act as dental nurse in institutions or for dentists. Instruction was included in pediatrics, endocrinology, nutrition and diet, anesthesia, and pre- and post-operative surgery of the nose, throat, and mouth. Graduation from an accredited high school or equivalent was needed for admission. Over 1,000 hours of instruction, laboratory, and clinical and in-service work were required for a certificate. Most of the training was received in the Forsyth Infirmary. By 1926 the Training School (which by then had become known as the Forsyth School for Dental Hygienists) had produced 440 graduates. The existence of both the Infirmary and the Training School, as unique assets to dental education, provoked enthusiastic approval from the compilers of the Carnegie Report on Dental Education in 1926. Dispensary and hospital facilities in which dental students could receive accredited instruction or perform stated clinical service by the mid-1920's were the Boston City Hospital, the Boston Dispensary, the Massachusetts Homeopathic Hospital, the Massachusetts School for the Feeble Minded, and the Roxbury Hospital. No accredited instruction was provided at the Forsyth Dental Infirmary after 1923–24.

All told, the Tufts Dental School was a strong school with an excellent reputation when the Carnegie Report was made. It had graduated an average of seventy students annually since 1900, with a total of 1,840 by 1925. Although the bulk of its student body were still from Massachusetts (over 60 per cent), the proportion was declining. Enrollment had averaged well over 350 for the past decade and there was no indication that the numbers would decline. The dental school was maintaining the Class A rating that had been granted in 1918 by the Dental Educational Council of America. Since 1921, one year of approved work in an accredited college had become the minimum requirement for admission, and in September 1927 the minimum for admission to the three-year curriculum went up to two years of approved college work. The number of teachers of dental students in 1924–25 was 131 (of whom only six were full-time instructors of exclusively dental subjects; sixty comprised an unsalaried "visiting staff" which was in process of reduction). Absence of endowment, lack of scholarship aid, and too great a proportion of part-time faculty were considered the main deficiencies. The problem of greatest concern to both the Carnegie investigators and the College was financial. This was reflected in many ways, notably in the limitation imposed on the amount of research being conducted. For several years the dental school produced a profit that helped support the medical school, but after the readjustments made necessary by the First World War and the raising of admission requirements in 1921–22, the school was conducted at a loss, and the annual deficit made up by the College had increased to almost $35,000. The indebtedness on the medical-dental building also meant that interest charges had to be paid from current income. The picture might have been dark, but it was not black. The quality of the school's output, measured in terms of the reputation it had achieved and the low percentage of failures on the licensing examinations (less than 11 per cent and less than the national average in the fifteen-year period from 1910 to 1925), did much to brighten the outlook. The story of the Tufts Medical School during the period after 1900 was considerably more complicated, and not quite so encouraging.

§   §   §

The dean of the Tufts Medical School had reported with some pride in 1903 that, with a teaching staff of 105 and an enrollment of 403 students, the school was the largest such institution in New England. By 1906 the school was seventh in size of the 175 medical schools in the United States. Enrollment in both medical and dental schools had climbed steadily in the years preceding the First World War. There seemed to be nothing to hinder their growth. The opening of new buildings for the Harvard Medical School in 1905–6 close by the Tufts schools was acknowledged to be an important event in medical education but was considered no threat to Tufts, for Harvard's principal efforts were aimed at research, while

Tufts continued its practical aim of educating the general practitioner rather than the specialist.

However, quantity and quality are not always synonymous, and some individuals concerned with the medical school could not shake off the nagging feeling that the large enrollments might be due to low admission standards as well as the attractiveness of the school's teaching facilities and professional stature. Likewise, lack of endowment, difficulties inherent in employing a largely part-time faculty, and the failure to obtain a hospital for exclusive Tufts use raised questions and created problems that refused to be downed. The first of many calls for endowment to finance clinics, laboratories, research, and a hospital connected with the school had been heard within two years of its establishment. A member of the medical faculty, in an article in the *Tufts College Graduate,* had called attention also to the lack of scholarship aid. "The department at the Hill boasts of about seventy scholarships, while the medical department . . . has not a single scholarship or other endowment of any sort." Plans were made to launch a drive for endowment funds for the medical school as part of the celebration of the semicentennial of the College in 1905, but nothing of great significance was accomplished. The first important endowment for research was made in 1908, when Herbert L. and Mary Crane Johnson established a fund in memory of their daughter Elizabeth, who had died of streptococcus meningitis. The five-year grant ($1,000 each year) was made to Dr. Timothy Leary to aid in the discovery of antidotes and possible cures for streptococcus infections. It greatly aided the work already undertaken at the medical school in the field of serum and vaccine development.

When a petition was granted by the state legislature in 1901 to remove the ceiling on annual income receivable by the Tufts Corporation, a petition was also granted to allow the College "to establish and maintain a hospital." The hope was expressed repeatedly that a hospital might some day be acquired. One member of the medical faculty suggested in 1903 that the ideal would be a thirty- or forty-bed hospital built on land adjoining the school on Huntington Avenue, and with provisions for future expansion. The possibility of obtaining control of the Emergency Hospital in Boston appeared in 1908, but nothing came of that.

The problem of having numerous part-time staff members

faced all medical and dental schools in some degree. The Tufts Medical School had come in for its share of criticism on this count from officers of the College. The chairman of the Board of Visitors to the medical school in 1897 had been unhappy over the arrangement. He used the dean of the school, Dr. Hildreth, as an illustration. The dean served also as Professor of Clinical Medicine, had a private practice, and besides, held a service commitment to the Cambridge Hospital.[7] Physicians were so intent on keeping up their own practice that in 1897 the chair of Clinical Surgery had to be declared vacant "on account of non-fulfilment of duty" by the incumbent. A problem closely allied to the dependence on part-time instruction was "the great want of teaching ability" among the staff. The staff members may have been competent physicians, but they were often unable to communicate their knowledge effectively.

The most basic and persistent problem, and the one that was mentioned most frequently in connection with both medical and dental schools, was admission standards. The Board of Overseers, during its life-span of eight years (1899–1907), and the Boards of Visitors that it appointed during this period were constantly concerned. The president of the College expressed his views on the subject more than once. In their first formal report to the Trustees, the Overseers noted "with great satisfaction" the increase in the requirements for admission to the dental school and were inclined to approve the idea (soon put into effect) that the first year's work be made identical for both medical and dental students. A year later (in 1902) the Overseers expressed concern over medical school standards. "With the end in view of eliminating the least desirable material so that the entire work may be raised to a higher plane, we suggest that a substantial increase be made in the requirements for admission. The present definitions are far below the requirements for graduation from a good high school." The Committee on Education of the Trustee Executive Committee followed up this complaint and made a personal examination of the entrance papers in the medical school in the fall of 1902. They noted "with pleasure a tendency gradually to increase the requirements" and assured themselves that the catalogue statements were being "faithfully applied."

[7] Dr. Hildreth resigned as dean in 1898 and was replaced by Dr. Harold Williams; however, Hildreth retained his post in clinical medicine.

A small step was taken in 1902–3 to advance admission standards in the medical school when examinations were required in
English, Latin, algebra, geometry, and physics of applicants who
were graduated from high schools not on the "approved list." The
fact that nearly 20 per cent of the applicants were rejected that year
was produced to show that the medical faculty was "holding stiffly"
to the admission requirements; in 1903–4, 37 per cent met a similar
fate. The Boards of Visitors to the two schools were still not satisfied. It seemed to them something of an anomaly that a student
could enter either the medical or the dental school on the strength
of a diploma from a good high school or academy, while to take the
medical preparatory course at a college, he was expected to be prepared to enter the A.B. or B.S. course. They were not yet ready to
consider a college degree either wise or expedient as a requirement
for either school, but they believed that "entrance requirements
should be very high indeed to insure a reasonable chance of success
for the applicant." The system of academic probation already in use
in the Hill schools was adopted by the medical school in 1907 as one
device for weeding out weak students. It was not until after the report was made on the medical school by the Carnegie Foundation
in 1910 that any substantial change occurred in admission requirements. This did not mean a disregard of the problem before 1910,
however. National trends in medical education could not be
ignored.

President Hamilton had recognized in his annual report in
1908–9 the mounting efforts to improve standards for those entering the medical profession. The Johns Hopkins University and
Harvard had gone so far as to require a college degree. A considerable number of schools had either adopted or given notice of intention to adopt the requirement of one or two years of college
work as a prerequisite to admission to medical training. Standards
varied, of course, from section to section within the United States.
President Hamilton was sure that a New England preparatory education was equivalent to two years of college in most southern
states. He believed that if any change were to be made, it ought to
be in the direction of extending the medical course a year or more
rather than requiring collegiate preparation. The lengthening of
the time before a physician obtained his license to practice had been
brought about already by the growing tendency to require a year of

internship. Adding a college requirement at the other end would impose financial hardship and postpone completion of formal education to the age of twenty-six or twenty-seven. Much of "the spring and momentum of youth" would have been lost by then, and such individuals would be at a distinct disadvantage as compared with those who had been fortunate enough to get an earlier start on their professional careers. Medicine was not an isolated instance. Hamilton predicted that engineering schools might soon be forced to require more than four years' preparation by either lengthening their courses or transforming themselves into graduate schools. The remedy, he thought, for the pressure to invest additional time and money in professional preparation lay with the lower schools rather than with the colleges. Proper organizing and financing at the secondary level would make possible division of large heterogeneous classes hitherto beamed at the mediocre student or the lowest common denominator into interest, ability, and achievement groups that would permit the brighter students to be prepared for college at sixteen rather than eighteen. If the combined undergraduate and graduate curricula could also be streamlined to a total of seven years, students could become economically productive sooner, and with less sacrifice and financial investment. As it turned out, Hamilton was both right and wrong. Professional education was extended in *both* directions.

It is no exaggeration to say that medical education in the United States was shaken to its foundations in 1910. Two years before, the Carnegie Foundation for the Advancement of Teaching had instituted the most thorough and far-reaching investigation of medical schools in the United States that had ever been undertaken. The report, prepared for the Foundation by Abraham Flexner, a prominent educator, became one of the most controversial landmarks in educational history.[8] The Flexner Report, as the Carnegie-sponsored investigation soon came to be called, was not the first survey of its kind in the field of medical education. The initiative had been taken by the Illinois State Board of Health in 1881. Up to then, only scattered statistics existed about medical schools, buried in the reports of the United States Commissioner of Educa-

[8] Abraham Flexner, *Medical Education in the United States and Canada* (New York: Carnegie Foundation for the Advancement of Teaching, Bulletin No. 4, 1910).

tion. The Illinois agency made a more comprehensive follow-up report in 1891, which was used as the basis for evaluation of schools by the thirty-two state licensing boards then in existence. The *Journal of the American Medical Association* adopted the practice of publishing the statistical results of state Board examinations taken by graduates of medical colleges and thereby established a basis for grading schools by classifying them according to their number of failures. Class I schools were those with less than 10 per cent failures; Class II schools, with between 10 and 20 per cent failures; and Class III, with over 20 per cent.

This publicity, unwelcome as it was to many schools, performed a valuable service and no doubt strengthened the hand of a new and powerful agency created under the auspices of the American Medical Association after its reorganization and incorporation in 1901. The Council on Medical Education, which came into being in 1903 and held the first of its annual conferences in 1905, undertook to establish standards for medical education by setting, as a minimum, graduation from a four-year high school plus four years of medicine and recommending as desirable a five-year medical curriculum of which the first year would include physics, chemistry, and biology. The first inspection of medical schools by the Council, reported in 1906, was severe in its criticism of poorly equipped and inadequately staffed institutions; for example, of fifty-four schools in five states, less than ten were giving what the Council considered adequate training. For the next inspection a year later, the Council established a Class A, B, and C rating, each based on a ten-point factor on a ten-point scale. Schools achieving a Class A rating required seventy points; Class B ("doubtful" schools) ranged from fifty to seventy points; and Class C ("unacceptable" schools) were those assigned less than fifty points.

The results of the survey of 1907 were prompt and effective. Thirty-eight additional schools had decided by 1910 to require one year of preparatory work in college (including chemistry, physics, and biology), and several inferior schools surrendered their charters when licensing boards refused to examine their graduates. The next inspection paralleled the Flexner Report and was overshadowed by it. The coincidence of the two reports, one from outside the profession, gave rise to understandable controversy.

The story back of the Flexner Report represented in itself a record of controversy. In 1905 Andrew Carnegie had established a $10,000,000 fund to endow a system of pensions for college teachers.[9] The idea was planted in Carnegie's mind by Henry S. Pritchett, president of the Massachusetts Institute of Technology, who broached the subject of pensions on behalf of his faculty in 1904. Pritchett resigned to accept the presidency of the Carnegie Foundation and dominated its policies and operations until the First World War. Carnegie originally conceived of his Foundation, which was chartered in 1905 and rechartered under act of Congress in 1906, as simply a device for aiding needy and deserving professors who had been retired because of age or ill health. In fact, Carnegie was quite willing to have his incorporated beneficence known simply as "The Carnegie Foundation for Pensioning of Teachers." However, he had turned complete control of the Foundation over to a Board of Trustees who, under Pritchett's influence, broadened the scope of the Foundation far beyond Carnegie's intention. The president of the Foundation turned it into an organization "dedicated to the betterment of American education." Professorial pensions were to be restricted to staffs of institutions that had achieved the standards set by the Trustees of the Foundation. In this way it was hoped that colleges and universities that did not meet certain requirements would be forced to look elsewhere for faculty pensions, to raise standards, or to close their doors if need be. The Foundation, as Pritchett saw it, was to use its free pensions as a lever (or, as some critics said, a bludgeon) by which the whole level of American higher education would be raised.

In order to make a determination of what institutions deserved Foundation favors, its Trustees undertook the self-appointed task of investigating and making public its findings. The justification for this ambitious and possibly audacious plan was Pritchett's conviction that all colleges and universities, whether public or private, were "in truth public service corporations," and because they were vested with a public interest, the public was entitled to be informed. Pritchett insisted that the Foundation "carefully refrained from attempting to become a standardizing agency" but he admitted that its influence was being used to make a differentiation be-

[9] The history of the stormy early years of the Foundation is to be found in Theron F. Schlabach, *Pensions for Professors* (Madison: State Historical Society of Wisconsin, 1963).

tween the secondary school and the college, and between the college
and the university and its professional schools. After making a start
by surveying colleges, the Foundation turned to universities and
their relation to professional schools. The first report was on medical education.

The investigations of medical schools were as comprehensive
as it was possible to make them in less than two years. Personal visitation, interviews, college catalogues, information in the files of the
American Medical Association and the Association of American
Medical Colleges were all used as bases for evaluating the 150-odd
schools surveyed. Data were then cross-checked by independent ob-
servers to assure accuracy and completeness. The conclusions to
which the Foundation came boded ill for many a medical school.
They called, in fact, for a complete reconstruction of medical education. Confusion bordering on chaos seemed to prevail in the field.
There was no uniformity in standards, which were for the most
part disgracefully low. A disturbingly high proportion of medical
faculties that claimed some relationship to an academic institution
represented "only a license from the college by which a proprietary
medical school . . . was enabled to live under its name." As
Pritchett viewed the results of the Foundation study, the situation
which was uncovered seemed nothing short of scandalous.

The Tufts Medical School was visited in October 1909. Flexner found it "administratively an integral department of Tufts
College, though actual scientific intercourse [was] not intimate."
Enrollment was 384 and there was a teaching staff of 103, one-third
of whom held professorial rank. Entrance requirements left much
to be desired. Even though the school professed to accept at face
value diplomas only from "approved" or "accredited" high schools
(i.e., those on the list of the New England College Entrance Certificate Board), it allowed also an "equivalent." Under this rather
ambiguous provision, in 1909–10 the school had accepted a total of
151 first-year students of whom only slightly more than half complied with the announced standard. Of the others, thirty were accepted from non-accredited schools on the strength of diplomas
and certificates that, according to the catalogue statement, were not
acceptable. The remaining thirty-eight were accepted under the
heading of "equivalent" by taking entrance examinations that ap-
proximated about half of the subjects usually taken in high school.

Six examination papers were required; the student was accepted "on condition" if he passed three. The low standards of admission were considered even less defensible considering the enviable reputation that New England schools were supposed to have attained, for 97 per cent of the total enrollment came from New England and 80 per cent from Massachusetts.

The Flexner Report noted a close correlation between high drop-out rates and schools that allowed "equivalents." Tufts was cited as a glaring example. The entering class of 1908–9 was 141; of these, seventy-five were promoted (some with conditions) into the sophomore class. Of the remaining sixty-six, only fifteen departed before the final examinations, leaving fifty-one who were neither advanced nor dropped. It was painfully clear to Flexner that a high proportion of that particular class should never have been admitted in the first place. Even though Tufts was considered in the report to have one of the seven strongest medical schools in the United States that operated on the "high school or equivalent basis," the statistical evidence of academic mortality for the seven schools taken together was of great concern.[10] To make matters worse, medical schools indulged in the pernicious habit of admitting each other's rejections or failures. Tufts, for example, admitted (as "specials") failures from Dartmouth, Queen's College (Kingston, Ontario), and the Medico-Chirurgical College of Philadelphia. Likewise, failures from Tufts appeared in the student body of the Baltimore Medical College. Tufts could take some small comfort from the fact that at least it was not guilty, as were so many of its fellow medical schools, of advancing students who had been refused promotion in other institutions with even lower standards.

The Carnegie survey found the laboratory facilities of the Tufts Medical School "entirely adequate to the teaching work," but the failure of the school to have its own hospital was noted with disapproval. There was one extenuating circumstance that allowed it to be classified among "the best of the schools without a hos-

[10] Of 2,280 students in 1908–9 in the seven (Jefferson Medical, New York University, University of Maryland, the Medico-Chirurgical College of Philadelphia, Yale, the University of Pennsylvania, and Tufts), 11 per cent dropped out before taking examinations, 38 per cent either failed or were conditioned, and only 51 per cent passed without conditions of some kind.

pital." Like Harvard (also without its own hospital in 1909), Tufts could share in an abundance and variety of clinical material lacking in some areas even where medical schools had their own hospitals. Nonetheless, Tufts, like Harvard, which was also clinically handicapped, suffered from the disadvantages inherent in the need to depend on outside facilities. Conditions of access were not under the control of the school and militated against both continuity of educational policy and complete freedom of research so essential to medical advance. Even more unfortunate was the necessity of drawing primarily on local personnel for teaching and clinical staff. As Flexner pointed out, this restriction would be considered "intolerable" in most other academic departments. In Boston, neither Harvard nor Tufts could take the initiative in filling staff positions in the hospitals used in teaching, and most of the larger hospitals had their own specialized departments in which it was difficult if not impossible to obtain privileges or from which to draw teaching personnel. Again, Tufts was more fortunate than some schools for it had "an imposing array of clinical facilities." However, its medical clinic in 1910 was limited to the Boston Dispensary and one service in the Boston City Hospital, and many of the "imposing array" referred to above represented contact with the Tufts Medical School through only a single doctor who might be on an annual appointment. Dispensaries open in Boston to Harvard and Tufts students were considered "adequate in all essential respects."

Possibly the most serious weakness of the Tufts Medical School, as both the College and the Flexner Report viewed the situation, was the lack of a *bona fide* endowment and the resulting dependence on tuition and fees to support the school. Medicine, said the author of the Carnegie Report, could not be and was not being properly taught on the basis solely or largely of receipts in the more than thirty university-affiliated medical schools or departments where this situation existed. Something had to be sacrified in the way of buildings, improvements, staff, or other requirements. Too many schools had to siphon off part of their income to pay off indebtedness. Tufts was used as an example of this unfortunate situation; the medical school, with an annual income of not quite $60,000, was paying off in yearly installments the debt incurred for the building it shared with the dental school.

The theme of the Flexner Report was simple but profound in its implications. It called for a complete overhauling of the whole field of medical education. Low standards, wasteful duplication of effort and facilities, undignified scrambling for students, and what appeared to be a callous disregard for the public welfare all had to be eliminated if medical schools were to meet in even a small way the demands of a society that was being weakened by unprofessional and sometimes downright unethical standards of education beyond the high school. The nation was being short-changed.

Several conclusions emerged from the nation-wide study of medical education. There was "an enormous over-production of uneducated and ill trained medical practitioners." This was due in the main to the "very large number" of commercially operated schools interested only (or primarily) in profits. As the expenses of operating medical schools mounted with the shift from didactic to laboratory-based teaching, the inadequacies of the weaker schools became alarmingly evident. Too many universities had annexed medical schools without either assuming responsibility for their standards or providing them with the resources they desperately needed, and had let the medical department become an *imperium in imperio* through neglect or weakness. The argument that catering to the poor boy justified a poor school was specious, fallacious, and insincere. Finally, a hospital connected with a medical school was as indispensable as a laboratory in chemistry or pathology. The long-range goal should be a much smaller number of medical schools, better equipped and conducted, and, as an end-product, fewer but better-trained physicians. Closer articulation than existed in most instances had to be provided between medical schools and universities to which they were attached or related in some degree. One trend approved in the Flexner Report was the articulation of the curricula of medical schools with the first two years of college — a tendency already evident in the North and East (but not including Tufts).

According to the blueprint prepared by Flexner, of the some 150 medical schools in existence in 1909–10, about 120 should be "wiped off the map" by closing or merger.[11] He called for thirty-one

[11] This was more than a figure of speech. Flexner included in his report two outline maps of the United States showing the actual and proposed distribution of schools after reduction had taken place.

medical schools to serve the United States. They had a current annual output of about 2,000, which could be increased to 3,000. The Tufts Medical School was to have been one of the schools eliminated. Flexner found that 85 per cent of the enrollment at the reputable schools in New England (including Tufts) was local, that the section was "badly overcrowded" with physicians, and that the population of the area was increasing too slowly to absorb the surplus. Requiring a thorough knowledge of physics, chemistry, and biology as the minimum basis for medical education and tightening the licensing requirements by the state Boards of Medical Examiners would automatically shrink the number of students and improve quality.

If the proposals in the Flexner Report were taken seriously and were actually carried out, one immediate result would be to wipe out "a thoroughly wretched institution, like the College of Physicians and Surgeons of Boston." Whether even Boston should continue to support two regular schools (Harvard and Tufts) was "decidedly doubtful." The Tufts enrollment, even on the high school basis, was "much swollen." If strict enforcement of even that relatively low standard took place, it would greatly reduce attendance. The school had no resources but fees. Legitimate financial demands for the near future could not possibly be provided from this source alone. The "remarkable prosperity" the school had shown had "depended to no slight extent on the inducement held out by low entrance standards." Its "only hope of escape" lay through endowment so that its laboratories could be developed independently of tuition income and a hospital could be secured. This was an expensive step that would take years to achieve and would still not solve the dilemma of overproduction. There was no alternative, in Flexner's view, but to close out the Tufts Medical School as well as all similar schools in Maine, Vermont, and New Hampshire. There was no good reason, said Flexner, why Dartmouth, Bowdoin, and the University of Vermont should be concerned with medicine at all. He did suggest that the Tufts Medical School be merged with Harvard rather than be as summarily disposed of as the College of Physicians and Surgeons. This might have seemed a less drastic alternative, and at least recognized that there was something worth salvaging, but in any case the Tufts school would have disappeared as an institutional unit.

No one school had been singled out as the target of the monumental Flexner Report. All medical training institutions in the United States were subjected to the same scrutiny and not one escaped criticism of some sort. But no matter how devastating the report might have been, and no matter how many institutions sent out howls of anguish, the intent of the Flexner study was worthwhile. It might be said in historical perspective that the Flexner Report represented what the author himself designated as the third stage in the development of American medical education. As he expressed it, the apprenticeship ("preceptorship") stage had been passed, the didactic method was on its way out, and medical education should be ready for the third step — the recognition of medical training as a "scientific discipline" that took the principle of the first stage, refined it, and added to it half a century of accumulated medical knowledge. The Flexner Report was a conscious attempt to usher in a new era.

Some of the repercussions and reverberations of the Flexner Report were heard and felt at the Tufts Medical School almost immediately; others took longer to show their effects. The implications of the report could not be swept under the rug either at the Boston-based school or by the medical profession at large. Nationally, the impact of the report was explosive. The Association of American Medical Colleges bestirred itself; there was a rush for university affiliation; the number of medical schools declined precipitately.[12] Controversial or not, the Flexner Report had launched a revolution in medical education.

The reactions of Tufts and its medical school staff were varied. Most of the sensitive points in the Flexner Report had already been discussed or had provoked some amount of concern although agreement was not always to be found or to be expected. Probably very few individuals felt as strongly as Edwin Ginn, who served on the Board of Overseers from 1899 to 1907 and was later elected an alumni Trustee. He had been "very doubtful" in 1900 about the advisability of "annexing so many schools when the funds are so limited" and in 1904 had declined to serve on the Board of Visitors

[12] Medical schools had been reduced to ninety-five by 1915, of which sixty-five held a Class A rating. Five years later the total number was down to eighty-five, and in 1927 there were eighty, with seventy-one Class A schools (of which nine taught only the first two years of medicine).

to the dental school, partly because he opposed the affiliation of that and the medical school with Tufts as a matter of principle. "I regard them as a detriment to the College, both as regard standards and also financially."

One prompt reply to the Flexner Report was the resignation of eight members of the medical school staff. Some of the resignations were merely a coincidence so far as timing was concerned, but at least three were not. The disaffected faculty who did depart were led by Dr. Horace D. Arnold, Professor of Clinical Medicine, who had been associated with the school since 1897. He proposed that the entire staff of the medical school be dismissed and that he be made dean with a free hand to reconstruct the whole school. The existing Tufts buildings were to be left for the use of the dental school and students in the first year of the medical school curriculum. Advanced work was to be done at the Harvard school under Harvard instructors. The new arrangement would be known as the Harvard-Tufts Medical School, and Harvard degrees would be awarded to those who could meet Harvard requirements; those who could not would receive Tufts degrees. President Hamilton's reaction to these suggestions was a masterpiece of restraint and understatement; Dr. Arnold's whole proposal was "inadmissible." The Department of Clinical Medicine was to be reorganized (without Dr. Arnold), and clinical facilities could still be maintained at the Boston City Hospital, even without his presence.

The sentiments of Ginn and Arnold were strictly minority expressions. It was up to Dean Williams to voice the views of the majority of the medical school staff and to undertake the none too pleasant task of making some sort of reply to allegations and the factual evidence embodied in the Flexner Report. He devoted parts of several annual reports to the subject. His first reaction was defensive, as it should well have been in view of the fact that the very existence of his school was conceivably at stake. Some of his arguments were well taken while others had an unconvincing ring about them. At least the Flexner Report had prompted some stocktaking. After commenting that the report had been compiled "by gentlemen not physicians, and hitherto professing no knowledge of medical training," he turned immediately to a piece of good news. Simultaneously with the publication of the Flexner Report there appeared a report by the Council on Medical Education of the

American Medical Association based upon an examination of schools by a physician and extending over a period of five years. In the latter report, American medical schools were divided into two classes. Of the 141 examined, seventy-three received a Class A rating. Tufts was among them.[13] In Dean Williams' view, another significant measure of the school's success was the placement record of its graduates. Hospital appointments after graduation were open to students from all schools, on the basis of competitive examinations. Sixty-six per cent of the Class of 1908 had received such appointments, and several individuals had received more than one offer.

The report of the Carnegie Foundation, in Dean Williams' opinion, was "ill-considered and based upon a superficial knowledge of the facts." It would, in his belief, work to the detriment of medical education instead of its betterment. He admitted that the Foundation exerted a great influence, and even some degree of control, particularly over Class A schools. The stiffening of requirements to "an arbitrary standard" would inevitably result in a decline of enrollment in the better schools and an increase in the enrollments of the weaker and inferior schools, to which students would flock who had been refused by the better schools.

Williams countered the allegation that the medical school existed on fees alone by calling attention to the affiliation of the dental and medical schools. This argument was perfectly sound but it proved very little inasmuch as the dental school had no endowment either. He pointed to the fact that both schools were well equipped and well financed. There was a sinking fund of $12,000 and $5,000 in annual income for research (the Johnson Fund). By his reckoning, the income of over $59,000 taken together with the other two items equaled the interest on an endowment of nearly $200,000. The dental school income the same year (1909–10) was over $50,000; its "endowment" (by adding in buildings and equipment) was $48,000; and its sinking fund was $5,000. Large savings were also being effected by combining several branches of medicine common to both schools such as anatomy, physiology, and chemistry, and by using the same laboratories, lecture rooms, and administrative services. This by no means meant that an endowment was

[13] This had followed on the heels of a similar report made in 1908 in which the Tufts school had received a Class I rating — among 64 such schools out of 149 investigated.

unnecessary; on the contrary, it was urgently needed. But the
school seemed to be not only holding its own but attracting increasing numbers of students. One of the greatest deficiencies continued to be a hospital under the direction and general management of the school.

No matter how upsetting the Flexner Report might have been,
there was no sign that the medical school was going to fold up its
tents. The best it could do was to continue on its way, but to recognize the weaknesses made so painfully evident in the Carnegie
study and to try where possible to do something about them. Even
if the Flexner recommendations had not been made, the Tufts
Medical School would have had to do something about admissions
out of self-defense. Bulging enrollments after 1910 made an upward
revision of requirements mandatory. Up through 1909–10, a
diploma from an accredited high school served as a ticket of admission. Beginning the next year, a diploma from a school not listed by
the New England College Entrance Certificate Board was supposedly unacceptable. Examinations were necessary for students
from such schools, and in any case students were required to be
proficient in physics, Latin, and chemistry.[14] A sharp reduction in
enrollment was correctly forecast, although it was a temporary phenomenon. The medical school undoubtedly lost some promising
potential students, as some high schools were not certified because
they had not sent sufficient numbers of graduates to New England
colleges to be entitled to certification by the Board. Graduates of
such schools preferred entering medical schools where their diplomas were acceptable to taking Tufts entrance examinations.

Dean Harold Williams noted with elation in his annual report for 1911–12 the affiliation of a hospital with Tufts. It had been
something long sought, and one of the needs prominently mentioned in the Flexner Report. The acquisition of the facilities of
Grace Hospital on Kingston Street in Boston gave the medical
school direct medical and surgical control over a hospital for the

[14] The medical school faculty struggled for some time over the chemistry
requirement. In the spring of 1910 it was voted that general chemistry be a requirement for admission beginning in 1911–12. But when the time came to put
the requirement into effect, chemistry was put in the Elective rather than the
Required group. The faculty reversed itself in the middle of the academic year
1911–12 and again voted to require chemistry for admission. Biology was similarly required after January 1, 1913.

first time. The use of this fifty-bed institution represented "one of the greatest advances in the history of the school" and even in a few months' time had proved to be "a step of enormous value." Gifts of several thousand dollars had been promised or committed by members of the medical school faculty, alumni, and other friends of the school to assure financial support for a two-year period. The arrangement sounded ideal, but very few people realized either the complicated negotiations that had made the hospital facilities possible or the doubt, hesitation, and trepidation with which the Tufts Trustees had given in to the constant urging of the medical school and to the pressures created by the Flexner Report.

The possibility of obtaining the use of Grace Hospital had been discussed for over a year by the Trustees after the hospital had been placed in receivership. They had been contacted by one of the receivers, who knew that the medical school was in need of its own hospital. The first reaction of the Trustees had been negative, for they had sufficient financial problems to solve without adding another. However, after extended conferences with the receivers, the Administrative Committee of the medical school, and the owners of the property occupied by the hospital, the Trustees reluctantly negotiated a two-year lease (April 1, 1912, to June 1, 1914). In presenting the report on which favorable action was taken by the Trustees, their special committee put their lack of enthusiasm on record. They had been "governed exclusively by what has been represented to us as the 'needs' of the medical school for facilities of this kind." Furthermore, those responsible for the conduct of the medical school and the dental school (which was also to use its clinical facilities) had to have impressed on them the fact that failure to bring and keep their school "within their financial responsibilities" would "make it necessary for the absolute and positive discontinuance of all efforts to maintain directly or indirectly any hospital accommodations." The skepticism of the Trustees as to the workability of the Grace Hospital arrangements was borne out, for the lease was canceled before the two-year period was up. Clinical needs were found to be sufficient through existing channels, and Mt. Sinai Hospital had been added in 1912 to the resources available to Tufts medical students.

The Tufts Medical School continued to pass muster at the hands of various accrediting agencies. It became a member of the

267

Association of American Medical Colleges in 1909, after the curriculum had been reorganized the previous year to provide the 4,000 hours of instruction recommended by the Association. Opportunity for practical training was increased at the same time by allowing hospital work to be counted as a substitute for certain electives. In 1911 the New York State Board of Regents made a very thorough investigation of medical schools in the United States and again put the Tufts school in its "acceptable" class. At the same time, the Council on Medical Education of the American Medical Association published an elaborate study of 116 American medical schools and again listed the Tufts school among the sixty Class A schools. The placement record of graduates of the Class of 1911 was even better than that for preceding years; ten received appointments in much-sought-after posts in the Boston City Hospital. In the opinion of its dean, the medical school was "doing a work of which Tufts College should be proud." He added the usual footnote that if an endowment could be provided, the school could become even more useful.

§ § §

Several other events of importance occurred in the history of the medical and dental schools in 1913 and the years immediately following. After fifteen years' service as the dean of both schools, Dr. Williams retired. He was succeeded by Dr. Charles F. Painter, who had been on the medical school staff since 1897 and was to continue as the dean of both schools until 1917. The medical school had grown sufficiently in numbers and complexity by 1913 to require a reorganization of its internal administration. The staff had been so enlarged, and so many courses and subjects had been added as medicine itself extended its boundaries, that the efficiency of the school's work was being impaired. The result was the division of the medical school into six departments: Medicine, Surgery, Obstetrics and Gynecology, Chemistry, Physiology and Therapeutics, Anatomy and Pathology, and Specialties. Each department had its own organization and provision for frequent consultations of its faculty and staff. Departmental needs were expressed through a Committee on Instruction, on which each was represented. The creation of this body relieved the Administrative Committee of much of the burden of settling purely educational matters and allowed it to concentrate on the business affairs of the school and the activities which required review or action by the Tufts Trustees. The Committee on Instruction met monthly and so made only two regular meetings of the whole faculty necessary each year. Another step was taken to streamline administration in both schools when the office of vice-dean was created in 1914 in the medical school and in 1915 in the dental school. On the recommendation of the Committee of Visitors to the dental school in 1917, the school obtained its own dean, in the person of Dr. William Rice. Dean Painter continued as dean of the medical school only, until 1921.

Of even greater importance in the field of medical education was the decision of the American Medical Association to refuse a Class A rating after 1913 to any school that did not require one year of college work in biology, chemistry, physics, and a modern foreign language. The rapidity of progress in medicine and surgery made the requirement inevitable. Neither the Tufts Medical School nor a majority of medical educators at large were yet prepared to require a college degree as a prerequisite to professional training, although a scattering of institutions had already taken this step before 1913. Whether a full college course was ever to be required or not, it seemed that the time had come for medical schools to turn over training in medical fundamentals to the colleges.

The requirement of a year of college preparatory work made mandatory the establishment somewhere in Tufts of a formal premedical curriculum. There had been concern already expressed about the long and expensive pre-professional and professional training period demanded of potential physicians. The Flexner Report of 1910, which was still very fresh in mind, also had had considerable to say about the proper basis for a medical education. Flexner's conclusions had been inescapable. Such fundamentals as biology, chemistry, and physics could not and should not be taught in the medical school proper. Some sort of preliminary technical education had to be provided, and the college was a more appropriate place for it than the high school. Because of the need for laboratory work, two years rather than one was desirable. This might have been too much to expect at the outset, but at least one year was required by over 80 per cent of medical schools by the time of the First World War; Tufts became part of this statistic.

One year of college work was added to the existing requirements for admission to the Tufts Medical School, beginning with the class entering in 1914. The decision was made only after much debate and questioning spread out over several years, and it was far from unanimous. A factor bringing a resolution to the dispute, which at times reached acrimonious proportions, was the persistent reminder by officers of the American Medical Association that the school's admission requirements were too low and that its Class A standing was in jeopardy.

In the fall of 1906 the medical school had been asked by the Council on Medical Education for its reaction to a proposal to require one year of college after 1910. The committee to which the matter had been referred waited over a year to return a reply, which was negative. The Association of American Medical Colleges had sounded out the medical school on the same question in 1909 and received the same reply, although the medical faculty commented that they would look favorably on a five-year course in the medical school itself. During the previous year the faculty had discussed (but not acted on) a proposal to request the Tufts Trustees to establish a program whereby a student who had successfully pursued a two-year medical preparatory course at Tufts could receive a B.S. degree at the conclusion of two additional years at the medical school and receive the M.D. upon completion of the four-year medical curriculum.

The officers of the Tufts Medical School and the College administration were kept on tenterhooks for most of 1912 by both the Association of American Medical Colleges and the American Medical Association. The former organization had put the Tufts school on its "doubtful" list because it admitted students in direct violation of the requirements of all approved medical schools, as judged by the American Medical Association; because it had no hospital; and because its clinical facilities were inadequate for its size. Throughout all this uncertainty, the medical school managed to hold on to its Class A rating, however precariously.

The question of requiring a preparatory college year received its first full airing in the medical school early in 1913; the resulting faculty report embodied all the arguments that could possibly be marshaled against the proposal. The reasoning went substantially as follows. Although the faculty fully realized the "magnificent work" done by the Council on Medical Education in eliminating poor schools, in raising the standard of entrance requirements, and in improving the standards of medical education throughout the country, it was their opinion that the action of the American Medical Association was "uncalled for and should not have been passed." They thought that it would be "a very serious mistake" to add one year of college work to the existing minimum requirements. One year of such study would not be worthwhile; if the student left at the end of one year, he would receive no diploma. He would simply be abbreviating his college course in order to shorten his medical education. If there was merit in requiring any college attendance at all, it should be at least two years and should terminate with an A.B. or B.S. after four years and an M.D. after six years. No higher education was really necessary for the study of medicine if the requirement of an approved high school education was rigidly enforced. This was not to disparage a college education but to recognize the unfairness of closing the doors of medical education to any intelligent young man who had received a good high school education but who, for financial or other good reasons, could not receive any college training.

The medical faculty reluctantly agreed to abide by the decision to require a year of college and so voted in the spring of 1913. In order to dispel any doubt as to their intention, they voted further that the pre-medical training "shall not be taken in a high school." But the debate was far from over. Dean Williams, for one, was unsympathetic to the change. As he made his last annual report as dean in the fall of 1913, he left the parting warning that a grievous mistake was being made in medical education. He felt that the establishment of higher entrance requirements was not the vital point. It was the results of medical training that were important, not the more or less arbitrary admission requirements, and the Tufts Medical School had an excellent record as a first-class institution. He believed that a high school education was sufficient, that the policy of weeding out weak students at the end of the freshman year was working well, and that many promising candidates for the medical profession would be excluded by summarily raising admission requirements at the demand of an outside agency.

Dean Williams' successor faced a faculty close to rebellion in 1914. The Committee on Instruction called for a full discussion of entrance requirements and suggested the alternative of rescinding or suspending the action of 1913 to require a pre-medical year, or

271

"reserving to the faculty the right to admit any student who satisfies the Committee on Admission, irrespective of whether or not he had fulfilled the one-year college entrance requirement." This gesture of defiance was modified when, after much debate, the faculty voted in May 1914 "that a pre-medical year be established in the school beginning next fall." However, the committee entrusted with the responsibility of presenting a revised set of entrance requirements in line with the faculty vote recommended that they remain unchanged and that the school continue to admit "such students as have had special advantages and possess special qualifications to begin the study of medicine, even though they have not had one year of college work." The persistent reluctance of the medical school faculty to approve the higher entrance requirements was not so much a refusal to recognize that reforms were necessary as a fear of what they might do to enrollment, on which the financial welfare of the school depended. Accompanying their recommendation for a delaying action was a plea for a publicity campaign which would result in an endowment. This, in turn, would make possible a reduction of tuition fees and would to some extent counterbalance the decline of enrollment which the faculty were positive would result from higher admission standards.

Actually, the ingredients of a pre-medical program were already available in the Hill departments of Tufts. The dean of the medical school had pointed out in his annual report for 1894–95 that training in the elementary courses taught in the medical school could be obtained under the supervision of the Department of Biology on the Medford campus. A four-year sequence of courses appropriate for prospective medical school candidates was first listed in the catalogue in 1895–96. While the Flexner Report was in the process of being prepared for publication in 1910, a one-year undergraduate science course was announced in the school of liberal arts. This was intended as an aid for those with insufficient background in subjects such as biology, chemistry, physics, English, or modern foreign languages, and was to supplement and not replace high school preparation. The medical school itself received permission from the Trustees in 1911 to open a summer school in chemistry "for candidates for admission to the medical school."

The next step in the evolution of a formal pre-medical program on the Hill was the adoption of a four-year sequence effective in 1910–11 designed to meet the objection that President Hamilton had voiced earlier, namely, that the training period for the medical profession was too prolonged. In the new program the last year of college coincided with the first year of medical school and enabled a student to earn two degrees in seven years. The first three years, for those entering the medical school by way of an undergraduate program at Tufts, were taken at the Medford campus and the fourth year at the medical school in Boston. The seven-year double-degree program continued as a parallel avenue by which one could enter the medical school after the one-year pre-medical program was instituted in 1914.

Neither Acting President Hooper (who succeeded Hamilton after the latter resigned in 1912) nor Dean Painter took as pessimistic a view as had Dean Williams of the effect of the increased medical admission requirements, although Painter had some reservations. The first-year enrollment in the medical school dropped sharply, as was to be expected, but Hooper sensed greater enthusiasm in the medical faculty, general approval within the medical profession, and more cordial relations between the school and hospitals providing clinical opportunities. As a matter of fact, in 1913 and 1914 the medical school obtained enlarged clinical facilities almost everywhere that connections were being maintained. The most important new clinical asset was the placing in charge of the medical school of an entire fifty-bed ward at the Boston City Hospital. This provided most of the advantages earlier thought to exist by using the Grace Hospital, but with none of the financial responsibilities and perplexities that had beset the Trustees. Increased access to the Robert Brigham Hospital was also obtained, as well as at the newly opened St. Elizabeth Hospital.

One of the firmest statistical grounds for optimism was a rapid rise in enrollment in the so-called "pre-medical year." Seventeen students had been enrolled in the last year of the optional one-year program in Medford in 1913–14, and 102 started out in the new required course. But the brightness of the academic atmosphere was clouded almost immediately when the medical school again ran afoul of the American Medical Association. Unlike the pre-1914 course, the new pre-medical program during 1914–15 was conducted by and at the medical school, where tuition was set at $100. At the close of the academic year the Association directed that the

273

pre-medical school (as it was officially designated) be placed under the supervision of the school of liberal arts. A compromise was worked out so that this requirement was complied with, but the teaching was actually continued on the premises of the medical school. It would have been impossible to conduct the courses on the Hill, for there were no laboratory facilities available for the students that poured into the new program. Chemistry courses were being conducted in a temporary building so inadequate that it attracted the unfavorable attention of faculty, administration, and innumerable Boards of Visitors. At least one advantage was salvaged out of the unusual geographical arrangement: the proximity of the students to the activities and personnel of the medical school exposed them, hopefully, to a professional atmosphere and motivated them to carry on their learning activities with greater industry and enthusiasm than would have prevailed if all of the program had been conducted on the Medford campus.

Throughout the period of rapid change and readjustment in medical education, Dean Painter maintained an attitude of cautious conservatism. While subscribing to all that had been said in favor of properly educated physicians, he thought there was still "reasonable ground for debate" as to whether the new methods were in all respects the best. The worst thing that could happen was to force changes too rapidly. He blamed inadequate preparation by secondary schools for the necesssity of installing a pre-medical curriculum, and state Boards of Examiners for exerting undue pressure to require college preparatory work. He believed that medical schools "should not be stampeded into calling for a two-year college preparation" for entrance to the Tufts Medical School until reforms were brought about in secondary education.

Dean Painter could scarcely have been more correct when in 1914 he included in his annual report the statement that "the last word has not yet been said" as to what was a proper standard of entrance requirement for a medical school or a proper medical school curriculum. After a year of discussion the American Medical Association adopted in 1917 a report of a special committee representing the Association, the Association of American Medical Colleges, and the Association of American Universities to require two years of college. A second year of college would provide opportunity for additional work in mathematics, foreign languages (French or German), advanced chemistry and zoology, and psychology besides the basic biology, chemistry, and physics already required. The Council on Medical Education in 1918 followed the recommendation of the preliminary study and made two years of college work a requisite for a Class A rating.

This new requirement threw the medical school into consternation. It had not yet even had the opportunity to complete the readjustments necessitated by the requirement of one year of preparatory education. It appeared that the school was being discriminated against or at least put at a distinct disadvantage competitively for Massachusetts was not among the thirty-seven states that had required even one year of college when the preliminary report had been made in 1917. Dean Painter accepted the new directive with as much resignation as he could muster and made the pointed remark that he assumed the public from which the medical profession was being recruited were aware of the added time and expense that the new program would entail. The Tufts Trustees made the new requirement for admission to the medical school effective September 1917. The customary loophole was left whereby a high school graduate could demonstrate the educational equivalent by special examination, but students were advised to pursue the full college program if possible. The new two-year pre-medical curriculum required sixty-nine credits, somewhat above the minimum of sixty requested by the American Medical Association. The responsibility for working out the program was placed by the Trustees in the hands of the president, the dean, and the faculty of the school of liberal arts.

Increased requirements or no, the enrollment in both the premedical program and the medical school swelled so rapidly that the staff and the facilities were literally swamped. Even the dislocations of the First World War seemed to have only a small net effect on the growth of both. Overcrowding, overused equipment, and building suffering constant wear and tear became chronic. Even an increase of $25 in tuition in the medical school seemed to make no difference. The medical school enrollment in 1920–21 was 452 and in 1921–22 was 470. The situation was neatly summarized by John A. Cousens, who had assumed the presidency of the College in 1919–20. "The enrollment is too large to be compatible with our ideals of medical education, but is fortunate for financial reasons."

A year later he admitted that the school had been "too large for a long time. . . . I am ashamed to say that this situation has been brought about deliberately with consideration for revenue." There were 281 students in the pre-medical program in 1922–23. Forty pre-medical candidates had to be rejected that year because there was no space for them. Typical was the situation in 1924, when 600 students applied for 145 places in the medical school. As a measure of desperation, the medical school Admissions Committee finally declared that it would accept from the pre-medical department only those candidates who had fulfilled all of the requirements for admission to the Tufts School of Liberal Arts.

One of the reasons for the strain on resources was the introduction of a one-year pre-dental program in January 1921 in compliance with the standards set by accrediting agencies in the dental profession, and in anticipation of a required rather than an optional four-year curriculum in the dental school which was to have gone into effect in 1921–22 but actually became operative in the following year. The pre-dental course was identical with the first year of the pre-medical school, consisting of biology, chemistry, physics, English, a modern foreign language, and mathematics. Like the pre-medical program, the pre-dental course was offered at the medical-dental headquarters in Boston but was under the supervision of the dean of the school of liberal arts. Even though the pre-dental school was opened in the middle of the academic year, there were already nineteen candidates on the waiting list the previous October, and the dental school enrollment correspondingly shot up to 525 in the fall of 1920–21 before the requirement of five years beyond high school was to have gone into effect.

President Cousens told the Trustees in the fall of 1921 that limits on enrollment had to be set until an expansion in physical plant could be provided. The maxima were to be 450 for the medical school, 500 for the dental school, and 400 for the combined pre-medical and pre-dental schools. The enrollment in the medical school the next year was twenty over the ceiling set the previous year and was justified on the ground that the dental school enrollment dropped sharply because of the requirement of one year of college. The "saturation point" in pre-medical and pre-dental enrollment referred to by the president was also exceeded immediately. To make matters more complicated, the requirement of a four-year dental course so drastically reduced enrollment (although temporarily) that the Trustees were informed that it would soon be impossible to finance the dental school. The only alternative that President Cousens saw in 1923 to lowering standards (and automatically losing a Class A rating) was conducting the dental school as a department of the medical school, requiring a two-year program identical with that of the medical school, allowing specialization in dentistry in the last two years, and graduating the students as "dental physicians."

The crisis brought on by the transition to a four-year dental course did not require such a step. Enrollment slowly climbed back to almost normal figures. Meanwhile, the swollen enrollment in the pre-medical and pre-dental courses and in the medical school became a matter of urgency. It appeared, in fact, as though matters had gotten out of hand. The fact that student fees were of "the utmost importance" meant an unfortunate tendency to accept too many applicants. President Cousens, unwittingly or not, put his finger on the basic problem in his annual report for 1924–25. "Emboldened by success in other years," the medical school advanced tuition in 1925 from $225 to $300.[15] The advance, which applied to upperclassmen as well as to entering students, "occasioned no unfavorable comment whatever and has increased the revenue of the school to such an extent that there is a substantial margin of safety as indicated by the budget." In spite of the increase, the number of applicants rose to over 600. This did not necessarily mean that admission standards were disregarded or that the quality of the product of the two schools became an embarrassment to the College. There was such a demand for the products of both medical and dental schools that the mere force of numbers of applicants resulted in a screening process that helped eliminate the weaker candidates. Nevertheless, there was dissatisfaction and concern in many quarters. Because of the very existence of the pre-medical and pre-dental curricula, well over half of first-year medical and dental classes came from the pre-professional programs. In 1922, only 25 per cent of the whole medical school student body held college degrees — far below the national average.

Dr. Stephen Rushmore, who had been associated with the

[15] The net increase was actually only $50, for laboratory fees were abolished simultaneously.

medical school since 1909 and had succeeded Dr. Painter in 1922 as its dean, became one of the most outspoken critics of the situation as it existed at Tufts and in 1927 finally resigned his position in protest at what he considered shortsighted and inexpedient policies. He became increasingly opposed to a two-year pre-medical program. It tended to reduce the number of men taking the four-year degree program in liberal arts colleges; it made for cutthroat competition among students; it exerted unhealthy pressures on those responsible for admissions; and it tended automatically to give preference to Tufts students and to discriminate against or even exclude candidates equally well or better qualified from other colleges and other areas than New England. At the time other professional schools about the country were tending to draw their student bodies from a wider geographical range, Tufts was becoming more and more provincial. True, the reputation of Tufts College as an institution was tremendously enhanced by the presence of the medical school, but the general public was rapidly acquiring the erroneous impression that the College and the medical school were synonymous. Dean Rushmore made constant pleas that the whole pre-medical program be scrapped and that the medical school accept only students who had had an opportunity for three, if not four, years of liberal arts background that would include some introduction to the social sciences and the humanities as well as the basic science courses. The College was not ready for his plan for good and practical reasons. Further, he had raised an issue that transcended Tufts and its financial problems and expressed a philosophy that was by no means agreed upon by the medical profession at large.

The College was able to retain Dean Rushmore's services as long as it did because President Cousens attempted to obtain financial support from the General Education Board, which administered funds allocated by the Rockefeller Foundation for medical education. Some token assistance was obtained on a matching basis, but the long-range proposals made by the Board were completely outside the capabilities of the College. Dr. Flexner, who served as the spokesman for the medical section of the Board during much of the 1920's, conferred with the president and the dean and made suggestions that Cousens described as "Utopian dreams." Flexner told them that he would recommend $5,000,000 in assistance if certain conditions were met. He required an overall plan that in effect would have created a completely new medical school which would be located on the Medford campus and would involve the securing of an endowment of "several million dollars." A special Trustee-medical faculty committee also considered the feasibility of moving the entire medical school to the vicinity of Boston City Hospital. Dean Rushmore favored an eventual move to the Hill campus, which would be, he pointed out, in harmony with national trends. He cited as examples the University of Colorado, Vanderbilt University, the University of Rochester, and the University of Chicago, which had all placed their medical schools on or near their main campuses.

The Board of Visitors to the medical school in 1926 also dealt at length with the problem of location. Existing facilities were notoriously outgrown and inadequate, and the school was not conveniently close to large hospitals that had on their staffs members of the Tufts teaching force. The idea of moving the medical school to the Hill and erecting a modern hospital there was a "magnificent. dream" that would require $10,000,000 to bring into actuality. "We have to deal with the facts as they are and not as we would like to have them." There seemed only one practical course: dispose of the holdings on Huntington Avenue and move the medical school as close as possible to a large hospital. The Boston City Hospital seemed to be the best choice, regardless of whether the dental school was also moved. Even this solution would have involved extraordinary expenses and readjustments; it was also opposed by Cousens, partly on the ground that such a move would mean the abandonment of "all hope that our school shall ever be of absolute first grade."

Dean Frank G. Wren, of the school of liberal arts, who was responsible for the administration of the pre-medical and pre-dental schools, suggested in 1923 that a partial solution to the many problems facing the two professional schools in Boston would be the raising of entrance requirements for the pre-medical program to make them comparable to those of the rest of the College. All that was required was a transcript and certification of graduation from an approved high school; there was no reference to the quality of the work. He was not, however, yet willing to abolish the program or to add or change course requirements that would make the two-year curriculum more difficult. A proposal of the Association of American Medical Colleges in 1925 to raise pre-medical standards did what the College had been unwilling or unable to do. Its recommendations spelled the doom of both the pre-medical and pre-dental programs. The College was informed that the Association's constitution was to be amended to require that all college instruction given to satisfy the requirements for admission to medical school be based on the same entrance requirements and the same quality of work required for the Bachelor's degree in the institution in which the student received his pre-medical training. Dean Wren was prepared by 1926 to recommend not only that this be implemented in the medical school but that the pre-medical program be gradually eliminated as a separate department. He suggested that publicity be given to the seven-year combined course which was still available and which would be a satisfactory way to secure a Bachelor's degree and save one year of preparation.

The medical school Admissions Committee recommended in 1926 that the proposed change be effected. Dean Wren suggested that the requirements go into effect in the fall of 1927, but the medical faculty postponed the effective date until January 1, 1929. This delay came on the heels of an inspection of the medical school by the Council on Medical Education in 1926. The points made in their report were hard to refute: that a two-year pre-medical education failed to equip the student as well as would attendance in a regular college or university, that more and more students were applying to medical schools who already had earned the first degree, and that Tufts College could do well to abandon the special program.

It was at this juncture that Dean Rushmore decided to do battle no longer. He submitted his resignation in 1927. He did not look favorably on the pre-medical curriculum as organized at Tufts and felt that the College had failed to cooperate with both the spirit and the letter of the various professional agencies to which the medical school was accountable. Consequently, the Class A rating of the school had seemed all too often to be hanging by a thread. Endowment and a hospital were still lacking, as every outside accrediting agency had tiresomely reminded him. Every effort to make a change had been an uphill struggle and somehow had seemed to him to stop just short of the goal. He was even more discontented and discouraged that his blueprint for medical education at Tufts, presented in December 1926 and summarized above, had not been translated into action. It seemed to him that the history of the medical school for the twenty years he had been associated with it had consisted of little more than one crisis and one makeshift arrangement after the other.

The history of the one-year pre-dental program since its inception in 1921 had followed a course almost identical to that of the pre-medical school of which it was a part, and admission requirements were the same. The decision was made in the dental school in 1926 to follow the medical school's requirement of two years of college work for admission, effective in 1927. Dean Wren was reluctant to have the requirement go into operation immediately because of the effect it would have on dental school enrollment, and President Cousens considered the new requirement unnecessary.[16] A two-year pre-dental program was arranged, nonetheless, with courses in English and American literature, psychology, elementary economics, and American history and civics intermixed with advanced work in biology and chemistry in the second year.

The problem of what to do about the pre-medical and pre-dental programs was solved by the Trustees in 1927. They seemed to have no other course. They voted to close the two pre-professional programs at the end of the academic year 1928–29. The last entering class (September 1927) was to attend the Huntington Avenue location. Thereafter, all pre-medical and pre-dental work was to be conducted by the liberal arts faculty in Medford, and a course within the school of liberal arts intended for medical and dental students and leading to the Bachelor's degree, if desired, was to be established within the existing framework of the College. The raising of medical and dental school admission standards made the continuance of the separate pre-medical and pre-dental school a needless duplication and a waste of precious resources.

There is little doubt that many of the difficulties surrounding the whole pre-medical and pre-dental experience, and many of the problems of the medical and dental schools, would have been alleviated or would never have risen at all if it had not been for the financial bind in which the College perpetually found itself, and

16 The enrollment in the pre-dental school was 123 in 1925–26.

for the great demand for doctors and dentists. One of the ironies of the situation was the very stature and popularity of the medical and dental schools, for it was in the 1920's in particular that both the reputation and the public image of the College became more firmly identified than ever with its two professional schools in Boston. Few people probably realized the dilemmas, the frustrations, the problems, and even the perils which faced those who were operating a twentieth-century university with the resources of a nineteenth-century college.

9. *A University:* De Facto

TUFTS COLLEGE ROUNDED THE CORNER of the twentieth century with solid accomplishment and with great hope. New men were coming to the fore. In 1901 death removed the senior member of the faculty. John P. Marshall had come to the Hill with the first president, had served temporarily as Ballou's successor, had laid the foundations for the impressive collections of the Museum of Natural History housed in the building donated by P. T. Barnum, and had taught nearly every student who had passed through the doors of the institution in his more than forty years of service. Only one member of the original faculty was still living in 1901; although William P. Drew had severed his connection with the College many years before and was residing in Pennsylvania, he was sufficiently interested to attend Tufts' Commencement exercises that year. He was probably a bit awed by what he saw and heard, for new buildings had sprung up everywhere, the campus had been fenced, many of the elms that he had seen planted as saplings had already attained great size and majesty and gave an air almost of antiquity to the once-barren hilltop. There were 312 students enrolled in the college of letters alone, and no less than 153 degrees were awarded that June day in 1901 as Professor Drew sat in Goddard Chapel — a building strange to him, and already taxed to capacity.

The members of the Board of Overseers looked "with pardonable pride" on the progress of Tufts. Most of them had been out of college long enough to have some perspective, and as the College entered the twentieth century they saw many grounds for congratulation. "In the increase of membership, in the higher standards of admission and graduation, in hospitality toward the changes necessitated by the advance of modern thought and disclosures of mod-

ern research, in elasticity of the conditions of admission and constantly broadening courses of study — we see the proofs of a success
as substantial as it has been surprising." As President Capen noted
with satisfaction in his annual report for 1900–1901, the College
had entered on a period of "substantial and steady growth." This
was most heartening to those who had worked hard and waited
long. The chief concern was that the growth might be too rapid.

Twenty-five years before, Capen had delivered his Inaugural
as the third president of Tufts College. The address was entitled
"The American University," and the major portion of it was devoted to the institution of which he had just been elected the
head. No one had suggested that the charter of the College be
amended to make it into a university; that would have seemed
presumptuous and premature. Yet the transformation of Tufts into
a university in fact if not in name was one of Capen's goals.

> But you will say I am talking all the while of a university,
> when this is only a college. To be sure we have given it in our
> modesty that name. Its chartered rights and therefore its possibil-
> ities in the realm of intellectual culture are as broad as the bound-
> aries of knowledge. . . . The principle, I am sure, is a just one, of
> bringing together in one spot as many colleges as possible. They
> act and react upon one another. Especially does the college proper
> exert an elevating and inspiring influence upon the professional
> school. It awakens within it the philosophic spirit, takes away in
> a measure the commercial and groveling desires which are too apt
> to engross its members, and leads them to regard their vocations
> not as temporary make-shifts by which they are to escape the drudg-
> ery of manual labor and keep themselves and their families from
> want, but as noble avenues through which they are to seize the
> truth and apply it to the necessities of men. It is the college that
> imparts a divine halo to the professions and enables them to be
> classed not as trades, but as liberal arts. Logically, therefore, the
> college precedes the professional school.

Capen called attention to the fact that the American university
was unique in one important respect: it established schools for
professional training under the same governing board as the college. Tufts had already shown that it was entering the mainstream
of university development by creating a divinity school. Other

professional schools were "yet to come. But they are coming, and I devoutly pray that somehow, through the providence of God, my hands may assist in placing their basal stones."

President Capen had reason to view his administration with satisfaction on that count alone. The medical and dental schools were already evidence of a partial realization of the aim of making Tufts more than a college. Some twenty years after he delivered his Inaugural, he was present at the opening exercises of new quarters for the medical school and heard Dr. Ernest W. Cushing, surgeon and gynecologist, make that very point. In referring to "the sagacious liberality of the Trustees of our University," Dr. Cushing said he was using the last word advisedly. With the addition of a school of medicine to its other branches of instruction, Tufts' had "become, and should be called a *university."*

There was even more justification to come in describing Tufts as a university *de facto* in the next decade. The Engineering Department went through such a phenomenal period of expansion that it became the largest undergraduate division on the Hill. Its resources were strengthened by the addition of a preparatory school that gave the College and its administrators a real taste of the problems of operating a university. Almost simultaneously, a graduate school was organized to grant the higher professional degrees becoming so popular and so much in demand in a society of increasing specialization and complexity. Within the same brief period at the turn of the century, the divinity school received its much-sought endowment, and under the name of the Crane Theological School offered augmented resources for the training of clergymen. All four of these institutional ventures at the turn of the century, whether initiated then or built on earlier foundations, proved sufficiently durable to continue into the era after 1954 when the institution had become a university *de jure* as well as *de facto.*

§   §   §

Expanded enrollment and the rapid growth of the sciences and particularly engineering in the late 1880's and early 1890's made additions to the physical plant essential. It appeared that never in the history of Tufts (or of any other college, for that matter) did the provision of buildings quite catch up to the need for

Professors Row in the 1870's

them. President Capen in 1875 had called for more academic facilities and had seen Goddard Chapel, Goddard Gymnasium, and
Barnum Museum rise in the 1880's. He had not called for more
dormitory space, but that was needed before his administration was
ten years old. In 1886 the Executive Committee was authorized
"to erect a dormitory on the lot of land between the houses occupied by Dr. Sawyer and Prof. Dolbear" on Professors Row.
The proposed dormitory was built, but not on the site specified.
Instead, it was erected behind the Goddard Gymnasium. The new
building, of red brick and undistinguished architecture, was intended to house twenty-four students and was named Dean Hall
two months after it was opened in the fall of 1887, in memory of
Oliver Dean, Tufts benefactor and president of the first Board of
Trustees. It served its purpose faithfully until it was razed in 1963
to make way for an enlargement of the Fletcher School of Law and
Diplomacy.

Dean Hall had proved inadequate by 1893, and so the decision
was made to remodel the interior of East Hall and increase the
number of rooms by moving the dining hall to another location. The new Commons Building was constructed at the corner

Dean Hall (later razed) and Goddard Gymnasium
both built in the 1880's

of College and Boston Avenues and was to provide rooms for students as well as the dining room and space for two or three stores. It was here that the Tufts Post Office was located as well as sundry other concessions intended to meet student needs. The building, named in 1904 for James Otis Curtis, Medford shipbuilder and Tufts Trustee from 1856 to 1890, was completed in 1894.

The two most urgent needs for strictly academic buildings in the 1890's existed in chemistry and engineering. Chemistry had expanded to such an extent even by the mid-1880's that the entire first floor of Ballou Hall, with the exception of one room occupied by the Department of Latin, had been turned over to chemistry. The chemistry laboratory had been enlarged sufficiently in the summer of 1890 to accommodate forty-three students, but no more space was available; the "absolute limits" had been reached. There was no other solution than "to erect a temporary structure of wood for a chemistry laboratory." The Executive Committee set a ceiling of $5,000 on construction costs, and the building was ready for occupancy in the fall of 1894. Erected east of Curtis Hall and conveniently close to the engineering school for those taking chem-

Curtis Hall (the "Commons Building") in 1902

istry, it was already so inadequate in 1906 that a Board of Visitors made it a special topic of concern. The president in 1907 called the attention of the Trustees to the fact that the building had served its intended temporary life, that it was in general disrepair, and that a replacement should be built close to Goddard Gymnasium at the earliest possible moment.[1] The "earliest possible moment" was longer than anyone anticipated. The Pearson Memorial Chemistry Laboratory was not completed and dedicated until 1923 and was built a considerable distance from the site originally suggested. In the intervening years the College made the best use it could of its "temporary" building, patched it up constantly, and after 1923 continued to use it for other than science purposes. It was the Music House for many years (until the Cohen Arts Center was provided in 1955) and, because of its location only a few feet from the tracks of the then-busy Boston and Maine Railroad, made a somewhat less than ideal headquarters for musical activities. After serving miscellaneous functions, the old chemistry laboratory became the

[1] The underpinnings had sunk so that the floors were badly out of level, the heating system was almost worn out, and the plumbing was in danger of total collapse at any time.

Research Building in 1963. It was still a multiple-purpose structure in the mid-1960's, seventy years after it had been erected and sixty years after it had supposedly outlived the purpose for which it had been constructed.

The Engineering Department faced the same housing crisis as did chemistry. Ballou Hall toward the end of the nineteenth century was jammed from attic to basement with engineering equipment. Beginning in 1892–93, the engineering curricula (civil and electrical) were extended from three to four years, which increased the number of students in residence accordingly. The introduction of the mechanical engineering course in 1894–95 also aggravated the problem. President Capen urged the Trustees to provide a separate building for the Engineering Department. Facilities on the Hill were so limited and so taxed that the College made arrangements both in 1891–92 and 1892–93 with Rindge Technical High School in Cambridge to offer some of the elementary engineering courses. This setup was "extremely inconvenient" because of the distance from the College. The opportunity to provide "the industrial and technical training now assuming so much importance in education," and at the same time offer many much-needed facilities to the engineering students and afford "some slight relief," came with the settling of the estate of Henry Bromfield Pearson. In anticipation of the Pearson bequest, the College charter was amended in 1890 to authorize the Trustees "to establish and maintain a preparatory school."

Henry Bromfield Pearson had been born in 1795 and had died at his residence in Boston in 1867. He was the son of Rev. Eliphalet Pearson, LL.D., the first preceptor of Phillips Academy in Andover and for twenty years Professor of Oriental Languages and English Literature at Harvard. His mother, Sarah Bromfield Pearson, came from a prosperous mercantile family in Massachusetts. Much of his life was spent at the Bromfield mansion at Harvard, Massachusetts, which had been the home of his parents and of his grandfather, Colonel Henry Bromfield.[2] By good fortune, Rev. A. A. Miner was the executor and trustee of the Pearson estate. He had undoubtedly been instrumental in persuading Pear-

---

[2] The mansion, built in 1733, had been purchased by the family in 1765 and was considered a showplace; it eventually came into H. B. Pearson's possession but was destroyed by fire in 1854.

son to add a codicil to his original will which not only made the College the recipient of part of his estate but included provisions that could be adapted to the special needs of the College.

Pearson was a strong believer in the efficacy of education for both sexes. His original will had provided for the creation of "The Bromfield and Pearson High School for Girls," to be located in the village of Harvard. The school was to be named in memory of three individuals: an uncle, Henry Bromfield; a cousin, John Bromfield; and his father, Rev. Dr. Eliphalet Pearson.[3] The original will was most explicit and detailed as to the type of instruction, regimen, and discipline to be provided in the school, and the reasons he gave therefore shed interesting light on the educational philosophies and practices of mid-nineteenth-century America. As knowledge of the Creator and His works was "the great end for which an institution of learning should be founded," Pearson specified that school exercises each day "should be opened by the reading of some portion of the Gospels of the New Testament, to be followed in every instance by the singing of a hymn from a collection of poetry of a liberal and devotional spirit, and closed by an affectionate and solemn reading of the Lord's Prayer, in which the pupils should have the privilege of uniting when considered desirable. At the end of the day, an anthem in harmony with the opening services, accompanied by the organ shall be sung. . . . At all times the preceptors and teachers in this School should impress upon the pupils committed to their care the principles of piety, virtue and morality, and by their exemplary conduct and judicious counsels, endeavor to persuade them to love and seek after those religious and moral excellencies of character, upon which more than all things else their happiness and usefulness in life will depend."

The College inherited various changes in Pearson's will which were to have an important effect on the future of the proposed school. "The Bromfield and Pearson High School" was to be co-educational, with the expectation that the boys were "to be fitted for college." However, Pearson stressed the point that the original

[3] For biographical data about the Bromfield family see the *New England Historical and Genealogical Register,* Vol. 25 (1871), pp. 334–335; Vol. 26 (1872), pp. 37–43, 141–143. The information about Pearson's plans was derived from extracts from his will.

plan had been for a girls' school, and that the boys were being allowed "in hopes that the girls may derive benefit from the connection." Therefore, the girls were "in no respect to be excluded from or deprived of any of the advantages of education" they would have received under the original plan. It was further ordered "that the boys shall in no cases exceed the girls in number."

The most important provision in the codicil was that the school was to become a part of the assets of Tufts College. The trustee under Pearson's will was directed, after obtaining suitable land and buildings, to turn them over to the Trustees of Tufts College. Any residue of the trust established for this purpose was to be set apart and invested, the income to be used for maintaining and equipping the school. The sum of $10,000 was established as the maximum to be expended for construction of the school, which was to provide facilities for approximately 100 pupils. The College Trustees were given the eventual responsibility of appointing "the principal teacher in said school" as well as administering and governing it. The staff of the school (both "male and female") was to be appointed by the principal, subject to the approval of the Trustees.

The first step to make the Bromfield-Pearson School a reality was taken in the spring of 1893 with the sale by the College of a parcel of land east of College Avenue to the trustee of the Pearson estate. The land was "sold" for $16,000 and this amount was immediately turned over to the Pearson estate "to aid in the erection of the Pearson School." This piece of bookkeeping was accomplished in order to further "certain interests of the College" which would "be thereby promoted." It also enabled the College to retain the approximately $65,000 of the Pearson estate virtually intact and at the same time provide for the possibility that construction of the building would cost more than Pearson had originally envisaged. By the summer of 1893 construction was well under way, and Gardner C. Anthony of Rhode Island had accepted the headship of the new school, with the understanding that he would also hold a professorship in the College without salary and would be dependent for his compensation on the proceeds of the school. Both the construction of the building and the negotiations with Anthony were initiated by Miner, as trustee of the Pearson estate. A careful reading of the will, however, disclosed that the choice of a head for the school devolved upon the Tufts Trustees, for the authority of the trustee under the Pearson estate ended as soon as the building was completed and turned over to the College. In addition, several matters of interpretation of the amended will left the Trustees in some doubt as to their responsibilities. Most important, the Trustees were determined, if possible, to turn the new school into a technical institution without violating the provisions of the will. So they petitioned the Supreme Judicial Court of Massachusetts for a series of rulings based on a six-point proposal and obtained what they desired.

The new institution was to be a secondary school, "to be open with equal privileges to young people of either sex," although the Court agreed that "neither girls nor boys shall be excluded from the advantages of education therein by reason of the excess in said school of either number." Compensation for the teachers was to be provided from tuition fees, or any other sources considered appropriate by the Trustees. Instruction was to be given "in elementary mathematics, ancient and modern languages, theoretical and practical science, mechanical and other drawings, music or other branches of study, literary or scientific, useful or ornamental, from time to time taught in the higher seminaries in the Commonwealth." The emphasis on scientific subjects and the vagueness about other areas was consonant with the plan approved by the Court, which ruled that the will and codicil, "constructed together," gave the College authority to operate the school so as to "substantially accord with the desires of the testator . . . which desires concerning such instruction, discipline and conduct are suggestive but not controlling upon the judgment and discretion of said Trustees of Tufts College." No doubt was left in the public's mind as to the purpose of the new school, for less than three months after its opening it was being referred to by President Capen as "The Bromfield-Pearson Technical School," in which "all the drawing and shop-work of the engineering courses will be given. . . . In addition to this, there will be courses preparatory alike to the engineering department, and to the various technical employments." [4]

The intent of the Trustees in establishing the new school may have been clear, but the organization and administration of

[4] "The Making of a College," *To-Day,* Vol. 1 (January 1894), p. 40.

it were another matter. What should be its relation to the College? Should there be both a dean and a principal? What kind of financial arrangements were to be made? The College had never before faced the problem of including a secondary school under its wing, and certainly not one with such a frankly vocational objective. A special Trustee committee appointed in the spring of 1893 to draw up plans for the new school were still divided over certain matters when decisions were finally made in October. The committee agreed that the school was a separate institution; but, because it was under the management of the Trustees, was located on the Hill, and "the condition exists that there will be more or less interchange of instruction between the School and the College," the relations between the two would, by their very nature, be close. It was the degree of integration that was in question. Trustees Miner and Robinson, the minority, argued that a dean should be appointed who would serve as the "principal teacher" for three years, receive and expend all fees, nominate staff members, and in general be totally responsible for the administration of the school, operating through a Trustee committee. The majority of the special committee, however, felt that the relationship of the two institutions should be closer; that because the Pearson will provided for a principal, the president of the College should serve in that capacity (without extra compensation); and that if the Trustees wished to appoint a dean he should be under the supervision of the president, as well as subject to the Trustees. If the dean should be made responsible for the finances of the school, it should be for one year only, on an experimental basis. The entire committee agreed that the dean should also hold a position in the College (without extra stipend) and that reciprocal enrollment privileges should be allowed students, with a financial adjustment at the end of each academic year.

Anthony was duly employed as Professor of Technical Drawing in the College (without compensation) in the fall of 1893 and served as *ad hoc* dean of the Bromfield-Pearson School until February 1894, while President Capen served as principal. But less than three months of experience indicated that administrative adjustments were needed. Anthony, who had actually taken over his responsibilities in July so that the school could be opened in October, found himself deluged with students from the College.

By December 1893 he was teaching as well as supervising eighty-six men in the Department of Drawing nineteen hours a week, with only seven hours of assistance from the Engineering Department. In addition, sixty-five students in engineering descended on him to do shopwork. The fourteen entering Bromfield students, to be the sole source of his income at a fee of $30 per quarter, brought him less than $1,700, out of which he was to pay all the expenses of the school. He contended that it would be "disastrous" to the interest of the school if an attempt were made to separate the two institutions. Further, a decrease in salary as compared to his employment before he came to Tufts, besides his unexpected teaching and administrative burdens, made him reluctant to continue unless the Trustees assumed complete operation of and responsibility for the school and employed a dean to act for the Trustees. The Trustees saw the predicament and promptly made new arrangements. The conduct of the school was assumed by the Trustees; Anthony was made dean, but was no longer responsible for the school's income and liabilities, and was to receive a salary as teacher in Bromfield-Pearson, with additional remuneration for the deanship. The latter was to be paid out of school revenue. The by-laws of the Trustees were amended to provide a five-man Trustee committee, including the president of the College, to have ultimate responsibility for the school, to act as a liaison body between the dean and the Trustees, and to submit periodic reports. Although reference was made to a principal for the school, no separate appointment was made to this post. The president of the College continued to hold his honorific office and made, through the Trustees, the necessary staff appointments in the school. All diplomas were to be signed by the dean and the secretary of the Trustees. The original staff included Frank T. Daniels, Instructor in Drawing; William H. Detwyler, Tutor in French; George H. Furbish, Teacher of Woodwork and Foundry Work; and Frank G. Wren, Tutor in Mathematics.

The Bromfield-Pearson High School was housed in a substantial three-story red brick building that presided in lonely splendor over a dense growth of bushes through which students made a path down from College Avenue. Although not yet finished inside, and far from completely equipped, the building was opened for use in October 1893. None of the upper flooring was laid, and much of the plastering remained to be done. The shops were not ready for use until the beginning of the second term, and preparations required working nights and Sundays in January 1894. When completed, facilities were provided for classes of fourteen to eighteen students in carpentry, pattern-making, forging, and foundry and machine work. The drafting rooms, which could accommodate over fifty students, were on the third floor, separated from the noise and vibration of the shops; light was provided by large skylights. A very busy dean presided over this establishment. By January 1894 he was responsible for the work of 172 students from the College and for direct teaching of about thirty hours per week. He described his position as "not an enviable one."

President Capen felt assured that the school would "be successful from the start" and that it would "fill an important place in our educational scheme." The facts seem to bear this out. At the outset, two programs were offered: a preparatory course for those qualified by previous education and maturity to enter the Engineering Department after one year of additional preparation; and a special engineering course for those able, for financial or other reasons, to devote only two years to formal instruction, and whose previous preparation was insufficient to enable them to enter the College. It was "not the object of the school to produce expert engineers or skilled draughtsmen, but to give such direction to the thought and afford such training in theory and practice as is requisite to every successful engineer." Unlike the College proper, the Bromfield-Pearson School followed the quarter system when it opened, and hence operated during most of the summer.

Before the school opened, a manual training course had been advertised, but it was abandoned in favor of a one-year preparatory course which it was thought would not only simplify administration and decrease expenses but open up "a unique and important field in preparatory work." The preparatory course, spread over four quarters, consisted of "academic" algebra, plane and solid geometry, arithmetic, French, English, and freehand drawing, with mechanical drawing elective for the first two quarters and required the third quarter; during the fourth quarter, trigonometry could be substituted for mechanical drawing. Sufficient instruction was given in mathematics, English, and French to enable the students to pass the College's entrance examinations. Properly prepared students could also pursue some of the basic College courses and thereby shorten their engineering program if admitted to Tufts.

The special engineering course was more intensive than the preparatory course and included mechanics, machine drawing, advanced algebra, spherical and descriptive geometry, differential and integral calculus, and three quarters of elective shopwork in the second year. The program was so arranged that students completing the first year or first part of the second year of this curriculum could be transferred to the College course without completing the two-year course. This was made easier by the fact that school and College students attended the same classes in most instances. Beginning in 1894–95, students in the second year of the special courses were allowed to elect College classes in either physics or chemistry.

Admission to courses in either program was in effect left up to the individual instructor, who could accept certificates from other schools or employ written or oral examinations. No diplomas or degrees were conferred, but Certificates of Proficiency were issued upon completion of either program. There was considerable interchange of students between the school and the College from the very beginning. Instruction in drawing and shopwork for all members of the Engineering Department brought part of the College to the school. In addition, engineering instructors promptly referred to the school those students considered deficient in basic engineering subjects. Before the end of the first year of operation, eight Bromfield-Pearson students were attending classes in the College, and three from the College had transferred to the school. Almost all of the students enrolled in elementary French in the preparatory course in 1893–94 expected to enroll in the College the following year. Many College facilities, including the gymnasium, the library, and various lecture series, were open to Bromfield-Pearson pupils. Dean Anthony, reviewing the work of the first year, felt confident that new educational ground was being broken, for the school was not simply "a new department in the College, but rather a new departure in preparatory and technical education." Most certainly, the school had departed markedly from the path that Henry Bromfield Pearson had originally marked out for it.

The Bromfield-Pearson School continued to exist into the

1960's although it enrolled in any one year only a handful of students.[5] It was officially listed in the 1960's as an institution "associated with the College of Engineering" intended to meet the needs of "a restricted group of young men who have spent a considerable time in practical work of an engineering character." The school maintained Henry Bromfield Pearson's original intent that it be a preparatory school, for enrollment in the school was for two terms only, and those who met the prescribed conditions were accepted by the College of Engineering as sophomores in regular standing at the end of the second term.[6] The close relationship between Bromfield-Pearson and Tufts existing at a later day had already been recognized in 1895 when the Trustees agreed that there was no need to keep separate accounts "in view of the commingling, and in many respects the identity, of interests between the school and the College." Historically, the school served a useful purpose by providing "a fitting school for the College," by furnishing desperately needed facilities for the engineering school in a period of rapid growth, and by enabling competent students who might otherwise have been lost to the College to make up deficiencies.

The Bromfield-Pearson School gave "some slight relief" to the housing problems of the engineering school, as President Capen had expressed it, but they were far from solved. In 1899, laboratory equipment for mechanical engineering was housed in two rooms in the cellar of Ballou Hall. They were badly lighted, without ventilation, and unheated, and in wet weather water frequently percolated through the foundation walls and settled in pools on the floor to such a degree that students were obliged to stand on boards or to wear boots. There was concern lest the whole mechanical engineering curriculum introduced only five years earlier might have to be abandoned if adequate staff, equipment, and space were not provided. There had been one glimmer of hope in 1894 when Mrs. Rebecca T. Robinson had offered $40,000 to erect a building

[5] The peak of enrollment had been twenty, in 1903–4; of these, fifteen entered the engineering school.

[6] The authorization for a one-year college preparatory course was given in 1894, but the two-year program remained officially available until 1904. The latter was abandoned when Dean Anthony pointed out that most of the students were qualified to transfer to the engineering school before the two years had elapsed.

"for giving technical training in engineering," to be known as the "Robinson Scientific School." The committee to whom the proposal was referred was hesitant to accept the gift because of the commitments it would entail. Such a sum was not considered adequate to construct an engineering building, the Trustees were in no position to contribute out of the College's strained resources, and the building would mean an estimated extra expense of $4,000 annually. They were also reluctant to accept an offer that might involve the establishment of another separate school. Mrs. Robinson's intention was to superintend personally the erection of "a building which would be worthy of the memory of her husband."[7] The Trustees agreed to construct the building, but were so dilatory that Mrs. Robinson's son (and attorney), Sumner Robinson, who had been elected a Trustee in 1892, warned that she was becoming impatient, and the College might receive nothing if construction were not started. Nothing was done during her lifetime, and in 1899 the needs of the engineering school were so urgent that an inquiry was made of her heirs to see if the offer was still open. By good fortune it was, and the Trustees agreed to spend $37,500 for a building. Neither the architect's fees nor the cost of a heating system were originally included. After the building was completed, makeshift heating was to be provided from the Bromfield-Pearson School.

The denizens of both Robinson and Bromfield-Pearson must have lived a Spartan life when using the two buildings, for the boiler in the latter was too small to service both buildings simultaneously and steam heat had to be furnished first to one and then to the other. The new building, although wired for electricity when constructed, was not connected at first with a commercial power line, and gas was piped into all rooms to furnish what artificial light existed. These somewhat primitive arrangements were not due to faulty planning or an attempt to reduce expenditures to zero, but to the fact that for some years a central heating and power plant for the campus had been hoped for, provided that

---

[7] Charles Robinson, who died in 1890, had been elected a Trustee in 1857 and after the death of Israel Washburn in 1883 had served as president of that body. He was a prominent attorney and served as legal adviser to the College (without charge) for many years; he was also counsel for several benefactors of the institution.

*The old combined foundry
and heating plant (later razed) and Robinson Hall*

the necessary $25,000 could be found. In the 1890's, the electrical engineering students received a goodly taste of practical experience and the satisfaction of knowing that they were contributing to the needs of the College, for their department until 1899 furnished light for both the library (Middle Hall) and Goddard Chapel.[8] The students of the Class of 1896 designed and partly constructed a 150-light dynamo capable of servicing the entire Bromfield-Pearson School. When Robinson Hall was completed, the Trustees appropriated a small sum to construct a temporary heating plant for the two buildings which was also to serve "for furnishing the necessary power to be used in said buildings for purposes of instruction." Fortunately, a gift to the College of about $8,000 from Ephraim Howe made possible something less modest than had been originally planned. Because the frame and stuccoed structure that was built in 1901 was to serve a double purpose, it was named the Howe Memorial Laboratory. The storage batteries and other equipment crowding Ballou Hall were moved to the new structure near the engineering buildings, and by 1904 an addition had been built to

[8] These were connected to the lines of the Somerville Light Company in 1899.

house the forge and foundry equipment originally located in Brom-field-Pearson. The "temporary" Howe Memorial Laboratory served many a heating, lighting, and instructional purpose until it was dismantled in the winter of 1960 when Anderson Hall, the new addition to the engineering complex, was completed.

As the Engineering Department grew from a handful of students and faculty occupying various corners of the then-unnamed College Edifice in the 1870's and 1880's to a school with over 100 students in new quarters in Robinson Hall, the Bromfield-Pearson Building, and the Howe Memorial Laboratory, there was a noticeable tendency for it to drift away from the so-called "academic" department. Matters concerning engineering coming before the general faculty were increasingly turned over to those teaching in the department. At first (in 1894) they comprised a standing "Committee on Engineers," but major policy decisions, including curricular concerns, were determined by the whole faculty. A school of engineering was formally created in 1898, with a dean (Gardner C. Anthony) and administrative board drawn from the engineering faculty.[9] The board was to formulate policies with the advice of the faculty of the college of letters on all matters affecting candidates for the Bachelor of Science degree in engineering excepting the conduct and dismissal of students. These remained under the control of the faculty of letters until 1903. The engineering faculty obtained even more autonomy over its own immediate concerns when the Faculty of Arts and Sciences was created in the fall of 1902 and the engineering faculty became a constituent body. Thereafter, only engineering matters having to do with administration affecting more than one of the Associated Faculties came before the parent group.

Simultaneously, course by course, the engineering students were separated from their fellow students in liberal arts. Part of this tendency to go separate ways was prompted by the growth of enrollment and the increase in the size of classes which necessitated division into sections. Part was due to the heightened awareness that the professional needs of the engineering students were different from those in the liberal arts curricula. The first separation oc-

9 However, it continued to be called interchangeably a "Department" in the official records until 1908.

curred in the basic mathematics courses, in which separate sections were created for "academic" and engineering students. Then came the division of the classes in French, and in 1903 the sections in the basic English course were likewise separated. The Department of Economics, created in 1902–3, started its career by segregating the engineers enrolled in Political Economy. Some liaison was briefly retained with the English Department, for much of the written work of the engineering upperclassmen was submitted to it for criticism. However, the engineering students were assigned their own English instructor, Professor Samuel C. Earle. As a member of the engineering faculty he attempted to impress on his students the importance of literate communication in general and in technical subjects in particular.[10] All the courses in French and German for freshman engineers were transferred to the jurisdiction of the engineering school Department of English in 1912–13. Dean Anthony justified this segregation of courses by insisting that the maximum cooperation and coordination was "rarely, if ever, accomplished between schools having very divergent methods and ideals." It appeared that liberal arts and engineering were two quite different species.

The only prescribed courses shared by the liberal arts and engineering students in 1903 had been the elementary courses in physics, chemistry, and German. President Capen was perturbed because it appeared that the engineering students were being trained in a narrower and narrower sense, and that the department was turning into a quasi-independent professional school. Dean Anthony also recognized this trend and told the Tufts College Club of Boston that he believed it "to be contrary to the desires of those who are entrusted with the administration of the department, and against the best judgment of the alumni." Yet Tufts was not alone, and over the years Dean Anthony changed his own viewpoint. The engineering school was being caught up in a nation-wide inclination to separate liberal arts and professional education. While on one hand there was pressure to reduce the time required for the

[10] The Tufts policy of teaching English to engineers was so successful that in 1913 the English Department of the engineering school was asked to recommend candidates for five positions in engineering schools outside of New England.

A.B. degree, engineering education was veering in the opposite direction. Because of the steadily rising standard of academic expectations and increased degree requirements it was becoming more and more difficult for the engineering student to complete the prescribed work in four years.

Dean Anthony had no simple or magic solution to offer, but he did suggest that the "academic" man needed to be led "to appreciate the educational value of technical subjects." One alternative discussed and tried briefly before the First World War was a combined liberal arts and technical program leading to the simultaneous award of the A.B. and B.S. degrees after five years. The experiment itself lasted only five years (1904 to 1909). In order to obtain both degrees the student had to offer a unit of credit in solid geometry for admission and choose engineering as his major department at the end of the freshman year. English, foreign languages, physics, and mathematics comprised the program of the first year, with history and philosophy intermixed with mathematics, shopwork, and drawing in the second year. The last three years of the sequence corresponded to the specific course in engineering elected by the student. Dean Anthony was never enthusiastic about the combined program and did not mourn its departure. It had appealed to too few students and was discontinued because it failed to provide for a unified technical training such as he had in mind. If there was to be any coordination or articulation, he thought it should be within the Engineering Department itself. The combined liberal arts-engineering degree program reappeared in substantially the same form approximately half a century later, and with the same appeal to only a small number of students.

Many aspects of the history of the engineering school from 1900 to the First World War bore a disturbing resemblance to the careers of the medical and dental schools. Enrollments increased beyond a realistic capacity to handle them; endowment, which was called for periodically after 1890, never materialized, and tuition became completely inadequate to finance the school even though it was raised more than once; the engineering profession grew so rapidly that almost without exception there were more requests for graduates of the school than could possibly be furnished; the faculty and other academic resources were so badly strained that morale dropped to the danger point and President Hamilton, for one, had to make plea after plea to the Trustees for assistance.[11]

Statistics told their own story. One of the most spectacular increases in enrollment in the College's history occurred in the Engineering Department. There were twenty students enrolled in engineering in 1887–88; a decade later, there were seventy-one. Enrollment in electrical engineering alone by 1894 had "nearly submerged" the Physics Department. In 1902–3 Dean Anthony argued that accommodations were adequate for a total engineering student body of 150. Yet in 1904 there were 187 enrolled. By constant rearrangement of offices, laboratories, and classrooms, student capacity was somehow increased, but the department had become so understaffed by 1905–6 that there was talk of abandoning the requirement of senior theses because most of them called for the construction of machinery or equipment for which there was no room. Serious consideration was given to abandoning the chemical engineering program, even though overflow quarters for lectures had been temporarily provided in Curtis Hall.

Both a special Trustee committee and the engineering faculty agreed that the best way to hold down the snowballing enrollment was to raise standards of admission. This was accomplished in part in 1907 by providing that all candidates for the Bachelor of Science in Engineering had to offer the same subjects for admission as the A.B. candidates except advanced work in an ancient language. The minimum graduation requirement for engineers was made ten credit hours greater than for A.B. candidates. The faculty also cut drastically the number of students allowed to be admitted with "conditions" of various sorts. The changes had some of the effect desired, for the faculty was both adequate and reasonably balanced in 1908 for the first time in many years, and the threat of faculty resignations was averted by salary increases ranging from $200 to $400. The increments were made possible by a vigorous and successful campaign by Professor Hooper to collect $1,700 from engineering alumni to tide the school over a serious crisis. Even with stricter entrance requirements, the sophomore class was so large in 1908–9 that a special summer school course in surveying was offered

[11] Tuition was increased to $150 beginning September 1906, over Dean Anthony's protest. It was raised again (to $175) in 1912–13.

to relieve the congestion in the regular term. The summer school was also offered in 1910 but had to be abandoned because of "limited income and insufficient teaching force."

Annual engineering enrollment until the First World War continued to be maintained slightly beyond the maximum of 200 that Dean Anthony thought the accommodations would allow by then. The hopes for a smaller student body after 1916 were counterbalanced by the departure of many of the faculty for military service. Even in 1915–16, academic housing was in such short supply that classes had to be held in the evening, and the once-sacred noon hour had to be desecrated with instructional activities. One English section had to meet in the pattern shop, and another recitation met in the hydraulic laboratory. As Dean Anthony stated the problem, "such arrangements are not conducive to the most efficient work and emphasize our great need of buildings and equipment if any further growth of the school is to be permitted." Turning a college into a university by expanding professional schools was no small matter.

The story of the Tufts Engineering School was not all grim and crisis-ridden between 1900 and 1916. The increased offerings after 1890 gave a great impetus to the growth of the department and helped heighten its reputation as an excellent training facility. Between 1893 and 1913, 430 engineering degrees were granted, representing over 80 per cent of the total awarded since 1869. Seventy per cent of the engineering alumni were engaged in the profession for which they were trained. Civil and electrical engineering led the list, and a respectable portion of the total graduate body were in positions of influence and responsibility in business and industry.

The engineering faculty were especially active in professional affairs and made a conscious effort to keep abreast (or ahead) of what other institutions were doing. In 1907 the custom was started of making an annual appointment from the faculty to serve as a "visiting delegate" to other schools. Tours covered the Middle West as well as the Atlantic seaboard, and the engineering school became through this channel "more widely known than by any other agency save that of its alumni." One by-product of these institutional visits was the election of several members of the engineering faculty to important posts in engineering organizations.

One became chairman of the Boston Section of Electrical Engineers and two others held high offices (including the presidency) of the Society for the Promotion of Engineering Education. Dean Anthony served on a joint committee of the Society and the Carnegie Foundation to make a nation-wide study of technical education comparable to the studies made or contemplated in the fields of medical and dental education. Professor Earle served on the Society's Committee on the Standardization of Engineering Nomenclature. It was on the initiative of another member of the engineering faculty that joint meetings were held in 1910 of the Boston Society of Civil Engineers and the engineering societies at Harvard, the Massachusetts Institute of Technology, and Tufts, to coordinate the interests of the profession and the schools. Cooperation between practicing engineers and technical school undergraduates was also fostered by engineering competitions, in many of which Tufts students excelled.

The curriculum of the engineering school was under continuous scrutiny by the faculty, and several studies were made of ways to improve technical education. Until 1909–10, the subjects of instruction during the first year were common to all four branches of engineering offered by the school, and consisted of English, a modern foreign language (French or German), drawing, mechanic arts, mathematics, and physics. The civil engineering course proved so popular that an optional curriculum was established, beginning in 1910–11, in structural engineering, although still leading to the degree in civil engineering. The entire curriculum reflected a large amount of prescription. A total of 140 credits was required for graduation, and the schedule was considered a demanding one, at least by the students. In 1905 the engineering faculty received a petition from virtually the whole student body requesting a longer period in which to take final examinations, "and in no case be required to take more than one examination during the same day." The faculty delayed their decision for a semester, but acquiesced. A curriculum common to all specialties was extended to two years in 1910–11 and included chemistry in the sophomore year. It was this requirement that placed such an unusual strain on the laboratory facilities in that subject and evoked the reiterated pleas for a new chemistry building.

As the First World War became imminent, the engineering

school launched the most comprehensive inventory of itself it had ever undertaken. Standards of scholarship, the curriculum, and the whole matter of the responsibility of the school to the community were among the topics reviewed by eight committees. The exigencies of war and the fundamental nature of the changes and policies considered in the self-study delayed the new program until after 1918, but there seemed to be little doubt that the Tufts Engineering School was making a substantial contribution both academically and professionally.

§   §   §

What is usually considered graduate work began at Tufts in 1876, with the accession of President Capen and the announcement that the Master's degree would no longer be given "in course" in accordance with time-honored usage. This seemingly innocuous statement meant more than it appeared to. It actually represented both a step in the direction of the modern concept of the earned graduate degree and a clarification of College policy regarding the whole subject of academic degrees. It was the occasion to review not only earned and honorary degrees but also a third category of Tufts degrees — neither earned nor honorary — that was awarded between 1861 and 1878 and had by the late 1870's apparently outlived any purpose it might have served.

In 1860–61 Tufts had joined the ranks of the majority of collegiate institutions by offering what for want of a better designation might be called the "unearned M.A.," although the euphemistic and somewhat misleading designation "in course" was often used. The requirements were minimal, the number of recipients impressive. It was provided that the degree of Master of Arts would be conferred on any alumnus who had been a holder of the Bachelor of Arts degree from Tufts for at least three years; had, in the interval, "sustained a good moral character"; and had paid a fee, including the diploma, of $5.00. The fee was payable (in advance) upon application to the president at least one week before Commencement.[12] Various explanations have been offered for the widespread practice illustrated by Tufts' policy before 1876. Systematic graduate study,

[12] The definitive work on the whole subject of degrees is Walter C. Eells and Harold A. Haswell, *Academic Degrees* (Washington: United States Department of Health, Education, and Welfare, Bulletin 1960, No. 28).

patterned to a large extent on German models, was not introduced into American higher education until after that date.[13] The Master of Arts "in course" was offered as a sort of substitute. Possibly colleges desired to have graduates reminded of their academic training or connection. Any degree beyond the first was considered to have real value in the professions; it had built-in prestige. President Charles W. Eliot of Harvard is said to have made the facetious (or cynical) comment that the requisites for the distinction of receiving an M.A. degree "in course" were "five dollars and continued existence." Tufts awarded seventy-three such degrees between 1861 and 1876, spread occupationally over most professions but with the preponderance going to teachers and clergymen. One attempt was made in 1870–71 to make the "unearned" M.A. a bit more meaningful by requiring "satisfactory evidence of having successfully pursued some professional or literary study." This was presumably to be determined by the president of the College, but there is no indication that any systematic attempt was ever made to implement it. Each such degree, however, was voted by the faculty and was usually followed by authorization from the Trustees.[14]

President Capen felt very strongly that all degrees conferred "in course" by the College should be truly earned. The M.A. "in course" was particularly offensive to him. He considered it a step forward, therefore, when the faculty voted to inaugurate a new M.A. program which required the following of a prescribed course in at least two departments for at least one year, the required attainment to be ascertained by examination. The new program, effective in 1876–77, was open to graduates of other schools whose courses of study were equivalent to those for which the same degree was given at Tufts. In order that no injustice be done those who were already members of the College, the faculty agreed to continue until 1878 to recommend M.A.'s under the old condition. In making the M.A. an earned degree, the College was indicating its "em-

[13] See W. Carson Ryan, *Studies in Early Graduate Education* (New York: Carnegie Foundation for the Advancement of Teaching, Bulletin No. 30, 1929). This work describes in detail the pioneer contributions of the Johns Hopkins University, Clark University, and the University of Chicago.

[14] Typical of the working of the system was the vote in 1874 "to recommend the conferring of the degree of A.M. in course to such eligible candidates of the Class of '71 as may apply." Three such degrees were awarded under this vote.

phatic approval" of similar measures already taken "by a few of the leading Institutions of the country." Approval of the new policy had already been expressed, for applications had been received from graduates of other colleges, and even some Tufts alumni had proposed to become candidates, feeling as they did that the degree as formerly conferred "was not worth even the five dollars required for the diploma."

Like other educational institutions, Tufts began the practice of awarding honorary degrees almost immediately after it was chartered, and individuals associated with the College both before and after its establishment have received a goodly share from other colleges and universities as well. Again following long-standing practice, any recipient of an honorary degree from Tufts automatically became an alumnus or alumna of the institution. Universalist leaders had been greatly pleased in 1845 when Harvard conferred an honorary D.D. on Hosea Ballou 2d. A writer in the *Trumpet* had been so bold as to suggest that, since a precedent had been established, there were great numbers of other deserving Universalists who might also be honored. Such unbridled enthusiasm was not unanimous, however. One of the very men suggested for such an honor objected strenuously to the whole idea of conferring honorary degrees — particularly D.D.'s — on anyone. The gesture might appeal to one's ego, but the degree was meaningless in substance, pretentious, and did not in any way "add to a man's talents, his learning, his piety, or any other good thing in his character; nor does it fit him to discharge the duties of his office with more ability, zeal, and fidelity." To make matters worse, requesting the bestowal of an honorary degree for anyone sounded like begging for honors — not a very upright thing to do.

President Capen expressed himself as forthrightly about the granting of honorary degrees as he had about unearned M.A.'s. No academic practice, he thought, had been so much abused as the granting of such degrees on the slightest provocation, and without any evidence of actual scientific or literary attainment.

The lavish manner in which such titles have been distributed among well-meaning dunces, has exposed our American institutions to ridicule among all who believe that learning is the very last province which shams and charlatans should be permitted to invade. The sooner, therefore, all degrees, even the higher ones of Doctor of Philosophy, Doctor of Divinity, Doctor of Laws, etc., shall be based upon actual attainment, to be ascertained, in all cases, by competent and impartial examiners, the better will it be, not only for our reputation at home and abroad, but for sound learning and genuine culture.

He thoroughly approved of the conservative policy so far pursued by the College in limiting its honorary degrees to those only who "were eminently worthy to receive them."

Tufts awarded its first honorary degree (Doctor of Divinity) in 1858 to Thomas Whittemore as the highest tribute the College could bestow on one of the men instrumental in bringing it into existence. The first honorary Master of Arts was bestowed the following year. The largest number of honorary degrees in the early history of the College went to Universalist clergymen, although they were more likely to receive M.A.'s than D.D.'s.[15] Several members of the faculty, such as Benjamin Graves Brown and Moses True Brown, also received honorary degrees from the institution in the nineteenth century. Rev. Charles H. Leonard, first Goddard Professor of Theology when the divinity school was opened in September 1869, was voted an honorary M.A. in August, and a special Trustee meeting had to be hastily called to approve the faculty action. The first LL.D.'s were awarded in 1872. Some individuals, including faculty members, received two or more honorary degrees from Tufts. Arthur Michael, a pioneer organic chemist who had attended several institutions in Europe but never received an earned degree, was given an honorary M.A. from Tufts in 1882 and in 1890 an honorary Ph.D., one of seven such degrees awarded by Tufts in the 1890's, when the practice was widespread among other institutions. William Leslie Hooper, of the Class of 1877, long-time member of the Engineering Department and acting president of the College between 1912 and 1914, received an honorary Ph.D. in 1898 and an LL.D. in 1915. Most benefactors of the College, as well as men who became its presidents or were especially active on the Board of Trustees, were likewise recognized by honorary degrees of some sort.

After the medical and dental schools joined the Tufts family,

15 Most of the early D.D.'s went to presidents of St. Lawrence University.

it became traditional to include a prominent physician or dentist on the list.[16] Tufts scored a "first" by awarding an honorary M.A. in 1895 to Otis Augustus Skinner, the first professional actor in the United States to be so recognized.[17] In the next year Mrs. Mary A. Livermore, active in feminist and humanitarian movements, became the first woman to receive an honorary degree (LL.D.) from Tufts. The College expanded its honorary degree offerings in 1900 by giving its first Doctor of Science degree to Frederick Stark Pearson, engineer, scientist, businessman, Trustee, benefactor of the College, and member of the Class of 1883.

As the College grew in stature and influence and broadened its horizons, it selected increasing numbers of honorary degree candidates from outside its own ranks, either religious or educational. Among recipients of such degrees before 1917 were Elbert Hubbard, the homespun philosopher; Edwin Ginn (Class of 1862), textbook publisher; Julia Ward Howe, author; Albert Bushnell Hart, historian; Henry S. Pritchett, one-time president of the Massachusetts Institute of Technology and first president of the Carnegie Foundation for the Advancement of Teaching; and Luther Burbank, horticulturist.

Tufts had awarded 297 honorary degrees by the time of American entrance in the First World War.[18] Thereafter, the number of prominent individuals so honored became even larger, and the persons selected tended to reflect the many-sided and changing patterns in American society, from Jane Addams and Evangeline Booth, of social service renown, to Van Wyck Brooks in literary history and Admiral Arleigh Burke of naval fame. Artists, businessmen, scientists, clergymen, scholars and educators, political leaders, and men of public affairs in innumerable professions, both civil and

[16] Such was Jarvis Wight, of the Class of 1859, who at the time he received an LL.D. (in 1894) was Professor of Surgery and Dean of the Long Island Hospital Medical College.

[17] Stephen E. Epler, *Honorary Degrees: A Survey of Their Use and Abuse* (Washington: American Council on Public Affairs, 1943), p. 100. Skinner was a member of the same family as Otis Ainsworth Skinner, who had raised the initial subscription for the College, and the actress Cornelia Otis Skinner, who received an honorary M.A. from Tufts in 1935.

[18] Master of Arts, 89; Doctor of Divinity, 57; Doctor of Humane Letters, 1; Doctor of Literature, 26; Doctor of Laws, 60; Doctor of Philosophy, 7; Doctor of Sacred Theology, 21; Doctor of Science, 16.

military, have been among those honored.[19] By the mid-1960's, Tufts had further expanded its list of honorary degrees to include the Bachelor, Master, and Doctor of Business Administration, Master and Doctor of Education, Doctor of Engineering, and Doctor of Fine Arts.[20]

The procedure for recommending candidates for honorary degrees changed over the years. In all cases, recommendations were acted on by the Trustees, but for many years the nominations originated with the faculty and the president. In fact, the Trustee by-laws of 1881 provided that "the General Faculty shall have the power of recommending to the Trustees candidates for honorary degrees." For almost thirty years the Trustees merely rubber-stamped the recommendations already voted by the faculty; there is no evidence that any of the honorary degrees voted by the Trustees during that time were suggested initially by that body. When the appropriate section of the by-laws was amended in the winter of 1885, the general faculty still had the power to originate recommendations for honorary degrees, but in order that the Trustees might have some opportunity to inquire into the qualifications of the candidates, it was provided that all faculty selections were to be submitted first to the Executive Committe and at least ten days before being acted on. The first indication that a change of this sort might be made had come the previous June, when one candidate recommended by the faculty was not approved, and another candidate was substituted by the Trustees. The privilege of the faculty to make nominations was never removed by a specific prohibition, but in 1889 the Trustee by-laws were again amended to provide that "honorary degrees may be conferred by the Trustees upon such persons as may be recommended by the Executive Committee." This step was taken after a special Trustee committee had found

[19] It is always dangerous to generalize, but the writer calls attention to the unusual ability of the Trustees to select as honorary degree recipients men who were later destined to become Presidents of the United States: Calvin Coolidge (1919); Herbert Hoover (1920); John F. Kennedy (1954); and Lyndon B. Johnson (1963). The danger of the generalization is illustrated by the award of honorary degrees to Thomas E. Dewey (1937) and Adlai E. Stevenson (1962).

[20] It had not, however, gone so far as to imitate a large mid-western university which in 1960 bestowed the degree of Doctor of Athletic Arts on a baseball manager and two football coaches after an unusually successful season.

"the present system of leaving all nominations to the Faculty . . . in open meeting . . . open to objection." The president was to make his nominations through the Executive Committee, so there was still an avenue by which the faculty could express its views if the ear of the president could be bent; it meant that candidates were no longer to be the subject of debates on the floor of faculty meetings. When the Trustee by-laws were amended in 1889, it was also provided that an honorary degree could be conferred on nomination by any Trustee, as long as the vote of the Trustees to confer such a degree was unanimous. Persons who had been voted honorary degrees were expected to be present at the Commencement or other occasion when the degrees were awarded, but more than one honorary degree was conferred *in absentia*.[21]

Not much ceremony accompanied the early awarding of honorary degrees. Until 1916 a brief citation in Latin was read; such a citation had first been used in 1875, when A. A. Miner received a Doctor of Laws degree. When the granting of honorary degrees was resumed after the First World War, the citations were read in English.[22]

§　§　§

In deciding in 1876 to grant the Master's degree only upon completion of a full year's work in residence under supervision, or its equivalent done *in absentia* during two or more years and approved by the appropriate College authorities on examination, Tufts fell into line with the practice of other New England institutions. The earned M.A. degree announced for 1875–76 was to be conferred on graduates of either the regular or the philosophical curriculum, or on graduates from other institutions with equivalent courses of study. The program began with three graduate stu-

[21] The first such instance occurred in 1902, when the recipient of an honorary M.A. was unable to be present because of illness. Eight of the fifty-seven honorary degrees bestowed in June 1905 celebrating the semicentennial of the first Tufts Commencement were awarded *in absentia*. The late John Holmes, well-known Tufts poet and faculty member, received his honorary Doctor of Literature in this fashion in 1962.

[22] Honorary degree recipients were furnished with caps and gowns after both the faculty and Trustees voted to appear in academic regalia in 1902–3. President Hamilton first suggested the idea in 1910 that honorary degree recipients should receive hoods as well, but this practice was not consistently followed until after 1923.

dents in residence who complied with the requirement that studies had to be pursued in two departments.[23]

The first earned Master of Arts was awarded in 1876 for a year's work in residence in the Departments of Chemistry and Physics to a graduate of the preceding year. From this modest beginning, the number of Master's degrees in arts and sciences rose in thirty years to 140, with 20 in the first decade, 40 in the second, and 80 in the third. About half of the unusually large number granted in the fifteen years preceding 1906 were awarded incidentally — that is, on work included in the requirements of the divinity school for the professional degree of B.D. Of the 100 advanced degrees awarded on the basis of specific work, the division was almost exactly equal between work done in residence and outside the College. Of the fifty degrees given for a year's work in residence, in twenty-five instances both Bachelor's and Master's degrees were given at the end of four years under the system based on the number of courses satisfactorily completed and not on a fixed number of years. In actuality, the first such "accelerated" earned degree (three years) was awarded in 1868. The A.B. and M.A. were first given simultaneously, at the end of four years, in 1894. There seems to have been no consistent policy at first in requiring a thesis, for passage of an examination was for many years an alternative at the discretion of the instructor. After 1891 an M.A. candidate could do his work in a single department.

Yet another set of degrees was introduced by Tufts at the end of the nineteenth century, in this instance in connection with its Engineering Department. The degrees of Civil Engineer and Electrical Engineer were created in 1892–93 to be conferred on Bachelors of Civil or Electrical Engineering to encourage professional activity.[24] These professional degrees were to be conferred on the

[23] Typical combinations under this requirement were English and German literature; mathematics and chemistry; or chemistry and natural history. Less typical were such combinations as Latin and mathematics.

[24] The undergraduate degree of Bachelor of Civil Engineering was created in 1892 to replace the original degrees of Civil Engineer and Bachelor of Mechanic Arts. In 1913, Acting President Hooper made an unsuccessful attempt to have the degree of all the engineering graduates who had received the Bachelor of Mechanic Arts prior to 1884 changed in the Official Register of the College to read "Civil Engineer." The Executive Committee insisted that the degrees as published in the Register remain "exactly as they were voted."

basis of either one year's residence and a thesis or three years of professional work, one of them "in a position of responsibility." After the earned M.A. degree was created in the school of letters, the Master of Mechanic Arts was provided for engineering students in 1883–84, to be granted under the same conditions as the M.A. The same provision was made for holders of the Tufts A.B. who enrolled in the divinity school. In the 1880's, students who "pursued with distinction" the B.D. program received simultaneously an M.A.[25]

The first recorded inquiry as to whether the College offered the earned Ph.D. came in 1879 from William Leslie Hooper, who had been graduated from Tufts in 1877 and had received an M.A. the following year. He was informed that "the college does not offer the degree and that the faculty does not at present consider it expedient to confer it." Four years later a faculty committee was appointed "to consider the subject of arranging a course of study for the degree of Ph.D.," but after taking the matter under advisement for several months they reported that they were not prepared to make any recommendations for such a program. The same policy prevailed until 1892, when it was announced that Tufts would award the earned Ph.D. degree in the Departments of Biology, Chemistry, "and such other departments as the faculty may determine." A three-year minimum was presupposed, with two years' residence or its equivalent required and all academic effort to be concentrated in one field. The same fees were to be charged as for undergraduates ($100), one half to go to the faculty as compensation for "laying out and supervising the work."[26] Higher degrees were to be open to both men and women.

The occasion for the decision to offer the Ph.D. was the strengthening of the Department of Biology by the appointment of Dr. John S. Kingsley in 1892 and the return of Dr. Arthur Michael to the Department of Chemistry. Four Ph.D. degrees had been conferred by 1906 on students in biology (1895, 1897, 1899, and 1905) and four in chemistry (1898, 1901, 1904, and 1906). The Department of Classical Philology added its announcement in

[25] Twenty-two combined B.D.-M.A. degrees were awarded between 1885 and 1901.

[26] Extra compensation for graduate school instruction was abandoned in 1913.

1893–94, but no candidates appeared, and the program was withdrawn when Professor Frank Pierrepont Graves left Tufts to become president of the University of Wyoming. The Department of History and Public Law announced a Ph.D. program in 1902–3 and had produced one doctorate by 1910. Between 1892 and the end of the First World War, Master's degrees had been offered in fifteen departments, ranging from Philosophy to Civil and Structural Engineering.[27]

Arrangements for graduate work were strictly informal until after 1890. A candidate would work out a program, usually in consultation with the president and one or more members of the faculty. Very little notice was given in the catalogues. Until 1891–92 not even the $100 tuition fee levied on undergraduates was applied to graduate students, and charges were scaled according to the number of courses taken. The casual attitude of the College toward graduate students in the early period was reflected in a faculty vote that an alumnus who wanted to "enter upon an optional postgraduate course [was] at liberty to return, making what private arrangements he may be able with the several instructors." Not until 1882 were the names of recipients of earned M.A.'s even listed on Commencement programs; not until 1887–88 were candidates for the Master's degree formally recommended for their degrees by vote of the faculty; not until after 1890 was any consideration given to establishing graduate courses or even to organizing a graduate faculty. Nothing resembling a system for handling graduate instruction appeared until 1891–92.

The decision to offer the Ph.D. degree coincided with the realization that some sort of administrative machinery had to be established to supervise graduate work. The first move in this direction was the creation in 1892 of a committee of seven, headed by the president, one of whose duties was the appointment of a board of three to examine each candidate for an advanced degree. The original committee was officially designated the "graduate faculty," but before another year passed, it was also being informally referred to as the "graduate department," until 1898 as the "execu-

27 Between 1895 and 1906, five of the eight Ph.D.'s were earned by Tufts graduates; the other institutions represented were Brown, Colby, and the University of Nebraska.

tive board," and from 1898 to 1903 as the "administrative board." The designation "graduate department" was first used officially in 1903 when the office of dean of the graduate faculty was created, with Professor Kingsley as the first incumbent. This had been done after Kingsley had urged the creation of "a graduate school and of graduate scholarships." At the same time (1903) one tuition scholarship was established for each department offering graduate instruction, with the understanding that a faculty member supervising the work of graduate students would relinquish his share in the charge otherwise made. The term "graduate school" was not officially used until 1909. The original graduate faculty was composed of the heads of undergraduate departments plus all instructors, regardless of academic rank, who supervised graduate work. Between 1914 and 1918 the deans of the Crane Theological School, Jackson College, and the engineering school were added as members *ex officio*.

Administrative details associated with graduate instruction were gradually worked out after 1903, when the Faculty of Arts and Sciences was created and the staff of the graduate department became one of the Associated Faculties. Thirty term (credit) hours were established as a requirement for the Master's degree, to be taken in one major department with related work in another. Whether or not the required thesis was a part of or in addition to the thirty hours was left up to the major department. No fixed minimum grade was at first set for graduate students; the various departments concerned made their own decisions, except for the expectation that the work was to be "of a higher grade than that demanded for the pass mark of undergraduates." Because of the policy adopted in the 1890's of allowing a student to work for both the first and the second degree in four years, undergraduates were allowed to undertake certain work which could subsequently be counted toward the Master's degree but could not be counted for both. Such students were listed in the catalogue as Master's candidates after they had completed 118 term hours of undergraduate work and had filed application for the combined degree program.

The expansion of the graduate program of the College had by 1906 brought into sharp focus a problem that had bothered some individuals almost from the day the earned Master's degree was introduced. What was the legitimate role of the College in regard to the relationship between undergraduate and graduate instruction? Did the institution have the resources to sustain both programs? Had the resources of the College been diverted, and, if so, to what extent, from strictly undergraduate work to the supervision of graduate students and the granting of advanced degrees? The Board of Overseers in 1905 recommended "that the resources of the College be devoted primarily, if not entirely, to strictly undergraduate work" and considered the issue such a fundamental one that it solicited the opinions of the faculty.

In replying to the Overseers' request, a representative faculty committee indicated that to their knowledge no financial resources had been drawn upon to any significant extent for either equipment or instruction in the graduate program, even in the decade preceding 1906 when the graduate degrees awarded averaged eight a year. On the other side of the coin, there was no doubt that "much time and labor" of instructors had been given to the supervision of graduate work "which should have been devoted exclusively to undergraduates." The addition of graduate work merely pointed up the fact that many instructors were overworked already. From the first, advanced elective work offered to undergraduates in any department of the college of letters was open to graduate students and could be counted for advanced degrees. It was difficult, if not impossible, to measure precisely the exact cost of graduate work in time and energy of instructors. Most graduate students took about half of their work in existing undergraduate courses, but no two students (or departments) had the same experience. If an average were to be struck for the years 1901–5, graduate work added the equivalent of one additional undergraduate course to the load of each teacher providing advanced instruction.

The faculty wanted it generally understood that, as a constituted body, they had exerted no pressure on any department to offer graduate work. Not until the staff of a department had "united in announcement" that they were prepared to receive graduate students had such students been admitted to undergraduate classes. The same neutral policy prevailed if a department deemed it best to withdraw its graduate program. Consultation with the heads of the nine departments offering such instruction in 1906 made it clear that the offering of graduate instruction had been a departmental prerogative for thirty years, although there was wide disagreement among departments as to whether it was advisable to continue or to expand graduate work. The faculty committee appointed to study the whole matter defended the offering of graduate work if a department saw fit to do so. There was no ground for criticizing the Tufts graduate program by arguing "that the ambition to do graduate work after the manner of a university" had caused "a burdensome and worse than useless multiplication of courses of study, with the necessity for many additional instructors." The faculty committee intimated that the Board of Overseers and other alumni perturbed about the introduction of graduate work were living too far in the past and had not been keeping abreast of developments in the educational world. Those who recalled the instruction given at Tufts thirty or forty years before and who "regret the passing of the 'good old days' " had better inform themselves as to what was actually going on. "No college could stand today on its administration of thirty years ago."

The list of advantages of graduate study compiled by the faculty committee consulted in 1906 differed not one whit from a list that might have been drawn up in the 1960's or in any other decade. Although a few instructors had found the supervision of graduate students a burden and a drain upon the energy they believed should have been expended on undergraduate instruction, a majority of the faculty found graduate supervision not a debilitating task but "a creator of energy." They believed that because they were involved in graduate work they could "do more for the undergraduates." Furthermore, "the presence of graduate students acted as a stimulus to all others."

Professor William L. Hooper of the Electrical Engineering Department had supervised some fifteen graduate students and regarded the effect of graduate work "as in the highest degree beneficial." Among other things, it kept him intellectually stimulated and had delivered him from "the daily grind." Professor Kingsley of the Biology Department felt that graduate work at Tufts should be "fostered and encouraged." He regarded the supervision of twenty graduate students over a thirteen-year period "not as a drain upon the department but rather as a distinct gain to it." Oversight of original investigation by graduate students into unsettled or unsolved problems kept him "out of the ruts which are so apt to trouble the mere following of routine work." A considerable number of students of biology were entering the teaching profession, and Kingsley felt that the College had an obligation to assist them in increasing their academic competency and enhancing their employment opportunities by offering graduate work. The chairman of the History Department, Professor Lawrence B. Evans, added his voice to the majority in favor of offering graduate instruction. Between 1901 and 1906, ten students had undertaken graduate work in his department and one of them was a candidate for the Ph.D. His arguments echoed those already given; like Professor Kingsley, he emphasized the growing demand for teachers who held more than the first degree. The influence of the College was extended by offering graduate instruction. He noted also the psychological effect on the campus. "The fact that the college offers graduate instruction is itself a wholesome corrective of the perspective of the undergraduates." He felt also that justice to the undergraduates seemed to demand that the opportunity should be left open for the more capable and enterprising students to complete the undergraduate work in less than four years and devote all or part of their senior year to work for the second degree.

The faculty committee saw no imminent threat to the principal work of the College — the instruction of undergraduates — when no more than fourteen graduate students (only half of them in residence) were receiving instruction side by side with over 350 undergraduates. It was the conviction of the committee that "whatever may be the wise policy of Tufts with regard to the most advanced degree, at least the Master's degree in Arts and Sciences should continue to be provided for." The head of a department should continue to be allowed to judge whether he and his staff could best serve the interests of their classes and of the College by devoting themselves to strictly undergraduate work and encouraging their more promising and ambitious students to do graduate work in a thoroughly equipped university, or administering a graduate program so long as it could be done without detriment to their primary obligation to undergraduates. If Tufts did have the capability of offering work at the Master's level and refused to do so, it would threaten its own existence as a "living institution [which] must continually advance or continually and hopelessly fall behind."

The College continued to offer the Master of Arts degree, with one-half to two-thirds of the departments participating. The Master of Science (M.S.) degree was introduced in 1897.[28] It was another story with the Ph.D. In 1907 the graduate faculty voted to accept no more candidates for that degree. Dean Charles E. Fay explained that the offering by Tufts of the highest degree had been "a new departure and an extension of the field of college work beyond what later developments showed to be feasible and expedient." It was almost half a century before the College felt that it had the resources to reestablish Ph.D. programs in any departments in the division of arts and sciences.

Doubts continued to be expressed even about the advisability of offering graduate instruction at the Master's level. Dean Anthony of the engineering school spoke for many of his colleagues when he called attention in his annual report for 1911-12 to the fact that no graduate students were listed in the registration statistics for his school. He "hoped that the practice of receiving such students may be entirely discontinued," for the engineering school, at least, could not carry on graduate work "even to a limited degree without severely taxing the departments involved, and we need to conserve all available funds and teaching force to maintain the present high standards, and to make an undergraduate school without a superior." The same sentiments were being echoed by some of the faculty fifty years later.

§　§　§

The Departments of Biology and Chemistry had taken the early leadership in offering graduate work, and a strong faculty had helped account for this. There were such men as John S. Kingsley, who succeeded John P. Marshall as Director and Curator of the Barnum Museum in addition to carrying on his research and teaching activities in biology; Fred D. Lambert, who joined the faculty in 1900 after having served as an assistant in the Biology Department since 1896; Herbert V. Neal, who succeeded Kingsley in 1913; and Arthur Michael. The latter served on two occasions as

[28] The first recipient of an M.S. was a graduate in electrical engineering. In 1907 the advanced degrees of Civil Engineer, Electrical Engineer, and Mechanical Engineer were abandoned in favor of the Master of Science. In the first few years after the introduction of the M.S. degree no clear distinction was made between arts and sciences; M.A.'s continued to be granted in such fields as mathematics for several years. By 1906–7, the M.S. was offered in biology and chemistry as well as engineering.

Professor of Chemistry between 1882 and 1907 and raised numerous eyebrows because he spent much more time in the laboratory doing research than in the classroom teaching undergraduates.

Laboratory resources were also steadily strengthened in both chemistry and biology. *Bona fide* laboratory work had been made possible for students of chemistry for the first time in 1875–76, with the purchase of considerable apparatus from Germany. President Capen had enthusiastically approved the move, for he was insistent that the College had to keep pace with the trend toward greater amounts of practical work to supplement traditional instruction by textbooks, lectures, and demonstrations. In the same academic year (1875–76) the first summer school in the history of the College was held.[29] Courses were offered in both physics and chemistry and were intended primarily for graduates who were preparing to become science teachers. A second summer school in chemistry was operated for six weeks under the direction of Professor Durkee in 1896. Sixteen students were enrolled, and the experiment was considered sufficiently successful to repeat in subsequent summers. Enrollment had increased to twenty-one in the summer of 1899. Most were Tufts undergraduates, but there were also high school teachers and students. Four courses were offered at the college level, and Professor Durkee was confident that by concentrating on only one or two subjects "the same student accomplishes more in a course taken in the Summer School than he does by taking it in the college year."

The Biology Department was equally active in supplementing the classroom instruction of the regular year. Its first summer sessions were rather unique, for they were conducted a considerable distance from the campus and became research as well as teaching enterprises. In the summer of 1898 a school was opened at South Harpswell, Maine, on the shore of Casco Bay. A cottage which served as a laboratory was acquired, and supplies and apparatus were brought from the College. The laboratory, furnishing facilities for ten workers supervised and assisted by three members of the Biology Department staff headed by Dr. Lambert, operated from

[29] A special Summer School of Oratory was conducted in 1883 and 1884 by Professor Moses True Brown, who also operated the Boston School of Oratory on Beacon Street. These summer offerings were a special project of the instructor and cannot be said to have established a precedent for operating a more or less continuous summer school in one department.

late June until early August and was considered a complete success. The sea yielded great quantities of marine life and an opportunity for research at firsthand. As a result of the first summer's efforts, nearly 100 specimens were added to the collection of Barnum Museum and supplemented the material for dissection that had been obtained from the marine laboratory at Woods Hole on Cape Cod since 1892.[30]

The experiment of summer work at South Harpswell in 1898 was so successful that it was continued on a semiprivate basis for over a decade. Land was purchased and a laboratory was constructed and equipped by a combination of private contributions and small allotments from the Olmstead Fund, which had been given to the College to encourage work in natural history. Thirteen students were enrolled in the summer of 1901, drawn from half a dozen institutions besides Tufts. As word of the laboratory spread, graduate students and faculty members from several colleges tended to replace the Tufts undergraduates, and in a few years the installation became almost exclusively a research center. President Hamilton considered the laboratory so important that in 1908 he called for an endowment of $10,000 to provide increased accommodations. The funds were not forthcoming, and the buildings and equipment deteriorated visibly over the years. The College had expended only $800 on the project by 1913 but was in no financial position to erect a new building or even to put the existing one in usable condition. The laboratory had become so useful to so many biologists that a plan was devised to continue it as a joint operation, owned and supported by several institutions including Knox College, Columbia University, Princeton, Johns Hopkins, and the University of Pennsylvania. In the summer of 1913 the Harpswell Laboratory became an incorporated body, and the Tufts Trustees deeded the property to it with the understanding that the College would have representation on the governing board and the use of

---

[30] During the 1880's and 1890's, the collections of the Museum grew by leaps and bounds. No one could complain that they were not diversified, for along with specimens of fish from Puerto Rico and dozens of gifts continuing to pour in from Barnum himself (including "a large giraffe" and "a fine stuffed baby camel" which undoubtedly aggravated the housing problem) came semiprecious stones from Canada, Confederate money, and fragments of battle flags from the Civil War.

the laboratory. The arrangement lasted until the early 1920's, when the facilities were transferred to other owners.

The same fund that had helped to establish the laboratory of marine biology was also used to strengthen the sciences at Tufts in other ways. The Olmstead Natural History Fund financed the first fellowships in the graduate school in the 1890's. It also made possible the existence for several decades of an agency frequently associated with a university rather than a college, namely, a means for publishing scholarly research. In 1893 the Trustees allocated part of the Olmstead Fund to launch a series known as the "Tufts College Studies." The faculty created a five-man Board of Editors in 1894 and announced an ambitious plan for publishing papers in four fields: language and philology; history, civics, and philosophy; physical and mathematical science; and natural science. The president served *ex officio,* and one faculty member was elected to represent each of the four fields.

The College was able even to publish under its own imprint beginning in 1901 and for many years to boast its own press on the Hill. Arrangements were made with H. W. Whittemore of the Class of 1886, who did much of the College's printing. He at first rented space in the basement of Curtis Hall and operated the "Tufts College Press" as a branch of his commercial printing firm, which had headquarters in Malden.[31] Business was so brisk that in 1908 he erected a one-story concrete-block building off College Avenue below the Boston and Maine Railroad bridge and on the site of the original Tufts College railroad station.[32]

The so-called Scientific Series was the most prolific and successful of the Tufts College publications. During the first decade (1894–1904) eight issues were published, and by the time the series became a casualty of the economic depression of the 1930's fifty-seven articles had been published.[33] Most of the early publications

[31] The Executive Committee had suggested that he use the designation "College Press and Printing Office" but he elected the name indicated.

[32] The building remained the headquarters of the College's limited printing facilities. For many years the *Tufts Weekly* was printed there. In the 1960's some of the printing for the institution was still being done at the same location under contract with a private firm.

[33] The last of the series, written by Professor Kenneth D. Roeder of the Biology Department, appeared in 1937.

were master's theses, doctoral dissertations, or faculty projects. After the First World War the series consisted mostly of reprints of articles by the Tufts faculty that had originally appeared in scientific journals. One of the most valuable by-products of the series was the exchange service that it made possible. Even before 1900 the transactions of over 100 scientific societies throughout the world were being received.

Publications in the other series that had been projected fared less well, for preference was given to subjects in natural history. Only one article appeared in the language and philology series, and none at all were published in the physical and social science series.[34] The faculty editorial board had little to do after 1937, although it continued to exist as a standing committee of the Faculty of Arts and Sciences until the committee system was reorganized in 1953–54. During its period of greatest activity the Tufts College Press, besides doing most of the printing required by the College and offering its facilities to the faculty, helped spread the word of Tufts' research endeavors in science. In the 1960's requests were still being received for reprints of some of the titles in the Tufts College Studies series.

The activities of the science departments in the 1890's prompted experimentation in another direction besides publication. The summer schools first conducted by the Biology and Chemistry Departments in 1898 were so successful that consideration was given to extending the idea to other fields. Among those suggested were foreign languages, mathematics, and history. Summer classes were actually conducted in the latter two subjects, although the enrollment was not very large.[35] Occasionally an inquiry was received from outside organizations to see if College buildings could be used for special courses. One such request (which was denied) was made in 1901 by the American Institute of Normal Methods through Professor Leo Lewis to offer a three-week program in music for teachers.[36]

[34] The single publication in the so-called Literary Series was a study of Thomas Carlyle's *Sartor Resartus* (1899) by Professor David L. Maulsby of the Department of English.

[35] The first summer course in history, in 1900, enrolled two students.

[36] The sessions were to have been sponsored and financed by the publishing firm of Silver Burdett Company and would have cost the College nothing.

The first serious consideration to conducting a summer school under the auspices of the College was given in 1902 when faculty opinion was solicited. The consensus was negative, but before the decision was made to continue the practice of allowing individual departments of instructors to offer courses (with the approval of the president and the chairman of the Executive Committee), almost every argument for and against summer schools was aired. On the plus side were "advertising the College, attracting to it teachers and others who might thus learn what we are trying to do and our facilities for doing it"; using a plant which ordinarily lay idle for a quarter of the year; and helping "some of the instructors to add a few dimes — possibly dollars, to their incomes." Among the arguments on the negative side were the extra expenses required by an augmented teaching force and the opening of the library and possibly the dormitories. The most basic objection centered about the quality of the instruction. College credit had been allowed for degree candidates by precedent rather than by any formal vote. But if summer school courses were developed to any great extent, this policy might lead to trouble, "for there would be a tendency to lower the standards to the level of the non-matriculated students who might form the majority of the summer attendance."[37] After weighing the pros and cons, it was decided to continue the existing policy whereby those offering summer school courses assumed all financial responsibility and "quietly pocketed the profits." It was not until the period of the Second World War that Tufts went on a year-round academic calendar, and not until 1945 that a regular summer school program was offered as a matter of College policy.

§   §   §

Commencement in June 1891 had a special significance, for it was the twenty-fifth such event in the College's history. It was even more memorable for Tufts' oldest professional school. The announcement was made at the dinner following the ceremonies that former President Miner had made a gift of $40,000 for a building

The Trustees failed to approve the plan because they were afraid that legal complications might arise; one of the project's provisos was that no student rooms would be occupied without the express permission of the occupants.

[37] It was pointed out that at the time Harvard gave no credit for work done in summer courses.

to house the divinity school, which had shared the cramped class-room and office quarters of the main College building since 1869. Miner placed one limitation on his gift: that at least $12,000 be raised to provide a separate dormitory for the divinity school students, who were still being assigned to a section of West Hall. Two persons at the dinner, Trustee Charles Robinson and James T. Perkins, immediately pledged $1,000 apiece in response to Miner's request.

T. J. Sawyer, who retired as dean of the divinity school in 1892 and was replaced by Rev. Charles H. Leonard, saw one of his dreams finally come true. The cornerstone of Miner Divinity Hall was laid on October 25, 1891, and construction had progressed sufficiently to permit use of the main floor for the dedication ceremony. Paige Hall, as a dormitory for divinity school students, was ready for occupancy in 1892. In one way, the divinity school by the turn of the century was more fortunate than any other part of the College, for it had the most commodious physical facilities of any department. Unfortunately, however, it lacked more fundamental assets: an endowment, and a growing and flourishing student body who met the educational standards of the rest of the institution. The latter deficiency was no reflection on the caliber of the faculty but was the result of a combination of circumstances arising out of the state of the ministerial profession over which the College had no immediate control. Likewise, efforts were not lacking to solve the three chronic problems of financing, increasing the quantity of the student body, and elevating the standards of both admission and academic performance.

The divinity school had reached one of its peaks at the time the two new buildings were provided. Student morale was high, for in 1889 the graduating class had successfully petitioned that their ordination take place in Goddard Chapel.[38] Appropriate arrangements were made with the Massachusetts Committee on Fellowship and Ordination, and the ceremony took place one week before Commencement.[39] Dean Leonard noted with satisfaction in his

[38] The precedent for this had been set by T. O. Marvin, who wanted to be ordained where he had received his training.

[39] The first such ceremony was especially noteworthy because it was attended by the venerable Lucius R. Paige, who had served in the Universalist ministry for sixty-six years.

Paige Hall (divinity school) in 1892

annual report for 1891–92 that all thirty-six spaces in the new dormitory were occupied and that yet another building might soon be needed, as well as a chapel for the use of the school. The completion of Miner Hall made possible the beginning of a departmental library and the transfer of the Universalist Historical Society Library from Middle (Packard) Hall to new quarters. There were forty-four students enrolled in 1892–93, representing twelve states. Dean Leonard was in a reminiscent mood after the twenty-fifth anniversary of the school was "silently celebrated" in August 1894; he "found it good to count up into result the work done." The divinity school had begun with two professors and three students in a small room with one window in the original College building. Twenty-five years later it could boast of a faculty of nine resident teachers and three non-resident lecturers and a student body of forty. It was many years before such a glowing picture could be painted again.

Dean Leonard's predecessor had always expressed concern that so few young men were entering the liberal Christian ministry. At the time when divinity school enrollment was averaging twenty a year (in the 1880's), Dean Sawyer had seen the entire Universalist denomination increasing its clerical force by only ten a year when thirty would have been more appropriate. The enrollment after 1895 seemed to justify Dean Sawyer's fears. It dropped to below twenty and remained there almost without exception. In 1906–7, only one student entered the school, and in the following year the total enrollment was only nine. No wonder the Board of Overseers was unhappy to see the "excellent facilities" so little utilized.

The steady drop in enrollment was not only discouraging but alarming. Almost everyone had an explanation or a suggestion to make. The Overseers thought that more special courses should be provided to appeal to individual needs and interests. But the majority of those concerned with the decline in enrollment looked outside the school for an explanation, if not a remedy.[40] They found it in the increasing secularism of American society; in the failure of organized religion to adjust to new conditions; in waning interest in the technical aspects of theological education, and the corresponding failure to provide divinity students with a broad, humane education; and in the enhanced appeal of other vocations and professions such as teaching and social work.

Certainly the decline in enrollment could not be blamed on an overly traditional or hidebound curriculum. Divinity school students were kept abreast of developments in many fields outside the strictly religious. Professor Dolbear of the Physics Department delivered a series of twelve lectures in 1882–83 to the divinity school on molecular physics. Dean Leonard did his best to keep the divinity school curriculum up with the rapidly changing times. Society needed clergy who could "do something besides write and preach fine sermons." He suggested training in settlement-house work and courses in the (then) new discipline of sociology as appropriate, and President Capen in the 1890's offered a course in Political Economy required of divinity school students.

President Hamilton, himself a Universalist clergyman, displayed particular interest in the theological curriculum when he took office in 1905, and urged the school to remain alerted to new

---

[40] Dean Leonard blamed part of the decline on the charging of tuition. This does not seem to have been a major contributor to declining enrollment, for no charge was made for either tuition or use of rooms for divinity school residents of Paige Hall beginning in 1905, and the student body still continued to shrink.

areas of activity germane to ministerial training. Investigations in medicine and psychology by 1908 had brought to public attention the new subject of psychotherapy — "the cure of diseases of certain types by influences brought to bear upon the mind of the patient, and through that upon the physical organism." What a later era might call "psychosomatic therapy" was thought to have particular effectiveness "when associated with the religious interest and religious sentiments." This was considered by Hamilton "directly to concern the College" and particularly the curriculum of the theological school. He recommended that a one-term course be offered jointly by a clergyman especially competent in this field and by a neurologist. It would be open only to divinity students and to others by special permission. The basic course in psychology was to be a prerequisite. Some of the Trustees were dubious about such a new course, and one Trustee, who was not able to be present when the proposal was voted on, sent a letter expressing his disapproval of such a newfangled idea. The course was finally authorized by a vote of eight to seven and went into the catalogue for 1908–9.[41] The students journeyed to the Tufts Medical School on Huntington Avenue twice a week to hear Dr. Morton Prince and spent part of an additional day in a clinic held at the Boston City Hospital. New courses in parish administration and "The Application of Psychology to the Work of the Christian Ministry" were added in 1907–8.

The problem of endowment dogged the divinity school for almost all of its first fifty years, and the decline in enrollment merely aggravated the problem. President Capen expressed his concern with annual regularity. A few special funds had been provided up to 1900, but they covered only a fraction of the total expense of the school. A bequest of $60,000 from Mrs. Mary T. Goddard in 1899 had helped, but half of it was earmarked by her will for the use of the college of letters, and the principal could not be touched. Enrollment in the divinity school had declined so significantly by 1900 that there was talk of closing Paige Hall and accommodating the few students in other dormitories. The eventual decision was to fill the building with non-divinity school students. The burden

[41] The course, listed as Philosophy 18, was described as follows: "Psycho-Pathology — The mental and moral origin of functional nervous disorders, and their treatment by methods of suggestion."

of operating the school was "causing a permanent disablement of the other departments." There was no expectation (or intention) that the College would ever be operated at a profit; but somehow it had to break even. The income from the $10,000 remaining of the Miner gift and from the residue of his estate in 1901 were also used for the school but failed to solve the problem. A bequest of $20,000 from Mrs. Mary A. Richardson in 1904, with a second $20,000 to be added, was welcome but likewise inadequate.[42] Something approximating Capen's hopes for substantial endowment came in 1906.

The donor of $100,000 to the divinity school was Albert Crane, of the Class of 1863. The gift was made as a memorial to his father, Thomas Crane, a Trustee from 1852 until his death in 1875. The benefaction was immediately accepted by the Trustees, and the suggestion was made that the divinity school bear the name of Thomas Crane. After consultation with the son, the Trustees voted to designate the divinity school as the Crane Theological School. Welcome as this gift was, it served only to accentuate the need for even more, for the College found itself in the most serious financial plight in its history. Even the release of funds for use elsewhere that the Crane bequest made possible represented a palliative, not a solution.

Another problem at which President Capen had hammered away was the admission standards of the school. Only a year after assuming office he was upset to discover that of the eleven students who had entered in 1876–77 not one was a college graduate. Even after due allowance was made for those with excellent natural ability who could not for some reason attend college prior to undertaking professional training, there were entirely too many admitted who were not qualified. Capen was afraid that the academic standards and reputation of the entire College were in danger when it undertook "to give a second degree to those who could not take the first degree." According to Dean Leonard, of the twenty applicants in 1888–89, one-half were rejected "on account of imperfect preparation." Only four students were graduated in 1889 in the regular course, and only two of these earned a Bachelor of Divinity degree because the Trustees refused to vote such degrees unless the recipient also possessed a baccalaureate degree.

[42] Unlike the Goddard bequest, the income of the entire gift, known as the Richardson Theological Fund, was to be used for the divinity school.

As has been pointed out earlier, some effort had been made to remedy the situation by requiring higher standards for admission, but the system somehow tended to fall short of the ideal when put to the test. Capen had insisted in 1877 that requiring a three-year course for holders of the A.B. and only four years for non-degree holders was not a proper arrangement, even if admission examinations were required for students in the second category. Four years in a professional school alone was no substitute for a combined seven-year collegiate and professional school course. Yet the conditions of admission did not really change until 1903–4. There were actually two interrelated aspects of the problem. One was the raising of standards for admission; the other was the relationship of the divinity school and its students to the rest of the College.

Capen argued for some time that the divinity school needed a separate endowment "so that it may stand apart from, and be independent of, the College" and that the students should be removed "from close and immediate contact with the College" — hence his justification for separate buildings. But over the years he modified his stand, realizing more and more clearly the desirability of closer liaison between the school and the College. One move in that direction was discussed by a joint committee of the college of letters and the divinity school in 1900. It was decided to require all candidates for the B.D. to earn also an A.B. No immediate action was taken on this proposal, for it was feared that the student body of the divinity school would be reduced still further or that it might disappear altogether.

A compromise was worked out, effective in 1903–4, that seemed to answer several criticisms that had been leveled at the school — from inadequate admission standards and degree requirements to the growing complaints that the curriculum was too narrowly focused and the students "too completely fenced off from the other departments of the College." The revamped admission and degree requirements did not affect those who entered the school with an A.B. degree.[43] They did provide specifically that undergraduate candidates for the Bachelor of Divinity degree had to conform to the regular conditions of admission to the college of letters. The

[43] The number of A.B. degree holders in the school always remained small; until 1913 the student was required to have studied Greek as an undergraduate.

most important single change was the introduction of a combined A.B.-B.D. program in which the students would matriculate in the college of letters and spend a terminal (fifth) year in the divinity school after completing four years of liberal arts courses selected for their relevance for the ministerial profession.[44]

The new curriculum had a larger significance than providing another way to meet degree requirements. It was a conscious effort to integrate the divinity school more effectively into the context of the whole institution. Dean Leonard had suggested this two years before the new program went into operation when he prepared a statement for the 1901–2 catalogue stressing the fact that those entering the four-year course of study were required to take work in psychology, logic, literature, and history "in addition to the strictly theological subjects." The new curriculum was based on a twofold philosophy: that theological students should be exposed to as wide a range of liberal arts preparation as possible, and that some courses in the divinity school were "properly regarded as culture studies" and should be open to all students in the College. Tufts, according to President Capen, had an obligation to give all of its students "the stamp of university training" by breaking down departmental barriers.

Capen had explained the new degree program to the Board of Overseers in the fall of 1902, one year before it went into operation. Novel as the plan might have been, the Overseers saw nothing but advantages from the program. It would more closely articulate the College and the school, tend to turn toward the ministry a larger number of college men, broaden the theological student's preparation, bring the studies taught in the divinity school into the college curriculum and make them available to a wider range of students, and eliminate overlapping and duplication of course offerings in such fields as philosophy. The combined degree program, if properly administered, would achieve a desirable balance between integrating the two sets of students and maintaining distinctiveness in aims and training for ministerial candidates. A practical benefit of the combined five-year program would be the shortening of the time between college entrance and receipt of the Divinity

[44] It is frequently difficult to ascertain the single person responsible for initiating new policies, but the evidence seems clear in this case that the idea emanated from President Capen himself.

degree. The timing of the new divinity school program was particularly good, for in 1903 the Faculty of Arts and Sciences was created, and the divinity school staff became one of the Associated Faculties. Closer relations between the parts of the College resulted at the faculty as well as the student level. Ten of the fifteen instructors involved in teaching theological school students in 1905–6 were members of the faculty of the school of liberal arts.[45]

The new degree programs by no means solved all of the problems besetting the Crane Theological School. Enrollment failed to increase significantly and remained, as President Hamilton expressed it in 1910, "pitiably small." When the school opened for the academic year 1911–12, only ten students remained; there was no one in the entering class. In spite of the Crane bequest and other smaller benefactions, the school continued to be a financial liability. The five-year combined course for undergraduates had to be extended to six in 1907 because students could not complete the shorter program satisfactorily.[46] In short, the Crane School was faltering badly by 1910. Only one new professorship had been created in a period of several years (the chair of Hebrew and Old Testament Exegesis in 1910), while another (the Woodbridge Professorship of Applied Christianity) was left vacant upon the holder's resignation. Dean Leonard was ready for retirement after forty-one years of continuous teaching; Professor Knight was seriously ill.

The Trustees reviewed the situation and found it not to their liking. They authorized the use of part-time instructors to fill gaps, and President Hamilton agreed to do the administrative work until a new dean could be selected. A committee was appointed to confer with representatives of the Universalist General Convention about the whole future of the Crane School. Rev. Frank Oliver Hall, a graduate of the school in 1884, prominent Universalist leader, and later a member of the Crane faculty, offered consolidation of the denominational theological schools as the best long-range solution. He felt that there was need for but one such school in the denomi-

[45] During the transition to the new program that year, five of the fifteen theological students were under the old program, seven were enrolled in the new program, and three were already holders of the A.B.

[46] The Divinity degree had, in 1903, been temporarily redesignated Bachelor of Sacred Theology (S.T.B.); it again became B.D. in 1905, and the S.T.B. was reinstituted in 1915-16.

nation and suggested that those at Lombard University and St. Lawrence University be joined with the Crane School at Tufts. President Hamilton also recognized the problems facing the school. In 1906 he had sent one of numerous personal appeals to several clergymen to interest youth in the ministry and circulated a plea from Dean Leonard that had appeared in the *Universalist Leader*. Hamilton pointed out that "no one would think of dropping the Theological School. . . . We remember . . . that the School is intimately related to the original purpose of the founders of the College, and that its graduates have been among its most active, enthusiastic and efficient supporters. If the influence of the Universalist ministry were withdrawn the College would suffer severely." This statement was made on the eve of Hamilton's own departure from the College. He resigned in 1912, the last clergyman to hold the office.

There was one ray of hope for the Crane School in a situation that otherwise looked bleak indeed. One of Hamilton's last acts before he left office was to invite Rev. Lee Sullivan McCollester to become dean of the school. The man chosen to succeed Dean Leonard was an alumnus of Tufts and of the divinity school, having received his A.B. in 1881 and his B.D. in 1884. He had started his college career at Buchtel College in Akron, Ohio, when his clergyman-father was president. The son transferred to Tufts at the end of his sophomore year. After serving his first pastorate in his native New Hampshire, he accepted a call from the Church of Our Father in Detroit. He had been there for some twenty-four years before accepting the deanship of the Crane school in 1912.

For several months there was doubt as to whether the College would be able to secure McCollester's services. He held an eminently successful and well-paid post in a large urban church and was reluctant to take on a new set of responsibilities for a theological school with a depleted staff, four students, and an uncertain future. But he accepted the challenge, after reviewing the potentialities of the school and after heeding the importuning of alumni. He made it very clear, however, that he would accept only under certain conditions, in which he would accept no compromises. He was to have a completely free hand to carry out any policies he considered essential to the rehabilitation of the school, insofar as finances would allow. He was to have freedom for outside work in the Universalist denomination to recruit students, to create interest in both the school and the ministry, and to assist churches whenever called upon; he refused to be "a recluse teacher of theology." Finally, he was to receive a specified salary, plus moving expenses. Even then, he reminded the Trustees that he was making a sacrifice. He added that he planned to buy or build his own house on the campus and that he would throw it open to theological students to foster their social life and solidarity.[47] McCollester's *quid pro quo* on salary was too much for the College to meet, but Trustee Austin B. Fletcher, who was much interested in the theological school, offered to guarantee personally $1,000 a year until it could be provided from other sources.[48]

Dean McCollester stated in his first annual report that he had been working out a new program to be announced for the next year and that he contemplated changes which would give the Crane School "a new place among professional schools in the training of men for efficient religious leadership." The combined A.B.-B.D. course was temporarily abandoned, although students were still encouraged to work for the A.B. Parish and social settlement work were emphasized in the final year of both programs. Undergraduate theological students continued to take their preparatory courses (English, science, history, philosophy, and psychology) and a limited number of electives with students in liberal arts, but the Crane faculty was responsible for all professional training and the programming of all theological students.[49]

In crisp and businesslike fashion the new dean introduced two revised curricula in 1913–14 which emphasized the practical rather

[47] After he arrived at Tufts, he proposed to construct his residence next door to Miner Hall, near the top of the Hill. Officers of the College dissuaded him from that somewhat unorthodox plan, but he did live as near the campus as he could. He purchased the house on Professors Row built by Professor John P. Marshall in 1857 and used since 1941 as the home of the vice-president.

[48] Rev. Alfred S. Cole, a member of the Crane faculty from 1931 to 1955, wrote a brief history of the school in 1947 in which he reported a conversation with Dean McCollester. The latter had said that Fletcher went so far as to outline a plan for a new theological unit to have cost $500,000, which he would presumably have donated. He did not change his will, however, and his substantial benefactions to the College went to other sections of the institution.

[49] This accounts for most of the students listed twice in College enrollment statistics.

than the academic. They were intended "to turn out, not men distinguished for varied and curious learning, but men thoroughly informed as to the problems of the hour, in sympathetic touch with modern needs, trained and equipped for moral and religious leadership in the seething life about us." The Crane School continued to offer the three-year course for college graduates but allowed substitutions for the traditional Greek or Hebrew. The undergraduate B.D. course was returned to five years, with increased emphasis on strictly professional subjects.

For the next several years, Crane experimented with various modifications of the undergraduate B.D. program, in which virtually all the students in the school were enrolled. The old A.B.-B.D. course was revived as a six-year program, and the freshman year was designated as a "try-out" or "professional guidance" period. Rev. Clarence R. Skinner's appointment to the faculty in 1914 greatly strengthened the school. The aggressive student recruitment campaign announced by Dean McCollester in 1913 increased the enrollment only slightly. It appeared that Crane was destined to remain small. There were only fifteen students enrolled on the eve of the First World War, and in the years immediately after 1916 the school almost disappeared. It survived largely through the efforts of its capable dean, who held classes in the living room of his home after the theological facilities had been assigned to military units during the war. The handful of students dispossessed from Paige Hall lived, appropriately, in the home of the late Charles H. Leonard, the second dean of the school. Plans for an expansion of Crane were postponed until the mid-1920's, when renewed hope for an enlarged school, both in numbers and in buildings, could be made into a reality. There was something a bit ironic in the fact that Tufts' first professional school became its feeblest.

10. Academic Indispensables: Curriculum and Faculty

I
T HAS OFTEN BEEN SAID that the library is the heart of an academic institution. If the analogy were carried a bit farther, it might be said that the faculty is the nervous system and the curriculum the vertebrae. It might be further posited that, once established, both the curriculum and the faculty organization tend to change but slowly. Educational institutions, by their very nature and by virtue of the tasks historically assigned them, have usually been conservative. The machinery once in operation, it seems to grind inexorably; alteration comes only after great and prolonged deliberation and is not as earth-shaking as it seems to be at the time the academic *status quo* is disturbed.

A review of the changes in curricular structure and faculty organization at Tufts over the years would seem to support this generalization. Not that change failed to take place, but, in the perspective of time, tradition and precedent (notably in the first half-century or so) bore heavily on these two facets of educational operations at Tufts. At the same time, the history of the College reveals that many of the "innovations" of a later day — especially in the area of curriculum — had roots much deeper in the past than the present-minded individual is likely to realize.

§ § §

The traditional classical curriculum introduced at Tufts when it opened in 1854 lasted, with minor changes, for almost exactly twenty years. Most courses had been prescribed. There were no such things as credit hours, letter grades, majors, minors, or foundation and distribution requirements. President Capen's major contribution for the next twenty years (after 1874) had been to recognize and to extend the elective principle. Greater variety had

337

been introduced into the liberal arts curriculum, but there was no wholesale review of the entire structure until 1892. The mandate given to a faculty committee in 1878 "to take into consideration the whole character of our course, and after comparison with those of the other colleges and after due consideration of all the circumstances, to report," produced less than spectacular results. The programs of the first two years remained unchanged; the only alteration in the junior and senior years was a reduction in the number of required courses and an increase in electives in the normal fifteen-hour program.[1] There was other minor tinkering with individual courses over the next fifteen years, but no thoroughgoing revision. Freshmen were required for the first time to take English composition (one hour for a half-year) in 1888–89.[2]

Intimations that more significant curricular changes were in the offing came in 1891, when a committee was appointed "to prepare a scheme of study for candidates for the degree of A.B. without Greek." Greek as a requirement either for admission or for the A.B. was dropped, effective in 1892–93, although it remained an optional offering.[3] Thereafter, there were two programs for the A.B.: for those who entered with Greek and for those who came with elementary training in one modern foreign language (French or German) and advanced (a minimum of two years) training in the

[1] The closest approximation to a concentration requirement between 1879 and 1893 was the provision for seniors that six hours of elective work were to be divided between two departments and the nine hours of required work among three departments.

[2] Proficiency in English grammar and composition had not been required for admission until 1876.

[3] At the same time, courses began to be numbered. Between 1915–16 and 1939, each department was assigned a code number, followed by the number of the course; e.g., English 12-1. Since 1939–40, courses numbered 100 or above have been open to both undergraduates and graduates. "Program" (credit) hours were introduced in 1892–93. A grading system based upon letters (A, B, C, D, E) rather than percentages was adopted in 1899, on the ground that accurate marks "on an exact numerical scale" were "an impossibility." In 1908 the grades of A, B, C, L, F, and FF were substituted, and this system lasted exactly half a century. In 1958 the grades of A, B, C, D, and F were adopted. The grade of F ("conditional failure)," which could be made up as an L or became an FF ("failed completely" — facetiously known as "failure with distinction"), caused no end of confusion. The difference between the F and the FF had to be explained periodically to the faculty as well as to the students.

other. Not until 1928–29 was the ancient language requirement (Greek or Latin) dropped as an A.B. requirement.

The most momentous and far-reaching academic change in the college of letters in the nineteenth century was the introduction of a new curriculum in the fall of 1893. Although the terminology and some of the details changed over the years, the basic structure was still intact as the College continued into its second century.[4] If President Capen had returned to the campus in the 1960's the system of majors, degree requirements, and credit (term) hours would all have sounded very familiar to him. The plan, something of an innovation when it was introduced, had a distinct philosophy behind it. President Capen explained it to the Trustees in his annual report for 1892–93.

> The new plan has been adopted in the belief that the true ground for promotion is intellectual attainment, and that the fixed requirement of a certain number of years of study, without regard to the mental power and achievements of the individual student, does not tend to encourage the highest scholarship. It is also believed that the series of compromises between the old prescribed course of study and the new elective system has produced a curriculum which is arbitrary in its arrangement and susceptible of great improvement in the direction of a system looking at once to the requirements of the general culture which should be the prime object of the undergraduate college course, and to the development of the individual on the lines to which he is especially adapted.

The new requirements for the A.B. degree, expressed in term hours, combined prescription and election in five areas: foreign languages (three from among Latin, Greek, French, and German: eighteen); English (rhetoric, composition, themes, and oratory: twelve); mathematics (six); natural science (one from among physics, chemistry, and biology: six); mental and moral sciences (one full subject or two half subjects from among psychology, logic, ethics, history, and economics: six).[5] Work in the latter group was

---

[4] The foundation, distribution, and degree requirements have been reviewed many times (e.g., 1907–8, 1915–16, 1931–32, 1939–40, 1960–61) and changes have been made, but the basic curricular edifice of 1893–94 withstood all onslaughts.

[5] The requirements in natural science and in Mental and Moral Science were increased by six hours each in 1900–1901. A proposal was made in 1897

not to be taken in the freshman year without special permission. At the end of his first year the student chose one major subject in which he was to complete eighteen hours and could include work already done in one of the prescribed groups.[6] Eighteen additional hours were to be taken in collateral subjects that tended "to strengthen and assist" in the work of the major field. The remaining forty-two hours of academic work could be made up by free election, subject only to prerequisites or restrictions of particular subjects.[7] The total requirement of 126 hours was to include two credit hours (four terms) of physical education.[8]

If the classical ideal of the harmonious development of body and mind proposed by the ancient Greeks was to be achieved, Tufts should have offered a program of systematic required physical education from the first, and for all seasons. But it did not do so; among other reasons, New England weather conspired against such a program. President Miner admitted that although the location of the College was "in one of the most salubrious and commanding in all this region of the country," it was subject to certain drawbacks during the winter months. He felt that at such times "a Gymnasium would be much used by many of the students and would greatly promote health and cheerfulness." Here was a need that "some thoughtful friend" might supply. The physical education requirement had been introduced in 1865–66 but was not consistently maintained even when facilities were provided by the construction of Goddard Gymnasium in the 1880's. Before outdoor apparatus was set up, such physical exercises were conducted in the chapel in the College Edifice "as could be made without injury to the building; this, of course, limited their content very much." The requirement that became a permanent feature of the curricu-

---

that mathematics be made optional but was tabled indefinitely. Mathematics was not dropped as a degree requirement until 1932–33.

[6] The requirement for a major was increased from eighteen to thirty hours in 1932–33.

[7] After 1895 no course listed in the catalogue as "Elementary" could be counted toward the major.

[8] In 1907–8 the degree requirement was reduced to 122 hours, with a minimum requirement of seventy-two hours of "C" work or better. After pluses and minuses began to be computed and entered on student records (1958–59), the minimum honor (quality) point requirement was changed to eighty-one credits of "C—."

lum in 1893–94 provided for meetings three times a week, "from about the middle of November to about the middle of March." Physical education almost became an elective in 1894 because of the full academic program and because of a shortage of space, but the problem was solved by scheduling the course on Saturday afternoons.[9]

Beginning with the second year, the student's major instructor was to be his official adviser for the remainder of his undergraduate program and was to assist him in selecting related subjects. Students had twelve departments from which to choose a major at the time the new curriculum went into effect.[10] Initially, students could change their major no later than the junior year, and only then by vote of the faculty. A double major was also permitted, effective in 1902.

The new plan was not intended to be obligatory until the fall of 1894, but the proposed changes met with such favor from the student body that it was put into immediate operation. President Capen was most enthusiastic. "Perhaps nothing has been done in the whole history of the College that has so powerfully quickened and strengthened the interest of students in their work." The students seemed much more strongly motivated than under the old system, in which so large a part of their work had been compulsory. The new curriculum found general approval and seemed to be working so well "on the classical side of the College" that the faculty were already considering the possibility of applying a modified version to the engineering course. However, Samuel W. Mendum, who served on the Board of Visitors to the college of letters in 1894, had some reservations. He approved of a fixed curriculum and was very critical of the elective system introduced by President Eliot of Harvard in the 1870's. It tended, in his opinion, to allow over-specialization and to result in an unbalanced and not truly liberal education. He was inclined to favor the more prescriptive curriculum to which Yale still tenaciously held.

[9] The system was revised in 1910–11 so as to require two hours a week from October through May, with out-of-door exercises when weather permitted. Regular practice with any team sport was accepted as a substitute.

[10] Engineering was at first listed as one of the departments in the college of letters in which a major was possible. After 1898 the Engineering Department became a separate division. Philosophy was added as a major department in 1895–96.

As might have been expected, the new curriculum had immediate effects on the departments of instruction. The required mathematics was now limited to algebra, solid and spherical geometry, and trigonometry. As the engineers required more advanced courses, they were thereafter taught separately from the liberal arts students. With the engineering course extended to four years and with mathematics continuing through all four years of the liberal arts program, it became necessary to create sections within courses and to depend more and more on teachers below professorial rank. Students, whether offering physics to meet their natural science requirement or not, flocked to hear Professor Dolbear lecture in Physics 1, which in 1900–1901 had an enrollment of 114. He also gave a well-attended extra course of lectures on the telegraph and telephone, in which fields he was a pioneer inventor. The basic work in chemistry (inorganic) was improved because it was no longer required of the junior class and tended to draw only students sincerely interested in the subject. Enrollment in biology decreased very little, but Professor Kingsley managed to maintain his requirement of two lectures and four hours of laboratory each week throughout the academic year by dividing his class into sections and employing an assistant. During the second term, students from the medical school at first did their laboratory work in histology in Barnum Museum.[11] Under the new program, biology majors developed sufficient sense of solidarity to organize a "Journal Club," which met regularly to discuss scholarly articles appearing in current professional publications. These students also took advantage of invitations to attend the Harvard Zoological Club.

The requirement of three foreign languages for A.B. candidates created something of a problem. Most students entered with German and French and "more or less Latin." But the first Latin course presupposed secondary school preparation, while Greek (which could comprise the third language) did not; hence, students with little or no preparation in Latin deserted to Greek, for which no preparation was expected and which could be taken as a double subject with double credit. In 1900–1901, half of the class were grad-

[11] Administratively, at least, the Biology Department was broader than its title indicated; for some years it included the instruction in geology and astronomy. The latter courses were taught by William Ransom, who also carried a full load in the Mathematics Department.

uating seniors who found this a comparatively easy way to complete this part of the degree requirement. The problem was alleviated, if not solved, when the foreign language requirement for the A.B. was reduced to two (one ancient and one modern), effective in 1915–16. Candidates for the B.S. needed only a modern foreign language.

With its system of majors and related fields, the new curriculum created a logical structure for the introduction of other degree programs. The advisability of establishing a course sequence leading to the degree of Bachelor of Literature was discussed in 1895–96 but was reported unfavorably out of committee. A proposal the same year to offer the Bachelor of Science (B.S.) degree was adopted. This new degree, in turn, reflected the growing nationwide stress on the function of the college as a training ground for the professions. Four combinations of courses were available: General Science, the "Biology Special," the "Chemistry Special," and the Medical Preparatory. From its very origins, the science degree allowed less election than the A.B.; in fact, those choosing to become candidates for the B.S. were assigned to a major instructor at the beginning of the freshman year. Forty-eight hours were specified for a major, with twenty-four hours in collateral studies. The four programs were frankly pre-professional in their objectives; they were intended for those who wished "to prepare themselves for specialized scientific work" and, like the engineering courses, were "placed upon a technical basis." English, history, and two foreign languages were the only non-scientific courses required. The diplomas of those enrolled in any one of the four programs indicated the specific field (e.g., Bachelor of Science in General Science). After the other programs lapsed or were incorporated into the general major, only one remained a distinctive degree by 1915–16. The Bachelor of Science in Chemistry continued to be listed as a separate degree, with its own prescribed curriculum, until 1957–58.[12]

[12] No candidates were accepted after September 1957 because a reorganization of the Chemistry Department offerings made the degree no longer distinctive or necessary. The last candidates for this degree (two Tufts students and one Jackson student) were graduated in 1960. A comparison of the catalogue statements of 1915–16 and 1956–57 indicates that virtually no change had taken place in the requirements in the forty years in which the degree was offered.

One trend in Tufts undergraduate enrollment watched with growing concern by College officials after 1900 was the steadily diminishing number of men in the A.B. curriculum. This tendency, by no means limited to Tufts, was occurring while enrollment in the B.S. programs increased markedly and the engineering school had grown to the limits of its physical plant. President Hamilton discerned several causes for the decline of liberal arts enrollment. Coeducation, in his estimation, was partly responsible. There was also the drift toward vocational training, particularly in the laboratory sciences, that seemed more attractive than linguistic, literary, historical, or philosophical study. This was being reflected at all levels of the educational system and was illustrated by the steps taken in Massachusetts to develop an ambitious state-wide tax-supported system of industrial education. It seemed that "the Age of the Engineer" had arrived with rapid technological advance and the need for specialists.

Another cause for decline in the so-called humanistic studies at the college level was the growing difficulty of obtaining a classical education in the secondary school. Greek in particular and Latin in general were being edged out of the curricula by greater emphasis on modern languages and science. President Hamilton laid the blame — if blame it was — for the decline of appeal of arts courses on the widespreaed use and misuse of the elective system, which tended to be much less commonly found in scientific and technical areas. In the latter, even though some choices were allowed, the curricula in the main were prescribed, and the student felt from the beginning that he was "being trained for something"; he had a goal and a definite path before him to achieve that goal. This was not the case with the students in the arts courses. They were usually left to their own devices and were wont to wander more or less at will through the academic offerings. The student with non-scientific leanings was more likely than his more technically oriented classmates "to follow fancy and convenience, student fashions, and the lines of least resistance" in making up his course program. At base, "the Arts course seems to promise an education, the scientific or technical course seems to promise an education for something."

There was no simple solution to this rather complex problem, but the president offered a possibility that was apparently favored by the faculty. A rearrangement of the A.B. courses to counteract some of the less desirable effects of the elective system without sacrificing the principle of election was undertaken, to take effect in the academic year 1910–11. This was less an overhauling of the arts curriculum than a reshuffling of course listings to make it appear that a certain combination would lead to a certain vocational objective. Just as in the engineering school there were basic courses in the freshman year from which students followed divergent paths leading to civil, electrical, mechanical, and chemical engineering, so also were there several liberal arts courses above the common freshman level that, if properly grouped, could be considered preparatory for law, teaching, journalism, social service, business, and the like. There were still abundant free electives both for those students with a specific vocational or professional aim in mind and for those who had not yet settled upon a life calling. This plan was intended to give a focus to the potential usefulness of an A.B. degree.

Only one area of instruction required particular strengthening to carry out the plan as Hamilton outlined it. Teacher training had been neglected by the College, and what courses in education were then being offered were an adjunct to the main efforts of the instructor.[13] On Hamilton's recommendation, a chair of Psychology and Education was established in 1910–11 to remedy this deficiency. From that date until the mid-1920's there was no independent Department of Education. Instead, it was listed, in various combinations, with philosophy, and psychology, and for many years was not considered a "major" department. President Hamilton's hope for pre-professional classroom training for potential teachers was realized in 1912–13, when arrangements were made for "observation and practice teaching . . . through the courtesy of the Somerville School Department." Within the next five years supervised teaching for Tufts students was extended to the high

---

[13] The first education course taught at Tufts was Pedagogics, offered in the Philosophy Department as a substitute for Ethics. The enrollment was large, for a high proportion of liberal arts students entered the teaching profession. Professor Cushman gave two lectures a week on "the ethical and psychological principles involved in teaching." They were supplemented by lectures by teachers in the Greater Boston area. Pedagogics (The Theory and Practice of Teaching), as it was designated in 1902–3, was taught infrequently for the next decade, and was first known as Education 1 in 1908–9.

schools of Arlington, Medford, and Winchester. The facilities of other public school systems were provided in the next few years. Hamilton's emphasis on "efficiency" and "practical training" was recognized in the stipulation in 1915–16 that "no student will be recommended by the Department of Education for a teaching position, unless he has shown teaching ability in the course in practice teaching." A combination of liberal arts education and professional and pre-professional training had become a fixed part of the Tufts philosophy by the time of the First World War.

There was no busier man on the campus throughout the period of curricular change in the 1890's than President Capen. He insisted that one of his prime duties was to keep in as close touch as possible with the students. In the very first year of his administration (1875–76) he introduced the progenitor of "Freshman Orientation." He delivered a series of lectures on "Education, and Methods and Objects of Study." He continued to teach from seven to ten hours a week, but found his administrative duties increasing at such a rate that he hoped someone else could be found to take over the teaching of Ethics, and Ancient and International Law. He taught Political Economy (alternately called Political Science after 1893) for several years, and in order to reduce the size of his classes the faculty had ceased to require the subject for seniors. But this did not appreciably diminish the number of students in the course, for many of the thirty-one enrolled in 1893–94 elected Political Science as their major field. Further, Political Economy was made a required subject for all engineering students beginning in 1895–96. The days when the president of Tufts was primarily an administrator were still in the future.

President Capen was strongly opposed to a lock step curriculum. He argued that the time element as a condition of graduation should be eliminated. "The College no longer says that a man must remain in college four years before he shall be entitled to its honors. . . . Those who can, . . . may take enough to make eighteen, twenty-one, and even twenty-four hours a week, and, receiving credit for all they do, may be advanced toward their degrees as rapidly as their work will carry them." This was no idle talk or empty promise. Announcement was made in 1893–94 that a student could be awarded the A.B. degree after he had completed the aggregate requirements. At first no specific number of courses was required in any one term.[14] If the student wished to receive his degree in three years, he was encouraged to do so provided he could maintain a "B" average for his entire course.[15] Even more was possible under the new curriculum, and was a natural outgrowth of the three-year A.B.

There appeared in the catalogue in 1899 a statement indicating that the Master's degree was not to be reserved solely for graduates who desired to continue or to resume their studies. It was provided that the Master's degree could be awarded simultaneously with the Bachelor's degree at the end of four years' work to those who had enriched their program and intensified their work so as to have completed the undergraduate degree requirements in three years with a "B" average. Between 1898 and 1913, twenty-three students completed the combined program. At least eleven, representing a variety of fields, entered the academic profession. Among them were Samuel P. Capen, son of President Capen and at one time chancellor of the University of Buffalo; William R. Ransom, teacher of mathematics at Tufts for some fifty years; Arthur B. Lamb, prominent chemist at Harvard; and Vannevar Bush, for many years associated with the Massachusetts Institute of Technology and internationally known as scientist and engineer.[16] The opportunity to receive combined degrees lasted until 1924–25 and formal provision for completing the baccalaureate degree in three years remained in force until 1938–39, but few students elected to follow either program.

The new liberal arts curriculum sought to provide a judicious balance between the required and the optional, between general education and specialization. Its elasticity made for durability, for the groups, and subjects within groups, could (and were)

[14] Capen's optimistic plan for a "ceiling unlimited" on course programs for all students had to be modified in the light of experience, although the principle of acceleration was still approved. The faculty put a limit of nineteen term hours on first-semester freshmen and a sixteen-hour limit on those who made below a "B" in more than six hours (two courses) or below a "C" in as many as three hours (one course). A twenty-one-hour limit was placed on those who had a certain proportion of work below "B."

[15] The first student to take advantage of this new program was Orren Henry Smith (Class of 1896), long-time editor of the *Tufts College Graduate*.

[16] It was also possible to obtain the Master of Science instead of the Master of Arts under the combined program. Bush was one such recipient.

changed from time to time as new subjects were introduced or old ones discarded, without altering substantially the foundation on which the whole curricular edifice was constructed. The only part of the original plan modified to any extent was the period within which "the mark of the scholar, the degree" was obtained. It tended to remain at the customary four years for the vast majority of students in spite of Capen's hope to the contrary. But "acceleration" had at least become an officially approved parallel to "enrichment." Tufts was willing to experiment.

§   §   §

Like any other educational institution, Tufts sought in various ways to reward meritorious academic achievement by special recognition. The first such method (introduced in 1877) was to confer "Special Honors" at Commencement on a student who excelled in the required work of the study in which he desired honors and in two "cognate studies," passed with distinction a comprehensive examination (oral or written), and completed a special project of some kind — all to be supervised and administered by a special faculty committee.[17] Such a student would probably have been invited to prepare a "Commencement Part" anyway, but if he elected the "Special Honors" (and achieved it), this fact was designated as *cum honore* after his name on the Commencement program.[18] The faculty made the first distinction between *summa honore* and *cum honore* in 1887. It was also possible after 1892 to achieve various degrees of honors through regular course work. They ranged from "Honorable Mention" up through "Final Honors," depending on the student's cumulative average.[19] After 1894 students could receive "Double Honors" if they had fulfilled the

[17] At first, application had to be made by the beginning of the senior year, but in 1880 it was advanced to the junior year in order to allow more time for the selection and execution of special projects and the making up of any course deficiencies.

[18] At the time the program was inaugurated, there were eight departments in which Special Honors work could be done. The first "Special Honors" was conferred in 1878 on a student who elected mathematics.

[19] "Final Honors" was reserved to those who attained an "A" (87 per cent) average in their major subjects and a "B" (75 per cent) average in collateral subjects. At first, "Honorable Mention" required the equivalent of a "B+" (80 per cent) average; in 1899 nine term hours of "A" in one department were required.

requirements (including collateral work) in two major subjects.[20]

One matter concerning honors about which the faculty had great difficulty in making up its collective mind was how students should be listed on Commencement programs. For many years they appeared in order of academic rank; then they were listed alphabetically, by degree, and in some years by type of honors earned. Even though a student might have been a candidate for only one degree, it was possible for his name to appear as many as three times on the Commencement program — as the deliverer of a Commencement Part, as the recipient of a stated degree, and as the possessor of some gradation of honors. Over the years the practice eventually became uniform of listing the degree recipients in alphabetical order within divisions and by degree, with honors (if any) indicated after the student's name.[21]

The same indecision characterized the Special Honors program, which had a most erratic career after the First World War and even in the 1960's was offered in only a scattering of departments. President Cousens, in the 1930's, questioned the soundness of the whole idea at the undergraduate level. He looked favorably on a plan to allow qualified students who desired advanced work to enroll in a special curriculum elected at the end of the sophomore year that would have bypassed the A.B. and ended in a Master's degree after three years of specialized work. Some of the proposals submitted to the Faculty Governing Board of the Experimental College established in 1964 reflected the continuing problem of combining acceleration and the liberal arts tradition.

§   §   §

The adoption of the new curriculum in 1893 made inevitable a review and reconsideration of admission requirements, which had not changed significantly since the College opened. New knowl-

[20] Engineering students did not need as high an average as letters students to be eligible to deliver Commencement Parts, but the minimum academic average was the same for all students for other degrees of honors.

[21] One group in the faculty in 1895 felt so strongly that academic achievement should be recognized that they recommended that only those graduating seniors ranking in the upper half of their class should have their names printed on the Commencement program at all.

edge, new subjects, and a growing public demand for a departure from the rigid pattern that had been inherited from the past made readjustment at the college level mandatory if institutions of higher learning were not to lose touch with the leading secondary schools and were to provide a "scheme of liberal education that seeks to be more than medieval." Many felt that the least the colleges could do was meet the preparatory schools halfway and recognize new educational developments in admission policies. Tufts had already assumed the leadership among New England institutions in offering, through the philosophical curriculum, modern languages as a parallel avenue to the traditional Greek requirement for admission, although it continued to require Latin for the A.B. degree for those who did not elect Greek. The liberalization of admission requirements in 1892 which allowed the substitution of French or German for Greek anticipated the plea made in 1897 by the Massachusetts Association of Classical and High School Teachers that the colleges of the state make greater allowance in their admission policies for the curricular limitations of the smaller high schools that attempted to prepare students for college. The College now determined to take an even more advanced position. Revised entrance requirements would allow a wide range of options that recognized diverse secondary school programs without lowering the standards of the institution at the same time.

In attempting to solve its admission problems, Tufts was in no sense "going it alone." From the day it had accepted students, the institution had cooperated and consulted both formally and informally with its sister institutions in the Northeast. At no time did it endeavor to lead an isolated existence, outside the mainstream of educational currents. Tufts was, in fact, a charter member of the Association of Colleges in New England, organized in 1858 and operating for many years (for largely geographical and practical reasons) as the Association of Southern New England Colleges. At its first meeting, held at the residence of President Woolsey of Yale, the membership and objectives of the Association were outlined. Each participating institution was to be represented by its president and one faculty member. The purpose of the organization was "to take into consideration various matters of common interest to the several colleges." President Ballou and Professor Marshall were Tufts' first delegates, and for the two succeeding years (until his death in 1861), Ballou took a different member of the faculty each time. Presidents Miner and Capen continued the same policy, and on several occasions Tufts played host to the Association.

In like manner, Tufts was represented, beginning in the 1860's, at the informal meetings of the Association of College Officers, which was officially constituted the New England College Officers Assocition in 1907. Whenever professional and scholarly organizations met in the Boston area in the nineteenth century, they could count on an invitation to visit the College.[22]

The twin problems of raising secondary school admission standards and achieving some measure of uniformity in college admission requirements occupied increasingly prominent places on the agenda of meetings among college representatives. Minor changes in the Tufts requirements in Greek and Latin were effected as the result of one set of recommendations made by the Association of Southern New England Colleges in 1878. Another proposal of the Association which the Tufts faculty unanimously supported in 1885 was the establishment of a Commission on Entrance Examinations for preparatory schools.

The committee that was created confined its activities to drawup lists of secondary schools that wished their students to be admitted to college by certificate. The New England Association of Colleges and Preparatory Schools was established in 1885. When it was proposed in 1892 that its Committee on Admissions be empowered to extend activities beyond establishing uniform requirements for secondary schools and include "the whole subject of requirements for admission to college, and methods of examining," a solid wall of opposition by the colleges appeared as if by magic. Institutions of higher learning were quite willing to set secondary school standards but jealously guarded their prerogative to establish their own admission requirements and conduct their own examinations.[23] Tufts, like many other institutions, made an exception in the case of Regents' Examinations in New York State. The long-time direct control and strict regulation of secondary education there (since 1784) had made it possible to admit students to

[22] Two such organizations were the American Association for the Advancement of Science and the American Historical Association.

[23] The faculty at Tufts were among those who voted down the proposal.

college by "Regents' cards" in lieu of the examinations ordinarily taken. The Tufts faculty finally (in 1894) agreed to the principle that uniform requirements for admission and examination might safely be placed in the hands of an outside agency, namely, the Committee on Admission Examinations of the Association of Colleges in New England.[24]

One admission policy (adopted in 1900) related specifically to the degree program then in operation that allowed a student to complete the A.B. and M.A. requirements in four years. Students could obtain both advanced standing and credit for work done in secondary school. In order to take advantage of this alternative, the applicant had to pass an entrance examination with a grade of "B" or better in the subject in which credit was desired and continue the subject in college for at least one year, maintaining a grade of "C" or better. Only courses "higher than those for which advanced standing has been granted may count towards the degree."[25]

New admission requirements were embodied in the recommendations of a special faculty Committee on Entrance Requirements appointed in January 1896. It labored until October and produced a plan that was adopted by the faculty of the school of letters. Each candidate for admission was to pass examinations in two groups of subjects, known respectively as Primary and Secondary. The Primary Group consisted of English, elementary preparation in a foreign language, history, and mathematics. These were considered prescribed subjects, a basic knowledge of which was regarded as fundamental to college study. Except for English and mathematics (arithmetic, algebra, and geometry), there was some choice allowed within the Primary Group: German, French, Latin, or Greek was acceptable for the foreign language requirement; candidates were allowed to take examinations in two of four fields of history: Greek, Roman, English, or American.

The innovation came with the so-called Secondary Group, which provided a range of options in both breadth and depth. The students were allowed to offer, for example, advanced foreign lan-

[24] The path was undoubtedly eased by the presence of Professor Charles E. Fay on the committee. Uniform requirements were first adopted in languages (English, French, and German).

[25] This program, which lasted for over a decade, is particularly interesting in view of the highly publicized Advanced Placement program organized through the College Entrance Examination Board in the 1950's and operating in twelve fields a decade later.

guage; intensive study in history (defined as a two-year course or a one-year course in a limited area either geographical or chronological); advanced mathematics (plane trigonometry, solid and analytic geometry) and advanced algebra; and physics, chemistry, botany, zoology, and drawing. All of the subjects were, for the first time, listed in terms of entrance units, computed on the basis of time spent in the high school on each subject. The formula, which assumed four years of college preparatory work, resulted in a total requirement of twenty-four entrance units. Eight were to be in the Primary Group and sixteen in the Secondary Group. The latter included a requirement of advanced foreign language. Anyone familiar with the system of "Carnegie units" of a somewhat later day will easily recognize its general outline here. Applicants for admission were to be allowed conditional standing (i.e., deficiency) on no more than one entrance unit in the Primary Group and no more than four in the Secondary Group. Three of the four deficiencies had to be made up before graduation. Work taken to fulfill entrance requirements could not be counted toward the degree requirements.

An alternate route to admission was still provided by the certificate system that had been introduced to a limited extent in 1886–87 but had never been considered with enthusiasm. In fact, when admission by certificate was introduced, it was intended only for special cases and was, as frankly stated in the catalogue, "regarded with disfavor." Candidates so admitted were considered automatically to be on probation, and admission could be withdrawn at any time if the students' preparation was found to be inadequate.[26] The certificate had to specify which of the subjects had been pursued and to what extent they differed from the requirements laid down for admission by examination.

The new entrance requirements for admission by examination became optional in 1897–98 and mandatory in 1898–99, but an attempt was made to regularize and enforce admission by certificate before the new program went into effect.[27] School principals were

[26] The first group of women admitted to Tufts came by way of certificate rather than examination.

[27] A faculty committee screened all applications, but candidates for admission by examination had to run the gamut of a full faculty vote, and the decisions of the committee were frequently challenged and sometimes reversed.

required "to state with exactness the time in years and in weekly periods given to each subject certified, with the standing of the candidate in each subject, according to the records of the school; and in addition a brief statement of the ground covered by the instruction, books, and method used, and such other particulars as department examiners of this College may see fit to require." No certificate would be accepted that covered a course of study of less than four years (although the four years could be taken at more than one secondary school), or from a school which had not filed with the College a full statement of its teaching force and its course of instruction. The tightening up of admission by certificate was a recognition that there had been a tendency to receive certificates too liberally and without a real check on the issuing school. A natural sequel to this new effort was the compilation by the College of a list of "acceptable" schools. Many a principal or superintendent was informed that his school was not on the approved list. The College made it clear in its public releases that "the acceptance of certificates is regarded as a favor to the candidate and a courtesy to the certifying school."

The long struggle to achieve some semblance of uniformity in admission examinations in American colleges and universities came at the very time that Tufts was revising its liberal arts curriculum and reviewing its own admission policies and procedures. The College Entrance Examination Board, created in 1900, was built on the foundations laid by the New England Association of Colleges and Preparatory Schools and the Association of Colleges and Secondary Schools of the Middle States and Maryland, and on the efforts of such educators as Charles W. Eliot of Harvard and Nicholas Murray Butler of Columbia.[28] The College Board, created originally as an instrument of the Middle States Association and developed eventually as a nation-wide organization, was intended as an agency by which uniform college entrance examinations could be conducted simultaneously at many locations and through

[28] The background of the CEEB is detailed in Edwin C. Broome, *A Historical and Critical Discussion of College Admission Requirements* (New York: Columbia University Press, 1902). For an informal history of the CEEB, with much attention to personalities, see Claude M. Fuess, *The College Board: Its First Fifty Years* (New York: Columbia University Press, 1950). See also I. L. Kandel, *Examinations and Their Substitutes in the United States* (New York: Carnegie Foundation for the Advancement of Teaching, 1936).

which certificates could be issued that would take the place of examinations traditionally given by individual institutions. The Board had the long-range and indirect effect of promoting the standardization of secondary school curricula that was more explicitly undertaken by various national and regional accrediting agencies.

Tufts promptly agreed (in 1901) to accept certificates of examination issued by the Board and in 1902 joined forces with twelve other northeastern institutions to form the New England College Entrance Certificate Board as a regional organization. One by one the New England colleges joined the College Entrance Examination Board. When Tufts became a member in 1910 it followed a policy shared by many other institutions. It abandoned its local entrance examinations administered in June but retained its own examinations administered in September. Not until after September 1940 did the College give the last of its own admission examinations and depend on a combination of College Board examinations and certificates.[29] Academic credentials in terms of so-called Carnegie units (fifteen) were adopted by the faculty in 1915.[30] Tufts showed a continued willingness to use the major tests developed by the College Board, including the Scholastic Aptitude Test (SAT), first developed in 1926.[31] During the Second World War, President Leonard Carmichael headed a Special Advisory Committee on Research and Development appointed by the Board to review the entire testing program when the nation returned to peacetime.

§   §   §

The professionalization of academic life today, with its specialization and division of labor, concern over academic freedom, tenure, rank status, teaching loads, and productive scholarship, and the hierarchical organization through elaborate faculty struc-

[29] However, the College continued to give its own placement and exemption examinations in several departments.

[30] One advantageous result of adopting these standardized criteria for admission was the reduction of the bulkiness of the annual catalogue. At one time over fifteen closely printed pages were devoted to describing the intricacies of admission requirements for liberal arts students alone.

[31] Some edition of this test, first subdivided into verbal and mathematical sections in 1929–30, has been familiar to almost all Tufts undergraduates since the Second World War.

tures, committee systems, and by-laws seem on the surface to bear little resemblance to their nineteenth-century counterparts.

A reading of the "Doings of the Board of Instruction of Tufts College," as the first volume of the faculty records was called, generates an initial reaction of amusement tempered with a fleeting twinge of nostalgia for the "good old days." Academic life in the past seemed to be uncomplicated, with the goals of higher education explicit and unquestioned, unafflicted with the pluralism, multiplicity, even confusion, of the twentieth century. The rigidity of departmentalization had not yet almost completely fragmented the unity of knowledge. The original faculty of four was notified by the Executive Committee of the Trustees on the eve of the formal opening of the College in the late summer of 1855 that they were expected to "distribute among them the necessary branches of instruction." The early faculty represented in the educational realm something approaching Eli Whitney's concept of interchangeability of parts in the industrial realm. After three years' experimentation, the faculty determined that Professor Marshall, who ostensibly taught natural science, should devote more time to junior and senior classes, so Professor Schneider, who was teaching only French and German, was assigned also the work in Latin and Greek in order that Professor Keen, who had previously taught these subjects, could take over the mathematics taught by Professor Marshall.

Student attendance was carefully supervised, and complete records were kept by the early faculty, who applied the same unyielding standards to their own deliberations. Even with such a small group, tardiness and absenteeism at faculty meetings became a problem. Professor Schneider, who at first commuted from Boston, was a chronic offender. The faculty thereupon imposed on itself a severe set of rules in 1858. "If any member of the faculty be tardy, he shall pay a fine of 25 cents, — if absent, 50 cents." [32] Obtaining a quorum was frequently impossible, but as long as the faculty met

[32] Professor Tweed was the first offender, at the very next meeting, and meekly paid a 25-cent fine. Such fines were collected for less than a year, although a record of faculty "excused" and "unexcused" absences comparable to that for students was kept for two more years, and lack of promptitude in arriving at meetings was faithfully recorded. The penalty of paying fines remains on the records today for it was never rescinded.

either once or twice weekly, as it did for several years, the wheels of the institution never ground completely to a halt because of the failure of the faculty to do business.

The faculty for many decades performed all of the routine work of the College without benefit of secretarial or clerical assistance. One member served as recorder for faculty meetings, another as "statistical secretary and superintendent of rooms," while still another made out student term bills. The secretary of the faculty received and acted on all student petitions until 1875, when other than routine cases required action by the whole body. The duties of the secretary became so time-consuming by 1878 that additional compensation was voted by the Trustees. Inasmuch as the teaching load ranged from seventeen to twenty-three hours a week until long after 1900, the faculty found their day a full one.[33]

No faculty rules were adopted until 1882, at which time the total teaching force was designated as the "General Faculty" in accordance with Trustee by-laws adopted the previous year. The school of letters and the divinity school comprised this ancestor of the Faculty of Arts and Sciences.[34] At the first of its three regular meetings each year the General Faculty was to choose a secretary and determine the academic calendar. At spring meetings preceding those of the Trustees, the faculty was to recommend candidates for honorary as well as earned degrees "on the usual conditions."[35] The letters faculty created its first standing committee in 1885; its task was "to consider cases of men doing unsatisfactory work" and it was

[33] The teaching load of the Wade Professor of Modern Languages in 1893 was typical. He taught 101 students three hours a week in seven courses (German, French, and Italian at several levels).

[34] The proceedings of this body were kept in a volume separate from the records of the theological, engineering, and graduate departments between 1882 and 1895. The dean and secretaries of the medical and dental schools were made members of the General Faculty in 1893 and 1899 respectively but seldom attended meetings on the Hill. Most divisional faculties met monthly. After the faculty of the school of letters was unable to transact business at an announced meeting in 1895 because of absenteeism, a quorum of ten was established, with the majority to be full professors.

[35] This phrase was first used in 1873. There was never a requirement that the names of degree candidates had to be recited, although it can be presumed that they were read aloud. Candidates for each of the Bachelor's degrees were acted on *en bloc*.

357

to report periodically to the faculty.[36] This committee, known until 1892 as the "Committee on the Standing of Students," was redesignated as the "Committee on Promotions and Recommendations for Degrees." In the same year, a Committee on Programme was also established. The faculty, on petition by the students, created in 1891 an Athletic Association composed in part of members of the faculty and the alumni. Out of this grew an Advisory Committee (or Board) on Athletics with joint faculty-alumni representation. The secretary of the faculty at this point had so much to do that he was authorized to employ an assistant (at $100 per year) and acquire a typewriter.

Expanded enrollment in almost all departments, the broadening of curricula, additions to the physical plant, continued flourishing of the medical school, and the addition of the dental school in 1899 had all increased the administrative activities of the College and had made necessary the creation of new positions and the provision of new services for faculty and students. In 1894 the faculty created a standing Committee on Books and Supplies and began the practice of appointing a student to manage the supplying of textbooks and other school needs. This one-man business, operating out of a dormitory room, was replaced by an outside concession when the Commons Building (Curtis Hall) was opened. In 1896 the man operating the Post Office in the Commons Building was given the privilege of selling books and stationery in return for a rental paid for his quarters in the building. Almost simultaneously, in the fall of 1894, the office of registrar was created, with Professor Dearborn as the first incumbent, and a year later William A. Start became the first bursar. A "Tufts College Bed" was provided by the Trustees beginning in 1896 in the Somerville Hospital for students requiring sustained medical attention. Student spiritual needs were served in organized fashion in 1905, when Edwin Courtlandt Bolles, Professor of English and American History, was made the first chaplain of the College.[37]

[36] After 1894 all standing committees were appointed by the president rather than elected by the faculty. Only one exception to this rule existed as late as the 1960's (the Advisory Committee on Faculty Personnel). Continuity of personnel rather than change characterized standing committee membership until 1953, when rotation became more the rule than the exception.

[37] After Professor Bolles had served in this capacity, it became traditional to appoint the dean of the Crane Theological School as chaplain.

In 1900, for the first time the college of letters had a separate dean.[38] William R. Shipman, for many years librarian as well as Professor of Rhetoric and Logic, was a logical choice to fill this position. The effects of the appointment were to secure a more efficient organization of the faculty, to relieve the president of many details hitherto devolving upon him, and to centralize the individual reports made annually by the instructional staff.

Standing committees in the college of letters had increased to nine by 1896. In addition to those already mentioned were committees on Catalogue, Glee Club, Freshman Plans of Study, and the Department of Engineering.[39] Until 1896, when a separate Committee on Admissions was established, undergraduate admissions both by certificate and by examination were supervised by the Committee on Promotions. The first standing Committee on the Library was created in 1898 on the recommendation of the Trustees. Many years' experience with a similar Trustee committee had made it evident that the faculty were in a better position to select books than the Trustees. Numerous complaints had also been registered about the slowness of acquiring library materials and the perpetual mystery surrounding the amount of money available for library purchases.[40] A Committee on the Use of College Buildings was created in 1900, also at the request of the Trustees, and a Committee on Information (first referred to as an "Intelligence Committee") was established the same year with the rather nebulous assignment of acting "as mediating board between graduating students, graduates, and schools and other positions."

The faculty had grown sufficiently in size and its activities had become so varied that a proposal was made (but not acted on) that a Faculty Senate, Administrative Board, or Executive Board be constituted. The faculty committee appointed to consider this possibility had gotten no further than writing a Preamble by 1902 because they could not agree on whether such a body should be

[38] Until that date, the Trustee by-laws (of 1881) provided that "the Senior Professor of the Faculty of the College of Letters, unless otherwise ordered by the Trustees, shall be the Dean of said Faculty." Professor Marshall had served in this capacity until 1899.

[39] The latter committee was abolished in 1898 after an administrative board for the engineering school was authorized by the Trustees.

[40] The faculty were never informed, apparently, but the total income available for the library for the three-year period 1895–97 was $1,173.93.

359

created at all. It was clear that a complete reorganization of the faculty structure had become advisable. Standing committees had proliferated to fifteen, and the number and functions of special committees had become unwieldy and overlapping. Standing committees by 1902 included one on Examinations; one on Curriculum; and one on Excuses (student) which had to have a subcommittee on Chapel Attendance. By 1902 there were forty-two full-time faculty members on the Hill, and the divinity school, engineering, and graduate departments had developed their own specialized needs and concerns. A plan for reorganization was submitted to the Trustees in 1902 and was approved (with minor changes) in time to go into effect in the middle of the academic year 1902–3. It took several faculty meetings to become accustomed to the various new channels of communication, but business was being transacted without serious complications when the College opened in the fall of 1903.

The "new plan," as it was called for several years, created a Faculty of Arts and Sciences composed of the members of the faculties of the school of liberal arts (previously called the school or college of letters), the engineering school, the divinity school, and the graduate school, and having jurisdiction over all matters common to more than one constituent school. The appointed dean of the school of liberal arts was to be *ex officio* dean of the Faculty of Arts and Sciences, and the elected secretary of the Faculty of Arts and Sciences was to serve *ex officio* as secretary of the constituent faculties. A brief experiment was tried in 1910 of giving the secretary (who was also a full-time teacher) more than purely clerical duties. On the initiative of Austin B. Fletcher, an aggressively loyal alumnus, the arts and sciences secretary was assigned the additional tasks of serving as general liaison agent between the College and the alumni and supervising publicity. This turned out to be too demanding an assignment for one man. Until supplemented (and eventually superseded) by a Department of Publicity organized in 1920, student newspaper correspondents handled most of the publicity and the Alumni Association maintained official contact between the College and its graduates. Only those of professorial rank were entitled to vote on matters of policy or general administration except in the case of those of lower rank who happened to be the sole representatives of their departments. The following standing committees were created in 1902–3: Absences and Petitions; Scholarships and Aids; Library; Program; Examinations; Catalogue; Books and Supplies; Student Organizations; and Use of College Buildings. Three faculty representatives were to serve on the Board of Directors of Athletics. Between 1904 and 1906, the following committees were added: Admissions; Student Employment; Commencement Parts (consisting of the president and the four deans); and Common Interests (the ancestor of the Committee on Administration).

The basic structure of the Faculty of Arts and Sciences and the relationships among constituent faculties underwent very little change after 1903.[41] The Crane Theological School faculty were temporarily removed from the Arts and Sciences faculty in 1962 at their request and became a separate faculty comparable to those of the medical and dental schools and the Fletcher School of Law and Diplomacy.[42] The Crane faculty thus briefly enjoyed the status they had had when the divinity school was established in 1869. In 1965, however, the Crane faculty rejoined the Faculty of Arts and Sciences because of a new program instituted by the school. Although standing committees of both the Arts and Sciences faculty and the constituent faculties were added or subtracted or renamed after 1903, the by-laws of the general faculty underwent no significant alterations. Dean Wren suggested in his annual report for 1934–35 that it was time the entire organization of the faculties was reviewed. The system adopted in 1902–3, when the entire enrollment on the Hill was 333, was still being used to administer a student body of nearly 1,300. Neither the administration nor the faculty took the hint, however, until 1953. Even then, the new by-laws adopted on June 1, 1954, did little more than incorporate minor changes that had been made in the previous half-century. It was not until 1964 that any of the Associated Faculties made any important changes in their organization. In that year the graduate school faculty rewrote their by-laws to clarify membership and to establish a new committee system.

Like most American colleges in the early and middle nineteenth century, Tufts was primarily a teaching institution when it

41 They were designated "Associated Faculties" after June 1, 1954.

42 This action was approved by the Executive Committee of the Trustees on April 4, 1962.

was established. The scholarship of the faculty was more likely to be exhibited in the classroom than in published research. The perpetuation and transmission of learning rather than its advancement was emphasized. Tufts' first president, Hosea Ballou 2d, was that rare combination of outstanding teacher and productive scholar, but the bulk of his published investigations, including his sermons, appeared before the multitudinous duties of college administration absorbed most of his energies. A. A. Miner and E. H. Capen excelled as orators, usually on religious and general educational subjects, and their sermons and addresses frequently found their way into print. Very little publication of faculty research took place before 1890, and with the exception of the laboratory sciences, the field was left largely to the alumni, who wrote on a great variety of subjects.[43]

The first systematic attempt to compile information on both faculty and alumni publications was made by the editors of the *Tufts College Graduate,* although the *Tufts Collegian,* an early undergraduate newspaper, had an occasional review. The alumni journal carried reviews of books (and even of articles) and notices of publications received, beginning with its first issue in the spring of 1903. Among the scholarly productions to which attention was called in the early issues was *The American Merchant Marine,* written by Winthrop L. Marvin of the Class of 1884 and published by Charles Scribner's Sons. Early graduates of the divinity school, including several of its alumni faculty, wrote or edited numerous collections of sermons. Leo R. Lewis, linguist and musical scholar and composer of Tufts' "Alma Mater," began early in his career at the College to publish manuals and handbooks dealing with the

[43] Illustrative of the early publications in science were several articles that appeared in the *American Journal of Chemistry* in 1882–83, summarizing thirteen experiments in organic chemistry worked out in the Tufts laboratory. In the years between 1892 and 1896, after Professor Kingsley had taken charge of the biology laboratory, eighteen scientific papers were published from that department. A convenient summary of the work of some of the leading scientists associated with Tufts from the nineteenth century to the Second World War (e.g., Amos E. Dolbear, Arthur Michael, Arthur Lamb, Norbert Wiener, Vannevar Bush, and Leonard Carmichael) can be found in Nils Y. Wessell, "Tufts Men of Science," *Tuftonian,* Vol. 3, n.s. (March 1943), pp. 102–106. See also Leonard Carmichael, *Tufts College: Its Science & Technology: A Centennial View, 1852–1952* (New York: Newcomen Society of North America, 1952).

technical aspects of music. The undergraduate Engineering Society for a brief period at the turn of the twentieth century sponsored *The Tufts Engineer,* which carried contributions by alumni on such subjects as the system of pneumatic tubes used by the Boston Post Office and the work of the Metropolitan Water and Sewerage Boards of Greater Boston.[44] Professors Sanborn and Hooper published books in 1901–2 that were outgrowths of their engineering courses. Frequently the activities of the faculty and alumni reflecting special non-professional interests resulted in significant editorial work or publication in addition to their contributions in scholarly fields. Professor Charles E. Fay, a talented linguist and founder of the Department of Modern Languages, and for a time dean of the Tufts Graduate School, was also an accomplished mountain climber who for many years edited *Appalachia* and participated in numerous exploring expeditions. The naming of Mount Fay in the Canadian Rockies and Fay's numerous publications relative to mountain-climbing are indicative of his special competency in this challenging area.

When a reasonably complete list of faculty publications began to be published as part of the president's annual report to the Trustees in 1909–10, there were thirty-two faculty members represented by one or more books or articles. The number of faculty on the list was equally divided between the departments on the Hill and the medical and dental schools.[45] By 1940 the list included the publications of ninety-six faculty members.[46] The "Faculty Annual," as it was redesignated in 1958, carried for 1962–63 an impressive sixty-nine-page listing of faculty publications and professional activities.

§ § §

The story of the evolution of policies relating to the rank, salary, and tenure of individual faculty members resembled that of

[44] Only one volume of the *Tufts Engineer* was published, comprising several issues between 1901 and 1904. The *Tuftonian* also published occasional engineering issues.

[45] There were no printed lists of faculty publications between 1917 and 1939, partly because president's reports were no longer printed and generally made public, and partly because of the First World War and a change of presidential administrations.

[46] The numerous publications of the faculty of the Fletcher School of Law and Diplomacy, which opened in 1933, were included in this total.

faculty organization in many respects. Over the years, as the College grew in size and scope of operations and the faculty increased correspondingly, appropriate decisions governing personnel matters were made, largely in piecemeal fashion. It is difficult to trace many of them because they were considered so much a part of academic tradition that they were taken for granted and were sometimes not even put down on paper. Until 1958, when a study of faculty personnel was included in the Tufts-Carnegie Self-Study and when a Faculty Manual was prepared by the dean of the college of liberal arts, there was no single place in which a reasonably complete statement of either policies or procedures could be found. Even in the 1960's questions of interpretation were being raised.[47]

The formal assignment of faculty rank at Tufts followed in general the practices of other academic institutions. The original faculty of 1854 (all professors) was augmented in 1856 by a "teacher" who in 1858–59 became an instructor, and the position of tutor was introduced in 1861–62 to provide instruction under the Walker endowment for mathematics. Four years later, the first Lecturer was appointed (in the field of history). For almost half a century, the two ranks of instructor and professor were the only ones used for full-time faculty members. Toward the end of the nineteenth century the rank of assistant professor began to appear. Associate professors were not customarily appointed in the Hill schools until 1939–40, when six faculty members were promoted to that rank. The latter rank was used quite extensively before the First World War in the medical and dental schools. It first appeared in 1898, when Dr. Martin Prince was elected Associate Professor of Nervous Diseases (without salary). In 1905–6 two members of the medical school faculty were promoted from assistant to associate professors. The first instance of Hill use was in 1911, when Arthur Irving Andrews was elected Associate Professor of History.[48] As late as the administration of President Cousens (1920–37), the rank was still largely unused on the Hill, although

---

[47] Historically, the best sources prior to 1958 were the by-laws of the Trustees, but they were published infrequently, contained relatively little on the subject of the faculty, and in most cases were in skeleton form only. The first edition of the Trustee by-laws was not printed until 1881, after the College was over a quarter of a century old.

[48] He was promoted to full professor the following year.

the medical and dental faculties continued to employ associate professors.[49] It was President Leonard Carmichael, Cousens' successor
in 1938, who made the associate professorship a meaningful rank
at Tufts.

Rules governing appointment, promotion, salary, tenure, and
retirement of faculty members were not very explicit in the early
days of the College, and within some of these areas a conspicuous
lack of uniformity prevailed. Professor Benjamin Graves Brown became a full professor in the Mathematics Department at the age of
twenty-seven and Professor Schneider was still teaching Greek at
the age of eighty. For many decades there was no particular channel
by which promotions were recommended, although they usually
came by way of the president. Several faculty members presented
their own cases directly to the Trustees, and more often than not
they received what they requested. Professor William Ransom of
the Mathematics Department followed this route in 1908 and received not only the promotion from assistant professor to full professor which he requested but a salary increase of $200 into the
bargain. However, there were certain items of academic procedure
established and maintained with little or no change over the years.
It was customary for the Executive Committee of the Trustees to
appoint all assistants, proctors, and minor administrative officials.
Full-time instructors were appointed by the Trustees on recommendation of the Executive Committee, and those of professorial rank
were elected by the Trustees by formal ballot after prior nomination.

The Trustee by-laws of 1881 provided that full professorships
"in all departments of the College . . . shall be held without express limitation of time." Until the Walker Professorship of Mathe-

[49] The question arose in 1921 when Dr. J. L. Conel, of the Department
of Anatomy of New York University and Bellevue Hospital Medical College,
was offered a position on the Tufts Medical School faculty. When he received
notification of appointment as assistant professor he wired the College, protesting that he had been promised an associate professorship by the head of the
Department of Anatomy. President Cousens replied that he was neutral on the
matter, having felt that there was "no clear distinction between Assistant and
Associate." Therefore, the recommendation of rank was entirely up to the
medical school and the question of title was not to influence Professor Conel's
decision. When the appointment was confirmed, he was listed as an associate
professor.

matics was created, the Walker Special Instructorship in Mathematics was a three-year appointment. All others with the rank of instructor or lecturer were for one year.

The phrase "without express limitation of time," as used in 1881, in no sense gave a professor tenure. When those sections of the Trustee by-laws that dealt with faculty personnel were amplified in 1884, it was provided that the Trustees might "at any time without previous notice remove from his office any professor or other person employed in any educational department of the College, for such cause as they may deem sufficient, and they may terminate his office at such time as they may determine, provided that it shall not be less than three months from the time when they shall give him notice of such intended termination."[50] There seems not to have been any wholesale perturbation among the faculty about these provisions, but President Capen started using the term "permanent appointments" in 1894 in his official (and public) communications to clarify the status of those members of the faculty considered to have tenure.[51]

No written rules governed leaves of absence until 1884. Professor John P. Marshall was the first regular faculty member to receive a leave of absence (in 1871–72), and the conditions under which it was granted remained in effect until well into the next century. There was no indication that leaves of absence were intended to encourage scholarly or professional activity. "Pleasure, travel, or partial illness" were the expected reasons for taking a leave of absence, and the applicant was required to make proper provision for his classes "without expense to the College." Every edition of the Trustee by-laws published through 1923 stipulated that a substitute teacher was "to be paid by the absentee." Occasionally an exception was made to the rules. Professor W. R. Shipman, after thirty-five years of uninterrupted service at the College, was granted a one-year leave of absence in 1899–1900. He was prepared to have one course not provided for deducted from his salary, but the Executive Committee, in view of his "long and devoted serv-

[50] Written contracts were introduced at the same time. Resignations required sixty days' notice. The Trustees also established the year of faculty employment as September 1 to August 31 in 1884; the faculty were originally paid five times a year, and then quarterly.

[51] Leo R. Lewis and Frank W. Durkee were among those so designated in the published *President's Report* for 1894–95.

ice," voted to give him full pay. Only two or three instances of leaves of absence granted before the First World War were intended to serve purely academic purposes. Professor David L. Maulsby, of the English Department, was granted leave in 1900 to complete his Ph.D. at the University of Chicago. He had started it at Harvard five years before but had been unable to finish because of a heavy teaching schedule. After 1900 the president or head of department rather than the leave-taker assumed responsibility for finding temporary replacements. Leaves of absence for personnel on annual appointments were not permitted. Professor Dolbear was the first faculty member granted a year's leave (1905–6) with full pay and without the obligation to employ a substitute.[52] Provision for what was to become a "sabbatical leave" in terms of intent and eligibility (although not in designation) was first made in 1908.[53]

That precious commodity, academic freedom, held dear by all teachers, was in copious supply throughout the history of Tufts. The institution had an enviable record in this respect from the day it was chartered. Faculty have come and gone for a variety of reasons, and in the mid-1930's two men resigned in protest over the loyalty oath first required in 1935 of all teachers in Massachusetts, but no cases involving the issue of infringement of academic freedom at the College were ever recorded. Even when McCarthyism swirled over the nation in the 1950's, the teachers at Tufts were considered sufficiently competent, loyal, and responsible to be left to their own devices in the classroom and on the campus. There is no doubt that President Ballou and his Universalist contemporaries would have thoroughly approved this adherence to the principle of academic freedom, for they steadfastly insisted on the unrestricted pursuit and dissemination of truth.

[52] Acting President Hamilton was given the responsibility of arranging for his courses, at a cost not to exceed $250.

[53] Professor Frank B. Sanborn of the Department of Civil Engineering was granted a leave on the grounds that he had "just finished nine years of continuous service to the College." Professor Lane of the Geology Department was the first faculty member to receive a "sabbatical," designated as such. His leave "during 1916–17 with half pay" established the tradition that a faculty member was to receive one-half salary for a year's leave and full salary for a leave of one-half year. Procedures for "sabbatic leave" were first elaborated by the Trustees in 1946 and were restated with minor modifications in 1959.

When the Trustees revised a portion of their by-laws in 1884, one amendment would have provided that "the course of study in the different departments of the College shall be subject to the control of the Trustees; and no essential change shall be made in the same by any Faculty without first obtaining the approval of the Trustees thereto." The proposal was decisively voted down, and no attempt was ever made to revive it. Less than a decade later, the faculty erected walls around their right to preside over the academic destinies of students which have never been seriously broached by colleagues, administrators, or Trustees.

> Each individual instructor shall determine in his own subjects the value of the work done by each student. He shall determine the effect of absences upon the students' work, and shall have power, after a warning which has been previously referred to the Faculty, to exclude from his classes a student whose work is unsatisfactory, either because of its quality or because of the number of absences.

Faculty disciplinary control over students, provided in the Trustee by-laws of 1881, was extended in 1908 to cover the whole area of admissions. It was not until after the First World War that the Trustees took a hand, and the purpose then was to set ceilings on enrollment for practical reasons rather than to dictate the criteria by which students were to be measured.

It was almost three-quarters of a century before any faculty members who had considerable service at the College and held professorial rank were forced by the Trustees to resign. The first such case occurred in 1911–12, and dismissal was preceded by censure and a warning. The faculty member in question was found "by his officious manner and by presuming without authority to represent the College before the public" to have "rendered himself obnoxious to many of the Trustees and friends of the College." No hearing was held, but the professor was warned by the president (at the request of the Trustees) that he was expected to guard his conduct and utterances in the future so as to make formal action unnecessary. The faculty member apparently did not heed the admonition, for the Trustees requested (and received) his resignation.

The second case had more than local ramifications. It involved a member of the faculty who was caught up in the toils of the Enemy Alien legislation of the First World War. Karl Schmidt, a

German by birth, served on the Tufts faculty from 1912 through 1918 and established an international reputation as a psychologist and pioneer in mental testing, which was first used on a large scale during that period. He was highly respected by the Tufts community, but his very prominence brought about his dismissal. As a professional psychologist he was asked to fill out a questionnaire for the Psychology Committee of the National Research Council, which was inventorying specialized manpower. He had to disqualify himself for government service because he was an enemy alien; to make matters worse, one of his statements was taken out of context in such a way that he appeared to refuse to aid the United States in time of war.[54] The Trustees felt that they had no alternative but to dismiss him. Trustee A. W. Peirce regretfully recognized the dilemma into which the College had been thrust. "I should be sorry to have Prof. Schmidt go, for I believe him to be a very valuable man. I realize the situation and am only anxious that we should manifest and keep absolutely plain our fairness and freedom from prejudice in this matter." If Professor Schmidt had not been dismissed when he was, pressure from other quarters would probably have brought about the same result. Less than a month after the Trustees had acted, President Bumpus received a copy of a letter sent to the United States Marshal's office in Boston by the captain in charge of an infantry detachment of nearly 275 men stationed on the Tufts campus. The captain expressed great concern when he discovered that an enemy alien was residing on Professors Row in a house "not over 300 yards from West Hall, the sleeping barracks of the men." The drill grounds were also dangerously close to Professor Schmidt's residence. In short, the captain did "not feel safe in having this man so near my detachment." Although Professor Schmidt was spending the college vacation at his summer home in Tamworth, New Hampshire, when his questionable status was uncovered by the military commander, the captain requested that "this man be removed." An agitated faculty wife lent her support to the necessity of getting the enemy alien off the campus by contacting the officer in charge of the Tufts College Training Detachment. The College had already fulfilled its duty and dismissed

[54] The full documentation for the Schmidt episode is to be found in the Presidential Correspondence, Tufts Archives.

Professor Schmidt, but he was invited to return after the crisis was over, and served as a Lecturer in the Crane Theological School for two years (1924–26).[55]

Faculty salaries at Tufts for most of its history followed patterns that did not deviate markedly from those prevailing in comparable institutions. They were usually considered too low by both the recipients and the majority of the officers of the institution who were responsible for providing them. Salaries almost invariably lagged behind upward swings in the cost of living, and by the time adjustments were made, another round of increases was called for, although not necessarily obtained. Both Presidents Capen and Hamilton were sympathetically aware of the problem. The latter president was the least able to do anything about salaries because of the grave financial crisis that came in the middle of his administration for which he, individually, was not to blame. Until a chapter of the American Association of University Professors was established at Tufts in 1917, the faculty had no outside body to promote their economic betterment, and even then the principal function of the AAUP was to serve only in an educative and prodding capacity by calling attention to the low economic status of the profession. Tufts lost a scattering of its faculty in the nineteenth century because of salary considerations, but the bulk of the regular members stuck by the institution in its periods of financial travail with a loyalty and devotion that frequently brought tributes from both administrative officers and Trustees.

The aggregate salaries of the four original professors (including President Ballou, who carried a full teaching load) was $2,800. This total figure was not significantly increased until the inflation accompanying the Civil War made an upward readjustment imperative. In mid-1864 the faculty received an individual across-the-board increase to $1,400. This step was taken, as the Executive Committee explained to the rest of the Trustees, "in view of the enhanced cost of the necessaries of life." The five full-time faculty with professorial rank were receiving the rather substantial stipend of $2,500 apiece by 1870.[56] The downswing in the national business

---

[55] Professor Schmidt was also a productive scholar while associated with Tufts; eight of his publications in professional journals are in the Tufts Archives.

[56] The two instructors were receiving $1,500 each.

cycle in the 1870's was soon reflected in faculty salaries. Professors were given a 20 per cent reduction to $2,000 in 1877 as a "temporary" emergency measure. Thirty-three years later, that figure was still the maximum salary.[57] It was no wonder that time after time the faculty petitioned for increases. President Capen presented such a request on behalf of the faculty in 1882. The gloomy reply of the Executive Committee was all too often repeated in the next decades.

> While your Committee recognize the justice of the request . . . and appreciate the sacrifices which the underpaid instructors have made and are making for the College, they do not see how in the present condition of the College finances such an increase can be justified. The alarming annual deficit seems to call for a reduction rather than an increase of expenses. They therefore recommend no changes, trusting that another year may find the College in better financial condition.

President Hamilton told the Trustees in no uncertain terms in 1910 that the problem of faculty salaries had reached a critical stage. The College's ability to replace staff or to fill new positions was made possible only because the faculty had private resources or were allowed time to do considerable outside work to supplement their incomes. "The time is past when we can expect to get the full service of men fit to be professors in Tufts College for the salaries now paid." He made salaries the subject of a special report to the Trustees in the spring of 1910 and told them that restiveness among the faculty was increasing and would not be quieted without substantial salary readjustments. He was even more urgent six months later in a second special report, proposing that the Trustees adopt and distribute to the faculty a resolution to the effect that it was "the intention and expectation of the Trustees . . . to establish in the fall of 1911 the rule that the salary of a Professor in the School of Liberal Arts or the Engineering School, who has been holding the rank of full Professor and a salary of two thousand dollars for five years, shall be established at twenty-five hundred dollars, and that the salary of an Assistant Professor in these schools shall be established at sixteen hundred dollars." But the best the

---

[57] In the same interval, salaries of instructors averaged $1,000 and the maximum for assistant professors (after the rank was introduced in the 1890's) was $1,500, preceded by three annual increments of $100.

Trustees could do was to express "the intention and expectation . . . to increase the salaries of professors and assistant professors . . . at the earliest possible moment that the funds of the College will allow."

Because nothing had been accomplished by 1916, twenty-two of the senior members of the faculty requested immediate action. They reminded the Trustees of several unhappy circumstances, all of which added up to the fact that the majority of the faculty were unable to live decently on their salaries. Tufts had "the unenviable distinction of paying smaller salaries than it did a generation ago," while salaries in other New England colleges had increased. The minimum salary of a full professor at Brown was 50 per cent greater than the maximum of his counterpart at Tufts. The answer of the Trustees was to vote a $100 Christmas bonus to each professor in the Hill departments who was not then receiving over $2,000, and to appoint a committee to study the problem. Nothing immediately came out of this, for still another committee was charged with the larger and all-too-familiar task of increasing the funds of the entire institution. Its efforts were, in turn, submerged by the involvement of the College in a nation at war. Some upward adjustments were made in the decade bridging the First World War, including the establishment of a $3,000 minimum for full professors, but the problem of adequate salaries for all ranks and the development of a coherent and long-range salary policy remained items of unfinished business for many decades to come.

One policy established immediately after the College opened that gave some of the faculty a measure of security and convenience if not increased take-home pay centered around the use of College property for faculty benefit. Professors Marshall and Tweed bought lots from the College in 1858 on what became Professors Row. Before many years had gone by, over a dozen such transactions were arranged and houses were constructed, often with mortgages held by the College. Fraternities such as Delta Upsilon made similar arrangements. Many variations developed in the agreements made between the faculty and the College that worked to mutual advantage. Professor Tweed was offered his lot in 1855 as partial compensation for his services; the provisions of his deed established a precedent which has been followed ever since, with only a few exceptions. If the land had been bought from the College, the institution was to have first option on the purchase of it (and any improvements thereon such as buildings) if and when it came on the market.[58]

Some of the faculty sold their equities in their homes to the Trustees and paid rent. Still others received use of their homes in lieu of a portion of their salaries.[59]

One benefit eventually acquired by faculty members on the Hill who had children was free tuition at Tufts for their offspring. President Capen received the first inquiries as to this possibility in 1876. One local argument in favor of such a practice was "the remoteness of the Professors' houses from the schools of the neighborhood," which put the faculty "at a disadvantage with respect to educational facilities."[60] He investigated the customs of other New England colleges and found no commonly accepted practice. About half of them gave free tuition to faculty sons or dependent wards. The Executive Committee discussed the matter but took no action. Twenty years elapsed before the subject was considered again. The Trustees received a petition from twenty faculty members in 1896 suggesting that as long as the reduction of faculty salaries in 1877 was still in effect, perhaps the Trustees could alleviate the financial problems of some families by permitting faculty children to attend Tufts without payment of tuition. This faculty effort attracted sufficient attention to result in a statement of policy by the Trustees four years later. The Executive Committee agreed to remit tuition

[58] This provision in Tweed's deed was invoked when he resigned in 1865. In accordance with the agreement, the appraised value was determined by three men — one selected by the Trustees, one by the seller, and one agreed on by both parties. Tweed's house was purchased for $3,500 and conveyed to Professor Heman A. Dearborn at the same price the following year.

[59] These arrangements, which were made a matter of record by the Trustees in March 1882, existed with such faculty members as Sawyer, Leonard, Tousey, Fay, and Shipman. Still another variation was a provision in many deeds to property near the College but not owned by it, that the Trustees should have the first opportunity to acquire it if it changed hands. All faculty members who lived in College buildings were charged for their heat and light as well as rent beginning in 1892. Effective in 1898, taxes were paid by all tenants occupying houses owned by the College.

[60] Three Tufts families would have benefited from free tuition at this time.

because "the presence of the children of the Faculty in the College is distinctly advantageous, . . . their education does not appreciably increase the expense of carrying on the College . . . [and] the salaries paid by the College are necessarily small." The tuition already paid by the five faculty children then enrolled was refunded or translated into scholarships. This policy adopted in 1900 became a permanent one and was later extended and adapted for Tufts faculty children attending other institutions.

Until 1905 the Tufts faculty retiring from their teaching careers shared with the majority of their academic colleagues all over the United States an uncertain and sometimes bleak financial future. Very few colleges or universities provided pensions or retirement benefits of any kind, and poverty (genteel or otherwise) and even destitution lay in store for many teachers who had been put out to pasture. It was not until college administrators interested Andrew Carnegie in the plight of the economically insecure retired college teacher that a system of sorts was devised under the auspices of the Carnegie Foundation for the Advancement of Teaching.[61] Brief and passing consideration had been given to the problem of the retired professor at Tufts only once prior to 1905. Edwin Ginn, of the Class of 1862 and head of the flourishing textbook publishing firm bearing his name, had been approached on this matter by Trustee A. A. Miner in 1894. After "thinking the matter all over, about establishing a fund for the benefit of retiring professors at Tufts," Ginn agreed to contribute $500 toward it, providing the amount raised reached $10,000.[62] The total sum was completely outside the financial capabilities of the College and nothing came of the idea. The so-called "Carnegie Plan," made public in 1905, appeared to be the answer.

The Carnegie Foundation had to determine what institutions were eligible for its free pensions, for there were two restrictions of considerable importance written into the rules of the Foundation. Faculties of institutions that were either state-supported or sec-

[61] The background of this organization is summarized in Chapter 8. The story of the early years of the Foundation is given in Theron F. Schlabach, *Pensions for Professors* (Madison: State Historical Society of Wisconsin, 1963).

[62] Ginn also specified that Professor Schneider was to have been the first beneficiary.

tarian in character were excluded.[63] There was no problem about Tufts' eligibility on the first count, but there was a delay in adding Tufts to the approved list because of the doubt about its relationship to the Universalist denomination. The existence of the divinity school was also a complicating factor.

The Tufts Trustees promptly sent a communication to the Foundation in 1905 "informing them as to the unsectarian character of Tufts College, and asking to have its Instructors regarded as eligible for aid in the distribution of the income of said fund." But this did not suffice. The first reaction of the Carnegie Foundation was that Tufts faculty could not be eligible because the College conducted a theological school under the auspices of a religious denomination. Furthermore, the Trustees had failed to comply with the requirement that a resolution be formally adopted and certified to the Foundation. The Foundation asked for clarification the next year, and the Tufts Trustees adopted and transmitted a statement of policy regarding religious teaching at the College. The statement that was prepared merely reaffirmed, reemphasized and made more explicit what had already been provided in the College charter. The resolution reassured the Carnegie Foundation that

> no denominational test is (or shall be) imposed in the choice of Trustees, officers or teachers or in admission of students, nor are distinctly denominational tenets or doctrines taught to the students in Tufts College; except that the Divinity School, having its separate Dean and Faculty and separate endowments, is primarily designed for the education of candidates for the ministry of the Universalist Church, although students are not required either on admission or at any other time to make profession of the particular beliefs of that denomination, and teachers in this School as well as in the College of Letters, Engineering School, Medical School and Dental School are appointed under the provisions of the Charter.

The resolution repeated the charter prohibition of a religious test of any kind for teacher or student.

The Carnegie Foundation ruled that the faculty of the theological school were not eligible for pensions but that the rest of the

[63] Whether or not Carnegie himself intended to exclude state-aided or state-controlled institutions is not germane here; however, this was a great matter of controversy in the early history of the Foundation and is treated fully in Schlabach.

College could be recognized as non-sectarian. Tufts thus became one of the 105 institutions in the United States and Canada that were eligible for participation. Faculty at eligible institutions could receive Carnegie benefits upon retirement if they had accumulated twenty-five years' service, or fifteen years' service and had reached the age of sixty-five. The pension was computed on the basis of a percentage of the professor's salary during his last five years of active service, with a sliding scale to benefit those with unusually low salaries. Allowances were also made to widows. The pensions were customarily paid through the institution, which had to file a certificate of eligibility for each faculty member. Professor Schneider was the first recipient at Tufts, with $540 annually from the Foundation. The retirement allowances under the Carnegie system were usually so small that some colleges (including Tufts) occasionally added a supplemental grant. With the $260 contributed by the College, Schneider was made Professor of Greek Emeritus with the munificent retirement stipend of $800 a year (raised by the College to $1,000 a year in 1908).[64]

No more institutions were admitted to the "Carnegie List" after 1913, and no individuals who started teaching after 1915 were eligible for pensions. The philosophy of the free pension system gave way to the contributory idea out of which emerged the Teachers Insurance and Annuity Association in 1919. It was many years, however, before Tufts became a participant in the annuity plan of the TIAA. In the interval it made retirement contributions to faculty or their widows on a strictly individual basis. The faculty member of the 1960's, surrounded as he was by a vast array of fringe benefits unheard of (or unthinkable) before the Second World War, would not be likely to have envied his colleagues of earlier generations to any great degree.

[64] Other early recipients of Carnegie pensions were Dolbear, Shipman, and Charles D. Bray; their pensions from the Foundation averaged over $1,200. In 1913, eleven alumni and friends of the College quietly banded together and pledged sufficient money over a five-year period to increase Professor Fay's salary so that $315 a year could be added to his Carnegie pension.

11. *Academic Indispensables:*
Students and Alumni

THE COLLEGE CONSISTS OF alumni, Faculty, students, and Trustees. These are not separate bodies with divergent interests, but one body bound together by interest in a common cause and engaged in a common endeavor." These words of President Hamilton, written in 1908, were not very startling or profound in themselves, and they said nothing that was not already known. Yet they needed to be placed in the record, for it often was — and is — all too easy for one group to forget that the other three existed. Whatever Tufts has been, is, and will continue to be, both to itself and to the world outside, involves an inextricable intermingling of all of these components. Bricks and stones, laboratories and libraries, and all of the other physical accouterments of a college, are not very useful or meaningful outside the human context. Students and alumni are as indispensable as faculty, staff, governing bodies, and curriculum. They are, of course, the *raison d'être* of an academic institution.

§ § §

A review of the Tufts undergraduate population, particularly in the nineteenth century, reveals a set of rather well-defined characteristics. The great majority of students lived in New England, came preponderantly from middle-class rather than wealthy homes, and reflected a religious diversity uncommon for the time. In 1865 Tufts published its first separate directory of officers and students (with all names more or less awkwardly transposed into Latin). It revealed that of the first eighty-five degree recipients the number of students from Massachusetts about equaled those from the other New England states. There was only a handful from New York State, and one graduate each from Ohio, Pennsylvania, and Wisconsin. Of the 224 students connected with the College since its

opening, only 59 came from outside New England. Tufts was destined to retain its basically regional character until the Second
World War worked a major revolution in the geographical origins
of the student body.

Most of the Tufts clientele in the nineteenth century were
modest in circumstances. In the course of seeking reasons for the
relative decline of enrollment in liberal arts in the decade preceding the First World War, President Hamilton found part of the
explanation in the nature of the student body. Students tended to
be drawn from families of "very moderate means." Tufts had
"many poor, very few rich." Consequently, most of the students
came from a stratum of society that was particularly sensitive to
fluctuations in economic conditions. Hamilton believed that all of
the engineering students and "very many" of the other students
came to college from purely economic motives. They were at Tufts
mainly, if not solely, because they thought a college education
would bring in a sure and quick financial return, for the sake of
which they and their parents were willing to make a considerable
investment or even sacrifice in money, time, and effort. The dull-
ness evident in the business world when he made his analysis was
immediately reflected in the size of the Tufts student body. The
hesitancy to make the financial commitments necessary for a college
education, the decreasing ability of parents to furnish the assistance
and of the students to obtain summer employment — all had an
adverse effect on enrollment.

Although the College was open to all young men who could
meet its admission requirements, the expectation was that most of
them would come from preparatory schools under Universalist
auspices. This was not to be uniformly the case. Universalist academies had furnished a high proportion of the students during the
first decade or so, but as the public high school movement gathered
strength and as the Universalist-sponsored schools declined relatively in numbers and output of graduates, the College drew from
an ever-widening circle of secondary schools outside of denominational influence. A scant one-third of the students entering between
1870 and 1875 came from Universalist preparatory schools.[1]

[1] Nine of the thirteen students who had entered Tufts in August 1855
(out of the thirty enrolled) came from Green Mountain Liberal Institute (later
Perkins Academy). Dean Academy and Goddard Seminary furnished the

An important factor making for a religiously heterogeneous student body at a time when "orthodoxy" of some kind was the rule rather than the exception in private colleges was the insistence that the article in the Tufts charter prohibiting any religious test for admission be strictly adhered to. At first, by the nature of things, the students tended to be overwhelmingly Protestant. The required attendance at chapel — a feature of every nineteenth-century college — probably acted as something of a deterrent to those of some faiths, but it served as a block in only rare instances.[2] President Capen reaffirmed the College's stand in an article reprinted in the Boston papers: "We have never been narrowly sectarian — we have students of all sects, including Roman Catholics." He was expressing both the spirit and the letter of Tufts policy then and later. Neither the race nor the national origin of either students or faculty was ever a primary concern; students from Puerto Rico and China, for instance, attended Tufts long before the First World War. Nonwhites were always a small minority of the student population, but that was more a reflection of the social milieu in which the institution found itself than the result of a deliberate policy of the College.

The student body by the opening decade of the twentieth century was clearly reflecting the liberal principles of Tufts' founders. It was attracting men and women from virtually all religious backgrounds. At the same time, however, the College continued to consider itself a Universalist institution by looking to that denomination for financial aid as well as for at least a portion of its students.

largest numbers of any of the Universalist schools in the 1870's, followed by Westbrook Seminary, Clinton Liberal Institute, and Perkins Academy. There were also several transfers from Buchtel College in Ohio. In his first annual report to the Trustees (1875–76), President Capen recommended that a special "fitting school," in the neighborhood of the College but not organically connected with it, be established by some alumnus, but no one came forward.

[2] One student in 1880 asked "to be excused from attendance upon Morning Chapel on the ground that it was contrary to the rules of his Church for him to attend any religious services other than those of his own communion." His petition was denied, and was denied a second time when he returned the following year. He thereupon dropped out of Tufts. Two things should be noted about his case: it was the only such instance of record in the history of the College, and the faculty was not unanimous in its vote to deny either petition.

Tufts was still being referred to in the late 1880's as "one of the leading educational forces in sympathy with and under the control of the Universalist denomination." The idea of maintaining a "community of interest" was also continued by the Trustees for a considerable time.[3]

When financial difficulties threatened to require a curtailment of the divinity school, a special Trustee committee in 1902 urged that "we do everything to hold and strengthen our Universalist support."

> Most of us probably would welcome the day when Tufts shall have become a prosperous non-sectarian college which no one will confound with the theological school or refuse a gift because he believes it strongly denominational. That day however is not yet come, nor is it even in sight. Those who are now showing their love and loyalty to Tufts by making it the recipient of gifts and legacies are doing so because they are Universalists and because they believe that it is a Universalist College, standing for and carrying out the purposes of its founders. The number of great donors who have given to it, not because it was a Universalist institution but wholly because it was a progressive, promising college can be counted on the fingers of one hand. The time has not come to cut away from denominational support. We should rather if we are to be guided by experience, do everything to make the denomination feel that Tufts is today, as in the past she has been, its principal intellectual stronghold and object of denominational pride.

In succeeding decades both the support and the direction of Tufts gradually broadened and shifted to include others along the religious spectrum. Methodists and Jews, Unitarians and Episcopalians, Roman Catholics and Congregationalists, contributed their patronage, their money, and their talents. Universalists continued to have a special affection for the College; they sent generation

---

[3] Typical were the proposals in 1906 to fill vacancies. William Fuller, a master in the Mechanic Arts High School in Boston, was a graduate of the Class of 1879. Mayor Charles Neal Barney of Lynn, Massachusetts, was a lawyer and alumnus of the Class of 1895. Rosewell Bigelow Lawrence, a lawyer and resident of Medford, was a Harvard graduate but was " prominent member of the Universalist Society in that city, and interested in Tufts College." William Lewis Douglas of Brockton, ex-governor of Massachusetts, was not a college graduate, but he had received an LL.D. from Tufts and was "an earnest and active Universalist."

after generation of their sons and daughters to Tufts and supported the institution in innumerable ways. But after the First World War they found themselves more and more in the minority and seemed to mind it very little. Their open-ended and unusually tolerant philosophy of letting each man be the keeper of his own conscience was translated into reality time and time again.

§ § §

No self-respecting collegiate student body, past or present, would exist and flourish long without organizing in some fashion. Tufts students were no exception. Literary societies, fraternities, athletic groups, and other manifestations of the gregarious tendencies of humankind appeared almost simultaneously with the opening of the College in 1854. Organizations and groupings, both formal and otherwise, rose and fell as the tides, disappeared and reappeared, often under new names, and reflected the changing social and intellectual needs of a long sequence of student generations. Class rivalries, hazing, and student antics all added to the variety and (at times) the excitement of college life. Rules and regulations there always were, furnished often by the students themselves, and equally often by elders who generally had the best of intentions in their recognition of the duty of the College to serve *in loco parentis*. Students from time immemorial have protested the apparent obfuscation that lies back of all attempts to regulate their activities and general behavior and have insisted that the faculty and administration are unenlightened and paternalistic at best, oppressive and downright tyrannical at worst. But somehow both the makers and breakers of said attempts at student governance and control have survived down the years, and the undergraduates, despite occasional threats to law, order, sobriety, stability, and the sanctity of life and property, have managed to leave the social fabric with only an occasional loose or dangling thread.

The first society formed among the students owed its name to Thomas H. Angell, of the Class of 1858.[4] Created within the year

[4] The bulk of the material in the sections of this chapter dealing with student organizations and activities has necessarily been drawn from student publications which were uneven in coverage and not always of unimpeachable accuracy. The records of the organizations themselves have not always been available. The reminiscences of many alumni, although of great interest, tend

that the College opened, the Mathetican Society, headquartered in a room reserved for it on the third floor of the College Edifice, became a literary organization typical of those that flourished on almost every college campus in the nineteenth century. Its meetings were serious and its programs were heavily weighted with intellectual content — debates, essays, orations, and poems on such topics as the tariff, women's suffrage, world peace, the income tax, and Nature, Truth, and Beauty. Mock trials and model legislative sessions conducted according to the strictest parliamentary rules were also within the society's province. The society held special exercises on its anniversary in October and on Commencement Day, and for many years its programs shared space with the names of the graduating classes on the printed Commencement folder.

As fraternities and other organizations grew in numbers and in strength, literary societies, so called, began to wane. The Mathetican was one of the casualties. After two resurrections, the organization became so moribund and the difficulty of obtaining a quorum so great that it was disbanded in 1896. But that did not mean the end of the oratorical endeavors it had encouraged. In a matter of weeks the treasury of the old organization ($9.95) was transferred to the newly created Tufts Debating Union, which in turn became a vehicle for forensics then enjoying great popularity among colleges everywhere. After the Union became comatose and then expired, the Capen Club and the Knowlton Club carried on the local debating tradition. The first intercollegiate debate in which Tufts participated was held in Goddard Chapel in 1903, with New York University as the opponent. The question was a timely one: "Resolved: That the United States Should Hold the Philippines as a Permanent Possession." The Tufts team, which took the affirmative, won the debate.

The Mathetican Society could not exist without a rival. Several members of the Class of 1860, dissatisfied with the management of the Society, created their own in 1857–58. The Walnut Hill

---

frequently to be surrounded by a certain haze engendered by the passage of time and the sometimes limited angle of vision of the viewer. These sources have been drawn upon wherever they could best serve a particular purpose or make a special point. Wherever doubt or contradiction appeared as to the origin, date, disappearance, or rebirth of an organization, activity, or tradition, the source closest to it in point of time was used.

Fraternity, even though it too received housing privileges in the main College building, lasted less than three years. With a degree of specialization and division of labor comparable to that so evident in American industrial society after the Civil War, yet another literary group appeared on the Tufts campus in the early years. After the divinity school was created in 1869, a Theological Society was organized among students planning to enter the ministry. In 1871 it became the Zetagathean Society. It held weekly evening meetings (including religious services) and for many years paralleled the more secular, but nonetheless elevated, Mathetican Society.

Secret societies (fraternities to later student generations) appeared promptly and fluctuated widely in numbers and strength. The first Greek-letter fraternity to appear at Tufts was Zeta Psi; the Kappa Chapter was founded in 1855 on the initiative (or with the assistance) of a chapter at Harvard. After its first meeting in student quarters in October 1855 the fraternity was based in Medford for nearly forty years; in 1894 it acquired rooms in Odd Fellows Hall in North Cambridge. The Civil War was a near disaster to the fraternity, for all but two members of the local chapter served in the armed forces and it suffered many casualties. No men were initiated during the first years of the conflict, but after 1864 the fraternity regained its strength and had by 1896 an undergraduate membership of over twenty, with six graduates serving on the Tufts faculty.

The founding of the second Tufts fraternity with national associations, Kappa Charge of Theta Delta Chi, took place in 1856, through the efforts of a transfer student from Brown University. This fraternity likewise contributed its share of membership to the Civil War but was able to live a continuous existence and to furnish at least one member to each Tufts graduating class during the conflict. It had the distinction of having on its rolls Elmer H. Capen, the first alumnus of Tufts to serve as president of the institution, and one of the charter members of the fraternity. The chapter acquired a house in 1893 built for its use on Packard Avenue.

For slightly over thirty years Zeta Psi and Theta Delta Chi had the Greek-letter fraternity field at Tufts to themselves. Rivalry was keen, but they cooperated long enough to publish the original *Tuftonian* (the first undergraduate publication) from 1864 to 1872. The Tufts chapter of Delta Upsilon was established in the winter of 1886 and in 1894 moved into quarters on Sawyer Avenue. Professor Frank W. Durkee, long-time chairman of the Chemistry Department, was a member of this fraternity.

Three local fraternities appeared between 1858 and 1869. The first, intended for upperclassmen (the last two years), was the Order of the Coffee Pot. Its motto, QUUM NOBIS PLACEAT CUJUS REFERT, was engraved on one side of the silver watch-fob which was a token of membership. The other side carried an engraved symbol of the organization. The fobs were displayed at all public occasions at which coffee was served. The Order of the Coffee Pot managed to exist for six years without a rival, but in 1864 the Order of the Round Table put in an appearance. The symbol of this secret society, with the motto UTILITAS PARITERQUE DELECTATIO, belied its name, for the silver fob was octagonal. The Round Table disappeared, along with the Coffee Pot, in 1868. Nothing is known of So Fa, the third local secret society, except that it was established in 1869 and lived a life too short to have been adequately recorded.[5]

A member of the Delta Tau Delta fraternity at Buchtel University and a graduate of the Tufts Divinity School in 1891 was responsible for the founding of the Beta Mu Chapter at Tufts in 1889. Its first chapter house was opened on the Hill in 1893, and two years later the fraternity moved to Curtis Street. Like Theta Delta Chi, it furnished a president to Tufts College — John A. Cousens, of the Class of 1898. The fifth national Greek-letter fraternity to appear on the campus was Alpha Tau Omega. The Gamma Beta Chapter was organized in 1893 as the first chapter of the fraternity in Massachusetts. Its best-known local member in the 1890's was Frank G. Wren (Class of 1894), who held many positions of responsibility on the Tufts staff, serving for over thirty years as dean of the school of liberal arts. His name was memorialized in the faculty dining hall opened in 1963 as a part of the growing complex of the Tufts Graduate Center. Not to be outdone by their fraternity-minded classmates in the classical, philosophical, and engineering courses, students in the divinity school organized in the fall of 1891

---

[5] A fourth society, Epsilon of Pi Kappa Chi, appeared in 1863 and claimed eleven members in 1864. That was the first (and last) statistic available. The fraternity undoubtedly became the victim of an overorganized campus, for the two principal Greek-letter societies already claimed a membership of close to two-thirds of the student body.

a Hebrew-letter society, Heth Aleph Res. It was able within five years to establish itself in its own house on Sawyer Avenue but disappeared not long thereafter, when enrollment in the divinity school declined.

Socially minded students who by necessity or preference remained outside fraternity bounds concocted their own organizations, mythical or otherwise. Among the tongue-in-cheek societies existing between 1865 and 1875 were the Old Gimlet Fraternity, which had among its officers Ye High MugWump, a Great Mogul, a Great Magoffigin, a Gorilla, and a Grand Putty Gumpus; and the "Augers" which had among its officers a Master Borer, a Little Bit, a Center Bit, and a Big Bore.

The introduction of coeducation in 1892 almost immediately brought sororities to the Hill. Alpha Delta Sigma was organized by six young ladies in the fall of 1895 and before the first academic year was over had increased its membership to fifteen. A second sorority had been in the planning stage less than a year after women were admitted to Tufts, but the number of women did not at the outset justify two sororities. However, the stimulus of the establishment of Alpha Delta Sigma was sufficient in 1895 to make the idea of a second local secret society for women practicable. Eight coeds constituted the charter membership of Alpha Kappa Gamma.

The merits and demerits of "secret societies" have been argued since the species evolved out of the misty past. Debate at Tufts over the subject did not erupt into undergraduate print until the fall of 1882, when the two fraternities then on the campus became the target of the "non-society" men because of "aggressive raids into territories to which they have no title." The rivalries between Zeta Psi and Theta Delta Chi and the favoritism allegedly shown to members of one group or the other had, it seemed, brought about the decline of football and had adversely affected every activity from elections for Class Day to the financially ailing *Tuftonian*. The perennial debate was far from over in 1882; by the 1960's, eight more Greek-letter fraternities and three more sororities had been organized (although they did not all survive) and furnished more grist for the continuing conversation over the advantages and disadvantages of brotherhoods and sisterhoods on the campus.

Fraternities and sororities, local or national, appearing at

Tufts in the nineteenth century were by no means limited to the social category. The Delta Chapter of Phi Beta Kappa, national honorary society, was chartered in 1892 through the efforts of Thomas Wentworth Higginson (whose institutional connections were much more closely associated with Harvard than Tufts); Professor William R. Shipman, who was long associated with the Tufts community; and Prof. Frank Pierrepont Graves, a classicist while briefly on the Tufts faculty, and an educator and college administrator of later renown at other institutions.

No one should have complained, even when Tufts was very young and very small, that there was no organization to appeal to the most diverse tastes, talents, and energies of students. If fraternity or sorority membership was unavailable (or unattractive), there were sports of all kinds, not to mention societies and clubs to appeal to those whose proclivities did not run in athletic directions. A student at Tufts between 1860 and 1900 might have belonged to the Tufts Chess Club (founded in 1873); the Tufts Amateur Dispatch Company (to practice telegraphy); the Reading Room Association, which subscribed to three Boston and three New York newspapers and such periodicals as the *Atlantic* and *Harper's*; the Pentagon Society (mathematics); a Bible Society; or the Shakespearian Club. In fact, there were already twenty student organizations on the campus in 1864, with membership ranging from three to thirty-five. The total membership in the six most important organizations alone that year was 129. If one considers the fact that there was a total student body of fifty-three in 1864 it can readily be seen that participation in extracurricular activities was widespread.

§   §   §

Music has always played an important part in the life of Tufts students. For many years at the turn of the century the institution was known as "the Singing College."[6] Quartets and quintets (including the Silver Bells) were the first musical organizations, providing everything from barbershop harmony to operatic selections. A Glee Club was formed in 1867, but, as with many another student group, the fatal mistake was made of selecting all the members from one class; their graduation put an end to this musical en-

[6] The definitive work is Harry Adams Hersey, *A History of Music in Tufts College,* published by the Trustees of Tufts College in 1947.

President Capen, using the facilities of the Reading Room

deavor for several years. After the passage of time and the arrival of another college generation, another organization took its place. During the mid-1870's a "private" Glee Club known as the "East Hallers" held sway, but vocal music did not take on great vitality until Leo R. Lewis, of the Class of 1887, appeared on the scene and organized the chapel choir into a Glee Club which gave public concerts in the late 1880's and 1890's and traveled extensively.[7] A Banjo Club, organized in 1888, was superseded by a mandolin and Guitar Club, which often accompanied the Glee Club. An orches-

[7] "Dear Alma Mater," the music for which was composed by Lewis in 1898, was first rendered in full choral form, with organ, at a concert in 1900. Professor David L. Maulsby of the English Department wrote the words. Discipline for the Glee Club was strict. There were four or five rehearsals a week, formal dress was required at all concerts, and members were fined for making mistakes and for letting their eyes wander too far in the direction of ladies in the audience. Smoking by members was prohibited at all times.

tra of five members was organized in 1871 but died out periodically and was now and again revived. The group sometimes erroneously referred to as the "Original Tufts Orchestra" actually existed from 1883 to 1890 but did achieve distinction in its day for its size (varying from eleven to over twenty members), the high quality of its performances, and its numerous public appearance. There was never enough talent on the campus in the nineteenth century to produce a full complement, so players from neighboring communities were frequently included. Only one brass band (organized in 1884) served the campus briefly before the First World War.

Aside from optional instruction in vocal music between 1869 and 1876, there was nothing approaching a Department of Music or provision for instruction until 1895. Albert Metcalf subsidized the first Professorship of Music (held by Leo Lewis) and obtained for the College between 1895 and 1897 many valuable works on the history and theory of music. He also secured the working library of Frederic Louis Ritter, which consisted of over 2,000 volumes, including 500 orchestral scores of standard works.[8] Orchestration was completed for five of the most popular Tufts songs as a part of regular class work in 1901. They were first publicly performed by sixty members of the Boston Symphony Orchestra on a May evening in 1901, thus inaugurating the annual spring custom of "Tufts Night at the 'Pops.' "

Dramatics was another student enterprise that attracted considerable interest. The Tufts Dramatic Club, formed in 1876, was among the first (and short-lived) Thespian organizations and performed on a stage constructed for the purpose in the chapel of the main College building. The Stuft Club, founded in 1886, lasted until 1892, when its chief promoter became an alumnus. Three years later, the Modjeska Club was formed, with the purpose of producing serious drama; it had but a brief career. The Eranos Club enjoyed a similarly abbreviated life. Until 1910 no organization interested in dramatics survived the graduation of its members, and except for an occasional special all-College production, individual classes presented what plays were given.[9] Out of this

[8] For many years most of the Ritter Collection has rested in dust-covered splendor in the recesses of the library.

[9] The great dramatic event in 1895 was a presentation of Nicholas Udall's *Ralph Roister Doister,* under the direction of the English Depart-

practice arose the custom of having the junior class produce and act a play each year. Out of this, in turn, came the only student dramatic group to have a continuous history into the 1960's. Founded in the spring of 1910, Pen, Paint, and Pretzels (3 P's) was an honorary society at first limited to seniors but extended after a time to juniors. Its original purpose was to "encourage dramatic interest at Tufts College by the production of original plays by students or graduates of Tufts or Jackson."[10] The "temporary" stage provided in Goddard Gymnasium in the 1880's was replaced by similar facilities in the remodeled headquarters of the Somerville Golf Club which in 1909 became the women's gymnasium. The same building, redesignated the Tufts Arena Theatre after the Second World War, was still serving as headquarters for dramatics in the 1960's, Jackson College having acquired a new gymnasium in 1948.

The 3 P's did not confine their productions to original plays, although they were in good supply. As scenery, lighting, and student interest grew, the organization became more and more ambitious and in 1913 went outside its own circle of authorship for the first time by offering Henrik Ibsen's *Enemy of the People*. Producers and sponsors varied from year to year, working in more or less close cooperation with the 3 P's. In some instances it was a particular Tufts freshman or sophomore class that put on the play; in others, it was the Masque, the official dramatic society of Jackson College, organized in 1915–16 and united with the 3 P's in 1930. During and immediately after the First World War the 3 P's went on the road, entertaining troops at Commonwealth Pier and the Navy Yard in Boston, and at Fort Devens, and civilians in such nearby communities as Winchester and Everett. Among the undergraduate leaders in the 3 P's in the immediate postwar years was Leonard Carmichael. He became president of the College less than twenty years after he played leading parts in several 3 P's productions and served as the society's president in 1921. The leading

ment. An even more impressive offering was the joint production of John Milton's *Masque of Comus* by members of the Departments of Music and English in 1901. Thomas Dekker's *Old Fortunatus* was the third major College-sponsored effort before 1910.

[10] Charles R. Gott, of the Class of 1911, and one of the five charter members, later returned as chairman of the English Department.

dramatic organization had no more qualms about presenting Shake-speare, Shaw, and a host of other prominent playwrights in 1916 than in the 1960's.

Events, organizations, and worthy causes in the non-collegiate world have always been reflected to some extent on the Tufts campus. A branch of the National Young People's Christian Union was established in 1891. In the following year a Prohibition Club appeared; it experienced various fortunes until it suffered a perceptible (and permanent) decline after 1932, with the repeal of the Volstead Act and the Eighteenth Amendment to the federal Constitution. Politically concerned students have organized local clubs to support national presidential candidates from one four-year period to another, following the tradition established in 1876 when rival organizations were created to support Rutherford B. Hayes and Samuel J. Tilden. The potential Republicans on the campus then outnumbered the Democrats almost four to one — a situation completely reversed by the 1960's.

Isolated as the College may have seemed in the nineteenth century, located on its hilltop northwest of Boston, there were numerous opportunities for contact — academic and otherwise — with the outside world. Students could make trips by boat (via the Mystic River), rail (the Boston and Maine), or streetcar (the Boston Elevated) to see the sights or enjoy the cultural — and other — advantages of the Big City. Or they could be treated to many forms of intellectual stimulation offered by outside speakers or special programs of various kinds made available on the campus The oldest endowed series was the Russell Lectures, established by James Russell of West Cambridge (Arlington), Massachusetts, in 1867. The lecturers, selected annually by the Trustees and usually after consultation with the faculty, spoke on a topic relating to Christianity, in accordance with the provisions of the donor's will. In only one year in the long history of the Russell Lectures was there no speaker.[11] Numerous other programs under the sponsorship of either the institution or some division or department, or one or more student groups, have enriched the regular offerings of the College and have appealed to almost every taste and interest imaginable.

[11] Rev. Massena Goodrich delivered the first address in 1868. No lecture was given in 1918 because of wartime conditions.

*The audience for this speaker in 1885 in front of Packard Hall
comprised half of the student body*

§   §   §

One of the student organizations that had ramifications extending far beyond the confines of the campus was the Tufts College Wireless Society, organized in 1910. It was the outgrowth of a freshman essay competition on "Why Tufts College Should Have a Wireless Club." Wireless communication, still in its infancy then, had already been the subject of experimentation by Professor Amos E. Dolbear of the Physics Department, in the early 1870's. He had obtained a patent in 1882 for a device for wireless signaling, on the basis of successful sending of messages to and from various locations on and near the campus. Students had become interested in the possibilities of this new means of communication and in 1899 had watched a demonstration by a student of the Tufts Engineering Society at a meeting in the main College building. News of the success of the experiments of Marconi and others also spurred the organization of the local club.

Quarters for the Society were first secured in Robinson Hall, and through the efforts of a faculty member who was a captain in the Army Signal Corps a portable wireless set was obtained. The students showed considerable ingenuity in building their own transmitting and receiving apparatus and soon established themselves in a first-floor room in Paige Hall. Before they had to suspend amateur operations because of the First World War, they engaged in such activities as transmitting national football scores to the Tufts Oval while home games were in progress, experimenting with various kinds of antenna, and receiving daily weather reports from Washington, D.C.

The moving spirit behind the early interest in wireless at Tufts was Harold J. Power, of the Class of 1914. While still an undergraduate he had served during vacations as a wireless operator on several vessels, including J. P. Morgan's yacht *Corsair*. With backing from the famous financier, Power organized the American Radio and Research Corporation (AMRAD) in June 1915 and with the permission of the College built a small laboratory on the hillside north of the College buildings. This structure became the nucleus of the building known as North Hall, which was built literally on the installment plan, with numerous additions and renovations that turned it eventually into an academic building.

One of the most interesting physical aspects of AMRAD was the 300-foot lattice-steel transmission tower topped with an umbrella-type antenna erected next to the AMRAD building in the late summer of 1915.[12] A dramatic episode temporarily delayed the completion of the tower. On the morning of September 26, 1915, the day before permanent guy wires were to have been installed to steady the tower, a sudden windstorm sent the structure crashing down the hill and across the street, and onto the Boston and Maine railroad tracks, just in time to derail the front trucks of the locomotive of the crack Montreal Limited inbound to Boston. The tower was soon rebuilt and was put to use in the early fall. Its sending range, originally about 100 miles, was much increased within a year as more powerful equipment was housed in an addition to the original AMRAD building. Power's pioneer work in controlling static electricity in radio transmission and his experimentation with

[12] There was also to have been a 500-foot tower nearby, but it was never constructed.

The Wireless Tower
and original Research Laboratory ("North Hall") in 1915

directional antennas as well as other contributions attracted national attention to his company and to the College.

Special quarters were provided in the AMRAD building for the Wireless Society, and special training opportunities were made available to furnish radio operators, many of whom served in vital military posts during the First World War. The Society was revived in 1923 under the leadership of Professor Raymond U. Fittz of the engineering school, who had been active in it as an undergraduate. Amateur radio communication was developed with a radius of several thousand miles and operated first as Station 1 DZ and in 1924 as 1 DZ-1XAW, with international contacts. After several moves about the campus, the Society died in the basement of West Hall in 1927 after having operated as WIKN (for the amateur) and W1XAW-W1XA1 (for the experimenter). Individual licensed students operated out of fraternity and dormitory rooms from time to time in the 1930's.[13] An attempt was made in 1933 to revitalize what was then known as the Radio Society, but it failed because of inability to raise the money needed for equipment. After other brief revivals amateur radio reappeared in the mid-1950's as the Tufts Amateur Radio Society, operating as WIKN. A closed-circuit student-operated broadcast station, WTCR, operating out of the basement of a classroom building between 1956 and 1961, represented another type of radio communications.

The AMRAD Corporation remained on the Tufts campus until 1931, after which it merged with the Magnavox Company. In its fifteen years on the Hill, AMRAD engaged in a variety of manufacturing operations and conducted numerous experiments. During the First World War it rendered valuable services for the armed forces and continued its transmitting station in full operation. In addition, it gave exceptional laboratory facilities for the Tufts Electrical Engineering Department and unique training opportunities for the Wireless Society.[14] Radio communications history was made on the Tufts campus on the evening of March 18,

[13] One such was Philip C. Noble, operating as Station W1JX8 out of the Theta Chi house.

[14] Among those connected with both the College and AMRAD for a time was Vannevar Bush, of the Class of 1913. One of the founders of the Raytheon Company invented the cold cathode rectifier tube while doing research at AMRAD. One of Power's most important inventions, a submarine detector, was in use in the North Sea at the time of the armistice in 1918.

1916, when AMRAD, working with the Wireless Society as Station 1 XE, broadcast three hours of phonograph music, picked up in an area of over 100 miles, and interspersed with the customary code of ship-to-shore messages.[15] The station continued to broadcast regularly, at first every two weeks and then once a week, until 1917. Programs were resumed in 1919, and in 1920 the station offered daily broadcasts. In May of the following year the experimental station (1 XE) became Station WGI and broadcast both daytime and evening programs.[16]

The educational as well as the entertainment possibilities of radio by means of the speaking voice were soon realized by both AMRAD and the College. The "Tufts College Radiophone Lectures," delivered at scheduled times during the academic year 1921–22 by several members of the Tufts faculty, were the first such talks known to have been broadcast in the United States. Fifteen minutes in length, they were delivered from the AMRAD studios twice each week at eight in the evening to an audience estimated at 100,000. They were given advance newspaper notice arranged by the newly created Department of Publicity.[17] Variety was added to the radio menu in 1924 when recitals were broadcast from the organ in Goddard Chapel and Shakespeare's *Romeo and Juliet* was aired by the Masque, the Jackson College dramatic society.

Broadcasting activities under AMRAD sponsorship came to a halt in the spring of 1925 when the company extended its manufacturing operations and moved to a new location on the campus. Under the original agreement with the College, AMRAD agreed to give its building on Medford Hillside to the institution in exchange for occupancy and use of the land. After the leases expired,

---

[15] One of the persons with earphones clamped to his head was J. P. Morgan, who was then aboard the liner *Philadelphia* off Cape Cod inbound from Europe. He had been notified of the special broadcast in advance by Power.

[16] WGI began scheduled broadcasting approximately one month before the better-known Westinghouse station KDKA in Pittsburgh, although the latter had been airing test programs for several months, and WWJ, the station operated by the *Detroit News*, began broadcasting intermittently in August 1920.

[17] The lectures ranged from "Athletics" by Professor Clarence P. Houston, through "Dramatics" by Professor Albert H. Gilmer, to "Bridge Building" by Professor Edward H. Rockwell. During 1922 approximately thirty lectures were delivered.

AMRAD built in 1920 a new reinforced concrete structure across the Boston and Maine Railroad on property acquired by the College many years before from the Stearns family.[18] The structure on the hillside vacated by AMRAD became the headquarters of the Electrical Engineering Department in 1925, and the radio tower was used briefly in the fall of 1927 as a transmitter for WBET, the station of the *Boston Evening Transcript*. There had been plans in 1925 to reduce the height of the radio tower by 100 feet in the interests of safety, but they were delayed until after WBET moved out. After the Electrical Engineering Department introduced instruction in radio engineering in 1927 and constructed a high-voltage laboratory in the building, the tower was replaced by two short steel poles, which were removed in 1931 when the Electrical Engineering Department moved to the manufacturing building constructed by AMRAD eleven years before. The stuccoed building on the hillside that had already seen so many occupants was designated the "Electro-Technical Building" and during much of the 1920's the Electrical Engineering Department shared it with an engineering firm organized by Frank C. Doble, of the Class of 1911, who leased space from the College. Between 1931 and 1947 the Doble Engineering Company occupied the entire building. The pressure for classroom and office space after the Second World War gave the old AMRAD building a new set of functions. It was renamed North Hall and became the headquarters for a wide variety of departments at one time or another, few bearing any relationship to the purposes for which it had been originally constructed.

§ § §

The Tufts student body would not have been normal if it had not developed its campus customs and traditions and had not indulged in escapades of varying degrees of seriousness. The tradition of Class Day, as a senior class activity, started in June 1876, two days before Commencement. On this gala occasion the exercises, which lasted more or less continuously from 12:30 P.M. to 5:00 P.M., were climaxed by a "grand reception" in the evening, with music furnished by the Germania Band of Boston. Among the cere-

[18] This building, which became a wing of Cousens Gymnasium in 1932, was originally to have been the first unit of a five-unit factory to manufacture radio and other electronic equipment.

monies during the day were deliveries of orations and poems, the burying of a box containing mementos at the foot of a tree near the main College building, and the smoking of "the pipe of peace" to denote the end of class rivalries for another year. As student-sponsored activities were wont to do, the Class Day tradition died out after a period of years and was resurrected by the Class of 1891. The Class of 1892 was credited with reestablishing the annual Field Day, which had also temporarily disappeared.

There were tangible senior "privileges" in the nineteenth century, such as carrying canes and wearing beaver hats. A sign of manliness (in the nineteenth century at least) among all classes was the production of some form of facial adornment. Mustaches, "side tabs," goatees, full beards and gradations thereof were the rule rather than the exception. The faculty in the 1870's and 1880's either set the style or conformed, judging from the graphic evidence of photographs, portraits, and class albums. One statistically minded student in 1864 found less than half of the student body *imberbe* and less than a quarter of the faculty likewise unadorned.[19]

Extracurricular traditions in the nineteenth century which took greater conscious effort than growing beards included the annual contest for the class pennant between the traditionally rivalrous freshman and sophomore classes. So much life, limb, and property was endangered by the "flag rush" customarily following the fall freshman-sophomore football game that it was abolished in 1900 by vote of the students (and at the request of the faculty). The first incident requiring faculty disciplinary action occurred shortly after the College opened, when a freshman allegedly attempted "to use a pistol upon a room-mate."[20] The frequent disappearance of the Bible from the chapel, or the substitution of a dictionary (unabridged) for The Book, was at least not as noisy as the firecrackers which now and again exploded under the platform or pulpit. There is no record that a cow was ever ensconced in any of the upper floors of the College Edifice, but at one time a

[19] The first president of Tufts was among the few completely clean-shaven inhabitants on the campus in his day; he did not have a like-minded successor in Ballou Hall until 1920.

[20] The culprit was suspended for a year for "intemperance, falsehood, disobedience, and for having dangerous weapons in the college and for using them." Neither the wielder of the pistol nor the intended victim completed his course or received a degree from the institution.

baggage wagon peacefully reposing in the College barn back of Middle (Packard) Hall was completely disassembled and subsequently reassembled in the "Mathematical Recitation Room."[21] When students received written admonitions in the early days of the College for various infractions of the rules of behavior and discipline, the vast majority quickly mended their ways. One, however, became so inured to the plentiful supply sent him that he papered the inside of his dormitory door with them and still managed to graduate. A somewhat more gruesome collection of mementos resulted from the excavations for a street to the Mystic Water Works Reservoir near the top of the Hill in 1879. A large Indian burial mound was uncovered and yielded nine skeletons and various artifacts. "Many of the students have tastefully decorated their rooms with vertebrae, teeth, ribs, and similar cheerful objects from the graves. The effect is quite striking to a stranger of nervous constitution."

Bonfires and other incendiary activities were a special source of anguish for over sixty years because of the isolated location of the College and because of the reluctance, for reasons unknown, of the faculty or Trustees to provide efficient fire extinguishers. The insurance coverage on campus property was never quite adequate in the nineteenth century, and only prompt action by the students prevented the burning of both the College Edifice and East Hall more than once. The former building was almost lost on July 4, 1858, when a student lit a pile of shavings nearby in order to explode firecrackers. His self-righteous explanation to the faculty was that "he had always been allowed to make all the disturbance, noise, and confusion he pleased on the 4th of July." The introduction of baseball created another hazard, for broken windowpanes in the dormitories became a chronic nuisance. The 100-foot tower

[21] By means of certain techniques not recorded, the names of the five guilty parties were ascertained by the faculty. The ringleader was suspended from the College for one semester and, like his pistol-toting classmate, failed to earn a Tufts degree. There is no record of how long the system lasted, but the first effort by the faculty to give the students a measure of self-government was taken in the spring of 1900 and arose out of cases of student discipline. A student jury was created, with the president of the College as judge, to hear and act upon "all cases of public disorder and all offences committed by students against each other." The faculty was to serve as a court of last resort in cases of conflict over jurisdiction or a hung jury.

A student room in East Hall in the late 1880's

No. 8, West Hall, in 1881

Goddard Chapel and Ballou Hall in 1884

constructed as part of Goddard Chapel in the 1880's gave rival classes unparalleled opportunities to lay siege to each other, and the flagstaff erected in 1903 near the top of the Hill tempted students to utilize it for impromptu antics, usually in the dark of the moon. Rolling stones down dormitory stairs, emptying buckets of water on unsuspecting passersby, and similar activities not included on the College calendar brought disciplinary action when the occasion warranted. Student demonstrations of sympathy for those "under sentence of punishment" often caused more excitement than the original offense. Students usually accepted the punishments meted out to them, but in rare instances an entire class would protest against some faculty or administrative action that they deemed unfair (such as failure to extend holiday periods) by the device of "concerted absence" from recitations. This "cutting" *en masse* usually brought faculty retaliation. An often-used countermeasure was to schedule makeup classes on Sunday morning. One student in the 1860's was deprived of the privilege of delivering his Commencement Part "for entertaining improper company in his room, at unseasonable hours."[22] The Trustees had to take a hand in proceedings in 1914 by employing a police officer "from noon to ten P.M. on Sundays for the balance of the academic year to keep objectionable women off the College enclosure."

Hazing of some sort was an ancient tradition (with freshmen the usual victims) and was most difficult to eradicate. From time to time the practice became sufficiently serious to require Trustee as well as faculty action, and the students issued policy statements regularly. The Class of 1869 unanimously adopted a resolution (at the suggestion of President Miner) on the eve of Independence Day in 1866 stating that "we regard the College custom of hazing as unnatural and barbarous, since it meanly takes advantage of inexperience and offers hostility to those entitled above all others to our sympathy and kind attention." Reportedly, the celebration of the July 4th holiday that year was as boisterous as ever. The resolution was passed on to the Class of 1870 in the hope that hazing would become extinct. Needless to say, it did not, for class rivalries were frequently spirited and sometimes tempers ran high. The faculty was commended by the Trustees in 1894 for condemning hazing "in all its forms, as unworthy of young men engaged in the pursuit of the higher education." It was "to be eradicated at whatever cost." More than one student lost his scholarship aid for having "come under . . . grave censure in the course of the year." The editor of the *Tuftonian* in 1911 assured his readers that "hazing is no longer a universal institution; horse-play is being tabooed." Probably no more inaccurate statement was ever made, for student exuberance and animal spirits in general have never been conspicuously absent on any college campus.

Among the matters of concern to the Overseers in 1902 was student conduct. They were highly critical of student behavior and the code of morals "which thoughtful men would repudiate at once in the domain of business or of society." Ostensibly, this student code tolerated cheating in examinations, justified the destruction of private property in the celebration of athletic victories, encouraged boorish manners and various forms of reprehensible

---

[22] In another instance, two young men "warranted the penalty of dismission" for having "brought two young women from Boston on Saturday evening, and provided them with room and entertainment till the following Monday."

conduct, and caused strained relations between professors and students, campus and community. The Overseers put part of the blame on the inflexible curriculum and "paternal form of college government" of an earlier day. But even with more liberal and enlightened administrative policies the situation still seemed to be bad around the country, and there was "reason to fear that the moral atmosphere at Tufts College is not essentially different from that in other institutions." The Overseers charged the faculty of the College to do something about the problem and suggested drastic measures if necessary. "The arrest and conviction of a few bumptious youths, followed by their prompt dismissal from college, would prove an object lesson in citizenship of incalculable value to the entire student body."

The faculty dutifully reviewed the report of the Overseers regarding student discipline and took a significantly more tolerant attitude than did the alumni board. The faculty pointed out that youthful energies needed a certain amount of outlet in shenanigans anyway, and that most of the difficulty had stemmed from exaggerated reports made in Boston newspapers by copy men who saw advantage in a bit of sensationalism. The Overseers considered it necessary in their annual report of 1903 to allude again to student behavior, particularly because of newspaper reports of hazing and immoral conduct. They were relieved to learn from President Capen that the reports regarding the first were "grossly exaggerated" and that the statements regarding immoral conduct were "absolutely without foundations." The Overseers, it is clear, were concerned about the image of the College created in the public mind. Problems arising out of newspaper publicity, "town and gown" conflicts (complicated by the location of the College astride two communities), and unorthodox student activities within the confines of the campus were never absent in any decade of Tufts history but somehow were surmounted without seriously threatening the survival of the institution, its inhabitants, or its neighbors.

§ § §

Class organizations were a normal part of student activity, and class officers were elected from year to year practically from the moment that a student body was created. Among the class societies that endured were Tower Cross, organized as an honorary senior society in 1897; the Ivy Society, created in 1901 for the junior class and originally christened the Ivy Leaf; and Sword and Shield, founded in 1902 to represent the sophomores. The charter members of Tower Cross, election to which was "considered one of the highest honors that can be accorded to an undergraduate," were selected by the faculty and were inducted in a formal ceremony which included the wearing of caps and gowns. The Ivy Society was intended to further the somewhat contradictory aims of "doing away with any factional feeling which may exist on the Hill, and . . . increasing of class spirit in the Junior class." One of its greatest contributions over the years has been the preparation of a "Handbook of Tufts College." This pocket-sized publication, known as the "Ivy Book," became a veritable bible for incoming students from the appearance of the first issue in 1902–3. The creation of Sword and Shield reflected the intense class rivalries of the day. It was intended to promote good fellowship and, more immediately, "the political and social interests of the Sophomore class." [23] One of Sword and Shield's historic functions was to provide what might be called the student version of "Freshman Orientation." In later years, the society became the keeper of Tufts undergraduate customs and in the 1960's was officially known as the Sword and Shield Traditions Society.

One area of collegiate and institutional symbolism which fell to the lot of student officers and societies to determine was class and College colors. The problem of selecting the latter apparently attracted far more attention from the undergraduates (and later the alumni) than from the faculty, administrative officers, or Trustees. Not until 1960 did the Trustees officially adopt the brown and blue that the student body had selected in 1876. The original Board of Trustees had not been color-conscious; when the corporate seal was adopted on July 7, 1857, no mention was made of colors in the official description. There were no recognized colors at Tufts prior to 1875, although cherry red was informally used and occasionally displayed. This color, however, presented two difficulties: there was no standardized shade of red used, and it was too much like Harvard's crimson. Early in 1876 the undergraduates decided to

[23] After Sword and Shield was organized the facetious suggestion was made that, in self-defense, the freshman class should also close ranks as the "Fist and Fender."

settle the question of colors by holding a special meeting to deal with the problem. There was considerable difference of opinion; the committee that had been appointed to report to the student body produced two conflicting recommendations. One faction argued for seal brown and pearl white; the other stood by seal-brown and gold. Seal brown and pearl white won by such a narrow margin that a second meeting was called at which blue was substituted for white, and brown and blue emerged as winners.[24]

The governing body of the College remained officially silent on the subject of College colors until 1904, presumably concurring in the meanwhile with the student choice. The greatest problem that faced the users of the colors was the shade of blue. "Seal-brown" was specific, but "blue" could mean almost anything. The first yearbook bearing the name *Brown and Blue,* published jointly in 1878 by Zeta Psi and Theta Delta Chi, boasted a baby-blue cover and chocolate brown trimmings, but the College song, "The Brown and Blue," produced in 1888, sidestepped the issue. A student poll, in which slightly over half the undergraduates participated, was conducted in 1904. They reaffirmed the use of the two colors and requested that "an attempt be made to standardize the shades on the basis of expert opinion."[25] The Trustees were asked to hand down a ruling, and reported that "the proper shades are those used for the lining of hoods by Cotrell and Leonard."[26] This was the closest that the Trustees came before 1960 to making brown and blue "official." The ruling was honored as much in the breach as in the observance, for technical and practical problems, and failure to adhere to the letter if not to the spirit of the decision, resulted in a bewildering array of shades of both colors for everything from bunting to athletic uniforms.

[24] The decision was by no means unanimous among the students, for only thirty-two of the sixty-nine students then in the regular course exercised their franchise, and those who contended for the original choice of brown and white insisted that the second decision was not binding on the student body.

[25] A further suggestion was made that the matter of an official flag for the College be considered, but there is no indication that this was ever acted on.

[26] The reference here is to the firm in Albany, New York, which became the official distributors of academic regalia to the College following a decision in 1902 that faculty, Trustees, and Overseers should appear in appropriate costume on academic occasions.

The institution continued to live with this ambiguity for over a half-century more. The Alumni Council finally took a hand in 1959, appointed a Colors Committee, arrived at a decision, and recommended their findings to the Trustees.[27] At long last the institution obtained an official color combination of brown and blue, in two specified shades which were selected after the most exhaustive investigations, including spectral analysis. Blue was to be the dominant color and brown was to accompany it "where appropriate." It was comparatively easy to paint a mental picture of the officially adopted "chocolate brown," but the shade of blue was still difficult to translate into the language of the layman. It has been variously described as "between a light and a middle blue" and "a dusty sky blue." The Trustees did not become involved in this problem of lay terminology for they identified the authorized shades as those listed on the standardized color scale of the Athletic Association of America as "Athletic 6" (brown) and "Athletic 40" (blue).[28] The story of class colors and class flags (when used) at Tufts was not as complex as the one for the institutional colors in spite of the fact that they were used much earlier. Long tradition established a four-year rotation of blue and gold; red and white; blue and white; and red and black. Display of class colors was usually confined to Senior Week activities and class reunions.

§   §   §

Organized athletics at Tufts had a slow, erratic, and inauspicious beginning and a haphazard development that was characteristic of collegiate sports at many institutions in the nineteenth century. Students had to wait some thirty years for a gymnasium; the rocky and uneven nature of the terrain on the campus, and the absence of money, manpower, and motivation played a part in delaying the appearance of team sports. Baseball, or "the New York sport," as it was first called, arrived on the Tufts campus in 1863,

[27] The leading spirit in this enterprise was Grace Neal Trefry, Class of 1935, who served as chairman of the committee and expended some six months of research effort. She prepared a sound-slide film, "Rainbow on the Hill," to publicize the problem. She donated to the Tufts Archives the considerable body of material she collected.

[28] At the same meeting, the Trustees voted to revise the colors of the Carmichael Shield (first used in 1939) to conform to the new official Tufts colors.

some fifteen years after it had begun to take shape as a game. Football appeared at Tufts in 1864–65 and became popular among the sophomores. Rival baseball teams were organized in 1864, as the "All Nine of Tufts" and the "Ballou Club," and competition soon became traditional between the sophomore and freshman classes. The All Nine was made up of the abler and more experienced players and played all the match games. Between 1865 and 1870 enthusiasts for baseball had organized the Tufts Base-Ball Club (with more officers than players), had appeared in gray uniforms, and had lost two games to Brown.[29] Arrangements for games with neighboring teams were strictly informal, and contests with town teams were at first more numerous than with college nines.[30]

Football was less popular at first than baseball, but by 1874–75 the latter went into a state of dormancy, reappearing three years later. A "College Eleven" was formally organized in 1875 and played only one match game. Those accustomed to considering baseball as a spring game and football as a fall activity would have had some readjustments to make when the two sports were introduced at Tufts. Baseball was first played from September through November (or as long as the weather permitted), and the first intercollegiate football game was a spring event. The traditional baseball contest between the freshmen and sophomore classes was played in the fall until 1892. The one football game with another college, played in 1874–75 on the afternoon of an "uncomfortably warm" June 4, went down in the annals of the College as a memorable event. Tufts defeated Harvard in Cambridge, having scored the only touchdown and goal.[31] After less than a year's experience,

[29] The freshmen jubilantly triumphed over the sophomores in 1867 with a score of 47 to 35; no freshman scored less than four runs. The sophomores trounced the freshmen in 1870 with the resounding score of 65 to 16.

[30] The record of games played during the 1871 season indicates matches with teams from Charlestown, Chelsea, Boston, Natick, Somerville, and Stoneham. Dartmouth, Brown, and Harvard were the only colleges on the list. During this year Tufts won eleven games and lost eight. M.I.T. had been added to the schedule by 1873–74.

[31] The so-called "McGill Rules," imported from Canada, were first used; there were three "innings" of half an hour each, and a touchdown was not counted unless a goal were kicked. If no goals were made, the team accumulating the greater number of touchdowns was declared the winner.

The 1875–6 Football Team, wearing distinctive attire for the first time.

both Tufts and Harvard adopted a modified version of Rugby rules. This may not have been a wise decision on Tufts' part, for the second game with Harvard, played in the fall of 1875, ended in a defeat for the Medford institution. The athletic reputation of the College was at least partially redeemed that year, for its "Second Eleven," organized in 1875, won over Bates. Tufts challenged Brown, Bowdoin, and Dartmouth in 1875 and added Cornell in 1877, but no games were played with these schools for several years. There was no such thing as a regular football schedule for several more decades. One difficulty was the lack of anything approaching uniformity of rules; every school played largely according to its own inclinations. The College Eleven failed to tempt a single opponent to a match game in 1876–77 and was driven in May of that year to play "a picked team" from among their classmates.[32]

In the late 1870's and early 1880's the novelty seems to have worn off both baseball and football, for there were no teams at all in either sport for some years. Three football games were played (and lost) in 1877–78 to Harvard, Yale, and Amherst, and the

[32] The regular team could take some comfort from the game; they not only won but appeared for the first time in new uniforms (blue shirts, blue hose, and white trunks); the color combination bore little resemblance to the College colors adopted a year earlier by the students.

freshmen who played Andover lost by fifteen touchdowns and a goal. The best the sports-minded alumni could do for the next few years was mourn the fact that there were no teams of any kind in intercollegiate competitions. The baseball team came out of hibernation long enough in 1881 to win a victory over Boston University and then relapsed into inactivity until trounced by Harvard in 1882. The blow was softened somewhat the latter year by wins over M.I.T. and the Boston Law School. Two losses to Bowdoin and one to Colby completed a rather mixed season.

The baseball picture looked brighter in the spring of 1883, for sufficient manpower was recruited to provide two substitutes in addition to the regular team and to schedule seven games, five of them played with other New England colleges. The high point of Tufts baseball success in the nineteenth century was acheived in 1889, but two years later interest in the sport had so far declined that not even a captain was provided for the 1891–92 season. In 1895 the baseball team recovered itself by winning over Harvard for the first time. Football had suffered the same unpredictable career; in 1890 the team had been disbanded, yet two years later it was reconstituted in sufficient strength to enjoy one of the best seasons in the game's erratic nineteenth-century history.[33] During the 1890's football enthusiasts had to compete with track athletics, which experienced a brief burst of popularity. Even with the coming of the twentieth century, Tufts belonged to no intercollegiate football league but played teams from all New England institutions on a strictly independent basis.[34] Even systematic coaching for football was not provided until 1892. The attention that eventually came to be focused on intercollegiate sports at Tufts certainly did not exist until well after the First World War.

When athletics took form in the 1860's, games were first played on a makeshift field on the Stearns estate beyond the northern boundaries of the College, and then on the field known as the "old campus." After this location was made inadequate by the extension

[33] The 1892 season was also the first one in which all games were played with colleges and not with a mixture of local town and city teams.

[34] Tufts joined Amherst, Williams, and M.I.T. in 1885 to form the "Northern Football Association," which lasted exactly two years. Tufts enjoyed its best football season before the First World War in 1913–14, when it won seven out of eight games; its only loss was to West Point (0-2).

of Professors Row in the 1870's, parts of the faculty cow pasture on the southern side of the campus running to Powderhouse Boulevard were gradually taken over for athletic activities. These areas were at first marked by a series of wooden fences (which made excellent bonfire material) and eventually by a wire enclosure. The first serious attempt to turn the pastureland into athletic fields was made after the "gallant record" of the football team in 1892, and as part of a deliberate effort "to invigorate and dignify athletics in Tufts College." Sports-minded individuals came to the embarrassed realization that no intercollegiate games of any kind could be played until a fenced athletic field existed. The result was a decision "to lay out a large oval, with grounds for base-ball, football, tennis courts, and general athletics." The alumni were asked to contribute $2,000 to fence off the "oval" and to provide seating accommodations. This had been accomplished in time for the opening of the fall term in 1894.

The Oval was still being used for Varsity football in the 1960's, although the enclosing wooden fence that had given the field its name had long since disappeared, together with the entrance archway donated in 1908 by Trustee Thomas Cunningham. The original Oval was rather extensive and included a large (and active) spring in its lower reaches. As the baseball diamond proper was the only part graded at first, it was not unusual for players fielding balls to engage incidentally in aquatics as they emerged dripping from the watery outfield.[35] Acquisition of a fourteen-acre combination of abandoned clay pit, brickyard, and city dump after the First World War made possible playing fields for baseball, soccer, and lacrosse; practice fields for football and track squads; and drill and parade grounds for military units.[36]

[35] The source of this moisture was Two Penny Brook which, when dammed sometime in the 1860's and known as the "Artificial" by the 1870's, made an excellent swimming hole in summer and skating rink in winter. It was still in active use at the time of the First World War, and until 1958 there was sufficient water available to provide a respectable skating area in the wintertime. But underground drains and the raising of the grade eliminated this campus landmark familiar to the students and townspeople of an earlier era.

[36] This area, known frequently as "College Acres," is located on the northerly side of the campus, across the Boston and Maine Railroad, and conveniently close to the Cousens Gymnasium.

The "Rez" (1865–1945), looking west from Ballou Hall

Baseball and football were quite literally innovations when they were introduced on the Tufts campus in the 1860's. The more conventional athletic contests, classified as "track and field sports" and compared by contemporaries to Sunday School outings, were supervised by the Tufts Athletic Association, which was founded in the fall of 1874. These equivalents of intramural sports, climaxed by an annual Field Day, were organized by classes and consisted of running and walking races, high and broad jumping, hammer throwing, wheelbarrow, sack, and potato races, and wrestling matches. The Field Days were usually held in the fall, and a barrel of cider awaited the class winning the largest number of events. For many years the contests took place on the grassy areas surrounding the giant reservoir at the top of the Hill. The fate of the losers can readily be imagined, with a body of water so convenient. Field sports suffered a complete eclipse for the ten years after 1882, and running was confined to attempts to outdistance Medford or Somerville policemen or irate owners of neighboring apple orchards. A general revival of enthusiasm for sports in the 1890's included the first indoor meet in Goddard Gymnasium in 1892 and membership in the New England Intercollegiate Athletic Association in 1896. The construction of a cinder track in the Oval in 1899 was a welcome addition during good weather, and a running track provided in the enlarged Goddard Gymnasium in 1900 served for the winter months.

The proximity of the Mystic River brought yet another outdoor activity to Tufts soon after it opened. Two boat clubs were organized in 1864, the "Theta" and the "Undine," and became a means by which the competitive spirit of Theta Delta Chi and Zeta Psi could be expressed. Each fraternity erected a boathouse a short distance from Medford Square and acquired a six-oared boat. The "Tufts Flotilla" was born. Enthusiasm for boating was uneven because of the inconvenient distance from the College and the chronic inability to raise sufficient funds to keep the project afloat. Fraternity rivalry in boating disappeared after 1866 and was replaced by an all-Tufts boat club that existed for several years and could in 1874 boast of twenty-five members, three crews, and a practice rowing machine installed in the basement of West Hall. Lack of funds was responsible for the demise of organized boating on the Mystic River. In the late 1890's sailing became popular on the Mystic Lakes, on the border of West Medford and Winchester. The tradition was continued with the organization of the Tufts Yacht Club in 1936.

Somewhat less popular in the early days of Tufts than baseball and football, but equally demanding in its way, was fencing, which took organized form as the Order of the Foil and the Mask in the winter of 1873–74, under the supervision of William Homer of Boston. Two members of the faculty were honorary members in the mid-1870's. Because there was no gymnasium at the time, fencing practice was permitted in a room at the main College building (Ballou Hall). In spite of later sporadic attempts to revive it, fencing never attained the status of a major extracurricular activity because it failed to appeal to more than a fraction of the student body. A Rifle Team was organized in the spring of 1878, with weapons lent by the state for a drill team. "Training was kept up until the members of the company could actually keep step, and some of them could even hit the target." However, just as a degree of proficiency was being developed, the team collapsed when the arms it was using had to be returned. Tennis, which had appeared as a local game in the mid-1880's, became an intercollegiate sport in 1900–1901. In the same year, renewed interest in athletics was heralded by the organization of a class in boxing, and "a modest beginning" was made in "scientific basketball."

No one could argue that athletics at Tufts was in a privileged position in the nineteenth century. It was not until the 1890's that any systematic attempt was made even to provide for effective supervision or that the alumni or Trustees took more than a nominal interest in the subject. The increasing attention paid to athletics all over the country after 1900 was mirrored on the Tufts campus, and something approximating a set of policies was finally developed. Throughout its history the College has made a sincere and usually successful effort to avoid the tendency to commercialize or professionalize its athletics or to give its team members special concessions or favors that would set the athletes apart from their peers and make them into priviliged characters. Now and again the institution came close to this and did make certain provisions and exceptions for which it could be (and has been) criticized.[37] But neither the incidence nor the magnitude of such occurrences should warrant feelings of shame, consternation, or defiance on the part of the faculty, governing bodies, or alumni. The athletic accomplishments of the Tufts students at the intercollegiate level have been for the most part unspectacular but solid. The faculty (the traditional enemies of organized athletics) have, over the years, been tolerant and sometimes downright enthusiastic about Tufts athletics; in return, they have been fortunately free from pressures of various kinds which could conceivably have distorted their academic vision or unduly interfered with the standards on which they have operated.

Aside from a student-operated Athletic Association organized in 1874 to arrange Field Days and the like, what little supervision there was at first came from the faculty. Their permission was required when any athletic team desired to visit another school. The football team was given "leave of absence" (for one afternoon) to play Harvard in the fall of 1877, but it was "granted with caution." Not until 1891 was an Advisory Committee on Athletics created, at

[37] In 1886–87 two non-Tufts men were hired to play a five-game schedule of baseball. However, this action by the Baseball Association was repudiated by the team captain and the manager, who both immediately resigned in protest. The two imports quickly disappeared, but the policy of hiring an occasional baseball player from outside the College was not abandoned until 1891.

the request of the students. It consisted of representatives from the faculty, the students, and the alumni. Team sports were placed under the supervision of the Instructor in Physical Education by the Trustees in 1900 "in order to secure the better discipline and higher efficiency of the teams." After 1900, students from the medical and dental schools contributed toward the expenses of Tufts athletics.

Some differences of opinion did develop from time to time between the faculty and students over athletic commitments. The faculty decreed in 1899 that no student on academic probation was to participate in intercollegiate athletics off the Hill. The timing of this announcement of policy was poor, for it came on the eve of a game with Bowdoin, and apparently with little or no warning. There was no question that the absence of no less than five members of the team because of the faculty ruling would have crippled its operations. On the petition of the Advisory Committee on Athletics the faculty agreed "to postpone the operation of the decree until after the game." In order to avoid similar complications and embarrassments, the Advisory Committee kept the faculty informed of the names of the members of each team, and the faculty in turn reported the standing of such students to the Advisory Committee in sufficient time to make necessary adjustments on the teams. The College thus faced for the first time in a serious way the problem of securing "faithful observances of student obligations, and a healthful and helpful conduct of athletes." [38]

The Board of Overseers, as an alumni body, felt called upon in their annual report in 1903 to express their views on athletics because sports seemed to be a topic of "ever increasing importance" on the campus. The Overseers were realistic enough to see the dangers of overemphasis on athletics and hoped for a coordinated balance between intellectual and physical training. Most of the difficulty on the campus seemed, in their opinion, to come from

[38] An alumnus (C. B. Southard of the Class of 1870) was apparently sympathetic to the problem. He swung his support to the side of scholarship by offering in 1892 a silver cup to the best player on each of the two teams (football and baseball) who also ranked in the upper half of his class. When the faculty representatives on the Board of Athletics made their annual report in 1907, they noted how fortunate the College was that the coaches employed for baseball, football, and basketball were "experts who have realized that athletics occupy a subordinate position in the College curriculum."

413

those members of teams who were "constantly upon the danger line in scholarship," and from those who were not athletes at all but thought they were being loyal to Tufts when they frittered away hours of valuable time talking and writing on the subject. As to the purported evils of professionalism in athletics, they saw no danger to the College as long as "every vestige" of it could be eliminated from College sports. "We hope that there is absolute and complete absence of professionalism at Tufts College. Whether teams are strong or weak, let them be genuine Tufts teams and let the athletic standing of the College be established in thoroughgoing honesty." The Boards of Visitors also had a word to say on athletics. Sumner Robinson, a Trustee and a man especially active in the affairs of the College, made an extended report on the subject in 1909. He expressed concern that Tufts was falling behind in collegiate competitions because it did not have winning teams. What to do about it posed a real problem. Should the College subsidize its players? Tufts had leaned over backward not to follow such a policy.

The introduction of hockey at Tufts illustrated some of the dilemmas in which schools sometimes found themselves in relation to athletics. A start was made in January 1907 at organizing an ice hockey team but it was not until seven years later that one actually came into existence. Although permission was secured to use the rink at the Boston Arena, the Committee on Athletics refused to recognize hockey as a Varsity sport. Enthusiasts for the game thereupon organized the "Tufts Independent Hockey Team," consisting largely of medical and dental students. This private enterprise, not under the control of the Athletic Association, brought down the wrath of Trustee Fletcher, particularly when it was discovered that a professional baseball player (a dental student on the reserve list of the Toronto Club of the International League) appeared on the Tufts team which won over Amherst in 1914. The team was immediately ordered disbanded by Tufts authorities. When hockey reappeared in the winter of 1918, this time as a sport officially recognized by the institution, it had strictly amateur standing. Its greatest handicap was the lack of a rink. The flooding of the lower part of the athletic field near the Oval never worked out satisfactorily, and the team was unable to play home games. This was one explanation for the fact that hockey never attracted as much attention among Tufts students as some other sports.

The first attempt at giving aid to athletes had been made in 1899, when several gratuities had been established by the Trustees for encouragement of extracurricular activities (including the Glee Club as well as athletics). But these had lasted for only a short time; they were too closely identified with the College to escape criticism. Trustee gratuities were temporarily abandoned on the recommendation of the Advisory Committee on Athletics. If financial aid was to be provided for athletes, it was believed that it should come most appropriately from the alumni. Nevertheless, the Trustees did feel justified in giving special assistance now and then, including direct subvention.[39]

The year-to-year operating expenses of athletics were financed on the eve of the First World War largely by an annual assessment of $10 entitling each student to a season ticket to all home games and sports; half of the assessment was earmarked to pay the expenses of physical education. Voluntary subscriptions were also solicited, but the amounts were always disappointing; one appeal to the alumni in 1913 netted only $365. Gate receipts were not sufficient to wipe out a continuing annual deficit of several hundred dollars. In 1909 Sumner Robinson, an outspoken champion of intercollegiate athletics, offered to "be one of ten to pay one hundred dollars per year for ten years" to finance the College bills of Varsity athletes, but the requisite number of benefactors failed to appear.

Tufts faced the same problem encountered by other relatively small institutions, namely, recruiting students competent both on the athletic field and in the classroom, and offering sufficient inducements to prospective athletes without being accused of favoritism and commercialization at the same time. A special Trustee committee in 1902 put the question directly. "How far a college may properly go in its encouragement of athletics is a mooted question. It was only after careful consideration and with some misgiving that the experiment of directly fostering athletic interests was undertaken. . . . Open college aid to athletics is tabooed and

[39] For example, nine team members in 1913 were allowed "to defer the payment of College charges without thereby incurring any disabilities as students of Tufts College." The Executive Committee in 1915 appropriated a total of $1,000 toward the expenses (tuition fees) of thirteen members of the football and baseball teams.

415

yet nearly all the smaller institutions are taking this method to make themselves prominent. If we have erred at all it is by being found out in doing more or less openly what others are doing secretly."

The decade before 1914 saw an emphasis on intercollegiate athletics all over the nation which many individuals considered most unhealthy. The number of intercollegiate sports had increased enormously, competition to develop winning teams had resulted in questionable recruiting and financing practices, and college calendars had become jammed with athletic events. There was considerable fear that a disproportionate amount of athletic energy was being expended, and at the expense of purely academic concerns. One of the first steps taken to bring order out of a rather confused athletic situation was the creation in 1906 of the Intercollegiate Athletic Association of the United States, of which Tufts immediately became a member. The Association was intended to be "a systematic attempt to improve the situation in intercollegiate athletics" and to bring about reforms in football in particular. A New England branch was soon organized, and Tufts became a charter member. Another major step to encourage cooperation and provide for consultation among institutions on matters of common interest was the organization of the Association of New England Colleges for Conference on Athletics in 1908. Dean Wren of Tufts was a member of the committee which drew up its constitution and nominated its first officers. Professor Clarence P. Houston, who served as a coach, Director of Athletics, and chairman of the Department of Physical Education at Tufts for much of the period from 1919 to 1946, was at one time president of the Conference. The sense of the first meeting was that intercollegiate basketball "as at present conducted" should cease and that the number of intercollegiate contests in other sports should be reduced. No more than twenty games per season in baseball and nine in football were suggested. Tufts adhered closely to the spirit of the New England Conference recommendations by discontinuing basketball as an intercollegiate sport in 1911, eliminating long and time-consuming trips for the Varsity football team, and encouraging intramural sports.

By and large, the policies expressed in the 1930's by President Cousens and Professor Houston could be taken as a summing-up of the prevailing attitude of the institution toward intercollegiate athletics for most of its history. Good athletes were encouraged to come to Tufts if they could meet its academic standards. It was the policy of the College "to maintain the teams upon an amateur basis, so far as is consistent with common sense." Cousens assured the Trustees that "there is absolutely no taint of professionalism in connection with any of the various sports at Tufts College." The rules in force at the time prohibited freshmen from playing on Varsity teams; students transferring from other colleges were not allowed to compete for one year. Students were limited to three years of undergraduate intercollegiate competition in any one sport.[40] Supervised intramural sports, which had started with baseball in 1909 and had been extended to six other games by the 1930's, were encouraged; however, no holder of a Varsity letter or member of a freshman squad was eligible. Most important of all in Cousens' view was the success in instilling "the idea not only into the students but into the faculty as well that intercollegiate athletics are an important factor in any general health program for a college."

§ § §

Tufts undergraduates, faculty, and alumni have been served over the years with various publications that bear a strong family resemblance to those found on any college campus. The functions performed and the problems faced by such emanations have been no more remarkable within the Tufts community than in other academic institutions. The first publication, known unofficially as the College "annual" and officially as the *Tuftonian,* appeared between 1864 and 1872. It contained much of interest in the way of descriptions of student organizations, sketches of faculty, and articles that would appeal to undergraduates.[41] The aspirations of the early editors to turn the publication into a "literary magazine" were an abysmal failure. The editor in 1865 came to the rueful conclusion that "the students of Tufts College are not eminently a Literary Class," for an urgent solicitation of creative works (including a College Ode) returned not a single contribution. Judging

[40] Any further participation by students in the medical and dental schools was prohibited by this ruling. Those in the graduate division were also ineligible to participate.

[41] The first volume, comprising seven issues (1864–70) was of tabloid size; thereafter it was published in pamphlet form.

417

from pleas for the next hundred years or so, this problem had not yet been solved to everyone's satisfaction in the 1960's. The two fraternities that sponsored the first *Tuftonian* (Zeta Psi and Theta Delta Chi) experienced a difference of opinion in 1872, presumably over the contents of the publication, and from that date until 1875 there were two rival magazines — the *Tuftonian* (continued by Zeta Psi) and the *Budget* (published by Theta Delta Chi). The latter, of which only two annual issues were published (1874 and 1875), was freighted with poetry and essays of a philosophical bent and can probably be called Tufts' first *bona fide* undergraduate literary effort. An ambitious attempt to broaden the base of student publications by organizing the Tufts College Publishing Association in 1874 produced the *Tufts Collegian,* which appeared monthly for four years and served as both undergraduate newspaper and vehicle for alumni contributions. In 1878, after the two fraternities had become reconciled and had agreed to share the journalistic field with others, the Publishing Association abandoned the name *Collegian* and resumed the name *Tuftonian.* Subscription rates were $1.00 for the academic year, the low price being made possible in part by the sale of advertising space beginning in the 1870's.[42] A high proportion of the early graduates who tried out their journalistic wings on Tufts publications as students had entered newspaper work by the 1880's and were either serving on the staffs or were editors of such papers as the *Springfield Republican, Providence Press, New York World, Chicago Daily News,* and the three leading Boston papers (the *Transcript,* the *Globe,* and the *Post*).

Between 1878 and the appearance of the *Tufts Weekly* in 1895, the *Tuftonian* continued to serve as the campus multi-purpose journal. After 1895 the latter was considered a "literary magazine," and after the First World War it became a quarterly (more or less). The *Weekly* and the *Tuftonian* were for many years under the same management, operating through the Publishing Association. Although the latter's constitution provided that the editor-in-chief of each was to be selected from the student board of editors

---

[42] It was not always feasible to accept offers to advertise; one western firm was willing to use the columns of the *Tuftonian* providing payment could be made in garden seeds.

by the faculty, the students exercised complete control over each publication and its editorial policies. The faculty's role in choosing the editors-in-chief was intended only to prevent competing societies from going to war over candidates. The combined staff of eleven editors of various degrees of specialization and authority was apportioned for many years among the fraternities and other student organizations according to the number of subscriptions furnished by each group. Keeping the Association solvent and free of campus politics posed recurrent problems. Financial difficulties usually made it necessary to call upon the faculty and even the Trustees at times for succor and support.

One of the resources most frequently drawn upon to help the Publishing Association out of its chronic difficulties was the Bookstore Fund. The College Bookstore, operating for years out of quarters in Curtis Hall, turned in almost annually a tidy profit which was earmarked for miscellaneous projects. There was sufficient surplus in 1905–6 to purchase a dozen electric clocks, which were installed in various buildings, to provide a drinking fountain in Ballou Hall, and to help finance a trip of the debating team to New York City. It was the Bookstore Fund from which was drawn most of the $300 needed to clear up the obligations of the Publishing Association in 1909.

The *Weekly* (with the sports reportage always on the front page) managed a continuous existence until after the last issue of Volume 16 on June 21, 1911. The next regular issue appeared on November 12, 1913. Between these dates the only approximation of a student newspaper was the *Tufts News,* sponsored by the Class of 1913 as "a temporary substitute." Even that modest contribution of four slender issues of less than conventional newspaper size lasted for only two months (April and May) in 1912. The *Weekly* was revived in 1913 only by dint of a two-year subsidy by the Trustees. The *Tuftonian* suspended publication for a much longer period. Thirty-six volumes had appeared by June 1911; then the magazine disappeared for fifteen years. When it was reborn in the spring of 1926, it bore a new format and was renumbered as a new series. The reappearance of this publication was prompted, in turn, by the demise of the *Tufts College Graduate* after its February issue in 1926. The latter reappeared in October 1927 as the *Tufts College*

Alumni Bulletin, which, after surviving the perils of the Second World War, became the *Tufts Alumni Review* in 1947.[43]

Of all the College publications, the *Weekly* was the one most immediately and sorely missed when it had to suspend operations. The precipitant for its temporary disappearance had been the failure of students to pay their subscriptions. The faculty Committee on Student Organizations had had to warn the Publishing Association in the spring of 1911 that failure to settle accounts (including a bill of $600 to the *Somerville Journal* Company which then printed the newspaper) would result in "discontinuance of undergraduate publications." In the fall of 1912 Acting President Hooper presented the problem to the Trustee Executive Committee, which conducted an extensive inquiry into the matter, including consultation with the faculty Committee on Student Organizations. The latter called attention to the fact that this was the third bankruptcy of a student publication because of poor management, and that on the other two occasions the alumni and faculty had assumed responsibility for getting the publications back on their feet. There were several explanations for the chronic difficulties, particularly as they applied to the *Weekly.* Subscriptions were voluntary, there was no *bona fide* list of subscribers (hence the publication was not eligible for second-class mailing privileges), and the price of $2.00 was considered too high. The deficit of $500 could be cleared off only by arranging for mass subscriptions and giving the faculty committee the management of the *Weekly,* at least for an experimental period. The inclusion of the cost of the newspaper in the student charges was also a possibility. If the Publishing Association, which had the responsibility for student publications, were given credit of $2.00 for each student in the College, and if the College made no payments for advertising, the newspaper might be revived. The Executive Committee recognized the importance of the *Weekly* but was unwilling to underwrite it completely. The whole matter was referred back to the acting president, with the suggestion that an attempt be made through the Committee on Student Organizations to find "a responsible and permanent means of conducting the business affairs of the under-

[43] During a portion of the war period (September 1943–July 1946) the regular alumni magazine was replaced by a multilithed newsletter, *Tufts Topics,* that was mailed to alumni all over the world.

graduate publications on the basis of volunteer subscriptions." Instead, a student petition to the Trustees to have the annual cost of the *Weekly* added to term bills was approved. Inclusion of the cost of student publications in the student activities fee paid as a part of College charges for those enrolled, and individual subscriptions for those who had left the Hill, became the ultimate solution.

Another of the places in which to enshrine memories of college days is the yearbook. From the founding of Tufts until 1867 it was the custom of each class to frame the pictures of its members and hang them in the College chapel. The Class of 1867 dropped the custom and donated a class album to be kept in the library. These bulky (and weighty) books, bound in leather and fastened by a heavy brass clasp, contained individual pictures of the faculty and autographed photographs of one's classmates, with perhaps six to a dozen views of the campus. The albums remained popular until the mid-1890's, when they were superseded by other means of remembrance.[44] In 1878 the traditional fraternity rivals, Zeta Psi and Theta Delta Chi, reconciled their differences long enough to publish the first book resembling the modern college annual. Christened the *Brown and Blue* in recognition of the College colors which had been recently adopted by the students after great debate and difference of opinion, the seventy-two-page pamphlet furnished the first pictorial description of and commentary on the institution. The tradition having been started, illustrated booklets, usually sponsored by the junior class, appeared more or less regularly until 1904 and matured into bound volumes. The junior class in 1894, wishing to display a measure of originality, published a collection of Tufts songs that year in place of the conventional yearbook. After a gap of twelve years, the Class of 1916 published a leather-bound annual that was continued in 1917 as *The Jumbo*. After a three-year lapse, the class book published by the seniors appeared as *Taps* in 1920. The *Tufts Elephas,* published by the junior class, served as the yearbook for 1921. The seniors published their own *Jumbo Book* in 1922, and after another interval the 1925 *Jumbo Book* was sponsored by the senior class. The seniors two years later called their annual merely the *1927 Class Book.* It was the Class of 1928 that revived the designation of *Jumbo Book* used con-

[44] There is a reasonably complete set of these class albums in the Tufts Archives.

sistently thereafter. No yearbook appeared in 1944 or 1945, but the Class of 1946 celebrated the end of the Second World War with a small paperbound "Victory Edition" and resumed a series not again interrupted by financial difficulties or wars.

§ § §

College publications, whether newspapers, literary magazines, or yearbooks of some sort, have always been one of the strongest bridges that could be built to close the gap between one's relatively brief undergraduate days and one's relatively lengthy days as an alumnus. Attempts to build and maintain such a bridge were made before Tufts was five years old. The organization that became the Tufts Alumni Association was born at seven-thirty on the morning of July 2, 1860, in a third-floor room of the College Edifice. The idea of organizing the alumni originated with William A. Johnson (Class of 1860), one of the four graduates representing the four classes that had so far received degrees and who were given the responsibility of drafting a constitution and by-laws.[45] When the second meeting was held a year later, the new association could boast of eighteen paid-up members. A brief frame of government was adopted for the "Association of the Alumni of Tufts College," and officers and directors were chosen who comprised an Executive Committee. In the preliminary draft of the constitution, those who had entered upon the second term of their senior year, as well as graduates, were to have been eligible for membership. The article finally adopted provided that anyone who had received the A.B., M.A., D.D., or LL.D. was eligible for membership upon payment of $1.00 and enrollment on the secretary's record book. In 1864 consideration was given to admitting the faculty into the Association, but the idea was abandoned at the next annual meeting.

The next proposal to enlarge potential membership was made in 1868, after the first graduates of the philosophical course had become alumni, but efforts to include them were unavailing. Repeated attempts for over a decade to have the constitution amended to include recipients of the B.Ph. degree were defeated. It was Professor Dearborn, whose classes in Latin were being bypassed by the

[45] Unless otherwise indicated, the material on the early history of the Association was derived from the minutes and other record books of the organization which are in the Tufts Archives.

Philosophicals, who championed their eligibility as prospective Association members. After the philosophical course had been extended to four years, its graduates were finally made eligible for membership in 1879. Alumni of the civil engineering course were admitted unanimously at the same time. Membership in the Association was thrown open in 1887 to all holders of Tufts degrees.

The functions of the Association provided in the constitution combined the academic and the social: to arrange for suitable exercises at the annual meeting, and to arrange for a dinner "and make such other arrangements for its happy celebration, as shall seem . . . advisable." Among the early customs of the Association was listening on the afternoon of Commencement Day to a formal oration and a poem, both delivered by members of the Association selected a year in advance, with alternates provided. Between 1865 and 1880 the alumni exercises were held every other year, the program being presented in alternate years by the Mathetican Society, the campus literary and debating club. For several years after 1880 the alumni program came annually, and in 1891 it was merged with the alumni dinner, usually held in a Boston hotel. The poems and orations gave way at the same time to after-dinner speeches. The alumni were also represented for many years at the Commencement dinner held by the College for the graduating class, their families, and officers and friends of the College. It was President Capen who in 1882 concentrated all of the academic ceremonies of the various departments on one day, so that Commencement was made more impressive for the increasing number of graduates returning each year.[46] Until the practice was abandoned in 1885, one alumnus was selected by either the president of the College or the Trustees from several candidates suggested by the Association to deliver a speech on behalf of the alumni. It was in this way that the alumni first participated in the affairs of the institution.

The alumni dinner authorized in the constitution of the Association was slow to become a reality. The first suggestion to have such a gathering was made in 1866, but it was considered "inadvisable" to carry out the idea "as so few members of the association could conveniently attend." For the next several years suggestions were made and planning committees were even appointed, but not

[46] Until 1882 the divinity school had held their own exercises, and candidates for the degree of Master of Arts were not included at all.

until 1875 was the first dinner authorized by the constitution actually held. It was preceded by the laconic announcement that it would be held in the Revere House "provided a sufficient number of the alumni express an intention to be present." A sufficient number did appear — forty-six — and the affair was a financial success, although not spectacularly so; receipts exceeded expenses by six cents.

The idea of an Alumni Field Day, to consist of athletic events and social festivities, was broached in 1909, to be held on a day preceding Commencement. By 1914 five Field Days had been held, and the whole matter was reviewed by the Association. There was great debate over the desirability of continuing the festivities on an annual basis and similar argument over what day of the week would be most convenient for the greatest number of people. These crises were somehow surmounted, and the annual Field Day was continued long after the First World War and became an occasion on which members of each year's graduating class were welcomed into membership in the Association. One of the means developed to bring the alumni into closer contact with the College was the plan inaugurated in 1906 to have the traditional Commencement dinner serve as the alumni dinner and to have the annual meeting of the Association on the campus. A much younger custom, and one that came to be associated with the football season in the fall, was started in 1925 as Homecoming Day. It began as an informal alumni reunion following the game with Middlebury that year, with a social program arranged by the Association of Tufts Alumnae. By 1926, Homecoming was on its way to becoming a tradition.

A less happy undertaking assumed by the alumni group was the recording of deaths among the graduates and in the College community. Before the Association had completed its second year of organized existence it was called upon to prepare resolutions to the memory of President Ballou, and to Thomas Harris Angell of the Class of 1858. The latter represented "the first instance where Death has entered the circle of the College students." Within the next three years the grim reports from battlefields indicated that the Civil War was taking its toll of Tufts alumni. The first such casualty among the alumni was Smith Goss Bailey, of the Class of 1859. The first undergraduate who had volunteered and lost his life was

Ezra Newhall Fuller, of the Class of 1863. It was the Association that in 1865 initated a move to erect a monument at College Hill to perpetuate the memory of those associated with the College who had lost their lives in the great conflict. At the same time, a move was made to provide a suitable bust or portrait of the late President Ballou to be located at an appropriate place on the campus. As for the first project, the Association found itself with too limited membership and means to provide a suitable memorial, but President Miner informed the group in 1866 that a plan was being discussed to build a hall "for chapel and literary purposes," to be known as Packard Hall. If this possibility materialized, the alumni were promised that the name could easily be changed to Packard Memorial Hall, and tablets could be installed in it that would honor the dead of the Civil War. Such a building was constructed in 1882–83 and became Goddard Chapel. It did serve as a repository for plaques, busts, and other tangible memorials of those associated in some way with Tufts.

The decision to obtain a bust or portrait of President Ballou resulted in 1866 in an assessment of $10 on each member of the Association, and the so-called "Ballou Fund" was started, with a five-year period provided to accumulate it. Contributions were so slow in coming in that insufficient money had been collected at the end of the five years. The treasurer offered to return the money so far sent in but requested that the various amounts be retained for one more year in hopes that the additional funds would be donated. Although a portrait was finally produced in 1874, it was considered unsuitable and was discarded. No further action to memorialize the late president was considered advisable until at least $500 had been collected. The Rev. Henry Blanchard, of the Class of 1859, was given what undoubtedly appeared to be the thankless task of raising that sum as a committee of one; two years later he was joined by President Capen and Professor H. A. Dearborn. The augmented fund-raising committee had obtained $800 by 1877, and if $200 more could be added, it was thought that a very acceptable bust of Ballou could be provided. After two more members had been added to the Ballou Memorial Committee, success seemed imminent. A bust was ordered and accepted from the sculptor W. W. Story, although some delay was encountered in its receipt because it had been executed in Italy. It was destined to grace Goddard Chapel. An unexpended balance of $40 was left in the Ballou Fund to accumulate interest. In 1899 the augmented fund was turned over to the library for the purchase of books on history, as an appropriate remembrance of President Ballou's interest in that field. At the same time, the Association presented to Professor Shipman a purse of over $800 in behalf of his former students, to spend while on a year's leave of absence. Two years later President Capen received a similar gift from the alumni graduated since his accession to the presidency. The gift was to be used to help defray expenses for a proposed vacation trip to Europe.

It was the Alumni Association, with the prompting of Eugene B. Bowen, Class of 1876, that in 1908 provided a memorial to the late Professor Shipman in the form of a portrait hung in the new library that had just been opened. President Hamilton had suggested in 1909 that the College needed a Professorship of Psychology and Education and intimated that the endowment of such a chair would be a fitting memorial to Professor Shipman. The Association, however, elected to provide the portrait as first planned, and to divide equally whatever remained thereafter of the Shipman Fund between a sum for the purchase of books for the library and a loan fund for worthy students. The portrait, costing $1,000, was painted by Mrs. Marie Danforth Page of Boston and was hung in Eaton Library as planned.[47] The Shipman Fund amounted to about $3,000 by 1912. A slight change was made in the original plan for the disposition of the money. The income of the first $3,000 was to be placed at the disposal of the Library Committee of the faculty; the Class of 1892 pledged an amount sufficient to bring the fund up to that amount.

The practice of recording the demise of alumni that had been instituted in the dark days of the Civil War was systematized in 1871. The secretary of the Association was authorized to make a record of deaths, collect as much biographical data as possible, and report to the annual meeting. Arrangements were also made to have the necrology published as a part of the triennial catalogue which appeared during a good part of the nineteenth century. A

[47] The wall on which the portrait was placed was retinted at the request of the artist so that it would harmonize with the portrait. This expense, it might be added, was borne by the Association and not by the College.

necrologist was made a permanent officer of the Association in 1885.[48]

Almost half a century went by before the Association revised the sketchy but workable constitution that had been adopted in 1861 to govern the organization. The number of alumni had increased from a mere handful to over 1,500 by 1906, and graduating classes were numbering over 150 annually. The medical and dental schools had been added, and the College had become coeducational. Local groups of graduates had begun to organize, and the time had come to recognize these and many other changes. The result was the adoption of a new constitution in 1906 for what became officially the "Tufts College Alumni Association." The document provided for "an association of the women graduates, and such local associations as the Executive Committee may establish or accept." The suggestion made in 1905 to provide secretaries "in order to unite the interests of the classes" was incorporated into the new constitution. However, systematic reporting by class secretaries was not started until 1911.

In order to recognize the role of local groups, or constituent associations, the constitution provided that one member from each of the associations or clubs in Maine, Boston, Rhode Island, New York, Chicago, and two members from the association of women graduates were to serve on the Executive Committee for 1906–7. Representatives from all the associations except Chicago were present at the first meeting of the reconstituted committee in December, although a Chicago delegate was able to attend in 1907. Ruth Dame of the Class of 1902 represented the "T.C. Alumnae Association" at the first meeting. It was considered desirable to encourage the formation of local associations "as fast as it seemed possible for them to become permanent organizations." An organization of alumni in the Connecticut Valley was suggested specifically. Associations in Minneapolis and California were also thought probable, and in the fall of 1907 a group in Pittsburgh expressed a desire to organize and be represented. The Pittsburgh Association was accepted as a constituent organization in 1908 and was given representation on the Executive Committee.

[48] Samuel W. Mendum was elected to that post in 1892, just as he was entering the door where the Association was meeting. In spite of his protest that he did "not feel competent to do the work satisfactorily," his resignation was not accepted for twenty-two years.

The constituent associations recognized by 1912 were the Tufts College Clubs of Boston, New York, Chicago, Philadelphia, Maine, Rhode Island, Pittsburgh, Connecticut, Lawrence (Massachusetts), and Vermont.[49] The Tufts Club of Western New York was recognized in 1914, and of Northern New York and Washington, D.C., in the following year. The ever-widening range of Tufts was illustrated by the recognition of the Tufts Club of Puget Sound in 1918 and the organization of many other alumni groups about the country.

The possibility of enlarging the scope of the Association by including the alumni of the medical and dental schools was discussed on numerous occasions, and they were invited in 1909 to apply for membership in the general alumni body of the College. Medical and dental graduates, however, tended to go their separate ways and to participate in their own organizations. The Boston Dental School Alumni Association had come into existence in 1872; in 1900, after the Boston Dental College had become part of Tufts, it was renamed the Boston and Tufts Dental Alumni Association. The Tufts College Medical Alumni Association was created in 1894 by the first class graduated from the medical school but was not active until 1902. In 1915 the Executive Committee of the Alumni Association invited "any reasonable proposition" that would result in closer affiliation with other degree holders from the institution. One of the difficulties was that many of the medical and dental alumni did not hold their first degrees from the College and hence encountered the problem of divided allegiance.

The women graduates of Tufts had already organized when the constitution of the Alumni Association was revised in 1906. Two years earlier, 104 undergraduates and alumnae had held their first annual luncheon on April 2 at a Boston hotel under the auspices of the All Around Club (the organization including all women undergraduates). It was then and there decided to organize a group with the somewhat redundant title of the "Tufts Girls' Alumnae Association." The mission was accomplished in May 1905

[49] Like other alumni clubs, the Vermont group lived an unstable existence. It became inactive shortly after it was recognized, and had to be reaffiliated in 1916. The Connecticut and Maine clubs were also dormant for several years; the former was recognized in 1916 after new boundaries were drawn for it. The problem of geographical coverage recurred in the case of the New York Club.

with the adoption of a constitution for the Association of Tufts Alumnae, and Ruth P. Capen, of the Class of 1902, become the first president. Any woman who had been a student at Tufts College for one year was eligible for membership. Annual meetings were held during the Christmas holidays. The women's group agreed in 1906 to appoint permanent class secretaries comparable to those for the men's classes, although this was not actually accomplished until 1911. The idea that women graduates should organize branch clubs and associations was rejected. The alumnae organization pursued a different course from that of its male equivalent by involving faculty wives and personnel of the medical and dental schools in its activities from the very start. Dr. Olga Cushing Leary and Dr. Ella G. Stone in medicine and Dr. Marion Woodward in dentistry were among the early participants.

The alumnae group was incorporated on March 30, 1910, and continued to be separate from the Alumni Association.[50] An initiation fee of $1.00 and annual dues of the same amount were levied on those entering the organization after the date of incorporation. After 1910 the Association became more of a *bona fide* alumnae group; any woman who had been for at least a year "a former member of a class in Tufts College" was eligible for membership. Holders of any of the six major offices of the Association were required to be graduates. In keeping with the policy of "segregation of the sexes" of which Jackson College was the visible symbol, the Association of Tufts Alumnae refused to be told by the Alumni Association how to run its affairs. When the alumni suggested that the alumnae raise their dues to $1.50 to include a subscription to the *Graduate,* the latter not only refused to bring their by-laws into conformity with the proposal but voted on December 30, 1911, to withdraw from the Alumni Association altogether. Reaffiliation of the two groups was not completed until 1921. The alumnae published their own *Bulletin* for several years but abandoned the project after the editor of the *Graduate* urged that the alumnae use its columns, and after alumnae coverage was extended in the *Weekly.*

[50] Among the advantages of incorporation and of the appointment of a dean of women for Jackson College was eligibility for membership in various College clubs through the Association of Collegiate Alumnae. The Tufts group was admitted to the latter in 1917.

The Jackson freshman class in 1915

The meetings of the alumnae, like those of the alumni, were at first mainly social in nature and intent. The first project undertaken by the women graduates was the raising of a fund in 1908 to assist undergraduates. An annual prize of $20 was established the following year, to be awarded to an undergraduate woman who wrote "the best essay on some subject of general interest to the College community." The coincidence of the incorporating of the Association and the establishment of Jackson College in 1910 appeared at first glance to give the alumnae an opportunity to have a hand in the selection of the first dean, but before they had done more than initiate correspondence with the heads of several colleges and universities soliciting suggestions, they were informed that Mrs. Caroline S. Davies had already been selected by the Trustees.

The financial contributions of the Association of Tufts Alumnae to the College were small when the organization was established but were given with sincerity and good intent. When Acting President Hooper appeared before the Association in 1912 to make a plea for funds to help the College out of financial difficulties, 125 alumnae immediately made pledges of $5.00 a year for five years.[51] The Association also assisted Dean Davies in various ways, including the holding of receptions for prospective Jackson students. An alumnae representative served on the Athletic Committee of Jackson College commencing in 1914, and until regular infirmary facilities were provided by the College, the Association paid for the services of a nurse for the Jackson undergraduates. It was through the efforts of the alumnae in 1916 that Mrs. Cora Polk Dewick became the first woman appointed to the Board of Visitors to Jackson College and that she also became (in 1920) the first woman to be elected to the Board of Trustees. Preparation of rosters of alumnae periodically by the Association was another activity of great value to many offices in the College. During the First World War, the Association bought its share of Liberty Bonds and contributed to Red Cross projects of various kinds.

The failure of the alumni to have, *qua* alumni, a voice in the government of the College had become a matter of increasing concern in the 1890's. President Capen, always sensitive to the needs of the various components of the institution, called attention to this deficiency in his annual report for 1893–94. The time had come, he told his fellow Trustees, to give the alumni a more active role in Tufts affairs than encouraging class reunions and alumni dinners. Even though some of the Trustees were alumni, they were not selected by the graduates of the institution. He suggested the possibility of having two sets of governing boards: one, about one-third the size of the regular Board, could handle the financial affairs and general administration of the College; the other, made up of alumni, could supervise the academic work and have a voice in the selection of staff. The closest equivalent to this proposal that was actually carried out was the establishment in 1899 of a Board of Overseers, which lasted until 1907, when formal representation was provided on the Board of Trustees.[52] There was also a measure of

---

[51] This was a remarkably good response in view of the fact that even a year later there were only 131 paid-up members, of 456 eligible for membership. Within a year the pledges amounted to over $1,000 and the effort was designated the "Alumna Fund."

[52] The history of the Overseers is related in Chapter 5. The strictly alumni character of the Overseers was illustrated by the fact that when the constitution of the Alumni Association was revised in 1906 it provided that

dissatisfaction among the alumni with their own contribution to the College. As H. Austin Tuttle noted in 1903, only 490 out of more than 1,500 living alumni belonged to the Association, and the organization itself met but once a year and then largely for social purposes. The only communication with members was the annual balloting for Overseers and an invitation to the annual dinner.

The hoped-for increase of alumni participation in the election of alumni Trustees did not occur. The alumni cast 374 ballots in their first election in 1907. The number of ballots cast in 1908 was 478, still considerably short of the number of alumni eligible to vote. One of the reasons for the relatively light vote was thought to be the lack of machinery whereby the alumni might register their choices for nominees before elections took place. To remedy this deficiency, the secretary of the Association was authorized to solicit from each local alumni organization the names of at least two and no more than four alumni eligible for Trustee membership. Such suggestions would be sent out with the request that nominations be made from the list. If the votes in 1909 were any indication, the plan was not notably successful. Only 463 ballots were cast for alumni Trustees that year, and the total hovered around that figure for some time. For several years the Association's Executive Committee struggled with the machinery of nominating and electing alumni Trustees, at various times recommending nominations by petition and the use of a preferential ballot.

The elaborate, cumbersome, and restrictive method of nominating alumni Trustees provided in the amendment to the Corporation charter in 1907 was replaced by a simpler procedure in 1919 which provided that the ten alumni-elected members were to "be nominated and elected in accordance with rules and regulations formulated by the alumni association . . . acting through its executive or other governing board or committee." It was further specified that the rules and regulations could "be altered or amended at any time in the same manner in which they were originally adopted."

---

the election of its officers be in the hands of the Overseers. However, because of the imminent dissolution of the latter body, the Association elected its own officers that year.

Having an official voice in College policy-making and cooperating informally and keeping in touch with Tufts affairs were different matters. In the two latter areas, considerable progress was made. A registration bureau for alumni was opened on the Hill in 1900 "in order that all possible aid may be rendered graduates in securing positions." The following year, the first alumni directory was published under the co-supervision of the secretary of the faculty and the secretary of the AlumniAssociation, under authorization from the Trustees.[53] The *Tufts College Graduate* (later the *Alumni Bulletin* and then the *Alumni Review*) served to keep graduates informed both of their own organization and activities and of events on the campus. The Association's annual dues were increased in 1911 to $1.50 to include a subscription.

One plan that failed of accomplishment was proposed in 1903. It was decided to commemorate the fiftieth anniversary of the founding of the College by raising funds to support an Alumni Professorship. A collector was secured for each class, but actual subscriptions never amounted to more than a trickle. A goal of $50,000 was set in 1904, with the intention of endowing the chair of physics, but the greatly reduced goal of $5,000 was still several hundred dollars short in 1914. The Finance Committee of the Trustees thereupon applied the interest to general faculty salaries. The Association was represented for many years before 1917 on the Athletic Advisory Board and took an active interest in organized sports. A Committee on Alumni Affairs was created by the Association in 1918 "to confer with the College officers, Trustees, and other interested parties and to recommend . . . such action as it deems for the best interest of the College and alumni."

The history of the Association from its founding in 1860 until 1920 was one of modest accomplishment in spite of some organizational difficulties. No decision had yet been made on a proposal in

[53] Similar directories were prepared in 1905, 1911, 1917, and 1923 by the secretary of the College and were published as College Bulletins. The editions of 1942 and 1950 were prepared under the auspices of the Alumni Council. Cost was the major factor in determining that the 1950 edition would be the last one printed. However, a locator index was established in the Office of Records and Administrative Services, and current files were maintained in the Alumni Office, which was moved from Ballou Hall in 1962 to the home donated by Professor Emeritus Houston.

1913 that life memberships be established (at a fee of $50), and no solution had been offered to the problem suggested in 1914 of whether to establish a permanent alumni secretaryship as a full-time position. Some lines of communication had been established and maintained with the College, especially through official representation on the Board of Trustees; but the heart of the matter was the failure of the majority of the alumni to join the organization. When the secretary of the Association made his annual report in 1919, there were only 173 members of the General Association and only 401 members in ten clubs. A major step in strengthening its structure and providing more unified support for their Alma Mater was the incorporation of the Association on June 19, 1920, with permanent headquarters in Medford.

No significant changes were made in the newly constituted Association. Dues were raised from $1.50 to $2.00 to help make up the chronic deficit of the *Graduate*. The membership on the Executive Committee continued to provide a "constituent committee," on which each of the twelve local associations or clubs then in existence had one place. The secretary-treasurer was authorized to draw $25 a year "as compensation for the faithful performance of his duties." J. Porter Russell, of the Class of 1898, was the first president elected under the new by-laws. Professor Clarence P. Houston, of the Class of 1914, served as secretary-treasurer for the three-year term specified and was succeeded by Joseph W. Morton, of the Class of 1911. Professor Houston became the first custodian of the official seal adopted at the first meeting of the Executive Committee under the new by-laws. The first annual meeting in June 1920 under the new organization was notable because it was announced that Mrs. Cora Polk Dewick, of the Class of 1896, had been elected a Trustee. In the same year, the Association of Tufts Alumnae was accepted as a constituent organization. Changes in provisions in membership and dues for alumni were made in 1921. Membership for alumni became automatic, and a levy of $2.00 for a subscription to the *Graduate* was substituted for the conventional dues. Local clubs were free to make their own assessments.

The period of the 1920's was one of decline for Tufts clubs. Membership in the general Association, as gauged by subscriptions to the *Graduate,* went up (to 550 in 1922) but the number of paid-up subscriptions in the constituent organizations went down sharply. The Connecticut Club produced sixty-four subscriptions and the Washington Club but one. There was a total subscription list of 690 in 1922. On the other hand, the number of alumni voting for Trustees achieved a new high of over 1,200 in 1923.

The idea of creating a fund financed by the alumni to increase the resources of the College had had nineteenth-century origins but had not enjoyed an uninterrupted existence. The so-called Alumni Fund known to graduates in the 1960's came into being as a result of Executive Committee action on June 13, 1925, when it was voted "to appoint a temporary committee to organize a permanent Tufts College Alumni Fund Association to be organized immediately by the alumni." The Sustaining Fund, as it began to be called in 1927, was the source from which the Alumni Gate and several sections of fence were financed during the same year. Subscriptions to the fund had reached over $20,000 by Alumni Day in 1929. Among the projects undertaken that year was the provision of War Memorial Steps between Miner and Paige Halls to commemorate those associated with Tufts who had offered their lives in wars in which the United States had been involved. The idea of a Placement Bureau that had been established in 1900 and had ceased to function was also revived in 1929. However, its activities were limited, for most departments on the campus desired to handle their own placements and make recommendations in their respective fields. The Placement Bureau's main function was to serve as a clearinghouse and referral agency. At the same time a recruiting committee operating through the Bureau of Alumni Service was appointed to interest prospective students and to provide for interviews conducted by alumni in various areas. The Association was also responsible in 1929 for taking under advisement a plan for a new physical education plant for men that less than four years later became Cousens Gymnasium.[54] This became the most important project of the many sections into which the Alumni Fund had been divided by 1930. Contributions and pledges totaled over $17,000 in that year. In spite of the nationwide depression that had reached ominous proportions by 1933, almost $7,000 was contributed that year by Hill alumni for scholar-

[54] It was Charles R. Marvin, of the Class of 1899, who suggested that the new facility bear the name of President Cousens.

ship aid. Meanwhile, the alumnae started their own fund to provide what, many years later, became Alumnae Hall.

An area of growing interest to the alumni in the 1930's was adult education. A committee was appointed in 1931 to survey the subject and to make recommendations concerning those phases that might be of special interest. They found considerable activity already under way, expressed through such interest groups as the Scribbler's Club, the Graduate Dramatic Society, the William Harvey Society lecture series at the medical school, and even an alumni gymnasium class. Further undertakings were encouraged, and discussions took place about the possibility of establishing courses in music appreciation, current events, modern languages, and so on.

By far the most lively topic engaging the attention of interested alumni in 1933 and 1934 was the structure of their own organization. For several years a feeling had been growing that the various groups of Tufts graduates were functioning in too uncoordinated a fashion; they should be welded into a closer union. There was also criticism of the way the Executive Committee had been organized under the by-laws of 1920.[55] The total problem was discussed at length at the annual meeting of the Executive Committee in June 1933, under the leadership of President Robert W. Hill, of the Class of 1904. Judge Hill's many services to the College were recognized by an honorary degree awarded in 1964 by his Alma Mater on the sixtieth anniversary of his graduation. The deliberations centered around "the desirability of instituting what might be termed an Alumni Council to take the place of the present Executive Committee." The proposed change was no mere shuffling of terminology. It was intended to bring about "a complete reorganization of alumni activities (and powers)" of sufficient scope to necessitate an amendment to the College charter. The president of the Association, as the sponsor of the plan, outlined the need for it. "Our alumni body has never been welded

[55] Only minor changes were made between 1920 and 1934. The most important was the transfer of the office of secretary-treasurer to the jurisdiction of the College in 1927. Thereafter, the financial reports of the Association became a part of the report of the treasurer of the College, and the office was known as "Alumni Secretary of the College." This arrangement was confirmed as part of a slight rewording of the Association's constitution in 1933.

together or sufficiently organized to secure maximum results. A strong alumni body will mean a strong undergraduate body, and a well developed and enthusiastic student body will in turn help to produce a loyal and enthusiastic group of alumni in years to come."

After numerous meetings, investigations, and consultations in 1933 and early 1934, the plan was unanimously ratified by the Executive Committee and enthusiastically endorsed by President Cousens. By an amendment to the Tufts charter the newly created Alumni Council was given the right, as a representative body of the alumni, to elect alumni Trustees. The new system went into effect immediately, for those alumni Trustees whose terms commenced on July 1, 1935, were elected by the Council. The new alumni agency, organized as a continuing body that was scheduled to meet regularly, was intended "to take active control of alumni affairs and to organize the Tufts alumni of all departments into a more closely welded and more aggressive body." [56] The twenty-one-member Council, representing all divisions of the College, became the first really integrated and truly coordinated body to administer alumni affairs. Judge Hill had recognized that the success of Tufts — and indeed of any college — depended on three elements: "the maintenance of an efficient and capable teaching body; the maintenance of a high class, intelligent, and loyal student body; and the maintenance of a well organized and efficiently operating alumni body." There was every indication that in their new Council the alumni had one of the important elements of success listed by Judge Hill.

[56] Arthur B. Newhall, of the Class of 1908, president of the Hood Rubber Company, and Stanley C. Wilson, Class of 1901, governor of Vermont, served as the first chairman and vice-chairman, respectively. The secretary-treasurer continued to be Joseph W. Morton, and an Executive Committee of eight was created, together with nine standing committees (Alumni Education, Alumni Fund, Alumni Room, Nominating, Placement Service, Prospective Students, Publicity, Trustee Election, and Alumni Activities). The committees were authorized to add alumni who were not members of the Council if they so desired.

12. From a Semicentennial
Through a World at War

Goddard Chapel was jammed beyond capacity early in the afternoon of April 21, 1902. Promptly at 2:00 P.M. a procession consisting of President Capen, the Trustees and Overseers, the mayors of Somerville and Medford, the presidents of several New England colleges and other specially invited guests, and the several faculties of the College marched down the path from Barnum Museum with the senior class acting as escort. The president took his official chair in the center of the chancel, flanked by Henry B. Metcalf, president of the Trustees, and George S. Boutwell, former governor of Massachusetts and the guest of honor. After an anthem by the College choir and prayer by Rev. Charles H. Leonard, dean of the divinity school, President Capen conferred the honorary degree of Doctor of Laws upon former Governor Boutwell, who then addressed the assemblage at some length.

It was a peculiarly fitting and even dramatic occasion, for the academic convocation was the climax of the celebration of the fiftieth anniversary of the signing of the College charter. Fifty years ago that day, Governor Boutwell had affixed the final signature to the document that had brought Tufts into corporate existence. At the conclusion of the ex-governor's address, the hymn composed by Mrs. Mary T. Goddard for the laying of the cornerstone of the College on July 19, 1853, was sung by the assemblage. A reception followed at the Capen residence, and the memorable day was closed with a reunion concert in the chapel, where nearly fifty alumni added their voices to the Glee Club, and the Mandolin Club exhibited its musical talents.

The celebration of the semicentennial of the opening of the College followed closely on the heels of the ceremonies marking the fiftieth anniversary of the signing of the charter.[1] The decision was made to have the celebration coincide with the anniversary of the formal opening of the College in August 1855, but a sorrowful event intervened, and the celebration became a commemoration. President Capen attended a meeting of the Trustees on March 14, 1905, and as chairman of a special Committee on Nominations he presented the names of three men to fill vacancies on the Board. Eight days later he was dead. A sense of unreality and of loss permeated the College. A series of gay and festive events scheduled for the spring and early fall of 1905 gave way to services of remembrance and appreciation for a departed leader. A sober Commemoration Sermon was preached on June 18 in Goddard Chapel by Rev. William H. Ryder, of the Class of 1869. Two days later, the forty-ninth annual Commencement took place, and the next day (June 21) a solemn academic ceremony marked the anniversary of the opening of the College. Austin Barclay Fletcher, of the Class of 1876, delivered the principal oration. The College then conferred the largest number of honorary degrees given at any one time in its history.

Tributes to the late president poured in from every direction. Resolutions adopted by faculty, Trustees, Overseers, and the Alumni Association expressed with varying degrees of eloquence the magnitude of the loss the Tufts community and the larger educational world had suffered. The Overseers summed up the man and his accomplishments by paying homage to his "judicious, liberal and progressive policy . . . and . . . the tactful and persistent quality of [his] efforts. Under his guidance the alumni have been brought more and more into sympathetic relationship with the College. They have been made to feel that, with him at its head, the institution was intimately concerned with their interests . . . he was dignified, courteous and affable, patient in explana-

[1] A certain amount of confusion has arisen about the distinction between the two events. When the Executive Committee of the Trustees undertook in 1901 to make arrangements "for the proper observance of the Fiftieth Anniversary of the charter of Tufts College," President Capen suggested that it be distinguished from the semicentennial, which was to be an observance of the anniversary of the convening of the first faculty on October 9, 1854. The Trustees voted originally to begin the semicentennial celebration on the second Sunday in October 1904.

tion, tolerant of differing opinions, and considerate of every call for information or advice." Some of the most striking tributes came from clergymen representing faiths other than Capen's own. Leaders in the Protestant Episcopal Church sent in messages side by side with those of educators at Boston College and Holy Cross. On the Sunday following Capen's death, the priest in the Roman Catholic Church in Medford made special mention during Mass of the late president, and reminded his parishioners "that they should honor one who been the friend of Catholics at a time when they had few friends." Capen's broad and liberal Universalist principles were more than mere verbalisms.

The coincidence of the fiftieth anniversary celebration, the semicentennial, and the passing of President Capen made particularly timely a review of the past and present of Tufts. The College had been the 163rd such institution chartered in the United States. It had opened formally in 1855 with thirty students and had graduated its first class of three in 1857. Since then, some 2,000 alumni had gone out from the College, which had grown from one building to eighteen, had added four professional and pre-professional schools that gave it grounds to call itself a university, and could boast of an instructional staff of 175 and an enrollment of almost 1,000. Excluding the professional departments, Tufts had grown to be thirty-eighth in the nation in size of student body. Statistics, however, could not tell the whole story. Professor Kingsley, in an address to the students in 1900, had come much closer to the truth than mere numbers could reveal. "How do I know that a tree grows? I cannot go out today and measure one on our campus and then measure it again tomorrow and see that it has increased in girth or height. Yet I cannot but believe that the tree is growing." So it was with Tufts College.

Much of the tangible evidence of growth in the College had resulted from Capen's efforts and from his flexibility and his willingness to encourage change. The extension of the elective system after 1875 had brought a great increase in the range of departments already existing and in the introduction of new subjects. When the first catalogue was published in 1854–55, a thin pamphlet of fifteen pages had been sufficient to outline the entire scheme of a Tufts education. In 1904–5, a volume of nearly 300 pages was required to do the same. Tufts had likewise kept pace with the phenomenal growth of the public high school movement, particularly in Massachusetts, by adjusting its admission requirements to new situations. As the number of high schools in Massachusetts increased from 60 to 260 in the half-century between 1852 and 1902, and as the preparatory school curricula changed in response to popular needs and demands, the College adjusted to the changes. It was largely through Capen's efforts that Tufts became the first New England college to challenge the rigidity of the traditional admission requirements.

In like manner, Tufts had been in the forefront of the movement to recognize the educational value of scientific instruction and to give science a leading place in the curriculum. When presenting his annual report for 1882–83, President Capen had suggested ways by which endowment funds could be most wisely spent. At the top of his list was the establishment of a scientific school where advanced experimentation could be conducted. Throughout his thirty years as president he had tried to promote the kind of growth and expansion that would "give Tufts College a place in the front rank of the progressive institutions of our time."

§   §   §

A committee of seven Trustees appointed to seek a new president was created at the same meeting (March 31, 1905) at which F. W. Hamilton, chairman of the Executive Committee, was made acting president. The committee was given no special instructions and was presumably free to consult whomever it wished. It was not until October that it made a preliminary report. Several persons were under consideration and a "voluminous correspondence" was in progress with some individuals, but no results had yet been achieved. The committee contacted the Board of Overseers as the logical body to represent the alumni; the Board immediately set to work to obtain suggestions from every graduate of the College for a successor to Capen. A circular was distributed, "countless" personal letters were written, and numerous interviews were held. The alumni were assured that all letters received in reply to the Overseers' request would be treated confidentially if desired by the writers.

A detailed report of the Overseers' findings and recommendations was forwarded to the Trustees in October 1905. The candi-

dates whose names were submitted ranged from men eminently fit
(but not available) to "radical suggestions and some few that might
be considered extraordinary." Out of the welter of ideas there did
come a consensus. Certain academic qualifications were recognized
as indispensable. The new president should be a man

> of ample scholarship, acquainted in the professional sense with
> modern educational thought, a competent business man or admin-
> istrator along educational lines; he should be a man of large
> executive ability; he should be magnetic, courteous, affable, force-
> ful, tactful in his dealings with men, so that he may represent the
> College in a large way in all financial, educational, and social
> circles; he should be one who by temperament, personal force
> and broad sympathy, should command the confidence and esteem
> of those about him; a man above all of large power of leadership,
> who shall rally to his support the loyalty of the oldest and the
> youngest of the college constituency.

Certain other qualifications that seemed of special relevance
to the situation at Tufts were spelled out. President Capen had
established such a harmonious relationship with the alumni that
the Overseers were particularly insistent that his successor be one
who would be "widely acceptable" to them, for "sooner or later the
future of the College must lie in the hands of the graduate body."
The Overseers had, in consequence, been led to the conclusion that
the new president ought to be a graduate of the College, if one
could be found having the necessary qualifications. They marshaled all the reasons that could ever be offered for making such a
recommendation.

On another point the consensus of the alumni was unequivo-
cal. The new president should be a layman rather than a clergyman.
This was partly a matter of following a national trend, of which
Yale was cited as an example. "The training of the clergyman is no
longer, as in former years, the ideal for the president of a College."
The general demand was for an experienced educator. Another argument centered around the desirability of removing any hint of
sectarianism in Tufts' operation, control, or admissions policy. A
third reason for avoiding a clergyman was the objection voiced by
"a large part of the alumni" to Frederick William Hamilton, Class
of 1880, Universalist pastor, and long-time chairman of the Executive Committee of the Trustees, who was "the clergyman most often

mentioned in connection with the position." It was surely no pleasant duty to report this fact to a group of which the person himself was a member and which had to make the ultimate choice for the presidency. The Overseers were as blunt as they could be under the circumstances and still handle the problem diplomatically. The judgment of the alumni added up to only one thing: Hamilton did "not have the all important support of the alumni sentiment of the College" and "would enter the office against alumni sentiment so strong as to handicap seriously the success of any man in the office."

In the opinion of the Overseers, speaking for the majority of the alumni, the alumnus who most nearly met all the conditions set down was Dr. Charles M. Jordan, of the Class of 1877. He was a man "in the prime of life" who had been engaged throughout his career in the practical affairs of education. After graduating from Tufts, Jordan had served as principal of the high school in Bangor, Maine, and then in the same capacity in Minneapolis, Minnesota. He had completed his thirteenth year as superintendent of the Minneapolis public school system, comprising approximately 1,000 teachers and 45,000 pupils. He had demonstrated his capacity as a good organizer, administrator, and speaker, and made a most favorable impression among other able men, judging from the correspondence received by the Overseers. He had declined such important positions as the presidency of Buchtel College, the state superintendency of education in Minnesota, and the superintendency of schools in Cleveland, Ohio.

The Overseers urged that the choice of a president should not be made in haste. They were "unanimously of the opinion that the largest latitude as regards time should be taken and that the field may be thoroughly covered and that the best man and the most acceptable to all interested should be chosen for the place." The Overseers were understandably upset when it was reported at their meeting in January 1906 that the Trustee nominating committee was about to make its report and that immediate action on the selection of a president was contemplated. Such a summary disposition of the problem of filling the presidency would alienate the alumni and might cause "irreparable harm."

If Dr. Jordan were not considered a suitable candidate, the Overseers were quite willing to suggest one of their own number, H. Austin Tuttle, of the Class of 1891. Even though he persistently refused to be considered a candidate, the overwhelming majority of the Overseers and many alumni would have considered him "a most fortunate selection." Overseer Henry Blanchard filed a dissent. He objected strongly to the allegation of "summary" and "precipitate" action by the Trustees, for they had been anxious to make a decision the preceding October and had yielded only on the importuning of the alumni. He had no objection to Mr. Tuttle, whom he did not know very well, but he did know Dr. Hamilton and supported him wholeheartedly. Blanchard considered groundless the fear that Hamilton would not win the regard of the undergraduates and alumni.

The Trustee nominating committee finally made its report to the parent body on March 1, 1906. The committee had held ten meetings averaging three to four hours each and had conducted, besides interviews, a correspondence "aggregating many hundreds of letters." It had consulted with the Overseers both informally and formally. A joint committee had spent five hours on an evening in February exchanging opinions. The committee had also solicited suggestions from the faculty and had ascertained the sentiments of "the Universalist body, which has contributed so generously to the maintenance of the College — which has, indeed, given it pretty much all the support and endowment that it has ever had." The committee had started its search with no common agreement on a suitable person and with no specific individual in mind; it was "open to suggestions from any quarter." In serving as a sort of clearinghouse for dozens of suggestions, the committee's task, not unexpectedly, was "difficult and perplexing." Quite contrary to a widespread impression, it reported that it had never contemplated precipitate action, and offered its delay of nearly a year before taking action as evidence of its deliberate intent.

The committee was quite frank in explaining the dilemma it faced in weaving some kind of middle way between conflicting views.

> There were many who thought we should go outside our alumni body and our Universalist constituency and select a man for the eminence of his name, someone with a record of public service which would reflect a luster upon the College. To others it was clear that we ought to find someone, even if he lacked a national reputation, who knew the traditions, the constituency and the

needs of the College from association and education. Some urged that we must secure a money-getter; others called for an administrator; others yet for a great educator. In some quarters there was strong opposition to the choice of a clergyman; to many others a minister seemed peculiarly fitted for the work.

One by one, each view was assessed. The committee eventually came to certain conclusions. The new president had to be someone, distinguished or not, who would consider the administration of the College a serious responsibility, not merely "as a feather in his cap." What the College needed most was "hard, tense work and serious, aggressive thinking on the part of its head." The committee felt throughout their deliberations that if a layman could be found who had the other desired qualifications the choice should have gone to him — "chiefly out of deference to the feeling of so many of the alumni." But such a person was not to be found. Further, they did not consider the selection of a clergyman intrinsically objectionable. Except for Harvard and Yale, every college in New England at the time had a clergyman for a president. If the new president could make the College strong and successful, then it made no difference whether he was a specially competent money-raiser or not, for the endowments would come. (This rather circular reasoning might not have represented the strongest of arguments.) Much more effective was their contention, arising from "decided and firm conviction," that it was essential to have a man with "intimate knowledge of the Universalist body, sympathy with its thought, and acquaintance with its membership." That he be an alumnus was desirable but not indispensable. It would have been an affront to "the great body of men and women who stand solidly for the support of Tufts College" if the committee had gone outside the Universalist fellowship and had recommended a man without knowledge of and sympathy for Universalist antecedents and ideals.

The committee recognized the fact that both of the persons recommended by the Overseers were Universalists, laymen, and alumni. The committee considered it unwise to nominate one (Jordan); the other (Tuttle) "absolutely refused to allow his name to be used." The committee believed it had deliberated long enough, and six more months or even a year of further consideration would not produce any better solution to the problem than they had to offer. The College needed leadership, and needed it without further delay.

Frederick William Hamilton, D.D., was the committee's choice. He was "the most eligible, qualified, and able" of those considered. His ability, his conscientiousness, his loyalty, and his scholarship were unquestioned. His experience as a Trustee had acquainted him with the inner workings of the College and had prepared him "in a marked degree" for the presidency. The committee admitted that he was "a clergyman indeed," but pointed out that he had had "an unusual business training." He was an alumnus and had won distinction as a Universalist clergyman. The committee admitted that they had found "a strong and persistent opposition" to Hamilton's nomination on the part of a "large majority" of the Overseers, who claimed in turn to represent a majority of the alumni. On the other hand, there appeared to be "strong support" of his candidacy from "many of the influential graduates of the College." In the committee's estimation, he had "in large degree" the confidence of the faculty and of his fellow Trustees.

In response to a request from the Trustees that the faculty suggest candidates, a secret ballot had been taken in June 1905 in which twenty-four of the thirty-five votes cast were for Hamilton. There is no indication in the records that the faculty ever prepared a formal slate from which to choose candidates.[2] At a meeting of alumni in New York in December 1912, after Hamilton had resigned, E. B. Bowen, of the Class of 1876, asserted that Hamilton's election had been "brought about principally by the efforts of the Faculty, combined with the Trustees."[3]

Before they had completed their lengthy report and had made a formal nomination, the Trustee committee returned to the mat-

[2] Some of the ballots were blank; Frank Oliver Hall, a graduate of the divinity school and a recipient of an honorary degree from Tufts that June, was the only other person who received votes.

[3] The editor of the issue of the *Graduate* in which Bowen's remarks were reported added his own parody of Rudyard Kipling's famous words as a footnote to Bowen's statement.

> "Some one has blundered:
> Ours not to make reply,
> Ours not to reason why,
> Ours but to print and die."

ter of alumni opinion. They recognized that unanimity had never existed among the graduates regarding College policies and probably never would exist. So it was "perhaps inevitable" that they should not be in entire accord. There was sufficient unity and solidarity, however, to be counted on to give the new administration "a cordial goodwill and a hearty helpfulness" once the presidency was filled.

The nominating committee's elaborate report was not acted on by the Trustees when it was presented on March 1. Two more weeks of doubt, hesitation, and maneuvering intervened before a decision was made on the presidency. The vote was postponed until March 13. When the Trustees convened on that date, twenty of the twenty-four were present, including the nominee. The president of the Corporation, Hosea W. Parker, was "detained by an important engagement" and the vice-president (and chairman of the nominating committee), Thomas H. Armstrong, presided. The election of a president of the College was the first article on a long agenda, but consideration of it was postponed until the very end. After Hamilton had retired from the room, a series of communications was read and discussed. The first was a letter from Trustee F. S. Pearson (who was not present) "dissenting from the report of the nominating committee so far as it related to the nomination of Dr. Hamilton to be president of the College." The second came from the chairman of the Board of Overseers, Edward H. Clement, asking for further delay. Next came a letter from Minton Warren, a member of the Overseers who had asked that his letter be read before the full Board of Trustees. Then came a motion for a four-week postponement of the vote, supported by a petition signed by thirty alumni. The motion to postpone was lost and after "a prolonged discussion" the Trustees proceeded to ballot. Hamilton was elected by a vote that was unanimous by the time the election was completed. The Trustees thereupon voted to send each graduate of the College a printed copy of the nominating committee's report, together with the action of the Trustees.[4]

Nobody is likely to have envied President Hamilton his new position. The committee's letter of notification included the per-

[4] These documents, with the committee's letter of notification and Hamilton's letter of acceptance, were published in the April 1906 issue of the *Tufts College Graduate*.

447

Frederick William Hamilton
Acting President, 1905–6; President, 1906–12

fectly accurate statement that he had been elected "by the affirmative vote of each and every Trustee present" and in his letter of acceptance Hamilton had repeated the phrase. Yet he could not
possibly have accepted the office without some intimation at least
that he was by no means the unanimous choice of the Tufts constituency. Minton Warren sent an indignant letter to the secretary
of the Board of Overseers within forty-eight hours of the report of
the Trustee nominating committee in which he tendered his resignation. He felt that he could no longer retain his self-respect and
remain a member of the Overseers "in view of the recent action of
a committee of the Trustees, ignoring and treating with contempt"
the "earnest request" of the Overseers to delay the choice of a
president or at least consider more seriously the selection of Jordan.
Within a few weeks, Edwin Ginn also submitted his letter of resignation from the Overseers; he was even more explicit in his reasons than Warren had been. The recommendations of the Overseers
were ignored in the selection of a president, wrote Ginn. If there
was any excuse for the existence of the Overseers, "their wishes

448

should have had recognition in this the most important action by the College on which their advice could be asked." Ginn was "not in sympathy with the new president nor with the general administration of the college." The crux of the matter to Ginn was the lack of any authority by the Overseers to make any decisions. They had "acted simply as an Advisory Committee with but a very limited influence. This was proved to me beyond question in the selection of a president. I was so disappointed over the outcome that I felt the time had come for me to withdraw entirely from the Board of Overseers."

A defensive note had crept into the report of the Trustee committee that had nominated President Hamilton. Was it justified? A review of the evidence available and of the situation confronting the Trustees (and the College) would seem to indicate that their choice of Hamilton was by no means an illogical one. The committee had settled on no one candidate at the outset and had certainly welcomed and considered suggestions from every quarter and of every complexion. It was inevitable under the circumstances that not everyone would be satisfied with the result, especially the alumni, who expected, or at least hoped, that the first choice of the Overseers would receive favorable consideration.

Hamilton had the qualifications and experience that most individuals agreed were necessary for a president of Tufts to possess. He represented a unique combination of clergyman and businessman. In the nine years between his graduation from Tufts and his acceptance of a pastorate in 1889, he had filled various executive and financial positions in the offices of the Portland and Ogdensburg Railroad in Maine and had gained the business experience that was coming more and more to be expected of college presidents. Hamilton had entered the ministry at the suggestion of President Capen and in 1889–90 had been one of the special students in the divinity school. He held pastorates in Pawtucket, Rhode Island, and Roxbury, Massachusetts, and held offices in numerous philanthropic and social organizations. He was a director of the Boston Associated Charities at the time of his election to the Tufts presidency. He had already written prize-winning essays on contemporary social issues (such as the immigration question and the Venezuelan boundary dispute of 1895) and had published a collection of his addresses. He had served as president of the Alumni As-

449

sociation for a two-year term and since 1896 had been a member of the Board of Trustees.

The task of winning the unqualified allegiance and support of the alumni was made even more difficult by the grave problems facing the College. The committee's letter of notification was less of an invitation than a series of challenges that the new president was expected to meet. Hamilton was reminded that the College had, in the past, experienced "a good measure of success," had done its share in the betterment of the world, and had a future of "as great and ample opportunities for continued growth and usefulness." He was then told that there were "serious problems of finance, administration, and education to be solved" which required a president who could assess the situation accurately and exercise "a wise and tactful judgment, a zealous watchfulness, a prudent foresight, and a resourceful management." He was being entrusted with a commission which, at base, demanded the building up of the endowment of the institution.

The new president promised to do what he could. In his letter of acceptance he gave assurance that he would hold the line and would not venture into new educational paths unless they were accompanied by the wherewithal to make them successful. He opposed the meeting of increased educational costs by raising tuition. "Tufts College, like every other college, must continue to be a philanthropic institution, giving education for fees far inadequate to meet the necessary expense involved." It was up to the friends of the College and public-spirited individuals to fill in the gap. The gap was widening and had to be closed if there was going to be any future at all for the institution.

President Hamilton echoed the same sentiments in his Inaugural Address, delivered on June 19, 1906. After a brief mention of the purposes of the College — to train the intellect for practical pursuits, to make "human minds instruments of precision," and to develop spiritual and moral values — he went to the heart of the matter. If the goal of the institution was "to fit young men and women for life," certain means were necessary. Money was one of them. Tufts had never had a single great financial patron and had depended on a few generous benefactors and many small ones. It was "the first duty" of the president to see to the financial welfare of the College. "We cannot do our work unless we can pay our bills." The watchword had to be "efficiency." The address was not particularly inspiring; it lacked the warmth and enthusiasm of his predecessor's Inaugural. But its pragmatic tone seemed to be what was needed at the time.

The financial clouds that hovered over the College at all seasons and threatened time after time to dim if not to extinguish its prospects became the darkest yet at the turn of the century. A note of warning that all was not well had been sounded in 1898 when the Education subcommittee of the Trustees was asked to consult with President Capen and "some of the leading professors" to see what could be done "to accomplish a saving of ten thousand dollars in salaries for the coming year." The Finance Committee simultaneously received a similar assignment covering the administration of the College grounds and buildings. It took no financial wizard to see what had happened to the resources of Tufts by 1900. As of that year, $719,000 of the College's total funds of $1,600,000 were invested in buildings and land used solely for educational purposes and therefore were productive of no revenue in themselves.[5] Annual operating deficits for the Hill departments increased from $15,000 in 1900 to $31,000 two years later, and thereafter the figure became even greater. When the Finance Committee refused to concur in a recommendation for additional appropriations for the school of letters in 1902, they put the problem baldly. "In our present financial conditions . . . our policy should be to annually cut our garments according to our cloth — and leave undone some of those things which, however desirable, would nevertheless not be matters of necessity." Time after time the Executive Committee reviewed every niche and corner of the College's operations to see whether a dollar could be saved here or another one there, but the basic stumbling block of finances refused to be budged. Expenses had already been cut to the bone by 1903, but that did little good. The Executive Committee, solely in compliance with an order by the Trustees, presented some "suggestions" that they refused to translate into formal recommendations because they saw no possi-

[5] Rental from dormitory rooms at this time barely paid for the cost of repairs and general maintenance. Dormitories were not always full; in 1900-1901, the Finance Committee raised the question of whether to keep all three of the men's dormitories open, "when two will more than accommodate the people."

Patrick Burns, who was (in his younger days)
the "Department of Grounds and Buildings"

bility of further reductions. If the "suggestions" had been carried out, they would have involved the dismissal of the one-man Department of Grounds and Buildings (Patrick Burns), drastically reduced salaries in the divinity school, closed one department in the college of letters and cut in half the personnel of four others, and stopped the purchase of all books for the library not acquired through the Joy Fund. After a two-hour discussion, the Trustees discarded all of the suggestions.

It was not as simple a matter as leaving the grass uncut during the summer months or allowing a leaky drainpipe to rust the walls of East Hall. Everyone in any way associated with the institution had to realize that Tufts was growing out of the horse-and-buggy era. College administration and instruction had changed radically by 1903 and had become more expensive. To keep up with her sister colleges, Tufts had had to offer a greatly expanded curriculum, and this meant enlarged expenditures. "Whatever we may think of the desirability of these conditions, they exist, and Tufts College must face them as other colleges have done." The Trustees

452

were not personally at fault for the constantly increasing expense of running the College, but they had to recognize that expense must be incurred and provided for, "or the College must go out of business."[6] The commitments of the College had increased more rapidly than the capacity to meet them.

The worst thing that could happen to Tufts, financially speaking, had to be faced up to by 1906. The College had encroached on its endowment to the extent of $199,000. The Finance Committee suggested reducing the indebtedness to permanent funds to $47,000 by charging off every unrestricted fund that could be found in the assets of the College.[7] Even with this bookkeeping legerdemain the encroachment was still there. What could be done? The situation was grave. There was no prospect of replacing the reduced principal out of current revenues. Some $200,000 of the values on the books represented a number of educational buildings constructed out of free funds of which nothing was left to produce income. One partial and short-range alleviation suggested was "a material increase in tuition charges." Another was strict enforcement of the program load of students and the levying of a charge of $20 per course on those above the limit. Still another would have required in the Hill departments the payment of tuition in advance, such as was already done in the medical and dental schools. This system would obviate the need for the posting of student bonds and the making of deposits and would hence save clerical costs.

The Finance Committee threw down the gauntlet in the fall of 1906. The estimated loss for 1906–7 was $35,000. The budget for that year was $216,000 and receipts from students were estimated at $140,000. From then on, every expenditure in excess of income would have to be charged against endowment — an immoral and thoroughly reprehensible procedure in the eyes of the committee. The time had come to take a step dreaded for years. The faces of the eight Trustees who attended must have been rather grim as they

[6] The comparative costs per student in the four major divisions of the College, and the receipts for each (not counting scholarship aid) were as follows in 1905: divinity school, $651.75, $42.95; college of letters (including engineering), $319.75, $86.91; medical school, $116.60, $121.32; and dental school, $153.40, $117.56.

[7] A readjustment, on paper, of the resources by the end of 1906 had actually reduced the impairment of the capital funds to $90,000 by borrowing from the principal of the permanent funds.

emerged from the regular meeting of the Board on March 12, 1907. After they had transferred another unrestricted fund amounting to some $35,000 to the profit and loss account to help reduce the deficit, they voted to approve the recommendation of the Finance Committee to sell off, in whole or in part, the wedge-shaped block of land bounded by Broadway, Packard Avenue, and Powderhouse Boulevard in Somerville, on the south side of the campus.[8] The loss of the land was a blow in itself, but the timing of the decision was even more unfortunate. The College entered the real estate market at a most inauspicious moment. The Panic of 1907 on the national front merely dramatized the economic uncertainty that was already reflected in depressed urban and suburban land values. It was in this sphere that endowment income was already reduced, and the very conditions that made it desirable to sell land made property unattractive to buyers. The Boulevard property, as it was called, was sold in bits and pieces over a period of more than ten years. Meanwhile, the impairment of the permanent funds of the College climbed to $120,000 at the end of the 1907 fiscal year. To cap off that dismal meeting in March, the Trustees had had to listen while President Hamilton related the woes of the engineering school, which had reached crisis proportions. He then lectured his fellow Trustees on the inevitability of continually mounting expenses if Tufts was to do a decent job. Better faculty salaries were absolutely necessary. He was "amazed at the loyalty and pathetic devotion of the men who at miserably inadequate salaries have stood by Tufts College loyally and patiently."

The nub of the problem in the Engineering Department was the relentless increase in enrollment, which called for additional staff, appropriations, and salary increases that the Trustees had for months been unable to provide. The numbers of students in 1904–5 were 177; in 1905–6, 188; in the current year, 218; in 1907–8, expected to be still larger. The entrance limit of ninety freshmen in the Engineering Department and ten in the Bromfield-Pearson School had already been reached. The consequences were inescapable: an overburdened teaching force, overcrowded laboratories, and already inadequate salaries made so much more so that the morale of the entire staff had been adversely affected. If any or all

[8] The parcel consisted of 85,000 square feet of land; there were no buildings involved.

of the staff saw fit to resign, it would be impossible to fill their places at the salaries being paid and the work load being carried. The situation was temporarily saved in 1906–7 by a special subscription among the alumni, but that was only a staying action. The closing of the overburdened shops to thesis work and the virtual elimination of the chemical engineering course during 1906–7 were most unfortunate, for these steps meant a lowering of the standards of the department and the turning away of qualified applicants. Simultaneously, tuition was raised and less was being offered. This was a situation that the Trustees should no longer perpetuate. It was a question of the very existence of the Engineering Department.

Three courses of action seemed possible: retain the existing faculty by paying them at least "living salaries" and furnishing them with at least a little more classroom assistance; permit the faculty to seek greener pastures and be prepared to pay much higher salaries to their successors; or reduce the enrollment to a figure comparable to what the instructors were originally employed to handle, and expect a decrease of about $10,000 in tuition fees. President Hamilton realized that none of these prospects sounded very attractive, but the first alternative seemed the only possibility. By increasing salary appropriations among the ten members of the faculty and staff by $3,400 and the laboratory and equipment appropriation by $1,000, the department could probably survive. According to Hamilton's reckoning, if it were not necessary to curtail enrollment, the enhanced tuition fees would provide $7,000 more in income than in previous years. Therefore, the increase in expenditures would not add to the deficit. Closing the Engineering Department should be only a last resort, and the College would unquestionably be even worse off without it. The issue thus squarely presented, a copy of Hamilton's report was mailed to each Trustee for him to ponder.

Fortunately it was not necessary to close the engineering school, for the deficit was lessened somewhat by increased student income following a raise in tuition, and by reduced salary commitments for faculty who retired by way of Carnegie pensions. The remainder of the money to build Robinson Hall was received in 1908, and the Crane gift added to the endowment of the divinity school. The outlook appeared even brighter in the same year when news was received that one Henry J. Braker had provided $500,000 for the College in his will. Tufts was able also to open its new library that year.[9]

§ § §

The circumstances surrounding the opening of Eaton Memorial Library in 1908 illustrated all too vividly the financial handicaps under which the College operated in the early twentieth century. With not a cent to spare for a desperately needed building, the Trustees were forced to solicit aid from outside and to accept certain disadvantageous conditions attached to the gift that eventually made the new library possible. Tufts was so severely limited in funds that the new building sat forlornly vacant for almost two years because there was no money to equip or staff it properly. The story of the Tufts Library between 1886, when it was moved from Ballou Hall to Middle (Packard) Hall, and the summer of 1908, when it was installed in its own building, unfortunately reflected the fate of similar undertakings on many another college campus. It struggled along with inadequate resources, an underpaid staff, unbalanced and out-of-date collections, cramped quarters, and a permanent place at the bottom of the priority list for expenditures. Space was at such a premium in 1899 that a notice was posted "that students must not use the Library for purposes of study." This prohibition, fortunately, did "not apply to those who are engaged in research work under the direction of their respective instructors." President Miner had made the statement in his report to the Trustees in 1874 that the Tufts Library was deficient, in some way, in practically every field. Professor Shipman, then in charge of the library as an additional duty, was apparently resigned to the idea that it was destined to be an orphan. He considered a "liberal selection of the best periodicals" an excellent investment "should any appropriation be made for the benefit of the Library for the coming year."

For the first three-quarters of a century, the Tufts Library depended almost entirely on gifts and donations, exchange of duplicates, and appeals to the alumni for the books and funds with which to operate. It could afford to subscribe to but few newspapers and

[9] The Braker bequest was not received for many years. It is dealt with in Chapter 14.

periodicals and relied for decades on the Reading Room Association to meet this need. This association, a student-sponsored group organized in 1859, subscribed to a dozen or so daily and weekly papers and magazines and donated its dog-eared back copies to the library after their immediate purpose had been served. The first drive for library funds aimed at the alumni took place in 1884–85. It was sufficiently successful to be continued for another year, and in 1886 had brought in gifts totaling $1,100. The Joy Fund, the only library endowment for many years, was of considerable aid, but only one-half of the income from what eventually became $25,000 was available directly for the purchase of books; and that was reduced after 1897. Many of the monetary gifts, both large and small, had strings attached. The Tabor Ashton Fund donated in 1899 (and later increased) excluded any books of a religious or theological character, and any work of prose fiction. One bottleneck in purchasing library materials from the $500 to $600 available each year from general and special funds was broken in 1906 when the Library Committee of the Trustees relinquished its control to the faculty. The latter were allowed for the first time to order books directly through their own Library Committee.

A list of books needed by the library was distributed to the alumni in 1897 and resulted in over 300 donations. But the continuing paucity of general funds for the library prompted President Capen in 1899 to try a more ambitious experiment. He suggested to Professor Shipman, chairman of the faculty Library Committee, that an attempt be made to raise $1,000 for immediate use by appealing to alumni and friends. Acting on this suggestion, Shipman (at his own expense) wrote about sixty letters, which netted $1,530. He was on leave the following year, but through the joint efforts of Byron Groce for the Library Committee of the Trustees and Professor Knight for the faculty, a more ambitious solicitation was made by circularizing the alumni for contributions to what became known as the "Shipman Fund." The amount was somewhat less than the previous year ($620) but a tradition was established, and for the next three years Professor Shipman sent out a similar circular. Over $3,000 was collected in that period, making a grand total of over $5,600 received between 1899 and 1904, given by some 350 persons. About one-third of the total was designated by the donors for the special needs of certain departments. The individual gifts ranged in amount from $50 to 25 cents. All were received gratefully, but Professor Shipman was particularly appreciative of the dozens of alumni who contributed from $1.00 to $5.00 year after year, as their means allowed. He quietly made his own contribution by paying personally for three years all bills for printing and postage. The responses to donations brought in, at interest rates then prevailing, the equivalent of the income of a permanent fund of $25,000.

Another expedient to raise money that was considered by the Trustees but discarded was to charge a fee for use of the library.[10] A modification of this proposal was adopted in 1896, on the suggestion of the students themselves. A charge of $1.00 was added to term bills to provide newspapers and periodicals through the Reading Room Association, which shared space with the library in Middle Hall.[11]

The size (and salaries) of the staff reflected the chronically impoverished state of the library for many decades. Helen Mellen, successor as full-time librarian to Professor Shipman in 1884, served until 1896 with no more than an occasional student assistant.[12] Ethel M. Hayes, of the Class of 1896, was appointed assistant librarian immediately after her graduation at a starting salary of $25 a month, which was increased to $30 after four years' service.[13] Miss Blanche Hooper, daughter of William L. Hooper of the Electrical Engineering Department, started her long career in the Tufts Library in 1905 at no salary at all. In 1907 she was advanced to $300 a year. After Miss Mellen's retirement in 1907, Miss Hayes served first as acting librarian and then as librarian until well after

[10] There was ample precedent for this policy if it had been adopted. For many years immediately after the College opened, students paid an annual fee of $1.00 for this purpose. A certain amount of money was no doubt collected as a result of a faculty rule of 1899 imposing a fine of 10 cents, in addition to the cost of retrieving the book by messenger, on "all students who fail to return an 'over-night' book to the library."

[11] The original Reading Room Association lasted until 1910, and a combined faculty-student committee made the selections.

[12] The academic year 1886–87 brought an unusually large number of gifts to be accessioned. Miss Mellen still had 1,000 volumes waiting to be catalogued at the end of the year.

[13] Her base salary was augmented by $6.00 a year for servicing the material acquired through the Reading Room Association.

the First World War.[14] When she retired as reference librarian she had accumulated a half-century of service to the College.

President Hamilton hoped that, with the opening of the new library, an experienced male librarian could be employed with the rank of professor and given a seat on the faculty. It was not until 1928 that the College carried out at least part of his wish by appointing Raymond L. Walkley to the post. One of his most noteworthy contributions was the reclassification of the collection according to the Library of Congress system. This in no way confused Miss Hayes, who was reputedly able "to carry the entire library around in her head." In 1919 the recently established Tufts chapter of the American Association of University Professors suggested to the Trustees that "the Librarian be given a place on the appropriate faculties of Tufts College." Although Miss Hayes and Mr. Walkley did attend faculty meetings, no librarian was formally assigned an academic rank until 1956, when Joseph S. Komidar was elected University Librarian and Associate Professor of Library Science.

The enlarged quarters in Middle Hall, which were to have provided for almost 50,000 volumes, were never intended to be more than temporary and were soon outgrown. Gifts of several hundred volumes each were particularly numerous after 1880, and in the 1880's the Tufts Library became a partial depository for government documents.[15] When the Trustees in 1901 cast about for assistance in providing a new library, there were over 42,000 books and more than 30,000 pamphlets in the collection. One practice inaugurated in 1892–93 that reduced the congestion in the main library was the establishment of departmental libraries. The first such branch library was created by Professor Kingsley in the Biol-

[14] Miss Hayes' initial salary as acting librarian was $600. Miss Mellen retired on a Carnegie pension of $450 a year, to which the Tufts Trustees added $50 annually in recognition of "her long and faithful services."

[15] By 1901 the library was entitled to receive over 500 volumes per year from the Superintendent of Documents, not to mention scores of pamphlets. No material received from the federal government could be disposed of in any way without authorization. Some of the valuable early legislative series, including the *Annals of Congress* and the *Congressional Globe,* which preceded the *Congressional Record,* were received as private gifts from Thomas G. Frothingham and Newton Talbot, both Tufts Trustees.

ogy Department and was housed in Barnum Museum.[16] Similar collections were established in the engineering school in 1900 after Robinson Hall was opened, and in the Crane Theological School.[17] However, this policy did not solve the central housing problem, and by 1901 space was so limited in Middle Hall that all the operations involved in unpacking, cataloguing, and otherwise processing books had to take place in a corner of the general reading room.

The gift from Andrew Carnegie that made a new library possible did not come unsolicited or as a complete surprise. The Trustees carefully laid the groundwork by relaying the needs of the College to that affluent gentleman in a letter written in February 1901. The communication, after stressing the non-sectarian character of the institution and its "remarkable success" notwithstanding "its limitations and struggles," referred to the glaring inadequacies of the existing library building, which had originally served as a dormitory. The College promised to make such arrangements as would allow the use of a new library to the high school students and members of the community of Medford and Somerville if Carnegie saw fit to provide it. The Trustees made reference to the numerous public libraries he had already donated, and hoped that "we may have a 'Carnegie Library' to alike honor your name and serve the best interests of humanity." Somewhat over three years later, the request was honored with a gift of $100,000, but with certain conditions attached.[18] The plans and specifications were subject to the donor's approval and were to include open-shelf public reading rooms. None of the money could be spent on furnishings, equipment, or staff, and the last installment of the gift would not be paid until the building was completed and all bills were paid.

The new library, for which ground was broken in the fall of

[16] It was through his efforts that the College received, without charge, a collection of some 3,000 volumes of scientific books worth about $5,000. This bargain was made possible by the consolidation of two libraries in Salem, Massachusetts.

[17] The existence of departmental libraries has never been unanimously approved at Tufts. Librarian Mellen in 1901 ventured the opinion that departmental libraries were "of doubtful utility" unless they could be housed in one building and duplicate copies could be acquired for the main library.

[18] Rev. Frank Oliver Hall, an alumnus of the divinity school, was instrumental in securing the Carnegie gift.

Eaton Memorial Library when it was opened in 1908

1905, was designed by the architectural firm of Whitfield and King. It was the better part of valor to have selected this particular company, for Mr. Whitfield was Mrs. Carnegie's brother. The stack area was designed for 200,000 books, although shelving for it was not completed for thirty years.[19] A large room on the right of the entrance was originally designed (and used for several years) as a lecture hall intended to accommodate 160 persons. The structure neared completion in the fall of 1906 and under ordinary circumstances would have been put to use at the end of the Christmas holidays. But that desirable event had to be "considerably postponed" because the College had no funds to make the building usable. The only alternative was to create a special Library Fund and to induce friends of the College to contribute.[20] Meanwhile, the receipt of the final installment of $5,000 from Carnegie was de-

[19] The books transferred from Middle Hall were originally shelved in the reading rooms. The first tier in the stack area was installed in 1915, and the installation of the remaining four tiers was not completed until the 1930's.

[20] The total cost of the new library (including equipment) as of 1908 was $102,849.49. The cost of equipping the library was slightly over $11,000, of which Tabor Ashton contributed almost half.

layed into the fall of 1907 because the College had not yet paid all
of the construction bills. During the spring of 1907 a plaque was
installed in the entrance hall identifying the benefactor, but Mrs.
Carnegie decided on a change. She wanted the building to stand as
a memorial to Rev. Charles H. Eaton, of the Class of 1874, so a
new tablet was installed and the building became officially the Eaton Memorial Library.

The new building, opened just before Commencement in
1908, was an impressive structure, centrally located near the top of
the Hill, with its red brick walls set off in the front by stone steps
and elaborate columns and friezework in the Greek classical style.
Two cast-iron curving staircases in the main hall and wooden fluted
columns with ornately carved pediments lent an air of spaciousness
and grandeur to the edifice. Tungsten electric lamps installed at
the last minute added a finishing touch.[21]

§   §   §

Andrew Carnegie's gift may have added much-needed facilities
and a new and dignified building to the campus, but it in no way
solved the pressing problem of finance. In fact, it aggravated the
situation by requiring additional maintenance and upkeep. Only
$15,000 had been realized on sales from the Boulevard land by
1908, and some $150,000 was still charged against the permanent
funds of the College.[22] Even though the Crane Theological School
earned more than its expenses in 1909 for the first time in its history, the engineering school went sharply into the red, and overall
operating deficits continued to be as large as ever. The financial picture was not at all brightened when the city of Somerville, following a decision handed down in 1896 by the Supreme Judicial Court
of Massachusetts, not only levied but steadily increased taxes on

[21] Less impressive were some of the costly repairs made immediately
necessary because of departures from original specifications. No provision had
been made for inspection by the College when the building was constructed.
The leaky copper roof had to be repaired and dank basement rooms had to be
waterproofed before the building was open a year. Termites appearing in the
1960's added their own brand of complications. One of their more successful
targets was a large and rather expensive volume on information retrieval.

[22] The net total from the Boulevard land after the residue had been sold
during the First World War was $155,000. Taxes, fees, and various other ex-
penses gobbled up over $50,000 of the gross receipts.

College-owned property occupied by faculty members.[23] The tax initially imposed in 1896 was almost enough "to pay the salary of a high-class instructor." President Capen protested that the argument used by cities and towns where colleges were located, that important tax revenues were lost through exemptions of educational property, was vitiated by the advantages gained by the community. The very existence of Tufts caused a rise in the value of surrounding properties because it enhanced residential attractiveness. Its campus was the equivalent of a public park and drew larger numbers of people than nearby Powderhouse Park, maintained by the city of Somerville. Capen also hastened to point out that Tufts was most generous in admitting students from Medford and Somerville and that some had received tuition grants. All of these arguments were to no avail, for in 1909 Somerville raised its tax assessment again, to the highest point yet reached.

The financial picture until the First World War remained one of unrelieved pessimism. Annual operating losses continued unabated. The Finance Committee warned their fellow Trustees repeatedly and "as strongly as possible" of "their unanimous disapproval of the plan of conducting the College upon a plane which is known in advance to be so greatly in excess of all income from all possible sources." Thomas Cunningham, Trustee since 1903, submitted his resignation in 1912 in protest against what he considered to be the unwise financial management of the institution. The budget for Grounds and Buildings was singled out for special attention because it was exceeded for several consecutive years by as much as $4,000 annually. The superintendent of Grounds and Buildings was replaced as a result. President Hamilton was advised to confer with the officers of the Carnegie Foundation, the Rockefeller Institute, and every other potential source of outside aid. The Department of Psychology and Education which Hamilton had so proudly brought into existence was temporarily abolished, and the positions of retiring teachers in several departments were not refilled. Among those affected were English, Modern Lan-

[23] "Lands with dwelling-houses thereon, owned by a college and occupied as residences by persons engaged solely in the instruction or government of the college or in the care of its property, under parol agreements whereby each is to receive as salary a stated sum monthly and the use of the estate while in the service of the college, for which use a certain sum is deducted from the amount of the salary, are not exempt from taxation. . . ."

guages, and Biology. No department was to acquire any new equipment or appliances or to install any that were donated if they entailed extra expense.

A special Committee on Finance consisting of representatives from the Trustees, the faculty, and the alumni was created in 1911 and given a triple assignment: to obtain a $1,000,000 endowment for the engineering school; to raise money "to carry on the work of the College adequately and efficiently"; and, after the first two tasks were completed, to endeavor to secure endowments for the medical and dental schools. President Hamilton gave the committee its instructions and sketched in the background. The College needed more money than the alumni could or would contribute; gifts were *not* to be solicited for new departments, new chairs, or new buildings not already on the needed list. The College was not trying to expand but was attempting to care for what it already had. The priority list included "a large gift" to the engineering school, $150,000 for a new chemistry laboratory and its maintenance, an endowment for chapel services (to furnish part of the president's salary or to pay "a college preacher" if or when the president happened not to be a clergyman), $75,000 to endow existing professorships, and funds for scholarships. Dean Anthony agreed to canvass the engineering alumni; Professor Durkee, those in chemistry; Professor Hooper, those in electrical engineering; and President Hamilton and Professor Harmon, the theological alumni. President Hamilton, in turn, was instructed by the Trustees to request the resignations of some members of the staff if that would help balance the budget.

Professor Hooper served as *ad hoc* chairman of the special fund-raising drive. He made a study of eight "near neighbors and competitors" and found the average productive endowment per student to be about $4,500, while the figure for Tufts was about $1,200. That was a major factor explaining his willingness to try his hand at fund-raising, for he was stubbornly convinced that the solution to the College's financial plight was to increase productive endowment rather than to attempt constantly to cut expenses, as many of the Trustees urged. He showed no hesitation in calling to the students' attention the sober fact that in 1911–12 Tufts spent "on every Liberal Arts student $187.91 more than that student paid in, and on every Engineer $28.36 more than he paid back."

William Leslie Hooper
Acting President, 1912–14

By the time he was commended by the Trustees in the fall of 1912 for his "excellent work" in raising more than $100,000 on behalf of the institution, he had become acting president of Tufts. President Hamilton had submitted his formal resignations as president and as Trustee on June 19, 1912, although they were not acted on until the annual meeting in October.[24] He was granted a six-month leave of absence beginning July 1, 1912, and the Executive Committee was authorized to appoint an acting president. The Trustees voted that Hamilton's resignation from the Trustees was "to take effect at once" and unanimously confirmed the Executive Committee's choice of Professor Hooper to head the College until a new president could be found. A five-man committee appointed on June 16 "to nominate a President of the College" made its first re-

[24] This item was not on the printed agenda of either of the meetings in June or October. Hamilton resigned twice from the Executive Committee, once on June 7, 1911, and again on July 2, 1912. The first resignation was accepted by the Executive Committee at their next monthly meeting, and A. W. Peirce was elected to take his place. However, Hamilton continued to serve and to be present at meetings until his second resignation, which took place after he had severed his connection with the Trustees.

port in October but had no candidates to submit.[25] It was over two years before they found a replacement for Hamilton.

The official records of the College give but slight indication of the reasons that prompted President Hamilton's sudden resignation. Very little was put on paper by the Trustees themselves. Yet a careful reading of Hamilton's annual reports and an action of the faculty in 1912 would seem to bear out the statement that he himself made public. Thirty members of the Faculty of Arts and Sciences presented to the Trustees in time for their May meeting a long memorial expressing dissatisfaction with the relationship they believed had come to exist between the faculty and the Trustees, as personified by President Hamilton, who also signed the memorial. The faculty argued that insufficient cooperation and "solidarity of interests" existed between "two of the bodies upon which rest the success and usefulness of the College as an institution of learning." In brief, the faculty were unhappy because they had been excluded from any opportunity to consult with the Trustees about matters of College policy with which they were much more conversant than the Trustees. The latter had overridden, drastically modified, or simply ignored some of the requests of the faculty presented through President Hamilton. The memorialists asked the Trustees "to entertain the question, whether the time has not arrived for a reasonable measure of influence to be exercised in your councils by the body of men to whose technical experience as educators, to whose judgment and loyalty you commit the day-by-day administration of the immediate concerns of the institution." The faculty mentioned two specific areas in which consultation would be profitable: the preparation of the budgets of the constituent schools and the selection of those members of the instructional staff who were given department chairmanships and professorial rank. There were "numerous other matters" that were not listed for which conferences were thought to be advantageous.

The signatories had definite procedures to recommend. The Trustee by-laws of 1908 (Article 17) had provided for a general

[25] The committee, chaired by Austin B. Fletcher, vice-president of the Trustees, consisted also of William W. McClench, Arthur E. Mason, Charles H. Darling, and Charles N. Barney. All were graduates of Tufts except Mason, who had received an honorary degree in 1904. Fletcher succeeded Hosea W. Parker as president of the Trustees in 1913.

faculty, to consist of the president, deans, and secretaries of the various Medford divisions of the College to "deal with all matters of a general character not provided for in the faculty of Arts and Sciences." The provision had remained a dead letter; the general faculty had never been convened. The memorialists recommended that this inoperative section be replaced by one authorizing a twelve-member Advisory Council to consist of the president, the deans, and seven members of professorial rank representing the Hill schools and appointed by the president for staggered terms. The Council was to serve as adviser to the president and to the Executive Committee of the Trustees and was to have authority "to initiate and discuss questions of administrative policy and to bring its conclusions" to their attention. The apportionment of funds for the constituent schools and candidates for positions of professorial rank were also to be reviewed by the Council before being acted on by the Trustees. The Trustees remained silent on the faculty proposal for six months. When the faculty inquired as to the fate of their memorial, they were informed that it had been referred to a special Committee on By-Laws. There the matter rested.[26]

The editor of the *Tufts College Graduate* requested that Hamilton furnish him with a statement of the reasons for his resignation so that the alumni could be informed. Hamilton submitted the following letter for publication.

... My action comes as the logical result of mutual loss of confidence between myself and the Trustees. I am not, and have never been, able to approve certain educational and financial policies of the Trustees. I have not believed, and do not now believe, that the management of the college property has been wise; and only a cursory examination of the Treasurer's Report is needed to show that it has not been profitable. Under the organization in use, the President has been for many years practically excluded from this side of college administration.

The Trustees, on the other hand, have felt that the great need of the College was a successful solicitor of funds, and point out the fact that under my administration only $100,000 has been added to the endowments of the College through direct action on my part, though other sums have come in during that period.

[26] A printed draft of proposed changes in the Trustee by-laws was prepared in 1912 but never adopted. The faculty proposal was not included.

A mere statement of these two positions, without argument, shows clearly that my usefulness to the College is at an end, unless conditions in the Board of Trustees would be very materially altered. I therefore retire to make a place for some other man who can establish and maintain those relations of mutual confidence which are essential to that welfare of the College which is dear to us all. Personally I hope to find opportunity to be useful to the College as a loyal Alumnus, though I can no longer serve it to its advantage in an official capacity.[27]

No one event is known to have precipitated his action; it was the climax of an accumulation of differences with the Trustees that had resulted in a virtual breakdown of communication. Put as briefly and as bluntly as possible, President Hamilton's plans for Tufts and his visions of its future were beyond realistic accomplishment, given the resources with which the Trustees had to work. In his second annual report he had expressed the hope that Tufts would aspire to rank third (after Harvard and Yale) among New England colleges. He wanted Tufts to advance much more rapidly on all fronts and chafed when almost every effort he made even to maintain the *status quo* seemed to result in orders to retrench. Even the creation of Jackson College, which he considered the only act of his administration "which could be called expansion," had not worked out before he resigned. As Acting President Hooper summed it up in a special report to the Trustees in the fall of 1912, "theoretically, Jackson is a separate institution, practically segregation is little better than a farce . . . a phantom." Hamilton considered himself an educator, yet his task made him into a money-raiser, for which he was not temperamentally suited. Even his successful efforts to endow the divinity school seemed not, in his estimation, to have been sufficiently appreciated.

Hamilton was a conscientious president who kept in touch with both the College constituency and trends in higher education. Knowing that he had not enjoyed the unanimous support of the alumni when he was elected, he had made a point of soliciting suggestions, criticisms, and advice from graduates. He had told the

[27] In reference to Hamilton's complaint that he had been "practically excluded" from participation in financial decision-making, it might be pointed out that the Trustees in 1916 amended their by-laws to make the president a member *ex officio* of the Finance Committee.

alumni in his Inaugural Address that he could not guarantee results, but he did promise to listen. As both a clergyman and college president he was in constant demand as a speaker at alumni affairs and public occasions. He served as a substitute for Theodore Roosevelt in 1910 as one of the principal speakers at a meeting in New York. It was at Hamilton's suggestion that the first scheduled "get-acquainted" meeting was held, for the Trustees, Overseers, and faculty in 1907. He took a special interest in the welfare of the divinity school, where he taught a one-term course in Administrative Religion.

Far from becoming the third of the "Big Three" among New England colleges, Tufts by 1911 was "doing barely enough to keep in the same class of colleges as Bowdoin, Amherst, Dartmouth, and Williams." Whatever measure of success and reputation Tufts had won had come "by taking the boys of the great middle class and making them efficient and useful members of society. She has had few rich men's sons to educate, and few gilded youths to furbish. Her work has been done with sturdy fellows who sought an education for the economic advantages it would confer and who were willing to work hard and sacrifice much to get it. She has done that work successfully. Her future lies along the same lines." It was useless, said Hamilton, to become involved in "the contest between the culturists and the vocationalists." Much more pressing was how to provide the means that would enable Tufts to fulfill its task in the educational world. It was not, in his view, doing this adequately. He felt that someone else might have better success than he.

The ex-president of Tufts also became an ex-clergyman. After he had served temporarily in the North Cambridge Universalist Church not far from the Tufts campus, Hamilton left the ministry permanently in 1912 and returned to the life of business that had been his first calling. In an interview reported in the *Boston Globe* he announced that "I shall not preach again, as I believe business and the pulpit should be kept entirely separate." He became business manager of a forestry company in Boston and until his death on May 22, 1940, at the age of eighty, he resided in nearby Cambridge. He continued to serve until 1920 on the state Board of Education, of which he had been a member since 1909. For several years he served as National Apprentice Director of the United Typothetae and Franklin Clubs of America and wrote articles on the history of printing. After 1915 he served as secretary of the Grand Lodge of Masons in Massachusetts and let others run the affairs of the College.

§　§　§

For over a year the Trustee committee, headed by Austin B. Fletcher and charged with nominating a new president, made no written report of any kind to the Board, and only an occasional verbal report, although they were hard at work. They remained officially silent for so long that the Boston papers began to become curious and to raise questions. The Executive Committee went on record in July 1914 that the "Trustees should elect a president of the College as soon as possible and that the Committee heretofore appointed for the purpose of nominating a President be notified of this vote." The nominating committee was prepared to report by September. Hermon Carey Bumpus, the unanimous choice of the committee, was in turn unanimously elected president of Tufts and simultaneously elected a Trustee.

The selection of Bumpus had been made only after suggestions had been solicited and received from alumni, faculty, and "friends of the College." Dozens of individuals expressed their views both orally and on paper. Some forty names were submitted and each was investigated.[28] A goodly number of the alumni took the request for suggestions seriously, and page after page of the *Tufts College Graduate* in 1913 was given over to their responses. Very few possibilities were mentioned by name, and most of the correspondents confined their communications to statements about the requisites for the ideal president. Although individual opinions differed widely in particulars, certain refrains seem to have been recurrent: "He should not be a clergyman; he should be a business man. . . . he should be the active business manager of the College. . . . Should he be a clergyman? That should certainly not bar him. . . . Should he be a Universalist? This should not disqualify him. . . . The all-important thing is his intellectual and educational

[28] There is no need to detail all of the candidates considered. They ranged from the most obscure to the most prominent. One person supported by Trustee Fletcher who was offered the presidency was James Hampton Kirkland, second chancellor of Vanderbilt University, who in 1913 "intimated that he might be in a position to consider the presidency of Tufts College at a later date." He was still being considered a possibility in the summer of 1914.

Hermon Carey Bumpus
President, 1914–19

size. . . . He should be a man of recognized executive ability and, in this particular instance, should not be chosen from the ministry. . . . Candidates should be confined neither to the list of our own graduates, nor to any sect nor profession. New blood is sometimes very helpful. . . . He must be a man who does things. . . . the need of the clergy in the collegiate education of youth is no longer apparent. . . . we must have an educator." There were but few who insisted that the new president should be an alumnus, even among the alumni themselves. The consensus was that the best person available should be chosen, regardless of his affiliation.

There is little question that if Acting President Hooper had made himself available he would have received the enthusiastic backing of both colleagues and alumni, but he let it be known "for the sake of the record" through the *Graduate* that he would not be a candidate for permanent appointment. His great love was his teaching and his Electrical Engineering Department. There is no doubt at all that his devoted services to Tufts in a trying interim period were fully appreciated. The Trustees made clear their own indebtedness to him on behalf of the College in frequent expressions both formal and informal. It was "in consideration of eminent qualifications and distinguished service" that the honorary degree of Doctor of Laws was conferred on him in 1915.

The faculty were given an opportunity to express their views on the presidency in a joint meeting with the Trustee nominating committee in March 1913. The faculty member most active in assisting in the selection of a new president was Professor John S. Kingsley, senior member of the Biology Department and at the time dean of the graduate school. In fact, he was apparently the person who initially suggested Bumpus for consideration.[29] Kingsley not only served on the five-man faculty committee "to formulate the qualifications important for the office of President" but conducted an extensive correspondence soliciting estimates of Bumpus several months before the faculty were officially consulted by the Trustees. Kingsley had known Bumpus when the latter was an undergraduate at Brown University and had worked at various marine biological laboratories where Kingsley spent several summers. The Tufts professor was also influential in helping Bumpus work out his plans for graduate work and in securing a position of responsibility for him at the Marine Biological Laboratory at Woods Hole, Massachusetts.

The report of the faculty committee on "prime essentials" for any candidate for the presidency dealt in principles rather than personalities. After referring to the "unusually critical juncture" at which the College had arrived, the report listed (in order, and among others) the following desired qualities: high moral ideals, wide educational experience, "a man of the world," scientific as well as classical training, "the ability to raise money," singleness of purpose, and optimism.[30] A non-Tufts man was to be preferred to an alumnus. Because the College was decidedly undenominational in spirit and student population, it was "far from imperative" that the president should be even a Universalist. The faculty was most

[29] This material has been drawn largely from the correspondence between Kingsley and Fletcher in the Tufts Archives.

[30] The "ability to raise money" was at the top of the list in the original draft of the report. The reference to scientific training was justified by the fact that over three-fourths of the Tufts student body at the time was interested in "the scientific and professional" rather than "the humanistic side."

emphatic that the Trustees realize that it was the teaching force above all who had to live with the president; therefore, his educational and administrative qualifications were fully as important as his assets "as a public man and a man of business."

The request of the faculty that they be allowed to express their opinions on "the several candidates" so that they "shall have had a hand in selecting" was not carried out to the letter, for the field was soon narrowed to two candidates — Bumpus and Chancellor Kirkland of Vanderbilt — and the latter eliminated himself on the ground of unavailability. There is no indication in the faculty or Trustee records that an opportunity was ever formally presented to the faculty to pass on specific candidates. However, it can be presumed that Professor Kingsley kept the faculty informed of the progress of negotiations, for in March 1913 they voted that he "be requested to name the candidate he favors." The faculty concluded their report with the remark that in the difficult work that would lie before him, the new president would "need all the support he can get from every quarter."

Dr. Bumpus, called to the Tufts presidency at the age of fifty-two, was neither a clergyman nor a graduate of Tufts, although he had received an honorary Doctor of Science degree from the institution in 1905. He was not even a Universalist, although he fully subscribed to the tenets of liberal religion. The new president, the ninth generation of French Huguenot ancestors who came to Plymouth, Massachusetts, in 1621 (the family name was originally Bon Passe), was born in Buckfield, Maine, in 1862. He had received a rather miscellaneous primary and secondary education in Boston, where his father was a self-ordained minister and social service worker and had Baptist connections. Bumpus was an alumnus of Brown University and held the first Ph.D. awarded by Clark University. It was through his father's acquaintance with influential Baptists that he selected Brown for his undergraduate education. Trained as a biologist, zoologist, and botanist, he had extensive teaching experience at several institutions between 1886 and 1901. After serving as Assistant Director and then as Director of the Marine Biological Laboratory at Woods Hole, he served for ten years (1902–11) as Director of the American Museum of Natural History. He was called to Tufts after three years as business manager of the University of Wisconsin while holding membership or office in dozens of professional and scholarly organizations. Bumpus was also the author of numerous monographs and articles on biological subjects.[31]

The nominating committee was actually indulging in understatement when they told their fellow Trustees that "the College will be fortunate in securing the services of Doctor Bumpus." Very few individuals connected with the College were probably aware of how difficult it had been to obtain the new president and how overwhelmingly impressive had been the dozens of testimonials received by the Trustees in his behalf from scientists, university presidents, and officers of such organizations as the Carnegie Foundation. President Bumpus had served with distinction at the University of Wisconsin as its first business manager at a most critical period in its history.[32] Letters from members of the Board of Regents to the Tufts Trustees made it most evident that Wisconsin's loss was Tufts' gain. President Charles R. Van Hise of Wisconsin, in outlining the qualifications for the holder of the post of business manager, in effect listed what he considered to be the qualifications of a good president. G. Stanley Hall, prominent psychologist and president of Clark University, in an unsolicited letter to the Tufts Trustees in support of Bumpus, expressed the same view. He wrote that the office of business manager was "an entirely new position, which was really an understudy for the presidency, for which they required a business organizer, who should also be a professor and in touch with everything inside the university." Possibly the most extravagant praise of Bumpus came from E. Benjamin Andrews, ex-presi-

[31] The most complete biography has been written by his son, Hermon Carey Bumpus, Jr. (*Hermon Carey Bumpus, Yankee Naturalist,* Minneapolis: University of Minnesota, 1947). Biographical data and tributes to his numerous services are plentiful. After his death, memorials and resolutions were prepared (among others) by the National Park Service, Brown University, the American Association of Museums (which he was instrumental in founding), and the American Museum of Natural History. An appreciation was prepared by Alice Hall Walter following his death in 1943 and was published by the Audubon Society of Rhode Island, of which Bumpus was the first president (1897–1901) and honorary president (1941–43).

[32] A full treatment is to be found in Merle Curti and Vernon Carstensen, *The University of Wisconsin, A History, 1848–1925* (Madison: University of Wisconsin, 1949), Vol. II, especially Chapters 1 and 5.

dent of Brown University, who informed Professor Kingsley that "there could not be a better man for the head of Tufts for the simple reason that God doesn't produce any better." [33]

In his last annual report to the Trustees in 1914, Hooper was quite frank to express a great feeling of relief in turning the responsibility of his office over to another. The "long period of suspense, uncertainty, and anxiety" appeared to be over. The new president, "admirably fitted by nature and by long and varied training," assumed his official duties on November 16, 1914. It was Bumpus' unfortunate fate to have become among later generations one of Tufts' lesser-known presidents; he deserved far better. He was the victim of circumstances surrounding the First World War. It was due largely to his competency and untiring effort that Tufts College not only survived the critical war years but emerged "with its prestige enhanced and its foundations strengthened." [34]

There were more urgent problems for Tufts in 1914 than war clouds and conflict in Europe. Bumpus was called upon immediately to use the administrative talents and business ability for which he had been selected. The *Boston Transcript* reviewed the situation of the College and put its editorial finger on the key challenge to the new president.

> Tufts in some respects is an overgrown college. From an educational standpoint it is really a university. To the original arts department have been added several professional schools, all of which continue to impose such a severe strain on the institution's treasury that Tufts has on hand a financial problem of no mean proportions. It is not overstating the facts to say that the college at this very minute needs an expansion fund of $1,000,000 and as large a

[33] This letter and others cited here were quoted in the biography written by Bumpus' son. The originals are in the Tufts Archives. Professor Kingsley had followed a rather unorthodox policy. After collecting the letters of recommendation and turning them over to Acting President Hooper so that copies could be made for the Trustees, Kingsley sent them all to Bumpus at the University of Wisconsin. When Trustee Fletcher requested the originals for filing with the College records, Hooper had to retrieve them. Kingsley had apparently become convinced that the prospects for the selection of Bumpus were not hopeful and that Chancellor Kirkland was going to be the choice of the Trustees.

[34] A. D. Mead, "Hermon Carey Bumpus," *Science*, Vol. 99 (January 14, 1944), p. 29.

sum for additional endowment. New buildings are urgently required, faculty salaries must be raised to a decent level, and some
additions to the teaching staff made. To effect all these improvements will undoubtedly be the first task to which the new president
will devote himself. And in this work he will have the undivided
support of all friends of the college. . . . A two years' open search
for a president has at least had the effect of acquainting the world
with the full extent of the financial problem facing the college.

President Bumpus was inaugurated on June 12, 1915, before
more than 2,000 persons. It was an important occasion, highlighted
by guests from over sixty American and European universities and
scholarly and professional groups. Trustee Fletcher took a personal
hand in selecting many of the notables, for "this inauguration will
be the greatest opportunity that the College has ever had or is likely
to have for some time, to properly bring itself before the public."
Among those from outside the College who delivered addresses
were President Abbott Lawrence Lowell of Harvard, Governor
David I. Walsh, President Alexander Meiklejohn of Amherst, and
President G. Stanley Hall of Clark. Samuel Paul Capen, son of the
former president of Tufts, represented both the Alumni Association (of which he was president) and the United States Department
of Education, in which he was serving as Specialist in Higher Education. Dean Painter, representing the medical and dental schools,
expressed gratification that the new president was a biologist, who
would be especially aware of the needs of medical and dental education. He took the opportunity to decry the overemphasis on specialization which seemed to be weakening the case for the general
practitioner and to deplore the lack of preparatory education, particularly in the sciences, of would-be dentists. Professor Fay, representing the Hill faculties as their senior member, pointed to the
precedent-shattering choice of Bumpus. Not only was he the first
layman to be called to the presidency of Tufts; he was the first
president selected because of his educational and administrative
experience. "Our previous presidents had all come to their duties
as amateurs in education. The measure of their success proves that
they did not remain so. But the day of the expert is with us."
Capen's remarks reinforced Professor Fay's comments. "College
education is no longer a parochial affair. It has become a national
enterprise. No college can live to itself alone, shut up within its

own traditions, limited for counsel to the wisdom of its own officers. To do so is to become mired in provincialism."

A new era seemed about to dawn for Tufts. The very theme selected for the symposium which followed the inauguration ceremonies reflected this: "The Obligations of the College to the State." This was no less true of Bumpus' Inaugural Address. Entitled "The Obligation of the Trustees, Faculty, and Alumni to the College," the bold and unmistakable theme was that a college is a public trust. Service "to community and commonwealth" should be Tufts' goal. An educational institution, even one privately endowed, was affected with a public interest. Tufts should be "a college for the people." Bumpus also had a piece of advice for each Trustee: His duty is "not discharged when he merely shows good stewardship so far as handling of funds is concerned." He must recognize a larger responsibility; and the only way to fulfill it was to create and maintain an active partnership with the faculty. Bumpus already sensed in his few months as president that too great a gap existed between the two bodies at Tufts, and called for Trustee initiative to close it.

President Bumpus' first annual report to the Trustees was crisp and businesslike. He had reviewed the establishment for which he had been given immediate responsibility and found it to his liking. Enrollment was going up steadily in most departments, there was "an awakening enthusiasm on the part of both students and faculty," and there had been an encouraging number of gifts. He cited ten "features that have characterized the period under report (January 1915 to January 1916)." The last one he listed must have been the most welcome of all: "We have paid our bills and closed the year without deficit." The president gave proper acknowledgment to the success of Professor Hooper's drive for the $100,000 "Deficit Fund"; he noted that receipts from tuition had increased by $30,000; he reported that the continuing sale of Boulevard land was slowly but steadily reducing the accumulated debt. He might have added that he was responsible for two economies — small in themselves but indicative of his practical approach to problems. He introduced a system of "continual maintenance" and did away with the expensive system of "summer repairs," which had allowed small needs to be postponed until they had frequently grown into large ones. Just prior to his arrival at Tufts the Trustees had become uncomfortably aware that laxness in collecting overdue student charges and loans had cost the College almost $25,000 by 1914. The greatest offenders were students on the Hill. Bumpus immediately investigated and issued instructions for more efficient collection of back bills; $9,000 was received in 1914–15. He inventoried the assets of the institution and found the total endowment (exclusive of educational buildings and grounds) to equal $2,000,000. If academic buildings and eighty acres of Medford campus were added, the total corporate property and investments aggregated $3,202,317. Here was a solid foundation on which a truly outstanding institution could be built.

The new president's penchant for statistical analyses and graphical representation was manifested in his first annual report. Charts were included showing the source and amount of every cent of special solicitation and a tabular view of the geographical distribution of the student body. In his second annual report (1915–16) he bombarded the Trustees with similar materials. He used the five years preceding to compare enrollments, endowments, receipts, and expenditures of several New England colleges with those of Tufts. Even the distribution of students from eastern Massachusetts enrolled in Tufts was shown on an elaborate graph. His conclusions were "that there is a real and a growing demand in this neighborhood for the kind of instruction that Tufts College is giving, that the College is operating efficiently, and that it is worthy of support more nearly commensurate with its usefulness."

Bumpus was particularly interested in strengthening secondary education and in maintaining close ties between the College and the community. He was the moving force behind the organization of the Tufts College Teachers Association, created in 1916 as a means for the many alumni engaged in educational work to meet, to exchange information, and in general "to bring about closer relations between Tufts College and those engaged in the profession of teaching." The Association, still active in the 1960's, continued largely to sustain the goals set for it by President Bumpus.

From all appearances, Tufts College was out of the financial woods by the fall of 1917. The Finance Committee reviewed the situation with satisfaction. They found "economy, large attendance, Prof. Hooper, kind friends, and the Good Lord responsible." The accumulated deficit, which had reached over a quarter of a million dollars in 1912, was reduced by 1917 to less than $100,000. About $700,000 more came in between 1912 and 1917 from bequests and legacies. Perhaps the College could again indulge in the luxury of some long-range planning.

The president of the Trustees made crystal clear to the incoming president his plans and hopes for the College. In June 1915, less than two weeks after the inauguration took place, Fletcher sent Bumpus a long memorandum listing ten ideas that he expected to become "accomplished facts as soon as possible." Some, dealing with fund-raising, revision of the Trustee by-laws, and plans for future buildings and campus development, were of basic importance and needed serious consideration. One of Fletcher's proposals on which Bumpus remained silent illustrated the categorical attitude of the president of the Trustees that frequently brought him into disagreement with some of his colleagues on the Board as well as with officers on the Hill. "I wish to see a statement in our catalogue that the College will not receive any young man who uses spirituous liquors in any form or uses tobacco and that their use will not be permitted at the College or elsewhere by any young man who is a student at the College. This necessarily means that the professors should also desist from its use." However, the long-range planning for the College, including the future use of tobacco on the campus, had to be shelved when the First World War intruded. By 1918 the College had taken on the appearance of a military post and had to face problems it had never encountered before.

The first official act of the College recognizing the possibility that the United States might become involved in the war in Europe had occurred in May 1916 when over 1,000 students, faculty, and alumni had participated in a monster Preparedness Parade in downtown Boston. Early in 1917 the faculty created a special Committee on Preparedness; its first act was to take a census of the student body to see what special qualifications might be available for national service. Almost a month before President Woodrow Wilson delivered his war message to Congress, the Tufts faculty had voted unanimously to allow up to three term hours of credit for satisfactory completion of a military training course having one lecture, two hours of recitation, and five hours of drill a week.[35]

[35] Major James C. D. Clark was appointed Instructor in Military Tactics at $25 per week to provide a ten-week course.

On the very day that Wilson delivered his fateful message, the faculty on the Hill voted to recommend to the Trustees that seniors in good standing called into service were to be given their appropriate degree at the June Commencement. Full credit would be given for the half-year if undergraduates were called into service. With commendable foresight the faculty also provided that for students returning to the College after the war, arrangements would be made "as though no interruption had taken place and that the advanced subjects will be adjusted to meet these conditions." Tufts joined other Massachusetts colleges in liberalizing the entrance requirements for students whose secondary school preparation had been interrupted for military or agricultural service, and War Certificates were awarded, starting in 1918, to seniors who had accepted a "Call to the Colors." The faculty, looking to the immediate emergency, then created a Committee on National Service to arrange for cooperation with the national and state governments. They also voted to petition both the President of the United States and Congress to prohibit "the manufacture and sale of all intoxicating liquors during the period of the war, as a logical and necessary conservation measure." Trustee Fletcher's hopes that alcoholic beverages would disappear seemed to have received official support.

The summer of 1918 was an exceptionally busy one for the College. The institution went on an around-the-clock schedule, offering special "War Emergency Courses" for civilians in chemistry, industrial electricity, and civil engineering.[36] Probably no one in the Tufts community lived a more hectic civilian life that summer than President Bumpus. On the importuning of officials in Washington, he became chief of the Organization Branch, Methods Control Division, of the Quartermaster Corps. In his work with the transportation division in particular he showed his unusual administrative abilities. He had already helped to organize and develop the War Department Committee on Education and Special Training, and as an ardent supporter of the Allied cause decided

---

[36] The faculty received extra compensation for their services. A special summer school was continued in 1919 in which mathematics, chemistry, and engineering courses were offered. The stipend for faculty of professorial rank was $200 for one six-week course and a maximum total compensation of $300 for more than one course.

that if he could "be of greater service by leaving the College and going to Washington to undertake a piece of constructive work, I propose to go." He found his duties at Tufts "very confining" and earnestly wanted to be of greater service to the war effort than he thought his tasks at the College provided.[37] Keeping in touch with Tufts affairs and maintaining an office in the nation's capital simultaneously was a demanding assignment. As he wrote a friend at the Museum of Natural History, he was "spreading [his] time rather thin at Tufts and thick at Washington." When he returned to Tufts in the fall of 1918, he was called upon time after time to speak in the Greater Boston area on subjects "pertaining to our War situation," and he complied whenever time and energy permitted. Among his most widely reprinted speeches was "The Demand of the Government for Efficient Men."

When autumn came, there were already on the Hill, or in the planning stage, an Army Collegiate Section of 500 men, an Army Vocational Section of 230 men, a Naval Section of 100 men, and at the Boston branch of the College a War Training Section of 900 men, all under the command of a major and eleven lieutenants. The first actually to arrive on the Hill (May 1918) was a contingent of 100 men to receive special training as carpenters, machinists, and automotive maintenance men. This group, one of many assigned to numerous colleges across the country, was under the Army Vocational Section and was known as the Tufts Training Detachment. The group was allotted to Tufts in response to a request of the Committee on Education and Special Training which President Bumpus had helped to organize and one of whose members was Samuel P. Capen, of the Class of 1898. The trainees were to remain at the College for sixty days and to receive military as well as technical instruction.[38] A second group (150 men) arrived in mid-June, and the campus hummed with activity.

In the meantime, a new project was undertaken by the federal government which involved Tufts directly, although briefly. A Re-

[37] "Memorandum to Thorkelson and Steeb," June 29, 1918, Tufts Archives. Halsten J. Thorkelson was Bumpus' successor as business manager at the University of Wisconsin; C. E. Steeb, a close friend, was at Ohio State University.

[38] It was this group that built an extension to the Howe Memorial Laboratory (the Power House) and constructed a separate building used for automotive training.

serve Officers Training Corps (ROTC) had been established under the authority of the National Defense Act of 1916. By mid-1917 it was operating at thirty-seven colleges (mostly land-grant) and nine military and other schools. The Tufts faculty recommended in June that President Bumpus and the Trustees "consider the advisability of establishing a Reserve Officers Training Corps at Tufts College." Instead, the College received units of the Student Army Training Corps (SATC), which was organized in the late summer of 1918 to take the place temporarily of the ROTC. The purpose of the SATC was to train enlisted men for special military assignments. After a twelve-weeks' term, men from each unit were to be sent to officers' training camps, non-commissioned officers' schools, or cantonments, or were assigned to assist in instructing others at SATC units.

When word was received that the War Department was organizing units of the SATC at selected colleges, Tufts immediately applied for a unit. By October the Hill was covered with marching men in military uniforms and draftees in fatigue clothing being trained under the Army Vocational program. West Hall, ordinarily housing about sixty-five men, became a bustling barracks for 320. Curtis Hall was remodeled as a mess hall in which 750 men could be served at one time. Jumbo, the College mascot, was boarded up in one corner of Barnum Museum, and his first-floor quarters became a post exchange. Part of the upper floor of the building became the distributing center for Quartermaster supplies. Goddard Gymnasium became a YMCA furnishing entertainment and social amenities for the 238 students in the SATC. Part of Eaton Library was set aside as barracks, and a reading and writing room was provided in it for the use of military personnel. The facilities of the Crane School were used by the SATC while theological classes met at Dean McCollester's residence.[39] The housing and feeding of pre-medical, medical, and dental students in the War Training Program in downtown Boston were made possible by the lease and conversion of Mechanics Hall, which provided facilities for 900 men. Captain Milton S. Bowman, who had been assigned to the Tufts Training Detachment in May 1918, was promoted to the rank of major and was placed in charge of the whole military operation at Tufts. Dean Anthony of the engineering

[39] He was reimbursed $150 by the Trustees for this service.

*The first military unit trained at Tufts during the First World War
leaving the Hill for service overseas*

school directed War Training Courses on the Hill, and Dean Wren
of the school of liberal arts directed the equivalent for the departments in Boston.

The war crept into every nook and cranny of the Tufts campus. Soon after the United States entered the conflict, the College
organized a course of weekly lectures required of all students. Academic credit could be earned if students presented within a week a
written synopsis of each lecture and showed "some acquaintance
with the subject and its literature." There were talks on such subjects as food conservation, the League to Enforce Peace, and relief
work in Belgium and Poland. A special secretarial course was introduced for Jackson students, who could also receive college
credit for Red Cross-sponsored courses in nursing and first aid.
Many a Tufts student and faculty member shivered through the
winter months as fuel conservation was rigidly enforced, and many
a waistline was presumably trimmed by those who followed Herbert Hoover's "Gospel of the Clean Plate." Many students paid
their College charges with United States Government bonds purchased by their patriotic parents.

Scarcely had the College made the abrupt transition from an
academic institution to a quasi-military establishment in six weeks

*This service flag, made by Jackson students, was hung
in Goddard Chapel during the First World War*

than it had to change gears again. The SATC began training in
mid-October, after the opening of the College had been delayed by
an influenza epidemic. The armistice was signed less than a month
later. The immediate post-armistice status of the SATC unit gave
as much trouble as any single activity. No one seemed to know from
day to day (either in Washington or at Tufts) when the program
would be liquidated, except that the financial obligations to the
College would eventually be met by the government. There was a
"strong probability" in November 1918 that students enrolled in
the SATC program would "be given the privilege of returning to
civil life if they so elect." This seemed to Treasurer Mason to
make Tufts' difficulties in formulating any plans all the greater, for
he assumed that most of the men released from the SATC would
"simply go" and would not transfer to other courses in the College.
On November 27, orders were received to demobilize the SATC
as soon as possible. The College had the opportunity in the winter
of 1918 to consider the establishment of an ROTC unit following
the disbanding of the SATC but the Executive Committee
"deemed it not advisable."[40] In December, demobilization had

[40] The ROTC did appear on the Tufts campus, but not until the period
of the Second World War.

484

been completed and the College found itself in the unenviable position of trying to resume a peacetime stance almost literally overnight. Somehow, in little more than two weeks, it managed to reconvert itself into an academic institution in time to open for the second semester in January 1919. The Trustees and administrative officers must have aged visibly as they lived through the weeks of uncertainty as to the very future of the College.

The disarrangements resulting from a nation at war and from demobilization, reconversion, and a general return to the *status quo ante bellum* after November 11, 1918, had innumerable repercussions on the campus, some involving serious financial problems. The fraternities, whose houses had been closed or taken over by the College and who wanted a home on the campus again, had to renegotiate their property arrangements.[41] The student body, although it did not disintegrate, did shrink noticeably in the fall of 1918, and with it went precious revenue. Faculty by the dozens (especially the medical and dental school staffs) became involved in military obligations and were given leaves of absence without pay; at the same time the question arose of how to occupy the remaining faculty. The expenses involved in adapting the buildings on the campus to military use were complicated by the fact that the cash balance in the College coffers toward the end of 1918 was "almost zero," according to a report of Arthur E. Mason, the harried treasurer. Government compensation to the College ($1.6481 per day for each SATC student on the Hill and $1.5555 for those quartered in Boston) came in long after services had been rendered. Treasurer Mason, in September 1918, predicted that the College would have to have a loan of nearly $200,000 to meet its immediate obligations; he had already been forced to borrow $25,000 to meet current expenses. The most crucial period in the wartime history of the College came when the demobilization of the SATC was ordered and before any estimate could be made of how many students would register after the military contingents withdrew.

The enrollment in midyear of 1918–19, when the College sud-

[41] Typical were the problems faced by Zeta Psi when the Trustees at first decided in the fall of 1918 to terminate the fraternity occupancy of the house located at the corner of Professors Row and Packard Avenue, but later changed their minds. The Delta Tau Delta house had been taken over by the SATC as an infirmary, and the Delta Upsilon house had served as a Jackson dormitory.

denly returned to peacetime status, exceeded all expectations. Jackson College, whose enrollment had increased during the war, set a new record with 174 enrolled, and created an acute housing problem which was alleviated by converting the president's house into a dormitory.[42] The most astounding statistics were for the school of liberal arts and for the engineering school. There were 521 students in all in the two schools by January 1919, including approximately fifty who had already returned from military service to resume their interrupted studies. Over 900 students registered in the pre-medical, medical, and dental schools. The author of a feature article in the *Tufts College Graduate* gave the lion's share of the credit for the prosperous condition of the institution to President Bumpus. He cited enrollment and financial figures to support his enthusiastic statement that the president had "made good," and said that if it had not been for his leadership and executive ability, the College might have foundered. Bumpus had apparently set it on the road to new heights and had fully vindicated his promise to make Tufts of maximum service "to the community and mankind."

Over 1,000 Tufts men served in the armed forces during the First World War. Twenty-one lost their lives in the nation's service, of whom fifteen were commissioned officers. Many received citations for bravery, including the Distinguished Service Cross.[43] If the members of the SATC who received their training at Tufts are counted, the total manpower contributions of the College were most impressive. Over two-thirds of the regular Tufts students, faculty, and alumni, ranging from the Class of 1878 through the Class of 1921, served in the Army; there were over 200 in the Navy; and a few served in the Marines. More than half the Tufts

[42] The home built by Capen in 1876 had been occupied by Presidents Hamilton and Bumpus until the latter's departure in 1919. Capen House was still a Jackson dormitory in the 1960's. Paige Hall and Curtis Hall were proposed in 1919 as girls' dormitories but were not so used at the time because the Trustees thought it "highly inadvisable on account of the relation of the buildings to that part of the campus occupied by the men's dormitories." No such doubts assailed the officers of the College in later years, for Paige Hall was used as a Jackson dormitory in 1926–27, the first half of 1927–28, and again between 1946–47 and 1953–54.

[43] One was Professor Houston, of the Class of 1914, who served for many years on the Tufts faculty.

men who served in some capacity were from the medical and dental schools. In addition to those in the regular armed forces, over 100 individuals were in various branches of auxiliary services such as the American Ambulance Field Service, the Red Cross, and the YMCA.

Several arrangements growing out of the war continued into peacetime. The YMCA remained on the Hill for another year, financed by a joint appropriation from the College and from the funds of the Crane School. David Cheney, the general secretary of the YMCA at the College, became Tufts' first Director of Publicity in 1920. The dental school provided instruction in dental mechanics to disabled veterans by arrangement with the Federal Board for Vocational Education.

§   §   §

The annual meeting of the Trustees had taken place as scheduled on October 8, 1918. After a sizable amount of routine business had been transacted, President Bumpus threw consternation into the ranks by submitting his resignation in a prepared statement.[44]

> The needs of any large educational institution are manifold. During the four years of my service with you I have endeavored to meet certain of these needs — always conscious, however, that there were many things which were left undone. It seems to me that a fair appraisal of Tufts College at the present time would show that there is now need for some one to take a directing hand who has qualifications different from those which I possess. Under these circumstances and after giving the matter careful consideration I am asking you to provide for my successor at some time no later than a year hence.

After the initial shock had worn off, a three-man committee was appointed, including Austin Fletcher, the president of the Trustees, "to consider the letter of resignation."

Bumpus' announcement came at a rather gloomy time in 1918. The campus had reached its maximum point as a military establishment, and officers of the College were beginning to be concerned about what its fate would be when the war was over. On the

[44] There was a certain irony in the fact that the president's salary was increased substantially at the same meeting.

home front, Tufts had lost, less than six months apart, two of its best-known and best-loved faculty members on the Hill. At the same meeting that the committee appointed to consider Bumpus' resignation reported that it was "with deep regret that the College is called upon to again fill a vacancy in the office of President," memorials were presented in memory of Charles H. Leonard, Dean Emeritus of Crane Theological School, and William L. Hooper, the man who had served so selflessly as acting president between 1912 and 1914. Notice was received during the same period of the death of Albert Crane, chief benefactor of the theological school. In accepting Bumpus' resignation, the Trustees recognized the services he had rendered the College at a most difficult time and expressed appreciation for his willingness to continue in office for as much as a year. Trustees Fletcher, Darling, McClench, and Mason were immediately appointed to recommend a successor. However, at the same meeting it was voted to enlarge the committee to include three other representatives of the Tufts community. For the first time in the history of the College, the alumni, the Faculty of Arts and Sciences, and the faculties of the medical and dental schools had an official place on a combined committee to nominate a president of Tufts.

Expressions of dismay and regret, intermixed with notes of appreciation for Bumpus' services to Tufts, began to pour in almost from the day that the news of his resignation was made public. An alumnus who was serving as an assistant surgeon in the Navy voiced the sentiments of dozens of alumni when he wrote "to personally express my regret at your going, my appreciation of the fact that you ever came, my thanks for your personal interest in the medical school, and my pride in the fact that I was graduated from the medical school during your term of office as president." Arthur B. Coolidge, lawyer, state senator, and member of the Class of 1903, acknowledged the "very unwelcome news" and expressed the view that "all of us who have watched the progress of the College during your administration have admired your handling of its educational and financial affairs."

As soon as the Faculty of Arts and Sciences were officially informed of Bumpus' action, two special faculty meetings were called at which resolutions were adopted expressing the sense of loss of his "leadership and inspiration." They paid tribute to his "untiring activity," his "courtesy and consideration," and particularly his harmonious relations with the faculty. The resolutions were reciprocated by an equally cordial acknowledgment by the outgoing president, who made a point of the fact that he had been "as much invited by the Faculty to become the President of Tufts as I was appointed by the Board."

The alumni were equally appreciative of Dr. Bumpus' efforts on behalf of the College during four years of "public storm, stress, and confusion." A testimonial dinner was given in January 1919 by the Tufts Club of Boston, the very first meeting of which he had attended in 1915. More than 250 alumni were present for the occasion, which was climaxed by the presentation of a series of resolutions, a gold watch, and a telephone message of good will from alumni in Chicago.

The one sour note injected into the Bumpus resignation came after it had taken place and originated with Austin B. Fletcher. His extensive correspondence with President Bumpus indicated that their relationship during the first three years, at least, had been reasonably cordial, but as the war progressed and as Tufts became more and more deeply enmeshed in governmental affairs, Fletcher became increasingly restive and dissatisfied. When the resignation was offered, Fletcher accused Bumpus of deserting the College when it needed his services most. Actually, Fletcher apparently had some reservations about the president from the beginning of Bumpus' administration. Bumpus was an "outsider" who could never really be completely attuned to Tufts' traditions and spirit.[45] Fletcher was also disturbed because he thought Bumpus had personally plunged too deeply into the war effort at the expense of College interests. When Bumpus assumed his duties in the Quartermaster Corps in the summer of 1918, Fletcher warned him that he was taking on too much, that he would find the labor involved "excessive and the methods of living exhausting." When Bumpus returned to the campus that September, Fletcher acknowledged the fact by informing the president that "it is the desire of every one to be thoroughly patriotic, but at the same time we must look

[45] The "community of interest" among the Trustees previously referred to was still noticeable in 1918. Of the twenty-eight members then on the Board, sixteen were not only alumni but divided equally in their fraternity affiliations between Zeta Psi and Theta Delta Chi. Fletcher was a member of Zeta Psi.

out for the College. I do not want to find that we are in a position where the Government has made use of us to the extent of crippling our regular work and then abandoning us."

During Bumpus' tenure, Fletcher kept an eye on as many of the details of administration as he could. He complained when the wrong class was attached to his name in the Register of Alumni and Officers published in 1917 and remarked that "it is claimed by some that this same slip-shod attention runs through the whole institution." Bumpus countered with the observation that "the per student cost of operating the college is only a fraction of that of other institutions in our neighborhood," and that in spite of inadequate administrative funds, "there is good work being done by Tufts sufficient in amount to warrant the commendation rather than the criticism of those who are acquainted with the difficulties under which we are operating." Bumpus' independence of spirit was also illustrated by his reply to Fletcher when the latter heard in 1917 that a chapter of the American Association of University Professors was about to be established on the Tufts' campus. Fletcher had no use for "such labor unions" and hoped it would not infiltrate the Tufts faculty. Bumpus replied that any effort that would result in protecting the rights of the academic profession and raising the professional stature of teaching was good, and that he might consider joining the organization himself.

Existence for President Bumpus and other officers of the College had been complicated during the war by the presence of an articulate pacifist in the person of Professor Clarence R. Skinner, holder at the time of the chair of Applied Christianity in the Crane Theological School. President Bumpus was constantly concerned also about "the element of pacifism and socialism" which he was sure was growing among students in 1918. They were solicited for funds to defend Scott Nearing, nationally known for his agitation against the military draft and under indictment in 1918 for violation of the Espionage Act. Professor Skinner was one of the subscribers. In the summer of 1918, when it had become apparent that both Bumpus and the College were becoming deeply committed to the war effort, Dean McCollester, who staunchly supported Skinner but was more tactful and diplomatic in expressing his views, requested the Trustees to "consider some plan by which Crane Theological School of Tufts College may become a separate institution in its management and operation." He had come to the conclusion that the aims and spirit of the College, with its technical and vocational leanings and the "emphasis laid upon material values," were no longer compatible with the goals of the theological school. The Trustees were so involved in what they considered more pressing matters that they took no action on McCollester's request until he reminded them six months later. A Trustee committee was appointed in December 1918 to confer with a special committee of Crane alumni and consider "future plans for the School." Several of the Crane faculty became convinced that Bumpus had "a destroying influence" on the theological school and that his resignation gave "new hopes" for it. This information, growing out of clashes between Bumpus and Dean McCollester, was relayed directly to Fletcher and may have had a part in the growing negative attitude that Fletcher developed toward the president.

There is no conclusive evidence in the records that Fletcher's criticism of his conduct of College affairs was the deciding factor in Bumpus' resignation, although he was sufficiently upset by a sharp letter from Fletcher, after he had announced his decision to resign, to consult with Trustee William McClench. McClench expressed sorrow that "any unpleasantness" had arisen between the two but felt sure that Fletcher had "no intention" of injuring Bumpus in any way in any statements he made concerning the reasons for Bumpus' resignation. Bumpus had, in his opinion, carried the College safely through the war and longed to return to his scientific pursuits.[46] After a brief interval spent mostly in Duxbury, Massachusetts, he returned to the field of natural history to which he had devoted so much of his life. He took a leading part in organizing the educational program of the National Parks Service and created the system of over 200 "trailside museums" which dot the United States today and are familiar to thousands of touring Americans. After serving as chairman of the National Parks Ad-

[46] This explanation was reiterated in several letters written to acquaintances and associates in 1918 and early in 1919. It is also supported by Dr. Bumpus, Jr., in his biography of his father. One gets the impression that the Tufts presidency was considered by Bumpus himself to have been only an interlude in a distinguished scientific career; it becomes a matter of perspective.

visory Board for many years and living to see his dream of "teaching Americans to know their heritage" come to pass, he retired at the age of seventy-eight, full of years and honors. In May 1943, just a few weeks before his death, he resigned as Senior Fellow of Brown University, on whose board he had served for almost forty years. That institution departed sufficiently from precedent to elect him the first Fellow Emeritus. As the American Association of Museums summed it up, Bumpus "lived the good life, and the world is lastingly better for his having lived."[47]

William W. Spaulding, who served as a Tufts Trustee from 1889 to 1929, noted in 1919 that "up to the time of President Bumpus, the institution had been distinctly under the Universalist auspices and I have always regretted the apparent necessity of selecting a president from the *outside field.*" Those who felt as Spaulding did could have had no grounds for complaint about the next president of Tufts College. John Albert Cousens was not only a leading Universalist layman but an alumnus of the Class of 1898 whose devotion to the College was difficult to surpass. He took office as acting president on September 1, 1919, and on June 5, 1920, became the head of his Alma Mater without benefit of a formal inauguration. He was to serve in the presidency until death ended his career seventeen years later.

[47] Quoted in Bumpus, *op. cit.,* p. 131.

13. "A New Era Dawning . . ."

THE UNIVERSALIST GENERAL CONVENTION met in Baltimore in October 1919. Tufts alumni who were present gathered informally to discuss the desirability of closer ties between the denomination and the College. The upshot of their conversations was a request to the Trustees that in the deliberations preceding the choice of a permanent president to replace Bumpus they "try to find a man who knows the history and traditions of Tufts, preferably an alumnus who is proud of the former and will cherish the latter, who is a strong Universalist and who will endeavor to keep the College and the denomination side by side." John Albert Cousens was just such a man, and his service as acting president in the busy months bridging 1919 and 1920 soon convinced the Trustees that they need look no farther for a head of the institution.[1] Austin Fletcher was strongly opposed to the choice at first, arguing that Cousens was not sufficiently well known in the educational field, but even he became reconciled after he had seen Cousens in operation for a few months. This does not mean that no other candidates were considered. The qualifications of several men were reviewed, and one person actually approached was Payson Smith, state Commissioner of Education.[2] He declined to be considered, on the ground that he had been in office only three years and felt responsible for carrying through several programs that he had initiated.

Cousens seemed in every respect to be admirably suited for the presidency. He had been born in Brookline, Massachusetts,

[1] It was Trustees Harold E. Sweet and Guy Winslow who had suggested Cousens.

[2] Smith had attended Tufts as a member of the Class of 1897 but did not graduate; he received an honorary M.A. from Tufts in 1903 and served as a Trustee from 1922 until his resignation in 1943.

John Albert Cousens
Acting President, 1919–20; President, 1920–37

and had received his college education at Tufts. After a period of indecision characteristic of many a freshman, he had selected English as his major and then had switched to chemistry when he decided to train for a medical career. He had entered with the Class of 1898 but his father died during his senior year and he had had to withdraw from school in order to enter business. He received his A.B. *extra ordinem* in 1903. The John E. Cousens Coal Company, which had been operated by his father, prospered under the son's direction. After it was merged with the Metropolitan Coal Company he became vice-president of the larger concern. His interest and competency in business, banking, and finance were reflected in his selection as vice-president and chairman of the Investment Committee of the Brookline Savings Bank, whose board he later headed until his death. He was also a director of the Brookline Trust Company and organized the Brookline Board of Trade, of which he was the first president.

494

Always an active alumnus, he was president of the permanent alumni organization of the Class of 1898. It was through his initiative that the 1898 Scholarship had been established, the first such effort made by an alumni class. The Class of 1898 also had the enviable distinction of having produced five graduates who became Trustees. As president of the class with which he had not been able to graduate, Cousens commemorated its tenth anniversary in 1908 by presenting the large bell hung in the tower of Goddard Chapel.[3] He was the leading spirit in raising a fund from his class on its twentieth anniversary to renovate Dean Hall. He was elected a Trustee in 1911 and served at various times on the Finance Committee, the Executive Committee, and the Board of Visitors to the medical school. Whether he needed it or not, he was given a good glimpse into collegiate financial affairs when he served on the committee to handle the intricate problems of "salvage, changes, reconstruction, restorations and in settling with the Government" after the liquidation of the Student Army Training Corps.

Those associated with the College who might have had qualms because Bumpus had not been a Universalist by formal church membership had their minds set at rest by the religious affiliation of his successor. Cousens was a staunch member of the denomination that had founded the College. The Board of Trustees had long since lost most of the clerical tinge it had once had, but when vacancies occurred on the Board in 1922, Cousens not only wanted a Universalist as one of the replacements but would have welcomed a Universalist clergyman. The Board received a judge instead.[4] However, President Cousens had his way when Rev. Vincent Tomlinson, a graduate of the divinity school in 1884, became the only clergyman on the Board in 1923; he served until his death in 1938. Rev. Mr. Tomlinson was joined on the Board in 1928 by Dr. Louis C. Cornish, president of the American Unitarian Association. When Cornish was elected, Cousens called attention to the financial contributions of "certain important Unitarians" to the funds

---

[3] This was supplemented in 1926 by a chime of ten bells given by Trustee Eugene B. Bowen of the Class of 1876. Ten years later Bowen expressed the wish to have a clock placed in the chapel tower but the Executive Committee considered such an installation "undesirable."

[4] The judge was W. W. McClench, who had already served two five-year terms as an alumni Trustee.

used for improvements in Miner and Paige Halls.[5] In 1923 the Executive Committee recognized the historic ties that still bound the College, however loosely, to the Universalist denomination by establishing tuition scholarships for students from the three leading Universalist preparatory schools: three for Dean Academy and one each for Westbrook Seminary and Goddard Seminary.

The Trustees and the College constituency in general were spared the long period of search, indecision, and debate that had preceded the election of Hamilton and, to a lesser degree, of Bumpus. The faculty had taken seriously their invitation to participate in the selection of a candidate and had elected Professor Fay to serve as their representative on the nominating committee. A faculty resolution was also prepared in the winter of 1918 expressing their views as to the qualifications of whoever was to succeed Bumpus, but it was never acted on or sent to the Trustees. The proposal was made that, because it seemed "improbable that all the qualities hitherto sought in a Head of the College should be found in one man," the Trustees should consider dividing the duties of the office. A business manager could be appointed, to operate through the treasurer's office and be responsible to the president. The professional schools in Boston could be administered by a chancellor, likewise responsible to the president, while the latter could concentrate his efforts on the Hill schools.

The vast majority of officers and alumni seemed immediately to react to Cousens' election as did Samuel P. Capen, a classmate and in 1919 director of the American Council on Education. "I believe that the man, the time and the job have come together now. What Tufts needed above everything else was genuine and enthusiastic leadership." They were not disappointed. In fact, the Trustees were so pleased with Cousens' administration of the College that they doubled his salary after he had been in office little more than five years.

[5] When President Hamilton resigned in 1912, the practice of opening Trustee meetings with a prayer was abandoned. In spite of the fact that there were clergymen on the Board after that date, the custom was never resumed and Trustee Fletcher was still lamenting the fact in 1922. It was Cousens who finally abandoned the first part of the traditional salutation, "The Honorable and Reverend, the Trustees of Tufts College," in 1932, when his annual reports had become so bulky that they were duplicated and distributed to the Trustees rather than being read at the annual meeting.

The new president kept an eagle eye on every detail of the administration of the College from enrollment and endowment to the contents of broom closets. He gave advice to the treasurer on how to keep his accounts. He personally reviewed every requisition for materials and supplies, however small. He went on the road time after time to stir up and maintain alumni interest and contributed a communication of some sort to almost every issue of both the alumni magazine and the undergraduate weekly newspaper. He felt so strongly the need of close relationship between the alumni and the Trustees that at one time he proposed that the president of the Alumni Association be made a member of the Board of Trustees *ex officio*. He tracked down every lead that might result in funds for the College. He had an opinion on everything concerning the institution, although he always welcomed suggestions and ideas from every source. In his loquacious (and often repetitious) annual reports to the Trustees he reminded them unfailingly of projects that needed attention. It is doubtful if any collegiate administrative body was ever kept better informed than the Tufts Trustees or that there was a more tireless college president than John Albert Cousens.[6] Cousens was always sensitive to the financial needs of students and had all cases involving suspension of the rules for payment of student charges transferred from the bursar to his own office. Many an undergraduate received private assistance in the form of a small loan from the president's capacious pocket. John Holmes, "poet laureate" of Tufts until his death in 1962, was among those who received indispensable aid and encouragement from the president. Cousens cherished "the tradition that Tufts College offers exceptional opportunities for poor boys and girls."

As to the size of the Hill divisions of the College, he wanted them kept relatively small. In his annual report for 1920 he suggested an optimum enrollment of 200 for Jackson and a total of

[6]In 1923 Cousens reinstituted the practice that had been abandoned in 1917 of including reports of the deans of the Associated Schools in his annual report to the Trustees. Until 1927, when the complete reports became too complicated and covered too many subjects to allow it, Cousens read the entire report to the patient Trustees. After 1927 he contented himself with reading only "certain selected paragraphs" from reports that were by then totaling over fifty typed pages. They were to become even longer.

800 men in the schools of liberal arts and engineering.[7] Five years later he still considered 1,000 the desirable maximum on the Medford campus. The Trustees in 1925 set the limits of under-graduate enrollment at 900.[8] "Under no circumstances" did he want to see the proportion of young women increased. He changed his mind on this from time to time. In 1923-24, when Jackson en-rollment had increased from 213 and corresponding male Hill enrollment was 675, he told the Trustees that he would "not be disturbed if the number of girls in Jackson increases to 250."

The immediate effects of the Trustee decision to limit enroll-ment were not very noticeable, for the registration in most divi-sions of the College had not yet quite reached the ceilings set. In 1927–28 the policy was directly operative only in the school of liberal arts and the medical school. In the long run, the policy of limiting numbers and announcing that fact publicly tended to bring earlier applications and some improvement in academic quality. The time had not yet been reached, in the 1920's and 1930's, when multiple applications (and multiple acceptances) by prospective students created a serious problem for those responsi-ble for admissions, although even as early as 1928–29 the ratio of students applying to those admitted in the school of liberal arts had risen to five-to-one.[9] The tendency for large numbers of stu-dents from relatively few schools to apply led Cousens to make a plea to the alumni to encourage promising students in their com-munities to apply to Tufts.[10]

[7] The actual Hill enrollment in 1920–21 was: liberal arts, engineering, and Crane, 686; Jackson, 173. Whenever he mentioned possible limitations on enrollment (which was frequently), he was referring to the undergraduate schools. Neither Crane nor the graduate school had sufficient students during his administration to justify any curbing of their size.

[8] It was distributed as follows: liberal arts, 350; Jackson, 250; engineering, 300. Enrollment in only the engineering school was then below the figure set.

[9] Typical was the case in 1929–30 when, out of 108 applicants considered "fully qualified" from three Boston high schools (English High School, Boston Latin School, and Dorchester High School), only 19 could be granted ad-mission.

[10] One result was the establishment in 1920, under the supervision of the Alumni Association, of up to fifteen tuition scholarships for students in as many secondary schools. The recipients were to be nominated by local alumni groups.

498

The effects of the Great Depression of the 1930's on enrollment were not nearly as great as some had feared. The full quota of students was registered in almost every undergraduate division of the College in the early and middle thirties.[11] Sustained enrollment was made possible in part by overdrawing the student scholarship and loan accounts. The most noticeable trend was the higher proportion of students who lived at home rather than on the Hill. While this meant some loss of revenue, it made possible the presence of students who might otherwise have been financially unable to attend at all. In order to encourage qualified students to enter the College, seven regional prize scholarships were established by the Trustees in 1933 at the suggestion of President Cousens. This action meant a modification of the traditional policy of the College not to offer financial assistance to any freshman until his second semester. The scholarships, covering tuition for the entire college course, were designed "to attract students of high grade, thus raising the level of the student body."[12] Six additional competitive scholarships, covering tuition, were created by the Trustees in 1935 and were known as "New England Scholarships." They supplanted the so-called Regional Scholarships after 1936–37.

Tufts and its students shared in the benefits provided in the 1930's under federal emergency relief legislation, and specifically through the National Youth Administration. Under the program, 12 per cent of the total enrollment of each undergraduate and professional school were entitled to assistance, with individual sti-

[11] In 1933–34, which was in many ways the lowest point in the trough of the depression years, the entering classes on the Hill were the largest in the history of the College. There were 199 first-year students in the school of liberal arts, 99 in Jackson, and 102 in the engineering school; there was a decline (less than ten) over the preceding year in the engineering school only.

[12] To encourage a wider geographical distribution than had traditionally prevailed, seven eligible students were to be selected annually, on a four-year rotation, from one of four districts in New England, Canada, and the Middle Atlantic states: Massachusetts and Pennsylvania; Maine, New Hampshire, New Brunswick, and Nova Scotia; Vermont and New York; and Connecticut, Rhode Island, and New Jersey. Scholarships were to be awarded the first year (1933–34) to students from Massachusetts and Pennsylvania. Applicants were limited to those in the upper half of their class in secondary school. Winners were selected after candidates had taken a three-hour examination in English, mathematics, and history, and after interview.

pends of $15 a month.[13] The quota of federal funds for Tufts students exceeded $20,000 in 1934–35, although the work which was required had to be supervised by College personnel and a considerable amount of material for some of the projects had to be furnished at the College's expense. In 1935–36 there were over 200 students receiving assistance, and the payroll amounted to well over $3,000 a month for that academic year. The wages, small though they might have been, often meant for the students the difference between continuing in college or dropping out, and Tufts was able to start or complete numerous projects ranging from inventorying library materials to constructing stage scenery and tennis courts. President Cousens was able to report officially that the program worked satisfactorily in all respects, although he had to struggle at times to keep students equitably distributed among divisions of the College competing for their services.

The Trustees made a further upward adjustment of enrollment in 1937, when the undergraduate maxima were established at 600 for the school of liberal arts, 350 for the engineering school, and 300 for Jackson College. It was a source of great satisfaction to the officers of the College to be required to limit enrollment. This not only signified a growing appeal and reputation for the institution but also gave it an opportunity to be increasingly selective. During his administration President Cousens sent many a member of the faculty on the road to explain "The Values of Education" to secondary school students. He was himself engaged constantly in a voluminous correspondence with headmasters, school principals, and superintendents and accepted every request to speak to secondary schools that he could cram into a well-filled schedule.

§ § §

Fund-raising had again become an urgent project of the College in 1919, and the device of employing a financial agent such as had operated in the nineteenth century was again considered by the Trustees. Rev. John Sayles, a resident of Buffalo and a graduate of the divinity school in 1892, was one of those suggested. There was some hesitation about using his services, but

13 Graduate students could receive from $10 to $30 a month, depending on their classification. The bulk of the recipients of federal aid at Tufts were undergraduates, and medical and dental students.

Trustee Fletcher urged his immediate appointment, partly on the ground that the "chief obstacle" to finding a permanent successor to Bumpus was the failure of the College to secure funds and the natural unwillingness of any candidate to assume the financial responsibilities of the institution. The Executive Committee, after having decided to employ Rev. Mr. Sayles, rescinded its vote twenty-four hours later. Acting President Cousens and Fletcher disagreed over the matter. The latter had insisted for several years that securing the services of a financial agent was the best solution, while Cousens argued equally vigorously that funds should be raised from the alumni, and by alumni initiative and effort, without the prodding of a professional money-raiser, alumnus or not.[14] Cousens and the majority of the Trustees prevailed, and Sayles was not employed; this failure Fletcher considered "the most colossal blunder" that had ever been made during the time he had served as a Trustee.

The vehicle used to organize the fund appeal was the Tufts Foundation Association, approved by the Trustees in the fall of 1919. It was both necessary and timely. President Bumpus had carried the College successfully through the war years, but the margin of financial reserve was a narrow one and postwar adjustments had to be faced squarely. In 1919 the operating deficits in both medical and dental schools exceeded the 10 per cent reserve that had been set apart annually and added to the sinking funds.[15] The College barely broke even when the SATC accounts were settled with the federal government, and the total amount paid out for operating expenses in 1919 was over $600,000 — the largest yet expended by the institution in a single year. Gifts and bequests were the smallest that had been received for some time (only $13,000), and both the men's and women's dormitories lost money. Austin Fletcher continued his long-standing practice of making generous annual donations ($10,000 in 1919) but continued also to reserve the right during his lifetime to control both the investment and the income of the fund comprising his gifts. The money collected through Professor Hooper's diligence had

[14] Fletcher aired his plans to employ a solicitor in a letter to the *Tufts College Graduate,* Vol. 17 (June-August 1919), pp. 151–152.

[15] The practice of setting up as a reserve 10 per cent of the receipts from students in the medical and dental schools was discontinued after 1921–22.

been almost exhausted by 1919 and amounted to less than $9,000.

Immediate as well as long-range action had to be taken to provide revenue. The salaries of full professors had been raised $500 (to $2,500) in 1918 and of most assistant professors to a maximum of $2,000 but were still conspicuously inadequate in relation to the inflationary economy that the nation had inherited from wartime. All tuitions were raised by $25, effective in the fall of 1919. Liberal arts and Jackson went to $150, engineering to $200, and Bromfield-Pearson to $175. Medical and dental school tuition went to $175, and the pre-medical charge to $150. Scarcely had these upward adjustments been authorized than another round of increases was voted by the Trustees for the following year. Tuition was further raised in some divisions of the College, dormitory rentals were increased, a fee of $7.50 was levied on all undergraduates not residing on the campus, and assessments were increased for such student activities as athletics and the weekly newspaper.[16] Part of the anticipated increased revenue, estimated at $100,000, was intended to go into further salary increases for full professors in the Hill schools.[17] A tuition increase of $25 in the Associated Schools of Arts and Sciences went into effect September 1921, and at the same time tuition for all four years of both the medical and the dental schools was established at $200.[18]

Cousens set the ideal target of the Tufts Foundation at $2,000,-000 for productive endowment and $500,000 for additions to the physical plant, but the sights had to be lowered to $1,000,000 for practical reasons. Trustee Fletcher, disgruntled by the failure of the Board to approve his plan to employ a professional fund-raiser, sniffed in disdain at the one-million-dollar goal and told Cousens

[16] Tuition in the school of liberal arts, Jackson, Crane, the graduate school, the pre-medical and medical schools, and the first two years of the dental school was raised at midyear in 1920 to $175. Tuition for the third and fourth years in the dental school was set at $160. Engineering school tuition remained at $200, but the Bromfield-Pearson charges were raised to that figure.

[17] The minimum salary for those holding permanent appointments was set at $3,000, to take effect not later than September 1920. Cousens had raised his goal to $4,000 for full professors by that time and five years later expressed his desire that the salaries of departmental chairmen reach $5,000. By 1927 this had been partially achieved by a distribution of a portion of the surplus which the College then enjoyed.

[18] Medical school tuition was again raised (to $225), effective September 1922, and more increases were yet to come.

in 1922 that "if Tufts had laid out a carefully planned campaign, with a man behind it who knew his business . . . we should have been well toward the two million mark by this time." A few months later Fletcher expressed the decided opinion that Tufts "should have started out to raise three million dollars instead of one million." Realizing that alumni contributions alone would never suffice, Acting President Cousens applied in 1920 for "immediate assistance" from the Rockefeller-based General Education Board. He requested $100,000 a year for five years. His efforts to obtain foundation support appeared to have been successful, for in June 1920 the Trustees were informed that the Board would commit up to $300,000 to an endowment fund of $1,000,000 provided the College would raise the remaining $700,000, the total amount "to be set aside and maintained inviolate by Tufts College as endowment, the income to be used in providing permanently for the increase of teachers' salaries." [19] The General Education Board also pledged for the same purpose the equivalent in interest of $60,000, scaled over a three-year period.

The conditions prescribed by the General Education Board came close to wreaking havoc with the Tufts Foundation drive. Among other things, it meant that money pledged without condition and "usable for any purpose whatever including payment of running expenses" (as stipulated in the original endowment drive) was automatically removed from funds available to pay current expenses; only the income of the Foundation funds could be so used, for the Board had added the proviso that a reduction in the principal below $1,000,000 would mean a corresponding decrease in pledges from the Board. The College set September 1925 as the deadline for attaining its goal. Certain other restrictions were included in the agreement made by the General Education Board in 1921. No legacies could be counted toward the endowment, and no part of the income from the fund could be used "for specifically theological instruction." Receipts were agonizingly slow in coming in at first. Slightly less than $60,000 had been received in six

[19] Cousens informed the General Education Board in 1920 that the Tufts salary scale was as follows: professors, $3,000 to $4,000; assistant professors, $2,500 to $3,000; instructors, $1,800 to $2,000; assistants, $1,200 to $1,500. This scale included increases totaling slightly over $45,000 made possible by the General Education Board grants.

months, and was credited to the "Tufts Salary Foundation." A year later the fund was still less than $150,000. Cousens told the Trustees in his annual report for 1919–20 that upon them "rested the final responsibility for the financial condition of the College." He chided them for having known "for years" that Tufts lacked endowment, and yet they had made "little effort" to secure it. They had an opportunity and a responsibility which they could not avoid. He issued a virtual ultimatum: each member of the Board should pledge either to get or to give at least $25,000 before another year had passed. He saw no other solution.

Much to the relief of all concerned, the Tufts Foundation campaign had accomplished its task by June 1923, with $15,000 pledged beyond the goal. A special "Jumbo Bond Drive" had been responsible for raising over $450,000 of the amount needed; the completion of the Foundation represented "a notable personal achievement" by President Cousens.[20]

As in most of the College's history, the bulk of the contributions consisted of many small donations rather than a few large ones. The largest single contribution was $50,000, and the total number of subscribers (as of October 1, 1923) was 5,812. Actual collection of pledges and commitments by the General Education Board totaled over $650,000 by the end of the next year. A gift of $7,500 from the Board in 1923–24 to enhance faculty salaries also added unexpectedly to the resources of the institution. Just as soon as the Tufts Foundation drive was completed, Cousens persuaded the alumni that a Sustaining Fund should be created. The Foundation pledges had gotten many of the alumni into the habit of making yearly contributions, and an annual fund of about $50,000 could be drawn upon to meet unforeseen deficits or be allowed to accumulate as part of the endowment if there were no unusual drafts on College operating funds.

The prosperity that was experienced in most sectors of the national economy in the mid-1920's was reflected in the financial fortunes of the College. Budgets, expenditures, and income all

[20] Harold E. Sweet, Fletcher's successor as president of the Board of Trustees, contributed the sum that made possible the success of the final effort to complete the Foundation drive on schedule. The Alumni Professorship Fund, which in 1931 was still less than $6,000 (including accumulated interest) was added that year to the Tufts Foundation Fund.

reached new highs. The total budget for 1926–27 was $800,000 and the estimated surplus was $35,000. In 1927, for the first time in its history, the College's operating expenses for a single year exceeded one million dollars. Tufts had become an educational enterprise of no mean proportions and had long since outgrown the financial provincialism of the nineteenth century. The returns from all general investments and the income from numerous gifts and bequests in the 1920's more than matched the immediate needs of the institution. In 1927, returns averaged 8 per cent.[21] In the midst of this prosperity, tuition was raised $50 in all but the pre-medical and pre-dental schools, effective September 1927.[22] Another round of increases, effective in 1930–31, brought the totals to $300 in the school of liberal arts and in Jackson. The undergraduate increases were not justified because the College was in financial difficulties — far from it in the mid-1920's — but because President Cousens held firmly to the conviction that students (or, more appropriately, their parents) who were able to do so should contribute a larger share of the cost of their higher education than prevailing tuition required.

The stock market crash of 1929 and the more prolonged and much more serious depression that followed in the 1930's had inevitable reverberations at Tufts. Cousens' greatest nightmare was that the operating expenses of the College might some day tip the ledger to the wrong side. He and the other officers responsible for the financial administration of the institution used almost every device available to prevent deficits. "Prudence" became the watchword. In 1929–30 the budget was balanced by canceling the president's expense account for traveling, by drawing for the first time upon the Alumni Sustaining Fund, and by charging against the funds of the Fletcher estate certain administrative expenses. The budget for the following year was kept in equilibrium largely

[21] This unusually high figure included extra dividends on the profitable Eppinger and Russell stock which the College received as part of the estate of Austin B. Fletcher, who died in 1923. Without this, the earned rate was still a comfortable $5\frac{1}{2}$ per cent.

[22] The numerous increases in tuition in the 1920's did not always apply to the graduate school. The tuition in that division had been set at $100 in 1921–22 and had been increased to $150 in 1927–28. It was raised to $250, effective in 1929–30, at which time the semester-hour fee for special graduate students was also raised from $7.50 to $8.50, and later to $10.00.

because of a "substantial increase" in revenue from student fees and a paring down of the budget for maintenance.[23] Of greatest concern in terms of anticipated revenue was the continued depressed state of enrollment in the dental school, which had never completely recovered from the period of slump apparently entered by the entire field of dental education in the mid-1920's. The increase in dental school tuition from $300 to $350, effective in September 1931, was in no sense a solution to its financial problem.

The securing of more adequate endowment for the whole institution, as well as any special endowment for some of its parts, seemed still to be the unattainable goal. "Our resources," said Cousens to the Trustees in 1930, "have never been commensurate with our ambition; indeed the exigencies of our situation have often compelled us to assume financial obligations before adequate financial foundations have been laid. The history of the College is full of such instances." Unfortunately, nobody could truthfully contradict him. However, the short-range prospects for the institution continued to look promising. Even without substantial increases in endowment in sight, the College managed to do very well in maintaining a slight balance in the black. In fact, in the fiscal year 1931–32 the treasurer was able to set up two reserve accounts totaling $25,000 — one for contingencies and one for the Department of Grounds and Buildings, to be used at the discretion of the president. At the March meeting of the Trustees in 1933 President Cousens was given a rising vote of thanks and congratulations "for the excellent financial condition of the institution."

The Trustees had "every expectation" that the College would continue to function as usual through the dark financial days of the 1930's and that even a balanced budget could be reported. They nevertheless saw fit to make all faculty appointments between 1933–34 and 1935–36 for one year only, "upon the express conditions that no contract is to be implied from or established by this vote" and that the College would assume no liability except for services already rendered if it became necessary to terminate an appointment. These provisions at first glance might have seemed to justify panic in the ranks, but there was another side to the story. So far as can be determined, no person considered

[23] The average income per student in 1930–31 for all divisions of the College was $436 and the expenditures were $433.

a permanent member of the faculty or staff either lost his position or suffered a reduction in salary directly because of the state of the Tufts treasury during a critical period in the nation's economy. The financial picture was sufficiently satisfactory by the spring of 1936 to make possible the discarding of the one-year limitation on all appointments.[24]

The long-range financial needs of the College were not neglected during the 1930's. In fact, the pressures of outside accrediting agencies on the engineering school and the medical school made endowment a more pressing requirement than ever. President Cousens reminded the Trustees periodically that the proportion of the total expense for operating the institution supplied by tuition and student fees was "altogether too large in relation to the amount received as income from endowment." The worst of the depression seemed to have passed by 1937, and the Trustees approved in principle three proposals: to raise an endowment for the engineering school; to approve the expenditure of $25,000 to conduct a campaign for an endowment of $2,000,000 for the medical school, to be conducted by its alumni; and to "organize an office under the direction of a qualified official of the Corporation to undertake the raising of an endowment for the College and its various departments."

§   §   §

The specter that had haunted the Tufts Medical School ever since the Flexner Report of 1910 — that of losing its Class A rating — refused to disappear in the period after the First World War. President Cousens strove mightily to exorcise the specter, and the problem was a source of constant worry to him. The inflated enrollments of both medical and dental schools had been aggravated by the lengthening of their courses and by the establishment of pre-medical and pre-dental schools. Laboratory space had been at such a premium during the war that the first section of an Anatomical Building had been constructed during President Bumpus' administration, but only one-third of the structure had actually been completed and put to use when Cousens became president.

[24] The credit for the sound financial state of the College was not due to President Cousens alone. The Finance Committee of the Trustees and particularly Richard B. Coolidge, treasurer of the Corporation from 1934 until 1952, merited a goodly share, not to overlook the many generous contributors.

The imperative need for additional space had resulted in 1920 in the construction of part of the second section. Only two floors of the three called for by the specifications were completed because of "the extraordinary cost of materials and labor." Even with this partial alleviation of a critical housing problem, physical facilities and instructional staff were still not adequate for the student body. These deficiencies were especially sensitive problems in 1920 because the president had made application to the General Education Board for assistance from Rockefeller funds earmarked for the benefit of medical education. Action on the petition for aid was dependent on the results of an inspection by the Foundation, and the College had to be prepared not only to justify itself but to present a convincing case for help.[25]

Dean Rushmore, Painter's successor, wrote letter after letter to President Cousens asking that the medical school be made less of a commercial operation and that the number of students be brought more realistically into line with the capacity of the school. What the medical school needed, in his estimation, was "improvement in the quality, rather than increase in quantity." The burden of fund-raising rested, in his opinion, on the Trustees of Tufts College, not on the teaching and administrative staff of the school. The dean remained unsatisfied with the continuing low percentage of medical students who had earned Bachelor's degrees, and put much of the blame on the existence of the two-year pre-medical course, which automatically reduced the number of students willing and able to pursue a four-year college course. Dean Rushmore was even less pleased to see the Trustees, instead of curtailing enrollment, vote another tuition increase, effective in 1925–26.[26]

[25] The inspection was conducted by Dr. N. P. Colwell in the fall of 1920 after consultation with Flexner, who represented the Rockefeller Foundation, and Wallace Buttrick, who represented the General Education Board. Dr. Colwell's report was generally favorable. One possibility discussed at length by Cousens and Buttrick was to secure the services of Dr. Thomas A. Storey, head of the United States Interdepartmental Social Hygiene Board in Washington, D.C., and subsequently on the staff of the College of the City of New York. Storey would replace Dr. Painter, who had resigned as dean of the Tufts Medical School in 1921. Storey's salary would be paid by the Board while it was engaged in a comprehensive review of medical education in New England, in which the Tufts school would have played a major part.

[26] The tuition became an inclusive fee of $300, which meant actually a net increase of $50. Rushmore had been so upset by the conditions in the

After Dean Rushmore had resigned from the deanship in protest against the College's medical school policies, Dr. A. Warren Stearns was selected to head the school. Stearns was himself a graduate of the medical school (Class of 1910) and had served in the Department of Neurology since 1921. By the mid-1920's he had already established a reputation as a leading criminologist. One of his areas of special activity was psychiatry, and he had served in numerous responsible positions in both private and public capacities. He was for a time medical director of the Massachusetts Society for Mental Hygiene and psychiatrist for the Massachusetts State Prison. During part of his tenure as dean he served as State Commissioner of Corrections. Dr. Stearns inherited a host of thorny problems when he assumed the deanship in September 1927. Increases in tuition seemed to have no effect on the large number of applicants; the entering class in 1928 (totaling 135) was selected from more than 1,200. While the school enjoyed apparently phenomenal prosperity in the 1920's, its very future nevertheless became a matter of serious and prolonged discussion.

The secretary of the Council on Medical Education of the American Medical Association had visited the medical school in 1926 and had not liked what he found. He told the College that certain recommendations would have to be carried out within two or three years. If they were not, the school would probably lose its Class A standing. The bill of particulars required the elimination of the pre-medical school, a separation of the medical school from the dental school, an increase in the staff of laboratory departments, the application of all revenues derived from medical school students to the expenses of the school, and the establishment of a special endowment. President Cousens sought a resolution of at least some of these problems by appealing again to the General Education Board. This, in turn, meant a reconsideration of the location of the medical school, which had become an item of Trustee business in 1925.

If the moving of the medical school were considered advisable, two possibilities were open. There was persistent talk that it might

medical school, and particularly the Trustees' policy of siphoning off medical school profits to other parts of the College, that he submitted an undated resignation to Cousens after having been in office less than two years. He was prevailed upon to remain as dean until 1927.

be moved to the Hill, but that would prejudice the prospects of substantial Rockefeller Foundation support for the school unless clinical facilities, and preferably a hospital, were available in the new location. The other alternative was to move the school closer to the Boston City Hospital so that a larger service could be rendered and foundation support more easily obtained, but Cousens was categorically opposed to any such move. If any geographical change was to take place, he wanted both medical and dental schools located on the Hill. The Board of Visitors to the medical school in 1926 made the matter of location a special item for consideration. They ruefully admitted that Tufts did not have the contacts that would provide the $10,000,000 needed to move the school to the Medford campus and construct a hospital in conjunction with it. The Visitors were insistent in recommending better accommodations, whether the dental school was moved or not.

It appeared in the winter of 1926 that Cousens' hopes had been carried a step nearer to realization. After an interview with Dr. Abraham Flexner of the General Education Board, the president obtained from the Executive Committee approval of a "general plan," yet to be formulated in detail, to move the medical school to the Hill and to construct buildings and a hospital. President Cousens also made arrangements, at the suggestion of Dr. Flexner, for a review by Dr. G. Canby Robinson, former dean of the medical school at Vanderbilt University and director of the Cornell University-New York Hospital Medical Center. Dr. Robinson, in a report made after a brief visit to the Tufts Medical School in the summer of 1928, recommended either that it be completely reorganized or that "Tufts College should retire from the field of medical education" and concentrate its efforts on dental education. As Dr. Robinson saw it, the wiser course for Tufts was to concentrate its efforts on collegiate education and to leave the field of professional education in medicine to be developed by other institutions unless it could acquire at least $13,000,000 to start anew. If this were possible, then the Medford campus would be the proper location. Even if the new hospital were eliminated in the new plan, the cost would remain over $5,000,000.

Dr. Robinson found the Tufts Medical School isolated, operating with antiquated buildings and equipment better adapted for high school instruction, with an impossibly large student body, and no endowment. It was, in fact, the only Class A medical school in the nation operating without any financial resources assigned to it from the parent institution.[27] All the other criticisms of the school made time and time again were repeated by Dr. Robinson. They ranged from overworked and underpaid part-time faculty to clinical facilities inadequately organized for teaching purposes. It was an all-too-familiar list of deficiencies.

The threat of the Council on Medical Education to reclassify the Tufts Medical School as a Class B facility was not scheduled to be carried out (if at all) until the spring of 1929. This gave the Trustees time to effect at least a few of the required changes. The closing of the pre-medical school was voted, and a few new appointments were made in the laboratory departments; this remedied somewhat a basic weakness, but it did not accomplish in any real sense the separation of the medical and dental schools. They continued to occupy the same quarters, and medical school staff still taught some dental school courses. Cousens was as blunt as he could be with his fellow Trustees. Tufts did not really have a first-class medical school, in his estimation, and he knew that the Trustees in their own hearts agreed with him, and they might as well face up to the facts. It was "in effect a Class B school . . . whether so labelled or not." A second-class medical school "in name as well as in fact could not be endured." Cousens proposed to solve the problem by following Dr. Robinson's compromise proposal of moving the school to the Medford campus, but without a new hospital, and at the same time paring down to the bone every cost estimate that was made. Cousens would have all but the clinical facilities located on the Hill and ready for use by the fall of 1930. Some kind of medical center, possibly with the Boston City Hospital at the core, could be provided, but would not be needed until the third-year class of the "new medical school" registered in 1932. The dental school would, under this plan, remain at the Huntington Avenue headquarters in Boston.

[27] This criticism was met, at least in part, when a new accounting procedure was established in the treasurer's office in 1928–29 by which deficits from the operations of any of the schools were considered as general College expense and charged on a per capita basis against those parts of the institution operating at a profit. Whatever net surplus remained was made available for divisions showing a deficit.

The president saw only two choices for the College; there was no "middle ground." Either the medical school had to be closed immediately, or Robinson's second proposal could be adopted so far as possible. The Trustees agreed and, like Cousens, elected to pursue the latter course. It was a difficult one to follow, for the long-sought and tantilizing offer of assistance from the General Education Board was abruptly withdrawn in 1928. Cousens attempted to obtain a definite commitment of assistance by presenting a detailed plan for the reorganization of the medical school along the lines recommended by Dr. Robinson, together with a request for $2,000,000. The president received a "flat refusal," on the ground that a reorganization of the General Education Board itself had resulted in a new policy that precluded direct aid to any medical school. Frustrated in this direction, Cousens snatched at another opportunity. A member of the Board of Trustees of the Boston Dispensary approached Cousens in the winter of 1928 and suggested that Tufts and the Dispensary might join with the Boston Floating Hospital in establishing a medical center.[28] The three institutions could be the nucleus of a comprehensive unit that in 1929 was already being referred to as the "New England Medical Center." Plans were made for a campaign to raise $1,500,000 by March 1929. Tufts agreed to advance $65,000 toward its share of $500,000 in order to acquire land, build a hospital, and alter and enlarge the Boston Dispensary. The new facility was to be supervised by a Joint Administrative Board.[29]

[28] The Boston Dispensary, dating back to 1796, was originally intended to provide home medical care for the poor. By 1930 it had expanded its operations to include diagnostic clinics for ambulatory patients and extensive laboratory facilities for training technicians in several specialties. The Boston Floating Hospital for Infants and Children was founded in 1894 by the Rev. Rufus Tobey. It started aboard a rented excursion steamer that was towed around Boston Harbor by a tug and was intended to give ailing children in the city an opportunity to enjoy fresh air. Funds were later raised to construct a steamer equipped especially for the care of sick children. The "floating hospital," placed in service in 1905, lasted until 1927, when it burned at the dock shortly after having been overhauled. Land-based permanent hospital facilities were developed in Boston between 1929 and 1931. The hospital became an important research unit for the study of pediatrics.

[29] The state legislature approved the creation of the medical center on February 13, 1930, and the College charter was amended accordingly. *Acts and Resolves,* General Court of Massachusetts, 1930, Chapter 40.

The "new Tufts Medical School" that Cousens and the Trustees had in mind was about to become a fact, although not in exactly the way it had been conceived. The improved clinical facilities would come first, and the removal of the rest of the medical school to Medford would have to wait. The new medical center presupposed an associated medical school. Here was Tufts' great opportunity. And while this exciting new prospect was being opened, the College complied with the "command" of the American Medical Association by releasing the contingency fund into which the profits of the medical school had been deposited and spending the money by reorganizing and strengthening the Departments of Physiology, Pathology, and Bacteriology. The start having finally been made, other improvements were scheduled but at a time when income and expense were almost in balance. Another increase in student fees was voted, effective in 1930–31. Tuition in the medical school became $400 — $100 higher than in the school of liberal arts and in Jackson College. There would be no difficulty in finding uses for the new income. Almost every paragraph of Dean Stearns' annual report for 1928–29 included the phrase "more personnel and equipment will be needed next year or in the near future." A Department of Psychiatry was created in 1930, and in the following year the school's offerings were greatly strengthened by the creation of the Department of Preventive Medicine through a grant from the Commonwealth Fund of New York which also provided a scholarship-loan fund for students. The fourth year was completely reorganized so that each student could serve the entire year under instruction at various hospitals for one-month periods. In 1931 two members of the medical school staff were given, for the first time, leaves of absence at full pay for research and study in Europe, on the recommendation of the Research Committee of the medical school.[30] A new spirit and sense of purpose seemed to have been infused into the school.

[30] They were Dr. Attilio Canzanelli and Dr. Benjamin Spector, at the time Instructor in Physiology and Associate Professor of Anatomy, respectively. Grants for medical research for both students and faculty were also made possible in the 1930's through income from the trust estates of Earle Perry Charlton of Fall River, Massachusetts, which became available to the College after prolonged litigation.

Before the creation of the New England Medical Center in 1930, the medical school had also added new ties of various degrees of closeness with hospitals and clinics in the metropolitan area. Neither the ill-fated efforts to make Grace Hospital a permanent facility under the direct control of the medical school nor the Tremont Dispensary had given the school exactly what it needed and wanted.[31] The first hospital actually to be staffed completely with Tufts medical personnel was the Evangeline Booth Hospital, which had been opened in 1920 as the Roxbury Hospital, to handle maternity cases. The clinical opportunities which it offered after association with Tufts in 1922 became invaluable for teaching obstetrics and pediatrics. Facilities of the new Beth Israel Hospital opened in 1928 gave Tufts students opportunities for instruction in such specialties as neurology, orthopedics, and gynecology as well as in general medicine and surgery. Teaching privileges in pathology were given to Tufts students for the first time in 1929-30 in the Massachusetts General Hospital, traditionally the bailiwick of the Harvard Medical School. Within a short time after the New England Medical Center was opened, valuable assistance from the outside was received. In 1931 the medical school received a grant of $50,000 from William Bingham of Bethel, Maine, who was particularly interested in developing rural medicine. This gift, like subsequent contributions by the Bingham Associates of $25,000 for X-ray equipment and maintenance, and an additional $25,000 for a hospital unit, was intended to strengthen the new Center. Part of the Bingham gifts was used to finance the work of Dr. Joseph H. Pratt, who served as Professor of Clinical Medicine from 1929 to 1947. By the fall of 1932 facilities were such that the amount of teaching in the Center was second only to that in the Boston City Hospital. Another important relationship was established when, in 1936, arrangements were made with the Carney Hospital that all the teaching there would be done by members of the medical school staff.

The continued excess of applicants of good quality even during the depression years prompted Dean Stearns to express the be-

[31] For a summary of the major facilities available to the medical school, see Benjamin Spector, *A History of Tufts College Medical School*, pp. 317-326. The Tremont Dispensary and the Massachusetts Dispensary for Women were taken over by the medical school in 1924.

lief in 1932 that the medical school could be made into "practically a graduate institution" and to recommend that only holders of college degrees be admitted.[32] It appeared by 1934 that the dean's hopes had been almost realized, for the medical school faculty ruled, effective in 1935–36, that its Committee on Admissions was to select, with only individual exceptions, candidates who were graduates of colleges of liberal arts or sciences which had been approved for pre-medical education by the Council of the American Medical Association. The attempt to carve down the excessive enrollment was finally made in 1935, when the Trustees, on Dean Stearns' recommendation, voted to limit the entering class in September 1936 to 100.[33]

The organizing of a graduate school of medicine was also discussed in the early 1930's. Nothing concrete was done at the time, but arrangements were made for post-M.D. work for short periods of study in nearly all subjects. A decade later (in 1943–44), graduate study in the medical sciences was made available through the cooperation of the medical school for students who were not candidates for a medical or dental degree.[34]

The Tufts Medical School took two important strides in the 1930's — one forward and one backward. The creation of the New England Medical Center was a most welcome event. Not at all welcome was the action of the Council on Medical Education and Hospitals of the American Medical Association in 1935. On the recommendation of an inspection team which visited the school, it lost its Class A rating and found itself on probation. The fact that it was one of nine schools receiving such treatment was no comfort at all. Even less comforting was the realization that, in coming to its decision about the Tufts school, the Council listed not a single criticism that had not already been made repeatedly. The student body was entirely too large; the pre-clinical depart-

[32] In 1931–32, 85 in the first-year class of 127 held college degrees.

[33] Tuition was raised from $400 to $500 to help compensate for the resulting loss of revenue. Tuition in the dental school was raised, effective the same date, from $350 to $400.

[34] Persons wishing to earn the M.S. degree in one of seven medical sciences could do so by meeting the same requirements as for the degree in the natural sciences. Courses could be taken both in the science departments on the Hill and in the medical school. The work was to be administered under the general supervision of the graduate school faculty.

ments, functioning in grossly inadequate quarters, were under-staffed as to both quantity and quality; clinical training in the third and fourth years was too widely scattered and unsatisfac-torily supervised. The library was too small and its collections were underdeveloped.[35] Laboratories were too crowded and in-sufficient in number; some of the teaching was "unstimulating and stereotyped"; there was insufficient time and space devoted to re-search. The Department of Pathology was handling a dispropor-tionately large amount of hospital pathology and was "virtually functioning as a commercial laboratory."

Cousens immediately informed the Council that the College not only was aware of all these (and other) deficiencies, but with isolated exceptions had already undertaken to remedy them. The quota of entering students had been reduced for future classes. A campaign to secure a special endowment was already in the process of organization. Plans for adding a third story to the Anat-omy Building were being "definitely developed."[36] He explained that the delay had been caused by the prolonged discussions over whether or not to move the entire plant to the Hill. The depart-ments, Cousens told the Council, were being strengthened one by one by additional staff. Improvements had already been made in the Department of Physiology (which had fared relatively well at the hands of the inspection team), and the Department of Anat-omy was receiving special attention. The inspectors had been dis-turbed to find that the bacteriological laboratory was being super-vised by a person with the rank of assistant professor who did not possess even one academic degree. Cousens hastened to de-fend the appointment, explaining that it was only temporary while the regular teacher was on leave of absence to study at the Uni-versity of London, but that in any case the person in question was

[35] No real attempt had ever been made to establish a comprehensive or definitive collection because of the accessibility of the Boston Medical Library, to which Tufts made periodic token contributions. The combined medical-dental library, housed in the main building of the school, was serviced by a full-time librarian by the 1920's but had never received generous appropria-tions.

[36] The addition was authorized by the Trustees in the fall of 1935, but plans were revised in the following year to create additional space for the bac-teriology laboratory by remodeling the amphitheater rather than building the third story.

"extraordinary" and was "an example of what may be achieved without the benefit of the usual opportunities for academic training." The president disagreed with the negative report on the Department of Pathology and argued that it was performing its basic educational function admirably. He likewise disagreed with the criticism of the clinical training, although he admitted that supervision could be improved and that the system of spreading students over a considerable number of hospitals was probably not ideal, but was necessary because of the "special situation" in the medical school. The fact was that Tufts still did not have a hospital to call its own, even though it had been authorized by the state legislature to establish and maintain one since 1901. Part of the criticism of the clinical aspects of the curriculum was met in 1937 when Dr. Dwight O'Hara, Professor of Preventive Medicine since 1931, became the vice-dean of the medical school, with special responsibility for supervising third- and fourth-year students.

The medical school had apparently reached another crossroads. Cousens categorically refused to countenance the possibility of operating a Class B school and just as stubbornly refused to discontinue it, on the grounds that such a step would mean even more than the dislocation of the entire structure of the College. As the president saw it, "the Tufts Medical School is not merely the concern of the Trustees and alumni of Tufts College, but its future is of consequence to the whole of New England." Dean Stearns, with the criticisms of the Council on Medical Education at hand, reviewed the strengths and weaknesses of the school at some length and was frank to concede that the majority of the adverse comment was justified. He was not happy to see an increasing number of failures of Tufts medical students on state and national Board examinations but considered the trend an outgrowth of the philosophy on which the school was being operated and not necessarily the result of poor teaching and overcrowded laboratories. He defended the emphasis on clinical experience rather than "pedagogy" during the third and fourth years. The staff and administration had stood from the beginning on the ground that the primary function of the school was not to operate "as an isolated institution whose sole function is to train a selected group of students to the highest degree possible in the scientific aspects of medicine." Its basic task was to meet the practical medical needs of the community, and for that reason it had made "certain concessions" in the area of theory and "classroom" medicine in favor of experience. The dean, like the president, saw the imperative need for new sources of revenue besides student fees, even though by 1936 over $100,000 had been received as gifts for special purposes.

§   §   §

The Tufts Dental School had weathered the crises and uncertainties of the First World War in spite of increased costs for maintenance and for materials necessary to fulfill its obligations to its students. Two developments under the leadership of Dean William Rice were particular sources of satisfaction. During the war the federal government, recognizing the importance of dentistry to the welfare of military personnel, gave dentists rank and pay equivalent to those of doctors. Then followed an investigation and classification of dental schools throughout the country, made on the recommendation of the office of the Surgeon General. The Tufts school received the highest rating (Class A); this entitled its graduates to take examinations for commissions in both the Army and the Navy. As a result, 280 men connected with the dental school entered military service. The quality of the training at the dental school also resulted in election to membership in the Dental Faculties Association of American Universities, in which there were only eight universities at the time. The Tufts school became the first department of a college to be thus honored. The Dental Educational Council of America placed the school in the Class A category in 1923.[37]

The enrollment of the dental school had dropped sharply when the requirement of one year of college work had become effective in the fall of 1922. The smallest entering class in the history of the school (twenty-one) had resulted, and enrollment had not approached what was considered normal until 1924–25 when the number of entering students rose to seventy-eight. Tuition was set at $250, effective the following year. President Cousens' concern in the mid-1920's about the dental school was centered around the relatively low academic and professional standards that seemed to prevail in the school proper; he put most of the blame on the pre-

[37] Tufts was one of the twenty schools out of the forty-eight examined that received such a rating.

dental program. Even then, the dental school was showing an embarrassing deficit in the mid-1920's, while the medical school was producing an equally embarrassing profit. In the last analysis, the College was reaping the bitter harvest of a vicious cycle. With no endowment for the dental school, standards of both admission and performance were depressed in both the school and the preparatory program in order to maintain sufficient enrollment to make the enterprise something like a paying proposition. One result was a double standard for the two pre-professional schools in Boston; the requirements of the pre-medical program were higher than for the pre-dental. Part of the responsibility for this seemed to lie in a tendency to stress dental mechanics at the expense of dental medicine.

To make matters worse, the dental school found itself caught between the demands of the Dental Educational Council of the American Dental Association and the plan recommended by the Carnegie Foundation. The Carnegie Report on Dental Education recommended for entrance two years in an accredited liberal arts college, a professional course of three years, and the organization of a one-year graduate course in dental specialties. The Dental Educational Council recommended, on the other hand, two years of college and a four-year professional course. New York State elected to adhere to the so-called "two-four" plan, which automatically made graduates of schools following the "two-three-graduate" plan ineligible to take the state licensing examination. Because the proportion of New York students in the Tufts Dental School was very high, the dental school reluctantly decided to conform to the New York requirements.[38] No one knew what plan would eventually become the standard for a Class A rating until 1934, when the members of the American Association of Dental Schools voted to adopt the "two-four" plan, effective in 1937–38. Doubt was also cast on the status of the dental school by the insistence of the American Medical Association that the work of the school be completely separated from that of the medical school. Cousens vigorously disapproved of this policy of separation and was inclined "to take a rather firm stand" and continue to allow at least some dental school

[38] In 1926–27 there were ninety students from New York. In the following year, more entering students came from New York than from any other state; New Yorkers comprised one-third of the total enrollment that year.

classes to be taught by men on the medical school staff. He was reinforced in such an attitude because he believed that within a short time the first two years of the dental school course would become identical with the first two years of the medical school.

The Tufts Dental School underwent some important changes in the early 1930's, although deficits continued to accumulate during the depression period. A complete modernization of the dental infirmary in 1931, involving the replacement of much equipment over thirty years old and expenditures of over $30,000, was made possible only by an appeal to dental school alumni; over 400 contributed or pledged to the Dental Alumni Fund. The dental school lost, by death in 1932, its dean of fifteen years, Dr. William Rice. Dr. Howard M. Marjerison, Associate Professor of Prosthetic Dentistry, after serving as temporary head, became dean in 1934.[39] Under his leadership the teaching staff was reorganized and consolidated from fifteen semiautonomous departments into four major coordinated divisions: Operative Dentistry, Prosthetic Dentistry, Oral Surgery, and Orthodontia. A new Department of Clinical Medicine was also organized, in line with a renewed emphasis on the biological aspects of dentistry and a decreased emphasis on dental technique and mechanical procedures. Dean Marjerison was strongly in favor not only of developing dentistry as a branch of medicine but of encouraging clinical research. He felt that facilities offered through the cooperation of the Departments of Clinical Medicine, Dental Pathology, and Oral Medicine would be a satisfactory equivalent of conventional hospital facilities. The greatest and most immediate personnel need seemed to be sufficient adjustment in teaching loads to enable research to be carried on.

Although the dental school did not experience the same pressure as the medical school to require college degrees of its matriculants, the proportion of holders of a Bachelor's degree did increase markedly. Almost one-half of the entering class in 1936–37 had already earned an academic degree. Yet there was the uneasy feeling, expressed by both Dean Marjerison and President Cousens, that dental education still had some distance to go before losing its status as a "trade school" and gaining full university recognition.

§   §   §

[39] The infirmary at the dental school was named "The William Rice Infirmary" by the Trustees in honor of the late dean.

The sixth president of Tufts College had not been long in office before he let faculty, students, alumni, and Trustees know that he had wide-ranging plans for the College. At the first faculty meeting in 1923–24 and again at the opening exercises for the students that fall, he announced that "the College is entering upon a new epoch," that "a new era is dawning." He sensed change in the air and promised that he would be in the midst of it. He had informed the Trustees in his annual report for 1923 that the time had come for "a radical change in the organization of the College, the time for an experiment in education of extraordinary importance." There was, he said, no way in which Tufts was basically different from a score of other educational institutions except possibly that in some respects its work was not as well done as elsewhere. If Tufts strove for quality, not quantity, it might become "one of the outstanding centers of learning in America." To this end, he offered a blueprint for the future.[40]

Cousens proposed to organize the College into three sections. The first would consist of a course of two years leading to the degree of Associate in Arts in which most of the work of the school of liberal arts, engineering, and the pre-medical and pre-dental programs would be carried out. Students prepared to do the prescribed work could be "received rather freely" from any regular high school, and the "artificial machinery" which currently encumbered college entrance could be dispensed with.[41] Secondary school preparation and college performance could then be realistically correlated. The two-year sequence would be an end in itself for those unable for academic or other reasons to complete four years, and would allow students with greater academic talents to find themselves. Nine out of the fifteen semester hours for which the typical

[40] He went so far as to send a copy of his plans to the president of the General Education Board in 1921, but received only a courteous acknowledgment.

[41] In a memorandum which Cousens prepared for his own use, some of the important items he listed under the heading of "College Entrance Requirements" were: "(1) Statistics show that specific preparation for college is not necessary. (2) To impose on the high schools special college preparatory courses distorts the curriculum and diverts the general purpose. . . . (5) Graduation from an accredited high school should be the only college entrance requirement. (6) It is the business of the college to do its own sifting of material."

student enrolled each semester would comprise a common core, and six hours of electives could be carefully controlled to assure unity of purpose.[42] Cousens believed that a coherent goal was lacking for students in the conventional curriculum who dropped out after preparing "for something that never followed."

Students "rigidly selected" from those earning the A.A. degree would complete two years of more specialized work leading to the Bachelor's degree, such curriculum to include also what ordinarily comprised the first two years of professional training. The third section of the College, the professional schools proper, would offer one- or two-year programs, depending on the field. This capstone of the educational system, with from only twenty-five to no more than one hundred students in each division, would require "a superlative quality of work," and be "the prize for which students compete throughout the first and second sections." He suggested, besides the existing schools of medicine, dentistry, theology, engineering, and the graduate school, schools of law, business, and teaching. This three-step pyramidal academic structure, based strictly on survival of the academic fittest, would all be housed on one campus so that a true university could be said to exist. Cousens was the first to acknowledge that his plan revealed "staggering proportions" and that it would take millions of dollars and probably the span of a generation to create. "A new educational objective" was the great task for the years ahead, and here it was.

The president realized that determination of educational policy was primarily within the province of the faculty, but in what he perceived to be "the present crisis" of higher education, Trustees and faculty had to work together. Possibly a joint committee might criticize and develop his plan. Whether he knew it or not, the way had already been paved for such a procedure. The faculty during Hamilton's administration had been concerned about the lack of close relations between faculty and Trustees, and Bumpus had pointedly called attention to the need for improved communication between the two bodies. There had been little opportunity to con-

[42] The philosophy back of the first two parts of Cousens' proposal was much like that of the "General College" and "University College" movement so popular in the 1930's, particularly among large universities. This movement, in turn, reflected the concept of the "core curriculum" then popular in secondary schools.

sider this subject seriously during the critical years of the First World War. After more normal conditions returned, the Executive Committee in 1919 had taken up the question and had recommended that a standing Trustee Committee on Faculty and Curriculum be created, to confer and consult at least twice a year with a similar committee selected by the faculty. Its purpose was "to promote mutual knowledge, confidence, and co-operation . . . in all matters pertaining to the welfare of the College." The Board took no action on this proposal at the time. Cousens' reorganization plan, presented to the Trustees in 1923, failed to produce even a resolution.

The president did his best to get the faculty interested in general educational problems by appointing a committee to arrange for a series of informal meetings in 1925–26. That effort having produced no tangible results, a Committee on the Reorganization of the College was created in the spring of 1926; a year later a Trustee committee was appointed to work with the faculty committee, but no action was forthcoming from that arrangement either. Cousens reported ruefully to the Trustees that the faculty were "definitely opposed" to reorganizing the undergraduate program as a two-year unit, and there the matter rested.

Cousens' next attempt to introduce educational innovations occurred in 1928–29 but did not represent as radical a set of changes as his previous unsuccessful attempts. He proposed this time to reorganize the curriculum for seniors in liberal arts by relieving them of conventional course requirements, introducing the tutorial system and individual projects in their field of major interest, and requiring a general examination. Nothing having come of this proposal in terms of faculty response, Cousens then used the Trustees as a sounding board and intimated in 1930 that their basic obligation was to study "the ultimate objective of education," while that of the faculty was to make changes "in the methods of education." He was still hopeful that some day he would be able to convince a sufficient number of the right people that a large part of the senior year, at least, in the school of liberal arts could be devoted to distinctly professional training.

The numerous recommendations made by President Cousens for an overhauling, or at least a rethinking, of the curriculum in the school of liberal arts and Jackson may not have fallen on completely deaf ears, but those parts of the Associated Faculties on the Hill failed to be stirred to any great degree. Continuity seemed to have more merit than change. The Hill faculties did review the A.B. and B.S. degree requirements in 1931–32 and did agree to some changes. The most drastic was in the science and social science requirements. Each was reduced from twenty-four semester hours to twelve, and mathematics, a required subject from the day the College opened, now became an optional alternative in meeting the science requirement. President Cousens was "a little sorry" to see the mathematics requirement abandoned, because it seemed "the surest means by which the fact that a student possessed a college mind could be established." He reconciled himself to the change by expressing a belief that curriculum requirements should be expressed in terms of group rather than single courses anyway.[43]

Tufts had always been a source of supply for secondary school teachers, but it was not until the 1930's that pressure was noticeable from state agencies, professional educators, and public school systems to require a significantly large number of education courses to meet certification and accrediting requirements. President Cousens looked with distinct disfavor on the mounting number of so-called professional courses required in education, considering them a distinct threat to "the fundamental principles of a Liberal Arts curriculum." At the same time, in fairness to both the students and the educational system, these requirements had to be satisfied and adequate teacher preparation provided. After much discussion, the faculty in 1933 forbade a student to earn more than eighteen credits (including practice teaching) in the Department of Education.

The most controversial item on the agenda of the faculty in the fall of 1934 was the retention of the classical language requirement for the A.B. degree. Either Greek or Latin had always been required of a candidate for the A.B., and for almost fifty years both

[43] Freshman English remained the exception. The reductions in the so-called "distribution" requirements in the revised curriculum were made up in part by increasing the major concentration to thirty credits. There were unsuccessful efforts to require three sciences for all, including mathematics or logic for B.S. candidates. The latter course, "The Organization of Precise Thinking," was to have been offered by the Mathematics Department for those who found "difficulty, either real or fancied," in mathematics. A move to add psychology to the list of social science options was defeated.

had been required. The requirement by the early 1920's had become a *pro forma* affair, usually completed in the freshman year, and with very few taking any courses in either language beyond the prescribed minimum. The College had been faithful to the idea of the A.B. as a symbol of a classical education, but the latter had become largely a fiction. For some twenty years prior to 1934, only about 10 per cent of the graduates of the school of liberal arts had received the A.B. The overwhelming majority of the students had elected the B.S. degree, if only to escape the classical language requirement. After much debate, it was proposed that the requirements for admission for both the A.B. and the B.S. degree program, so far as the language requirement was concerned, be made identical; as a concession to those students who had earned four units in Latin or three in Greek in high school, they were to be admitted with fourteen units instead of fifteen. It was the consensus of the faculty that both A.B. and B.S. degrees should be granted and that the distinction between the two should rest on something more meaningful than a classical language requirement. But when it came to an actual vote, the faculty at first failed to agree on the specifics and considered no less than five plans for revision of degree requirements. It was finally agreed that the classical language requirement should be dropped both for admission and for either degree program.[44]

President Cousens was receptive to experimentation in yet another direction besides curriculum, but again his plans were not received as enthusiastically by the faculty as he would have wished, and the Trustees did not become sufficiently interested to take any formal action. He had decided by 1932–33 that the academic calendar might be overhauled with profit to all concerned. The two-semester system was, in his estimation, a wasteful and expensive anachronism that resulted in duplication of accounting records and an elaborate plant left idle for much of the year. He came to the conclusion that the division of the academic year into two terms was "a mistake." Because of it, the catalogue was too full of short courses, time was lost at midyears, and grades were being re-

[44] The distinction between the A.B. and the B.S. degrees was determined by the subject in which the students chose to do their major work; they were to indicate at the end of the sophomore year the degree for which they expected to be candidates.

ported more often than necessary. He suggested that the time between semesters in January and February be used partly by the
faculty for individual student conferences instead of for an exces-
sively prolonged examination period.[45]

§   §   §

During his seventeen-year tenure, President Cousens had to
face a multitude of administrative and personnel problems that
arose out of both routine and unusual conditions. Dean Wren
urged in 1933 that a Department of Personnel and Vocational
Guidance be established. He recommended that a psychologist be
employed to assist students with personal problems such as orientation to college life, methods of study, principles of mental hygiene,
and choice of vocation. The president, however, backed away from
such a suggestion, admitting that he was "a skeptic with regard to
much that is being done in the name of personnel work and guidance." He would not object to "an investigation of the subject,"
but that was as far as he would go. The College did introduce a
freshman counseling system in 1936–37 by which each first-year
student was assigned to a member of the faculty, who was to assist in
solving academic and personal problems. The program was so well
received that it became a permanent service offered by the institution.[46] For several years following the First World War a faculty
Committee on Student Employment operated an office primarily to
assist undergraduates in obtaining part-time positions. In order to
render a similar service for alumni, the Trustees in 1936 approved
the creation of a Placement Service "on an experimental basis" for
a six-month period, selecting Lester W. Collins, of the Class of
1901, as director. The experiment was so successful that the Placement Office was continued; it performed a valuable service in
bringing Tufts graduates and prospective employers together. The

[45] This idea bore an interesting general resemblance to the so-called
"reading and consultation period" (optional with the instructor) which went
into effect in 1964–65 as a substitute for regular class work during the "lame
duck" period after the end of the Christmas holidays the first semester and
after the spring holidays the second semester. However, the two-semester academic year was left unchanged.

[46] A double standard at first prevailed in assigning students. No men students were to be assigned to faculty women, but women as well as men could
be assigned to male faculty members.

possibilities of creating the posts of Dean of Men and Director of Admissions were discussed during Cousens' administration, but his opposition to anything that smacked of bureaucracy was a factor in discouraging any action at that time.

The decision to close the pre-medical and pre-dental schools in Boston at the end of 1928 naturally brought important personnel problems, but none proved insurmountable. The matter of how to dispose of the twenty-man faculty of the two preparatory schools raised some questions. All but one of the faculty were on annual appointment, and within a year most had been settled in new positions, largely through the efforts of Dean Wren, who had been responsible for the administration of the two programs. A few were assigned to the Hill schools and some to the medical and dental schools, but the majority, who did not hold advanced degrees, resumed graduate study at various institutions. Dean Wren recognized the wisdom of discontinuing the schools but hastened to point out that due credit had not always been given for the good work done by the staff of the pre-professional programs.[47] The building used for so many years on Mechanic Street in Boston was vacated in the summer of 1928, and the remnants of the pre-professional program were transferred to the so-called Anatomical Building of the medical-dental school.

The most difficult problem arising from the liquidation of the two pre-professional programs was the adjustment of the relationship between the school of liberal arts and the professional schools. This was a particularly vital matter because in 1927 over one-third of the students in the former were enrolled in the combined course, which, after three years on the Hill and four in the medical school, led to the simultaneous award of the B.S. and the M.D.[48] Cousens resolved the problem, at least in his own mind, by af-

[47] A check of the records of the medical school indicated that all of the holders of the M.D. who had received their degrees *summa cum laude* during the period of the two-year pre-medical school's existence had come from its student body and that 80 per cent of all other honors awarded at Commencement to graduates of the medical school were received by those who had been enrolled in the pre-medical course.

[48] The seven-year combined degree program, which had been in effect before the First World War, was reactivated in the mid-1920's but withdrawn in 1929 because relations between the medical school and the school of liberal arts were not sufficiently close to make the arrangement practical.

firming that these two major divisions of the College should be kept separate. Those undergraduates interested in medicine should be restricted in proportion to the total student body. He had already become concerned that in much of the public mind the Hill components of the College were merely adjuncts of the medical and dental schools. He feared that the school of liberal arts would lose its "essential characteristics" and would become "too much like a vocational school." Nevertheless, he was willing to raise to a maximum of 500 the ceiling on liberal arts enrollment in order to absorb at least part of the student population hitherto enrolled in the premedical program. One of the consequences was the perpetuation of the tradition that the College offered a separate and formal premedical curriculum.[49]

A personnel problem that troubled President Cousens greatly and reached considerably beyond the confines of the Tufts campus in 1935–36 was precipitated by a state law requiring a special "loyalty oath" for those teaching in the schools of Massachusetts. It provoked much controversy and resulted in the resignation of two members of the faculty who protested against what they considered to be a violation of the broad principles of academic freedom. Professor Alfred Church Lane, long-time head of the Department of Geology and a prolific scholar of more than local reputation, and Professor Earle Micajah Winslow, chairman of the Department of Economics since 1929, resigned their positions rather than "submit to obligations which in their opinion were subversive to the dignity and freedom of the teaching profession."[50]

[49] Although technically the separate pre-medical course such as existed before 1930 no longer existed, in actuality there was a distinctive curriculum for those planning to enter medical school. During Cousens' administration a separate section in chemistry for pre-medical students was listed in the catalogue, and after 1937 there was provision for "majors in chemistry (pre-medical) and biology (pre-medical)." A new major, "Biology-Chemistry," was created in 1939. A "pre-medical curriculum" was also listed in the catalogue, beginning in 1940.

[50] The Trustees, who accepted with regret the two resignations in the middle of the 1935–36 academic year, expressed their appreciation for valuable services rendered by voting each man a bonus equivalent to his salary for the remainder of the year. Professor Lane immediately made the College a gift of part of his bonus, to be distributed among the remaining members of the Geology Department who were called upon to do extra work because of his retirement from the department.

The law that provoked all the excitement was approved on June 26, 1935. It required all teachers in the state to swear or affirm that they would "support the Constitution of the United States and the Constitution of the Commonwealth of Massachusetts" and would faithfully discharge the duties of their positions according to the best of their ability.[51] The legislation contained the reassuring statement that it would in no way interfere "with the basic principle of the constitution which assures every citizen freedom of thought and speech and the right to advocate changes and improvements in both the state and federal constitutions."

Tufts faculty members were administered the "oath of allegiance" in the fall of 1935 by an officer of the College, in compliance with the new law, but they did not let it pass without comment. The Faculty of Arts and Sciences, after expressing for the record their regret that the law, which they considered "both unwise and unnecessary," had forced the resignation of two men, proceeded to adopt a resolution protesting its enactment and urging its repeal. The faculty argued that "patriotism cannot be fostered by compulsory legislation of this type," that the law had "failed to reveal a single teacher of subversive doctrines," and that it was "mistaken in principle and already deplorable in its results." The protests of the Tufts faculty, of President Cousens, and of the heads of most institutions of higher learning in the state were unavailing. The law stayed on the statute books.[52]

§   §   §

The engineering school, which had undertaken on the eve of the First World War a thorough review of curricula, aims, and philosophy, introduced some changes after a measure of normalcy had been reestablished. The "new type of education," as Dean Anthony described the regime that went into operation in 1919–20, centered around the basic principle that "early training in shop, field, and laboratory for experience and observation" should pre-

[51] *Acts and Resolves*, General Court of Massachusetts, 1935, Chapter 370. The oath, to be signed in duplicate, was made effective in October; all teachers already in service had sixty days to comply with the new law.

[52] A Committee for Peace and Freedom and a student-organized Association for the Repeal of the Teachers Oath Bill were active in tumultuous hearings on a bill to repeal the law in the spring of 1936. The committee compiled a scrapbook of relevant material which is located in the Tufts Archives.

cede detailed study of theory.[53] Experience with the intensive war courses that were opened to promising high school seniors during the war period demonstrated that many could do work which had formerly been reserved for college juniors. These findings, to which were added the recommendations of a Carnegie-financed report of a Committee on Engineering Education on which the Tufts Engineering School was represented, resulted in a simplification of the school's course structure, the organization of an introductory course required of all students, and a general raising of academic standards. The survey course given in the freshman year introduced the student to the nature of the special field of his choice within engineering and was conducted by the project method, which involved design and layout work. Departmental courses, those involving theory, and electives comprised the upperclass years. The requirement of a modern foreign language for an engineering degree was voted out in 1919.

Sufficient time had elapsed by 1924 to evaluate the results of the new engineering curriculum. Dean Anthony found them much to his liking. The giving of the introductory course combining theory with laboratory practice directly related to the field of engineering had maintained the initial interest of students that had led them to choose the profession. "Sophomore slump" had not been eliminated but had been significantly reduced, and the general level of performance had risen noticeably in all classes.[54] The academic level of progression from year to year had been raised to the equivalent of at least one semester. The concentration on the essentials of the sciences during the first three years also gave students greater freedom in choosing electives from among the social sciences and humanities during their senior year. The greatest cause for concern was the chronically high academic mortality rate in the engineering school, which between 1922 and 1924 ran to one-third of the freshman class and to 50 per cent over the four-year curriculum.

[53] Dean Anthony made a report of the new program to the alumni in the *Tufts College Graduate,* Vol. 18 (September-November 1919), pp. 24–29.

[54] Four years of experience led to the raising of the degree requirement to 140 credits and the transfer of chemistry from the sophomore to the freshman year. Mathematics, graphics, and English remained as requirements in the first year.

A perceptible slowing down in the increase of engineering enrollment in the 1920's and a chronic deficit in the school's operations evoked an explanation from Dean Anthony. At the top of the list was the "antiquated and inefficient method of admission" (particularly the foreign language requirement), which might be well adapted to liberal arts but which was quite unsuitable for technical students.[55] Too much stress was being laid on the "misleading paper records of the certificating and examination boards" and not enough on the real abilities and character of the students. A second factor making for lagging enrollment was the failure to advertise. The third limitation of the school, as Dean Anthony saw it, was the need of a head of the Electrical Engineering Department who had the professional reputation outside the College enjoyed by the late Professor Hooper. A new man to head the Civil Engineering Department was also needed, but not as critically. The dean hinted that the appointees should have "administrative ability and a personality such as would be suitable to serve as dean of the Engineering School." Anthony resigned in September 1927, after an association of thirty-three years with the College. Professor Edwin B. Rollins of the Electrical Engineering Department became acting dean of the engineering school and of Bromfield-Pearson until George Preston Bacon assumed his duties in the fall of 1929.[56]

The professional field receiving the greatest attention in the 1930's fell within the province of the Electrical Engineering Department, where much valuable research was conducted in the so-called Electro-Technical Laboratory located in what became known as North Hall. The bulk of the research was financed by commercial firms and was made virtually a self-supporting unit. It might be said that in this field Tufts really began the practice of conducting sponsored research which became so important after the Second World War. The larger educational problem facing the engineering school in the 1930's was how to strike a balance between general

[55] When Dean Anthony submitted his last annual report before his retirement in 1926, he reiterated the need for continuing the Bromfield-Pearson School so that deserving young men who were not allowed to pursue a college course because they could not meet "the arbitrary standards for admission to college" could still receive an engineering education.

[56] At the same time, Start House, a faculty home which had later served as a dormitory, was set aside as the residence of the dean of the engineering school.

education and technical training for the prospective engineer. This engaged the attention of both Dean Bacon and President Cousens. They concurred in desiring to deemphasize the technical aspects of the curriculum, particularly in the first year or so, and to place greater stress on broad preparation than on narrow specialization. The introductory course established immediately after the First World War had been abandoned in 1930, and electives of any kind almost completely disappeared.[57]

There was another aspect besides educational theory involved in a reconsideration of the engineering curriculum. The enrollment in the engineering school continued to decrease in the 1930's, and the chronic annual deficit in its operations continued to average between $25,000 and $30,000. A general course in engineering might appeal to a category of potential students not otherwise interested in specialized training. Dean Bacon recognized two practical problems under the existing system of providing more opportunity for "cultural studies." One was schedule conflicts, arising from the fact that programs were arranged in the arts and sciences and engineering divisions quite independently, without any attempt to coordinate or cooperate. The other was the discouraging barricade of prerequisites the engineering student had to hurdle before he could take most liberal arts courses of his first choice. President Cousens also insisted that liberal arts courses should not be offered both in the school of liberal arts and in the engineering school, for this produced wasteful duplication. Consequently, if a general course were organized, much of the work would have to be conducted by teachers with primary appointments in the school of liberal arts.

The engineering school in the mid-1930's embarked on the most thorough self-assessment it had yet undertaken. The prompting came from two directions. One was the creation in the 1930's of a nation-wide Engineering Council for Professional Development, which undertook to set up standards for licensing engineers

[57] The standard freshman program became physics, chemistry, mathematics, graphics, and English for all engineering students, who then chose their specific field of concentration at the beginning of the sophomore year. One hour of surveying was also added for all programs in the engineering school, and the modern foreign language requirement (French or German) was temporarily restored in 1930 for the chemical engineering program only.

and arrange for the accrediting of schools of engineering. The other moving force, coming from within the school itself, was the appointment of a new dean in the fall of 1936 to replace Bacon, who retired at the age of seventy. Professor Harry Poole Burden announced at the outset that he had "some rather definite ideas concerning the future of the school" and proceeded to outline some of them before he had held the deanship two months.[58] The first requirement was to formulate a set of aims and objectives for the school. A comprehensive study was naturally in order.

Both the new dean and President Cousens looked with mixed feelings on the new Engineering Council's efforts. Cousens was particularly agitated because he was positive that his goal of liberalizing the engineering curriculum by including a higher proportion of non-technical courses would be doomed. He feared, judging from the College's experiences with the accrediting agencies in medicine and dentistry, that the engineering school curriculum might be forced by an outside agency into a straitjacket quite contrary to the philosophy of permissiveness which he favored. The engineering school was visited in the fall of 1935 by representatives of the Council. They found the staff generally adequate but too prone to carry professional autonomy to an extreme. There was insufficient attention to such subjects as English, mathematics, and economics and too great an emphasis on applied subjects, such as drawing, too early in the program of study. The buildings and equipment drew the most criticism. They were "said to be the worst with but one exception of any engineering school in New England." Dean Burden not only considered the adverse comments of the visiting committee "justifiable to a marked degree" but proceeded to lengthen the list of weaknesses. He would have no difficulty in putting to good use some $350,000 if that amount could be found.

Three of the four branches of engineering (civil, mechanical, and electrical) received certification for a probationary period of two years. Chemical engineering, the most popular course in the engineering school at the time, did not pass muster. The satisfaction of engineering needs involved an amount of money so far beyond the capacity of the current budget for the school that the only

[58] Professor Burden had joined the staff of the school in 1913 and since 1930 had held professorial rank in the Department of Civil Engineering.

recourse was a campaign, endorsed by the Trustees in 1937, to secure a special endowment. The engineering school was given two years to put its house in order if it wished to receive unconditional certification. The new dean had a challenging situation on his hands.

§   §   §

Other parts of the College on the Hill during the Cousens administration led a much more placid existence than fell to the lot of the engineering school. After the campus had returned to something resembling routine in 1920, Jackson College maintained the increased enrollment that had marked the war years. The most important administrative changes were the creation of the office of vice-dean in 1922, which was capably occupied by Mrs. Caroline M. Robinson, and the resignation of Dean Davies after fifteen years of service as the first head of the women's division.[59] A joint Trustee-faculty committee was appointed in the winter of 1924 to find a successor. Tufts was fortunate in its choice. Miss Edith Linwood Bush came from a family overflowing with Tufts graduates and was herself a member of the Class of 1903. She had served as housemistress at Start House for many years before assuming the deanship in 1925 and had taught mathematics since her initial appointment in 1920.[60] She served Jackson College and the Tufts community with devotion and high competency for a quarter of a century — the longest tenure of any dean of Jackson for its first fifty years. The contributions of this distinguished graduate with honors in mathematics and French were well put when her Alma Mater awarded her the honorary degree of Doctor of Letters in 1942. "As a wise leader in our campus life," the citation read, "you accomplish with quiet deftness the magic of solving constructively with mathematical exactness and sympathetic human insight the living problems of your important office."

President Cousens' policy of integrating all Hill divisions of the College was illustrated by his attempt to identify Jackson more closely with the rest of the institution. At his suggestion, a Trustee

[59] Mrs. Robinson served as acting dean for the second semester of 1921–22. She was for many years supervisor of Metcalf Hall and Jackson dining facilities. The office of vice-dean was created in part as a means by which the College could express its appreciation for her services.

[60] It was at the time of her election as dean that the Dearborn house on Professors Row was set aside as the residence of the dean of women.

committee investigated the possibility of changing the name of the women's division. The upshot of their deliberations was the decision to retain the name "Jackson College for Women" in compliance with both the wishes of Cornelia Maria Jackson and the legislative act that had created it in 1910, but to add in official publications and in publicity the subheading "The Department of Women in Tufts College." The history of Jackson College during Cousens' administration was notably stable. With a curriculum identical to that of the school of liberal arts, and with its own residential housing and administration, it lived a life of coexistence with remarkably little friction or crisis.

One important service for Jackson students, developed during Cousens' administration was an infirmary, which for forty years was located in a frame building constructed in 1894 as a fraternity house.[61] Not until 1922 was Jackson served by a resident nurse, who spread her efforts over the seven dormitories then used for women and attempted to follow the instructions of as many as twelve doctors at a time who were called at the individual preference of the students. In 1927–28 the medical supervisor for the men was employed also to oversee the health needs of Jackson, assisted by one or two nurses.

§　§　§

After experiencing many of the same difficulties that beset other divisions of the College during the First World War, the Crane Theological School returned to peacetime conditions with hope and confidence for the future. The enrollment (twenty-four) in the fall of 1923 was the largest since Dean McCollester had taken up his duties in 1912. The relations between the Crane School and the rest of the institution had become so close that it was in reality

---

[61] This structure, on Sawyer Avenue, was built to house Heth Aleph Res, a divinity school fraternity. Between the late 1890's and 1915 it was used for various purposes, including faculty residence. It became a combined Jackson dormitory and infirmary in 1916 and was known as the Gamma House until it became a dormitory of the Eliot-Pearson (Nursery Training) School in 1955; thereafter it was known as Bartol House. For over a decade after Hooper House on Professors Row became the men's infirmary (in 1949), an enclosed passageway connected the two buildings so that the same nursing staff could serve both. Between 1933 and 1949, Hooper House was the headquarters for the Department of Education, and in 1956 it was made the University Infirmary.

"a department of Tufts." The instructional staff taught some classes open to all students, and a few of the faculty of the school of arts and sciences such as Professor William F. Wyatt, chairman of the Department of Greek, offered special courses for the benefit of Crane students. Dr. J. A. C. Fagginger Auer was added to the faculty in 1923–24, as Professor of Church History and Philosophy of Religion, and also taught in the Department of Modern Languages in the school of liberal arts. Professor Bruce W. Brotherston, who resigned from St. Lawrence University to join the Tufts staff in 1930, taught courses in philosophy in both the theological school and the school of liberal arts.

At a conference in the fall of 1924, alumni of the Crane School agreed that a better name for the school would be "Tufts College School of Religion, Crane Foundation." President Cousens also favored the change of name. There were two justifications given for the proposal. The identification with Tufts, which had become much closer over the years, should be recognized in the name of the school. The growing emphasis on social service work and the development of the field of religious education also made a more comprehensive description than "theological" appropriate. In 1925 the school became officially the "Tufts College School of Religion — Crane Theological School," after extensive discussions, including a conference with the widow of Albert Crane. Offerings in religious education were greatly expanded when Rev. John M. Ratcliff was added to the faculty in the fall of 1927.

Dean McCollester, always on the alert for means by which Crane could broaden its services, suggested that the scope of the school could be easily enlarged if an undergraduate Department of Religion staffed by Crane faculty were created and if the school concentrated on professional training at the graduate level. Dean McCollester in the mid-twenties saw a larger field than ever before opening for the school in liberal religious training with the location of the Meadville Theological School in Chicago and the increasing emphasis placed on theological research rather than on the ministry as a profession by the Harvard Divinity School. The dean recognized an opportunity thereby to help educate those in the Unitarian and Congregational Churches respectively. The work of the Universalist Church would always be the "first responsibility" of Crane, but associated ministries would be welcome. Like the en-

*The War Memorial Steps with Fischer Arcade
connecting Miner Hall with Paige Hall and Crane Chapel*

gineering school at about the same time, the Crane School saw the advantages of increased advertising. Students from denominations other than Universalist had begun to put in an appearance by 1926.[62]

Housing for the Crane School was a sore point for many years after the First World War, for Miner and Paige Halls were diverted to other uses when the College was turned over largely to military uses and were not returned to the school after the war. Crane headquarters remained in Packard Hall until 1927 and in the midtwenties Paige Hall became temporarily a Jackson dormitory; Crane students were housed in Dean Hall. Both the dean and the Board of Visitors to Crane were strongly in favor of having a new building constructed for the exclusive use of the school, but its size

[62] Most of the students enrolled in the school in 1928–29 intended to enter the Universalist ministry, but there were several training for the Unitarian, and one each for the Episcopal, Methodist, and Congregational ministry. The growing cordiality and cooperation between the school and the Unitarian denomination was sufficiently important to deserve special mention in Dean McCollester's last annual report, in the fall of 1932.

did not seem to warrant such an expense.[63] Instead of a new building, the Tufts School of Religion received, between 1927 and 1929, the first floor of a renovated Miner Hall, a chapel attached to Paige Hall, and the Fischer Arcade connecting the two main buildings.[64] It was at the same time that the enlarged gateway and the Memorial Steps leading down to College Avenue on the easterly slope of the campus were authorized. The addition of the wing housing the Crane chapel made possible the utilization of the ground floor for the Crane theological library which had been located in Packard. Dean McCollester had earlier proposed that the theological collection be housed in Eaton Library and that no distinction be made in the rules governing the use of books. This was another expression of the fact that Crane was an intimate part of the College.

The School of Religion, housed in rehabilitated and enlarged quarters and appealing increasingly to those outside the Universalist denomination, prospered in the 1920's under the leadership of Dean McCollester. The enrollment had climbed to thirty-six by 1928–29, and it was not necessary to raise tuition for new students until 1931 (from $250 to $300). The makeup of the relatively small faculty underwent but few changes. In 1931 Rev. Alfred S. Cole replaced Dr. F. O. Hall in the Department of Homiletics. Relations with the school of liberal arts remained generally satisfactory, although the Crane faculty, after reviewing its own curriculum, found that there were still areas of pre-ministerial preparation at the undergraduate level that needed more attention than was possible by adhering strictly to the A.B. requirements. Consideration was given in 1928–29 to creating a distinctive undergraduate degree (Ph.B.) for the Crane School's undergraduates, while con-

[63] President Cousens, like several of his predecessors, was in favor of razing Packard Hall but wished to use the space between East and West Halls for an Administration Building or a Student Union Building, or both, rather than building a new home for Crane. He contemplated the possibility of returning Crane to West Hall, where the divinity school had resided before Miner and Paige Halls were built.

[64] Rev. Theodore A. Fischer, a graduate of the divinity school in 1896, was a generous contributor to the College and provided the money for the arcade. The Department of Modern Languages occupied the second floor of Miner Hall and was still located there in the mid-1960's. Packard Hall became the headquarters of the Department of English.

tinuing to award the S.T.B. for those completing the professional course.

With an eye toward strengthening the work of the school in new directions and developing new programs, the Trustees created the office of vice-dean in 1929, on the recommendation of Dean McCollester, and elected Professor Skinner to the new post. The dean left no doubt that he was grooming the new vice-dean to take his place eventually, and Cousens added his blessing by noting that the elevation of Skinner was "wise and necessary and desirable." Dean McCollester submitted his resignation in the fall of 1932, effective the following February, and Vice-Dean Skinner took his place as planned.[65] The dean could retire with much satisfaction, for during his administration he had seen the Crane School develop from a group of four students in makeshift quarters to forty-five students in adequate and attractive dormitories and classrooms. The Trustees in 1935 approved a proposal by Dean Skinner in behalf of the Crane faculty to honor the retired dean by undertaking to raise a fund with which to endow the Lee S. McCollester Professorship of Biblical Literature.

Throughout his presidency Cousens maintained a sympathetic interest in the Tufts School of Religion and its problems, but he did not hesitate to recognize its weaknesses. One of the policies of the new dean which he enthusiastically approved was the admission of students who could pay "actual money for tuition." It had always seemed to the president that the extension of so much financial aid to theological students in the past had "tended to pauperize them and resulted in a general lowering of the calibre of the students while in college and in their professional standing after leaving college." Cousens was also dissatisfied with the combined School of Liberal Arts-School of Religion degree program, preferring the creation of a special degree for those registered in the Crane School who were "not ambitious to pursue the long course for the degree of Bachelor of Sacred Theology." He could not be satisfied until

[65] McCollester did not sever his connection with the College but continued on the staff as Professor of Biblical Literature and Dean Emeritus and adviser to the Crane staff until his death in 1943. He also continued for several years as the College chaplain. His work in Biblical literature was continued by Rolland Emerson Wolfe, who joined the Crane staff in 1934.

Crane became a *bona fide* graduate school. Cousens was heartened by the expressed determination of Dean Skinner to weed out those who did not seem intellectually or temperamentally suited to the ministry. The dean promised that the final result would be "a better grade of student than we have had in recent years." Skinner was perfectly aware that the peculiar system of double enrollment resulted in the admission of students who did not always possess the formal academic qualifications expected of liberal arts students, but he was positive that some of the School of Religion students who did not meet conventional requirements were among the best men in the school. The outspoken dean not only stood as the champion of his students but called to the president's attention the latter's own criticism of rigid entrance requirements that blunted or even blocked the chance of promising students to obtain an education beyond the secondary school.[66]

§ § §

The Tufts Graduate School, never very large in proportion to the undergraduate schools, was even further reduced in size after the First World War. There were only ten students enrolled in 1919–20, of whom half were in the Department of History. Five years later the number was twelve, registered in six departments; only seven were first-year students. The abandonment of the Ph.D. program in 1907 had been one factor, and the failure of the school to be known outside the walls of the College had been another.[67] A decision was made in the fall of 1921 to grant no more Master's degrees *in absentia,* and this was expected by some to be a further deterrent. The long-standing privilege open to alumni of obtaining a professional engineering degree (Mechanical, Civil, Electrical, or Chemical Engineer) after four or five years in the field, the presentation of a thesis, and an oral examination was therefore withdrawn.

Professor Fay, then dean of the graduate school, was so un-

[66] The Crane faculty in 1935–36 were proud of the fact that seven of the forty-five students in their school had attained superior academic averages that year — a much higher proportion of students than in the school of liberal arts.

[67] There was only one recorded instance during Cousens' administration when the re-offering of the Ph.D. was considered. The idea was voted down by the graduate school faculty before it could even be referred to a committee for consideration.

happy at this decision, which had been made by a bare majority of the graduate faculty, that he resigned. He was replaced in 1924 by Professor Herbert V. Neal of the Biology Department.[68] Fay argued that, aside from depriving qualified alumni in engineering of an opportunity to obtain a professional degree, the residence requirement automatically put an extra burden on the faculty, who supervised graduate work as an additional duty anyway. He believed that if the Master's degree *in absentia* were not restored, the graduate school would have to be eliminated. His fears proved groundless, for graduate enrollment held its own and in fact increased slightly in the next decade.[69]

Opinion was unanimous that the presence of the Braker and other graduate fellows, beginning in 1925–26, redounded to the great benefit of both the College and the graduate school.[70] The great majority of candidates for the Master of Arts degree in the 1930's intended to enter the teaching profession; in fact, such a high proportion became secondary school teachers that candidates were encouraged as a matter of course to take at least one semester's work in educational psychology. To accommodate even further such prospective candidates, including those handicapped by an eighteen-hour limit on education courses for undergraduates, the graduate faculty (with Trustee approval) began to offer the new degree of Master of Education in 1933–34. Thirty semester hours in the Department of Education and allied departments were required, twenty of which had to be earned in residence. Students had to attain a minimum grade of "B" in all courses to meet the degree requirements. Both a thesis and an oral examination were required, the thesis to be part of the thirty-credit requirement. A reading knowledge of one or more modern foreign languages was expected if necessary to develop thesis problems.[71]

[68] At the same time, the appointment of members of the graduate school faculty was assumed by the Trustees; this practice lasted through the Cousens administration. The number of graduate faculty in the 1930's averaged twenty-five, including the president and deans; all members had either Ph.D.'s or some degree of professorial rank, or both.

[69] In the fall of 1926 there were nineteen graduate students in residence, registered in five of the fifteen departments which then offered graduate work.

[70] The Braker Fellowship program is discussed in the next chapter.

[71] Admission to the graduate school in any department required "an average of 'C' or better during their whole college course and an average

The Trustees helped to counteract the effects of financial depression in the 1930's by allowing recent graduates of the College unable to secure employment to continue their education in the graduate school without payment of tuition, provided they were in residence. Tuition for other graduate students was raised from $250 to $300, effective in 1935–36. The graduate faculty also liberalized its entrance requirements in 1931–32 by admitting candidates of high quality from any institution on the "accepted" list of the Association of American Universities rather than imposing conditions because the applicant's undergraduate courses did not include precisely the subjects required for the first degree at Tufts. It had been customary up to 1933 to admit without conditions only graduates of liberal arts colleges.[72]

Enrollment in the graduate school remained at a satisfactory level even during the 1930's, but the whole development of the school represented a somewhat artificial situation. It was not so much strong and growing in itself as propped up by special arrangements of various sorts. The Teaching Fellows in the Economics, English, and History Departments added significantly to the numbers in the graduate school, but when these programs were curtailed, the school would have virtually disappeared if the Trustees had not provided free tuition to all unemployed graduates who wished more formal education, and if a high proportion of the registrants had not been secondary school teachers who received tuition readjustments because their schools provided practice teaching facilities for Tufts students. Of the fifty-five students enrolled in the graduate school in 1934–35, only seven paid any tuition, and

---

higher than 'C' during the last two years." No applicant could have considered this an unreasonably high expectation in view of the minimum grade requirement of "B" in all courses counted toward any of the three Master's degrees being offered by the mid-1930's. The graduate faculty had voted in 1923 that "no work shall be accepted for the Master's degree for which a grade lower than 'B' has been attained."

[72] Some local exceptions were provided. Beginning in 1920, holders of the S.T.B. from the Crane School could become candidates for the M.A. degree. At the same time, it was provided that holders of the Tufts B.S. degree could be admitted on the same basis as A.B. degree holders. With the introduction of the Master of Education degree, arrangements were made for graduates of the Tufts Engineering School who had not acquired competency in a foreign language to become candidates for the new degree.

nine were special students who were not candidates for a degree.[73] No extra financial burden was imposed on the College because of this, for the faculty merely absorbed the graduate students as an extra teaching load, without extra compensation. At the same time the graduate faculty, with a view toward raising standards, voted to grant credit only for work done in a graduate school, except by special vote of the faculty, and to allow no academic credit toward a graduate degree for work done by special students. This sharply reduced the number of special students (non-degree candidates), who in effect had been placed in that category because they could not meet the regular entrance requirements.[74]

Dr. Herbert V. Neal resigned as dean of the graduate school in 1935 and was replaced by Dr. Charles Gott, Fletcher Professor of English Literature and chairman of the Department of English. Dean Gott was as firmly convinced as his predecessor that the standards of the graduate school had to be raised as well as maintained, and was as disturbed as President Cousens about another trend that had become noticeable by 1935–36. A large number of the candidates for the Master of Education degree were teachers in service, many of whom were provisionally admitted and were discovered after further investigation not to be able to meet regular admission requirements. Twenty-five of the forty-five graduate students were enrolled in the Department of Education, and Cousens feared that such numbers from this department would overwhelm the graduate school. The eventual solution, as he saw it, was to establish a separate graduate department for the training of teachers, for in no other way could satisfactory standards be maintained in the regular graduate school. At the same time, such a step would create another

[73] Many of these special students were college graduates who had failed to be admitted to medical school and hoped that additional study would enhance their opportunities for eventual admission. Dean Neal was firmly opposed to allowing the graduate school to function as this kind of preparatory agency.

[74] These votes of 1935 and 1936 also brought to an effective end the combined Bachelor's-Master's program that had been adopted in the late nineteenth century, but for which there had been no candidates for several years. Prior to 1934 it had been customary to allow students who had accumulated more credits than were required for the Bachelor's degree to use the extra credits toward the second degree.

543

The Medford campus in the 1880's

dilemma by decreasing graduate enrollment below a "reasonable minimum." There seemed to be no easy solution at hand.

§　§　§

President Cousens had ambitious plans for the expansion and beautification of the physical plant of his Alma Mater. When speaking to the Boston Tufts Club in the winter of 1922, he expressed his desire that the campus might some day be described by the phrase "The Hill a Garden." The slogan was immediately associated with his plans for landscape improvements. Not all of his projects were carried out in his lifetime. Nonetheless, the record of accomplishment was impressive in spite of delays and difficulties created in almost every instance by that most effective of roadblocks — paucity of funds. Throughout the economically depressed 1930's the College conducted its building program with whatever private resources it could summon. The question was raised in 1935 as to the propriety of applying for aid from the federal government under one or more of the numerous public works programs, but the Tufts Trustees voted that "as a matter of principle" it was not desirable to seek such aid for the construction of new buildings. The College seems to have done surprisingly well in expanding and improving its physical plant during a period of economic malaise by following the philosophy of "Hooverism."

The first problems of campus planning and building utilization faced by the College during Cousens' administration were associated with the return to peacetime conditions after the First World War. Because Curtis Hall had been turned over to military uses, the College bookstore was temporarily housed on the second floor of Ballou Hall. To relieve the resulting congestion, the bookstore was moved to the basement of Eaton Library, where it remained until 1948.[75]

Less than six months after he had been unanimously elected president (June 8, 1920), Cousens was apprising the Trustees of the need for an additional women's dormitory and for a combined Administration-Student Union building. That portion of the Stearns estate north of the Hill came into the possession of the College in 1920. It consisted of vacant land and the decrepit remains of the old Stearns homestead, which were removed the following year. In 1921 it was decided to set the land aside for the use of the Physical Education Department.[76] The president also saw the advantage of obtaining several acres of abandoned clay pits across the street from the Stearns property — popularly known as the "Brick Yards" because of the manufacturing operations conducted there for many

[75] The quarters were so cramped, even in the library, that the expedient was tried in the spring of 1923 of selling textbooks directly in the classrooms, with bookstore staff in attendance. This experiment failed, largely because no one had thought to officially notify either faculty or students of the plan in advance. In 1922 the operation of the bookstore, which had been under the supervision of a faculty Committee of Books and Supplies, which in turn had been responsible for arranging for student management, was taken over directly by the Trustees. Under the new arrangement the facility was to be managed and conducted "without profit for the benefit of the students." Joseph W. Morton was the first bookstore manager; he was replaced in 1923 by Dirrell D. Sample. A bookstore was operated for many years in Boston for the convenience of medical and dental students but was closed in 1931 because it seemed "impossible to run it without a loss."

[76] A piece of vacant land adjoining the Stearns property and purchased as part of the property of the American Radio and Research Corporation (AMRAD) in 1925 was set aside for the same purpose. The AMRAD buildings were leased back to the Corporation until it moved from the campus in 1931.

years.[77] This area too could be converted (as most of it actually was) into athletic fields after proper filling and grading.

President Cousens, anxious to enclose as well as beautify the Hill campus, devoted much attention to the construction of gates and fences. The Gager Gate, dedicated in 1921, was placed at the head of the Campus Drive and across from the site of the old reservoir.[78] In 1924 Eugene B. Bowen, a newly elected Trustee from the Class of 1876, presented, for the west end of the campus, a brick and ironwork gate bearing his name. This became part of the brick and iron fence which had long been desired as an enclosure for the main campus and to which sections were contributed by the Class of 1899 as part of its twenty-fifth anniversary celebration and by numerous other classes beginning with the Class of 1924.[79] Simultaneously (in 1923–24) a six-hole golf course was laid out on the south side of the campus on the site of part of the old athletic fields, and Professor Robert C. Givler of the Philosophy Department became one of the leading organizers of golfing activities. The golf course, the number of holes of which varied over the years, finally disappeared when new buildings encroached on the former cow pasture after the Second World War. The Starkweather Gate was added to the easterly side of the Hill in 1926, and that entrance was completed within the next three years by terraced steps leading up to Miner and Paige Halls and the top of the Hill. In order to keep the campus as well maintained as possible and to care for the rapidly growing physical plant, the annual budget for the Depart-

[77] The College secured an option to buy in 1921, and the purchase was authorized in 1925 but was delayed until the following year. The 450,000 square feet was bought for $52,500. Additional property adjoining the clay pits was acquired in 1927 in order to improve and straighten existing boundaries. Cousens contributed the funds for this purchase out of his own pocket.

[78] The gate was donated by the parents of Harold A. Gager, who had been a member of the Class of 1921 but had died before his graduation. The brick-columned structure had to be removed in 1963 because of extensive construction on the Hill and because its narrow aperture no longer sufficed for conveyances which had to enter the campus.

[79] The Trustees voted in 1926 to construct ten sections of the campus fence to represent the Classes of 1857 through 1866. By the 1960's the fence had been almost completed around two sides of the campus and a part of a third, while at the same time parts of it were being removed to expedite both pedestrian and vehicular traffic.

A winter scene showing the Gager Gate (now razed) in the 1930's

ment of Grounds and Buildings had skyrocketed to more than $100,000 by 1926.

The problem of the ramshackle, unsightly, and completely inadequate old chemistry laboratory building had dogged the College for decades before Cousens became president. The complaints were as loud and as persistent in the early twentieth century as those voiced by President Capen in 1876 when the chemistry facilities in the College Edifice had been outgrown. "Some of the Professors can find no place for the soles of their feet, but are obliged to wander about in the peripatetic fashion, from room to room, as they may chance to find one vacant." There had been rumors in 1911 that Frederick Stark Pearson, one-time teacher at Tufts and a Trustee from 1892 until 1909, might have contributed "a gift of a chemical laboratory," but even if that had been the case, the financial state of the College at the time would have prevented it from taking advantage of the possibility.[80] President Bumpus had been very much aware of the need for a new building, but the estimated cost of $75,000 to $100,000 in 1916 was beyond the reach of the College. Even the idea of another "temporary" building constructed

[80] Professor Durkee had been the source of the Trustees' information.

alongside the existing structure at a cost not to exceed $15,000 had to be discarded. The efforts of a Trustee committee in 1916 to raise money for a new building were side tracked by the untimely intrusion of the First World War although they did make sufficient progress to consider a site for the new structure; it would have been located on the exact spot where the new University Library was constructed between 1963 and 1965. When the campus returned to peacetime demeanor and appearance after 1919, the Chemistry Department again found itself in the unenviable position of being forced to use part of Curtis Hall as a lecture room. The chemistry laboratory suffered a fire in the spring of 1919 and the *Tufts Weekly* voiced an opinion shared by many: "The firemen of Medford and Somerville very shortsightedly saved the Chem. Lab. from burning up last year, and now that building . . . with the aid of a few soap-boxes and a couple of old railroad ties has been completely remodeled."

After years of delay, a new chemistry laboratory was finally authorized late in 1919. The site selected two years before was abandoned in favor of a new location.[81] But progress in moving the plans off the drawing board was painfully slow, for much of the effort and money intended through the Tufts Foundation for capital outlay had to be diverted to an attempt to meet the pledge of the General Education Board to help raise salaries. As a consequence, the start of actual construction was delayed until the spring of 1922. In the interval, yet another site had been selected, on the southerly side of the campus and across from the faculty residences on Talbot Avenue.

The naming of the new building was left by the Trustees to the discretion of the president. On his recommendation, it became the "Fred Stark Pearson Memorial Laboratory" in 1926, three years after it had been dedicated (on Alumni Day, June 16, 1923).[82]

[81] The special committee to develop plans for the new building established as the tentative site in 1920 the corner of Packard Avenue and Professors Row. If this plan had been carried out, it would have meant the moving or razing of the Zeta Psi chapter house, which the Trustees had sold to the fraternity less than a year before.

[82] A separate account of $35,000, known as the Pearson Memorial Fund, had been created within the Tufts Foundation endowment fund. Trustee Robert Brown and Professor Durkee of the Chemistry Department were largely responsible for the success in raising the Pearson Fund.

Pearson Memorial (Chemistry) Laboratory, dedicated in 1923

Pearson had been an alumnus (Class of 1883) who had achieved international prominence in the field of electrical engineering and urban transportation. He had lost his life in the sinking of the *Lusitania* early in the First World War.

President Cousens drew heavily on the talents and services of the Tufts Engineering School faculty in campus planning, including the design and supervision of building construction, alterations, and repairs. Professor Edwin H. Wright of the Civil and Structural Engineering Department planned and supervised the addition to Richardson House (a Jackson dormitory), and he and Professor Edward H. Rockwell designed the Pearson Memorial Laboratory. They received extra compensation for their services. Professor Edwin B. Rollins of the Electrical Engineering Department and acting dean of the engineering school between 1926 and 1929 rendered similar services in regard to the heating, lighting, and power requirements of the campus.

The aging original chemistry laboratory building, instead of being torn down, received another series of face-liftings and new occupants. It was used for a time in the early 1920's by the SAVEM Economy Products Company and in 1930 became officially the

"Music House." Even though intended as only a temporary headquarters for the Department of Music, the building was far superior to the quarters formerly occupied by that department on the
third floor of Goddard Gymnasium. No one could say that the College had failed to get its money's worth out of the old chemistry
laboratory. In 1930 space was also provided in it for the use of the
Drama Department, and the basement was fitted up as the hydraulic laboratory of the engineering school.[83]

Cousens' constant aim was the unification and centralization
of the operations on the Hill to turn it into a more cohesive academic community. He wished to abandon the "cottage" system
of dormitories for Jackson College and to construct one large dormitory that would fulfill enrollment needs for at least ten years and
simultaneously release the frame dwellings occupied by women so
that a higher proportion of the faculty could live on or near the
campus.[84] Cousens had to remain content until 1927 with a con-
tinuation of the "cottage" system, for after the Delta Tau Delta
fraternity moved to Professors Row in 1920, the home built in 1895
by Professor Frank P. Graves became a Jackson dormitory, and an
addition was made to Richardson House in 1923 to accommodate
twenty students.[85] The need of a large dormitory to centralize at
least partially the scattered Hill residences of Jackson women was
met in 1925 by receipt of a bequest from Martha Stratton Ensign,
of which $50,000 was to be used to construct a dormitory to be
named "Stratton Hall."[86] Litigation involving the estate delayed
construction of the new women's dormitory until 1927. Pressure for
more dormitory space for Jackson College continued to mount,
even during the depression years, and in 1937 the Trustees authorized the construction of a new wing for Metcalf Hall which
approximately doubled the capacity of the existing building.

[83] Until 1930 engineering students had been required for several years to
make an annual pilgrimage to Worcester Polytechnic Institute in order to
study the application of principles of hydraulics.

[84] In order to encourage as many of the faculty as possible to live near
the College, the Trustees restated their long-standing policy of selling land to
the faculty under certain conditions and liberalized the provisions so that land
acquired from the College could be mortgaged by the occupants.

[85] Graves House became, in 1955, the residence of Dr. Clark W. Heath,
Director of Health Services.

[86] Mrs. Ensign's legacy was supplemented from the estate of her father.

When discussions were in progress in the winter of 1925 about building a men's dormitory from part of the proceeds of the Fletcher estate, the architectural firm of Andrews, Jones, Biscoe, and Whitmore were given permission "to make a general study for the development and expansion of the College plant at the Hill," on the presumption that they would become architects for the institution.[87] Fletcher Hall was completed in 1926 at a cost of a quarter of a million dollars and, with a new dormitory for women, helped to make Tufts more of a residential college and less of a "trolley-car university."[88] The president, with an eye to the future, saw the need in 1926 for at least two additional dormitories, a new gymnasium for men, separate buildings for the Departments of Music and Dramatics, a physics laboratory, more adequate housing for the Crane School, and better facilities for College assemblies for faculty, students, and outside speakers. An amount in excess of $2,000,000 was called for.

President Cousens' desire to make at least one addition to the physical plant each year during his administration was not always realized, although it came close to being achieved. The record was almost blemished in 1933, but authorization of a greenhouse behind Barnum Museum for the use of the Biology Department saved the day. In 1934–35 the east wing of Barnum Museum that had been projected in the donor's original gift in the late nineteenth century was finally constructed. The bulk of the total cost ($50,000) was financed by $38,000 of accumulated income from the Barnum Fund.[89]

[87] This was the second survey of the Hill grounds and buildings for which Cousens was responsible; he had had a survey made in 1921 to project possible developments for the next fifty years. Among the buildings designed by Andrews, Jones, Biscoe, and Whitmore were Stratton and Fletcher Halls and a new house for the Theta Delta Chi fraternity. In 1926 they prepared a set of drawings for a medical school on the Hill. As has been indicated elsewhere, the possibility of placing the school on the Hill was widely and seriously discussed in the mid-1920's.

[88] In 1923 the following percentages of students lived off the campus: liberal arts, 51 per cent; Jackson, 29 per cent; engineering, 62 per cent. There were no dormitories for students in the medical and dental schools at the time, and no provision for graduate students.

[89] The new wing was named for Fred D. Lambert, a long-time member of the Biology Department. It was to have been faced with red brick which would in no way have harmonized with the stonework of the original building.

In 1932 the firm of Andrews, Jones, Biscoe, and Whitmore prepared a long-range plan for the Hill grounds and buildings which made possible some interesting comparisons with what was actually done in later years. They foresaw the need for an enlargement of Eaton Library "before many years" and recommended that Packard Hall be moved back and two larger buildings constructed between East and West Halls. They suggested that one be the headquarters of the new Fletcher School of Law and Diplomacy, which was scheduled to be opened in 1933. It would be built directly across from Ballou Hall, which in turn would have a new portico on the north side to match the one originally constructed on the opposite side.[90] Barnum Museum and West Hall were considered "the poorest buildings on the campus, both in their construction and their interior arrangements as well as in their exterior design." The architectural firm advised "never spending money to remodel them," for they should be replaced by better buildings. They proposed the same fate for Curtis Hall, which in their estimation was "not well planned for any purpose and could some time well be given up and torn down."[91]

The architects suggested a "monumental building" at the foot of the Hill and across from the Memorial Steps. It was to include an assembly hall, theater, and student union. Although such a structure as both the architects and President Cousens desired was not built during his time in office, he kept the idea constantly before the Trustees and recommended in 1934 that a building to serve as a social center and a headquarters for student organizations and alumni offices be constructed between East and West Halls. Packard Hall would be either incorporated into the new building or demolished. At Cousens' suggestion the College architects prepared sketches for the building and presented them for consideration in 1935. It was to have been known as the Graduate Center, and the

Those interested in the aesthetics of collegiate architecture were relieved by the decision to use stone which matched the original as closely as possible.

[90] The College bookstore, or "Taberna," was constructed there in 1948. The new portico for Ballou Hall (the Bowen Porch) was provided in 1938.

[91] Instead, it continued to serve into the 1960's as a multi-purpose structure housing a branch of the United States Post Office, student activity rooms, sorority headquarters, and lounge and refreshment facilities. It also received an exterior coat of white paint in the summer of 1964 which altered its traditional appearance considerably.

Alumni Association was to have secured the estimated $500,000 needed from sources outside the College. Monetary considerations required that this project be set aside for some indefinite future date. Establishing a permanent home on the campus for the Association was a long and drawn-out affair after its constitution of 1906 had stipulated that the secretary-treasurer be selected from alumni living near the College. An Alumni Room had been provided for the use of the Association for several years in Goddard Gymnasium. The headquarters migrated in 1925 to Eaton Library, where Executive Committee meetings of the Association were held for some time. The annual meetings usually took place on the main floor of Goddard Gymnasium, which could be temporarily converted into an auditorium. After Cousens Gymnasium was constructed in 1931–32, an Alumni Room was provided there, furnishings having been contributed by the Class of 1932.[92]

Cousens' desire to consolidate campus operations and to integrate the total work of the institution was carried over into the curriculum. In 1919 Professor Durkee had urged the Trustees to establish a semiautonomous school of chemistry. All students enrolled in chemical engineering or in the curriculum leading to the B.S. in Chemistry would be registered in the new school. They would take courses in liberal arts and engineering only on request of the faculty of the school, but those meeting requirements of arts or engineering in chemistry would take such courses in the school. Durkee had been "forced to the conclusion that chemical education under existing circumstances cannot be developed satisfactorily or even long maintained at its present standard" without some such arrangement as he suggested. Professor Durkee's proposal had been tabled by the Trustees and was opposed by Cousens. There was, he said, "too much tendency toward division into schools already. Our effort should rather be in the direction of uniting some interests now too far apart than to create any more division." He thought that the "conflict of interest" that had ostensibly developed between the engineering school and the Department of Chemistry could easily be worked out by creating a special course for chemical engineers. In the field of the social sciences, integration was again the watchword. Cousens looked favorably on a proposal to offer a

[92] Alumni headquarters were then moved to Ballou Hall and eventually to the former home of Professor Houston on Talbot Avenue.

general introductory course basic to the social science group which would include materials drawn from history, government, economics, psychology, and philosophy. Students could then begin their "chosen work" during their first year.

Closer integration of the Department of Physical Education with the academic departments was accomplished in 1920 when it was placed upon "a comprehensive basis" and strengthened by emphasizing the two-year requirement for graduation and an additional one-year requirement in general hygiene. For the first time physical education was scheduled during the regular class hours and in that respect achieved the status of the regular academic offerings. Freshmen were required to take three hours a week, and sophomores two, except that war veterans were excused. Systematic lectures on hygiene were introduced for both men and women in 1913–14, given by members of the staff of the medical school. Hygiene as a degree requirement was introduced in 1920–21, and the number of hours necessary for graduation was increased accordingly for all undergraduates.[93] Professor Houston, who had served for several years as graduate manager of athletics and as alumni secretary, was also placed at the head of the Physical Education Department to coordinate the interests of both undergraduates and alumni. President Cousens was firm in his belief that the expression "a sound mind in a sound body" should be more than an aphorism. He was equally convinced that college athletics, both intramural and intercollegiate, were inseparable from the activities of the Department of Physical Education. In his annual report for 1921 he added a swimming pool to his ever-lengthening list of needed facilities and, faithful to his promise, reminded the Trustees of the need for it in every annual report thereafter. He considered the lack of a pool "almost as anomalous as a private house without a bathroom."[94]

As the years passed, a new gymnasium for men crept closer and

[93] Physical education for the Boston-based schools was also introduced in the 1920's, through a cooperative arrangement with the YMCA. The course in hygiene for Hill students lasted as a degree requirement until 1951–52.

[94] No discernible progress was made in providing for the swimming pool until 1935, when a plan was recommended whereby the Alumni Council would undertake within two years to raise $75,000 toward $120,000 to construct one. This proposal, however, was not followed up. The Department of Physical Education found the lack of a swimming pool particularly embarrassing, as

Cousens Gymnasium

closer to the head of Cousens' priority list, and in 1928 it reached the top. Three years later the lease by the AMRAD Corporation was terminated, and its building became part of the gymnasium when it was constructed in 1931–32. The structure was the most expensive building yet undertaken by the College, costing upwards of half a million dollars. It was financed in part from the income of the Fletcher estate and from special funds raised through alumni efforts. The Alumni Association also allocated part of their Sustaining Fund for the purpose, and it was at their suggestion that the Trustees voted to name the new gymnasium in honor of the president.[95] It became a fitting memorial to a man who had played Varsity football as an undergraduate and whose enthusiasm for athletics remained undiminished throughout an energetic lifetime.

ability to swim had to be demonstrated as a degree requirement. The College had to depend upon the Somerville YMCA pool.

[95] The five-stage plans for the new physical education plant which Cousens outlined were carried out much as he had hoped, except that the Department of Electrical Engineering was moved into the old AMRAD section, which was to have consisted of locker rooms and offices, and provision was not made exactly as he had anticipated for indoor tennis courts. His dream for a swimming pool was not realized until the Hamilton Pool was built in 1945.

§ § §

President Cousens was so busy and so immersed in the affairs of the College that it was difficult for him to realize in 1929, as he completed his tenth year as the head of Tufts, that he had come as acting president expecting to stay three months and had agreed to assume the presidency for only five years until "a better man could be found." No one in that decade had made any attempt to seek "a better man." Instead, the president of the Alumni Association circulated a brochure among the graduates reminding them that Cousens had served for ten years and that a word of appreciation might be in order. The alumni responded by flooding the president's desk with congratulatory messages. Samuel P. Capen, son of the former president of Tufts and Cousens' classmate and lifelong friend, put the administration of the College in historical perspective when he sent Cousens a note. Capen could see three well-defined periods for Tufts.

It was created and its status established under the leadership of Ballou, Miner, and my father. Then followed something very much resembling a Babylonian captivity. Certainly the pride which some of us felt in it had declined although our affection remained. Under you it has been recreated and made better and finer and more beautiful than ever before. You may be disposed to pass the credit around as liberally as you will — and there is plenty to go around. But yours has been the master hand and the personal inspiration. If ever I have seen an authentic exhibit of leadership you have shown it to me.

The Trustees recognized Cousens' "Ten Years of Good Stewardship" by conferring on him at Commencement in 1930 the honorary degree of Doctor of Laws. Many of those who sent a note to the president expressed the hope that another recognition could be arranged on his twentieth anniversary as president. But that was not to be.

Cousens attended a special meeting of the Trustees at the Exchange Club in Boston at 1:00 P.M. on July 2, 1937, to act upon an accumulation of routine business. Less than two hours after returning to his Chestnut Hill home in Brookline, he succumbed to a heart attack, at the age of sixty-two. A year and a half before, this man with seemingly boundless energy had been forced tempo-

rarily to slow down because of a faltering heart. He had taken a
leave of absence abroad, on medical advice, and returned apparently rested and refreshed. But his determination to continue
his work as if nothing had happened became a factor in his eventual
undoing. The College lost, with virtually no warning to those outside an intimate circle, one of the strongest leaders in its history.

Cousens had not escaped criticism during his administration.
Strong personalities seldom do. He had certainly not solved all the
problems of the College, and the status of both engineering school
and medical school were still in doubt in 1937. Many individuals
felt that he paid too much attention to detail that could better have
been left in other hands, and that on some occasions he interfered
unduly with departmental operations. Others believed that he
placed excessive emphasis on the outward and physical side of the
College and that some of the money expended on grounds and
buildings could more profitably have been used to thaw the almost
completely frozen salaries of the faculty, or to provide greatly
needed teaching equipment. Still others complained that he undertook to do too much, too rapidly. Yet in the long view the College
owed an incalculable debt to its sixth president. Of tributes to
Cousens there was almost no end. Deans and faculty, both individually and collectively, joined the alumni and other friends of
the College from near and far to express with all degrees of eloquence their appreciation of his character and services.[96]

Perhaps the most impressive tributes of all came from the
Trustees, with whom the late president had worked with unusual
harmony for just over a quarter of a century — and during over
half of that period while he was head of the institution. The resolutions they adopted caught his spirit admirably.[97] Cousens was an
exceptionally able administrator and organizer, with an unusual
ability to analyze problems and to deal tactfully and sympathetically even with those with whom he disagreed. He combined the
difficult roles of leadership and partnership with enviable ease and
earned the respect of all by sharing his ideas and feelings. But there

[96] Many of these tributes are to be found in special Memorial Issues of
the *Tufts Weekly,* Vol. 31 (September 30, 1937), and the *Tufts College Alumni
Bulletin,* Vol. 11 (December 1937).

[97] The resolutions on the death of Cousens were prepared by Robert W.
Hill (chairman), Ira Rich Kent, and Cora P. Dewick.

was another side to his character. He was a sentimentalist, in the best sense of the word. He had not only the dignity that befitted his office; he had warmth, and above all he loved his Alma Mater and everything connected with it. He literally devoted his life to the College. The Trustees who prepared the resolutions quoted Daniel Webster, who is said once to have spoken of Dartmouth College as "a small college, but there are those who love it." The resolutions were concluded with these words: "Tufts has been a small college, but it will be a great college in its ultimate achievement because John Cousens loved it, and because the inspiration of his life has caused both students and alumni also to love it."

President Cousens' contributions lay in several realms. He possessed, as one alumnus expressed it, a rare combination of business acumen and scholarly inclination. He had guided the College successfully through periods of financial stress and strain while continuously improving its plant and appearance. He tried, and with a large measure of success, to raise both the morale and the academic standards of the student body, from athletics to admissions. He was loyal to his faculties and frequently expressed the obligation of the College to those who served unstintingly in classroom and laboratory, often with inadequate tangible reward. He tried — with signal success — to maintain a judicious balance in the development of the numerous divisions of what was in effect a small university. He was in large part responsible for the creation of two new instruments of education, widely separated in their areas of operation — the New England Medical Center and the Fletcher School of Law and Diplomacy. The latter, an outstanding experiment in inter-institutional cooperation, "more than justified the efforts needed for its accomplishment," in the opinion of the Trustees. Cousens did live to see "a new era dawning" for the College.

14. The Fletcher School of Law and Diplomacy

I T WOULD BE DIFFICULT TO FIND a Trustee of the college generation of the 1870's and 1880's who was a more devoted champion, defender, and supporter of Tufts than Austin Barclay Fletcher. As he wrote to President Bumpus in 1914, "I carry the college with me night and day." A graduate of the Class of 1876, a Trustee since 1909, and president of the Board from 1913 until his death in 1923, Fletcher quietly paid bill after bill for small things and large. He financed a reader for Professor Bolles, long-time chaplain of the College and Dickson Professor of English and American History, who lost his eyesight in the closing years of his long life. He supplemented the meager retirement income of Charles H. Leonard, Dean Emeritus of the Crane Theological School. Fletcher knew the first man intimately and admired him greatly, referring to Bolles frequently as "The Grand Old Man of Tufts." Leonard he had not "spoken with a half an hour in his life," yet Fletcher realized his great value to the College. The Tufts Trustee confided to a correspondent that he had himself, in the one year of 1915, "contributed about $12,000 to the College and to various things connected with it, a very large part of which is quite unknown." Much better known than his smaller benefactions were his arrangement of the Braker bequest to the College and his own gift which made possible the Fletcher School of Law and Diplomacy. This pioneer venture in graduate education did much to make Tufts known far outside its New England boundaries.

It was public knowledge that Fletcher was a millionaire, although the exact amount of his fortune was not known until a considerable time after his death. Among his far-flung interests as a prominent New York corporation lawyer was the firm of Eppinger and Russell, of which he was long-time president and owner of nearly all of the stock. The firm, with headquarters in New York City, owned over 100,000 acres of woodlands in northern and central Florida and engaged in an extensive lumber, turpentine, and creosoting business.[1] As the trustee of the estate of Henry J. Braker, Fletcher also supervised during his lifetime the operations of the Gregorian Hotel in New York City, which served as headquarters for many meetings of Tufts alumni in that area. Both the Eppinger and Russell Company and the Braker estate became intimately involved in Tufts affairs.

Fletcher was a strong personality, as any person intimately associated with the administration of the College soon had reason to discover. There is no question that he liked to run affairs in the grand manner. On June 28, 1914, when the financial plight of the College was compounded by the continued failure to secure a president to succeed Hamilton, the *Boston Sunday Herald* carried a feature article on the problems of the institution which was sufficiently embarrassing to result in the action which brought Bumpus to the presidency. A purportedly authoritative (but naturally anonymous) informant close to Tufts affairs revealed in an extended interview the "inside story" of the difficulties facing Tufts and intimated that alumni who "knew the situation" would hesitate to consider an offer of the presidency because they would "have to adjust themselves to the characteristics of the chairman of the trustees." The newspaper played up the account with a headline which undoubtedly distressed many a loyal alumnus:

FUTURE OF TUFTS HANGS IN BALANCE
May Become Merely a College
Institution Faces Real Crisis Because of
Lack of Strong Head and Financial Shortage —
Differences of Opinion Among Trustees
as to Use of College Funds

[1] It was from this firm that the College acquired much of its lumber, including that used for the bleachers constructed at the Oval in 1915. The assets of the company were a mixture of property owned in the name of the concern and by Fletcher personally. The Mendon Tract, consisting of 40,000 acres, was located near Orlando and was listed among the assets of the company. The Olustee Tract, owned by Fletcher, comprised 80,000 acres in the vicinity of Jacksonville. Both became part of the Fletcher estate after his death; the assets of the company were listed as $1,500,000 in 1923, and the profit from the Mendon Tract was estimated at $500,000 in 1924.

*Austin Barclay Fletcher, Class of 1876, who provided
the initial endowment for the school of
law and diplomacy bearing his name*

Much of the responsibility for this unfortunate state of affairs was laid on the doorstep of the strong-willed president of the Board of Trustees. The informant was quoted as having said that

> Mr. Fletcher represents a certain type of New York business man. He is accustomed to sitting on boards of directors where he holds a majority of the stock, therefore is able to do what he pleases whatever the views of the others. Something of that spirit is displayed at times in the meetings of the college board. He has been heard to say many times that he has $4,000,000 of money which he would like to give sometime, perhaps by will, for educational purposes. . . . Trustees and faculty members are human. . . . Naturally, a certain amount of deference is bound to be paid to such a man under such circumstances. It makes it comparatively easy for him to have his way in the administration of a school, and especially of a school which is in serious need of large sums of money.

Like many such assertions, this one was an oversimplification although not necessarily a falsehood. Fletcher by no means had his own way in everything concerning the College's affairs. At the same time, those whose ideas ran counter to his, even though they might have won the argument, knew that they had been through a skirmish — or battle — before victory was achieved. President Cousens combined tact, diplomacy, persuasive talent, and the art of interpretation in such judicious and skillful ways that he managed to carry out Fletcher's basic wishes at least in spirit without unduly antagonizing the man who was as loyal an alumnus of Tufts as he himself was.

§   §   §

The Braker bequest to Tufts had come about in rather unusual fashion. Fletcher had among his clients and closest personal friends Henry J. Braker, a New York drug importer, real estate owner, and manufacturer who originally left in various trusts (most of them charitable) some $2,500,000, reduced, after several business losses, to $1,400,000. In 1905 Fletcher had interested Braker sufficiently in the College to persuade him to visit the Hill, meanwhile pointing out to him the need of the College to develop the fields of economics, finance, and business administration. Braker, who was not a college graduate, was impressed. He set foot on the Tufts campus long enough one afternoon to hear Fletcher deliver an oration at the celebration of the semicentennial of the opening of the institution. Braker's will, which was probated after his death three years later, provided half a million dollars for Tufts. The sum was to be known as the "Henry J. Braker Fund" and was to be "securely invested." The income was to be used for "the establishment and maintenance of a School of Commerce, Accounts and Finance in the said College"; or, if such a school, department, or course of study should already have been established, the income of the fund was to be used for "its maintenance and expansion." President Hamilton confidently informed the Trustees in his annual report for 1907–8 that the Braker School of Business Administration would be opened "in the near future," and the news was made public in 1910. The College was immediately flooded with inquiries, including requests for positions, catalogues, and course syllabi. A multitude of suggestions poured in for staff appointments, many of them from alumni in the business world, and included everything from deanships to those wanting to install steam heat in the new building that was to be constructed. The dean of the Harvard Graduate School of Business Administration was among the many who offered their services to help organize the school.

The announcement of the imminent opening turned out to be grossly premature; in fact, the Braker School never came into existence at all. Tufts received none of the Braker bequest until 1913, and the balance arrived two years later.[2] The income accumulated while one plan after another was worked out and eventually discarded. All kinds of possibilities were discussed. Hermon Carey Bumpus, who had succeeded Hamilton as president in the fall of 1914, engaged in an extended correspondence with Fletcher about the proposed school for the next two years. They considered also the idea of opening a separate school of public administration to train experts in local and municipal government. Fletcher began immediately to search for a dean for the Braker School. His most acceptable candidate was Henry C. Metcalf, who had held the Cornelia M. Jackson Professorship of Political Science at Tufts from 1899 to 1919 and who had resigned to accept a position in the New School for Social Research just established in New York City. Metcalf proved unavailable, and Fletcher was still looking for a dean to head the new school when he died in 1923. It was at first intended that when the school was established it would be located in Boston; to that end, the so-called Estabrook property on Huntington Avenue near the medical and dental school buildings was acquired by the College. Part of the property was to provide room for the future growth of the medical and dental schools. There was also some thought given to installing the Braker School in a building near the campus of the Massachusetts Institute of Technology in Cambridge. Neither idea proved feasible.

The Trustees took a positive step in the spring of 1920 by voting to establish the "Braker School of Business Administration in connection with the School of Liberal Arts," with students to be admitted in September 1920. The name of the proposed school was changed to the "Braker School of Commerce, Accounts and Fi-

[2] The first portion amounted to $350,000. Because the residue of the estate was insufficient to provide the remaining $150,000, property in New York City was accepted in lieu of the cash balance, on Fletcher's recommendation.

nance" a few weeks later (to comply with the exact provision in Braker's will), and it was to be established "in connection with the School of Arts and Sciences." Several curricula were worked out which were intended to mesh with the undergraduate program.[3] But the school did not open as scheduled. The reason given to the Trustees by President Cousens, who had inherited the project from his two predecessors in 1919, was failure to secure the proper man to head the school. The story was actually more complex than this. The strong-minded president of the Trustees had met an equally determined new president of the College. When Fletcher died the two men were still at odds over what the nature of the new school was to be.[4]

Fletcher was justifiably proud of the fact that it was he who had single-handedly secured the Braker bequest. It had to be understood therefore that it was to be administered under his explicit directions. The proposed school of commerce and finance, according to Fletcher, was his idea entirely. Because it was being established with "the largest gift of the kind ever made for a similar purpose," the school was to be "of the very highest class" and would not only redound to the benefit of the whole College but become so famous that it "would attract some of the foremost men in the country, who would be glad to lecture without charge." The income of the fund supporting it "could not, under any pretext, plan or scheme, be diverted from its own uses. It cannot be used to bolster up other departments, or to make up annual deficiencies." The annual income from endowment alone was expected to be $25,000, and the administration as well as the financing of the school was to be completely separate from the other parts of the College. Fletcher was insistent that it was not to be affiliated in any way with the school of arts and sciences, and that it was to be an exclusively graduate school. He had in mind an institution comparable to the Wharton School of Finance of the University of Pennsylvania.[5]

[3] Professor Harvey A. Wooster, then chairman of the Department of Economics, produced one of the most detailed plans. Another called for a minimum operating budget of $50,000 a year.

[4] It was principally because Metcalf feared that he would be caught in the crossfire between the two men that he declined to accept the deanship.

[5] At one time he considered the notion of opening the Braker School to high school graduates, again to those with two years of college. He discarded both possibilities. Shortly after President Hamilton had been informed of the

Cousens' ideas about the nature and purposes of the proposed school tended to change over the years, but they were distinctly not the same as Fletcher's. His original idea was to offer a combined course of five or six years leading to both a liberal arts and a professional degree. Immediately after the Trustees had voted to establish the school, Cousens sent a letter to the president and secretary of every Tufts Club informing them of the good news and expressing pleasure that it would now be possible "to offer courses in business administration to the students at the Hill." A few months later he announced that his conceptions had "crystallized somewhat." He decided that the school should make a "small beginning" rather than try to do everything at once. He was inclined to think that its efforts should at first be confined to the field of finance. Courses to prepare the student to take his place in the financial world were to be open for degree credit to undergraduates in the school of liberal arts, with special work of graduate level for students properly prepared. He saw the school not as an autonomous professional training facility of exclusively graduate level, drawing its students from far and wide, but as an adjunct to the school of liberal arts, with its central student body composed of Tufts undergraduates. When a vacancy occurred in the chairmanship of the Department of Economics in 1923, Cousens briefly entertained the idea that a man might be found who would serve at first as head of the department and later become dean of the Braker School.

Cousens and Fletcher sparred back and forth for four years, and no step was taken to implement the Trustee vote. Another reason for the delay in planning for the school was the introduction of Cousens' proposal for a general reorganization of the College into three parts. It was thought advisable to wait and see where the Braker School would fit into such a plan. Then Cousens announced that he was tentatively prepared to recommend the opening of the school in September 1925, with the work to be limited at first to advanced courses in the Department of Economics. Then another possibility occurred to him. Braker's will had left an alternative besides establishing a school *per se*. Why not take advantage of it? The bequest had provided that if a school, department, or course

bequest, Fletcher had made it clear that it was to be a graduate school, and when Hamilton assisted Fletcher in searching for a dean in the next few years, Hamilton made a point of that fact to all who inquired.

of study which offered the equivalent of a "School of Commerce, Accounts and Finance" already existed, the income of the fund could be used for it. President Cousens convinced both the Finance Committee and the Executive Committee that at the time of Braker's decease the Department of Economics offered "a broad group of subjects" which, in his opinion, "covered the subjects of Commerce, Accounts and Finance." Therefore the income of the Braker Fund could properly be used "for the maintenance of the Department of Economics and for further additions to the teaching staff of that Department, its equipment, scholarships and fellowships." The income was to be thus used, beginning in 1924–25, until the Trustees voted otherwise. The dilemma of the Braker School had apparently been resolved.

The president had, within a month, arranged for the enlargement of the Economics Department, including the creation of four graduate teaching fellowships for 1925–26. The fellows were to receive tuition and $1,000 a year while working toward the Master's degree and teaching part-time. The program was so successful that beginning the next year the number of fellowships was doubled. They were granted to qualified graduates of any recognized college, without restriction as to sex. Fellowship holders were not expected to complete their degree requirements in one year and were therefore eligible for reappointment for a second year. The fellows conducted two discussion sections each in the introductory course in economics. The system of Braker Fellows met with such enthusiastic response that similar positions were created in the Departments of English and History, and one graduate teaching fellowship was provided in the Department of Chemistry.[6] Between 1925–26 and the end of the program in 1937 (a victim of economic recession), seventy individuals from twenty-five states and forty-five colleges had participated in the various graduate fellowship programs, and several of them served as faculty residents in dormitories while

[6] Those outside the Department of Economics were supported from other than Braker funds. Five of those who held graduate fellowships in the 1920's or 1930's were serving in administrative or teaching capacities at Tufts in the 1960's, including Professor Lewis F. Manly, chairman of the Department of Economics, and Mr. Paul Wren, chairman of the Finance Committee of the Trustees. See "Teaching Fellows at Tufts — Thirty Years Later," *Tufts Alumni Review*, Vol. 10 (Spring 1964), p. 17.

earning their advanced degrees. The income of the Braker Fund was also used for the purchase of library materials for the Department of Economics.

Cousens did not abandon his hopes for a full-fledged school at some future date. He considered the steps taken by the end of 1925 as only "a beginning toward the establishment of the Braker School." However, it never came into being exactly as either Braker or Fletcher planned it. The Trustees did attempt to carry out the spirit if not the letter of the bequest. They established the Henry J. Braker Professorship of Commercial Law in 1926, and in 1927 constructed, with some $203,000 of accumulated income, a classroom and office building bearing the donor's name.[7] Braker Hall was built to house the Department of Economics and to provide space for the Braker School if it should ever be established.[8] The new building served the immediate purpose of enabling the Departments of Government, History, and Philosophy to move from overcrowded Ballou Hall, although the latter was used in part as a classroom building until it was renovated and turned over exclusively to administrative offices in 1955.

§   §   §

The death of Austin B. Fletcher in the summer of 1923 created one of the most complex legal tangles in which the College ever became involved. It had, by a will made in 1914, become the principal beneficiary of an estate estimated at well over $3,000,000. Fletcher had, in characteristic fashion, left no doubt as to his intentions. Five professorships of $100,000 each were to be endowed in Oratory, English, Music, Philosophy, and Public Speaking and Debate. A school of law and diplomacy was to be established with $1,000,000. The income of the residue, estimated in 1923 to be "at least $2,000,000," was to be available for new buildings and their

[7] Professor Clarence P. Houston was elected to the professorship and also resumed that year his post as head of the Department of Physical Education.

[8] The Braker Fund still existed in the 1960's, as provided in the original bequest, and its earnings continued to be used to support the Department of Economics. The department introduced the courses which Henry J. Braker specified, and in 1963–64 was authorized to grant the Ph.D. in Economics in addition to the M.A. it had given for many years.

maintenance.[9] The good fortune that appeared to be the lot of the College was marred, however, by a series of challenges to the will by several of Fletcher's cousins. They protested the allowance of the will on the grounds that it was not authentic, that Fletcher had been "unduly influenced," and that one of the two executors was not a fit person for the task.[10] Temporary administrators had to be appointed, counsel had to be arranged for the College to defend its interests, the case necessitated a jury trial, a key witness (Fletcher's valet) was in Europe when his testimony was needed; in short, every kind of legal delay and complication seemed to be built into the case.

Nevertheless, considerable progress had been made by the end of 1924. The suit brought by the Fletcher relatives was settled out of court (at a cost far less than had been anticipated); liquidation of the assets (stocks and bonds) revealed a substantial gain over inventory values, and sufficient cash had been accumulated to pay legacies preceding those marked for Tufts. The Eppinger and Russell Company, in which the legacy of the proposed law school and the residuum of the estate were then involved, had an unusually prosperous year. The next delay in settling the Fletcher estate was brought about by complications in the acceptance of the Braker estate, of which Fletcher had been a trustee. Fletcher and the co-trustee had made no returns to the probate court for over a decade. Meanwhile, many of the securities of the estate had declined in inventory value by 1924, and the Fletcher estate could not be settled until the Braker estate had been closed out.[11]

The Trustees had decided in 1925 to liquidate part of the

[9] The estimates of the amount anticipated from the bequest fluctuated widely. Cousens reduced the expectation to $1,000,000 in 1924 but raised it to $3,250,000 a year later. Whether due to erroneous newspaper accounts or to overoptimism, literally dozens of individuals flooded Cousens' desk with applications for teaching and administrative positions for a school that was far from being even created in 1923.

[10] The two executors were Charles S. Chadwick of New York and H. Austin Tuttle of Brooklyn, a Tufts alumnus of the Class of 1891. It was Chadwick who was challenged; he was president of the Eppinger and Russell Company, one of Fletcher's many business interests.

[11] The gift of $500,000 to Tufts was not involved in this litigation. It had been paid in two installments (in 1913 and 1915), largely out of cash assets. It was Braker's extensive investment holdings that were the center of controversy after 1923.

assets of the Eppinger and Russell Company (the Florida holdings) rather than use a commercial (and to some extent speculative) operation as an endowment for the projects undertaken under the Fletcher bequest.[12] Shares of Eppinger and Russell stock were accepted at various times as part of the residuary estate, and Cousens and Frederick C. Hodgdon became the agents of the Trustees of Tufts College to vote on such stock. In accordance with Fletcher's wish, Chadwick and Tuttle, who had been executors of the Fletcher estate, became managers of the company. All questions concerning the accounts of the Fletcher funds were settled by 1928.

One provision of Fletcher's will that was carried out strictly in accordance with his wishes was the establishment of endowed professorships bearing the donor's name. The Trustees acquiesced in Cousens' recommendation that men to hold the Fletcher Professorships should be selected from the existing staff rather than imported from outside. Aside from rewarding meritorious faculty members, this system resulted in a saving of $12,500 in salaries from general funds, according to Cousens' estimate. In order to honor also Fletcher's often-expressed wish that faculty salaries be raised, Cousens recommended that the money thus released be used for "horizontal" salary increases on a selective basis. Leo Lewis of the Music Department was the first faculty member to be elected to a Fletcher Professorship (in 1924). Then followed, in 1925, the election of Albert H. Gilmer, Robert C. Givler, and Newell C. Maynard to the Fletcher Professorships of Rhetoric and Debate, Philosophy, and Oratory, respectively. Each appointment was for three years. The fifth professorship authorized, Public Speaking and Debate, which reflected one of Fletcher's own special interests while an undergraduate, was not then created because there was no such department; but later in the same year Charles Gott was elected Fletcher Professor of English, and Gilmer became Fletcher Professor of Dramatic Literature.[13]

§   §   §

[12] One block of land was sold, but the Mendon Tract was received and retained by the College in 1926. The institution thus found itself in the then-profitable lumber business. Arrangements were made to sell over $1,000,000 in timber off the tract.

[13] Professor Givler ceased to be Fletcher Professor of Philosophy in 1931 and became Hunt Professor of Psychology when two separate departments

The endowment for the school of law and diplomacy provided in Fletcher's will began to trickle in as various parts of the estate were settled. The first installment ($100,000) arrived in 1925, and in the following year the Trustees authorized the setting aside of the income in accordance with Fletcher's bequest. President Cousens was also authorized in 1926 to start planning for "the Fletcher School of Law and Diplomacy." A few weeks later, Professor George Grafton Wilson of the Harvard Law School was appointed "Lecturer in International Law in the Fletcher School" for the academic year 1926–27. An assistant in the Government Department was also appointed and paid from the Fletcher School fund. These were somewhat misleading appointments, as the Fletcher School had not yet actually come into existence. They represented, however, more than bookkeeping sleight-of-hand. The appointments were quite in accord with Cousens' broad interpretation of the Fletcher bequest. Long before the estate had been settled, the Tufts president had insisted that the word "school" might "mean almost anything. . . . If we wanted to we could make the Fletcher School of Law merely a group of five or six eminent men who give courses of lectures on College Hill to those who care to listen." The two appointments were actually operative in the school of liberal arts, where Professor Wilson taught the course in international law in the Department of Government and International Law, following the resignation of Professor Arthur I. Andrews. In 1927, because Professor Wilson was otherwise committed, W. Penn Cresson was elected Professor of International Law and Diplomacy "in connection with the Fletcher School of Law and Diplomacy." This rather makeshift arrangement did not work out very well. In 1928 a substitute had to be provided when Professor Cresson served as a member of the United States delegation to the Sixth International Conference of American States in Havana. Illness then prevented him from fulfilling many of his academic duties the following year. As a consequence, instruction in international law by way of the school of liberal arts was temporarily abandoned.

---

were created in 1932. The Hunt Professorship was created in 1931 by a consolidation of the Ebenezer and Moses Hunt funds. Professor Bruce W. Brotherston became Fletcher Professor of Philosophy.

It appeared by 1927 that appropriate trust fund investments intended to finance the Fletcher School were in order, and a committee was appointed to investigate possibilities for the school. That part of the Fletcher legacy earmarked for the school was derived from the sale of part of the Florida lands, and by 1929 all but a $75,000 mortgage had been "conservatively invested in stock and bonds"; the mortgage was cleared away during the following year when the federal government purchased part of the land for reforestation purposes. The next step was to obtain clarification of the exact intent of that portion of Fletcher's will that provided for a school of law and diplomacy. This was made necessary because Boston University was an interested party to the Fletcher bequest. Fletcher had been a member of the Trustees of Boston University as well as of Tufts, and in his will he had stipulated that if his $1,000,-000 gift were not used by Tufts "for the purposes declared therein," Boston University would receive the bequest. Expert advice was obtained which removed any question that Tufts' plans for using the gift might be inconsistent with Fletcher's intention. According to the ruling handed down, Fletcher's purpose was not to be narrowly construed. More specifically, the interpretation was offered that he did not have in mind a school "of the usual kind, which prepares men for admission to the bar and for the active practice of the law."[14] Instead, according to legal advice, Fletcher envisioned "a school to prepare men for the diplomatic service and to teach such matters as come within the scope of foreign relations [which] embraces within it as a fundamental a thorough knowledge of the principles of international law upon which diplomacy is founded, although the profession of a diplomat carries with it also a knowledge of many things of a geographic and economic nature which affect relations between nations." Some research on the part of the law firm that offered the liberal interpretation of Fletcher's intent divulged the fact that Georgetown University in Washington, D.C., and the Walter Hines Page School of Diplomacy of the Johns Hopkins University offered such programs and that similar courses, in whole or in part, were also available at the American University in Washington, D.C., at Columbia University, and at Harvard. The

[14] Frank Knowlton, an alumnus of the Class of 1899 and a member of the firm of Choate, Hall and Stewart, acted as counsel for the College.

Wharton School in the University of Pennsylvania offered a four-year course for those interested in foreign trade. The conclusion was that there was "in process a development which has reached a point where it may well be said to have a recognized standing of its own," and that the Fletcher bequest could properly be used to establish a school of international law and diplomacy. The settlement of questions concerning the far-flung Fletcher estate in 1928 and the clarification of the Fletcher will at the same time led Cousens to plan optimistically for the opening of at least part of the school by September 1928.

The Fletcher School did not become a reality in 1928; in fact, it did not open its door for five more years. Yet considerable necessary groundwork was laid in the intervening period. One forehanded idea developed in 1929 and 1930 was to collect a group of eminent persons who could "be invited to consider themselves a Board of Advisers" during the preliminary stages and who might then become the Board of Visitors to the school when it actually came into being. Among those first suggested were Owen D. Young, Edith Nourse Rogers, Mrs. Roland B. Hopkins, and Manley O. Hudson. In 1930 Cousens' list had become a "Committee of Seven" which included several listed above, plus Frederick Hodgdon and Frank Knowlton (representing the Trustees), Christian Herter, Charles K. Webster, Roland W. Boyden, Daniel G. Wing, and James T. Shotwell. Cousens also had one or more conferences with literally dozens of other individuals whose judgment, by the very nature of their positions and reputation, would be of value. This list included President Lowell of Harvard and Sherwood Eddy.

The President offered tentative plans for the school to the Trustees in 1929 on his own responsibility, without having yet submitted them to the special Trustee committee on the Fletcher School which had been created some time before. The full Board nonetheless gave his plan their "general approval" and authorized the committee, "after checking the plan in detail," to submit it to the appropriate court to be sure that it was compatible with the conditions in Fletcher's will. After the Supreme Judicial Court of Massachusetts approved the Tufts petition in 1930, it appeared that the road was finally clear for the working out of detailed plans.[15] Boston University also gave its assent to the detailed draft of the plans for the Fletcher School.

The problem of interpreting Fletcher's will having been presumably cleared away, Cousens put on paper his thoughts as to the nature of the school.[16] He saw it as mainly (but not exclusively) graduate in character, offering the degree of Master of Arts in International Law to a highly selected student body that would attain a maximum of fifty. A building to accommodate the school was to be provided on the Medford campus, and the course would require the conventional minimum of one year in residence. If students were discovered to have deficiencies in certain basic subjects such as history, economics, and foreign language, they could satisfy prerequisites through courses in the school of liberal arts. Cousens emphasized the need of a Board of Visitors, machinery for which had long existed in the organization of the College. However, unlike the existing bodies of Visitors, the one for Fletcher would be composed of persons generally outside the Board of Trustees and having no connection with the institution; because of their interest in international affairs, they would render "real service in initiating the policy of the School." The Fletcher School was to be housed in a new building constructed on the Hill, next to Miner Hall, with access both from the main Campus Drive and by a short path from the corner of College Avenue and Professors Row on the southeasterly corner of the main campus.

After the building was provided for, Cousens estimated that an annual income of $50,000 from the Fletcher bequest, which in 1929 he allocated down to the last cent, would be sufficient to operate the school. The two chief members of the faculty were to be a Professor of International Relations, who was to serve also as dean

[15] The member of the firm of Choate, Hall, and Stewart who presented the petition on behalf of the College reported that the judge before whom the case was heard "entertained no doubts whatever about the complete propriety of the plan for the school as now outlined and of the further propriety of changing it from time to time to meet exigencies as they might arise." The basic outline of the course of study was prepared by Halford L. Hoskins, then chairman of the Department of History and later the dean of the Fletcher School when it opened four years after the court ruling was handed down.

[16] His proposals were embodied in his annual report to the Trustees in the fall of 1929.

of the school, and a Professor of International Economics. Both were expected to spend at least half of each year abroad and for this reason were allotted general travel expenses in Cousens' plan.[17] There would be four additional staff positions carrying professorial rank: a Professor of International Law, a Professor of Diplomatic History, and one Assistant Professor each in International Relations and in International Economics. Cousens never for a moment saw the school completely separated from the rest of the College. One-third of the salary of the Professor of International Law was to be contributed by the school of liberal arts, and the chairman of the Tufts Department of History was to serve as Professor of Diplomatic History, with the school of liberal arts contributing the majority of his salary. The high salaries for three of the four full professors (who were to be brought in from outside the institution) were, as Cousens noted, "entirely out of line with any other salary scheduled in the institution." This was, to him, "the crux of the whole plan"; only the very best men should be obtained, and their services came high. The division between Fletcher and College funds in the payment of salaries was made because it was "to be expected that certain courses in the School of Law and Diplomacy would be open to Seniors in the School of Liberal Arts." Likewise, the Professor of International Law would teach the undergraduate courses previously taught by Professors Wilson and Cresson. Tuition had yet to be considered, but he believed it would "not be very difficult to secure ten to fifteen scholarships of $500 each." There were also to be five Teaching Fellows giving service half-time, and a secretary-librarian. Cousens allotted the remainder of the $50,000 ($5,500) for a library and for building maintenance.

No attempt had been made in 1929 to prepare a detailed curriculum, but the president offered some general suggestions. The Fletcher School, as a graduate institution, was to be strictly professional in its objectives. At least four areas should be taken into account in working out a course of study: the consular service, the secretarial departments of the diplomatic service, teaching, and industry overseas. The uniqueness of the school would not lie so much in the courses to be offered as "in the stress laid upon the outstanding character of the three chief men, and the provision that

[17] Half of the traveling expenses of the Professor of International Economics was to come from the Braker Fund.

they must use the world as a laboratory to the end that theirs may be a contribution to education in international affairs in the broadest sense." Cousens had consulted sufficient experts by 1930 to present to the Trustees a "hypothetical" curriculum for the Fletcher School, organized for the most part along the lines he had suggested the previous year. The courses were grouped under four general headings and represented a combination of full-year and one-semester courses in International Relations, International Economics, International Law, and Diplomatic History.

In accord with his plans to find the very best man possible to head the school, Cousens selected Professor James T. Shotwell of Columbia University. Shotwell, a distinguished scholar and maker of diplomatic history and expert in the complex field of international affairs, had taken a great interest in the Fletcher School project and offered some suggestions for the curriculum.[18] He was unofficially offered the position of dean (with the equally unofficial consent of several of the Trustees) by Cousens, but the disappointed president had to be content with a refusal on the grounds that Shotwell was too deeply involved in other projects to accept. Shotwell added that if he were a few years younger and did not have so many other obligations (including commitments in the Carnegie Endowment for International Peace, of which he later became the head), he would have "seized the opportunity with eagerness." Cousens thereupon readjusted his sights. After coming regretfully to the conclusion that the search for a director who had Shotwell's qualifications, and who was at the same time available, was "hopeless," he decided to concentrate on finding "a relatively young man whose future lies before him and whose reputation has not yet been established." Meanwhile, he continued to seek advice about the school and turned to Harvard for counsel. There followed a series of conversations with Manley O. Hudson, George Grafton Wilson, and Roscoe Pound, dean of the Harvard Law School. The upshot of the informal meetings was the suggestion that the operation of the Fletcher School might be made a joint project of Tufts and the Harvard Law School. No such arrangement could be concluded without the approval of President Lowell and the Harvard Corporation, so Lowell was apprised of the dis-

[18] For an account of important aspects of his career, see James T. Shotwell, *Autobiography* (Indianapolis: Bobbs-Merrill, 1961).

cussions. As soon as he was informed by Dean Pound, who took the initiative and assumed "somewhat of a controlling hand," the Harvard president agreed to an expansion of the idea of cooperation to include utilization of all of Harvard's educational resources that might be appropriate.

During the first semester of 1931–32 Cousens was on leave of absence for a trip abroad, but officials at Harvard were sufficiently intrigued by the possibilities of the new school to approach Dean Wren, of the Tufts School of Liberal Arts, to discuss "the possibility of combining with Tufts in establishing a School of Diplomacy." No decisions were made at the time, any possible action being necessarily deferred until Cousens' return. Preliminary conversations were resumed between the presidents of the two institutions early in the spring of 1932. The end product was a memorandum submitted to the Tufts Trustees and to the Harvard Corporation outlining a proposal for joint administration of the Fletcher School. This seemed to offer a unique opportunity that would redound to the mutual benefit of both Tufts and Harvard, and Cousens predicted that a development of "far reaching consequences" was in store for the College. This proposal to cooperate formally with other institutions in the Boston area in conducting an academic program was not the first. At the same time, it did represent the most far-reaching such venture as well as the most durable, in spite of grave difficulties that developed over the course of years and threatened more than once to bring the experiment to an unhappy end.

§　　§　　§

At various times in its history Tufts had had the opportunity to engage in cooperative ventures with several neighboring institutions, including Harvard. In some instances fruitful arrangements were worked out, while in others the College found it to its best interests not to commit itself at all, or to do so for only a brief period. One proposal that would have gone even further than cooperation had come from the Emerson College of Oratory but died aborning. Charles Wesley Emerson proposed a union of his school with Tufts in 1899, the same year that the Boston Dental College became the nucleus of the Tufts Dental School. The Trustees declined to enter into negotiations with Emerson College because at the time they were dubious "whether the work done is on a par

576

with the work of Professional Schools having College or University affiliation."

The subject of university extension courses offered jointly by Boston-area colleges had been broached by Harvard in 1909–10. The idea was instantly approved, and a Commission on Extension Courses was created, consisting of representatives from Boston College, Boston University, Harvard, Massachusetts Institute of Technology, the Museum of Fine Arts, Simmons College, Tufts, and Wellesley. The program was financed by a combination of contributions from the Lowell Institute, the Boston Chamber of Commerce, and tuition charges. The courses, offered in the belief that many adults wished to extend their intellectual horizons, were given by members of the faculties of the cooperating institutions and corresponded as closely as possible to regular curricular offerings. The degree of Associate of Arts was established in 1910 by the Tufts Trustees on recommendation of the faculty for those who wished to take advantage of the adult education program and who wished to "avoid the technicalities of definite entrance requirements."[19] During 1910–11, a total of twelve late afternoon and evening courses offered by the seven institutions attracted 650 students. A member of the Tufts faculty offered the basic course in economics. Tufts' rather nominal participation in the university extension program lasted until the eve of the Second World War, when the College (in 1939–40) opened its own Extension Division. Comparatively few persons at Tufts took advantage of the cooperative program, although it was still listed in the catalogue until 1954–55. In the meantime, the degree had been redesignated "Adjunct in Arts" in 1935.

One experiment in inter-institutional cooperation that was tried briefly, languished, and was temporarily revived was initiated in 1904 by the dean of the Boston University Law School. Graduates of Tufts who had earned six to twelve credits in Public Law

[19] Tufts required that a candidate earn at least 30 credits of the 102 needed for the degree in "subjects given by officers of instruction of Tufts College or by authority of Tufts College." Although the student had to earn at least six credits in courses in each of four broad groups, one of which was Language, Literature, Fine Arts, and Music, there was no foreign language requirement *per se*. The first recipient of a Tufts Associate in Arts degree (1914) was enrolled in Jackson College.

were allowed to complete the course of study at Boston University leading to the degree of Bachelor of Laws in two years instead of the conventional three. Tufts students pursuing courses equivalent to any in the law school were allowed to take the regular examinations there and to receive credit toward a law degree. The Tufts faculty agreed to this arrangement but did not allow seniors to matriculate in the first-year class of the law school and to credit such work toward the A.B. Only a scattering of Tufts students took advantage of this program.[20]

The idea was revived in 1920 as part of a grand design suggested by President L. H. Murlin of Boston University. He proposed a whole series of combined schools including one in medicine, in dentistry, and one in law. They were to be known respectively as the Boston University-Tufts Medical School, the Boston University-Tufts Dental School, and the Union Law School. The latter was to be a joint enterprise of Boston University, Boston College, and Tufts. The dean of the Boston University Law School worked out an arrangement so that students in each of the participating colleges would be able to obtain training in law and receive their degrees from their home institution. A minimum of two years of college was to be required for entrance into the program and the curriculum was to be arranged so that a student might secure both his A.B. or B.S. degree and the degree of LL.B. in six years (or seven, if the law school course were extended to seven years). This plan failed to materialize, for authorities at Boston University raised objections to certain aspects of the proposal, and Tufts was unwilling to accept a compromise which would have given the College representation on a Board of Management but without an actual voice in the control of the affairs of the law school.

The proposals for jointly operated medical and dental schools were worked out in even greater detail than the plan for a law school. Each school was to have been administered by a committee of faculty and trustees representing both institutions, and graduates would have received a diploma signed by the presidents and

[20] The first recipient, A. W. DeGoosh, who had received a Ph.B. from Tufts in 1893, actually was enrolled in the special program before it was formally established and received an A.B. *extra ordinem* from Tufts in 1896 simultaneously with an LL.B. from Boston University.

deans of both. Pre-medical work would have been pursued in the respective schools of liberal arts by both prospective medical and dental students. The first two years of the medical courses (to be taken also by dental students) were to be taken at the Tufts Medical School and the last two at the Boston University Medical School. Clinical and research facilities were to be provided through existing affiliations of the latter with the Massachusetts Homeopathic Hospital, the Robinson Maternity Hospital, the Evans Memorial Hospital, Haynes Memorial Hospital, and the Westboro State Hospital. These plans came to naught for several reasons. The Tufts Dental School would have lost its separate identity, and Boston University would have been the sole beneficiary of this part of the plan for it did not have such a school of its own. Cousens also bristled at being informed that Boston University would "bring to the merger in medical education much more than you can bring." All told, the entire plan required too great a subordination of Tufts to Boston University. Their officials were given to understand that the position of the Tufts Medical School was such that its interests would have to be dominant. Negotiations thus came to an abrupt halt. Such were the perils that beset any plan involving more than informal cooperation. The Tufts president ran into this problem head on when negotiations were commenced with Harvard for the Fletcher School.

By the time the arrangement with Harvard had been worked out in relation to the Fletcher School, Tufts had already been involved in at least three joint programs with the institution in Cambridge. The first concerned the Forsyth Dental Infirmary, which had opened in 1914 and was intended originally to have been operated exclusively by Tufts, but became a project shared with Harvard.[21] Austin Fletcher, chairman of the Tufts Trustees at the time, never became reconciled to the cooperative arrangement. When he undertook to brief Bumpus on the College's affairs when the latter became president in the fall of 1914, Fletcher informed him of his sentiments in no uncertain terms. Fletcher explained that the Forsyth Dental Infirmary "started out as an attachment to our dental school, but it was too big a thing for Harvard to allow us to have." According to the disgruntled Tufts Trustee, the Tufts representatives on the original Forsyth Board of Trustees were asked to resign

[21] See Chapter 8.

so that they could be replaced by Harvard choices. Fletcher gave Bumpus the rather unwelcome charge of making "a careful inquiry of the whole affair . . . and possibly we may yet swing it back where it was originally intended to go."

The second attempt at cooperation with Harvard met a somewhat similar fate. President Cousens, who had succeeded Bumpus, had developed what he considered "very cordial relations" with President Lowell when in 1923 a "novel experiment" was tried of arranging a coordinate professorship in the two institutions for Dr. Frank Lahey, head of the Department of Surgery in the Tufts Medical School, and Dr. Harvey Cushing of Harvard. Dean Rushmore of Tufts was not at all enthusiastic, predicting (as it turned out, correctly) that the College would lose Dr. Lahey's services to Harvard. Dr. Lahey devoted so much time to the Deaconess Hospital that it was necessary for him to resign from the Boston City Hospital. This brought in turn his resignation from the Tufts staff because no other clinical facilities with which he was connected were available for teaching purposes. Lahey, however, maintained his connection with Tufts by becoming a Trustee in 1927.

A third experiment in cooperation with Harvard had been worked out in 1930, when the Crane School faculty voted to affiliate with the theological school at Harvard in certain respects. The proposal, received from Dean Willard Sperry of Harvard, went into effect in the middle of the academic year 1929–30. It involved the acceptance by the Tufts School of Religion of some students from Harvard and allowed the attendance by some Tufts students of courses at Harvard, all without payment of extra fees. The affiliation between the Tufts School of Religion and the Harvard Divinity School was still in existence when their parent institutions undertook the much more intricate task of operating the Fletcher School.

The memorandum of March 1932 drawn up between Tufts and Harvard was to become the basis on which the Fletcher School was finally organized, although many a change had to be made and many a delay recalled the Biblical statement quoted by Cousens to the Trustees in the fall of 1932: "Hope deferred maketh the heart sick." The memorandum provided that the name of the new facility would be the "Tufts College Fletcher School of Law and

Diplomacy, established and operated with the cooperation of Harvard University." The body ultimately responsible for the school was to be the Trustees of Tufts College, but its actual operation was to be in the hands of a Joint Executive Committee headed by the dean of the Harvard Law School and comprising one member of the Harvard Corporation, two members of the Tufts Trustees, one member selected from the faculties of Harvard and one from Tufts, and the presidents of the two institutions, *ex officio*. The staff was to consist of the president of Tufts, *ex officio*, a dean (selected from the Harvard faculty), a vice-dean (selected from the faculty or Trustees of Tufts), and a teaching staff selected "largely" from Harvard and "partly" from Tufts. A new building, to be erected on the Medford campus, was to house the school, and a special library was to be provided which would supplement those of Tufts and Harvard. Space would also be provided for the school in the buildings of the Harvard Law School.

The curriculum proposed for the school did not differ materially from that presented earlier to the Trustees by Cousens, but it was proposed in the 1932 memorandum to offer not only a Master's degree but also a Ph.D. At an organization meeting in June 1932, Dean Pound outlined a curriculum which was rejected by both Cousens and Lowell on the ground that it was too narrow. Pound admitted that he was thinking primarily in terms of a conventional law school which merely stressed international topics, but he had a reason for it. A short time before, he had warned Cousens of the danger of making the Fletcher School "too broad at the start. . . . I have a horror of ambitious paper programs at all times, and in my experience they seldom come to anything in the setting up of professional schools." The idea of allowing Tufts undergraduates who were not candidates for the second or third degree to take one or more courses in the Fletcher School was broadened to include both Harvard undergraduates and graduate students. Tuition for a full program (four courses) was to be $300, and fees for non-degree students were to be charged by the semester hour. Registration and payment of fees were to be handled by Tufts, and the institution bearing the expense of non-degree students taking a partial course was to benefit from the fees. Degrees were to be conferred in the name of the Tufts Trustees and at Tufts Commencements. Women were to be admitted to courses leading only to the Master's degree, such work to be done solely on the Tufts campus.[22]

The plan outlined above was unanimously approved "in general" by the Tufts Trustees at the same meeting it was presented. Cousens was authorized to work out the details, after which a definite decision would be made. Sufficient progress had apparently been registered by the summer of 1932 to appoint Mrs. Roland G. (Marguerite S.) Hopkins and Frederick C. Hodgdon to the Joint Executive Committee as the Tufts Trustee representatives. While waiting for other problems to be settled, the Trustees authorized their two representatives to spend up to $5,000 "to make a comprehensive survey with reference to what is being done in education in foreign relations in America and abroad, which may serve as a guide in determining the purpose of the proposed Fletcher School of Law & Diplomacy."

After having carefully laid the groundwork for the school with President Lowell by lengthy conferences and a mountainous exchange of correspondence in 1932, Cousens faced another discouraging prospect. The president of Harvard announced his resignation in November 1932, effective the following September, and the Tufts president apparently had to start all over again. For the moment it seemed that the long years of perplexity and the struggle to work out a successful plan for using Fletcher's gift had been in vain. Negotiations with Harvard, which had proved "very difficult and delicate," had apparently brought matters around in a complete circle. There was serious talk in the fall of 1932 of having Tufts try to proceed alone. Trustee Robert W. Hill, like Cousens, was afraid that during the transition period at Harvard, Dean Pound might exercise such influence on the character of the project that it might "develop into nothing more than an adjunct to the Harvard Law School." Cousens hoped to push the project sufficiently rapidly to have the cooperative effort of the two institutions as worked out in the memorandum of 1932 go into effect before Lowell actually left office.

[22] Cousens acceded regretfully to this denial of equal educational opportunity for women. Harvard in 1932 had no intention of reversing its historic policy of prohibiting women students from attending courses in its buildings. This rule was not relaxed even for Radcliffe students until 1943.

Cousens tried to turn the delay in deciding on the fate of the proposed school to advantage. If its opening had to be postponed, at least an additional year's income could be accumulated in the Fletcher Law School Fund and a careful assessment could be made of its worth. The sharp decline in security values during the depression had a pronounced effect on the Fletcher resources. Cousens had the College auditors divide the securities into two groups, one representing the principal, having a book value of $1,000,000 and comprising the soundest investments, and the other representing accumulated income, with a book value of $366,000 and made up of securities of less stable character. Tufts had sole responsibility for the Fletcher Fund both by the conditions of the original gift and under the proposed plan of joint operation with Harvard. Only by showing in the principal the soundest securities possible could Harvard be assured that estimated income would be available. Furthermore, the school had to be started in a new building appropriate to its needs, not in "makeshift, borrowed quarters," either at Tufts or at Harvard. An adequate headquarters "rather better built and furnished than any . . . so far constructed" should cost no more than $200,000. Delay in starting construction could be justified on several grounds. The translation of the book value into actual sale value of accumulated income would return less than $115,000; the dean or director, who should certainly have something to say about the proposed building, had not yet been selected; the security market would (it was hoped) improve; and approximately $70,000 in additional income would be available by waiting a year or so.

Negotiations with Harvard continued in the winter of 1932–33. Cousens' contact with Lowell's successor, Dr. James B. Conant, restored at least a degree of confidence that satisfactory negotiations could continue. The Tufts president told the Trustees that the new president of Harvard was "already vitally interested in the Fletcher School and may be depended upon to cooperate fully in its development." Meanwhile, sufficient progress had been made by April, while Lowell was still in office, to result in another "Memorandum of Understanding" between the two institutions, based on prior approval by the Corporation and Overseers of Harvard. Much of the memorandum was a reiteration of arrangements already embodied in the previous agreement, although certain additions and readjustments were made.[23] The $1,000,000 endowment in the custody of Tufts was to be held as a separate fund, "its investment never to be mingled with the investment of other funds." Since the Trustees were legally bound to be the custodians of the Fletcher endowment for the school, they were also responsible for executing contracts with its faculty.

It was decided that initially the courses of study should lead only to the Master of Arts degree, and that the majority of such work would be done on the Tufts campus. Eventually the Ph.D. would be offered, with the major part of the candidates' time to be spent at Harvard. It was proposed that the course of study for the first year of the school would be arranged on the basis of a full calendar year; that a student could complete the M.A. in the academic year (September to June); and if the candidate wished to receive a Master of Arts in his special field of study (e.g., Master of Arts in International Law and Organization), he could attend a summer session which would round out a twelve-month year. The summer quarter would give non-degree candidates from either institution an additional opportunity to enroll in the Fletcher School for special courses. The number of degree candidates was to be "strictly limited" to fifty. This figure was considered desirable because the school was to be on a very high scholastic level and because it was "likely that the demand for the product of the School [would] not be great." Tuition for degree candidates in the nine-months course would be $300, and for the full-year course, $400.

The memorandum of 1933 was to continue as the basis of operations unless terminated by written notice of either party, allowing sufficient time to enable the school to fulfill its obligations to accepted and enrolled students. Modifications in the understanding could be made under the same condition by mutual consent. The sum of $25,000 was appropriated by the Trustees to cover general expenses, and an additional $5,000 was provided for a limited number of fellowships and scholarships.[24]

[23] The memorandum, undated, was assigned the date of April 10, 1933, by the secretary of the Tufts Trustees, based on the time of the letter of transmittal to President Lowell.

[24] The first such awards were made to four students in 1933–34 and consisted of tuition for the academic year plus $200. One of the fellowship re-

Rules governing the admission of students and the granting of degrees were also adopted at the March meeting in 1933. Undergraduate preparatory studies were to have included a reading knowledge of French or German (although a reading knowledge of two or more modern foreign languages was "strongly recommended"), three years of history, and one year each in government and economics. The Executive Committee of the Fletcher School, taking its cue from the March agreement, decided in the fall of 1933 to grant, besides the conventional M.A., the special degree of Master of Arts in Law and Diplomacy (M.A.L.D.). This degree was introduced primarily for those contemplating careers in the Foreign Service or in business enterprises rather than for those interested in strictly academic pursuits. It called for at least one year in residence, presentation of a satisfactory thesis, and the passing of an examination before a committee of the faculty.[25] The number of groups from which students were to select one for concentrated attention was reduced to three in this version of the curriculum (International Law and Organization, Diplomacy and International Relations, and International Economics). Several courses were common to two or all three groups.

Although no mention was made of it in the 1933 memorandum, Cousens held tenaciously to the idea of a tie-in between the new school and the undergraduate school of liberal arts. The dean of Tufts undergraduates shared the same view. Even after the Fletcher School had opened, he hoped that "many of the properly qualified students in the School of Liberal Arts may take advantage of the opportunity of doing work in International Law and advanced courses in Government." He made a point of the fact that four of the courses in the Fletcher curriculum were already being offered in Tufts and were open for either graduate or undergraduate credit. In fact, "all of the subjects specified as necessary for candidacy for the Master's degree are now offered in our School of Liberal Arts, except a year of comparative government or political science." He still felt that some of the courses in the Fletcher

cipients in 1934–35 was Robert B. Stewart, who was also appointed assistant in the Tufts Department of Government and later became dean of the Fletcher School.

[25] The original plan for a twelve-month year, including a summer session, never materialized.

School could be opened to undergraduates. If the cost of subjects already offered in the undergraduate school were borne by that division, the Fletcher budget could be "considerably relieved" and the total annual expense which would have to be incurred for the first two or three years could be held below $20,000.

The Tufts Trustees in the summer of 1933 certainly seemed to be satisfied with the progress of negotiations that had led to the establishment of the Fletcher School. They not only ratified the action taken by the president and the Executive Committee but expressed their "sincere appreciation of the successful manner in which the president of the College conducted the negotiations with Harvard University, to bring this cooperative enterprise to a successful beginning." But not even they apparently appreciated fully the difficulties that Cousens faced in his almost daily concern for the welfare of the project so close to his heart. Problem after problem dogged the negotiations and planning for the new school.

Finances continued to be of paramount importance, and they affected almost every move that was made or contemplated. The determination to provide housing for the Fletcher School by way of a building constructed expressly for its use still held firm through the fall of 1932. But then the full effects of the Great Depression began to be felt. For the first time in the history of the Eppinger and Russell Company (the stock of which comprised almost all of the Fletcher residuum from which money was to come for new buildings), a substantial deficit occurred.[26] For years it had been necessary for the College to borrow in anticipation of receipts from students. It was the good fortune of the institution to be able in the 1930's to use the Eppinger and Russell cash surplus as the source of loans instead of having recourse to an outside bank. Convenient as this arrangement might have been, it had the natural result of reducing the potential resources from which building funds could be obtained. While President Cousens watched financial depression eat away at the Eppinger and Russell reserves, arranging a home for the Fletcher School was made imperative by

[26] The Florida timberland, which comprised a significant part of the Fletcher assets, dropped precipitately in market value during the depression. At one time Fletcher had prophesied that the Florida land would eventually be worth $20,000,000; in 1913 it was being carried on the books at $100,000 — and even that figure was "considerably in excess of present values."

The old Goddard Gymnasium of the 1880's was scarcely recognizable
half a century later as the headquarters
of the Fletcher School of Law and Diplomacy

the decision to open the school in the fall of 1933 and by the expectation that the library of the World Peace Foundation in Boston
would be located on the Hill in connection with the Fletcher
School. The Trustees, after having been apprised of the situation,
voted to approve the proposal to assign Goddard Gymnasium for
the use of the school and to authorize the expenditure of $50,000
from the Fletcher Fund for necessary alterations.[27]

Staffing the new school was even more tangled and frustrating
than being forced to house the Fletcher School in makeshift quarters. Among the appointments considered in the memorandum of
March 1932 had been George Grafton Wilson of Harvard, who
might serve at least temporarily as dean; and Halford L. Hoskins,
Dickson Professor of English and American History and chairman
of the Tufts Department of History, who might serve as vice-dean.
Eleven men were suggested for the faculty from Harvard and three
from Tufts (Professors Hoskins, Ruhl J. Bartlett [History], and
Earle M. Winslow [Economics]). It was understood "in general"

[27] The building officially became Goddard Hall in September 1933.

that faculty members from both institutions would serve on a part-time basis. The crucial personnel question was the choice of a dean or director, and on this the presidents of the two institutions failed to agree. Among those seriously considered by Cousens was Christian A. Herter, who declined a tentative offer in 1931.[28] Cousens had a person in mind in the fall of 1932 other than Professor Wilson but was unwilling to make his recommendation until he was "reasonably sure that President Lowell and Dean Pound will recognize him." After "some rather delicate maneuvering," he persuaded President Lowell and Dean Pound to commit themselves. The man with whom Cousens was negotiating was Dr. James Grover McDonald, chairman of the Board of the Foreign Policy Association, to whom Tufts had awarded an honorary LL.D. in 1932. Cousens' frustrations mounted when McDonald declined the invitation in February 1933 and decided to remain where he was.[29] Dean Pound was "not at all surprised" at McDonald's decision. Pound wrote Cousens that he was "convinced that we can hardly expect a first-class man to take this position in view of the relatively small endowment which precludes entire independence, and the connection with this institution [Harvard] which, I suspect, makes the type of man we desire feel that his light will be under the bushel of the Harvard Law School." The problem of the dean-ship remained unsolved.

The Tufts Trustees, not wishing to delay the opening of the school any longer, voted in March 1933 to enroll students that fall, with Professor Hoskins as acting dean.[30] The Memorandum

[28] Herter later became governor of Massachusetts and held important posts in the federal government. He was a Representative in the state legislature at the time Cousens' offer was made.

[29] Cousens' disappointment was compounded by the fact that he had been criticized for having in 1932 secured the authorization, at the suggestion of the Foreign Policy Association, of the generous sum of $5,000 to finance the preparation of a work by Dr. Raymond L. Buell on United States policy in the Caribbean. Buell was research director of the Foreign Policy Association. Cousens was frank to admit that the grant was partly "bait" to secure McDonald for the deanship.

[30] Because Hoskins still had duties as chairman of the History Department, the departmental headquarters was moved temporarily to Goddard Hall in the fall of 1933. It was returned to Braker Hill a year later.

of Agreement concluded with Harvard a few weeks thereafter removed some of the obstacles that had required the delay, and in the latter part of May formal announcement was made of the opening of the school so that a student body could be recruited.

The original Fletcher faculty were elected for one year by the Trustees on June 17, 1933, and in October their official titles were adopted. Halford L. Hoskins was appointed Acting Dean and Professor of Diplomacy and International Relations. The other Professors of Diplomacy and International Relations were George H. Blakeslee, Arthur N. Holcombe, and William L. Langer. Lauchlin B. Currie and Seymour E. Harris were appointed Professors of International Economics. Those serving as Professors of Public and International Law were Roscoe Pound, Josef Redlich, Julius Stone, and George Grafton Wilson. Albert E. Hindmarsh held the rank and title of Assistant Professor of International Law.[31] After seemingly endless negotiations, the problems of staff appeared to have been solved.

Another major stumbling block in putting the school into operation had been removed in the summer of 1933. If the school was to serve the purposes set out for it, the granting of the Ph.D. was a logical goal, and had been so assumed when the memorandum of 1932 had been prepared. However, by the spring of 1933 it had become unmistakably clear that there was insufficient money in the Fletcher Fund to establish the special library that would be indispensable for research at the doctoral level. The resources of Eaton Library were focused on undergraduate instruction and even in that respect were far from ideal. In 1930 Cousens had requested the College librarian to inventory the existing collection and to make some estimates of the expenditures necessary for a minimum working collection for the Fletcher School. The results were most discouraging. The library was already a partial depository of the documents of the federal government and of the publications of the Carnegie Endowment for International Peace. A start had been made in 1929 to purchase the publications of the

---

[31] Hoskins' existing salary continued to be paid entirely from the school of liberal arts until he was made dean the following year. Pound volunteered his services without compensation, but the Trustees did vote him a stipend; Hindmarsh was also appointed Visiting Assistant Professor in Government in

League of Nations, which would require at least $1,500 to complete to date and an annual expense of over $200 thereafter. The library had virtually none of the official publications of foreign governments, such as the British and Foreign State Papers. Many sets would cost many hundreds of dollars apiece to acquire. On the basis of only two lists of authoritative works on international affairs, at least $1,000 would be needed to fill only the most glaring gaps, not including periodical files of major importance.[32] No matter how the problem was approached, the library resources of the College would in no real way meet the needs of a graduate school in foreign affairs. It was the lack of library materials on the Tufts campus that explained in large part the provision in the memorandum of 1933 that the course of study would at first have to be confined to the Master's level.

The impasse over library needs was broken in the summer of 1933, when the director of the World Peace Foundation, at the prompting of Acting Dean Hoskins, formally proposed that its library, consisting of more than 40,000 books, documents, and pamphlets, be placed in the custody of the Fletcher School for an indefinite period, as soon as accommodations became available. This invaluable addition to the Fletcher School was in no sense an unheralded windfall. President Cousens had carefully and patiently started negotiations to that end in 1929, when he suggested to Raymond T. Rich, general secretary of the Foundation, "a possibility of cooperative effort" between that organization and the proposed school. The first tangible result of consultations with the Tufts librarian was the placing of orders for selected publications of the League of Nations, the World Court, and the International Labor Office, to be housed in Eaton Library.

The Foundation collection was transferred to Goddard Hall in the fall of 1933. The basement of the old gymnasium became the stack area, and what had been the basketball cage became the reading room. The research director of the Foundation, Mr. Denys P. Myers, was employed by the College as research librarian, in

---

the school of liberal arts for the second semester of 1933–34 and 1934–35.

[32] The librarian reported the disturbing fact in 1932 that the Tufts Library contained less than 35 per cent of approximately 500 titles in political science considered indispensable in the Carnegie List of Books for College Libraries.

accordance with the agreement with the Foundation.[33] The research librarian had been largely responsible for the selection of materials for the Foundation collection, and because he was thoroughly familiar with its contents, his presence was not only welcomed but absolutely necessary.

The curricular and degree requirements that had been outlined early in 1933 were further defined and amplified later in the year. The eleven courses comprising the first curriculum were divided among three groups, under the headings of Public and International Law, Diplomacy and International Relations, and International Economics. Candidates for the Master of Arts degree were expected to complete one year in residence, carry a program of four courses (two of them in the group in which the student wished to specialize), exhibit a reading knowledge of one foreign language (French, Spanish, or German), present a satisfactory thesis, and pass an examination before a committee of the faculty. The degree of Master of Arts in Law and Diplomacy required, in addition to one foreign language and a thesis, the passing of a general oral examination in four approved special fields of study selected from the three groups. It was anticipated that the requirements for this degree could not be met in less than two years.[34]

The Fletcher School of Law and Diplomacy opened its doors the second week of October 1933 to twenty-one students, all college or university graduates, four of them already holding a Master's degree. The first class represented twelve states and nineteen institutions and thus set the pattern for a cosmopolitan student

[33] One-half of his salary was paid out of Fletcher School funds; his term of service was at first "undetermined" but became an annual appointment. The same salary arrangement was provided for his combined secretary and assistant until 1936, when the Fletcher School became responsible for the entire salary. This came about because the Foundation's income had been "greatly reduced."

[34] The first act of the Fletcher faculty at its only meeting of record in 1933–34 was to establish academic standards. It was voted that "B—" would be the lowest acceptable mark in fulfilling the course requirements. It was also provided that in case of failure, a degree candidate had both to make up his course deficiencies and to repeat his oral examination. Degree recommendations the first year were made to the Joint Executive Committee, but thereafter directly to the Tufts Trustees.

body thereafter. Seventeen of the twenty-one received some amount of financial assistance. Because there were as yet no housing or dining accommodations for Fletcher students, eighteen of the new arrivals were housed in Tufts dormitories. Fifteen Fletcher students received Master of Arts degrees at Tufts' seventy-eighth Commencement in June 1934, and seven of the first class of twenty who completed the year expressed a desire to return for a second year of study. An enrollment of thirty-one in the fall of 1934, representing twenty-three American colleges and universities and three foreign institutions, was most encouraging. Fourteen men and women received the Master of Arts degree in 1935, and at the same Commencement the Fletcher School awarded its first Master of Arts in Law and Diplomacy. The dean of the school had already come to the conclusion by the fall of 1934 that, given the resources available, thirty-five students rather than fifty should represent the maximum enrollment. Fifteen of the thirty-three students in residence in 1935–36 had previously attended the school.

Austin Fletcher's dream had finally come true. It was, in Cousens' enthusiastic language, a "magnificent start" which seemed "incredible." He had ventured to predict in the fall of 1933 that "unless we are wholly deceived as to the future possibilities, it is reasonable to prophesy that the opening of the Fletcher School will prove the most important event in the history of Tufts College." He praised the work of Professor Hoskins, who, lacking "a wider reputation in international affairs," had the great assets of "enthusiasm and intimate knowledge of the situation of the College." The prospects of the Fletcher School looked promising indeed. With a uniquely valuable library of great renown and one of the most distinguished faculties that could have been assembled, the school might not only become the center of interest in international affairs in the Northeast but could serve the community of nations on a scale well outside the boundaries of the United States. President Cousens' optimism was based on events that occurred even before the school was formally opened on October 27, 1933, with keynote addresses by James T. Shotwell of New York and Professor Charles W. Hackett of the University of Texas. The Fletcher School almost immediately received a joint invitation from the Foreign Policy Association and the World Peace Foundation to collaborate in organizing national committees of experts who would discuss, at the policy-making level, significant problems in the realm of international diplomacy. The first such meeting — of a Committee on Latin American Policy — was held at the school the last week in October. Out of their discussions came an important report; parts of it were incorporated into the instructions to the United States delegation to the Seventh Pan American Conference at Montevideo which was significant in developing President Franklin D. Roosevelt's "Good Neighbor" policy in hemisphere relations. Plans were also under way for the first of the projected six-weeks summer sessions which were to be of particular value to teachers. Most signs pointed to an auspicious start for the Fletcher School for which Cousens had labored so mightily.

§   §   §

Operating a school such as Fletcher, with its interlocking and intricate relationships with both Harvard and Tufts, was no simple matter. Misunderstandings, conflicts of interest (and personalities), and embarrassments of one sort or another over both details of administration and larger matters could have been quite accurately predicted. Unfortunately they also came to pass.

The establishment of a working relationship between the Tufts and Fletcher libraries was one of the most important matters of concern. President Cousens had firm ideas on the subject. He insisted that the College librarian "should take responsibility as head of the library organization of the college for all departmental libraries." This was not only "good organization but the only one which could be adopted." He considered the newly acquired library of the World Peace Foundation "an integral part of the library of Tufts College." This inevitably created practical problems of administration, particularly as Research Librarian Myers found himself in a position subordinate to the dean of the Fletcher School and the librarian of the College as well as to President Cousens. Nonetheless, Cousens was "confident that any difficulties which may be inherent in the situation" could be satisfactorily overcome. The problem of the geographical separation of the College and Fletcher libraries became apparent immediately. Cousens had reluctantly been forced by financial considerations to abandon a proposal made in 1930 by Professor Ruhl J. Bartlett to construct an addition to Eaton Library to house the Foundation library and make accessible to Fletcher students the standard reference works already available in the College library. Such an arrangement would have provided maximum convenience and would have obviated the need for the purchase of expensive duplicate materials for Fletcher students.

Raymond Walkley, the College librarian, did his best to work within the framework on which the president insisted. An initially workable division of expenditures was arranged whereby the World Peace Foundation continued the subscription of periodicals needed for the school, and the Fletcher School purchased new books. It was hoped that the Fletcher library would "also prove useful to students here at Tufts College in advanced courses which may lead to work in the Fletcher School after they complete their undergraduate work." In order to concentrate in one building the books needed by Fletcher students, the College librarian arranged to transfer "several hundred" volumes to Goddard Hall as a loan from Eaton Library.

The Fletcher library was designated the Edwin Ginn Library in 1933 in honor of the Tufts alumnus who had founded the prominent educational publishing house bearing his name; he had also donated $1,000,000 to found the World Peace Foundation in 1910. A year's experience with the library required some readjustments of original plans. Because it was primarily a research collection intended for graduate students, it was anticipated that the use of the Ginn Library by Tufts students would "be confined principally to graduate work or work of graduate character."[35] Tufts graduate students were required to obtain special permission cards through their department chairmen, subject to the approval of the Fletcher librarian. Undergraduates were allowed to use the reading room "individually for approved, specific purposes." To avoid unnecessary duplication of material as between the Fletcher and Tufts libraries, book orders for the first few years were "executed in principle through the Librarian of the College." There was also a constant lending of books back and forth — a device which saved considerable money but which also resulted in considerable inconvenience. It was no small task to transform the Foundation library from a private institutional collection into an integrated

[35] Rules for the use of the Fletcher library were prepared in November 1933.

academic library; it took years to accomplish. The Ginn Library at first consisted "overwhelmingly" of the World Peace Foundation collection, but Fletcher funds were used to build up gradually the books needed for course work. Initially, some friction occurred at the administrative level over library relationships. The research librarian had to be called to task in one instance for requesting a library grant of $5,000 directly from the Carnegie Corporation, bypassing all of the authorities responsible for the Fletcher School. The dean of the school was similarly forcefully reminded "that the Fletcher School library and the Eaton Library will, of necessity, be built up together." Therefore, "except in rare instances," purchases for Eaton Library were not to be duplicated in the Ginn Library. One of the reasons for channeling all book orders for both libraries across the Eaton librarian's desk was to make sure that the books desired were not already available. The overlapping of the two libraries was to be a perennial source of discussion, particularly as Dean Hoskins' understanding was that materials to build up the teaching collection should usually be obtained through the order department of the World Peace Foundation rather than through the Tufts Library.

The personnel problems of the Fletcher School continued to be a source of difficulty after the school was opened. One of the penalties paid for depending on part-time faculty was a constant turnover of teachers from year to year. When the school opened for its second year (1934–35), there were five new appointments, all from the Harvard faculty: William Y. Elliott, Professor of Diplomacy and International Relations, who was also the chairman of the Department of Government at Harvard; Josef A. Schumpeter, Professor of International Economics; Philip W. Thayer, Professor of Public and International Law; John H. Williams, Professor of International Economic Relations; and Professor Richard V. Gilbert, who replaced Professor Lauchlin B. Currie. Professors Holcombe and Langer were not on the Fletcher staff that year, and in the following year three more changes were made. This became an all-too-typical situation in subsequent years. Virtually every appointment involving Harvard faculty required prolonged negotiation between Presidents Cousens and Conant and did not always result in complete harmony. The Fletcher School was able to obtain in 1936–37 the part-time services of Dr. Hajo Holborn, who was Visiting Professor at Yale.[36] Simultaneously, it lost Professor Manley O. Hudson, who had been elected by the League of Nations to a judgeship on the Permanent Court of International Justice.[37] Professor Julius Stone returned to Cambridge University. No person was more aware than Dean Hoskins of the drawbacks inherent in a system of part-time staffing, for he was himself required for the first year of his administration to split his responsibilities between the Fletcher School and the Tufts Department of History.[38] Even those of the Harvard faculty who were involved in and enthusiastic about the Fletcher program had their major academic commitments elsewhere. Consequently, they could contribute little more than classtime instruction. Hoskins considered the nucleus of a full-time faculty an absolute necessity as soon as possible — men who could "identify themselves completely with the School and share some of the duties of administration and student guidance." A beginning was made in recruiting a full-time resident faculty when Dr. Norman J. Padelford was appointed in 1936–37 as Professor of International Law and Organization.

President Cousens never succeeded in staffing the Fletcher School with the full-time faculty that everyone agreed was necessary. He summarized the dilemma in one sentence: "The kind of man whom we want as a full-time teacher in the Fletcher School is very hard to find and very difficult to finance after he is found." Even the minimum goal of only two full-time faculty members was impossible to achieve during Cousens' lifetime. The fields of international economics and diplomatic history seemed to be in most urgent need of strengthening. An effort was made in the summer of 1934 to obtain the services of a prominent young Cana-

[36] The traveling expenses of commuting faculty members became a sizable item in the Fletcher budget.

[37] The series of lectures he delivered at the Fletcher School in 1935 became part of a book (*By Pacific Means: An Implementation of the Pact of Paris*) published for the Fletcher School by the Yale University Press. The royalties were assigned to Fletcher.

[38] His appointment as dean, beginning September 1934, had repercussions in the undergraduate division of the College. It required adjustments in the Department of History, the most important of which was the appointment of Professor R. J. Bartlett as chairman. A new member of the department also had to be added.

dian scholar from Toronto, but he slipped through Cousens' fingers even after a contract had been signed with the Trustees. The Canadian government found it necessary to employ the young man. This turn of events greatly perturbed Cousens. He was confident that the school could "find men of reputation who have reached such an age that a comfortable berth in the Fletcher School at a good salary appears attractive." But men on the verge of retirement were not what was wanted. The ideal faculty were those in their middle years who had become recognized scholars and were of the highest caliber; but they were beyond the financial capabilities of the school. The remaining alternative was to select "young men of promise with the hope that their reputations may grow with the school." But this policy created its own disadvantages, for it was in its early years that the school most needed the faculty of highest stature.

Separate housing for Fletcher students had become imperative by 1935–36. Twenty Fletcher men in the fall of 1935 were residing in rooms designed for and sorely needed by undergraduates. In spite of his "high hopes to the contrary," Cousens found that the undergraduates and Fletcher students were like oil and water — they "will not mix." The answer to the problem was the purchase in 1936 of the so-called Bruce House opposite the western end of the campus and only a short walk from Goddard Hall.[39] Enlargement of the house by using adjoining property acquired by the College was authorized in 1937, and a wing was added that year. This first Fletcher dormitory was named the George Grafton Wilson House the same year, on the recommendation of Dean Hoskins. The relatively small number of women then enrolled in the school did not yet seem to warrant an additional building. They made what private arrangements they could until the fall of 1937, when quarters for six students were provided near the school. In 1939 a house for women students was obtained adjacent to Wilson House and was named Blakeslee House in honor of another of the original members of the Fletcher faculty.

Before the Fletcher School had been open three months, the problem of insufficient funds for fellowships and scholarships arose.

[39] The purchase was made in two installments because the house was divided into two sections. This curious arrangement prevailed because the two parts of the house were owned by different people.

Many of the students enrolled in the first year soon expressed their intention of continuing for the doctorate and needed continued financial assistance. Funds available for such purposes amounted to only $5,000. Cousens considered the total necessary for 1934–35 to be twice that figure and, because there was no money available, asked his friend Frederick C. Hodgdon to try to obtain a grant of at least $5,000 from the Carnegie Foundation. His efforts were fruitless. Cousens and Hoskins were fully aware that "large funds" were being established in the best universities for student assistance and that the keen competition for students of high caliber would increase rather than decrease. It was therefore incumbent upon the Fletcher School to make a relatively large outlay in this area. This policy was carried out in 1934–35, even though outside assistance was not forthcoming. Nine students were awarded scholarships equal to tuition, and fourteen others were awarded fellowship grants ranging from $500 to $1,000.[40] It was evident that tuition charges could never become a very material source of revenue. Tuition was advanced for new students from its original $300 to $400, effective in 1936–37. This step was taken not only to bolster the slim treasury of the school but also to make its charges equal to that of Harvard. A $100 differential in tuition between institutions in which there were course exchange privileges could create an awkward situation.

The dearth of fellowship aid for Fletcher students was alleviated somewhat in the fall of 1934 when Dean Hoskins negotiated a cooperative fellowship for the school with the Brookings Institution in Washington. By this arrangement, similar to that for fellowships already established by the Institution with five other schools, a pre-doctoral grant of $1,000 to a third-year student was provided; it also provided housing and access to research facilities in Washington. The first such fellowship was awarded in 1936.[41]

[40] The total expenditure was offset in part by the fact that fellowships did not carry exemption from tuition charges, and by the fact that two students were financed by traveling fellowships received from the institutions from which they were graduated. The net outlay for financial assistance was actually less than $3,500 in 1934–35, and that figure was not exceeded the following year in spite of the fact that over two-thirds of the student body received assistance in some amount.

[41] One-half of the cash grant was paid by the Brookings Institution and the other half by the Fletcher School.

Informal arrangements were also made with the Institute of International Education in New York so that one or more exchange fellowships abroad could be provided Fletcher students; in return, the school was to receive a foreign student which it would select. Tangible evidence that the Fletcher School was growing in stature and reputation in academic circles was provided in 1935–36, when Dean Hoskins was selected to serve on the American Coordinating Committee of the International Studies Conference.[42] Hoskins made a point of the fact that the school was selected for representation on the committee "as an independent unit, not as a school associated with Harvard University."

The creation by 1936 of a backlog of students who had completed their work at the Master's level and were anxious to continue for the doctorate became a matter to which serious attention had to be given. Again, the school was handicapped by a part-time faculty that continued to rotate with such rapidity that the students could not be encouraged to develop any long-range research projects. Initially, the students' only alternative was to transfer to Harvard to complete the doctorate, and several followed that path. Three students made formal application for Ph.D. candidacy in the Fletcher School in 1936–37, a development that necessitated the setting up of examining committees provided in the cooperative arrangement with Harvard. The Fletcher School awarded its first Ph.D. in 1941.

One noteworthy and valuable feature of the Fletcher School, introduced during its first year of operation and continued thereafter with great success, was the bringing in of outstanding scholars, public leaders, and diplomatic officials to deliver formal public lectures and to participate in informal discussions with the students and faculty of the school. Among the speakers in 1933–34 were Professor Alfred Zimmern of the School of International Studies at Geneva and President Charles R. Watson of the American University at Cairo. During the following year, the roster of distinguished speakers included Raymond L. Buell, by then president of the Foreign Policy Association; Stephen P. Duggan, director of the Institute of International Education; and Sir Herbert Ames, former treasurer of the League of Nations. The list of dis-

[42] The Conference had been established in 1928 by the International Institute of Intellectual Cooperation of the League of Nations.

tinguished speakers was impressively long for virtually every succeeding year.

The early products of the Fletcher School went into the most diverse occupations. For the first few years only a scattering of graduates entered the Foreign Service or held diplomatic posts of any kind. The majority went into college or secondary school teaching or into business. The high quality of the students admitted to the school was demonstrated in the early years in several ways. Not only did a high proportion come equipped with Phi Beta Kappa keys, impressive academic records, and strong recommendations, but many, after obtaining their Master's degree at Fletcher, went on to advanced work as holders of coveted fellowships in numerous prominent universities. Twice in the first three years of the school's history Fletcher students were selected as Rhodes Scholars.

§ § §

Cousens had his moments of doubt and hesitation — even regret — about the joint administration of the Fletcher School. Just a few days after the first memorandum with Harvard had been signed in 1932, he put his thoughts on paper. By bringing that institution into the project, Tufts had had to give up what might have been the greatest opportunity it would ever have to enhance its reputation single-handedly. In wording reminiscent of Hosea Ballou 2d's opposition in the early 1850's to the locating of Tufts so close to Harvard, Cousens expressed fear that Tufts would be more than ever "over-shadowed by the great institution which is our neighbor." He tried to convince himself that these were "rather emotional objections than intelligent ones" and that without Harvard's help it might have been impossible to have achieved "the fundamental purpose" of the Fletcher bequest at all. He had been tempted, before the negotiations with Harvard had taken place, to tell the Tufts Trustees that the College "had better delay the entire plan until the endowment amounted to at least $2,000,000." Cousens came to the shocked realization that almost every cent of the original bequest of $1,000,000 could easily have been spent for the Fletcher library alone. And there was always the possibility that Harvard would find the relationship with the Fletcher School insufficiently attractive to continue the arrangement. What was then to be done?

The worst seemed to have happened in the late spring of 1934. Cousens received formal notice from Harvard in May of its intention to terminate the agreement of April 1933. Harvard was, however, willing to negotiate a new agreement, effective in 1935–36, to which the Tufts Trustees agreed.[43] The new arrangement continued the mutual availability of library facilities, reciprocal course privileges, and the understanding that the enrollment would still be limited to fifty.[44] The heart of the brief memorandum of 1934 was the statement that "the entire control of the Fletcher School of Law and Diplomacy will be administered by Tufts College alone." Behind this barebones wording lay months of discussion, debate, and disagreement, aggravated by conflicts over personalities.

Anxious as President Lowell apparently had been to work out the cooperative arrangement with Tufts that resulted in the opening of the Fletcher School, he had disagreed with Cousens over the deanship. In the draft of the memorandum of April 1933 Cousens had listed Professor Hoskins as acting dean, pursuant to the action already taken by the Tufts Trustees in March, and had intimated that he might very well be considered for the deanship. President Lowell objected. "Grave doubt" had been raised whether Hoskins was "the best man for a permanent dean, and whether it would not be better to make him secretary and leave the position of dean open for the present." Lowell nonetheless accepted Cousens' decision to make Hoskins the acting dean. Unfortunately, the question of the deanship was raised again after Conant became president of Harvard. In February 1934 Kenneth B. Murdock, dean of the Harvard Faculty of Arts and Sciences and a member of the Joint Executive Committee, forewarned Cousens that, after informal discussions with Harvard faculty teaching in the Fletcher School, he could not see his way clear to support Hoskins' appointment as dean. The most he could favor would be the re-

[43] The Harvard Corporation approved the new memorandum on May 14 and the Tufts Trustees did likewise on June 16. Termination of this agreement required written notice three years in advance.

[44] Hoskins completed arrangements in June 1934 with the dean of the Harvard Graduate School of Arts and Sciences for mutual exchange of students. Only a few in either institution took advantage of the course exchange arrangements. Access to Harvard libraries was, according to Dean Hoskins, the most valuable of all the facilities for Fletcher students.

appointment of Hoskins for one year as acting dean. President Conant not only agreed with Dean Murdock but was given to understand that dissatisfaction and criticism were more far-reaching than Murdock had supposed and would require a careful review of "the whole situation." President Conant immediately appointed a committee to consider the relationship between his institution and the Fletcher School.[45]

The report, amounting in effect to an indictment of the whole Fletcher School as then organized, included a grim list of particulars which added up to the fact that the relationship was "not one which is advantageous to Harvard University." It was alleged that the courses offered at the school were almost all duplicates of those offered in the various schools and departments at Harvard, and that there seemed "to be little reason for continuing to maintain an institution which does not after all extend the possibilities of instruction available at the present time." The endowment of the Fletcher School was inadequate to secure full-time staff and because almost all the teachers were drawn from Harvard the end product was a serious diversion of their energies. The committee insisted that one unfortunate by-product of depending on part-time staff from outside was a lowering of academic standards. The Fletcher School was too ambitiously organized and was trying to do entirely too much too soon. It would be much wiser, reported the committee, to have the school specialize in some area, possibly in administrative law or international law or organization. Another suggestion was to operate Fletcher only as a summer school. In any case, the committee thought it unwise to try to conduct a school offering both the second and third degrees when it did not by any stretch of the imagination have the resources to do a decent job. The school had "great possibilities," but only if it concentrated on specific and limited objectives and secured a small full-time staff. It might then be possible to offer as much as a Master's degree, but no more. If the Trustees of Tufts College saw fit to establish realistic goals and to furnish adequate support, then the school's potential could count for something. Otherwise, unless the possibilities could be realized, Harvard could not "advantageously afford to continue its formal cooperation." As late as the fall of

[45] The committee, headed by Dean Murdock, consisted also of Dean Pound and Professor Arthur N. Holcombe and George Grafton Wilson.

1934 Cousens could get no assurance from Conant that he would allow any member of the Harvard staff, except for some in the law school, to teach in Fletcher. The school was at the mercy of Harvard. President Conant did leave the door ajar by intimating that he might allow "some few men" to teach in the school, but on a temporary Visiting Professor or Lecturer basis only.

Dean Hoskins prepared a spirited defense of the school and argued that quite naturally "an enterprise representing in several respects a new departure in graduate instruction and depending for its success on wholehearted cooperation of leading members of two educational institutions, including some having little personal interest in the undertaking, could scarcely hope to escape adverse comment, particularly during the experimental period." Yet it was all too true, as Cousens acknowledged to the Trustees in his annual report for 1934, that the Fletcher School could not exist without Harvard's cooperation, and that the plan he and President Lowell had worked out in 1932–33 implied "an equal partnership" which was actually impossible to maintain.

President Cousens' distress at the Harvard committee report was exceeded only by his astonishment that the four men who compiled it could possibly feel as they apparently did. It was "simply amazing" to Cousens that these men, who had been so influential in bringing the Fletcher School into existence and had apparently been so enthusiastic about its future, should now take the view that it was "an outside institution, to which under some circumstances, Harvard University might be pleased to lend assistance." Cousens conceived the Fletcher School to be "intrinsically a part of Harvard University"; to imply that it was otherwise could mean only a gross misinterpretation of the relationship established in the 1933 memorandum. No person teaching in both Harvard and Fletcher was to receive extra compensation; Fletcher duties were to be considered a normal part of a full academic load. Cousens knew that at least those faculty drawn from the Harvard Law School had so considered their teaching assignments and salaries. It was Harvard's responsibility to work out its own policies regarding faculty compensation. As to criticisms of the objectives, curriculum, and academic standards of the school, Cousens informed the Harvard president that it was the latter's own faculty who had helped to set up goals of the school and outline the three fields in which work was being given. He could not understand why the committee members had suddenly turned against their own handiwork and had not raised objections earlier.

As to the deanship, Cousens unwaveringly supported Hoskins; it was the president's refusal to compromise on that issue that had precipitated Harvard's announcement in May 1934 of its intention to terminate the 1933 agreement. Cousens justified his stand on several grounds. It would have been "impossible under the circumstances" for the Tufts Trustees to consent to have Hoskins replaced by "some man out of the Harvard Yard." To renew the search for a dean from outside would be "unwise"; two years of effort had already shown the futility of that. Even if someone were found, "it would be a disaster to the school to put in a new man as Acting Dean now." Finally, there was the matter of Hoskins himself. It would, in Cousens' estimation, be unfair both to the acting dean and to the Tufts Department of History to continue him indefinitely without assurance as to his future at the College. Cousens insisted that when Conant knew Hoskins better he would agree that "Dr. Hoskins is precisely the right man in the right place."

Cousens gave the Harvard president very little room to negotiate. The Tufts president suggested that Hoskins continue as acting dean for another year (1934–35), with assurances that his title would be changed to dean as of September 1935. The curriculum and faculty arrangements were to continue for one more year and then be subject to renegotiation. These arrangements were to be accepted with the reservation that "if Harvard University finds them incompatible with her own policies and purposes notice to that effect will be given on March 1, 1935, the cooperative arrangement dissolved as of September 1, 1935, and the Fletcher School continue from that date under the management of the Trustees of Tufts College alone." Cousens urged a prompt decision, for applications were pouring into the school. Word had also spread among the students, and a number of them were "clamoring to know what is to become of them."

The decision was not long delayed. In a conversation on March 7, 1934, Cousens was informed that if Hoskins continued as head of the Fletcher School Harvard would serve notice of intention to withdraw from the 1933 arrangement as of June 1935. In the meantime, Cousens was assured that arrangements for the school would continue for the academic year 1934–35 under the original agreement. Cousens reiterated his decision to recommend Hoskins' continuance in office and expressed the conviction that the question of the deanship could not possibly be the sole explanation for Harvard's decision. The committee report made him sure "that Harvard University would not be happy to go on with the present Fletcher School arrangements under any leadership unless radical changes in the purpose of the School contrary to the present agreement" were made. President Conant's reply was to let the subject "remain open for discussion." The outcome was the revised agreement which was signed early in the summer of 1934 and which remained the basis of Harvard-Tufts-Fletcher understandings thereafter. After mid-1935, all official publications reflected the changed relationship by carrying the explanation "Administered by Tufts College, with the cooperation of Harvard University."[46]

There is evidence that many Fletcher School alumni over the years received the impression that one of the greatest difficulties and handicaps besetting the school was the lack of cooperation and support given to Dean Hoskins by the Tufts College authorities. The documentation available indicates that the fault lay in the reverse situation, namely, that Hoskins actually received too much support from the College. Cousens' refusal to compromise on the deanship precipitated the breakdown of the 1933 plan of joint administration, which had been a source of friction in other respects as well. Other voices were heard from the Tufts campus itself that lent support to the need for a reassessment of Harvard-Fletcher relations but did not deal in personalities *per se*. At the very time that Presidents Conant and Cousens were in almost daily conversation or correspondence, Professors Bartlett and Albert H. Imlah of the Tufts History Department transmitted their views to Cousens.[47] They too expressed dissatisfaction with the joint administration of the school. It was in no real way integrated into the College even though housed on the same campus. The faculty, with two exceptions, were Harvard men, and their basic allegiance

[46] The appropriate change of wording was made in 1955 when Tufts officially became a "University" by change in its charter.

[47] Both of these men were destined to serve on the Fletcher faculty in later years.

was to Harvard and not to Fletcher. Some of the faculty seemed to view their work in the school as merely "an educationally unprofitable chore," and the broadcasting of this jaundiced view might be harmful to both the school and Tufts. The fact that only one member of the Tufts faculty was teaching in the school cast "a reflection on the abilities and worthiness of the Tufts faculty which is much too palpable for the good of the College."

It seemed that continued formal cooperation with Harvard could result in nothing but "a continued struggle." Was it worth the effort? Why not rely less on Harvard, bring the school into closer relationship to Tufts, and develop a faculty drawn primarily from the College itself, perhaps in some cases teaching in both Fletcher and the undergraduate divisions? Lessened dependence on Harvard would free the school to develop its own interests, would promote unity and centralized control under one president and one Board of Trustees, and would permit distinctive achievements of the Tufts faculty to redound to the credit of the school and the College.

The two Tufts faculty members were arguing, in brief, that the Fletcher School as then administered was but a pale and sometimes flickering shadow of Harvard. It needed its own identity, and if any association were to be emphasized, it should be with Tufts. But that was considerably more difficult to achieve than to talk about, even in the early years of the school. It had its own endowment from the start, and one of Dean Hoskins' continuing efforts was to create an *esprit de corps* among the student body so that it would consider itself a distinct unit. The preliminary decision to allow Tufts undergraduates access to Fletcher courses was abandoned even before the school opened, in spite of Cousens' hope. It was made clear when the Ginn Library opened that its use by undergraduates was to be considered a special privilege, subject to restrictions. In the fall of 1933 President Cousens was disturbed to discover that the first letterhead stationery of the school carried its name in large letters, with the reference to the joint administration by Tufts and Harvard in minuscule print underneath. Even more upsetting to that loyal alumnus of the College was the fact that the return address on the envelope did not even carry the name of Tufts. It seemed important to him that "we should not neglect any opportunity to indicate the connection of the Fletcher School with Tufts College and its location here."

The revised arrangement for the administration of the Fletcher School removed one advantageous channel of publicity which was enjoyed for only one year, namely, a section on the school in the Harvard catalogue. President Conant felt in the summer of 1934 that a description of the school would be "out of place" in view of the fact that it was to be administered solely by Tufts. More important, the return of full administrative responsibility for the Fletcher School to Tufts removed all official machinery by which Harvard could be kept systematically informed of the condition and progress of the school, for no mention was made of the Joint Executive Committee in the new memorandum. The problem of communication promised to become a serious one if no liaison at all were provided.

Dean Hoskins continued to affirm in 1934 that the school was a distinct success, in spite of all the difficulties already encountered and yet to be surmounted. He recognized that the Joint Executive Committee, as originally provided, was well designed as a general governing board but could not function successfully as a legislative body to handle the innumerable details of operation. Some kind of faculty organization was required. The personnel problem was a serious one, for the Harvard authorities were reluctant to release those members of their faculty teaching in the Fletcher School from their regular duties, and the school was unable to assume a proportionate share of their stipends. It appeared that no true cooperation could exist unless the work done in the Fletcher School was made an integral part of the teaching load of such faculty. Because of constant turnover, *esprit de corps* was lacking, the courses of instruction could be planned only one year at a time, and the students failed to receive the guidance they needed in planning both their course work and their careers. He acknowledged the basic criticism leveled at the school by the Harvard committee by recommending that the objectives "be confined to those which might most appropriately be pursued in a specially organized school with limited income." This meant specialization in those branches of international affairs not emphasized at Harvard. He agreed that the school should, until further notice, confine its degrees to the Master of Arts and the Master of Arts in Law and Diplomacy. Removal of the formal agreement with Harvard raised the serious question of the school's ability to offer the Ph.D. degree.

The Fletcher Committee on Curriculum and Requirements for Degrees undertook in the fall of 1934 to find some means of preserving effective contact with Harvard on Fletcher School matters.[48] They suggested a joint supervisory committee which would cease to exist after the academic year 1934–35. The aim was to work out some scheme so that Harvard could be assured of sufficient participation in the direction of the Fletcher School to justify calling it a cooperative enterprise. The new committee was to consist of the presidents of both institutions, the dean of the Harvard Law School, the dean of the Fletcher School, and one member of the Harvard faculty not connected with the school, to be nominated by the president of Harvard. The committee would perform dual functions: visitorial and supervisory. The Fletcher dean would make an annual report to the committee and the committee would be invited to visit the school at least once a year. Supervisory functions would include approval of nominees to the Fletcher faculty and approval of requirements for admission and the granting of degrees. These powers were assumed to be appropriate as long as Harvard continued "to give the Fletcher School the advantages of association with it, and consequently to assume in some degree responsibility for the work and standards of the Fletcher School." The creation of such a committee and the delegation of its powers would have to rest with the Trustees of Tufts College because of their responsibility for the administration of the school. To be assured that any Ph.D. awarded by the school represented standards acceptable to both Harvard and Tufts, a member of the Harvard faculty unconnected with the Fletcher School was to be selected by the committee to serve as an external dissertation reader and examiner.

Much to Cousens' relief, President Conant agreed to continue to cooperate on Fletcher matters and agreed to serve on the proposed committee and to appoint another Harvard representative. The name of the new body and its exact duties were subject to considerable fluctuation. Cousens conceived its functions primarily as

[48] The committee at the time consisted of Professors Blakeslee and Stone of Harvard, with Dean Hoskins as chairman.

those of a Visiting Committee or Board of Visitors which would also serve as a guiding and supervising body. As actually worked out, the body which was created in 1935 by the Trustees was known at first as the Committee of Visitors and then interchangeably as the Joint Advisory Council or Board.[49] Until 1955 the Board (usually referred to as the Council after 1939) was listed also as the Committee of Visitors. In the meantime, a Board of Counselors was created (in 1940), consisting originally of four distinguished public officials whose function it was to advise "on technical matters" and to assist "in maintaining liaison with the practical needs of a rapidly changing world."[50] Beginning in 1945 this body was redesignated the Board of Advisers and was greatly enlarged. It underwent another change of name in 1960, when it became the Board of Visitors. The Joint Academic Council continued separately, with the makeup as originally provided in 1935.

Cousens quite naturally had to use Harvard faculty on the terms laid down by Conant. The Tufts president had no other recourse than to agree to Conant's ruling that the salaries paid to Harvard faculty for services to the Fletcher School would be "over and above their full-time salaries here at Harvard," and that the use of Harvard faculty in any given year in no way bound that institution to continue the arrangements for another year. The Fletcher School was able to secure the services of Professor John H. Williams, of the Harvard Department of Economics, and of Professor George Grafton Wilson as Special Lecturers in 1937–38, with the understanding that they would be given no additional responsibilities at Fletcher beyond scheduled appearances. The amount of time

[49] This committee originally consisted of Presidents Conant and Cousens, Dean Pound of the Harvard Law School, Professor Clarence H. Haring, of the Harvard History Department, and Dean Hoskins. None of the original members of the Committee of Visitors created by the Tufts Trustees in 1931 for the (then) unborn Fletcher School appeared on the reconstituted committee. With the exception of Christian A. Herter, all members of the 1931 committee had been associated with Tufts in some capacity.

[50] The first Board of Counselors consisted of Dave H. Morris, former ambassador to Belgium (chairman); Christian A. Herter, then Speaker of the House of Representatives of the Massachusetts legislature; Pierrepont Moffat, chief of the Division of European Affairs of the State Department; and Henry M. Wriston, president of Brown University.

they could devote to the Fletcher School depended entirely on their other commitments.[51] But all in all, Cousens was happy with the new arrangements with Harvard. As he informed the Trustees, the prospect (if not the guarantee) of a faculty, even if part-time, and the continued availability of the Harvard libraries for Fletcher students gave the school, for all practical purposes, what had existed under the original formal agreement. A tie of sorts was also established with another part of the Harvard complex when the Tufts Trustees approved in 1937 a cooperative arrangement requested by Radcliffe College whereby courses in the Fletcher School might be opened by special arrangement to students in Radcliffe.[52]

In 1936 an engrossed parchment was forwarded to the officers of Harvard offering greetings and felicitations on the occasion of the 300th anniversary of its founding. Included in the statement was a reference to the "many neighborly courtesies" extended to Tufts and to "the cordial relation of which the administration of the Fletcher School of Law and Diplomacy is symbolic." Less than a year after this expression of good will was transmitted, the man at Tufts who had carried the principal burden on his own shoulders was gone. The Fletcher School had completed less than five years of an uncertain and sometimes stormy existence when President Cousens succumbed to his heart attack in July 1937. Yet there was already evidence that the school was serving a unique and valuable purpose. It had been established, as Dean Hoskins noted in his first annual report to the Joint Advisory Council in the fall of 1935, at a time when foreign concerns seemed less pressing than domestic problems. The increasing gravity of international affairs, witnessed by the rise of totalitarianism in Europe and the Far East and the creeping paralysis that was afflicting the League of Nations, seemed to make the need for an institution such as the Fletcher School more urgent than ever. The school, itself faced with one obstacle after the other, somehow weathered every academic storm

[51] Professor Williams had just been appointed dean of the Harvard Graduate School of Public Administration. It was impossible even to arrange for stipends in orderly fashion because when the time came to set up a schedule Professor Wilson was in the Far East.

[52] The arrangement was made reciprocal in practice, and an occasional Fletcher woman enrolled in Radcliffe courses.

and even showed signs of prospering. Its very existence was a monument to Cousens' determination and unremitting effort. Dean Hoskins penned a tribute in the fall of 1937:

> The loss of President Cousens is very keenly felt. Without his confidence in its potentialities and his constant support of the plan laid out by the original organizing committee, the School certainly could not have achieved its present organization, physical equipment and recognized position in the academic world. The satisfaction with which he viewed the accomplishments of four years establishes a criterion and enhances an obligation for the years to come.

The Fletcher School by 1957, twenty years after Cousens' death, had posted a truly remarkable record of accomplishment, particularly in view of its limited resources and its small size. Alumni numbered about 900, representing more than forty nations and serving in a wide range of professions. By far the largest single group (approximately 350) were in government service and other public service careers either in the United States or abroad. A significant number were engaged in such activities as foreign trade, banking, publishing, and public relations, and over 100 were in the educational profession as teachers or administrators. There seemed little doubt that Austin B. Fletcher's dream of over a quarter of a century before had been in large part realized, although no one would deny that there was still much to be done to perform a "practical service in a disordered world."

15. *Tufts and a Second World War*

THE DEATH OF PRESIDENT COUSENS on July 2, 1937, came as a shock to all who knew him. As had happened twice before in the history of the College, the demise of its chief executive brought sorrow to many but could not mean a cessation of normal activities. On the very day of Cousens' funeral, both the Executive Committee and the main body of Trustees met in special sessions and requested Professor George S. Miller "to serve, with reference to administration of the College, in the manner and to the same extent as he formerly has served in the absence of the President."[1] Tufts had always enjoyed the good fortune of having among its ranks at critical periods in the presidential succession a person who could step into vacated shoes and carry on the work of the institution. Professor J. P. Marshall had served in such a capacity following the death of Tufts' first president, Hosea Ballou 2d. Professor W. L. Hooper had served the College most ably after the resignation of President Hamilton in 1912. The selection of Professor Miller in 1937 could scarcely have been wiser, for he had assets not shared by the two individuals just mentioned: His teaching experience was extensive, for he had been on the staff of the pre-medical school and in the Department of History and Government in the school of liberal arts since 1917. He had also acted as assistant to both Presidents Bumpus and Cousens and, since 1920, had been secretary both of the Associated Faculties on the Hill and of the intown schools. As a graduate of Tufts (Class of 1906) he had been exceptionally active in the Alumni Association and had held numerous assignments of responsibility. There was, without question, no one connected with

[1] Trustees Ira Rich Kent, Vannevar Bush, Richard B. Coolidge, Sumner Robinson, Guy M. Winslow, and Harold E. Sweet (then president of the Corporation) were appointed as a committee to select a permanent successor.

George Stewart Miller
Acting President, 1937–8

the institution then who had a more intimate knowledge than he of the details, intricacies, and problems of its administration, or of the personnel associated with it. He had a finger on every movement of the College pulse.

The Trustee nominating committee, chaired by Ira Rich Kent, submitted its recommendations for a permanent successor to the late President Cousens on February 17, 1938. Dr. Leonard Carmichael, a graduate of the Class of 1921, was unanimously elected, to take office on September 1, 1938. If Cousens had been present, he would have not only enthusiastically voted for the new president but expressed great satisfaction that the successor he had himself selected was also the choice of the Trustees. In 1937, at the last Commencement over which he presided, Cousens had told Denys P. Myers, research librarian at the Fletcher School, that he took a special interest in the honorary degrees he had just awarded. Among the recipients had been Dr. Carmichael, a member of the first class over whose graduation Cousens had presided as president. Cousens' enthusiasm for the recipient of the honorary Doctor of

Science degree was so obvious that Myers commented that Cousens seemed to be describing presidential timber. "I believe that is so," was the Tufts president's reply. In a conversation with Trustee Kent in March 1937 relative to the candidates for honorary degrees at Commencement, Cousens had remarked, when Carmichael's name was mentioned, "This is a man I have in mind as my possible successor in the presidency of Tufts College."

The new president of Tufts, who was elected to his post at the age of thirty-nine, had already compiled an impressive record as an undergraduate, as a graduate student, and in the academic profession. He also had a family connection with Tufts that reached back well into the nineteenth century. His maternal grandfather, Rev. Charles H. Leonard, had helped to establish in 1869 what was then known as the divinity school. From 1892 until 1912 Leonard had served as dean of the school, and his residence on the Hill until his death in 1918 made possible a close personal tie with his grandson during the latter's first year at Tufts. Although Carmichael's official field of concentration while an undergraduate had been English, he took considerable work in history and biology and served as an assistant to Professor Herbert V. Neal in the latter department for three of his four undergraduate years. He became interested in psychology and found his professional career in that field. A brilliant student, he was graduate *summa cum laude* but found the time and energy to be a proctor in Dean Hall, president of Pen, Paint, and Pretzels (the undergraduate dramatic organization), editor of the *Tufts Weekly,* a member of Tower Cross (the senior honorary society), and Theta Delta Chi, a social fraternity. His academic excellence was recognized by election to Phi Beta Kappa and his selection as representative of the school of liberal arts on the Commencement platform in 1921.

After receiving the Ph.D. in psychology at Harvard in 1924 and a Sheldon Travelling Fellowship from that institution, he returned from Europe to teach briefly at Princeton. Between 1928 and 1936 he served on the faculty of Brown University, where he developed a research laboratory in psychology and sensory physiology. He developed similar facilities at the University of Rochester, where he was chairman of the Department of Psychology, beginning in 1936. He was serving as the dean of the Faculty of Arts and

Leonard Carmichael
President 1938–52

Sciences at Rochester when he was called to Tufts. He had also published widely in the field of psychology, had worked in several editorial capacities, and held the rank of Professor of Psychology at Tufts after 1939. His training and experience as both scholar and administrator were natural assets for a college presidency. During his busy professional career before 1938 he kept in close touch with Tufts affairs, engaged in an extensive correspondence with President Cousens, and served as class agent as well as historian of the Class of 1921.

The reaction of alumni to the announcement of Carmichael's election was typified by the resolutions of the Tufts Club of New York, presented to the Trustees in the spring of 1938. The Corporation was commended for selecting a man who was "ideally fitted by training, by experience, and by native ability to fulfill the duties of this office with honor and distinction." As he and his wife, Mrs.

Pearl Kidston Carmichael, prepared to move from New York State to Massachusetts, the new Tufts president explained his decision to his colleagues at Rochester. He was especially interested, he wrote, in the "remarkable development in strength" shown by Tufts under Cousens' leadership. "I only hope that I can help to maintain the momentum of this sound growth. In many ways Tufts seems to me to have one of the most attractive futures of any educational institution in this country." Here was both challenge and opportunity.

The wise and prudent interim administration of George S. Miller in 1937–38 made transition to new leadership almost effortless. The services of Miller were not, however, lost to the College, for he continued as assistant to the president and, in 1939, became the first vice-president of the institution. In his first annual report to the Trustees, President Carmichael had recognized Professor Miller's contributions by the simple statement that "no words of appreciation" could exaggerate the importance of Miller's effective service to the College. The Trustees also made their gratitude for Miller's services a matter of record.

Until well after the First World War the College managed to operate with a minimum of administrative personnel. President Cousens, who insisted on handling great quantities of detail himself in his eighteen-year tenure, had been ably assisted by the deans of the various schools and by Professor Miller. For some time Cousens had entertained the idea of establishing the post of dean of men, but decided in the early 1930's to delay its official creation. Informal arrangements seemed to be working out most satisfactorily. Professor Arthur W. Leighton served for many years as adviser to freshmen classes in the engineering school, and Professor Miller functioned admirably as an *ad hoc* dean of men in the School of Liberal Arts. Cousens had felt that the affairs of the College were not yet sufficiently complex to require such an office. President Carmichael took a somewhat different view and received considerable support from those members of the administration who were in office when he became president in 1938.

It seemed to be evident by the late 1930's that the burden of handling admissions was becoming too large a task for the deans and that there was a noticeable lack of uniformity in selection policies.[2] Cousens had admitted, near the end of his administration, that before many years passed a director of admissions, working with a joint faculty-administrative committee, would have to be established. Dean Wren, of the school of liberal arts, had suggested in 1935 the appointment of an assistant dean or vice-dean who would have charge of pre-medical and pre-dental admissions and curricula. Dean Bush of Jackson College added her voice the following year in favor of an admissions officer for that division of the institution.

The decision of Dean Wren in the fall of 1938 to resign became the first occasion for a series of administrative reorganizations that continued through the end of Carmichael's administration in 1952. The first involved a review of the functions of the office of the dean of the Faculty of Arts and Sciences. No one could deny that it was too demanding an office to be carried any longer by one man. The day had long since passed — some thirty years before — when Wren could serve simultaneously as dean of the School of Liberal Arts, teach a twelve-hour program (with over fifty students), and still find time for a round or so on the College golf course on a sunny afternoon. In 1939 Professor Miller's administrative title was changed from Assistant to the President to Vice-President of the College and Dean of the Faculty of Arts and Sciences. Nils Y. Wessell, who in less than fifteen years would be president of the institution, came from the University of Michigan in 1939 to become Assistant Professor of Psychology, the first dean of men in the school of liberal arts, and the first director of admissions for that school. He had been one of President Carmichael's students at both Brown and the University of Rochester.

The Committee of Visitors to Jackson College, ever mindful of the welfare of the students in that division, immediately requested the Trustees to create the equivalent office of dean of women to be in charge of student personnel matters. This request went unfulfilled, although additional personnel were added from time to time to meet the growing demands of the women's college. The vigilant Committee of Visitors to Jackson College, under the leadership of

[2] The direct responsibility for admission of undergraduates had been transferred from the faculty to the respective deans in 1916. Admission to the graduate and professional schools was by vote of the appropriate faculty, on the recommendation of the departments concerned.

Mrs. Cora Polk Dewick, made an effort in another direction in the late 1930's to assure that the non-academic needs of the women were not neglected. She urged training in correct social usage, social graces, and social amenities. She was not prepared to recommend the establishment of a Domestic Science Department in Jackson, but she did suggest that "there be offered some form of instruction and training in Household Arts and allied subjects" which would not count for degree credit but would give valuable instruction for prospective homemakers. This proposal was never carried out in the literal sense suggested by Mrs. Dewick. On a somewhat different level, she also expressed distress from time to time that the identity of Jackson College, in terms of public relations, tended to be submerged under the name of Tufts and did not stand out sufficiently as a coordinate women's college comparable to Radcliffe, Pembroke, or Barnard.

A review of the virtually identical curricula of the school of liberal arts and of Jackson College shared, with administrative rearrangements, a place on Dr. Carmichael's agenda early in his presidency. The Curriculum Committee was given a mandate in 1939 to assess the course of study, and the faculty busied itself for many months with degree requirements, electives, and required courses. After much discussion, the Liberal Arts and Jackson Curriculum Committee made its recommendations to the parent faculty early in 1940 and in so doing provoked even greater discussion and considerable difference of opinion.

If the recommendations of the Curriculum Committee had been adopted by the faculty, the foreign language requirement as such would have disappeared as a prerequisite for either the A.B. or the B.S. degree and maximum permissiveness would have been built into the entire course of study. A first-year student would have taken either English composition or English literature, his decision to be based on "his needs and interest," advice from the Department of English, and the results of placement tests. The student would have been required to take, instead of a foreign language, a one-year sequence in foreign literature, selected from the Departments of Classics, French, or German; one of three social studies (history, government, or economics); and a science selected from any one of six departments, including mathematics and psychology. The fifth course to round out a normal load would be an elective. One rather interesting aspect of the review of the curriculum in 1939 and 1940 was the statement of educational principles that accompanied it. There had been in actuality no important review of the basic philosophy behind the system of foundation, major, and elective requirements that had been adopted in 1892. Even the 1940 statement represented no change of philosophy except that greater emphasis was put on voluntarism.

> Each student is regarded as an individual whose training and experience in preparation for college, and whose aptitudes and plans may differentiate him from his fellows. Accordingly, the courses in which credits may be earned are not prescribed in any restrictive sense but are selected by each student to suit his own needs within a general framework designed to insure breadth and depth in his intellectual development. . . . Various professions have various special needs: in some, one or more modern or classical languages may be necessary or valuable; in others, mathematics, or special scientific training. A good general education, in the humanities as well as in science and the social studies, is a distinguishing characteristic of members of all the established professions. Tufts College does not consider it wise or necessary to require all students to conform to a uniform pattern. Its officers do feel it is their duty to point out as clearly as possible, however, that members of even the most specialized professions have a personal and social need for a common basis of understanding of modern civilization and culture and a well-developed capacity for clear thinking, as well as a mastery of the knowledge and techniques of their own vocational fields.

By the time the faculty had completed its review of the proposals, the degree requirements had settled very much into their old niches. The concentration requirement was left intact, except that it was increased from thirty to thirty-six semester hours. Students selected their courses and major fields from a broad three-way division of knowledge into humanities, social sciences, and biological and physical sciences, including mathematics. After struggling with the foreign language requirement for many months, the faculty retained it, emphasizing the desirability of choosing French or German because of their importance for admission to graduate or professional schools. The large amount of choice allowed in completing basic degree requirements was continued, although a literature requirement which had been removed by the Curriculum Committee was restored. It was expected that the typical student would complete his five general foundation courses by the end of the sophomore year. No serious attempt to review the entire curriculum was again made until after 1955. The system of foundation and distribution requirements and a broad spectrum of electives continued to reflect President Carmichael's conviction that attention to individual needs was more important than a rigid, prescribed course of study in the arts and sciences.

The period of the late 1930's and early 1940's was also one in which competition for unusually able students was exceptionally keen among institutions in the Boston area as well as elsewhere. Carmichael hoped that a flexible curriculum would attract students of outstanding ability. In his annual report to the Trustees in the fall of 1941 he laid great stress on the College's recognition of the individual *qua* individual. He emphasized this point time and time again. The central idea was that "college students are not alike. . . . we do our best to help the individuals who come to us to educate themselves." A premium was therefore placed on testing programs, and on the greatly expanded guidance and counseling functions of the faculty. He defended the principles of both election and some degree of specialization, even at the underclass level, as clearly preferable to the fully prescribed curriculum. He was aware that a "cafeteria-style" educational menu seemed to disturb such notable educators as Robert M. Hutchins (University of Chicago) and Stringfellow Barr (St. John's College) but vigorously defended Tufts' emphasis on recognizing individual differences as against Chancellor Hutchins' plan for common-core distribution subjects. The tremendous growth of knowledge made concentration in some areas necessary and neglect of others inevitable. Tufts, like many another college, had come a long way from its set nineteenth-century classical curriculum.

Another lively question in educational circles during the 1930's and early 1940's that attracted some attention at Tufts concerned the failure of most institutions of higher learning to emphasize the inculcation of moral and ethical values that had more or less automatically accompanied teaching in older days. The problem was particularly relevant at Tufts, for the faculty's engagement in a review of curricula between 1939 and 1941 was fresh in mind, and the emphasis on meeting individual needs threatened to leave the students without a common core of values, concepts, and ideals. In order to assess this problem (if not to solve it), President Carmichael, who as a psychologist was particularly interested in value theory, appointed a faculty committee in 1941 "to codify the values and objectives of the College." The task of the so-called Committee on Values was to see if agreed-upon "value scales" could be drawn up and made known to the students. There was some talk of planning a syllabus that might eventually become the basis for an elective or even a required senior course. Hosea Ballou 2d, the first president of the institution, would surely have greeted this proposal enthusiastically, for it was he who had had the responsibility of sending the seniors of the first five Tufts graduating classes out into the world equipped with the axioms of Intellectual and Moral Philosophy. Professor Bruce W. Brotherston, chairman of the one-man Department of Philosophy, headed the committee. But just as it was beginning to formulate its propositions, prepare an elaborate questionnaire on values, and solicit articles from the faculty on the subject to be printed in the *Tuftonian,* United States involvement in the Second World War thrust the enterprise into oblivion. More crucial and immediate problems were at hand.

As in the past, various devices were used during Carmichael's administration to recognize and reward undergraduate academic achievement. The Academic Awards ceremony was emphasized, and a special time was set aside each fall to salute students who were elected to honorary societies, both local and national, and to recognize those who received scholarships, fellowships, and prizes for a growing list of achievements. Following the practice already instituted by the engineering school, the school of liberal arts, Jackson College, and the Crane School created a Dean's List and a Freshman Honor Roll in 1939–40 to recognize superior scholarship.[3] An attempt was made in 1941 to revive the historic but almost defunct Honors program for qualified undergraduates, but the greater freedom of opportunity provided for highly gifted stu-

[3] There were tangible rewards for those eligible for such recognition. Students in such categories were allowed to take excess programs without payment of additional fees. Until the system of signing off and on the campus before and after vacations was abolished in the mid-1950's, students on the Dean's List or Freshman Honor Roll were excused from performing this duty.

dents failed to attract more than a small fraction of eligible students. Recognition of scholarship was also provided when, in 1943, the College was granted a chapter of Sigma Xi, the national honorary scientific society. It was President Carmichael who saw to it that the academic primacy of the College's functions was emphasized when he introduced the formal ceremony of Matriculation Convocation in the fall of 1947. Freshmen were thus formally received into the institution and were treated to an address by the president and their first glimpse of the faculty in formal academic attire.

As the Tufts undergraduates came and went in the course of time, many a student custom, tradition, and activity became only a memory. Classes graduated in the Carmichael era would have had no knowledge of the Junior Day "Horribles" of the decades of the First World War and the 1920's, when time out from regular class exercises was called so that students could watch the third-year class, dressed in all imaginable costumes, cavort about the campus and engage in contests. Neither would they have been familiar with such customs as the "Jumbo Rush," when from one to three dummies of the College mascot were thrown from the tower of Goddard Chapel. The men who returned them, albeit tattered and torn, to the chapel steps, received the first copies of the yearbook bearing Jumbo's name. Unfortunately, as a writer in the *Tufts Weekly* pointed out, the Rush for 1917 was overshadowed in the daily newspapers by "a revolution in Russia." Students on the campus between 1937 and 1959 would have recalled the "mayoralty" campaigns in which from two to half a dozen students competed each year for the purely honorary post of custodian of the "campus spirit" as mayor of the Hill. The springtime "mayoralties," imported by John Crockett (Class of 1937), a transfer from Bates College, became an outlet for energies pent up during a long winter and served, with parades, speeches, costumes, and variegated antics, as a welcome "break" before settling down to the serious business of completing laboratory assignments, term papers, and preparing for final examinations. On the more sedate side, there was the tradition, which lasted into the 1950's, of the seniors' "last chapel," when the graduating class assembled solemnly in caps and gowns in front of Ballou Hall to march in stately procession to God-

The Tufts Band at the "Oval" in 1928

dard Chapel to hear the president deliver an inspirational message.

The story of the decline and fall of required chapel exercises at Tufts is more than a fragment of local academic history. It is the story of the growing heterogeneity of college student bodies and of the increasing secular pressures exerted by society at large. The eventual disappearance of that hallowed institution was, in turn, a reflection of a latent rebelliousness characteristic of students the world over, built into young men and women who react against anything labeled "required," and admittedly aided and abetted at times by sympathetic faculty. The bastion of daily compulsory chapel at Tufts was not breached for almost half a century; the first weakening of the structure came with the provision of voluntary Sunday chapel in 1907. In 1911–12, week-day chapel was cut to three days a week, and the disruptions caused by the First and Second World Wars made further inroads. The experience of "no chapel" was not as extraordinary during the 1940's as before, because by 1928 the requirement had been reduced to twice a week

623

for all students, and by the following year to once a week for those privileged to be upperclassmen. Secularism had seemingly triumphed in the 1940's, when the traditional mildly religious service was made voluntary for all, and periodic assemblies and convocations took its place. By 1942–43, captive audiences for required assemblies had been reduced to freshmen only. President Carmichael used these occasions to introduce the first-year students to the nature of the educational process and to the intricacies of the academic lives they would lead for the next few years.

It should be pointed out that this sketch of the disappearance of the time-honored tradition of compulsory chapel gives not even a glimpse of the struggles that went on both overtly and behind the scenes — from periodic barrages in campus publications to lengthy and sometimes heated discussions among a usually divided faculty. Neither does this brief account make allowance for the network of regulations, the flood of paper work, the monitoring and proctoring, the experimentation with every kind of inducement (or penalty) for attendance or non-attendance, from allowed cuts to letter-grading and credit deductions; or for the constant migration of chapel hours all over the school day in a fruitless attempt to accomplish the impossible — namely, to avoid conflict with something else. The voluntary Sunday chapel services of the 1950's and 1960's represented the residue of a custom that had flourished, as a matter of course, in more religiously minded eras in the past. Students, however, continued to be encouraged to attend religious services of their choice in the Tufts neighborhood, and both chaplains and lay faculty representing a variety of faiths and denominations assisted in maintaining clubs and groups on the campus to meet student religious needs.

Debates and discussions about compulsory chapel in the 1930's and early 1940's, and about student activities at any time, received their share of attention. A subject not as likely to attract headlines but just as basic to the college community was the status and welfare of the faculty. Little or nothing concrete had been accomplished during Cousens' administration in the way of providing a pension system, setting up an adequate and rational salary scale, establishing uniform procedures for promotion or sabbatical leave, or adopting a policy regarding academic freedom or tenure. In many of these areas no formal action was considered necessary. The somewhat benevolent paternalism of a relatively simple administrative organization in a relatively small college seemed to make such legislation superfluous. It somehow would have given the impression that the faculty did not trust its superior officers. A faculty of fifty or seventy-five was likely to be well acquainted with the administrative personnel as well as with itself. The college community, fairly close-knit and easily identified, was often referred to as the "Tufts family," in which informal arrangements and understandings could take the place of more bureaucratic and less personal relationships characteristic of either a large business or a gigantic university. But times changed. Tufts by the late 1930's was steadily, if not spectacularly, expanding its size and responsibilities. Faculty pressures from rising costs of living, the problems of insecurity in old age, and growing professional awareness all played a part in bringing to the surface some of the matters of concern that had somehow been ignored or sidetracked in the past. It was during President Carmichael's administration that all of them had to be faced up to by faculty, administration, and Trustees.

Carmichael, when he came to Tufts, was not only cognizant of faculty needs both at the College and elsewhere but painfully aware of the limited financial capabilities of Tufts to meet those needs. Facing the manifold tasks of recruiting and retaining a first-class faculty amid the uncertainties and confusion of the depression-ridden 1930's and the war-ridden 1940's was an experience welcomed by few college presidents.

A personnel problem to which President Cousens had devoted much thought and investigation in the early 1930's was the provision of retirement allowances for members of the faculty who had completed active service. After the Carnegie Foundation had ceased to enroll additional names on its pension lists at the time of the First World War, no system had been introduced at Tufts in its place. Instead, the Trustees followed a policy of aiding individual cases as need arose, without any contractual commitment with the recipients. Cousens had contemplated the establishment of a funded pension system whereby a teacher retiring at the age of seventy after at least twenty-five years of continuous service would receive an allowance of one-half the salary received during the preceding ten years.[4] A similar arrangement might be made for those reaching sixty-five years, with a correspondingly smaller pension. However, Cousens did not yet think it wise to commit the College to such a system, and left cases to be considered on their individual merits. He did suggest that the Trustees might consider setting up a reserve fund to take care of such cases, but he consistently refused to countenance an across-the-board pension system. Cousens believed that there were too many fluctuations in the economy to provide stable retirement stipends; further, he had too much of the self-help philosophy built into his way of thinking to approve pensions for those who already had means and therefore did not deserve assistance. As the nation-wide depression continued well into the 1930's, Cousens reluctantly admitted that some kind of selective pension system was probably desirable. However, it was not until after his death in 1937 that a really strong plea was made. Acting President George S. Miller stressed the importance of providing some form of pension and called the Trustees' attention to the fact that most of the New England colleges had already done so. If Tufts did not do likewise, it would encounter mounting difficulties in securing able men for its faculty. Dean Wren echoed the same sentiments, adding that entirely too many of the faculty were being forced into extra-curricular jobs in order to make ends meet.

The growing restiveness of the faculty at the failure of the College to take any real responsibility for their long-range financial needs and academic security was brought to President Carmichael's attention before he had been on the Tufts campus a year. About 1930 a faculty group led by Professor Charles Gott of the English Department had planned to make a formal statement on the retirement problem, but the onset of the depression and the reluctance of President Cousens to commit the College to any particular pension plan had resulted in postponement. A second proposal to adopt a pension plan was shelved because of the administrative readjustments necessitated by Cousens' death. The financial problems associated with retirement were discussed again by the faculty in

---

[4] The immediate survivor would receive one-half of the retirement allowance. Cousens' decision to air his views on the whole subject was precipitated by the death of Professor Fred D. Lambert of the Biology Department and the survival of his widow "practically without any means of support." The Trustees voted her a retirement allowance.

1939 and 1940, but again no formal action was requested of the Trustees because President Carmichael had intimated that the contributory pension plan of the Teachers Insurance and Annuity Association would be adopted for certain categories of the faculty and would eventually be extended to others.[5] President Carmichael discussed the problems of faculty annuities and retirement with the Trustees in 1939 and notified them that the growing concern of the faculty about such matters, would also, in the near future, "require much more definite determination of tenure and appointment than has been true in the past."[6]

The timing of faculty agitation for increased salaries just prior to the Second World War was most unpropitious. The newly elected president pursued such a cautious fiscal policy that in 1939, on his recommendation, the Trustees voted that all the contracts of all teaching staff for the academic year 1939–40 be modified to release the institution from all obligations beyond one year. The reason given was the same that had prompted identical action between 1933 and 1936: "general business and financial conditions throughout the country." Fortunately, this limitation on contracts lasted only one year.[7] This decision of the Trustees served only to agitate the faculty still further. It seemed that not only were their requests for a retirement program and salary increases being ignored but their very job security was in jeopardy. The time appeared to have

[5] Arrangements had been made by the College, beginning in 1936, for faculty retirement coverage under the TIAA, but in 1939–40 there were only ten faculty members on the contributory pension plan, by which the College and the faculty member each paid 5 per cent of the individual's salary.

[6] The general rule of thumb when Carmichael became president was that those with the rank of instructor received annual appointments; assistant professors, three-year appointments; and some (but not all) with the rank of professor were listed as "permanent." The rank of associate professor was seldom used until 1939. There were many exceptions at all levels, and in some instances over the years the faculty received what were known as "dry promotions," i.e., advances in rank without increases in salary.

[7] It was at this juncture that the term "permanent" was replaced by "without limit of time" for selected faculty who were reelected. But even then it was understood that the dozen or so senior members of the faculty who received contracts with this designation in 1939 were not excepted from the possible modification or termination of their contracts. The word "tenure" has never been used in a faculty contract at Tufts.

come for the faculty to make a formal presentation of their case. Experience over the past fifteen or twenty years had demonstrated the fact that no occasion would ever be "opportune in every respect." The static situation with regard to faculty salaries and a sharp rise in the cost of living made the problem critical for many faculty members. Tufts in 1942 was the only New England college of high standing that did not have a general pension program for its instructional staff.

There were still other factors that precipitated the faculty request for a pension plan. Tuition in the School of Arts and Sciences was raised from $300 to $350 in 1941–42, and considerable publicity was given to the announcement that part of the augmented income would be applied to the improvement of faculty salaries. On the heels of this ostensibly welcome news, the faculty was notified that because of war conditions a summer school would be operated in 1942 in which the faculty would be expected to teach without compensation. The faculty was also disturbed to see a constantly increasing proportion of College income expended for purposes other than salaries.[8] This trend, coupled with recurrent postponement of any systematic step to improve the financial lot of the faculty, led the teaching staff to fear that their situation would deteriorate still further, a development that would be prejudicial to the entire institution as well as to the faculty.

In a report prepared by members of the local chapter of the American Association of University Professors and presented *in extenso* to the Faculty of Arts and Sciences in 1942, a faculty spokesman reviewed the practices then being followed and requested a review of the whole problem of faculty status. The decline in the number of faculty eligible to receive Carnegie pensions and the inadequacy of the provision of retirement stipends by the College

[8] On several occasions in the early 1940's an annual operating deficit was created by the transfer of several thousand dollars to a reserve fund for grounds and buildings. The deficits thereby created were made up by appropriations from the Alumni Fund. The reserve fund was used for such purposes as providing quarters for the Naval ROTC unit in a wing of Cousens Gymnasium in 1942 and for turning Davies House into a Jackson College dormitory. The College also lost almost $200,000 in investment funds, at least on paper, when in 1942 it divested itself of the common stock held in the Eppinger and Russell Company of the Fletcher Residuum Fund. At the same time, the $90,000 mortgage on Cousens Gymnasium was paid in full.

required a systematic pension arrangement. The retirement problem was aggravated, in turn, by the salary situation, which made it impossible for the average faculty member to put aside an amount each year sufficient to care for later needs. The president recognized the request of the faculty and relayed their report to the Trustees. The Executive Committee expressed sympathy for the plight of the faculty and agreed to refer the whole question to the full Board. Carmichael also urged the Executive Committee to "seriously endeavor" to include annuity coverage of all full-time members of the arts and sciences faculty in the two top ranks when the budget was made up for the next year. The urging of the faculty produced results, for annuities were arranged, effective in January 1943, for those holding a professorial rank.[9]

Provision for annuities in 1943 brought some comfort to the faculty, but the salary issue remained a sore point. Faculty petitions to the Trustees to receive compensation for summer school teaching in 1942 produced only additional expressions of sympathy from that body; the uncertainties of the war emergency by that date made such compensation "impossible."[10] Faculty entering active duty in the armed forces were given leaves of absence (without salary) and were promised reemployment for a minimum of one year, provided there were positions available when they returned. Individuals on annual appointment in thirteen so-called "non-critical" departments were warned that their contracts might not be renewed after 1942–43.

The local AAUP chapter registered dissatisfaction with the salary scale in 1943, and a year later Carmichael recognized that the token increases provided in 1944–45 were far from sufficient. The chapter thereupon made an analysis of the salary situation from the rather scanty information available and prepared a report, which President Carmichael transmitted to the Trustees "at length." He

[9] Faculty members holding such ranks in the Fletcher School and the medical and dental schools were also included.

[10] After the College shifted to a war-induced full calendar year, the Trustees did provide supplementary compensation for those teaching the full year, effective in the fall of 1943. The increase comprised one-third of base salary but could not exceed $1,000 annually. For the last semester of the preceding year (1942–43) the Trustees tried the expedient of scaling the increase from one-sixth to one-third, depending on faculty seniority and the number of Naval students enrolled in various classes.

did not, however, encourage them to take any action on the request
for salary increases, for he prefaced his remarks with a gloomy account of the disappointing prospects for enrollment in the 1945
summer session and the comment that the next financial year might
well be "the most difficult one that the College has had to face so
far." So the problem of "salary stabilization" was referred to the
Executive Committee for study. The result was a slight upward
readjustment of minimum compensation for each grade, effective
in 1945–46; this placed the Tufts salary scale closer to the "middle
group" of salaries of comparable New England colleges instead of
almost at the bottom, where it had been previously.[11] The only
other tangible result that came out of the discussions about salaries
in 1945 was the decision to pay extra compensation for summer
school teaching.[12]

A sizeable proportion of the faculty, operating through the
local AAUP chapter, was far from content with what they still considered markedly inadequate salaries, particularly in view of the
sharp rise in living costs after wartime controls were removed. They
undertook a comprehensive study of their whole economic status
and accumulated necessary salary data by means of questionnaires
to department chairmen. Only a few failed to cooperate. A report
was prepared and presented to the president in 1947.

The hopes of the AAUP chapter for Trustee action were at
least partially realized, for a review of the salary situation was made
by that body, and at least a scale for minimum salaries for each rank
was established.[13] The Trustees congratulated themselves that
Tufts had experienced so few losses of faculty because of compensation differential with other institutions, "although the unfairness
of expecting such sacrifice over a long period of time was emphasized." The president and Trustees were constantly reminded by

[11] The increases ranged from $200 to $500 (for department chairmen),
with an average of about $300 for the professorial ranks.

[12] Beginning with the 1946 summer school, compensation for a full program (two courses) was set at one-sixth of annual base salary, with a minimum
of $500.

[13] The minima recommended by the Executive Committee were: instructors, $2,500; assistant professors, $3,500; associate professors, $4,000; and
professors, $5,000. The minimum had been achieved for full professors only by
1947–48. Before the end of his administration, Carmichael admitted that
salaries for full professors should be a minimum of $8,000.

the AAUP chapter that the problem of adequate compensation for the academic staff was "very real" and that "certain upward adjustments" were necessary as well as desirable. In 1951–52 another salary study — the most elaborate up to that time — was placed in the hands of the Executive Committee. Their conversations in the latter part of 1952 led to the proposal to provide in the budget the sum of $20,000, to be used by President Carmichael's successor for salary adjustments.

Salary increments during Carmichael's administration may have come with agonizing slowness, but new or more generous fringe benefits were also provided after the Second World War. Medical and hospital insurance were made available at modest cost through a group plan in 1945. Tuition gratuities for faculty children were continued, although under certain limitations; and in 1947 the president was authorized to make arrangements with other colleges to exchange students of faculty and administration, with scholarship privileges.[14] The College's contribution toward faculty retirement annuity for those eligible was increased from 5 per cent to $7\frac{1}{2}$ per cent (of the total of 15 per cent of base salary) in 1948, and in 1951 to $12\frac{1}{2}$ per cent, with corresponding reduction of the faculty contribution to $2\frac{1}{2}$ per cent.[15] Collective-level insurance through the TIAA was added on a contributory basis in 1949, and in 1952 the faculty was authorized to participate, on a voluntary basis, in the College Retirement Equities Fund. Federal social security coverage for academic personnel became effective in 1951. The faculty in 1948 even received a "Faculty Club," used as a dining room and general gathering place.[16]

Like many other institutions of comparable age and size, Tufts was slow to provide a formal statement of policy regarding academic

[14] In 1945, the Executive Committee provided that faculty children would receive free tuition in the division of the College of which the parent was a member; half-tuition was provided for enrollment in any other division.

[15] Those not participating in the TIAA plan received a 5 per cent increase in salary. Full-time research personnel were placed on the same annuity basis as the teaching faculty in 1949.

[16] It was located on Professors Row, in the home built and occupied in the nineteenth century by faculty member Benjamin Graves Brown and leased to the College by his descendants. Other locations considered for the Faculty Club had been in Curtis Hall and in the new wing of the library constructed in 1949–50.

freedom and tenure. This was not because the College opposed either, but because there was thought to be no need for one. The first attempt to establish such a policy was made during the First World War, when the faculty created their half of a proposed joint committee with the Trustees in 1918. Their assignment was "to formulate rules governing tenure of office and dismissal and reappointment of teachers." The full committee never came into being because the Trustees failed to act. In the winter of 1922 President Cousens received a questionnaire from the Commission on Academic Freedom and Academic Tenure which was gathering information for a statement to be issued by the Association of American Colleges. In his reply he emphasized the large degree of academic freedom that had always prevailed at Tufts and concluded with the comment that formal statements and machinery did not exist at the College. He assured the Commission that "such a healthy and cordial relation'" existed among the Trustees, president, and faculty that no such provisions were necessary.

Fear by the Tufts faculty that the national preparedness program and the involvement of the United States in the Second World War might threaten freedom of expression and faculty security resulted in the adoption by the Trustees of their first formal policy on academic freedom and tenure in 1940. As in the case of salary readjustments, the local chapter of the AAUP was very active. Extended discussions were held by the chapter, with President Carmichael present at some of the meetings. The upshot of the chapter effort, after delays of over a year, was the adoption by the Trustees of the preliminary Statement of Principles of Academic Freedom and Tenure drawn up by representatives of the Association of American Colleges and the American Association of University Professors in the fall of 1938.[17]

The faculty, wanting still further assurance that they would have a channel by which to air any grievances they might have involving tenure, promotion, rank, or appointment, also created a

[17] The statement, as adopted by the Trustees, was also "spread upon the records" of the Faculty of Arts and Sciences, to which the policy first applied. Because of certain ambiguities and differences of interpretation, arising partly out of changes in wording between the preliminary statement and the so-called "1940 AAUP Statement of Principles," which the Trustees never officially adopted, a new statement of policy on academic freedom, tenure, and retirement was adopted in the fall of 1964.

five-man Advisory Committee on Faculty Personnel in 1940. Although the committee had no legislative powers, it was given authority to confer directly with the Trustees if communications with the president broke down. Dean George S. Miller considered the creation of the committee a "liberal and democratic procedure" which should give "ample protection for faculty members." Upon the urging of Dean Miller, the Trustees also fixed, for the first time, the faculty retirement age. It was made optional after the age of sixty-five and mandatory at seventy. This provision became a part of the Statement of Principles on Academic Freedom and Tenure adopted in 1940.

During most of its history, Tufts welcomed faculty who engaged in creative or productive scholarly work but until a decade after the First World War neglected to adopt anything approaching an official policy either encouraging or discouraging it. The College had, as indicated elsewhere in this book, been fortunate in the number of its faculty who had published work of stature in the fields of both science and the humanities. But, at base, this evidence of scholarly effort was incidental to what was considered the main task of that part of the institution located on the Hill, namely, to provide the best undergraduate instruction that its resources allowed. No serious or formal attempt was made to encourage faculty research at Tufts until 1928, at about the mid-point in Cousens' administration. In that year a special committee prepared a comprehensive statement which was adopted by the Faculty of Arts and Sciences. Several points were made. Research, the interpretation of research, and "direct creative writing" were considered "a reinforcement of teaching." Teachers should share research problems with advanced students; teaching loads, particularly of those who demonstrated "marked capacity for research," should be arranged as to number of courses, number of students, and classroom schedules to provide "the maximum amount of uninterrupted time for research." Other ways suggested of encouraging research and professional activity outside the classroom were the taking of sabbatical leaves, the provision of secretarial services and experimental apparatus, reimbursement for traveling expenses to meetings, and the printing of annual lists of publications by faculty members. Even the display of faculty publications in the library was suggested.

President Carmichael recognized the desirability of faculty research and publication and professional activity. In 1940 he reinstituted the earlier practice of printing annual bibliographies of faculty publications. The adoption of a formal Trustee statement in 1946 governing sabbatical leaves was another step in the direction of encouraging scholarly activity. The phenomenal expansion of contract research at Tufts during and after the Second World War was in large part the result of Carmichael's efforts. However, neither the faculty nor the administration enunciated any formal policy having to do with research and publication until almost thirty years after the faculty statement of 1928. Meanwhile, teaching loads in most departments remained sufficiently demanding to preclude extensive publication except by a small segment of the faculty.

§ § §

Unenviable as the distinction may have been, President Carmichael shared with President Bumpus the tremendous responsibility of seeing the College through a world war. Though the involvement of the institution in the great conflict between 1917 and 1919 had been great, it bore only a surface resemblance to the degree of participation and the effects on the College of the second holocaust. Probably few institutions of higher education in the United States threw themselves more completely into the war effort. It was largely through President Carmichael's leadership and energy that so much was accomplished.

It appeared in the fall of 1939 that once again the nation and Tufts College might have to face the possibility of another world war. Ominous clouds were gathering over Europe and a feeling of uneasiness seemed to be everywhere. President Carmichael was among those who sensed impending crisis. He confessed reluctance to discuss the question of preparedness at Tufts for such an eventuality but felt that it should be faced. A number of the science departments at the College were already in communication with various agencies in Washington to develop research and study programs that might "be useful in case an emergency does arise." Preliminary steps were also taken to participate in a program of college training for pilots sponsored by the Civil Aeronautics Authority. This did not have a direct connection with military preparedness *per se* but it did have important implications for the whole problem of national manpower. Late in 1939 the Trustees authorized the signing of a contract between the United States Government and the College which would utilize the institution's resources in certain phases of pilot training. The program was placed under the supervision of the dean of the engineering school, and during the 1939–40 school year twenty students received primary training. There was a class of thirty in the summer of 1940. A second group of twenty was enrolled in the fall of 1940, and advanced training was provided as the students progressed. Forty-six of the first fifty students enrolled in the preliminary training program at Tufts completed all of the ground and flight tests and received private pilot's certificates. Between 1939 and 1943, when the CAA pilot training program came to an end, 398 students completed their basic training at Tufts.

The engineering school was also actively contributing to national preparedness in another area by 1940. In that year the United States Office of Education organized a nation-wide Engineering Defense Training Program to provide specialized instruction in fields considered essential for national defense. The Tufts Engineering School, by the end of the academic year 1940–41, had offered such training to over 650 individuals through both full-time day courses and part-time evening courses. The program was extended the next year to science and management training, and by the fall of 1942 the number of enrollees had totaled over 1,200 in some forty courses. By the time the Engineering Science and War Management Training Program was terminated, in June 1945, some 2,000 enrollees had received college-level engineering courses at Tufts.[18] Simultaneously, the engineering school undertook other special programs involving government-sponsored research which remained classified information through the war period.

As pilot training under the direction of the engineering school continued, faculty members in various departments began to be called to national service, although the enactment of the Selective Service Act of 1940 and enlistment in the armed forces had no initial effect on undergraduate registrations in 1940–41. A few stu-

[18] The individuals were not degree candidates at Tufts but were, for the most part, graduates of colleges and technical schools who were employed in business and defense industries.

dents were called into the National Guard, and a few more enlisted in officer training courses, but their places were taken by other students from a rapidly growing waiting list for college entrance. When war finally involved the United States directly, President Carmichael was adamant that the total resources of the College be turned to the nation's service. In his report to the Trustees in the fall of 1942 he made his views crystal clear: "The present goal for Tufts is to use the important resources of the College for the good of the United States. . . . [Tufts] must in this year of our nation's desperate need be dedicated wholeheartedly to one aim and one aim only, that of serving the total war effort of our nation as effectively as possible."

As early as the fall of 1939, the president had raised the question of whether facilities comparable to the Student Army Training Corps operative during the First World War might be organized if it again became necessary to train large numbers of troops rapidly. He reminded the Trustees of the effective part played in this capacity by the College in the earlier conflict, when the Tufts contingent was rated as one of the five most effective units of the SATC in the United States. The first step to carry out Carmichael's suggestion was taken in 1941, when he requested the Navy Department to allocate an ROTC unit to the College. The request was honored, and Tufts became one of eight colleges in the United States granted a unit beginning in 1941–42. The headquarters of what was at first known as the Navy V-1 Program was installed on the second floor of a portion of the old AMRAD wing in Cousens Gymnasium. It began operations with three commissioned officers and a non-commissioned staff, and 100 students — the initial limit set by the Navy. Enrollment in the new unit was limited to freshmen in the schools of liberal arts and engineering, who were scheduled to take one course each year for four years in the Department of Naval Science and Tactics. After completing undergraduate instruction and passing appropriate examinations, the graduates were eligible to receive commissions as ensigns in the United States Naval Reserve or as second lieutenants in the United States Marine Corps Reserve. Membership in the unit was to be voluntary, but President Carmichael was positive that all students who met the physical qualifications would wish to join. The addition of this unit justified the admission of extra students. During 1940–41, be-

fore the NROTC unit was established, over fifty students had qualified and had been recommended for reserve commissions as officers
in the Army, Navy, or Marine Corps. Several had also taken the
Platoon Leaders' course in the Marine Corps and were destined to
participate in the famous Guadalcanal campaign during the Second
World War. Unlike the intention of the federal government during the First World War with its short-lived SATC to train junior
line officers, the policy some thirty years later was to concentrate on
preparing technically trained personnel. Hence Tufts, in the early
days of the war effort, had much less the appearance of an armed
camp, and there was a deliberate attempt to integrate military units
into the life of the College. Courses for the four-year sequence in
Naval Science and Tactics were adopted by the faculty of liberal
arts and Jackson in the spring of 1941, subject to review and revision by the Navy Department.[19] In order to point up the fact that
the Naval unit was not isolated from the institution, a Committee
of Visitors to the new department was created by the Trustees almost immediately.

The College was informed in the spring of 1943 that it was being assigned 1,000 uniformed Naval trainees, to be enrolled in one
of four special programs. The basic course, known as the V-12 Program until June 1946, included both Naval training and advanced
work in selected courses in the school of liberal arts. There were
also special curricula for engineers and pre-medical and pre-dental
students, as well as for the regular NROTC unit. All of the Naval
programs were in full operation on the campus by July 1943, and a
School for War Service was organized to administer them. When
the College received its quota of 225 Naval students in engineering
in 1944, President Carmichael reported to the Trustees with great
pride that this represented the third largest quota of any NROTC
program among the twenty-seven educational institutions then
participating. He went on to point out that Tufts had, by then,
trained more men directly from civilian life for commissions in the
Naval Reserve than had any other New England college.

Even as the Second World War was coming to an end, it had

[19] Students completing the first two years of the four-year sequence, including drill, could thereby fulfill their science, hygiene, and physical education requirements. This was modified in 1943 when the vote allowing credit
for physical education was rescinded.

been decided that an NROTC unit would be established permanently at the College. With victory over Germany and Japan a reality, the Navy merged its wartime V-12 Program with NROTC units established in fifty colleges throughout the country, of which Tufts was one. Under the new program the College's quota was 571 in the fall of 1945. Students in the Naval unit were to be enrolled for a full four years. Although they could obtain the necessary number of credits for a Tufts degree, Naval requirements were such that they could not at first meet the College's foundation, distribution, and major requirements. The problem was resolved by awarding the degree of Bachelor of Naval Science to NROTC students who earned the required number of credits and completed also modified foundation and major requirements. It was anticipated (and correctly) that this expedient would be only temporary, for there was general feeling among both civilian educators and those responsible for the Navy curricula that the latter's requirements were too narrow and would soon be broadened. The Navy readjusted its program, and the special Bachelor's degree was not needed after June 1946.

The Naval ROTC, which had been, in President Carmichael's words, "an absolute lifesaver for Tufts" during the war, was not only continued but expanded after 1945. There were almost 300 Naval students in either the "regular" or the "contract" program in the fall of 1951. At the same time, a new Air Force ROTC unit, for which President Carmichael had applied in 1949, was in operation with over 300 enrolled. Simultaneously, Army ROTC units continued in the medical and dental schools. During the Korean military crisis in 1951 almost 70 per cent of the male students in liberal arts and engineering were enrolled in one or the other of the two programs on the Hill, and Dean Burden of the engineering school served as liaison officer for the College. Space was at such a premium for the administrative staffs of the two units that the Trustees, in the fall of 1952, authorized the construction of a building for their use.

Dr. Carmichael was the organizer and first director (1940–44), and then consultant, of the National Roster of Scientific and Specialized Personnel, which had during the Second World War the responsibility for inventorying and allocating the best minds and most effectively trained individuals that could be recruited for war work. His activities in this post made him particularly sensitive to shortages that might develop in key areas requiring technically and professionally trained individuals. He took to heart the recommendation of a committee of the Roster, headed by Owen D. Young, that colleges should be encouraged to intensify training in all areas where shortages became most acute. Tufts seemed to be in a most favorable situation so far as training in engineering, chemistry, mathematics, physics, medicine, and dentistry were concerned. Certain fields of economics were also of special importance. The only major problem, as the president saw it, was how to channel the talents of those students majoring in the humanities into war work. He suggested that they enroll in one or more "technique" courses so that they would be useful in the war effort. College contracts with the Office of Scientific Research and Development, which was directed by Dr. Vannevar Bush, a distinguished graduate of the Class of 1913, had reached significant proportions by 1942. Two years later, government contracts with the College totaled over half a million dollars. Almost one-half of the funds in 1944 were being used by the Research Laboratory of Sensory Psychology and Physiology, which President Carmichael had organized after his arrival at Tufts and which represented an early example of sponsored research at the College.

The impact of the Second World War was felt everywhere in the College. The faculty, and many of the students, went on a round-the-clock schedule, beginning in 1942. At the height of the world conflict, during 1943–44, Tufts was not one institution but three. It was simultaneously training service personnel in uniform, educating civilian men and women, and providing educational opportunities for returning servicemen. In order to meet the needs of these diverse groups, the acceleration proceeded in different ways and at differing paces, depending on the needs and facilities of various divisions and departments. In the school of liberal arts and Jackson College, two six-week summer sessions were arranged for 1942. Students enrolling in both sessions could in this way advance by one semester. It was decided in the following year to divide the academic year into three terms of sixteen weeks each, beginning July 1, November 1, and March 1. The faculty was careful to point out at the same time that academic credit woud not be granted willy-nilly to students merely because they had served in the armed forces, without regard to actual educational achievement.[20] The engineering school at first required acceleration for upperclassmen during the summer months so that seniors could graduate in February rather than in June. The medical and dental schools adopted an eleven-month, three-semester academic year. Only the Fletcher School did not plan a formally accelerated program.

Physical changes and rearrangements were everywhere in evidence. East Hall, the oldest men's dormitory, was taken over in 1942 for the pilot training program, and sixty men were housed there in eight-week rotation. Part of West Hall, another men's dormitory, was leased by the federal government as a residence for enlisted men. When the normal resident population jumped from approximately 700 to over 1,200 in a matter of months, new dining and residence facilities had to be provided. Traditionally male quarters were invaded by women students when four fraternities on Professors Row became Jackson dormitories. The young ladies, in turn, had been ousted from Stratton Hall to make way for the Navy, which also occupied three men's dormitories and two fraternity houses. In 1944–45 there were so few civilian male residential students left on the campus that they were all housed in Richardson House, an ertswhile women's dormitory. One fraternity house became the "sick bay" for the Navy, and another served as a dining room for Fletcher students, who found their two dormitories occupied by undergraduate women. Until Curtis Hall could be converted into a Navy mess hall, the students in that training contingent had to be served temporarily in the baseball cage of Cousens Gymnasium by a catering firm. An area of rough terrain near the gymnasium became an obstacle or "commando" course for the rigorous physical regimen of the Naval students, and the various playing fields, tennis courts, and the golf course were thronged with classes in calisthenics and related activities. Jackson students were busy with extracurricular "war courses" which included Red Cross First Aid, Air Raid Precautions, and Motor Transport. They helped during the war to collect hundreds of books for donation to

[20] The College followed the practice used in the First World War of granting War Certificates to students who had been in attendance for two or more semesters and who left to enter the armed forces.

the armed forces. Tradition was shattered when the engineering school awarded a degree to a woman in 1943. In the same year Tufts graduated more women than men for the first time in its history. "Victory gardens" sprouted at strategic points about the campus as faculty-turned-farmers vied with one another in setting new production records in everything from radishes to rhubarb.

When the Board of Trustees met in the autumn of 1942, there were 188 students in uniform on the Hill. A year later, there were approximately 1,000, most of them in the Navy V-12 Program. If the several hundred in the medical and dental schools were counted, over 1,600 men were to be found in some phase of combined academic and military training. Taken together, they outnumbered civilian students by considerably more than two to one.[21] A concerted effort was made to continue regular student activities such as the dramatic society. A combined Navy-civilian student council was organized, musical activities were much in evidence, and the campus newspaper continued to appear. A new publication, *Tufts Topics,* in the form of a newsletter, was sent all over the world to the more than 4,000 Tufts men and women in service in 1943. The College was placed on the map in another way. Two ships bearing the Tufts name were constructed and launched during the war: the Liberty Ship SS *Charles Tufts* and the SS *Tufts Victory.*[22]

On the home front, intercollegiate athletics continued on a limited scale, and in 1943 Tufts not only was one of the few schools to play a full schedule of football but was able to achieve one of its infrequent victories over Harvard. Tufts resisted the change of policy of many colleges which, because of a shortage of athletic manpower, allowed freshmen to play on Varsity teams. The College managed admirably by replacing curtailed intercollegiate sports such as basketball with an enlarged intramural program. Physical fitness was the order of the day, and during the war both civilian men and women were required to take three hours of physical education per week for all four years. Almost all of the regular faculty

[21] Many civilians admitted in the school of liberal arts were high school seniors who were allowed, on special recommendation of their schools, to enter college before completing their secondary school work.

[22] The first was built in Portland, Maine, and the second in Wilmington, California.

taught forty-eight out of the fifty-two weeks, with more hours in the classroom and larger classes. Additional personnel had to be used on the staff of the engineering school to teach mathematics, physics, and engineering drawing.

An administrative mechanism comparable to the School of War Service was created in 1943–44 to handle returning servicemen; it was known as the School for War Veterans. Like its Naval counterpart, the new agency recommended no degrees and established no curricula. A Veterans Center was established in Braker Hall, and Professor Arthur Leighton became its head. Among his tasks was the advising of returnees and the evaluating of their educational plans as they became eligible for federal aid under Public Law 346 (the so-called "G.I. Bill of Rights") and Public Law 16, for disabled veterans. The School for War Veterans ceased to exist under that name after the war was over, but the reception center for veterans continued, with a peak of activity in 1946–47. It also kept the records of students registered under the Selective Service System. Tufts was also, beginning in 1944, one of the cooperating schools in the Veterans Administration Guidance Center at Harvard. The Center was transferred to Tufts in mid-1948, and Dean Wessell served as its executive officer as well as director of counseling.[23] The College thus became one of the many institutions to assist the Veterans Administration in furnishing educational guidance at the college level.

Even the traditional Commencement ceremonies were affected by the war. The innovation of as many as three special Degree Convocations a year was introduced, sandwiched in between the customary ceremonies in June. Until the custom was abandoned after the last regular Commencement in 1943, orations had been prepared by graduating students selected from among all the divisions of the College except the graduate school and the Fletcher School of Law and Diplomacy.[24] After 1943 the institution continued the tradition of having one of the recipients of honorary degrees, usu-

[23] The facility became the Veterans Counseling Center in 1952 and remained on the campus until the mid-1950's.

[24] Since 1932 only two were selected each year for actual presentation. Student orations were also scheduled for the special Degree Convocation in March 1943 and were delivered by students from the medical and dental schools.

ally from outside the Tufts community, deliver the principal address. Many were sorry to see the abandonment of the custom of
having the students participate. But it is usually impossible to
please everyone. Some might have shared the sentiments of one
undergraduate who complained in the *Tuftonian* in 1879 that it
was "very tedious" for an audience to listen to a succession of student speakers who, "as a general thing, say what their predecessors
have said before them, and in about the same manner." Even speakers of a later era may have considered their assignment a thankless task.

§   §   §

The College faced a mountainous set of problems as the Second World War drew to a close in 1945. There was the matter of
returning to the normal two-semester academic year. Should the
war-born summer school be continued? College buildings, worn to
the floorboards by continuous use, had to be restored and recon-
verted to their original uses or modified for new ones. A peacetime
student body had to be rebuilt and the faculty reconstituted and
strengthened. A return to prewar conditions in some areas was accomplished with amazing rapidity. Other adjustments took longer,
and inevitably there were more offices, more divisions, an enlarged
staff, and a more complex administration. The fraternity houses
leased by the College were returned to their occupants. The summer school system introduced in 1942 was continued and adapted
to peacetime, and the traditional two-semester academic calendar
was resumed in September 1946.

The problem of reassembling the scattered regular faculty and
releasing temporary personnel had to be faced long before the war
itself was over. The turnover of faculty because of war service or
other governmental commitments became bewildering in its complexity and rapidity. Some members, such as Professor Dawson G.
Fulton of the Mathematics Department, were originally "loaned"
by other institutions but remained on the permanent faculty after
the war. Several senior members of the faculty chose to retire during the war period, after having given long and faithful service to
the institution. In the one year of 1943, three faculty members (all
graduates of the College), with a combined total of 114 years on the

Tufts staff, retired.[25] Death, too, took its toll among the faculty in the 1940's. Leo R. Lewis, of the Class of 1887 and Fletcher Professor of Music, had been a member of the faculty since 1892. Melville S. Munro, of the Class of 1904, had been a member of the Electrical Engineering Department for many years and, with the collaboration of Professor Rollins, served as College photographer.[26] The early 1950's brought even more staff changes. Edith L. Bush retired in 1952, after an association of over thirty years with Tufts — twenty-eight of them as dean of Jackson College. In the same year William F. Wyatt, Professor of Greek and on the Tufts faculty since 1914, concluded his active service with the College. There had been 109 members of the Faculty of Arts and Sciences in 1941–42. In the one year 1946–47, thirty-seven new members were added to meet the needs of a record enrollment. In 1948–49 the number of faculty had risen to 170 in this division of the institution alone. There were changes among the Trustees, too, as Harold E. Sweet stepped down from the presidency of the Board after a service of a quarter of a century, and Arthur J. Anderson took his place in 1949. The invaluable services of Trustee Anderson were lost with his death in 1964.

Many academic departments needed special attention after the war. Some had to be rebuilt, others expanded, and still others created. The Economics Department had been reduced to two full-time faculty members by the fall of 1944.[27] Growing interest in the field of sociology warranted attention, and in the fall of 1945 Dr. A. Warren Stearns, after retiring from Naval duty and relinquishing the deanship of the Tufts Medical School, became the chairman

25 They were Ethel M. Hayes and Professors Edwin B. Rollins and Edwin H. Wright.

26 Thanks to the efforts of these two men, the institution possesses over 20,000 photographs, documenting the history of Tufts from 1912 to 1942. The so-called Munro Collection consists of over eighty volumes of mounted pictures of everything and (almost) everybody associated with the College during the thirty-year period.

27 In 1944 a one-man Department of Aesthetics and Creative Imagination was organized, with Professor Robert C. Givler as chairman. Professor Givler, on the faculty since 1919, was the only man in Tufts history to have held separate professorships in three different departments (Philosophy, Psychology, and Aesthetics) at one time or another. The Department of Aesthetics disappeared when the chairman retired in 1952.

of the new Department of Sociology.[28] Courses in government had been taught for many years, but a separate department offering a major in the field had never been created. In 1945 Dean Wessell called attention to the practical need for expanded course work in this area in a period of postwar political reconstruction on a world-wide scale. He also thought it a bit paradoxical that the College had, in its Fletcher School, a graduate institution in international law and diplomacy but no major in the field of government at the undergraduate level. The faculty remedied the deficiency by creating a Department of Government in 1946. An Institute of Applied Experimental Psychology was authorized in 1948.

Tufts, sharing an experience with most other educational institutions in the postwar period, was flooded with applications from returning veterans and did its best to prevent overenrollment and lowering of standards. The total student body jumped from 2,369, with 307 veterans, in September 1945, to 3,385, with 2,125 veterans, a year later. In 1946–47, 80 per cent of the student body in liberal arts and in engineering were veterans. Only 15 per cent of the Hill students were veterans in 1949. They were an unusually serious, mature, and able generation of students who not only did creditable work but took a prominent part in campus activities. President Carmichael insisted that the best way to achieve and maintain an ideal academic community was to "continue rigorously to limit the number of students admitted." Even before the peak of veteran enrollment passed, after 1948, a more systematic effort than ever before was made to select a superior student body from secondary schools. In 1946 Tufts joined other highly selective institutions in requiring College Entrance Examination Board tests of all applicants, and achievement tests of all but a few candidates. Under the leadership of Dean Wessell, admission procedures became more thorough and exacting, and personal interviews were used wherever possible. Much to the delight of Dean Bush, Jackson College finally obtained an assistant director of admissions in 1945 to help with the sharply rising tide of applications in that division.

[28] For several years prior to the war, sociology courses were offered in the combined Department of Economics and Sociology. The Professorship of Sociology which Dr. Stearns held was made possible by a grant from the Rockefeller Foundation. Stearns had already achieved a notable reputation as a pioneer in the field of social psychiatry.

Prize scholarship competitions for prospective students in liberal arts and Jackson begun a few years before the war were revived and intensified.

The effect of the Second World War on the composition of the undergraduate student body was nothing short of dramatic. In 1940 Dean Wessell had expressed the hope that in the future the students might be drawn from a wider geographical area than in the past. Over 80 per cent of the students on the Hill came from within fifty miles of the College in 1939 and 1940. Within five years after the war every state in the Union was represented, and in 1948 there were sixty-two foreign students in the various divisions of the institution. Tufts had lost, permanently it seemed, its characteristics as a "neighborhood" college.

Just as Tufts was settling into what appeared to be a period of uninterrupted progress, the national mobilization and readiness plans brought by developments in the Korean conflict between 1950 and 1952 threatened to disrupt long-range planning as well as the stability of the student body. President Carmichael was peculiarly aware of the demands that might be made on personnel because of his involvement in the work of the War Manpower Commission during the war and his services as consultant to the National Security Resources Board and Selective Service System, as well as membership on the Science Committee of the National Resources Planning Board. The president of Tufts, like many another person concerned with educational matters, was distressed by the "crisis-thinking" that seemed to dominate manpower policy-makers, and by the apparent lack of a well-defined national policy regarding inductions under the Selective Service program. He fretted because morale was lowered among draftable males and uncertainty was injected into admissions policies. One result of a wavering and sometimes inconsistent national policy was the interruption, across the nation, of the college careers of thousands of young men who had already served in the armed forces.

In the area of organized sports before the Second World War, the outstanding name in the annals of Tufts athletic history was that of Edward Dugger, of the Class of 1941. "Eddie," as he was known to all, achieved national prominence as a track star. By the time he was graduated, he had amassed the impressive total of twenty-four individual track titles and held several records in that

Eddie Dugger, Tufts' record-breaking track star between 1938 and 1941

sport. Athletics, naturally disrupted by the war, promptly resumed their customary place among student affairs as the College attempted to return to normal after 1945. Many intercollegiate sports had exceptionally favorable years in the late 1940's. In 1945 the lacrosse team won the New England championship and the track team was victorious in the New England Track and Field Games for the first time in fifty years. The Tufts teams completed the academic year 1949–50 with a most respectable record overall. Varsity teams engaged in 137 intercollegiate contests, in which Tufts won 88, lost 14, and tied 5. The basketball team was selected as one of the contestants in the final play-off of the New England championship and finished in third place. The baseball team was chosen to represent the New England section of the National Collegiate Athletic Association. It lost in the final play-off but took comfort from the fact that the winner (Texas) had an enrollment of over 17,000 students while Tufts was the smallest college, in terms of student body, in the entire tournament.

In the postwar period the College continued to follow a policy of avoiding professionalism in the particularly sensitive area of intercollegiate football. President Carmichael, in 1939, had pointed with satisfaction to the fact that Tufts was one of the handful of colleges having a policy "free from any possible taint of commercialism" — the exact phraseology used by President Cousens earlier in the same decade. Professor Houston, who served as head of the Department of Physical Education for many years (until succeeded by W. Stanton Yeager in 1947) could see the problems of athletics from a nation-wide perspective, for after the Second World War he was named chairman of a committee of the National Collegiate Athletic Association to draft a "sanity code" to encourage the amateur spirit in collegiate athletics. After the code had been adopted by the 375 participating colleges, Professor Houston was for three years (until 1951) chairman of a compliance committee to interpret and enforce the code. He was later honored by election to the presidency of the NCAA, in which capacity he served between 1955 and 1957.

The need to construct new buildings as well as to repair old ones appeared to have reached almost emergency proportions by 1945. No major academic structure had been provided since the end of Cousens' administration. The Trustees had voted to furnish President Carmichael with a house when he became president in 1938, and this was duly accomplished when a red brick residence was constructed not far from the site once occupied by the home of Tufts' first president.[29] Whatever plans for building that might have been in anyone's mind in 1938 were rudely dissipated by the ravages of nature and by the lean state of the College's pocketbook.

[29] Although the president was expected to reside at the College, an exception had been made in the case of President Cousens, who lived at his home in suburban Chestnut Hill. Capen House, where Carmichael might have resided, continued to be used as a women's dormitory.

*The old Tufts College railroad station
later made into the Drama Department workshop*

On the afternoon of the very first faculty meeting over which the new president presided, a disastrous hurricane swept up the New England coast and damaged the trees and the buildings on the Tufts campus to such an extent that repairs were not completed for a whole year. An emergency "tornado fund" of over $4,000 was raised by voluntary contributions, but it defrayed only a fraction of the costs involved in reconstruction.

The College treasury looked far from promising in 1938 and 1939. After only one year as president, Carmichael was convinced that "it is difficult to believe that there has ever been a time in the history of Tufts College when financial problems were more pressing." The institution eked out the fiscal year 1937–38 with an operating balance of $1,411, and a deficit was expected for the next year. Declining interest rates on investments were the principal culprits, induced in turn by events in a jittery world. As a consequence, additions and improvements to the College plant before the Second World War consisted of nothing more ambitious than providing improved facilities in 1940 for the Chemical Engineering Department (known officially as the "Durkee Memorial Laboratories") and acquiring the Tufts College Station (vintage of 1896)

649

from the Boston and Maine Railroad for use as a storehouse and workshop for the Drama Department.[30] The undergraduates also obtained a species of Student Union when a lunchroom and soda fountain, dubbed the "Kursaal," was installed in 1940 in a previously unused area of Cousens Gymnasium. In 1941 Barnum Museum acquired, through the generosity of Trustee Eugene B. Bowen, a pair of stone lions to flank the main entrance. The property of the old Tufts College Press was acquired in 1943 from the widow of H. W. Whittemore, who had operated it before 1938.[31]

When the Second World War came to an end, the Trustees found a towering stack of building requests to consider. Some immediate needs could be met with temporary structures; others represented offers or gifts for permanent buildings which could not be put to use until government restrictions on labor and materials were relaxed; still others were intended to meet expanded academic requirements and, for the most part, had to be paid out of investment funds. The emergency housing needs of returning veterans were met functionally (if not aesthetically) by the erection in 1945 of twelve two-story buildings on the site of the old Stearns estate adjoining Cousens Gymnasium. Known as Stearns Village, these contained apartments for eighty couples (undergraduates, graduates, and instructors), who added appreciably to the postwar "baby boom" in the ten years that the "Village" existed.[32]

President Carmichael listed nine top-priority building needs in his report to the Trustees in the fall of 1945: an addition to Eaton Library, a new mechanical engineering building, a powerhouse, an ROTC building, a student union or alumni-alumnae headquarters, a theater, a dormitory for men, a Jackson dormitory,

[30] The railroad station was to have been demolished in 1941 but it was turned over to the Drama Department in 1943.

[31] Samuel R. Moses was employed in the fall of 1948 to manage the press, the work being limited to items like posters, notices, and letterhead stationery; its most important responsibility was printing the *Tufts Weekly*. Larger and more complex printing tasks were handled by contract with outside publishing firms.

[32] The structures, obtained through the Federal Public Housing Administration, had already seen considerable use as housing for employees of an aircraft plant in Hartford, Connecticut, when they were disassembled, trucked to their new locations, and reassembled. They were to have been used for only five years, but there was too much demand for them to permit demolition before 1955.

Bray Mechanical Laboratory, constructed after the Second World War

and a bookstore. They were not actually provided in the order in which he listed them, nor did the list include other additions to the physical plant that were either planned or actually built. Some were not completed during his administration although they had been authorized for years. The first permanent construction completed immediately after the Second World War was actually the Hamilton Pool, attached to Cousens Gymnasium. It was built during the winter of 1945–46 and was opened the following summer.[33]

The building of the next postwar structure, the mechanical engineering laboratory, illustrated the difficulties of construction at a time when wartime shortages still plagued contractors. The story of the laboratory was in turn related to the acquisition by the College of the reservoir (the "Rez") that had stood at the western end of the campus since 1865. As early as 1938 rumors circulated that the Metropolitan District Commission, which had jurisdiction over it, might decide to give up the reservoir. It was used between 1914 and 1944 as a reserve for emergency use only. In 1944 the reservoir site was sold to the College for $1.00, drained, and dismantled shortly thereafter. The excavation was filled in, and flanked by four men's

[33] It was originally to have been named the "Fletcher Swimming Pool" because it was financed in part from the funds of the Austin B. Fletcher estate. It was named, instead, for Frederick W. Hamilton, of the Class of 1880, fourth president of the College.

Henry Clay Jackson Gymnasium, constructed in 1948

dormitories built in the 1950's and 1960's, became a mall and the locale for Tufts Commencements beginning in 1964. The bricks salvaged from the old reservoir were used to face the new engineering building, which was completed in 1946 and was designated the Charles D. Bray Laboratory of Mechanical Engineering, in honor of the first man on the Tufts faculty to have the words "mechanical engineering" in his professional title.[34]

While the laboratory was being constructed, extensive renovation and modernization of the men's dormitories was being undertaken. Part of the financing of these projects was made possible by one of the many special gifts quietly made to the College by Trustee Arthur J. Anderson. Plans were simultaneously being laid for other buildings on the priority list. The bookstore (Taberna) was constructed in 1948. Another building not on the list, but much needed and warmly welcomed, was also completed in the same year after many frustrations because of fluctuating costs and restrictions still imposed on materials. The Henry Clay Jackson Memorial

[34] The size and configuration of the new building were less the choice of the architect than of the contractor, who furnished what sizes and amounts of structural steel he happened to have on hand in 1945. The building was financed, like the Hamilton Pool in part, from Fletcher funds.

Gymnasium for women was ready for use in the fall of 1948.[35]

Four buildings in the planning stage after the Second World War had not yet been built when President Carmichael's administration was over. The Jackson dormitory, authorized in 1945, was to be named "Frothingham Hall" in honor of Richard T. Frothingham, one of the original Tufts trustees and third treasurer of the College. It was actually completed in 1954 and was named in honor of Tufts Trustee and benefactor Frederick C. Hodgdon. A similar delay was encountered in the construction of the new men's dormitory, which was also opened in the fall of 1954. The outgoing president was, however, still at Tufts when the Trustees voted in 1952 to name the building in his honor. Nine years elapsed before the Trustees were able to use for the purpose intended a gift from Edward E. Cohen, Boston industrialist and benefactor. He had proposed in 1943 to give $125,000 toward the construction of an auditorium to bear his name.[36] In 1952 the Trustees authorized the building of not only what became the Cohen Auditorium and Art Center but the long-talked-of Alumnae Hall, linking the Cohen complex and Jackson Gymnasium when completed in 1954.[37]

[35] This structure was made possible through a gift from the estate of a conductor on the New York, New Haven, and Hartford Railroad and was administered through the Paul Wilde Jackson Trust Fund established by the donor's brother. The original gift was $200,000, but $50,000 more was provided, at the College's request, to cover additional costs.

[36] He proposed at the same time a generous gift to the Tufts Medical School.

[37] The construction of Alumnae Hall represented the culmination of a twenty-five-year effort sponsored by the Association of Tufts Alumnae. Women graduates of Tufts (before 1910) and of Jackson had worked diligently to build up the Alumnae Hall Fund established in 1928. The effort was made under the initial leadership of such devoted alumnae as Mrs. Bella (Porter) Ransom, of the Class of 1907 and for ten years chairman of the fund. Among the money-raising devices used were teas, sales, subscriptions, and recitals; detailed reports of progress and pleas for funds were reported in a pamphlet entitled "The Little Beggar." The alumnae had raised in excess of $12,000 by the time Dr. Carmichael became president of the College. The original intention had been to construct a separate building, to have been known as "Ruth Capen Farmer House" as a memorial to the person who had organized the Association of Tufts Alumnae and had been its first president. The building as planned in 1930 would also have included sorority rooms and a "little theatre." Those interested in a place to stage drama had to be content with the old Jackson Gymnasium, which was vacated in 1948.

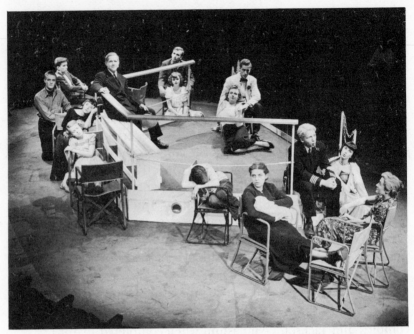

A scene from Victor Wolfson's Excursion, *presented
in the Tufts Arena Theatre in 1950
eight years after such productions began there*

There are always those projects, practical or otherwise, which never leave the drawing board (or never reach that stage), like the ambitious plan for a combined Student Union and Alumni Center; it had progressed as far as architect's sketches in 1935 but got no farther. The Carmichael administration saw its share of such unrealized plans. In 1945 the Trustees considered, but declined to act on, a proposal that a television broadcasting station be constructed at Tufts as a joint venture with the DuMont Laboratories. In 1946 Trustee Eugene Bowen offered a contribution toward the construction of a combined theater, student union, and art and music center, provided it be built on the site of the old reservoir. The new center, if Trustee Bowen had had his way, would have been a memorial to Leo R. Lewis and would have followed the architectural lines of Thomas Jefferson's "Monticello."

The Tufts Library shared in the effort made in the postwar period to make up for lost time, although it still lagged woefully behind many other parts of the College in important respects by the time the 100th anniversary of the institution was celebrated in 1952. Housing, staff, and the collections themselves were becoming embarrassingly inadequate for the expanded needs of a growing faculty and student body. In the fall of 1945 the librarian was calling for a new structure to replace the outmoded and overcrowded building erected almost half a century before; it had undergone no structural change in the meantime. The librarian very well knew that his hope was only "wishful thinking," as he expressed it, but he agreed to settle for at least a new wing for the building. Space for every activity from the processing of acquisitions to study areas was at a premium, and until 1948 the presence of the College bookstore in the basement compound the problem. Frequently-used teaching materials on reserve for undergraduate classes had, in the fall of 1945, overflowed into part of the auditorium of Goddard Hall, the home of the Fletcher School of Law and Displomacy, inconveniently located across the campus from the main library.

Cooperation with other libraries in the Boston area in 1941 had made possible the long-range plan of storing little-used materials in the New England Deposit Library in Brighton. Some 3,000 volumes from the Tufts Library had been transferred there by 1948, but the whole process had been delayed by frequent changes in cataloguing personnel. Between 1938 and 1948 there had been over a dozen replacements in a staff which never totaled more than six to eight full-time persons. The turnover occurred simply because the College could not match salaries being paid elsewhere. The notable exceptions of continuous service were Ethel M. Hayes, who had loyally completed forty-seven years of service at the College when she retired in 1943; and Blanche M. Hooper, whose service when she retired as assistant librarian in 1952 lacked only two years of half a century. The library somehow managed to process over 37,000 books in the ten-year period preceding 1948, with no more than one trained cataloguer on the staff at any one time. It was not until the fall of 1948 that the librarian was able to obtain (and retain) the services of a full-time professionally trained reference librarian.[38]

[38] Mrs. Dorothy Markle Union, the reference librarian, also served as acting librarian for one year, following the retirement of Raymond L. Walkley in 1955, and continued on the staff when Joseph Komidar became University Librarian.

The working collection of the library, which remained almost exclusively an undergraduate facility until after 1955, grew slowly and spottily in the decades before Tufts officially became a university. The number of volumes by 1948 had barely reached 150,000, and the library budget remained almost static over a period of almost twenty years. The amount charged students for laboratory breakage fees in chemistry alone in 1941–42 was more than was budgeted for all books and magazines for the library that year.[39] In the decade 1938–48, only 29,000 volumes were added to the main collection. Gifts accounted for one-third of the total, largely from the faculty and alumni and the United States Government. It was fortunate for the library that it had been a depository for government documents since 1896. The "starvation budget" for the library was all too characteristic of an institution whose total resources required the most careful establishment of priorities. Strengthening the library collection had not been one of them during the Carmichael regime.

The librarian did at least see his plea for enlarged quarters fulfilled. In the fall of 1945 the Trustee Executive Committee included the possibility of a wing for Eaton Library in their discussion of plant needs. The Alumni Fund for 1945–46 was devoted to raising money for the purpose, and by 1948 the Trustees had arrived at the conclusion that the total cost "must not exceed $170,-000." The new wing was dedicated and opened in the fall of 1950 and was designated as a memorial to the 7,232 Tufts students and alumni who had served in the armed forces during the Second World War, of whom 102 had lost their lives. The provision of a greatly needed reading and reserved book room, additional stack space for bound periodicals, and study carrels made possible the vacating of that portion of Goddard Hall used as a makeshift extension of the library. The original structure was also refurbished, and structural arrangements in the joining of the two buildings sup-

[39] The only increase in funds for library purposes between 1943 and 1948 came from the bequest of $3,600 by the late Professor Wade. In 1948–49, money was specifically allocated for the last time out of student fees to help support the Reading Room Association. This organization, from the days of President Miner, had helped finance recreational reading as a supplement to College appropriations. Since the 1920's, much of the money had been used to purchase extra copies of library books required in courses with large enrollments.

The War Memorial Wing of Eaton Library
dedicated on December 7, 1950

plied additional space for special uses. Part of it became a lounge, a memorial to Thomas M. Mark, a graduate of the Class of 1916 in the School of Religion who in 1941 lost his life while serving as a chaplain in the armed forces.[40] The new wing also made possible the housing in a separate room of a special collection of works of English literature and other literature in translation. In 1940, following a recommendation of the Faculty of Arts and Sciences, the Trustees had authorized President Carmichael to appoint a five-member committee to collect and administer a fund for what was known as the Charles Gott Memorial Library of the Novel.[41] Fifteen years after the Memorial Wing had been opened, the entire library was given a new and spacious home. Eaton Library, and the Memorial Wing, had failed to meet the needs of the College by the mid-1950's. The Nils Yngve Wessell Library, attracting nation-wide

[40] Among the principal contributors who made the lounge possible were Lieutenant Commander Mark's classmates and Donald R. MacJannet, who contributed part of his salary as fund-raiser for the medical school.

[41] The collection was a tribute to an outstanding member of the Tufts faculty who had served for many years in the Department of English and was both its chairman and dean of the graduate school at the time of his death in 1938.

attention for its architectural features, and named for President Carmichael's successor, was opened in the fall of 1965.

There were many other areas of activity besides building construction that kept the campus humming after the Second World War. The decision of George S. Miller to retire as vice-president and as dean of the Faculty of Arts and Sciences in 1951 produced a revised administrative structure, effective in 1951–52. Dr. Wessell, dean of the school of liberal arts, shouldered as an additional duty the vice-presidency vacated by Dean Miller as well as a Professorship of Psychology. John P. Tilton, who continued as dean of the graduate school, became the first provost. Miller assumed the title of Dean of Administration, while Richard A. Kelley became Assistant Dean of the Division of Special Studies, and a year later its dean; Clifton W. Emery became the Acting Director of Counseling. President Carmichael passed no judgment on the net increase of administrative staff but did forewarn the Trustees that even more such posts would be needed in the near future. Further administrative changes came promptly, effective September 1952. Grant Curtis, who had been Admissions Officer for the school of liberal arts and assistant to Dean Wessell, became Director of Admissions, and Emery became Assistant Dean of Liberal Arts as well as Director of Student Personnel, thus relieving Vice-President Wessell of some of his multitudinous duties. Professor Paul Flint became Assistant Dean of the graduate school, and Katharine R. Jeffers succeeded Edith Bush as dean of Jackson College following the latter's retirement. James R. Strawbridge took on the duties of assistant to the provost as well as registrar, following the retirement of Mrs. Nellie W. Reynolds after half a century devoted to the College.

There were still other offices created or enlarged during Carmichael's presidency. The Placement Office, which had been created in 1936 in the heart of the Great Depression, and had been operated for many years by Lester W. Collins, became a major operation after 1946 under the direction of Mrs. Viola Saltmarsh. President Carmichael's predictions about further administrative changes were quite correct. The days of multiple activities carried on by one or two offices were fast receding, and new lines of communication were established with a rapidity that bewildered the faculty and the students, if not the administrators themselves. Each set of expanding duties seemed to become more than one person could manage. The case of Joseph W. Morton can be used to illustrate the changes that had taken place between the 1930's and the early 1950's. One of the busiest persons when Carmichael became president, Morton figuratively wore a whole rack of hats later parceled out among half a dozen or more different individuals. In 1938–39, he was secretary of the Alumni Council and of the Association and all of its committees, treasurer of the *Tuftonian,* responsible as managing editor for five issues each year of the College catalogue, editor of the *Alumni Bulletin,* keeper of alumni records and the alumni mailing service, in charge of the weekly official College Calendar, and supervisor of the student-manned College news bureau.

Throughout his administration, Carmichael was eager to have the College before the public as much as possible. He spoke frequently and at length on "the very great importance of maintaining proper professional publicity for our entire educational enterprise." It was on his initiative that the format of the rather drab College catalogue was radically changed in 1939–40; he considered the more attractive product "one fundamental form of Tufts publicity." The public relations program was greatly intensified when Mrs. Cecilia Van Auken was appointed to the staff in 1943 and was made Public Relations Officer three years later. In 1947, David Geller, who had edited *Tufts Topics* during the war, was placed in charge of publicity for the medical and dental schools. A summer school equivalent of the *Tufts Weekly* during the regular term was first published in 1946. Known for two years as the *Tufts Summer News* and after 1948 as the *Tufts Hilltopper,* it also became a responsibility of the Public Relations Office. As the magnitude of the institution's operations grew, so did the need for administrative staff. It is probably safe to conjecture that Hosea Ballou 2d would have looked with awe and a bit of consternation, if not downright disbelief, at the once-tiny college he had helped to create and over whose first years he had presided a century before.

16. Professional Education:
Old Problems and New Ventures

TUFTS HAD BECOME MORE THAN A LIBERAL ARTS COLLEGE within two decades of its chartering in 1852. In the 1860's it had committed itself to offering undergraduate education in two professions: engineering and the ministry. Admittedly, both curricula — the first established in 1865 and the second in 1869 — had a large amount of what is generally considered "liberal arts" content. Yet both were intended to prepare students for careers requiring some degree of special training beyond that expected in the somewhat amorphous creature known as the "liberally educated man." The addition of the medical and dental curricula and the establishment of the graduate school in the 1890's and the Fletcher School of Law and Diplomacy in the 1930's reinforced the idea of preparing students for professional competency, whether at the graduate or undergraduate level, whatever lip service might have been given to the so-called liberal arts. On the eve of the Second World War, Tufts College embarked on a new series of academic ventures which committed it to a greatetr extent than ever before to professional education — this time largely at the undergraduate level. These new extensions of the College's responsibilities provoked considerable controversy among a liberal-arts-oriented faculty who were consulted on none of the major policy decisions involved. They also produced inevitably a tangled web of administrative relationships which remained a mystery to all but a few.

§　§　§

The Tufts Engineering School received its share of attention in the review of curricula and educational aims that took place shortly after President Carmichael's arrival in 1938. This part of the institution, unlike the school of liberal arts, had the problem of professional accrediting agencies to contend with. It had naturally been jolted by the report of the inspection conducted by the Engineers' Council for Professional Development in 1936. The Council had given only probational recognition to the Civil, Mechanical, and Electrical Departments, and the Chemical Engineering Department had not received accreditation at all. The school was given until June 1939 to review itself, its aims, and its role in engineering education. The Council had found, besides antiquated equipment and inadequate staff and instruction, too much of a "trade school" atmosphere and too much of a propensity for turning out mere technicians.

President Cousens and the dean of the engineering school had had a series of conversations which produced certain conclusions. One was that insufficient use was being made of the resources in the school of liberal arts. It was agreed that a "sound educational program" for engineers should include, besides the fundamentals of engineering, "a considerable election in the humanities, the social and natural sciences." To this end, an attempt was made to formulate a curriculum that would provide a common core of studies for the first three years (except for chemical engineering), with a degree of specialization permitted in the senior year. Among the opportunities provided in a suggested course of study were an increased amount of mathematics, more electives in non-engineering subjects, and reduction of emphasis on so-called applied subjects, particularly in the first two years. None of these proposals was very revolutionary, and all had been either recommended or attempted in earlier curricula but had always seemed to wither away with the passage of time. A curriculum for chemical engineering students was proposed in 1937 that made the first year identical to that of other engineering students but contained more chemistry and less engineering thereafter. It was suggested that the degree of B.S. in Chemistry be awarded on the basis of a four-year program and that a B.S. in Chemical Engineering be awarded upon completion of a fifth year. By the fall of 1937 no decision had actually been reached by the engineering faculty, although discussions were active and disagreements were numerous. A year later, Trustee T. S. Knight, of the Committee of Visitors to the engineering school, was disappointed that the school, in an attempt to meet the demands of the Engineers' Council, was concentrating on physical

661

plant and seeking to acquire new and better equipment. In his estimation this was misdirected effort; quality of education, not physical plant *per se*, should receive the greatest and most immediate attention.

Those who were concerned about the state of engineering education at Tufts could take heart, however. On the urging of President Carmichael and with the arrival of the deadline set by the Engineers' Council, the engineering faculty reviewed its curricula and made certain modifications in the degree programs in civil, mechanical, and electrical engineering. The most significant change, effected in 1939, was the adoption of a program in general engineering for those who preferred not to specialize in one of the four branches offered by the school; for purposes of carrying out this program, both physics and mathematics could be considered as major fields. A welcome physical rearrangement also took place in the fall of 1939; greatly needed space for the electrical engineering department was provided when it was moved to the old AMRAD wing of Cousens Gymnasium.[1]

The engineering faculty continued to wrestle with the problem of the chemical engineering curriculum. The lack of accreditation was an especially sensitive problem because for several years, in the late 1930's, approximately one-third of all engineering students wished to major in that department, preferring a chemical engineering degree to a Bachelor of Science in Chemistry. No attempt was made, however, to secure accreditation for the next several years, partly because of the effect of the Second World War and partly because of the lack of agreement about accrediting standards and requirements among various agencies such as the Engineers' Council for Professional Development, working through the American Institute of Chemical Engineers; the National Commission on Accrediting; and the Committee on Professional Training of the American Chemical Society. Part of the difficulty was reflected locally in differences of opinion over how much chemistry should be required in the engineering program, and over relations between the Department of Chemistry and the engineering school.

[1] It was named the "Hooper Laboratory" in honor of William Leslie Hooper, for many years a member of the Electrical Engineering Department and between 1912 and 1914 acting president of the College. The vacated space in Robinson Hall was immediately taken over for a new physics laboratory.

When the Civil, Electrical, and Mechanical Engineering Departments were accredited by the Engineers' Council for Professional Development in 1949–50, the general engineering curriculum was not accredited because insufficient engineering work was provided. No request was made at that time to have the chemical engineering program accredited, but this was finally accomplished in 1952. Meanwhile (in 1947–48), a somewhat revised curriculum for the entire engineering school went into effect. It included a common freshman year and the requirement of the equivalent of eight one-term courses in the humanities.[2] There seemed to be a continuing consensus that a prospective engineer, no matter how proficient he might be in his area of technical specialization, needed at least minimum exposure to the liberal arts tradition.

§　§　§

If enrollment had been the sole criterion, the Tufts School of Religion (the Crane Theological School) would have been experiencing a period of unprecedented prosperity when Dr. Carmichael became president of the College in 1938.[3] There were sixty students enrolled in 1937–38, the largest number in the history of the school up to that time. The Executive Committee of the Trustees even considered the advisability of curtailing enrollment. A high point in the affairs of the school was achieved in September 1941, when it played host to the Universalist Convention. This was an historic occasion, for it marked the first time that the denomination responsible for having founded the College had held a formal meeting on the campus. At the same time, denominational representation in the student body had continued to broaden; in 1942, individuals from seven different religious bodies were enrolled, including even the Greek Orthodox faith.

A tradition was established in 1940 which served a double purpose. The practice of dedicating various rooms in the school

[2] Beginning in September 1948, solid geometry and trigonometry were also required for admission.

[3] For the thirty years between 1925 and 1955, the Crane School was listed in all official publications as "The School of Religion . . . A Department of Tufts College." It was not again referred to officially as the "Crane Theological School" until 1955, when it was considered "an integral part of Tufts University." It was, except for one brief period in the 1960's, one of the Associated Schools of the College of Arts and Sciences.

memorialized outstanding faculty and benefactors and also helped
to finance physical improvements. The furnishing of the Vincent
E. Tomlinson Memorial Lounge in Paige Hall was made possible
by a gift from the family. Three classrooms in Miner Hall were
similarly refurbished in 1942 and 1949.[4] In 1950 the Clarence R.
Skinner collection of Oriental shrine and art objects, which had
been willed to the school, was put on display in Miner Hall.[5]

President Carmichael viewed the school with a less enthusiastic eye than some of its supporters and found it deficient in several
respects. It posed a continuing financial problem for the College,
and in 1939 the president told the Trustees that the school involved
"a deficit which may be inconsistent with its accomplishment." He
was also critical of the curriculum and called for increased attention
to "scientific social work" and similar "technical studies." His most
serious doubt concerned the continued admission of undergraduates to the school. He might have noted also that although eight
faculty members were teaching in the school, in 1937–38 only one
was actually full-time, and four were teaching half-time in the
school of liberal arts.[6] Dean Skinner, always the champion of his
school and of its students, was also dissatisfied with the position of
the school; his concern, however, was on quite different grounds
from those of Carmichael. Skinner wanted the theological students
identified as a much more separate and homogeneous group than
they were considered, and felt strongly that they should have their
own academic and social community in Paige Hall.[7] He was also
disturbed because the tuition charge ($350 in 1942) was the highest
of any theological school in the United States. He believed that,
for this reason, the Crane School was in a poor competitive position

4 The Frank Oliver Hall classroom was dedicated in the spring of 1942,
and the William George Tousey and George Thompson Knight rooms were
provided in 1949 by contributions from the families of the two long-time faculty members.

5 Skinner, who had been dean of the school from 1932 to 1945, had
died in 1949.

6 Attention was called to this by the Committee of Visitors to the school
in the fall of 1937.

7 He offered at one time to invest $2,000 of his own funds in a project to
provide a dining room, kitchen, and social area in the basement. This was
finally accomplished in the 1950's by the alumni.

and could not always secure the most desirable students. This argument by Dean Skinner was of less concern to Carmichael than the matter of academic preparation of the Crane students. The burden of tuition charges could always be lightened by the granting of Trustee gratuities. The president objected to the use of the Crane School as a "back door" to the school of liberal arts by students who could not normally meet the latter's requirements.

The School of Religion fared better, in some respects, than did some other parts of the institution during the Second World War. Theological students were deferred from military service by law, although about one-fourth of those at Crane left their studies to volunteer for military service. Paige Hall was taken over by the Navy, and the remaining Crane students were temporarily housed in a residence adjacent to the campus. During and immediately after the war the school's greatest losses were in the faculty. Dean Emeritus McCollester died, and Professor Bruce Brotherston, who taught half-time in the school, retired. In spite of repeated efforts to retain his services, Professor Rolland E. Wolfe, who had served on the faculty since 1934, accepted a position elsewhere. Dean Skinner announced his own retirement, effective at the end of the academic year 1944–45, after thirty-one years as a teacher and administrator. After his temporary replacement by Professor Alfred S. Cole, Dr. John M. Ratcliff, a member of the Crane faculty since 1927, was elected dean.

The school emerged from the war period in 1945 with thirty-four students, but with only one full-time faculty member and one serving half-time. The three remaining faculty gave but a single course each. The McCollester Professorship was still unfilled, and the school was farther than ever from meeting the standards of staff strength established by the American Association of Theological Schools, which required a minimum of four full-time faculty for accreditation. The situation was little better four years later. The school commenced the academic year 1949–50 with thirty-eight students, and Dr. Eugene S. Ashton, who had joined the faculty in 1947, had been appointed to the McCollester chair. However, he and Dean Ratcliff still comprised the only full-time faculty. At no time in over half a century had the school operated with so small a full-time staff. The curriculum was kept at a respectable level during Dean Ratcliff's tenure only by the expedient of using part-time faculty to offer courses in alternate years.[8] Students were beginning to desert the school because it had so few faculty and such meager course offerings. Ironically, one of the reasons was the renewal, in 1943, of the cooperative arrangement with the Harvard Divinity School, whereby Crane students maintaining a high academic average could take without charge two courses there. When some of the Crane students saw the opportunities at Harvard they transferred. The school even lost the residence facilities for its students when Paige Hall, to have been returned to it after the war, became a Jackson dormitory in 1946 and was not again made available for theological students until the fall of 1954.[9]

After the Second World War a thorough study was made of the entire Crane School — from the scholastic standing of its students over the ten-year period since 1934 to the fundamental objectives it sought to accomplish. Admission policy was a basic and long-standing weakness that had become increasingly noticeable over the years as professional and academic standards had risen. The traditional practice had been to admit students as freshmen in the school of liberal arts and to combine undergraduate with graduate and professional training offered by Crane. While the general procedure had been to admit only those who had completed secondary school and had met the standard entrance requirements, exceptions had been made "in a number of cases." Four categories of students resulted. One, designated as "Specials," included students ranging from those who had had only "irregular high school training" to an occasional student who already possessed a Ph.D. The second group included those with a high school diploma. A third was composed of transfers from other colleges. The fourth group was made up of those who had been admitted with a Bachelor's degree. Of the 135 students between 1934 and 1944 whose records were reviewed, forty-seven were "Specials," forty-five were

[8] Among the part-time faculty who had a long association with the school and who contributed greatly to it were Professor J. A. C. Fagginger Auer, who served as Professor of Church History from 1924 until his retirement thirty years later; and Rabbi Beryl D. Cohon, a Visiting Lecturer obtained through the Jewish Chautauqua Society, who taught from 1947 through 1961.

[9] Dormitory accommodations were provided for the displaced Crane men in Fletcher Hall.

high school graduates only, thirty-five came with some amount of college credit, and only eight possessed an A.B. degree. As might have been expected, the group with the most formal education and regularity of training compiled the best academic records. The heterogeneity of the student body was reflected in the wide range of academic achievement in each group. Both Dean Skinner and Dean Ratcliff were a bit defensive about the records of the students in their school as compared with those in the school of liberal arts.

President Carmichael and Dean Ratcliff were never able to agree on what the essential nature of the Crane School should be, in terms of its admissions and degree-granting policies. The dean of the school argued that it should continue to admit undergraduates who could obtain a combined A.B.-S.T.B. degree. He saw as its primary mission the training of all those interested in some phase of the ministry (taken in its broadest sense), college graduates or not. He put particular emphasis on the necessity for preparing young men and women who intended to enter the field of religious education and general parish work. Carmichael, on the other hand, opposed the policy of admitting undergraduates directly from secondary school and wished to see Crane achieve and maintain a professional level comparable to that of the medical school. Yet at the same time, no move was made to include the school in the Second Century endowment campaign between 1949 and 1951 — a fact that Dean Ratcliff called to the president's attention.[10] The president wanted Crane, if it were to continue as a professional school, to require a Bachelor's degree for admission, with academic standards and requirements to match.

An event at St. Lawrence University in Canton, New York, in December 1951 had a direct bearing on the Crane School. The interior of the headquarters of the Universalist theological school on the St. Lawrence campus was gutted by fire. The Trustees of the school, which body was separate from that of St. Lawrence Univer-

[10] In the extensive fund-drive publicity, the School of Religion was merely lumped in under the heading of "Tufts Undergraduate Schools" and was not mentioned in the statement of financial objectives. It did, however, conduct its own campaign, which was endorsed by the General Assembly of the Universalist Church in 1951. It had the threefold objective of augmenting the endowment of the McCollester Professorship, faculty salaries, and scholarships.

sity proper, immediately voted to rebuild the damaged structure. The New York State Convention of Universalists, which had founded the theological school in 1856 and continued to select its Board of Trustees, approved the decision. While the securing of funds for rebuilding was being discussed, the suggestion was made that it might be an opportune time to consider merger of the St. Lawrence and Crane theological schools. A formal invitation to the Crane School to merge with the St. Lawrence school on the New York State campus was extended in March 1952 by the New York State Convention. Further discussions took place, and President Carmichael was authorized by the Tufts Trustees to study the possibilities of merger. Representatives of each school then presented the most favorable case they could muster for locating on their respective campus.

There seemed to be a certain logic in combining two relatively weak schools (neither of them accredited) into one much stronger institution.[11] Dean Ratcliff, who heartily endorsed the idea of merger and had discussed the possibilities of some kind of close association of the two theological schools for over a decade, was given the responsibility for conducting the negotiations for Tufts. President Carmichael remained neutral and attended none of the meetings at which merger was discussed. The very prompt decision of the Board of Trustees of the theological school at St. Lawrence had, for all practical purposes, closed the door to any possibility that the schools could be merged, but conversations continued for several months. President Eugene C. Bewkes of St. Lawrence University, who was not directly involved in the decisions but was naturally interested in the outcome, expressed his hope that a broader representation than the New York State Universalist Convention could be brought into the negotiations, so that the decision to rebuild could be considered more carefully. The Board of Trustees of the theological school at St. Lawrence expressed no enthusiasm over merger or affiliation, particularly if the combined schools were located at Tufts. So the whole matter was dropped after the Trustees of the St. Lawrence school declined (in May

[11] At the time, each school had only three full-time faculty members. The school at St. Lawrence had an endowment of $440,000, while the Crane funds had, by 1952, shrunk to less than $300,000, including $35,000 for scholarships. Even then, part of the Crane funds were merely assigned arbitrarily to the school by the Tufts Trustees from other resources of the College.

1952) a tentative proposal prepared by Dean Ratcliff and approved by President Carmichael which would have merged the two theological schools on the Medford campus.

After the collapse of negotiations with the theological school at St. Lawrence, Dean Ratcliff returned to the yet unanswered question of the status of Crane as a professional school. He prepared a detailed memorandum embodying the arguments for and against making it an exclusively graduate school. He was highly dubious that there would be sufficient enrollment in a purely graduate school to justify the school's existence, in view of the experiences of similar schools in the denomination. However, he did take cognizance of the growing pressure to establish a *bona fide* graduate program, chiefly from the American Association of Theological Schools. He recommended that a compromise be worked out by extending the S.T.B. combined program from six to seven years and in that way meeting the requirement of three full years of graduate work. This naturally would require an increase in faculty and extension of curriculum.

A step was taken in the direction outlined by Dean Ratcliff when, in the fall of 1952, the Executive Committee of the Tufts Trustees approved a set of revised degree requirements for the combined A.B.-S.T.B. program. They went even farther by requiring the completion of a four-year undergraduate degree for admission to the B.D. program. Dean Ratcliff did not see the working out of the new program, for death cut short his career early in 1953, a few weeks after President Carmichael had himself resigned. Dr. Ashton, McCollester Professor of Biblical Literature and assistant chaplain in the College, served as acting dean until Dr. Benjamin Hersey was appointed. It was left to the new head of the school to see if a transition could be made, after 1954, to the status of a full-fledged graduate institution.

§   §   §

The story of the all-graduate Fletcher School of Law and Diplomacy between 1937 and 1945 was a grim and unhappy one, of almost unrelieved pessimism. During this critical period the school, almost bereft of a student body because of the exigencies of the Second World War, lost its original dean, about one-third of its library resources, and a large part of its faculty. There was a very real possibility that it might be forced to close or at least to suspend operations for a period of years. Somehow it managed to hang on, and experienced a revival and sense of renewed strength after 1945 that lent an air of unreality to the preceding decade.

Finances seemed to be, as in the entire history of the school, the crucial consideration. The limitation of enrollment to fifty meant that no other division of the College during the administrations of Cousens and Carmichael had as large a ratio of investment income to tuition income as did the Fletcher School. Dean Hoskins, and President Cousens until his death in the summer of 1937, had sought outside assistance that would remove the school from its unfortunate hand-to-mouth existence. The problem had become acute for several reasons. The modification in Harvard's policy of cooperation, arranged several years earlier, placed severe limits on the use of its faculty outside its boundaries and required the development by the Fletcher School of its own staff to a greater extent than before. The school had also to exploit as best it could the special talent that became available in the Boston area from time to time. The continuing attempt to build up a full-time faculty was marked by a degree of success when Dr. Leo Gross was appointed Lecturer in International Organization and Administration for 1941–42, with his salary furnished under a grant from the Rockefeller Foundation. This aid, welcome as it was, fell far short of the total needs of the school. What few gifts it received tended to be designated for special purposes, such as financing lectures. The problem of steadily shrinking income from the Fletcher endowment was aggravated by increased need for student aid.[12] Library costs were going up because of financial problems encountered by the World Peace Foundation, which until 1937 had paid a large part of library staff salaries and had provided valuable documents from foreign governments. There was no endowment at all available for establishing a John A. Cousens Professorship in International Economic Relations. This chair had been proposed after his death to memorialize Cousens' part in creating the Fletcher School and to recognize his special interest in the realm of finance.

As a result of a prolonged effort by the Fletcher dean and by

12 A Fletcher School loan fund was established in 1938, consisting originally of $30.30 contributed by the World Peace Foundation and $25.00 by an anonymous donor.

President Cousens, sufficient interest in the school and its prospects had been generated among the various Carnegie organizations (Endowment for International Peace, Foundation for the Advancement of Teaching, and the Corporation proper) to encourage submission of a statement of the school's endowment needs. No specific sum was mentioned, but $200,000 seemed to be appropriate.[13] Hoskins was told that the application for funds would receive "sympathetic consideration." The Trustee Executive Committee gave its blessing to such an application, and an elaborate prospectus was prepared by Dean Hoskins and forwarded to the Carnegie Corporation in January 1939, a few months after Dr. Leonard Carmichael became president of Tufts. The effort bore no fruit; neither did a proposal in 1941 for support of a program in American defense. Hoskins persistently called to President Carmichael's attention the fact that the school's finances were more precarious than ever, that its relative standing was beginning to decline, and that it was in danger of losing its position of leadership and becoming a second-class school. Unless the situation changed radically, some faculty and courses would have to be dropped.

The outbreak of the Second World War seemed to make bad matters worse for the Fletcher School. It was justifiably proud of the fact that in the fall of 1942, 75 of its 238 alumni were in government positions, 36 of them in the State Department alone. It was likewise noteworthy that a member of the Fletcher Class of 1943 became the first woman in fifteen years to pass the State Department examinations and to be accepted in the Foreign Service as a career diplomat. These facts did not, however, have much relevance to the problem of maintaining a student body of at least minimum size. Dozens of students who would ordinarily have stayed in the school to complete their degrees left for government or military service. There was no draft exemption or deferment for Fletcher students; there were no special programs comparable to the Naval

13 At the time the request was made, the annual income from the Fletcher endowment ($1,000,000) was less than $48,000. Receipts from tuition and fees ($17,500) almost exactly equaled those from other sources (dormitory rental, dining-hall charges, and the like). The operating deficit of the school for 1937–38 was almost $6,000. It was erased only after the Honorable Dave Hennen Morris, former ambassador to Belgium and for a time chairman of the Board of Counselors to the Fletcher School, offered $500 toward cancellation of the deficit; the Tufts Trustees agreed to raise the remainder.

units that had been established in the undergraduate departments of Tufts in 1943. Fletcher enrollment in 1943–44 dropped precipitately, from fifty to twenty-five, of whom ten were women. The Fletcher men's dormitory was taken over by the Navy V-12 Program, and the few males left in the school's student body were housed in the Phi Epsilon Pi fraternity house, which had been taken over by the College. Blakeslee House was used for a few Fletcher women and students from Jackson College and the Bouvé-Boston School of Physical Education, which had become affiliated with Tufts in 1942.

The Fletcher School was the only part of the College that did not go on an accelerated program during the war, although it adjusted its opening date to November 1 to conform to the undergraduate school calendar. So many of the Harvard faculty teaching in the Fletcher School had been engrossed in some phase of the war effort, even by 1942–43, that the only alternative, if the school was to be staffed to any degree, seemed to be the use of the undergraduate faculty of Tufts. Consultation with President Conant made it a certainty that the school could no longer count on using Harvard faculty, for they had committed themselves to a twelve-month teaching year in such a way that they could not be allowed to do "outside teaching." For the Fletcher School to remain open, the choice seemed to be between sacrifice of position and an unbalanced budget. If any further retrenchment were forced on the school, it would have to be accompanied by a lowering of standards of instruction or a reduction in the caliber of students admitted. These were alternatives to be avoided as long as possible.

Several efforts were made, as early as 1941, to explore ways in which Fletcher could contribute to the war effort and at the same time continue to serve academic needs. The Navy League suggested in that year that it might contribute to a special study group on the role of sea power in international affairs, and in 1942 the possibility of setting up a program for training intelligence officers was considered. Nothing came of either proposal, or of a scheme, also discussed in 1942, of establishing a program for preparing personnel to govern areas recovered from the Axis powers. When Dean Hoskins heard in the autumn of 1942 that Harvard was negotiating with the federal government for a similar program in international administration, he immediately inquired as to what role the

Fletcher School might play. President Conant's reply made it clear that he had no desire to involve the school. In fact, Hoskins was told in no uncertain terms that Harvard was "endeavoring not to interfere with your domain, but I am sure you will agree that this particular activity does not fall within the scope of your original activities." The best that Dean Hoskins could expect was to be kept informed of Harvard's plans. The Fletcher dean replied that he had been unprepared "for a by-passing of the Fletcher School entirely in the development at Harvard of a program of training in international administration." He admitted that Fletcher could not conduct such a program alone, but he felt that the school deserved "some consideration." He very well knew that the project at Harvard would have an adverse effect on the future prospects of the Fletcher School. Harvard did, however, invite Dean Hoskins to serve on its Committee on Military Government and International Administration. President Carmichael was also a participant in a conference held at Harvard early in 1943 to discuss training programs for personnel in occupied areas. The upshot of this meeting was the announcement by Harvard in February 1943 that a special School for Overseas Administration was being established "under the auspices of Harvard University with the assistance of the Fletcher School of Law and Diplomacy of Tufts College."[14]

The year 1944 was especially critical for the Fletcher School in several respects. One of the serious problems concerned its library resources, which consisted, in effect, of four parts. The two smaller segments were largely teaching materials borrowed from the Tufts Library and current materials acquired with Fletcher funds. The two major sections were not the property either of Tufts or of the Fletcher School but had been housed at the school and were subject to recall; the older collection was that of the World Peace Foundation, deposited when the school had opened, and the other was the property of the Diplomatic Affairs Foundation. This foundation, established in 1939 with headquarters in New York City, was organized by the Honorable Dave Hennen Morris and associates to assist in advancing "the orderly conduct of international affairs," to promote international economic relations, and to encourage the effective application of international law. Among its projects was

[14] Dean Hoskins and Professor Norman J. Padelford of the Fletcher School were listed as members of the staff.

673

the development of a special library which was deposited at the Fletcher School early in 1941 "for an indefinite period." Needless to say, the collection greatly strengthened the school's research capabilities, which were also augmented by some financial support from the Foundation.[15] Within a brief period in 1943–44, both the World Peace Foundation and the Diplomatic Affairs Foundation announced their intention of reassessing their policies regarding their libraries, with the probability that they would be relocated.

After the World Peace Foundation library had been placed in the Fletcher School, President Cousens had, in the 1930's, made sure that relations between the school and the Foundation were as close as possible. He saw to it that when a vacancy occurred in 1937 in the directorship Dean Hoskins' name was considered. One linkage that was maintained for almost a decade between the Foundation and the Fletcher library was Denys P. Myers, the research librarian of the Foundation. He severed his connection with both the Foundation and the school in 1942 and joined the staff of the Division of Special Research in the State Department.

Early in 1944 the World Peace Foundation reminded President Carmichael that its collection was on deposit only, and that if its integrity were not being maintained or if the library ever ceased to be used "for purposes of advanced instruction in the fields of international law and diplomacy," it might be withdrawn from Fletcher. Carmichael hastened to inform the Foundation that there was "in contemplation no change in the conditions under which the collection is maintained" and that the school very much hoped the collection would remain where it was. The next step taken by the College was to offer to purchase the collection for slightly over $5,000. The Foundation declined the offer, on the ground that the League of Nations publications in the library had a market value themselves of approximately $10,000. A compromise was eventually worked out whereby the Foundation repossessed sufficient works to comprise an effective reference collection in its Boston headquarters, and the main body of the library was acquired by Fletcher for $10,000. The settlement was made with the understanding that the collection in the Fletcher School would always be available to qualified investigators (including the staff of the Foundation) and

15 Contributions by the Foundation in the form of money or gifts provided more than half the Ginn Library accessions in 1941–42.

would be transferred to the Foundation "in the event that the Fletcher School is discontinued or the Library ceases to be maintained." Fortunately for the school, it received by gift the same year the extensive private library of Professor George Grafton Wilson, one of the original Fletcher faculty.

The wartime situation in which the Fletcher School found itself had become a matter of official concern to the Diplomatic Affairs Foundation in mid-1943. The status of its library on deposit at the school was the main issue at stake. Word had come that the residential facilities of the school were being taken over for other uses, and doubt had been expressed that the school would maintain its original character and direction. The Foundation requested a statement from the College, "as clear and detailed as may be," of its policies and plans affecting the Fletcher School. President Carmichael informed the Foundation that, although Wilson House (the men's dormitory for Fletcher students) was being taken over temporarily by the Navy as part of its training program, the Tufts Trustees expected to continue the Fletcher School during the war if at all possible, even though on a greatly reduced scale. Carmichael further assured the Foundation that its library collection would be kept intact. He also promised that, after the war emergency was over, the Trustees would "devote all possible energy to the general promotion of the program of the Fletcher School." An attempt to maintain it on a full scale while a world war was in progress would have seemed "doubtful both from an educational and from a patriotic point of view."

The specific reason for the Diplomatic Affairs Foundation's sudden interest in the future of its library was not far to seek. In 1943 there was established in Washington, D.C., an organization known as the Foreign Service Educational Foundation. Its official aim was "to promote the education and training of persons in the fields of government, business, international economic relations, international law, and such related fields as may fit them for better service in the foreign interest of this country at home or abroad."[16] The twenty-four Trustees included Presidents Conant of Harvard and Henry W. Wriston of Brown, with Congressman Christian A. Herter as president. The new organization immediately set about

[16] W. S. Rich and N. R. Deardorff (eds.), *American Foundations and Their Fields,* Vol. VI (New York: Raymond Rich Associates, 1948), p. 200.

establishing a Foreign Service Training Center with aims strikingly parallel to those of the Fletcher School. Dean Hoskins proposed to President Carmichael in the spring of 1944 that a cooperative arrangement be entered into with the Foundation so that the advanced work of Fletcher students could be taken in Washington through the new training center. The nation's capital would thus become a working laboratory for Fletcher students. In reply, President Carmichael instructed Hoskins that the Fletcher School would "go forward with approximately its present program here on the Tufts campus next year." Carmichael did, however, attend a conference in June at which representatives of ten other institutions were present. The possibility was discussed of establishing a Universities Cooperative Training Center in International Affairs in which institutions which were members of the Association of American Universities, plus the Fletcher School, might participate. Nothing came of the proposal after the directors of the Foreign Service Educational Foundation rejected the plan.

Dean Hoskins, in the meantime, had become treasurer of the Diplomatic Affairs Foundation and curator of its library deposited in the Fletcher School. He was instructed in May 1944 by the secretary of the Foundation "to proceed at once to remove the Foundation's possessions from their present location and to place them in storage pending an opportunity to transport them to their destination in Washington." When President Carmichael was apprised of this decision, he immediately contacted the acting president of the Foundation (Herter) and ordered Hoskins to leave the collection where it was, pending an investigation of its ownership. Legal advice requested by Herter made it indisputably clear that the Foundation had the right to withdraw its collection, and the Tufts Trustees promptly released it.[17] The seemingly precipitate departure of the Foundation library, of which the College had received no written notification until after the arrangements had been made, was followed in a matter of days by Dean Hoskins' resignation and his departure for Washington.[18] The intricate and close

[17] An inventory of the most important titles was kept so that the Fletcher School could replace as many as seemed necessary and desirable.

[18] His formal resignation was dated June 27, 1944, effective three days later. It was confirmed by the Trustees as of August 31, 1944, with the explana-

relationship of the ex-dean of the Fletcher School with these various groups did much to explain the circumstances under which he left the Tufts campus, but the factors that accounted for his decision to depart can be traced back well before 1943 and 1944. Dean Hoskins had become increasingly restive under the restrictions imposed by the limited endowment of the Fletcher School, and its worsened plight because of the Second World War. Its future was, to him at least, a matter of serious doubt. The school had become too small and too uncertain an operation with which to be associated, particularly when the vistas of Washington seemed so bright for postwar opportunities.

Whether justified or not, a cloud hung over Hoskins' sudden departure. It appeared to some that he was deserting the school when it needed most the directing hand of an experienced administrator, especially one who had seen the school born and nursed through its infancy. Others were perturbed that the Diplomatic Affairs Foundation library had been removed without sufficient warning but with the foreknowledge of the ex-dean.[19] Still others interpreted his well-matured advance plans to move to Washington as a deliberate attempt to become involved in establishing a school that would compete directly with Fletcher and weaken it correspondingly. Others noted that not only the dean's secretary

tion that his "full time seems to be required in his service with the Foreign Service Educational Foundation at Washington, D.C." Hoskins continued as treasurer of the Diplomatic Affairs Foundation and also became director (until 1948) of the training facility established by the Foreign Service Educational Foundation. The Diplomatic Affairs Foundation library formed the nucleus of the Center, which became known as the School of Advanced International Studies. The school, in turn, was incorporated into the Johns Hopkins University in 1950 as a graduate school of foreign affairs.

[19] At President Carmichael's request, the College librarian made an inspection, as best he could, of the already crated library in the summer of 1944. He found that a separate catalogue had been maintained of the collection, which was quite appropriate for a library on deposit only. The librarian was a bit more disturbed to discover that several miscellaneous gifts of books intended for the Fletcher School had been put in the Foundation collection. The Eaton and Fletcher libraries had over 40 per cent of the titles in the Foundation collection, but its removal left several important gaps that had to be somehow filled. The loss of the World Peace Foundation library would have been a much more serious matter.

but the registrar and also the acting librarian resigned simultaneously.[20]

President Carmichael immediately turned to the pressing matter of securing a new dean for the Fletcher School. He asked for President Conant's reaction if the post were offered to Dr. Norman J. Padelford.[21] Carmichael's choice met with Conant's full approval. The next task was to obtain Dr. Padelford's services. Meanwhile, Dean Hoskins had informed the alumni of the Fletcher School that he had resigned, and referred to the difficulty in securing a full complement of either students or faculty during the war. President Carmichael also felt constrained to send letters to the Fletcher alumni explaining the difficulties faced by the school in wartime and assuring them that the school would return to something approaching normalcy with the ending of the war and under the leadership of a new dean.

As President Carmichael feared might be the case, Dr. Padelford declined the deanship of the Fletcher School in the late summer of 1944. The work of the school, seriously curtailed as it might have been because of the dislocations of war and the resignation of its long-time dean, had to go on, and Professor Ruhl J. Bartlett, chairman of the Tufts Department of History, was appointed acting dean.[22] The unanimous choice of the Tufts Trustees for the deanship of the Fletcher School was Dr. Robert Burgess Stewart. He had received the Master of Arts in Law and Diplomacy from the

[20] It was alleged by some individuals that Hoskins "wanted to move the whole Fletcher School to Washington." There is no conclusive evidence to support the assertion also made that he took some of the Trustees, faculty, and students with him. Miss Priscilla Mason, the ex-registrar of the Fletcher School, did become secretary to the Board of the Foreign Service Educational Foundation when Hoskins became its director; she later became associated with the Johns Hopkins School of Advanced International Studies.

[21] The latter had received his Ph.D. from Harvard and had been Professor of International Law in the Fletcher School since 1936. He had been offered permanent posts of major responsibility in the State Department and had declined two offers of college presidencies.

[22] After relinquishing this temporary post in 1945, Dr. Bartlett continued as a part-time member of the Fletcher faculty, with the title of Professor of Diplomatic History. Beginning in the fall of 1956, he was a full-time member of the Fletcher staff, and Professor Albert H. Imlah became chairman of the Department of History; the latter served simultaneously on the staff of the Fletcher School on a part-time basis.

school in 1937 and his Ph.D. from Harvard. For the six years preceding his appointment he had served in various capacities in the State Department, including posts as assistant chief in the Division of European Affairs and in the British Commonwealth Division. He had also been a representative at a number of conferences. Immediately after taking up his new duties at the Fletcher School in March 1945, the dean-elect had participated, together with over a dozen other Fletcher alumni, in the San Francisco conferences establishing the United Nations organization. He had also maintained close ties with fellow Fletcher graduates and had held the presidency of the school's Alumni Association.

The imminent end of the Second World War in the spring of 1945 and the appointment of a new dean for Fletcher infused new life into the struggling school. President Conant of Harvard sent a cordial letter to Carmichael offering good wishes for the success of the school under its new head and expressed Harvard's willingness "to continue to share in the work of the School through representation on the Joint Academic Council." The Harvard president also reaffirmed the accessibility of that institution's libraries to the students and faculty of the Fletcher School and expressed the expectation that reciprocal course privileges for students would continue. The enrollment of the school, so greatly disrupted by international conflict, returned to the limit of fifty for the first time in mid-1946, after having reached a low point of seventeen at the start of the 1944–45 academic year. The faculty, which in 1945 could boast of only one full-time member, was rebuilt and strengthened, and new courses were offered. There was talk of raising the ceiling on enrollment because of the increased demand for graduates of the school. Operating income was increased when tuition was raised from $450 to $600 in 1949 and to $700 in 1952.

The Fletcher School received, in 1946–47, the first addition to its endowment fund since it had been established in 1933. Joseph Cummings of Somerville bequeathed $15,000 for the Edwin Ginn Library. Even though the school, in 1948, was operating with substantially the same financial resources it had possessed twenty-five years before, it was still able to perform phenomenally well. During its first fifteen years it had awarded only five Ph.D.'s; in the one year of 1948, there were thirteen candidates. The faculty was also more active than ever. Harry C. Hawkins was elected Professor of International Economics in mid-1948, after twenty-one years in the State Department. George N. Halm, who for many years held a shared appointment between the arts and sciences Department of Economics and the Fletcher School, became a full-time member of the Fletcher staff in 1950, as Professor of International Economic Relations. Both men were frequently called upon for expert advice. In 1948–49 they assisted the State Department Foreign Trade Council, the United States Chamber of Commerce, and the National Association of Manufacturers. The Fletcher School in the postwar period also assumed the unique task of giving special training to the diplomatic corps of the new nation of Pakistan, and to that of Siam. At the same time, two Foreign Service officers of the State Department were assigned to the school for special training in international trade and finance. Although substitution frequently had to be made in course offerings and gaps appeared and reappeared in special field and area coverage from time to time, individuals were somehow found to cover them and to augment and enrich existing offerings. Systematic instruction in the areas of eastern Asia and the Far East was made possible by the addition of Professor Allan B. Cole to the staff in 1949. The school was heartened in 1949–50 to receive an allocation of $600,000 in the Tufts Second Century endowment fund drive. Scholarly endeavor by the faculty in the field of international affairs was also made available to the public with the inauguration of a series of volumes published under the general title of Fletcher Studies in International Affairs. The first three works, appearing in 1951 and 1952, were George N. Halm's *Economic Systems: A Comparative Analysis,* Harry C. Hawkins' *Commercial Treaties and Agreements,* and Hans Kelsen's *Principles of International Law.*

As the Fletcher School approached its twentieth anniversary in 1952, another source of strength was added. The school had obtained its first endowed chair in 1949 when the William L. Clayton Professorship of International Finance was established.[23] Three

23 Harry C. Hawkins was the first occupant. The second endowed professorship resulted from a piece of business that remained unfinished for a quarter of a century. In 1958, after several attempts to settle the matter, the Braker Professorship, intended for the Fletcher School since 1930, after the Braker School of Commerce failed to materialize, was assigned to the school.

years later the endowment which made possible this position was enlarged to $300,000, largely through the efforts of Dean Stewart, and was funded as the William L. Clayton Center for International Economic Affairs. The Center, created to honor the nation's first Under Secretary of State for Economic Affairs, and under the sponsorship of the American Cotton Shippers Association, was devoted to research and training in an area of critical significance in world affairs. The Fletcher School thereby received not only its first endowed chair but also a fellowship program and an annual series of public lectures. The latter were delivered in the years immediately after 1952 by such distinguished individuals as Dean Acheson, former United States Secretary of State; Lester B. Pearson, a president of the United Nations General Assembly and leader of the Liberal Party in Canada; and J. William Fulbright, United States Senator and, at the time he delivered his series of lectures in 1962–63, chairman of the Senate Committee on Foreign Relations. There could be no doubt that the Fletcher School of Law and Diplomacy brought deserved luster to itself and, at least indirectly, to the institution of which it was a part on the Medford campus. Notwithstanding the handicaps under which it had been conceived and lived its early years, the Fletcher School had made remarkable progress, and looked with confidence toward its future.

§   §   §

The problems of the Tufts Medical School in the 1930's were serious and extended far back into the past; they all somehow centered around the word "finances." The school had been able to maintain its Class A standing but had "always been on the border line." Every inspection under the auspices of the American Medical Association had revealed a more or less disturbing list of shortcomings. In 1935 the Council on Medical Education launched a campaign more vigorous than ever to weed out weaker schools. The system of letter classification (A, B, and C) was abandoned, and schools were either recognized or not, usually after a period of probation in which it was hoped that they would mend their ways. The Tufts Medical School in 1937 had found itself in this

George N. Halm was the first recipient on the Fletcher faculty, although he continued to carry also the title of Professor of International Economic Relations.

unenviable probationary position. It became one of fifteen such schools out of a total of approximately seventy medical schools in the United States. The most recent inspection had resulted in three basic complaints: an excessive number of students in relation to the equipment, an undesirable teacher-student ratio in the laboratory sciences of the first two years, and insufficient supervision of the clinical work in the third and fourth years. The diagnosis and the remedy centered around the same word: money. The criticism of the Council was directed specifically against the policy of using medical school income for purposes other than for the medical school. Some $200,000 had been diverted to other College uses in the ten years between 1927 and 1937. The opinion of Dean A. Warren Stearns was bluntly stated: the school could never receive full recognition until the College ceased to use it as a source of revenue. This unfortunate policy was "absolutely opposed" to the standards established by the American Medical Association.

The school faced a crisis of major dimensions, and a year before his death President Cousens, fully recognizing the gravity of the situation, worked out in conjunction with the Medical School Alumni Association a campaign to seek substantial financial support for the school. The professional fund-raising team of Ward, Wells, and Dreshman was employed and immediately went to work in the spring of 1937.[24] The biggest difficulty seemed to be, not a paucity of potential sources for funds, but the lack of a general development plan that would attract gifts. The generalized goals of raising faculty salaries and increasing personnel were insufficient inducements to attract money. Prospective donors wanted to contribute to something less nebulous than "increased unrestricted income." One suggestion was to create a fifty-bed surgical unit at the Boston Dispensary and in that way establish the Department of Surgery on a permanent basis. This unquestionably would have been attractive as a money-raising project and would have strengthened the school. However, analysis of the project showed that it would be prohibitively expensive to maintain and would absorb the entire campaign effort; therefore, a compromise was worked out. It was proposed to use part of the Bingham gift, which was for a diagnostic clinic at the Dispensary, to enlarge the

[24] The College also availed itself of the services of the firm of Tamblyn and Brown in 1939.

building and equip a small surgical unit, and to earmark $150,000 of the proceeds from fund-raising to cover expenses for three years. An additional sum of up to $850,000 was designated for the construction of an "entirely new medical school" adjacent to the New England Medical Center. This meant the eventual abandonment of the old headquarters on Huntington Avenue. The other half of a total goal of $2,000,000 was to be used for endowment. The Trustees, approving the campaign in principle, guaranteed up to $70,000 toward the construction and equipment of an additional floor on the newly named Pratt Diagnostic Clinic, to be used as a surgical unit.

The results of the fund drive were disappointing. The campaign, which was the ultimate responsibility of the school's alumni organization, was left leaderless with the death of President Cousens in 1937. To complicate the situation, the nation at large experienced a so-called economic "recession" in its attempt to climb out of the trough of the post-1929 depression, and money was correspondingly hard to come by. Canvassing of foundations produced only minimal amounts, the largest of which was $35,000 contributed by the Charles Hayden Foundation. Only $422,000 had been given or pledged by the fall of 1940, the great bulk of it coming from alumni and faculty. During the period up to the Second World War, some support for student financial needs was made possible by the aforementioned Hayden Foundation, together with the W. K. Kellogg Foundation and the Charles H. Hood Dairy Foundation. Some important faculty appointments were also made possible by grants from the Rockefeller Foundation. By 1939 the school still had some distance to go in meeting the criticisms of the American Medical Association. The student body was gradually being reduced, although there were still too few instructors in the basic sciences. The greatest progress made in the two years since the American Medical Association's adverse report of 1937 was in the supervision of clinical work during the third and fourth years, a large part of it under the direction of Vice-Dean Dwight O'Hara. Clinical facilities were also greatly strengthened by the opening of the Pratt Diagnostic Clinic.

The coming of the Second World War had immediate and significant effects on the school as it plunged into the task of training hundreds of sorely needed doctors. Questions of fund-raising,

the move to a new location, and meeting professional requirement had to be subordinated for "the duration."[25] The school went
on an around-the-calendar schedule beginning in September 1941
and in three years had graduated four full classes, the majority of
whose members immediately entered military service. Acceleration became the order of the day. Faculty were in short supply,
and in February 1942 Dean Stearns was called to active duty as
a commander in the United States Naval Reserve. In spite of all
the dislocations accompanying forced-draft medical education, the
school continued to make plans for the future. The combined
medical-dental fund drive had netted $880,000 by the fall of 1944,
and Donald R. MacJannet had been selected to oversee the campaign. Plans to construct a building for the medical and dental
schools adjacent to the New England Medical Center were formulated, the acquisition of property was authorized, and an architectural firm had been employed by 1943 to draw up preliminary
plans. A year later the mortgage on the Huntington Avenue property had been paid off, and there was talk of moving into new
quarters by the fall of 1949.

The years between 1945 and 1952 were eventful ones for the
medical school. Curriculum, standards, physical plant, and finances
all had to be reassessed, and a student body reflecting the experiences of wartime dislocations had to be accommodated. One interesting by-product of the Second World War was the sharp increase in the percentage of married students in the fourth-year
classes, which for a short period had an average age significantly
lower than those who entered as first-year students. A tangible reminder of the continuing crucial need for specialized national
manpower, in war or in peace, was the establishment of an Army
ROTC unit in 1947-48. Military instruction, limited initially to
the first three classes, was extended to all four in 1948–49, as part

[25] The medical school was inspected in 1941 by the governing board of
the Alpha Omega Alpha fraternity and was authorized to establish a chapter,
the third such in New England; the others were at Harvard and Yale. The
school received, in the same year, a favorable report from the Approving
Authority for Colleges and Medical Schools for the Commonwealth of Massachusetts; and in 1943–44, in anticipation of a return to peacetime conditions,
the Council on Medical Education of the American Medical Association scheduled an informal inspection of the school. The exigencies of wartime and the
accelerated program precluded a thorough review such as was made in 1954.

of long-range government plans to train medical officers. Tufts thus became the first school in the Boston area to accept such a program, which was also extended to the dental school in 1948–49.

While the United States was still in the midst of war, considerable thought was devoted to the effect of acceleration on the student body and the course of study. The Tufts Medical School, like most of its counterparts, returned to an annual entering class in the fall of 1945. Although there were advantages in continuing the accelerated program, experience indicated that the middle group, academically speaking, was having a difficult time, and the performance level was distinctly lower than it should have been. The students at the bottom were "more of a problem than ever," pedagogically speaking, and if an accelerated program became a permanent policy, it was seriously doubted if border-line applicants should be admitted at all. Because Tufts, like most medical schools (according to Acting Dean O'Hara), had so few really superior students, he favored a return to prewar scheduling which would stress "character and stability quite as much as . . . scholarly aptitude and cleverness." He also called for stability in another direction: the adoption of some kind of policy that would provide minimum and maximum faculty salaries, particularly for those at the lower ranks. The obtaining and retention of a competent and responsible staff made such a policy mandatory.

There were matters other than curriculum and faculty to be considered in the busy years after 1945, and they represented a more positive side of the medical school. Completion of the new physical plant was a top priority, and after the delays and frustrations of the war period the expansion of the New England Medical Center proceeded apace. In 1946, the Bingham Associates Fund of Massachusetts became the fourth member of the Center, and the Pratt Diagnostic Clinic was transferred to control of the Associates.[26] The more than $2,000,000 made available through the Bingham group made possible the erection of a greatly enlarged surgical unit designated as the Pratt Diagnostic Hospital. During the same year (1946), the so-called Harvard Building adjacent to the New England Medical Center was acquired by the Tufts Trustees for the use of the medical school. The final decision to sell the old

[26] Tufts was in this way released from the agreements and obligations undertaken in 1937.

*A view of the Tufts Medical School
on the evening of its dedication in 1951*

Huntington Avenue property and move to the new center on Harrison Avenue in downtown Boston was made in the spring of 1948.[27] Many months of delay in making the move were yet in store, but by the time the Trustees assembled for their March meeting in 1950, all activities of the medical and dental schools had been transferred to the new headquarters. Both faculty and students surmounted the inconveniences built into the move, but the tem-

[27] The Trustees had hoped to realize $400,000 on the sale. In actuality, they accepted an offer of $200,000 from Northeastern University.

porary disruptions were considered well worth the effort. The "great event" in the history of the medical and dental schools had taken place. President Carmichael quite accurately called the completed Center "one of the greatest forward steps" ever taken by the College. Even though financial resources had to be strained to equip and furnish the new facilities, the institution managed to do it by borrowing approximately half a million dollars. Donations in many amounts helped greatly to ease the pressure. Five years before the move was made, the medical school had received a gift from Dr. William E. Chenery and Mrs. Marion L. Chenery, to be used to establish the Chenery Memorial Library. Another welcome gift was that of Mr. and Mrs. Harry Posner of Medford in 1951. These benefactors of the school contributed $1,000,000 toward the construction of the Posner Memorial Residence Hall for medical and dental students. No longer were the students obliged to find living quarters in the byways of Boston and environs. Additional financial sustenance was also provided when medical school tuition was increased from $500 to $600, effective in the fall of 1946, and to $675 for the academic year 1948–49. Tuition was raised again the following year to $800 and to $850 effective in 1952–53.

Dr. Dwight O'Hara, who had served as dean of the medical school and as Professor of Preventive and Industrial Medicine since February 1946, presented his final report as dean, as of the fall of 1952.[28] After reviewing his eleven years as dean, Dr. O'Hara could look with satisfaction on a record of solid accomplishment by the school. The move into a new physical plant, beset as it had been with delays and difficulties, had been accomplished. The Departments of Chemistry and Pharmacology had been thoroughly reorganized. Medical research on a scale undreamed of fifteen years before had been undertaken — and this in spite of the abnormalities and uncertainties of the war period. There was also a significant intangible asset acquired by the school, particularly after 1945. The attrition rate, always higher than most individuals like

[28] Although Dean O'Hara's resignation was to have been effective in September, he actually continued to serve until March 1953, when Dr. Joseph M. Hayman, Jr., assumed the deanship. Dean Hayman also held the rank of Professor of Medicine and Senior Physician at the New England Center Hospital.

to see, dropped sharply, especially in the freshman class.[29] Part of this happy consequence was due to a return to peacetime conditions, which enabled the school to set higher standards of admission. Part was due to greater resistance than ever before to "the natural pressures that are brought to bear through friendly sources" and to "importunate urging of undeserving candidates." Dean O'Hara detected "a new stability and industry in the student body as a whole." A higher level of scholarship than ever before was demanded when the minimum standard for continuing in the school was raised substantially and when completion of Parts I and II of the national board examinations was required before graduation. Makeup opportunities, beginning in September 1952, were denied any student who failed more than two major courses in the first three years.[30]

The Tufts Medical School, following a national trend, was emphasizing quality over quantity in the output of doctors. Even though there were many more internships than available interns, and over twice as many students knocking at the door than were being admitted, medical schools about the country were consciously creating bottlenecks. Numbers alone would not fulfill the needs of a profession devoted to high standards. It was partly for this reason that Dean O'Hara and others greeted with relief the legislative defeat in the summer of 1952 of a proposal for a state medical school.[31] His argument that the student bodies and faculties of the three existing medical schools in Massachusetts (Boston University, Harvard, and Tufts) would be "diluted" if such a school were authorized was reinforced by the inescapable fact that the Tufts Medical School was drawing 70 per cent of its students from within the state. Creation of a tax-supported medical school would have forced the Tufts school to abandon its "New England policy," for it would have had to compete in a much larger area. This revised policy might, in the opinion of the dean, have tempted, or even forced, the school to accept candidates who did not meet its aca-

[29] The attrition rate for first-year classes was less than 3 per cent for each of the years 1950 and 1951.

[30] Prior to that date, students might, with the approval of successive promotion committees, make up failures in two major courses each year.

[31] Such a school was finally authorized ten years later; it was not until 1965 that a site was selected.

demic requirements fully. A combination of commitment to professional standards and practical self-interest thus posed a recurring dilemma for the private as against the public educational institution.[32]

Closer home, in a sense, was another problem of long standing —the relation of the medical school itself, and its students and alumni, to the College. Still geographically separated, living much of its life as a distinct entity with, for the most part, only the most tenuous of associations with the College below the highest administrative level, the medical school tended to turn more and more to the medical profession than to Tufts for financial support and endowment. Although the medical school was well represented in the Second Century Fund goals, its needs were much greater than the amount provided there. Dean O'Hara felt that the primary allegiance of the professional school graduate was in reality focused there rather than on his undergraduate school, but that insufficient effort had been made to capitalize on this fact. The medical school graduate had to be "convinced that what he gives is going to his medical school, not to the college or university whose name it bears." The start already made by the National Fund for Medical Education, and the American Medical Education Foundation sponsored by the American Medical Association, seemed to be the "great hope" for future support rather than dependence on the parent institution. The establishment of an aggressive public relations office, located at the medical school, "not at the College in Medford," would be a move in the right direction. Dean O'Hara and President Carmichael, simultaneously stepping down from their respective offices in 1952, left this problem to be worked out by those who followed.

§ § §

The Tufts Dental School between 1937 and 1952 faced many of the same problems that beset the medical school, although their magnitude was not always as great or as apparent. The plan outlined in 1937 to move the medical school eventually to the New England Medical Center brought into sharp focus the long-stand-

[32] The American Medical Association had already exerted considerable pressure on schools not to restrict applicants geographically. In 1948, 109 of the 111 members of the entering class of the medical school were from New England, and 77 of those were from Massachusetts.

ing problem of the relationship between the medical and dental schools. The discernible trend of dentistry to become a medical specialty made imperative a close affiliation of the two professions. For many years the dental students had received basic instruction in the Department of Anatomy, with financial adjustments made on a per capita basis. Dean Stearns of the medical school felt that the two schools should occupy separate buildings, although it was obviously economical for the medical school to operate the departments in the fundamental sciences needed by both sets of students. Payment by the dental school of a service charge seemed to be an equitable plan. The Dental Alumni Association, not so confident that this could be worked out, asked the Trustees what would become of the dental school if the medical school did move to another location. The Association was much concerned that the provision of laboratories and teachers for the basic medico-dental sciences was beyond the capability of the dental school to furnish. The school was greatly relieved when the decision was made to house it, together with the medical school, in the vicinity of the New England Medical Center.

Dr. Marjerison, dean of the dental school in the 1930's, was wont to place the problems of the school in a large context and reiterated his plea that the school be developed as less of a "vocational school" and more of a professional educational activity associated with a liberal arts college and, specifically, with the medical school. There was no question in his mind that dentistry was no more than "a problem in human biology." He was of the opinion that for the dental school to meet the university ideal it had to be subsidized by the parent institution as well as by tuition fees and was obligated to encourage career teaching and research. These were, in Marjerison's opinion, as much the responsibilities of the officials of the College as of the dental school. Allowing or forcing the school to operate as a commercial venture should be made a thing of the past.

The dental school dean used his annual report for 1938–39 as a vehicle for discussing some of the broader problems involved in dental education. He paid particular attention to the inadequacies of the two-year dental preparatory program. He considered the so-called "two-four plan" entirely too inflexible and too conducive to the lowering of academic standards. The pre-clinical sciences in the first two years of dental school were acceptable for credit in neither the medical school nor graduate departments of the College. There was no sound reason, in his estimation, for considering the pre-clinical scientific training of the prospective dentist less demanding or somehow lower on the scale of academic values than similar training for medicine. Commitment to one narrow curriculum was no way to attract superior students. Eventually, entrance requirements for dentistry should, he felt, be the same as for medical school, namely, a Bachelor's degree. Some progress had been made in requiring a four-year degree, but the goal was not yet achieved. In 1939–40 every first-year student admitted to the Tufts Medical School was a college graduate; slightly less than 40 per cent of entering dental students in the same year were degree holders. Another major weakness in dental education, as Marjerison saw it, was the lack of well-administered teaching internships. It was unfair to expect the dental school faculty to turn out finished products. The addition of an intern year seemed to be the best solution. Although it was true that almost one-third of the graduating class in 1939 received hospital appointments, these internships were conducted independently of the dental school and hence were not part of an articulated curriculum. The dean's reiterated plea for support of full-time teachers and research workers lost none of its pertinence in repetition.

Only a year after he had offered his thoughts on dental education, and twenty-three years after his first appointment at Tufts, Dr. Marjerison resigned to accept the deanship of the dental school at the University of Illinois. At least some of his hopes for an even closer affinity of dentistry and medicine were realized in his successor, for Dr. Basil B. Bibby held a joint appointment in the two schools as Professor of Bacteriology.

Like other divisions of the College, the dental school bent all of its efforts to the special tasks that confronted liberal arts and professional education during the Second World War. Surmounting the complications associated with shortages of professional, technical, and clerical personnel and scarcities of material was little short of heroic. Curricular acceleration was immediately introduced, and faculty and students alike were scattered literally to the four corners of the world as others took their places in the crowded Huntington Avenue headquarters and sought to give and receive essential dental training. It came as no surprise that an informal report made after a visitation from representatives of the Council on Dental Education in 1943 called attention to the inadequate staffing. The school managed, in spite of the difficulties it had faced during the war period, to become one of the twenty-three dental schools given full approval by that same Council in 1945.

Some of the accomplishments of the dental school by 1945 undoubtedly contributed to the favorable report of the inspection, although even more progress was made after the national emergency had passed. During the academic year 1942–43, clinical opportunities for students were extended by an informal arrangement with the Oral Surgery Clinic of the Boston City Hospital, and in the spring of 1945 a formal affiliation with that institution gave Tufts students exclusive privileges in the Department of Oral Surgery. In January 1944 a new cooperative arrangement with the Boston Dispensary went into effect by which part-time instructors were employed jointly with the dental school. The Boston Dispensary Clinic was made an integral part of the dental school in the fall of 1949.[33] In the midst of the Second World War (1944) the dental school arranged with the Forsyth Dental Infirmary for the use of senior students who in effect served as interns. It had been during the First World War that Tufts' relationship with Forsyth had also been close.

Despite the increased work load of a badly depleted staff during the war, the dental school undertook new and important projects; after 1945, the expansion of research and postgraduate activities was even more impressive. One of the most significant studies undertaken in 1943 was an investigation of the value of fluorides in dentifrices, aided by a grant from the Procter and Gamble Company. A grant of $90,000 from the W. K. Kellogg Foundation gave much aid to postgraduate research. The first candidate for a Master of Science degree in the medical sciences began work in the dental school in January 1943, and in 1950 the Master of Dental Science degree was created. In the meantime (1945), postgraduate courses were being offered in cooperation with the Massachusetts Dental Society.

Dean Bibby did not remain to see all of his plans for a greatly

[33] The clinic was used for the Department of Oral Pediatrics during the daytime, and Tufts personnel continued to operate the evening clinic.

expanded graduate program come to fruition. He resigned, effective September 1946, to return to Rochester, New York, where he accepted an appointment as director of the Eastman Dental Dispensary. His successor for a brief period was Dr. Joseph F. Volker, Professor of Clinical Dentistry in the Tufts School, who resigned in 1949 in order to head the newly created University of Alabama School of Dentistry. It was under the leadership of yet another dean, Dr. Cyril D. Marshall-Day, who assumed his post in midyear of 1948–49, that the dental school made the long-awaited move to the New England Medical Center.

Even though the leadership of the school had changed three times in less than ten years, and it lost by death in 1948 Dr. John T. O'Rourke, who had built up the Division of Graduate and Post-Graduate Instruction to a position of national prominence, the Tufts Dental School maintained a record of consistent progress. A continuous effort was made, even during the war years, to increase the financial support so critically needed to strengthen teaching staff and to provide student assistance. A limited amount of scholarship aid was finally provided in the early 1940's. An increase in tuition in 1945 (from $400 to $500) and again in 1948 (to $600) helped in some measure.[34] Even more important as a source of income was the Development Fund Drive of $300,000, successfully completed in the spring of 1946. Meanwhile, faculty leadership in professional activities was signalized by the election in 1948 and 1949 of Dr. Philip Adams, Professor of Orthodontics, to the presidency of the American Dental Association; Dr. Murray Gavel, Professor of Clinical Dentistry, to the presidency of the Massachusetts Dental Society, succeeding Dr. Herbert Margolis, Professor of Graduate Orthodontics; and Dr. Irving Glickman, Professor of Oral Pathology and Periodontology, to the presidency of the Greater Boston Dental Society.

The move of the dental school to the New England Medical Center in 1949–50 was doubly significant, for it coincided with the completion of the first half-century of affiliation with Tufts. The new location also made the close relations with the medical school, so long sought by so many, more of a possibility than ever before. Dentistry was being more and more recognized professionally as a

[34] Dental school tuition became $800 in 1949–50 and was raised to $850 for 1952–53.

significant phase of preventive medicine.[35] As the academic year 1951–52 drew to a close, the dental school completed its eighty-fourth year as a training institution. Its record had been one of growth — in the quality as well as the quantity of its graduates, in its research activities, in the caliber of its faculty, and in its national reputation. It ranked among the top schools of the forty-two similar institutions in the United States. On the local level, it furnished the bulk of the dentists for New England. Its community services to dental health education and its graduate and refresher courses for practicing dentists were among its many contributions. The research division alone had a staff of over forty and an annual budget approaching $200,000 in 1952.

The road of the dental school had not been as rocky as that of the medical school, but it still had the challenges of the future to face. The increased requirements for the armed services and the competition of government agencies and of private practice posed serious problems in the field of faculty recruitment and retention. Like the medical school, the dental school calculated the probable effects of the creation of a state-supported school as proposed in the state legislature in 1952. What was the role of the non-tax-supported institution? There were, as well, more academically oriented questions to be answered and deficiencies to be remedied. The failure to correlate pre-clinical education adequately in the basic sciences with clinical experience was one example. Another fundamental problem of dogged persistence was the inability of students to communicate their ideas in effective and correct fashion. One distressed dental school faculty member deplored "the relative degree of illiteracy in the student body." There was concern expressed from time to time that competition for entrance into dental schools had become so intense that students were neglecting the liberal arts tradition in their haste to excel as specialists in science at the undergraduate level. There still remained the larger question, facing many another dental school besides Tufts, and schools in other professional areas as well, of how to produce educated men and women as well as narrow technicians.

[35] This close relationship was recognized in the terminology used when the College officially became Tufts University in 1955. The dental school became the Tufts School of Dental Medicine.

§   §   §

During President Carmichael's administration, the College negotiated affiliations with five undergraduate professional schools which were placed under the ever-growing umbrella of what was first known as the Division of University Extension and later as the Division of Special Studies. Many critics of the Extension Division and of the so-called "affiliated schools" were convinced that expansion of vocational training at Tufts was not in harmony with the liberal arts tradition; that the existence of such organizations, with the Tufts name attached, threatened the maintenance of collegiate academic standards and spread the resources of the institution entirely too thin. Defenders of these schools, notably President Carmichael, emphasized the community services that could be rendered "without expenditure of money on the part of the College"; pointed to the favorable publicity that would heighten the College's prestige and spread its name and influence; and called attention to the increase in student enrollment (and fees) that would "be profitable in a small way to our faculty," many of whom were beginning to chafe under a salary scale that had remained unchanged year after year. Notice should be given of the fact that the expansion of the Extension Division's operations between 1939 and 1951 coincided with a period of uncertainty and crisis in naional and world affairs that could have adversely affected both enrollment and income.

Tufts took the first step in broadening its field of operations in professional education in 1939–40 by creating a Division of University Extension. It was intended, when first organized, to serve several categories of individuals for whom attendance at college as regular students was impossible. Among these were elementary and secondary school teachers unable to attend regular weekly classes. Hence the Extension Division was organized to supplement the work of the Department of Education by offering late afternoon, evening, and weekend courses. Another group to which the new division expected to appeal consisted of adults who desired academic work as part-time students but who had no intention of earning a degree. Tuition was set originally at $10 per semester hour, plus laboratory fees where appropriate, and secretarial employees, and wives and members of the faculty were permitted to enroll in extension courses at one-half tuition. At first, all such courses carried two academic credits. A new degree, Bachelor of Science in Education, was authorized in 1940 for those enrolled in extension courses who wished to earn an academic degree. Completion of the customary fifteen high school units was required for admission, except that individual cases could be evaluated on their merits.[36]

The faculty of the Extension Division was made up of the heads of the major departments in the school of arts and sciences, the deans of all of the divisions of the College, and any others appointed by the president and the Trustees.[37] Beginning in the fall of 1940, graduate students were allowed to enroll in certain approved courses in the Division of University Extension and could receive graduate credit for such work provided they met the regular entrance requirements of the graduate school. The Extension Division thus gave graduate students additional opportunities to meet their degree requirements by enrolling in courses not offered in the regular liberal arts or graduate program. The coordination of the work of the Extension Division and the graduate school made it desirable to appoint one man to administer both. Professor Ruhl J. Bartlett, who had served for one year as dean of the graduate school, resumed his full-time duties as chairman of the Department of History in 1939, and Professor John P. Tilton, who had joined the Tufts faculty in 1927 in the Department of Education, was appointed in the dual capacity of director of graduate studies and director of university extension.

The new Division of University Extension prospered from the outset and almost immediately expanded its operations. Its director found himself also administering a wide miscellany of College activities for which there seemed to be no other administrative home.

[36] The degree requirements (120 semester hours, of which 72 had to be of "C" grade or better) included twenty-four hours of education and psychology courses, twelve hours of English, twelve hours of social sciences, twelve hours of science or mathematics, and thirty hours of concentration in a subject-matter field. The remainder of the degree requirements comprised electives. The minimum residence requirement was thirty credits earned at the College, thus allowing transfer with advanced standing from other institutions.

[37] There were forty on the extension faculty in 1940–41, when by-laws were adopted.

Enrollment in the Extension Division was 123 its first year (1939–40), with students registered in nineteen courses. The enrollees ranged from teachers to housewives, and their previous academic preparation from a Bachelor's degree to no college work at all. The first Bachelor of Science in Education degree was awarded in June 1941. Registration in 1941–42 jumped to 177, with over half of the individuals teachers in service.

In 1940 the intellectual fare on the campus was enriched by the organization of a series of evening University Lectures for the alumni and the general public, delivered (without charge to the listener or financial return to the speaker) by members of the faculties of all of the divisions of the College. The administration of this extracurricular activity also became the responsibility of the director of university extension. The University Lecture series was suspended during the Second World War but resumed in 1948–49. It lasted as an outlet for local talent and source of academic enrichment for only a short time and was replaced in the 1950's by a lecture series using people of note from outside the institution. Another community service project instituted by President Carmichael which used existing faculty resources and was likewise under the jurisdiction of the Extension Division was an Institute for Educational Guidance. The first sessions were held in the summer of 1940 and included two series of discussions, one for parents and one for high school students. Educational, personal, and vocational problems of adolescents were the main topics, and the students were tested extensively regarding abilities, interests, and aptitudes. The idea was followed up at Dean Academy, where members of the Tufts staff cooperated with school personnel in conducting a guidance clinic for its entering students. In the following summer the Institute also sponsored an intensive two-week workshop in educational guidance for thirty-six persons interested in problems of youth. The guidance workshops were discontinued during the Second World War because of transportation difficulties, but this special course was typical of literally dozens of programs offered in subsequent Tufts summer schools. The Institute was used during the Second World War to provide the testing program for veterans as they returned to civilian life.

The Extension Division likewise became the administrative agency for the Tufts College Nursery School, organized in the fall of 1940. Like the other projects under its aegis, this undertaking was established, as President Carmichael took pains to point out, "without cost to the College" by using the personnel and course offerings of the Departments of Education and Psychology. The nursery school was intended both as a service to the College community and as a laboratory for the observation of child behavior for Jackson students planning to enter the teaching profession. Eight children, most of them from faculty families, were enrolled in 1940–41. The school was discontinued after 1942 for the duration of the war, but with the hope that it could be reestablished as a demonstration school. The first postwar nursery school was actually organized on an informal basis in 1949 among the student and faculty inhabitants of Stearns Village.[38] The school went out of existence after 1951, when the Nursery Training School of Boston was affiliated with the College and many of the Stearns Village children were trained under its supervision.

In the spring of 1942, just as the disruptive effects of the Second World War began to be felt by the College, the Trustee Executive Committee approved in principle the affiliation of the Bouvé-Boston School of Physical Education with Tufts. The school, founded in 1913 as the Boston School of Physical Education, with Miss Marjorie Bouvé as its co-director, was intended for young women who were secondary school graduates and who wished to make the teaching or supervision of physical education their professional career. It had been chartered in 1914, and in 1930 merged with another school which had opened five years before. Between 1931 and 1942, the school was affiliated with Simmons College in Boston. Those who completed a four-year program received a Bachelor of Science degree from Simmons. A physical therapy curriculum was added in the mid-1920's and in 1928 was approved by the American Physical Therapy Association and the American Medical Association.

The affiliation with Tufts, operative in the fall of 1942, enabled qualified Bouvé-Boston students to receive a Bachelor of Science in Education degree, which in turn was made possible by course work in education and psychology necessary for certification for teaching purposes. The Tufts association gave Bouvé-Boston

[38] In spite of its *ad hoc* character, the school's existence was officially recognized by the Executive Committee of the Trustees.

students an opportunity to receive instruction in the liberal arts. The Bouvé-Boston School was placed administratively under the Division of University Extension, and those students able to qualify were, shortly after the affiliation began, enrolled as degree candidates during their third and fourth years if they were in the upper third of their classes. Upon completion of their Bouvé-Boston training, the students also received a certificate. Hence, beginning in 1948, graduates of this affiliated school who received both the Tufts degree and the certificate from the school became alumnae of both institutions.

Until the fall of 1944 no Bouvé-Boston students resided on or near the Tufts campus; they were forced to shuttle back and forth for their instruction between Medford and the Huntington Avenue headquarters of the school. The situation was even more complicated for those receiving training in physical therapy, for much of their clinical experience was obtained in Greater Boston hospitals. Transportation difficulties during wartime made the regimen even more demanding for the students. During the war the Bouvé-Boston upperclassmen were scattered in Jackson College dormitory residences, and some were housed temporarily in Wilson House, which had been turned over to the use of women students by the Fletcher School. Soon after the war Bouvé-Boston students were housed in dwellings near the campus. A multi-purpose classroom, office, and gymnasium building for the school was constructed on land donated by the College (but subject to return to it), and was occupied at midyear in 1950–51. In 1956 Ruth Page Sweet Hall was erected nearby as a dormitory. This structure was named for a person who had been associated with the school since 1929, had been its director since 1948, and until her death ten years later had attempted to raise the admission standards of the school and to integrate its student body, at least partially, into the total life of the Tufts campus.

As originally planned under the contract between the Bouvé-Boston School and the College negotiated by President Carmichael in 1942, approximately one-half of the projected four-year degree curriculum was to be taught by the faculty of the Tufts Division of University Extension. At least twenty-eight credit-hours of the total of fifty were to be given in the first three years. The proportion of Tufts instruction to the total program was to increase so that those students accepted for a degree program would take mostly Tufts courses by the time they were seniors. Tufts was guaranteed a certain amount annually for furnishing instruction and the use of facilities. Initially, eleven members of the extension faculty received additional compensation for teaching in the Bouvé-Boston program. The College thus received an assured income, part of which went to certain members of the faculty. Observant individuals noted that the Bouvé-Boston student body, as well as those of the other schools affiliated during the Second World War and Korean conflict, were either exclusively or preponderantly female; neither they nor the College, so far as the affiliated schools were involved, would be subjected to the hazards of the military draft.

Those responsible for the Bouvé-Boston and Tufts affiliation faced difficult tasks which were shared in some degree by the other schools later associated with the College, namely, to raise the admission standards of an undergraduate professional school to a level comparable to those of a liberal arts college and to establish reasonably satisfactory relations between the student bodies of the school and the College. At the time the affiliation was arranged in 1942, the normal program for a Bouvé-Boston student was three years. Very few could qualify for a Bachelor's degree.[39] The joint administrative committee established by the 1942 agreement decided that, beginning with the entering class in September 1945, students would be accepted only for the four-year degree program so that eventually the three-year diploma program would be eliminated. This determination to raise entrance requirements was reflected in the 1948 graduating class, in which the majority earned a Tufts degree as well as a school diploma. Recruiting Bouvé-Boston students with reasonably high College Board scores and other evidences of college preparedness was a continuing problem for the school's officials.

Relations between Tufts and Bouvé-Boston, particularly in the early years of affiliation, were tenuous at best and strained at worst. The school retained its own corporate identity and separate Board of Trustees, its own records, and its own admissions officers and ad-

[39] There were 164 Bouvé-Boston students in the first year of operation with Tufts. Fourteen in the graduating class earned Bachelor of Science in Education degrees. In 1943–44, twelve completed the four-year program, with a total of 129 students enrolled.

ministrative staff, even after the school was located entirely on the Tufts campus. The Bouvé-Boston students taking such basic courses with Tufts faculty as English, history, psychology, and biology were segregated in their own sections until after 1956. Bouvé-Boston seniors who wished to use their elective privileges to enroll in upperclass courses in Tufts were frequently frustrated by a high wall of prerequisites. The affiliated school students conducted their own student organizations and held their own diploma-granting ceremonies, although they also appeared at Tufts Commencements. Their entire academic orientation contrasted sharply with that of the students in Jackson College. The joint administrative committee had been charged in 1942 with the responsibility of determining all questions relating to "the participation of students enrolled in [the] Bouvé-Boston School in athletic, social, musical or other nonacademic functions at Tufts College or their eligibility to join teams, clubs, student governmental organizations or sororities otherwise composed of students of Tufts College or its affiliates." These, and a host of related problems, had to be somehow ironed out, and failures were more frequent than successes. Before the Bouvé-Boston students were provided with their own dormitory accommodations after the war, they were subject to the same general regulations as the Jackson students as to dormitory life and the payment of activity and medical fees. The director of the University Extension division, in whose office dozens of related problems landed, expressed the opinion that the Bouvé-Boston students should not be eligible for interscholastic sports (in which they were likely to excel by the very nature of their course of study and vocational choice). Whether Bouvé-Boston students could become members of Jackson organizations, such as sororities, or participate in numerous social activities was left to the organizations themselves. Regardless of the attempts made by sincere and well-meaning individuals on each side, the Bouvé-Boston students tended to remain a tightly-knit group. True social integration among Tufts, Jackson, and Bouvé-Boston undergraduates was far from accomplished when President Carmichael left office in 1952.

Only three years after the Bouvé-Boston School became associated with the College, another educational institution in the Greater Boston area joined the rapidly growing Tufts academic family. The School of the Boston Museum of Fine Arts became affiliated in the fall of 1945. The relationship between the College and the Museum School had begun during the academic year 1943–44, when Professor Russell T. Smith, head of the Huntington Avenue-based school in the Museum of Fine Arts, joined the Tufts faculty on a part-time basis after Professor Edwin H. Wright retired from the Department of Fine Arts. During the same year, arrangements had been made so that Tufts and Jackson students could take elective work in creative art at the school, and they were continued after the affiliation was consummated in 1945.[40] In addition, students registered in the Museum School were permitted to take courses in Tufts leading toward the Bachelor of Science in Education degree. This made possible, for those desiring it, certification to teach art. Four such students began work at Tufts in the fall of 1945. The affiliation between Tufts and the Museum School was not as elaborate as that with the Bouvé-Boston School, and fewer problems were encountered; nonetheless, occasional embarrassments over the meeting of Tufts academic requirements did occur, and in only a few instances did Museum School students become a real part of the Tufts community.

A third professional school in Boston was linked to Tufts in the same year that the arrangements with the Museum School were worked out. An affiliation, again administered through the Division of University Extension, with the Boston School of Occupational Therapy was approved in the spring of 1945 and went into operation that fall. This school, founded in 1918 at the request of the Surgeon General of the United States to meet rehabilitation needs of hospitalized service personnel during the first World War, had been incorporated in 1921 and was open to young women. Located at the time of affiliation on Harcourt Street in Boston, the school offered a so-called "diploma course" based on four semesters of professional technical training and approximately two semesters of clinical training which was received in one or more of a dozen or so hospitals and agencies in and near Boston. Affiliation with Tufts enabled those students who desired it to complete a "degree course" entitling them, after four years of academic and professional study and one year of clinical training, to receive both a diploma from the school and a Bachelor of Science in Education degree from

[40] Nine courses were available to Tufts and Jackson students; up to fifteen credits could be counted toward the Tufts degree.

Tufts. The nature of the affiliation was virtually identical with that worked out between Tufts and the Bouvé-Boston School in 1942. Academic courses were offered by the extension faculty and professional course by the school's own faculty. The school started its affiliated existence with thirty-nine students, and plans were laid to increase the number of students yearly until 1949, when all five years of the curriculum would become part of the degree program. Again, their courses at Tufts were taught in segregated fashion, and the students lived in their own residences near the campus. Their contact and association with Tufts and Jackson students were minimal.

During and immediately after the war, the Division of University Extension added several other special projects to its responsibilities. In the summer of 1944 it co-sponsored, with Mr. and Mrs. Donald R. MacJannet, a six-weeks "Vacation School of French," the theme of which was training for rehabilitation work in war-torn France. Two years later the Extension Division became the administrative agency through which Tufts cooperated in the Lowell Institute Broadcasting Council. The Council was established in 1946 to make available to the general public by way of radio (and later, television) some of the talent to be found in the numerous institutions of higher learning in the Boston area; each contributed a sum of money to make the programs possible. Several members of the Tufts faculty participated in panel discussions and classroom demonstrations and delivered lectures in an educational experiment considered eminently successful as it continued into the 1960's. Meanwhile, the evening and weekend courses which had been the chief reason for the creation of the Division of University Extension almost disappeared. In the years after 1946 the enrollment remained much smaller than at any time in the prewar period.[41] The time appeared to have come to reassess the role of the Extension Division, and its director, John P. Tilton, expressed the opinion that the prime emphasis should be placed on developing the programs of the affiliated schools. He feared that resumption of an ambitious program of extension courses for the general public might result in excessive demands on the faculty. Because the bulk of the work being offered by the Extension Division involved full-

[41] During 1947–48 there were forty-eight students enrolled in the three courses offered that year.

time students in the affiliated schools, he also felt that it was time to change the name of the division. Otherwise, the general public might be misled into equating the work of the affiliated schools with the part-time, often haphazard, and generally uncoordinated courses conventionally associated with extension work. His suggestion was heeded, for in 1949 the Division of University Extension was renamed the Division of Special Studies. Work of an extension nature continued, but on a greatly reduced scale, for two more schools were affiliated after 1948.

President Carmichael was authorized by the Executive Committee of the Trustees in the fall of 1948 to contract with the Forsyth School for Dental Hygienists to provide certain academic instruction, beginning in 1949–50. The Forsyth School had been organized in 1916, a year after the Forsyth Dental Infirmary for Children had opened, and graduated its first class in 1917.[42] Until the affiliation with Tufts, the school, intended to give training to young women in oral prophylactic treatment and to encourage general dental health education, offered a one-year course. A trend toward increased educational requirements resulted in a decision to extend the course to two years and, beginning in September 1949, to become associated with an institution that could provide college-level undergraduate instruction in academic subjects. Affiliation with Tufts met the need. After taking the major part of such basic general subjects as English and psychology on the Tufts campus in Medford during their first year, Forsyth students received their professional courses and clinical training at the school's Boston headquarters. Those completing the two-year course received a certificate, then took the board examination in the state in which they wished to practice under the supervision of a licensed dentist. It was possible for some students to continue their studies and to complete the requirements of the Tufts Bachelor of Science in Education degree. The faculty for teaching the professional curricula were drawn for the most part from the Tufts Medical and Dental Schools, although Harvard faculty were also included, as well as personnel from the Forsyth School itself. The enrollment

[42] For a period in its early history the Forsyth Dental Infirmary maintained close ties with the Tufts Dental School. In 1955 the Infirmary became affiliated with the Harvard School of Dental Medicine.

seldom exceeded seventy-five, of whom no more than about half were taking courses at Tufts at any one time.

The last of the five schools affiliated with Tufts during the Carmichael administration was the Nursery Training School of Boston, which became associated in 1951. Renamed the Eliot-Pearson School in 1955 to honor the two individuals largely responsible for its creation and early activities, it was the outgrowth of a project undertaken by a committee of the Woman's Education Association, of which Mrs. Henry Greenleaf Pearson was chairman. The committee had sponsored a trip to England in 1921 by Miss Abigail Adams Eliot to observe nursery school education. Upon her return, Dr. Eliot dedicated herself to the task of founding a training center and observation school for teachers of pre-school children. The end product was the opening of the Ruggles Street Day Nursery School as a combined school and training center in 1922. Mrs. Pearson served for ten years as the chairman of the Board of Managers of the institution, which later was renamed the Nursery Training School. Dr. Eliot, long-time director of the school, retired from that position a year after the affiliation with Tufts took place but continued to serve as a faculty member, adviser, and director of the school's Office of Development.

The agreement between the Nursery Training School and Tufts was almost identical to that made with the Bouvé-Boston School in 1942 and the Boston School of Occupational Therapy in 1945. It provided that students admitted to the school could take appropriate courses in the College. Reciprocal privileges were also allowed for Tufts and Jackson students. The oversight of the affiliated program was placed in the hands of a joint administrative committee, and the academic administration of the school became the responsibility of the Division of Special Studies. Students completing the requirements of both the school and the Division of Special Studies received both a certificate from the school and a Bachelor of Science in Education degree from Tufts. Like students in the other affiliated schools for women, those of the Nursery Training School who were degree candidates had a dual enrollment and upon graduation became alumnae of both institutions. When time came to make a choice of loyalties, the majority of graduates of the affiliated schools were likely to cast in their lot with their own professional school rather than with Tufts. Much the same phenomenon occurred in the other professional schools related in some way to the College — notably the medical and dental schools, and the Fletcher School of Law and Diplomacy.

§ § §

President Carmichael was no more able to escape the problems of institutional finances than any of his predecessors had been, and the presence of the numerous professional schools, both graduate and undergraduate, made his tasks no easier. He came to the College at a time when it was operating on the narrowest of margins. After reviewing the situation in his first annual report in 1938–39, he emphatically announced that *"the endowment of Tufts College must be increased."*[43] The College avoided an operating deficit in 1939–40 only because of gifts to the Alumni Fund. An upward readjustment of tuition became a necessity, and a sliding scale based on an ability-to-pay formula was discussed but not acted on. Tuition was raised from $300 to $350 effective in 1942–43, in the undergraduate schools.

Preparing budgets and estimating income from enrollment became exercises in guesswork during the Second World War. Although income went up sharply when the College changed to an around-the-calendar schedule, so did expenditures. Even then, the only net operating loss in Carmichael's administration occurred in 1944–45, because of the overhead costs created by the School of War Service.[44] Lack of confidence in what the postwar period might bring in the way of enrollments, the policy of returning the student body to something approaching a prewar size, and the increased costs of operating the institution resulted in the most rapid round of tuition increases yet seen. Five increases within seven

[43] In view of later struggles over faculty compensation and benefits during his administration, the following statement in the same report is worth noting: "For too many years, it has been necessary for the Administration of the College to deny able Faculty members the advances in salary which they not only need but most thoroughly deserve."

[44] The Navy was not authorized to pay the full costs of instruction for students in its programs. Even the deficit was not as bad as it appeared, for part of it was eventually made up by government payments which had been delayed. Furthermore, the deficit was overbalanced by reserves of over $250,000 which had made it unnecessary for the institution to borrow.

years, at the rate of $50 a year, brought Hill tuition to $600 by 1952.[45]

It was a well-known fact of financial life that tuition increases alone could never carry more than a part of the burden of running the College, particularly at the rate it was expanding after 1945. In 1948–49 endowment was slightly under $10,000,000 and the operating budget for the following year was over $4,000,000. By the time the endowment exceeded $10,000,000 (in 1950–51), the budget had topped $5,000,000. A comparison made by President Carmichael in 1945 with twenty other well-known institutions which had smaller endowments indicated, on the surface at least, that Tufts was faring quite well. Carmichael recognized, however, that such comparisons were very difficult to make and were quite misleading in some instances, for Tufts had "peculiar qualities as a university-college" setting it apart from almost every institution with which it might wish to compare itself. It had a larger student body than many and more numerous educational functions than most. Thus income from endowment funds had to be spread more thinly than at many other schools. This was one of the factors accounting for Carmichael's often-expressed hope that the wartime cooperation with government agencies and industry might be continued. It was for the same reason that after the war the College looked more and more to philanthropic foundations for support.

Long-range planning to provide unrestricted endowment for physical plant, the professional schools, and faculty salaries was essential. President Carmichael, after casting about for a worthwhile project to mark the upcoming 100th anniversary of the chartering of the College in 1952, suggested the creation of a centennial fund of $3,000,000 or more. Plans were laid in 1946 for such a campaign, the goal to be $3,500,000; almost one-third of it was intended for the medical school. The objective of the drive, as it evolved in 1949 and 1950, became $4,200,000.[46] The campaign, under the general direction of Professor Clarence P. Houston and designated the "Sec-

[45] The increase of $25 per term in 1945 had been applied to those already enrolled as well as to those entering.

[46] It was originally allocated as follows: $1,600,000 for two dormitories on the Hill; $2,000,000 for the medical school (a dormitory, two endowed professorships, and the expenses of moving to the New England Medical Center); and $600,000 for two endowed professorships in the Fletcher School. There was no provision for increasing faculty salaries.

ond Century Fund," was launched on a full scale in 1950, its financial objectives centered on the professional schools (medical, dental, and Fletcher); faculty salaries in the division of arts and sciences; student scholarship aid; and the completion of Alumnae Hall, to supplement the funds already raised by the Association of Tufts Alumnae.[47] The drive, successfully completed in 1953 with more than $100,000 beyond the goal, was unique in two respects: it represented the broadest base of giving for any fund drive yet conducted, with nearly 12,000 individual gifts; and it was conducted entirely by volunteer workers, drawn from alumni, faculty, and friends of the College.

The 100th anniversary of Tufts' chartering was marked in other ways than by fund-raising. A Centennial Pageant, "The Light Upon the Hill," depicting a century of the College's history, was presented during Commencement Week in 1952. The birthday celebration was climaxed by a three-day Centennial Celebration and Degree Convocation in October, attended by delegates from more than 400 colleges and universities and by statesmen and jurists from both the United States and abroad. The academic pageantry was highlighted with addresses by Dr. Vannevar Bush, of the Class of 1913 and at the time president of the Carnegie Institution of Washington, D.C.; Sir Hector Hetherington, principal and vice-chancellor of the University of Glasgow; President James B. Conant of Harvard; and the Honorable Erik C. Boheman, Swedish ambassador to the United States. The conferring of eleven honorary degrees was also part of the celebration. The Centennial observances were significant not only in and of themselves but also because they marked the closing weeks of President Carmichael's administration. On April 10, 1952, fourteen years after he had accepted the presidency of the College, he formally presented his resignation, effective December 31, 1952, in order to accept the secretaryship of the Smithsonian Institution.

[47] The allocations were actually as follows: medical school, $1,400,000; dental school, $600,000; Fletcher School, $600,000; arts and sciences, $1,500,000 ($1,000,000 for salaries and $500,000 for scholarships); and Alumnae Hall, $1,000,000. The necessity for making the residence halls "the main object" of the Second Century Fund was removed by the passage of the Federal Housing Act of 1950, under which the College was able to obtain loans at low interest rates to construct dormitories.

Dr. Carmichael made his last annual presidential report to the Trustees of Tufts College in October 1952. He took the opportunity to review some of the events and achievements of his long and active administration, and to make some suggestions for the future. He reviewed first the institution as a physical entity. In spite of his conviction "that glass, concrete and paint do not make a college," what he considered to be a disproportionate amount of attention and money had had to be devoted to the restoration, renovation, and improvement of plant. The most important addition, in his estimation, was the new home for the medical and dental schools, representing an investment of over $2,000,000. The association of these professional schools with the New England Medical Center made possible a level of teaching and research unparalleled in the history of either school. The departing president reported that "the always excellent faculty" had become stronger, showed remarkable stability in its makeup, and grown steadily in numbers.[48] Salaries had improved between 1938 and 1952, although admittedly not as much as desired. There had been, however, important retirement and medical insurance benefits provided for the faculty during his administration.

Endowment funds had risen from approximately $7,500,000 in 1937 to over $11,000,000 as Carmichael's administration drew to a close. The value of the College plant had risen from $3,600,000 to over $6,500,000 during the same period, and the operating budget had skyrocketed from $1,300,000 to well over $5,000,000. Borrowing for current needs had become almost a thing of the past, and in the fourteen years between 1938 and 1952 there was a deficit in only one year, in spite of his often-expressed fear that it would happen more often. Gifts and grants averaged $1,000,000 annually for the period of his presidency, and in 1952 the Second Century Fund was within half a million dollars of its goal of $4,200,000. He considered an effective and continuing Alumni Sustaining Fund indispensable to the future well-being of the College, and a yearly target of $200,000 not unrealistic.[49]

One of the most striking accomplishments of Carmichael's ad-

[48] There was a grand total of 568 faculty when Carmichael assumed office in 1938 and 985 when he resigned in 1952. He always included part-time faculty for all divisions of the institution when citing statistics of this sort.

[49] Alumni Fund contributions in 1965 exceeded half a million dollars.

ministration was the expanding scientific research program, financed in large part by grants from the federal government and from industry and comprising an important source of College income. In 1951 there had been assigned to Tufts a Naval research project on systems coordination (systems analysis) consisting of studies of basic military communications, with a budget in excess of $500,000.[50] Dr. Leonard C. Mead, who had joined the faculty in 1939 in the Department of Psychology and was later to become, in succession, dean of the graduate school, provost, and senior vice-president, was made Assistant to the President for Research Projects. In 1953 he became Research Coordinator for the network of sponsored research activities that had begun to spread over the institution. Instruction at Tufts, as Carmichael pointed out, was being carried out in more and more of a "university-research" atmosphere.

Yet with all of the research activity in progress, the president insisted that Tufts should remain steadfastly and primarily an undergraduate college, so far as both the academic and professional offerings on the Hill were concerned. Tufts was "an essentially teaching College in which research is also given real emphasis." He saw no merit in building up a large, formal graduate program in arts and sciences emphasizing the production of Ph.D.'s, particularly with two large and exceptionally well-staffed and well-equipped such schools nearby (Harvard and M.I.T.). It did not seem likely for many years that Tufts would wish to enter the graduate field at an advanced level except in special instances, already represented by such divisions as the Fletcher School. When the graduate faculty voted in 1947 to reinstitute the Ph.D. program in arts and sciences which had been in abeyance for exactly forty years, it was with the clear understanding that no department should venture into this phase of higher education unless its resources were sufficient to insure success.[51] President Carmichael thought it was

[50] During the brief period it was located on the Medford campus this research project was housed in a concrete-block building erected for the purpose near the Cousens Gymnasium. A Department of Systems Analysis was created in the graduate school and was authorized to award the Doctor of Science degree.

[51] Preliminary plans were made in 1946 to set up the standards and requirements. It was actually not until two years later that any department

far better to maintain and strengthen a first-class undergraduate college with affiliated undergraduate professional schools and sponsored research than to embark on a too ambitious graduate program that might overextend the institution's comparatively limited resources and turn it into a second-class university. The commitment of Tufts to the undergraduate was a measure of its uniqueness.

The undergraduate enrollment during Carmichael's administration had shown the same phenomenal change as the physical aspects of the campus and the growth of contract research. The total number of undergraduates in the school of liberal arts had been 615 in 1937; thirteen years later it was 1,175. In the immediate postwar period (1947) it had jumped to 1,561. Increases in student enrollment in the engineering school and in Jackson College for Women were less dramatic but fully as significant. President Carmichael viewed the total increases in full-time student enrollment in the entire College — from 2,104 in 1937 to 3,356 in the autumn of 1952 — with mixed feelings. Bigness for its own sake should never be the goal of the institution. The student might well be the loser if the College succumbed to pressures to become a large educational establishment. Tufts should, in the future, "do everything in its power to remain a strong and effective small institution. Unless quite unexpected funds are presented to the College it probably should not become a larger university than it now is." Quality and quantity were two quite different things. The slogan of the Second Century Fund — "A Better, Not a Bigger, Tufts" — was quite in harmony with the outgoing president's aspirations for his Alma Mater.

on the hill (Biology) felt prepared even to receive candidates. In 1952, Ph.D. degrees were actually awarded only in the medical school and the Fletcher School.

Epilogue:
"A Small University of High Quality"

IN A PARAPHRASE of what had once been said of President Eliot of Harvard, Dean Emeritus Lee S. McCollester of the Tufts School of Religion had written of President Carmichael in 1938: "His work is not to reproduce the Tufts of the past, but to produce the Tufts of the future." This was not to be the challenge for one man alone, but for his successor as well. At their fall meeting in 1952 the Trustees authorized the Executive Committee "to designate an appropriate individual as Acting President of the College." Vice-President Wessell was appointed, and a year later, by unanimous election, he became the eighth president of Tufts.

The dynamic new head of the College, like his predecessor, was only thirty-nine when he took office. Full of ideas and receptive to new ones, and thoroughly familiar with the workings of Tufts, from inside and out, since 1939, President Wessell set out with vigor and enthusiasm to make even more meaningful the charter change which, in 1955, finally made Tufts officially what it had been for generations — a university. But the institution was to be, in his often-repeated phrase, of a special kind: "A Small University of High Quality." What did this signify? It meant first a complete inventory of the new "university," accomplished under the immediate supervision of Provost Leonard C. Mead between 1956 and 1958. The Tufts-Carnegie Self-Study involved the faculty directly in the recommendation of major educational policy for the first time in decades and produced a series of projections for the future that was to keep the Trustees busy for a generation or more to come.

The concept of "university" meant a closer tie than ever between the branches and the main stem that was Tufts; this, in turn, called for such measures as the dismantling of the loosely con-

Nils Yngve Wessell
Acting President, 1953; President, 1953–66

structed educational edifice known as the Division of Special
Studies and erected during the Carmichael administration. Many of
the so-called "affiliated schools" were given the choice of losing
their semiautonomous status and casting their lot completely with
Tufts, according to Tufts standards, or leaving the family. The
term "university" meant also a larger and busier faculty who earned
much more money than ever before and spent less time in the classroom but not less time in the "community of scholars." There was
more research activity and greater attention to professional involve-

ment than heretofore. There was curricular experimentation to meet the needs of college generations more highly selected and more intellectually sophisticated than their forebears. Pressures to expand and proliferate were stoutly resisted (although, some thought, not always successfully). New demands stretched resources as tightly as ever.

With the new president came many changes — in physical plant, in faculty and administration, in student body, in relationships among all the intermeshed parts that went into making up the University. Yet two themes that were echoed repeatedly over the years were as much a part of the philosophy of the institution in the 1950's and 1960's as they had been at almost any time in its history. Both had been expressed by President Cousens, and neither of his two successors, at least, saw fit to challenge them. "Our view," wrote Cousens to Harold E. Sweet, long-time president of the Board of Trustees, "must reach far into the future, within the field of our endeavor there must be no limit to our ambition. . . . Tufts College is ambitious to be great because of quality and not because of quantity." The second theme was much older than the man who expressed it: ". . . with pride I say to you again we are rich with the riches most to be prized; rich in men and women, you will find them everywhere among the students, among the alumni, on the staff, in the Board of Trustees; men and women ready to grapple with each problem as it comes, and to solve it finally. Day by day, my faith in the College strengthens. . . ."

Bibliographical Note

ONLY TWO HISTORIES OF TUFTS have been written, neither since it became a university in 1955. In 1952, then-President Leonard Carmichael assembled a brief pictorial history in recognition of the centennial of the chartering of the institution. The other had been published in 1896, as a labor of love by the Class of 1897. From time immemorial, classes about to leave their Alma Mater have left something to remind incoming classes, and posterity, of their existence. Instead of donating a section of fence, a bell, a plaque, a bench, or the like, the Class of 1897 prepared, in their junior year, a history of their college. Bound in the school colors of brown and blue, and with an impressive 382 pages, their offering, on closer examination, is found to consist of only eighty-eight pages of narrative. The bulk of the book is devoted to alumni directories, reproductions of the course of study at the time, and the usual lists of faculty, Trustees, and miscellaneous statistical information. In spite of certain deficiencies, however, the 1896 history is generally accurate as far as it goes and has served as a handy reference volume for almost three-quarters of a century. The biographical sketches of the faculty up to that date and the information on the oldest fraternities are still of special value and have been drawn upon in the present work.

Since 1958, the writer has served as organizer of the archives of the University as well as its historian. He has thus had an unusual opportunity to become acquainted with the materials available. The collections of the Universalist Historical Society, located on the Tufts campus, have also been of great value. By good fortune, much of the personal correspondence of the early presidents has survived and is located in the Tufts Archives. The most valuable single primary sources for nineteenth-century Universalism are the weekly newspapers published by the denomination. From their columns can be pieced together a surprisingly complete story of most aspects of Universalist history in the United States. The leading newspaper was the *Trumpet and Universalist Magazine* which under variant titles was published from 1819 until it was merged with the *Universalist* after the Civil War. In the issues of the 1850's and 1860's can be found almost a week-to-week account of the origin and progress of Tufts, for it was established procedure to reprint most of the proceedings of Trustee meetings and even lists of library acquisitions in its columns. There were many other lesser-known Universalist papers, such as the *Gospel Banner* and the *Christian Ambassador,* but all newspapers followed the widely encouraged practice of copying from each other. The writer has had access to a complete file of the *Trumpet* and its predecessors and successors and has used it extensively for background and illustrative material, especially for the two chapters covering the period prior to the chartering of the institution.

The files of both the official records of the Corporation and of its constituent parts, and of student publications, are unusually complete. The most useful records have been the following (1) Trustees of Tufts College — minutes of the full Board and of its Executive Committee, and supporting documents and correspondence in the secretaries' files; (2) faculty minutes, official papers and supporting documents, and the secretaries' files; (3) the presidents' annual reports to the Trustees (when made in writing — printed, 1873–1917, mimeographed and on microfilm, 1932 to date); (4) presidential correspondence; (5) catalogues and other official publications and reports of the University; (6) files of student and alumni publications (including complete sets of the literary magazine, the campus newspaper, yearbooks, and the alumni magazine); (7) miscellaneous publications, press releases, scrapbooks, correspondence, and other memorabilia that form a vital part of any college archives. The bulk of the University Archives are housed in the central library. In the winter of 1963–64 the major records of the University were microfilmed for safekeeping, and sufficient copies were made to assure the preservation of documents vital to the history of the institution.

Index

717

Index

Index